THE DOMESTIC SPACE REA

Tune in to HGTV, visit the magazine section of your local bookstore, or flip to the 'Homes' section of your weekend newspaper, and it becomes clear: domestic spaces play an immense role in our cultural consciousness. *The Domestic Space Reader* addresses our collective fascination with houses and homes by providing the first comprehensive survey of the concept across time, cultures, and disciplines.

This pioneering anthology, which is ideal for classroom use and for the general reader interested in the home, features significant writing on the subject by senior scholars and seminal thinkers and writers, including Gaston Bachelard, Pierre Bourdieu, Mary Douglas, Le Corbusier, Dolores Hayden, Henri Lefebvre, Jean Baudrillard, Mrs Isabella Beeton, Edgar Allan Poe, Diana Fuss, Beatriz Colomina, and Edith Wharton. Among the many topics explored are: the impact of domestic technologies on family life; the relationship between religion and the home; the attitudes of nomadic peoples towards housing; domestic spaces in art and literature; and the changing meanings of the bedroom throughout history. *The Domestic Space Reader* demonstrates how discussions of domestic spaces can help us to better understand and challenge our perceptions of life in particular times and places.

CHIARA BRIGANTI is the academic director for British Programmes of the College of Global Studies at Arcadia University and a visiting research fellow at King's College London.

KATHY MEZEI is a professor emeritus in the Department of Humanities at Simon Fraser University.

The Domestic Space Reader

EDITED BY CHIARA BRIGANTI AND KATHY MEZEI

UNIVERSITY OF TORONTO PRESS
Toronto Buffalo London

Toronto Buffalo London
www.utppublishing.com
Printed in Canada

ISBN 978-0-8020-9968-6 (cloth)
ISBN 978-0-8020-9664-7 (paper)

Printed on acid-free, 100% post-consumer recycled paper with vegetable-based inks.

Library and Archives Canada Cataloguing in Publication

The domestic space reader / edited by Chiara Briganti and Kathy Mezei.

Includes bibliographical references and index.
ISBN 978-0-8020-9968-6 (bound) ISBN 978-0-8020-9664-7 (pbk.)

1. Dwellings. I. Briganti, Chiara II. Mezei, Kathy, 1947–

GT170.D64 2012 392.3'6 C2012-902650-6

This book has been published with the help of a grant from the Canadian Federation for the Humanities and Social Sciences, through the Aid to Scholarly Publications Program, using funds provided by the Social Sciences and Humanities Research Council of Canada.

University of Toronto Press acknowledges the financial assistance to its publishing program of the Canada Council for the Arts and the Ontario Arts Council.

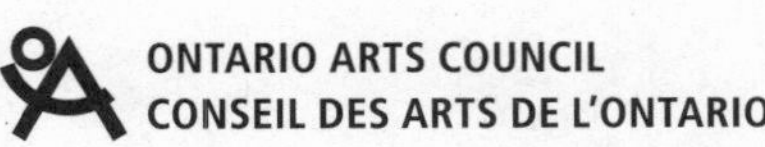

University of Toronto Press acknowledges the financial support of the Government of Canada through the Canada Book Fund for its publishing activities.

A Nina che fa casa
(To Nina who makes a space domestic)

To the memory of Eva in her final home

Contents

List of Figures xiii
Acknowledgments xv
Permissions xvii

Chapter 1: Introduction 3

Chapter 2: The Idea of Home 17
2.1 GASTON BACHELARD 'The House from Cellar to Garret. The Significance of the Hut' 19
2.2 MARTIN HEIDEGGER 'Building, Dwelling, Thinking' 21
2.3 HENRI LEFEBVRE 'Social Space' 26
2.4 TIM INGOLD 'Building, Dwelling, Living: How Animals and People Make Themselves at Home in the World' 31
2.5 PIERRE BOURDIEU 'The Berber House or the World Reversed' 35
2.6 JUAN EDUARDO CAMPO 'Domestications of Islam in Modern Egypt: A Cultural Analysis' 40
2.7 DAVID STEA 'House and Home: Identity, Dichotomy, or Dialectic? (With Special Reference to Mexico)' 45
2.8 MARY DOUGLAS 'The Idea of a Home: A Kind of Space' 50
2.9 LINDA MCDOWELL 'Rethinking Place: Thoughts on Spaces of the Home, Absence, Presence, New Connections and New Anxieties' 54
2.10 WILLIAM J. GLOVER 'A Feeling of Absence from Old England: The Colonial Bungalow' 59
2.11 ALAN PASSES Loud Women: Creating Community from the Domestic in Amazonia (An Anthropological View) 65

Chapter 3: Interiors 73
3.1 JOSEPH RYKWERT 'A House for the Soul' 77
3.2 CLIVE KNIGHTS 'The Spatiality of the Roman Domestic Setting: An Interpretation of Symbolic Content' 79
3.3 GEORGES DUBY 'The Aristocratic Households of Feudal France: Communal Living' 83
3.4 WITOLD RYBCZYNSKI 'Intimacy and Privacy' 88
3.5 MA THANEGI The Burmese House 91
3.6 FRANCES BORZELLO 'Looking for the Interior' 94
3.7 ROBERT KERR 'The Family Apartments' 100
3.8 WALTER BENJAMIN 'Louis-Philippe or the Interior' 103
3.9 ALAIN CORBIN 'Domestic Atmospheres' 105
3.10 SHARON MARCUS 'Seeing through Paris' 108
3.11 DOROTHY TODD AND RAYMOND MORTIMER The New Interior Decoration: An Introduction to Its Principles, and International Survey of Its Methods 112
3.12 DOLORES HAYDEN 'Nurturing: Home, Mom, and Apple Pie' 114
3.13 RITSUKO OZAKI Purity and Danger from a Japanese Perspective: Culture and House Plan 116

Chapter 4: House / Body / Psyche 121
4.1 MARJORIE GARBER 'The Body as House' 123
4.2 ANNMARIE ADAMS 'Childbirth at Home' 127
4.3 EMILY BURBANK Woman as Decoration 130
4.4 JEAN-CHRISTOPHE AGNEW 'A House of Fiction: Domestic Interiors and the Commodity Aesthetic' 133
4.5 CARL GUSTAV JUNG Memories, Dreams, Reflections 135
4.6 SIGMUND FREUD 'The Uncanny' 138
4.7 ANTHONY VIDLER The Architectural Uncanny: Essays in the Modern Unhomely 141
4.8 GEORGES TEYSSOT '"Water and Gas on All Floors": Notes on the Extraneousness of the Home' 147

Chapter 5: Gendered Spaces 151
5.1 BART VERSCHAFFEL 'The Meanings of Domesticity' 153
5.2 DEBORAH COHEN 'In Possession: Men, Women, and Decoration' 157
5.3 BASIL D. NICHOLSON 'The Architectural Consequences of Women' 160
5.4 CHRISTOPHER REED 'Taking Amusement Seriously: Modern Design in the Twenties' 162

5.5 RICHARD A.H. LIVETT 'Bronte House Scheme' 168
5.6 GEORGE WAGNER 'The Lair of the Bachelor' 170
5.7 MATT COOK Queer Domesticities 173
5.8 MARCIA STEPHENSON 'The Architectural Relationship between Gender, Race, and the Bolivian State' 180
5.9 RENÉE HIRSCHON 'Essential Objects and the Sacred: Interior and Exterior Space in Urban Greek Locality' 186
5.10 IRIS MARION YOUNG 'House and Home: Feminist Variations on a Theme' 190
5.11 ARITHA VAN HERK 'Cleansing Dislocation: To Make Life, Do Laundry' 194

Chapter 6: Home Parts 199
6.1 JOHN E. CROWLEY 'Chimneys and Privacy' 203
6.2 EDGAR ALLAN POE 'The Philosophy of Furniture' 206
6.3 JEAN BAUDRILLARD 'Structures of Interior Design' 210
6.4 EDITH WHARTON AND OGDEN CODMAN JR 'Bric-à-Brac' 214
6.5 CATHARINE E. BEECHER AND HARRIET BEECHER STOWE 'Earth-Closets' 217
6.6 KATHERINE ASHENBURG A Short History of the Newest and Sometimes Smallest Room 221
6.7 MRS C.S. PEEL 'The Nurseries and the Schoolroom' 224
6.8 NORBERT ELIAS 'On Behavior in the Bedroom' 225
6.9 MRS ISABELLA BEETON 'Arrangement and Economy of the Kitchen' 230
6.10 CHRISTOPHER WILK 'Frankfurt Kitchen, 1926–7. Designed by Grete Lihotsky (Margarete Schütte-Lihotsky; 1897 Vienna–2000 Vienna). From the Am Höhenblick Housing Estate, Ginnheim, Frankfurt' 233
6.11 IRENE CIERAAD '"Out of My Kitchen!" Architecture, Gender and Domestic Efficiency' 236
6.12 STEPHEN KLINE Interviewed by Kathy Mezei, 2009. The Telephone and the Radio Enter the Home 238
6.13 DAVID MORLEY 'What's "Home" Got to Do with It? Contradictory Dynamics in the Domestication of Technology and the Dislocation of Domesticity' 241

Chapter 7: Liminal Spaces 247
7.1 GEORG SIMMEL 'The Bridge and the Door' 249
7.2 BEATRIZ COLOMINA 'Interior' 251

7.3 OLIVIER MARC 'Birth of the House' 256
7.4 JOËLLE BAHLOUL 'Telling Places: The House as Social Architecture' 259
7.5 ROBERT MUGERAUER 'Toward an Architectural Vocabulary: The Porch as a Between' 264
7.6 CATHERINE ALEXANDER 'The Garden as Occasional Domestic Space' 268
7.7 EMMA ROBINSON-TOMSETT 'So Having Ordered My Berth I Lay Me Down to Rest'; Ships and Trains: Travelling Home 273
7.8 PATRICK CHAN Vancouver's Laneway Houses: Changing Notions of Home 278

Chapter 8: Contested Spaces 285

8.1 CHARLOTTE PERKINS GILMAN The Home, Its Work and Influence 287
8.2 PAIGE RAIBMON 'Living on Display: Colonial Visions of Aboriginal Domestic Spaces' 289
8.3 REBECCA GINSBURG '"Come in the Dark": Domestic Workers and Their Rooms in Apartheid-Era Johannesburg, South Africa' 294
8.4 LE CORBUSIER Towards a New Architecture 300
8.5 LARS LERUP 'Planned Assaults: Reflections on the Detached House' 303
8.6 RICHARD SHONE 'A Cast in Time' 305
8.7 DAVID MORLEY 'Heimat, Modernity, and Exile' 309
8.8 LESLIE ROBERTSON 'Taming Space: Drug Use, HIV, and Homemaking in Downtown Eastside Vancouver' 314

Chapter 9: Literary Spaces 321

9.1 CHIARA BRIGANTI AND KATHY MEZEI House Haunting: The Domestic Novel of the Interwar Years 325
9.2 CYNTHIA WALL 'Gendering Rooms: Domestic Architecture and Literary Arts' 330
9.3 KAREN CHASE 'Jane Eyre's Interior Design' 335
9.4 JULIAN WOLFREYS Dwelling with Dickens and Heidegger 339
9.5 PHILIPPE HAMON Expositions: Literature and Architecture in Nineteenth-Century France 343
9.6 DIANA FUSS The Sense of an Interior: Four Writers and the Rooms That Shaped Them 346
9.7 HANNA SCOLNICOV Woman's Theatrical Space 349
9.8 SUPRIYA CHAUDHURI Interiors and Interiority in Nineteenth-Century India 351

9.9 HOMI K. BHABHA 'The World and the Home' 358
9.10 JINI KIM WATSON A Room in the City: Woman, Interiority, and Post-colonial Korean Fiction 363
9.11 WENDY THOMPSON Domestic Spaces in Children's Fantasy Literature 367
9.12 MATTHEW REYNOLDS Designs for a Happy Home: A Novel in Ten Interiors 371

Bibliography 377
Index 411

Figures

1 Rudyard Kipling's bungalow in Lahore c. 1897 (destroyed) 62
2 *St Jerome in His Study* by Albrecht Dürer, 1514 90
3 *View Down a Corridor* by Samuel van Hoogstraeten, 1662 95
4 *Tappé's Creations* by Thelma Cudlipp 132
5 *The Eavesdropper* by Nicolaes Maes, 1657 155
6 *Fun Home* by Alison Bechdel, 2010 173
7 *Vivienda actual* by Jorge Saravia Valle, 1986 184
8 Proposed modernized house by Jorge Saravia Valle, 1986 184
9 Interior of a *vivienda actual* by Jorge Saravia Valle, 1986 185
10 Interior of an 'improved' dwelling by Jorge Saravia Valle, 1986 185
11 The Frankfurt Kitchen by Margarete Schütte-Lihotsky, 1927 234
12 The Moller house by Adolf Loos, Vienna, 1928 253
13 Greek-revival house, Austin, Texas 267
14 Craftsman-style laneway houses in the Arbutus Ridge area of Vancouver, British Columbia 282
15 Kwakwaka'wakw village at the Chicago Fair, 1893 292
16 *House* by Rachel Whiteread, 1993 306

Acknowledgments

A *Reader* like this requires the effort, good will, and contributions of many – researchers, editors, publishers, and first and foremost, our distinguished contributors. We are grateful to them all.

We appreciate the extra efforts of Robert Mugerauer and William Glover. For their invaluable and diligent help in researching and compiling the *Reader,* we thank Katherine Delany, Jeff Fedoruk, Emily Fedoruk, Daniel Kline, Wendy Thompson, Natalie Wong, and Arianna Dini. We are most appreciative of the assistance of Carole Goldsmith, Ivana Niseteo, and Donald Taylor from the Simon Fraser University Library. The Department of Humanities at Simon Fraser University provided not only valuable facilities but also cheerful encouragement – in particular, we thank Christine Prisland, Wendy Sjolin, Alice Hartley, and David Mirhady. For technical assistance, we thank Anita Mahoney. Bev Neufield was most helpful with our grant applications. We have benefited greatly from the services of Clare Hall, Cambridge, the British Library, the London Library, the Munby Rare Books Room and the Architecture and History of Art Library, Cambridge, and the Cambridge University Library. For skilfully preparing the final manuscript, we are indebted to Robin Anderson. Our editor at the University of Toronto Press, Siobhan McMenemy, has been unfailing in her advice and support. We also are grateful for the assistance of Frances Mundy and Kate Baltais. For their helpful suggestions, we thank Christopher Reed, James and Nancy Duncan, Angus and Arlene McLaren, Paul Delany, Stephen Kline, Richard Shone. For their thoughtful input, Kathy thanks her students in Domestic Space courses in Humanities and Graduate Liberal Studies at Simon Fraser University and the vibrant Home Invaders Research Group – Fran Moore, Patrick Chan, Emily Fedoruk, Jillian Povarchook, Margaret Archibald, and Keith Higgins. Chiara thanks the College of Global Studies at Arcadia University for library resources. Our husbands, Paolo Dini and Robert Anderson, have often advised us wisely and assisted us practically. Without Dave Gaertner's efficiency, persistence, diplomacy, and most of all, his good humour, the completion of this *Reader* would not have been possible.

We express our sincere appreciation to the Social Sciences and Humanities Research Council of Canada and the British Academy for the funds to research and prepare this *Reader*.

Permissions

Considerable effort has been made to trace and contact copyright holders and to secure rights prior to publication. The editors and publishers apologize for any errors or omissions. If notified, the publisher will endeavour to correct these at the earliest opportunity.

Adams, Annmarie, from Chapter 4, 'Childbirth at Home' in *Architecture in the Family Way: Doctors, Houses, and Women 1870–1900*, 103–28. © 1996 by McGill-Queen's University Press. Used by permission of McGill-Queen's University Press.

Agnew, Jean-Christophe, from 'A House of Fiction: Domestic Interiors and the Commodity Aesthetic,' in Simon J. Bronner, ed., *Consuming Visions: Accumulation and Display of Goods in America, 1880–1920*, 133–55. © 1989 The Henry Francis du Pont Winterthur Museum, Inc. Used by permission of W.W. Norton & Company, Inc.

Alexander, Catherine, from 'The Garden as Occasional Domestic Space,' Forum: 'Domestic Space,' edited by Kathy Mezei and Chiara Briganti, *Signs: Journal of Women in Culture and Society* 27/3: 857–71. © 2002 The University of Chicago. Used by permission of The University of Chicago Press.

Bachelard, Gaston, from *The Poetics of Space*, translated by Maria Jolas. © 1964 The Orion Press, Inc. Original © 1958 Presses Universitaires de France. Used by permission of Viking Penguin, a division of Penguin Group (USA), Inc. and Les Presses Universitaires de France.

Bahloul, Joëlle, from 'Telling Places: The House as Social Architecture,' in *The Architecture of Memory: A Jewish-Muslim Household in Colonial Algeria,*

1937–1962, 28–50, translated by Catherine du Peloux Ménagé (Cambridge: Cambridge University Press, 1996). © English translation, Maison des Sciences de l'Homme and Cambridge University Press. Used by permission of Cambridge University Press.

Baudrillard, Jean, from *The System of Objects* [1968] (London: Verso, 1996). ©1996 Verso. Used by permission of Verso.

Benjamin, Walter, from *Charles Baudelaire: A Lyric Poet in the Era of High Capitalism*, 167–9 (London: Verso, 1983). © 1983. Used by permission of Verso.

Bhabha, Homi K., from 'The World and the Home,' *Social Text* 10 / 31–32: 141–53. © 1992 Duke University Press. All rights reserved. Used by permission of the publisher.

Borzello, Frances, from 'Looking for the Interior,' in *At Home: The Domestic Interior in Art,* 16–25. © 2006 Frances Borzello. Used by permission of Thames and Hudson Ltd., London.

Bourdieu, Pierre, from 'The Berber House or the World Reversed,' *Social Science Information* 9 / 2: 151–70. © 1970 SAGE publications. Used by permission of SAGE.

Briganti, Chiara, and Kathy Mezei, revised from 'House Haunting: The Domestic Novel of the Inter-war Years,' *Home Cultures* 1 / 2 (2004): 148–68. © Chiara Briganti and Kathy Mezei. Used by permission of Berg Publishers, an imprint of A&C Black Publishers Ltd.

Campo, Juan Eduardo, from *The Other Sides of Paradise: Explorations into the Religious Meaning of Domestic Space in Islam,* 98–138. © 1994. Used by permission of the University of South Carolina Press.

Chase, Karen, from '*Jane Eyre*'s Interior Design,' in *Eros & Psyche: The Representation of Personality in Charlotte Brontë*, 47–65. © 1984 Methuen. Used by permission of Taylor and Francis Books, UK.

Cieraad, Irene, from '"Out of My Kitchen!" Architecture, Gender and Domestic Efficiency,' *Journal of Architecture* 7 / 3 (2002): 263–79. © The Journal of Architecture. Used by permission of Taylor and Francis Ltd. (http://www.tandf.co.uk/journals) on behalf of The Journal of Architecture.

Cohen, Deborah, from 'In Possession: Men, Women, and Decoration,' in *Household Gods: The British and Their Possessions*, 98–121 (New Haven, CT: Yale University Press, 2006). © 2006 Yale University. Used by permission of Yale University Press.

Colomina, Beatriz, from *Privacy and Publicity: Modern Architecture as Mass Media,* 1,737-word excerpt from pages 74–99, text only. © 1994 Massachusetts Institute of Technology. Used by permission of The MIT Press.

Corbin, Alain, from 'Domestic Atmospheres,' in *The Foul and the Fragrant: Odor and the French Social Imagination*, 161–75 (Cambridge, MA: Harvard University Press, 1986). © Alain Corbin. Used by permission of Berg Publishers, an imprint of A&C Black Publishers Ltd. and Harvard University Press.

Crowley, John E., from 'Chimneys and Privacy,' in *The Invention of Comfort: Sensibilities and Design in Early Modern Britain and Early America*, 22–36 (Baltimore, MD: Johns Hopkins University Press, 2001). © 2001 The Johns Hopkins University Press. Used by permission of The Johns Hopkins University Press.

Douglas, Mary, from 'The Idea of a Home: A Kind of Space,' *Social Research* 58 / 1 (1991): 287–307. © Social Research. Used by permission of Social Research.

Duby, Georges, from 'The Aristocratic Households of Feudal France: Communal Living,' in *A History of Private Life,* vol. 2, *Revelations of the Medieval World,* , 35–85, edited by Georges Duby, translated by Arthur Goldhammer (Cambridge, MA: The Belknap Press of Harvard University Press, 1988). © 1988 the President and Fellows of Harvard College. Used by permission of the publisher.

Elias, Norbert, from 'On Behavior in the Bedroom,' in *The Civilizing Process: The History of Manners and State Formation and Civilization*, 132–38. © 1994 Blackwell. Used by permission of Blackwell Publishing Ltd.

Freud, Sigmund, from 'The Uncanny,' in the *Standard Edition of the Psychological Works of Sigmund Freud,* translated and edited by James Strachey, published by the Hogarth Press. © 1955 James Strachey. Used by permission of Nation Books, a member of the Perseus Books Group, and by permission of The Random House Group Ltd. and Paterson Marsh Ltd.

Fuss, Diana, from *The Sense of an Interior: Four Writers and the Rooms that Shaped Them* (New York: Routledge, 2004). Used by permission of Taylor and Francis Ltd. (http://www.informaworld.com).

Garber, Marjorie, from *Sex and Real Estate: Why We Love Houses.* © 2000 Marjorie Garber. Used by permission of Pantheon Books, a division of Random House, Inc.

Ginsburg, Rebecca, from '"Come in the Dark": Domestic Workers and Their Rooms in Apartheid-Era Johannesburg, South Africa,' *Perspectives in Vernacular Architecture* 8 (2000): 83–100. © 2000 Vernacular Architecture Forum. Used by permission of Vernacular Architecture Forum; and Rebecca Ginsburg, and in *At Home with Apartheid* © 2011 by the Rector and Visitors of the University of Virginia. Published by the University of Virginia Press.

Glover, William J., from 'A Feeling of Absence from Old England: The Colonial Bungalow,' *Home Cultures* 1 / 1 (2004): 61–82. © William J. Glover. Used by permission of Berg Publishers, an imprint of A&C Black Publishers Ltd.

Hamon, Philippe, from 'Introduction' to *Expositions: Literature and Architecture in Nineteenth-Century France*, 3–13 (Berkeley, CA: University of California Press, 1992). Used by permission of Editions Corti, Paris.

Hayden, Dolores, from *Redesigning the American Dream: Gender, Housing and Family Life* – Revised and expanded by Dolores Hayden. © 2002, 1984 Dolores Hayden. Used by Permission of W.W. Norton & Company, Inc. and Dolores Hayden.

Heidegger, Martin, from 'Building, Dwelling, Thinking,' in *Poetry, Language, Thought,* translation and introduction by Albert Hofstadter (New York: Harper and Row, 1971), 145–61. © Martin Heidegger. Used by permission of HarperCollins Publishers.

Hirschon, Renée, from 'Essential Objects and the Sacred: Interior and Exterior Space in Urban Greek Locality,' in Shirley Ardener, ed., *Women and Space: Ground Rules and Social Maps* (Oxford: Berg, 1993), 70–86. © Renée Hirschon. Used by permission of Berg Publishers, an imprint of A&C Black Publishers Ltd.

Ingold, Tim, from 'Building, Dwelling, Living: How Animals and People Make Themselves at Home in the World,' in Marilyn Strathern, ed., *Shifting Contexts:*

Transformation in Anthropological Knowledge (London: Routledge, 1995), 57–80. © 1995. Used by permission of Taylor and Francis Books, U.K.

Jung, Carl Gustav, from *Memories, Dreams, Reflections,* edited by Aniela Jaffé, translated by Richard and Clara Winston (London: Collins, 1989). © 1953 Carl Gustav Jung. Used by permission of HarperCollins Publishers Ltd. Translation © 1961, 1962, 1963 and renewed 1989, 1990, 1991 by Random House, Inc. Used by permission of Pantheon Books, a division of Random House, Inc.

Knights, Clive, from 'The Spatiality of the Roman Domestic Setting: An Interpretation of Symbolic Content,' in Michael Parker Pearson and Colin Richards, eds., *Architecture and Order: Approaches to Social Space* (New York: Routledge, 1994), 113–45. © 1994 Routledge. Used by permission of Taylor and Francis Books, U.K.

Le Corbusier, from *Towards A New Architecture,* excerpted from a facsimile of the work originally published by John Rodker, London, 1927, reprinted by The Architectural Press, London; Frederick A. Praeger, New York, 1978, translated by Frederick Etchells from the 13th French edition, originally published in Paris by Editions Crès. Used by permission of Elsevier.

Lefebvre, Henri, from *The Production of Space.* ©1991 Blackwell. Used by permission of Blackwell Publishing Ltd.

Lerup, Lars, from 'Planned Assaults: Reflections on the Detached House,' Special Issue, 'L'inquieto spazio domestico / Disputed Domestic Space,' edited by Pierluigi Nicolin, *Lotus International* 44 (1984): 76–81. Used by permission of Lotus International.

Marc, Olivier, from *The Psychology of The House.* © 1977 Olivier Marc. Used by permission of Thames and Hudson Ltd., U.K.

Marcus, Sharon, from Part One, Chapter One, 'Seeing through Paris,' in *Apartment Stories: City and Home in Nineteenth-Century Paris and London*, 17–50 (Berkeley, CA: University of California Press, 1999). © 1999 the Regents of the University of California. Used by permission of the University of California Press.

McDowell, Linda, from 'Rethinking Place: Thoughts on Spaces of the Home, Absence, Presence, New Connections and New Anxieties,' *Home Cultures* 4/2

(2007): 129–46. © Linda McDowell. Used by permission of Berg Publishers, an imprint of A&C Black Publishers Ltd.

Morley, David, from 'What's "Home" Got to Do with It? Contradictory Dynamics in the Domestication of Technology and the Dislocation of Domesticity,' *European Journal of Cultural Studies* 6 / 4: 435–58. © 2003 SAGE Publications. Used by permission of SAGE.

Morley, David, from *Home Territories: Media, Mobility and Identity*. © 2000 Routledge. Used by permission of Taylor and Francis Books, U.K.

Mugerauer, Robert, from 'Toward an Architectural Vocabulary: The Porch as a Between,' in David Seamon, ed., *Dwelling, Seeing, and Designing: Toward a Phenomenological Ecology*, 103–28 (Albany, NY: State University of New York Press, 1993). Used by permission of SUNY Press.

Raibmon, Paige, 'Living on Display: Colonial Visions of Aboriginal Domestic Spaces,' Special Issue 'Domestic Spaces,' edited by Kathy Mezei, *BC Studies* no. 140 (Winter 2003): 69–89. Used by permission of BC Studies and Paige Raibmon.

Reed, Christopher, from 'Taking Amusement Seriously: Modern Design in the Twenties,' in Penny Sparke et al., eds., *Designing the Modern Interior: From the Victorians to Today*, 79–93 (Oxford: Berg, 2009). © Christopher Reed. Used by permission of Berg Publishers, an imprint of A&C Black Publishers Ltd.

Reynolds, Matthew, from *Designs for a Happy Home: A Novel in Ten Interiors* (London: Bloomsbury, 2009). © Matthew Reynolds. Used by permission of the author c / o Rogers, Coleridge & White Ltd., 20 Powis Mews, London W11 1JN, and by Bloomsbury Publishing.

Robertson, Leslie, from 'Taming Space: Drug Use, HIV, and Homemaking in Downtown Eastside Vancouver,' *Gender, Place and Culture* 14 / 5 (2007): 527–49. Used by permission of Taylor and Francis Ltd. (http://www.informaworld.com).

Rybczynski, Witold, from 'Intimacy and Privacy,' in *Home: A Short History of an Idea* (New York: Viking, 1986), 14–49. © 1986 Witold Rybczynski. Used by permission of Viking Penguin, a division of Penguin Group (USA), Inc. and Witold Rybczynski.

Rykwert, Joseph, from *On Adam's House in Paradise: The Idea of the Primitive Hut in Architectural History*. © 1981 Joseph Rykwert. Used by permission of Harold Ober Associates, Inc.

Scolnicov, Hannah, from *Woman's Theatrical Space* (Cambridge: Cambridge University Press, 1994). © Cambridge University Press. Used by permission of Cambridge University Press.

Simmel, Georg, from 'The Bridge and the Door,' translated by Michael Kaern, *Qualitative Sociology* 17 / 4: 407–13. © 1994 Human Sciences Press, Inc. Used by permission of Springer Science + Media B.V.

Stea, David, from 'House and Home: Identity, Dichotomy, or Dialectic? (With Special Reference to Mexico),' in David N. Benjamin, ed., *The Home: Words, Interpretations, Meanings and Environments*, 181–201 (Aldershot: Ashgate; Brookfield, VT: Avebury, 1995). Used by permission of David Stea.

Stephenson, Marcia, from 'The Architectural Relationship between Gender, Race, and the Bolivian State,' in Ileana Rodríguez and Maria Milagros Lopez, eds., *The Latin American Subaltern Studies Reader*, 367–82 (Durham, NC: Duke University Press, 2001). © 2001 Duke University Press. All rights reserved. Used by permission of the publisher.

Teyssot, Georges, from '"Water and Gas on All Floors": Notes on the Extraneousness of the Home,' Special Issue, 'L'inquieto spazio domestico / Disputed Domestic Space,' edited by Pierluigi Nicolin, *Lotus International* 44 (1984): 82–93. Used by permission of Lotus International.

Verschaffel, Bart, from 'The Meanings of Domesticity,' *Journal of Architecture* 7 / 3 (2002): 287–96. © The Journal of Architecture. Used by permission of Taylor and Francis Ltd. (http://www.tandf.co.uk/journals) on behalf of The Journal of Architecture.

Vidler, Anthony, from *The Architectural Uncanny: Essays in the Modern Unhomely*, 3–14, © 1992 Massachusetts Institute of Technology. Used by permission of The MIT Press.

Wagner, George, from 'The Lair of the Bachelor,' in Debra Coleman, Elizabeth Danze, and Carol Henderson, eds., *Architecture and Feminism*, 183–220 (New York: Princeton Architectural Press, 1996). Used by permission of the Princeton Architectural Press.

Wall, Cynthia, from 'Gendering Rooms: Domestic Architecture and Literary Arts,' *Eighteenth-Century Fiction* 5/4 (1993): 349–72. Used by permission of Eighteenth-Century Fiction.

Wilk, Christopher, from 'Frankfurt Kitchen, 1926–27. Designed by Grete Lihotsky' (Margarete Schütte-Lihotsky; 1897 Vienna–2000 Vienna). From the Am Höhenblick Housing Estate, Ginnheim, Frankfurt,' in Christopher Wilk, ed., *Modernism: 1914–1939, Designing a New World*, 180–1 (London: V&A Publications, 2006). Used by permission of V&A Publications.

Young, Iris Marion, from 'House and Home: Feminist Variations on a Theme,' in *Intersecting Voices: Dilemmas of Gender, Political Philosophy, and Policy*, 134–64 (Princeton, NJ: Princeton University Press, 1997). © 1997 Princeton University Press. Used by permission of Princeton University Press.

THE DOMESTIC SPACE READER

CHAPTER ONE

Introduction

What Is Domestic Space?

> Home is where one starts from.
>
> T.S. Eliot, *Four Quartets*

> A whole history remains to be written of spaces – which would at the same time be the history of powers [...] from the great strategies of geo-politics to the little tactics of the habitat.
>
> Michel Foucault, *Power/Knowledge*

This *Reader* gathers together significant writing on domestic space through history and across cultures and disciplines, ranging from anthropology to fiction. As its Latin source (*domesticus; domus*) suggests, 'domestic' signifies of/belonging to the home, house, or household. And so the concept, 'domestic space,' as presented in this *Reader*, takes into account the material, psychological, spiritual, gendered, social, cultural, and political aspects of house, home, and garden in the context of the everyday and of human relationships within and beyond the house.

Incorporating foundational sources as well as contemporary and occasionally controversial contributions, the *Reader* demonstrates how discussions of domestic space not only lead us to a deeper understanding of the individual and the inner self, but also to question traditional perceptions of historical periods, society, the public, and national ideologies and practices. As conceptualized here, domestic space looks both inward at interior designs, objects, technologies, and differentiated spaces inside the house and outward to gates, paths, laneways, and patios. It blurs the borders between inside and outside, private and public, physical and psychological; it also encompasses spaces beyond traditional ideas of home such as trains and ships, hospitals, daycares, prisons, shops, what Michel Foucault described as 'other spaces' or 'heterotopias.'[1]

Writing in 1995, anthropologists Janet Carsten and Stephen Hugh-Jones lamented that 'much of the more comparative and theoretical work on the anthropology of architecture has been done not by anthropologists but by architects and art historians [...] One reason for this neglect is that houses get taken for granted.'[2]

In the past decade, far from being taken for granted, houses have been the subject of growing and interested multidisciplinary inquiry. The immense reach and influence of global and transnational economies have provoked a contrary desire for the local and the domestic, which has increased the scrutiny of the home. This scrutiny inevitably generates a multitude of questions, which the following selections seek to address: how does one configure and interpret the home in relation to nation, political ideologies, the everyday, domestic rituals, built dwellings, and social relationships? How is the construction of self and subjectivity connected to one's domestic space? What does it mean to belong? And by what means do we distinguish between the domestic interior and architectural metaphors as representational or analogical and the architectural and domestic as epistemological and ontological, as ways of thinking, knowing, being? Might it be that, as Diana Fuss has argued, 'to attribute substance and materiality to architecture, and imagination and metaphor to literature, misreads both artistic forms'? And when we recompose 'the too easy bifurcation between literal and figurative space' that architecture and literature reinforce, 'the seemingly intractable distinction between literary metaphor and architectural reality [...] quickly falls away' (see section 9.6 in this volume). How, as Anthony King has suggested, do we find ways of writing about architecture and the built environment that pay 'attention to questions of meaning and the social, economic, political, and cultural as well as spatial processes through which the built environment is produced?'[3]

Given the pervasiveness of houses in literature, when is the house emblematic in itself and when is it a structure that shapes human actions? Could it be, as Philippe Hamon (see section 9.5 in this volume) claims à propos of nineteenth-century French fiction, that the extent to which the house lodged itself in the nineteenth-century realist tradition indicates that 'the writer henceforth would always have to provide housing for his characters, to make them inhabitants; no longer would he be able to describe any of his heroes' habits [...] without also mentioning their habitat'?

Domestic space as an increasingly pertinent subject of inquiry is obviously linked to the mid-twentieth-century 'spatial turn' in critical thinking. For, as

Foucault contended, our era 'seems to be that of space. We are in the age of the simultaneous, of juxtaposition, the near and the far, the side by side and the scattered.'[4] We see this turn to the spatial, and to buildings in particular, in the writings of Walter Benjamin (see section 3.8), Martin Heidegger (section 2.2), Gaston Bachelard (section 2.1), Henri Lefebvre (section 2.3), and Michel Foucault's study of prisons and the Panopticon.[5] Fredric Jameson and Jacques Derrida have examined architecture as a form of writing, way of thinking, and mode of being and the interpellation of space, power, knowledge, and politics.[6] Indeed, 'deconstruction,' Derrida's influential concept that seeks to expose the paradoxes in Western thought and discourse can be seen as a spatial concept emerging from architectural materiality. Jürgen Habermas, Nancy Fraser, Richard Sennett, and David Harvey further extended spatial meaning to analyse public and civic spheres, while Arjun Appadurai, Homi Bhabha (see section 9.9), and Anthony King have directed attention to post-colonial and transnational spaces and cultures.[7]

Although the *Reader* does not purport to be a complete history of spaces and power, it seeks to unveil the ways in which negotiation of space exposes negotiations of power from the 'great strategies' of nations and the global economy to the 'little tactics' of habitat and home. For, after all, one of the derivatives of the Latin word *domus* is 'dominate': 'in one French usage, *domestiquer* means quite simply the subjugation of a tribe to a colonizing power.'[8]

House and Home: Definitions and Challenges

Any discussion of domestic spaces naturally invokes two of its central components, *house* and *home*. Whereas the house is generally perceived to be a physical built dwelling for people in a fixed location, the home,[9] although it may possess the material characteristics of a built dwelling, implies a space, a feeling, an idea, not necessarily located in a fixed place. Noting that the history of the house is the history of the dialectic that emerges between the two imperatives of shelter and identity, Gerry Smyth and Jo Croft remind us that 'although protection from the elements would remain its [the house's] primary function, it could not have been long before the dwelling [...] became an arena for more complex human practices.'[10] It is these 'complex human practices' of the house that furnish the intricacies of the concept of home. As David Benjamin cautions, 'the home is a symbol, so that even though we recognize it, and "know it," it will always defy a rational deconstruction and complete explication of its meaning content.'[11] And despite Robert Frost's famous and debated lines in 'The Death of a Hired Man' – 'Home is the place where, when you have to go there, / They have to take you in'– Roderick Lawrence serves up the caveat, reflected in a number of contributions to this *Reader,* that 'the concept of home is ambiguous, and therefore, it cannot be taken for granted.'[12] Not only belonging but also exile, longing for home, homelessness, and homesickness are incorporated in the idea and experience of home. One has to agree with Angelika Bammer that 'perhaps [...] the best we can do about home at this point in time is to bring it, in all its complexity, out into the open.'[13] And once we bring home out into the open what we discover is its strikingly adaptive and resilient quality, its ability to be shelter and labyrinth, vessel of desire and of terror, Le Corbusier's 'machine for living' and the surrealists' 'convulsive theatre of the domestic.'[14]

Between Private and Public

> Perhaps our life is still governed by a certain number of oppositions that remain inviolable, that our institutions and practices have not yet dared to break down. These are the oppositions that we regard as simple givens: for example, between private space and public space.
>
> Michel Foucault, 'Of Other Spaces'

Foucault's 'simple givens' have not gone unchallenged. The idea of home as a fixed place, capable of connecting past and future, and separate from public space, has been queried by scholars who have pointed out how such an idea, absent from many pre-modern or non-Western societies, is predicated on settled and unitary communities and has been remapped by migration.

Thus, they have called for 'a future-oriented project of constructing a sense of belonging in a context of change and displacement'[15] (see McDowell, Raibmon, Morley, and Bhabha in this volume). Others, attending to cultures in which individual identity is inseparable from family or from the larger community, have focused on the way in which specific kinship structures bear upon the idea of boundaries that is foundational to 'privacy' (see Stea, Passes, Thanegi, Ozaki, Hirschon, Ginsburg, and Watson in this volume). To follow David Stea (section 2.7), 'the hard walls define a boundary between the private and public realm, but public and private to whom?'

The permeability of such boundaries is inscribed in what we have called the 'liminal space' (Alexander, Simmel, Marc, Bahloul, Colomina, Mugerauer, Robinson-Tomsett, and Chan in this volume), and is often challenged in the seemingly private spaces and home parts of bathrooms, bedrooms, kitchens, and domestic technologies (Baudrillard, Ashenburg, Elias, Wilk, Cieraad, and Morley in this volume).

This permeability as well as the inextricable connection between private and public, power and space, geopolitics and habitat, and the home and the world is embedded in the word 'economy,' whose origin lies in the Greek *oikos* (house) and *nomos* (rule, law). While in the seventeenth century *oikonomia* ceased to denote 'household management' and came to signify 'manage the resources of a country' (short for political economy), traces of the original remain. For instance, for Mary Pattison, writing in North America in 1915, 'the house was the nation [the family] administered.'[16] Insisting on this connection, Jon Hegglund has noted how in the Edwardian period, 'the future of England depended on the fitness of its houses.'[17]

Commenting upon the link between the proliferation of built forms and the emergence of a capitalist world economy – a 'global culture' – Anthony King has demonstrated how 'a particular type of individual and consumer-oriented suburban and resort development, represented by the bungalow, has developed – first in the countries of the English-speaking ecumene, but later, selectively round the world.'[18]

Marx had argued that the home provides the site for reproduction and thus for the production of future labour power. If it is economically viable, the house shelters parents and children, and stores and produces the food that will nurture them. But then during the 1920s and 1930s, particularly in North America, domestic space was dramatically impacted by capitalism and consumer culture. House, home, and 'housekeeping' were guided by laws of efficiency, the assembly line, and Taylorism, as well as by the imperative to consume the products of the assembly line – stoves, fridges, vacuum cleaners, washing machines – purportedly labour-saving devices. In 1950s Turkey, consumerism was promoted to stave off the danger of communism. Popular magazines, Hollywood movies, and advertisements all contributed to create a version of domestic space presided over by the 'modern' Turkish woman as a homemaker – a mother, a wife, a domestic manager, and a fashionably dressed Western figure.[19] More recently, in contemporary Britain, markets, migration, and political pressures have redrawn the boundaries of home (McDowell and Morley in this volume).

Unpacking Domestic Space

> She is the house; there is no separation possible.
>
> Alice Munro, 'The Office'

Just as the home is affected by and replicates national and capitalist ideologies and agendas in microcosm (see Stea, Glover, Stephenson, and Raibmon in this volume), the social geography of the house itself charts the course of relations between sexes and classes (see McDowell, Thanegi, Benjamin, Hayden, Ginsburg, and Morley in this volume). The house and home are frequently perceived as symbols of the self, the psyche, and the body. For example, the identification of the house with the female body gained noticeable momentum in modernity, as Alice Munro acerbically quipped above. This is strikingly evident in the correspondences between fashion and interior decoration that were so profitably exploited by Emily Burbank (section 4.3).

Although this identification of the decorative female body with the home, and of women as homebound and housekeepers, was perceived as detrimental to women's independence and selfhood in early feminism, Iris Marion Young (section 5.10) offers a more nuanced approach by arguing 'that while politics should not succumb to a longing for comfort and unity, the material values of home can nevertheless provide leverage for radical social critique.' She suggests that home can have a political meaning as a site of dignity, resistance, and preservation of values (see also Cohen, Hirschon, Stephenson, and van Herk in this volume). The home can also serve as a fertile site for the subversion of and resistance to convention, stereotypes, and dogma, whether sexual or ideological (see Reed, Wagner, and Cook in this volume), and thus elaborate the definitions and concepts of home and household.

Much recent research has implicitly agreed with Bart Verschaffel's (section 5.1) plea for the avoidance of reductive interpretations and for contributions that promote the discourse of domestic space in fruitful ways. Thus, for instance, the masculine premise of Bachelard's blindness to 'the suffocating house and the sick home'[20] has been taken to task, in particular by feminists, perhaps never more compellingly than by Louise Bourgeois in her installations, *Cells*, and in the iconic half-house, half-naked woman of her *Femme maison* sculpture series. As Homi Bhabha (section 9.9) argues, by making visible the forgetting of the 'unhomely' moment in civil society, feminism specifies the patriarchal, gendered nature of civil society and disturbs the symmetry of private and public which is now shadowed, or uncannily doubled, by the difference of genders which does not neatly map on to the private and the public, but becomes disturbingly supplementary to them.[21] (See also Freud and Vidler in this volume.)

Emerging and Multidisciplinary Interest in Domestic Space

The selections in this *Reader* demonstrate how increasingly complex analyses of gender, the unhomely, and the elasticity of the concept of home have unpacked simplistic, nostalgic, or sentimental understandings of house, home, and household.

From the popular to the academic and across national boundaries, the subject of domestic space has of late garnered enormous attention. Besides drawing the notice of the media (television home improvement shows, real estate programs, popular magazines, dedicated sections on the home in newspapers, Facebook, and YouTube), and inviting obsessive, even erotic attention,[22] it has become an important academic subject. For example, geographers James Duncan and David Lambert observe that 'with increased interest in the everyday, the production of space in a globalizing world [...] with feminist destabilizing of the private-public dichotomy [...] as well as renewed interest in the body [...] emotions [...] and psychoanalysis,' the home has become a main topic of interest for geographers.[23]

This flourishing interest is evident in the rise of new journals (*Home Cultures, Journal of Design History, Interiors, Design and Culture*); dedicated research networks such as Making Home; interdisciplinary discussion on domesticity; and specialized museums (e.g., Geffrye Museum, Design Museum in London, Museu do Design e da Moda in Lisbon), not to mention displays such as Rachel Whiteread's famous London installation, '*House* (see Shone in this volume), or the 'Surreal House' exhibition at the Barbican Art Gallery, London (June–Sept. 2010). A number of special issues of journals have been devoted to the 'home,' for example, 'Home: A Place in the World,' *Social Research* 58, no. 1 (Spring 1991); 'The Meaning and Use of Home,' special issue of the *Journal of Architectural and Planning Research* 8, no. 2 (Summer 1991); 'The Question of Home,' in *New Formations* 17 (Summer 1992); 'Espaces domestiques' in *Annales de Géographie* 110, no. 620 (July–Aug. 2001); Forum: 'Domestic Space,' *Signs* 27, no. 3 (Spring 2002); 'Domestic Spaces,' special issue of *BC Studies*, no. 140 (Winter 2003); 'Home,' *M/C Journal* 10, no. 4 (2007), available at http://journal.media-culture.org.au/0708//01. In addition, several important essay collections on the home have appeared such as Christopher Reed, ed., *Not At Home: The Suppression of the Domestic in Modern Art and Architecture* (1996); Irene Cieraad, ed., *At Home: An Anthropology of Domestic Space* (1999); Tony Chapman and Jenny Hockey, eds., *Ideal Homes? Social Change and Domestic Life* (1999); Daniel Miller, ed., *Home Possessions: Material Culture Behind Closed Doors* (2001); Jeremy Aynsley and Charlotte Grant, eds., *Imagined Interiors: Representing the Domestic Interior since the Renaissance* (2006); Gerry Smyth and Jo Croft, *Our House: The Representation of Domestic Space in Modern Culture* (2006); Mark Taylor and Julieanna Preston, *Intimus: Interior Design Theory Reader* (2006); Alison Blunt and Robyn Dowling, eds., *Home* (2006); Barbara Miller Lane, ed., *Housing and Dwelling: Perspectives on Modern Domestic Architecture* (2007); Penny Sparke, Anne Massey, and Brenda Martin, eds., *Designing the Modern Interior: From the Victorians to Today* (2009); and Ben Highmore, ed., *Design Culture Reader* (2009); Lois Weinthal, *Toward a*

New Interior: An Anthology of Interior Design Theory (2011). Elsevier's extensive *International Encyclopedia of Housing and Home* was published in 2012.

However, the very abundance of material in diverse locations, while testifying to a constantly growing interest in the field, has proven unwieldy for both scholars and students. In many cases the texts that are available are discipline specific; others have an almost exclusive Anglo-American or primarily modern approach. To provide a more exhaustive, historical, cross-cultural, and multidisciplinary coverage, our *Reader* includes material from the humanities, philosophy, literature, arts, interior design, media, gender studies, and architectural history, as well as the social sciences (geography, anthropology, and sociology). By dedicating a chapter to literary domestic spaces, as well as presenting a number of entries on artistic representations of and responses to domestic spaces and offering a wide-ranging array of material from the humanities, the *Reader* corrects an earlier imbalance in scholarship in this field, which focused on the social sciences to the detriment of the humanities and the arts.

The Structure of the *Reader*

This *Reader* is structured so that it can be studied effectively in conjunction with other primary materials such as novels, paintings, and buildings. Its aim is to provide an essential resource for scholars, instructors, and students in programs as varied as gender studies and design and art history, and to respond to the increasingly interdisciplinary nature of education and scholarship. The *Reader* does not propose to present the essays in comfortable cohabitation. While several of the essays gathered here gain their impetus from Martin Heidegger and / or Gaston Bachelard (such as those by Ingold, Bahloul, Wolfreys, and Fuss), others challenge Bachelard's universalism and Heidegger's attribution of a plenitude of meanings to dwelling. Charlotte Perkins Gilman (section 8.1), for instance, in deeming the myth of home to be a tenacious and deep-rooted superstition, anticipates much criticism of the unproblematic benignity of Bachelard's topophilia; Henri Lefebvre (section 2.3) historicizes Bachelard's (and Heidegger's) 'obsession with absolute space' by locating its raison d'être in the climate of insecurity and loss after the Second World War; Supriya Chaudhuri (section 9.8) notes the distance that separates Bachelard's rapturous phenomenological celebration of European domestic spaces from the spatial experiences of Indian cultural history; and David Morley (section 6.13) contends that diverse socio-economic factors inflect the ability to sentimentalize the home. Marcia Stephenson (section 5.8) demonstrates how the linking of womanhood and motherhood with the home is determined by a colonial imperative, while Irene Cieraad (section 6.11) goes beyond the commonly held argument that efficiency strategies were a solution to the domestic servant shortage.

The essays, which include specially commissioned as well as seminal published pieces, are arranged thematically in chapters with short explanatory introductions; the *Reader* concludes with a Bibliography of the field. The chapter topics are: The Idea of Home; Interiors; House / Body / Psyche; Gendered Space; Home Parts; Liminal Spaces; Contested Spaces; and Literary Spaces.

'The Idea of Home' (chapter 2) offers a cross-section of the diverse yet linked concepts of home, from the philosophical and phenomenological (Bachelard and Heidegger) to the sociological, anthropological, and geographical (Lefebvre, Douglas, and McDowell) to the post-colonial (Glover), touching upon the animal kingdom (Ingold), and exploring different religious and cultural approaches, as found among the Berbers (Bourdieu), in Mexico (Stea), the Amazon (Passes), and Islam (Campo).

In 'Interiors' (chapter 3), the selections demonstrate the historical and cultural evolution of the domestic interior from the primitive hut (Rykwert) to the Pompeian house (Knights) to the modern Japanese home (Ozaki), and probe different, at times unusual, aspects of the interior including odours (Corbin), communist experiences with communal kitchens (Hayden), and artistic representations of the domestic interior (Borzello). They focus on the evolving, shifting, and culturally determined concept of privacy and comfort (Duby, Rybczynski, Thanegi, Kerr, Benjamin, Marcus, Todd, and Mortimer).

'House / Body / Psyche' (chapter 4) offers examples of the deeply rooted connection between the home and human anatomy (Garber, Adams, Burbank, Agnew, and Teyssot) and the unconscious (Jung, Freud, and Vidler), and in particular, the haunted and unhomely aspects of home and household and modernity (Freud and Vidler).

In 'Gendered Space' (chapter 5), we present selections that expose the interpellation of gender, sexuality, and the home including the feminization of space (Verschaffel, Nicholson, Livett, Stephenson, and Hirschon), queer space (Reed and Cook), masculinity and the home (Cohen and Wagner), and a revisioning of traditional feminine household occupations (Young and van Herk).

Rooms and objects in the home are explored in 'Home Parts' (chapter 6), including chimneys (Crowley), furniture (Poe), bathrooms (Beecher and Beecher, Ashenburg), bedrooms (Elias), nurseries (Peel), knick-knacks and household possessions (Baudrillard, Wharton and Codman Jr, and Morley), kitchens (Beeton, Wilk, and Cieraad), and television, radios, and telephones (Kline and Morley).

Spaces that cross the boundaries of private and public and inside and outside are the focus of 'Liminal Spaces' (chapter 7): doors (Simmel, Marc, and Bahloul), windows (Colomina), the porch (Mugerauer), the garden (Alexander), trains and ships (Robinson-Tomsett), and Vancouver laneways (Chan).

Home as a site of controversy is examined in 'Contested Spaces' (chapter 8), with attention paid to Aboriginal homes (Raibmon), South African apartheid (Ginsburg), modern designs (Le Corbusier and Lerup), homelessness (Morley and Robertson), economic efficiency (Gilman), and controversial artistic installations (Shone).

In 'Literary Spaces' (chapter 9), we present a selection of literary genres: poetry (Fuss, Hamon), fiction (Briganti and Mezei, Wall, Chase, Wolfreys, Hamon, Fuss, Chaudhuri, Bhabha, and Watson), theatre (Scolnicov), fantasy (Thompson), and an excerpt from a contemporary novel (Reynolds) that offer models for reading and analysing the pervasive significance and role of domestic space in literary texts.

The concluding Bibliography contains many of the key works related to domestic space in a range of disciplines.

Each chapter connects the different disciplinary approaches and subjects. For instance, in 'Liminal Spaces,' doors are the topic of selections from the social scientist Georg Simmel, from the anthropologist Joëlle Bahloul who examines doors and memories in colonial Algeria, and from the cultural historian Olivier Marc whose psychological approach resonates with Carl Jung's articulation of the house as symbolic of the psyche presented in the earlier 'House / Body / Psyche' chapter. Thus the walls between the chapters are porous and allow the essays to enter into conversation with each other. In the 'Literary Spaces' chapter, for example, the trope of the door is also central to Diana Fuss's analysis of Emily Dickinson's poetry and letters.

Future Directions

The diversity and range of material in this collection suggests that the seemingly everyday practical space of the home offers a surprisingly rich resource to mine for the understanding of cultures, peoples, and histories. The essays draw attention not only to how humans (and other species) inhabit domestic space, but also to how domestic space inhabits us,[24] and to how potently and poetically it influences our ways of being, thinking, and discourse. They note that the domestic rather than being opposed to the outside is a kind of 'mediating skin'[25] through which the external world (food, clothes, furniture, and visitors) passes and enters the inner private domain of the home, and thus continually transforms it. They recognize that domestic space – the very idea of home – is changing to incorporate, once again, work spaces, salons, galleries, food production, and the home garden.

In the current turn to things and objects evident in art exhibits such as Tracey Emin's notorious 'Bed' at the Saatchi Gallery in London (see www.saatchi-gallery.co.uk/artists/.../tracey_emin_my_bed.htm), and publications such as Daniel Miller's *The Comfort of Things* (2008) or *The Object Reader,* by Fiona Candlin and Raiford Guins (2009), we see the desire to peel away the layered meanings of home.[26] Similarly, as the concept of 'citizen' shifts from the civic to the transglobal to the homeless, domestic space in all its ramifications and possibilities models a welcoming venue for a renewed and invigorated discourse on being and belonging. While this collection does not and cannot claim to be exhaustive, it does seek to offer its readers a fertile sampling of the many possible and engaging entries into domestic space. Here is an opportunity not only to step into other homes, but to come home again.

A Note Concerning the Format of Reprinted Excerpts

In the contributions that have been previously published, we have retained the original spelling and punctuation unless there were errors. Brackets around ellipses indicate deleted material; ellipses without brackets are part of the original text, and all material in italics for emphasis is in italics in the original unless otherwise noted.

NOTES

1 Michel Foucault, 'Of Other Spaces,' translated by Jay Miscowiec, *Diacritics* 16/1 (1986): 26.

2 Janet Carsten and Stephen Hugh-Jones, eds., *About the House: Lévi-Strauss and Beyond* (Cambridge: Cambridge University Press, 1995), 3.

3 Anthony D. King, *The Bungalow: The Production of a Global Culture* (London: Routledge, 1984), xiii.

4 Foucault, 'Of Other Spaces,' 22.

5 Michel Foucault, *Discipline and Punishment: The Birth of the Prison* (New York: Vintage, 1979).

6 Jacques Derrida, *Specters of Marx: The State of the Debt, the Work of Mourning, and the New International*, translated by Peggy Kamuf (London: Routledge, 1994); Frederic Jameson, 'Is Space Political?' in Neil Leach, ed., *Rethinking Architecture: A Reader in Cultural Theory* (London: Routledge, 1999), 255–69.

7 Jürgen Habermas, *The Structural Transformation of the Public Sphere: An Inquiry into a Category of Bourgeois Society* (Cambridge, MA: MIT Press, 1991); Nancy

Fraser, *Scales of Justice: Reimagining Public Space in a Globalizing World* (New York: Columbia University Press, 2008); Richard Sennett, *The Corrosion of Character: The Personal Consequences of Work in the New Capitalism* (New York: Norton, 1998); David Harvey, *Spaces of Capital: Towards a Critical Geography* (New York: Routledge, 2001); Arjun Appadurai, *The Social Life of Things: Commodities in Cultural Perspective* (Cambridge: Cambridge University Press, 1986); Anthony D. King, *Buildings and Society: Essays on the Social Development of the Built Environment* (London: Routledge and Kegan Paul, 1980).

8 Rachel Bowlby, 'Domestication,' in Diane Elam and Robyn Wiegman, eds., *Feminism beside Itself* (London: Routledge, 1995), 75.

9 The *Oxford English Dictionary* states that 'home' is derived from the Old English *hām* and the High German *heim* and that the Old English and Middle English meaning is 'a village or town; a village with its cottages'; other meanings include 'a dwelling-place; house; abode; the fixed residence of a family or household'; 'a place, region, or state to which one properly belongs, in which one's affections centre, or where one finds rest, refuge, or satisfaction' (1548); 'one's own country, one's native land' (1595); 'home' also means a reference to the grave (M.E.) and in games, 'the place where one is free from attack.' The origins of 'house' are equally interesting and complex – from Old English and Old High German *hüs*. Various meanings include a building for human habitation, esp. a dwelling-place; the portion of a building occupied by one tenant or family; a place of worship; an inn, tavern (1550); a religious house, a college in a university; a boarding-house attached to a public school (1857); the building in which a legislative assembly meets; a place of business; a theatre; the persons living in one dwelling (O.E.); a family, lineage, race.

10 Gerry Smyth and Jo Croft, eds., *Our House: The Representations of Domestic Space in Modern Culture* (Amsterdam: Rodopi, 2006), 13.

11 David N. Benjamin, 'Introduction,' in David N. Benjamin, ed., *The Home: Words, Interpretations, Meanings, and Environments* (Aldershot: Ashgate; Brookfield, VT: Avebury, 1995), 3.

12 Roderick J. Lawrence, 'The Meaning and Use of Home,' Special Issue, 'The Meaning and Use of Home,' edited by Roderick J. Lawrence, *Journal of Architectural and Planning Research* 8/2 (1991), 93.

13 Angelika Bammer, 'Editorial: The Question of "Home,"' *New Formations,* no. 17 (1992): xi.

14 See Kate Bush, 'Foreword,' in Jane Alison, *The Surreal House* (London and New Haven, CT: Barbican Art Gallery, in association with Yale University Press, 2010), 8.

15 Nikos Papastergiadis, *Dialogues in the Diasporas* (London: Rivers Oram Press, 1998), 7; cited in David Morley, *Home Territories: Media, Mobility and Identity* (London: Routledge, 2000), 43 (see also section 8.7 in this volume).

16 Mary Pattison, *Principles of Domestic Engineering: Or the What, Why and How of a Home* (New York: Trow Press, 1915), cited in Jennifer Craik, 'The Making of Mother: The Role of the Kitchen in the Home,' in Graham Allen and Graham Crow, eds., *Home and Family: Creating the Domestic Sphere* (London: Macmillan, 1989), 49.

17 Jon Hegglund, 'Defending the Realm: Domestic Space and Mass Cultural Contamination in *Howards End* and *An Englishman's Home*,' *English Literature in Transition* 40 / 4 (1997): 400.

18 King, *The Bungalow*, xi.

19 Meltem Ö Gürel, 'Woman as Representative of Turkish Modernization and the Modern Domicile in the Mid-20th Century,' paper delivered at the 9th Annual Dorich House Conference, 'Fashioning the Modern Interior,' Kingston University, London, 17–18 May 2007.

20 Bart Verschaffel, 'The Meanings of Domesticity,' *Journal of Architecture* 7 / 3 (2002): 294.

21 Turning to Freud to critique Bachelard's romanticization of the ideal childhood home, which finds no room for the *unheimlich*, Rachel Bowlby has pointed out that 'in psychoanalysis the home is no place of harmony' [...] [for] the house [...] is irredeemably driven by the presence of ghosts, its comforting appearance of womblike unity, doubled from the start by intruding forces [...] untimely and dislocated hauntings of other times and places and other presences' ('Domestication,' 75).

22 'Real estate today has become a form of yuppie pornography [...] Sex and real estate are two of the most erotic terms in the language. Especially when you put them together.' Marjorie Garber, *Sex and Real Estate: Why We Love Houses* (New York: Pantheon, 2000), 3. (See also section 4.1 in this volume.)

23 James S. Duncan and David Lambert, 'Landscapes of Home,' in James S. Duncan, Nuala C. Johnson, and Richard H. Schein, eds., *A Companion to Cultural Geography* (Oxford: Blackwell, 2004), 382–3.

24 Fuss, *The Sense of an Interior: Four Writers and the Rooms that Shaped Them* (New York: Routledge, 2004), 2.

25 Lisa Robertson, 'Citizenship and Domestic Space,' unpublished paper, May 2010.

26 See, for instance, the exhibition 'The Everyday Life of Objects,' University of Wisconsin, Madison, 2007, available at http://www.everydaylifeofobjects.net; Sharmila Samant's photographs of everyday objects that have been used as explosive devices (Lakereen Gallery, Mumbai, April–May 2010); Haris Epaminonda's displaced objects 'Vol. VI,' Tate Modern, London, May–Aug. 2010.

CHAPTER TWO

The Idea of Home

The diversity of ideas of home is indicated in the following samples, which range across historical periods, geographical locations, and cultures. Ideas of home are contingent on place and time, reflect religious and cultural practices, and are modulated by economic and social factors; they shape and are themselves shaped by kinship structures and gender roles. In one of the seminal texts on domestic space, *The Poetics of Space,* Gaston Bachelard evokes the phenomenological significance of the image of the house – its attics, cellars, doors, windows, hearths, drawers, corners, and nooks and crannies – and the 'primitive hut' – for our intimate being and imaginative life. Martin Heidegger's ontological meditation on the necessity to dwell in order to build and to think within his fourfold cosmology of earth, sky, divinities, and mortals permeates many of the contemporary contributions in this collection. In his Marxist and materialist approach, Henri Lefebvre situates the idea of the house within urban modernity and critiques Bachelard's quasi-religious, cosmological 'poetics of space' and 'topophilia' as well as Heidegger's ontology in which 'building' is close to 'thinking.' Drawing on Heidegger's distinction between building and dwelling, Timothy Ingold compares how humans and animals (molluscs, beavers, apes) design and execute their homes and shelters. From a sociological and structuralist perspective, Pierre Bourdieu minutely details the binary spatial organization of a Berber household into masculine / feminine, inside / outside, nocturnal / daylight, nature / culture, while Juan Campo's investigation of the sacrality of religion, in this case Islam in modern Egypt, demonstrates how the idea of home is connected to the ways in which religious symbols and practices are domesticated. From the perspective of ancient and modern Mexican households, David Stea shows how the house is not necessarily a high priority in all cultures, how homes replicate entire social systems on a household level, and how families strive to maintain cultural continuity in the face of social change.

In her classic essay, Mary Douglas maintains that home, while not necessarily fixed in space, is a localizable idea, which represents the organization of space over time and a form of exchange and transaction. Although, like hotel space, it has differentiated and allocated spaces, the space of the home differs in offering a much wider scope of intention (e.g., a space in which to raise children); it also enacts a tyranny over the mind and body of its inhabitants. Linda McDowell pursues these social and economic determinates of the idea of home in her analysis of the effects of contemporary social mobility, labour, and immigration practices on the interrelation of home, domesticity, and gender. In his examination of the 'bungalow' during the Raj in India, William Glover queries the assumptions that have shaped histories of colonial urbanism and explores the physical and social consequences of the intermingling of British Victorian concepts of domestic spatial organization with local Punjabi domestic practices and features. Alan Passes discusses a vital yet often unacknowledged aspect of the home by explaining how Amazonian domestic spaces and acts are deeply social and political and how the home, the basis of society, deliberately includes the domestication of destructive and antisocial beings.

2.1 GASTON BACHELARD
'The House from Cellar to Garret. The Significance of the Hut'*

I

À la porte de la maison qui viendra frapper?
Une porte ouverte on entre
Une porte fermée un antre
Le monde bat de l'autre côté de ma porte.

Pierre Albert Birot, *Les Amusements Naturels*

(At the door of the house who will come knocking?
An open door, we enter
A closed door, a den
The world pulse beats beyond my door.)

The house, quite obviously, is a privileged entity for a phenomenological study of the intimate values of inside space, provided, of course, that we take it in both its unity and its complexity, and endeavour to integrate all the special values in one fundamental value. For the house furnishes us dispersed images and a body of images at the same time. In both cases, I shall prove that imagination augments the values of reality. A sort of attraction for images concentrates them about the house. Transcending our memories of all the houses in which we have found shelter, above and beyond all the houses we have dreamed we live in, can we isolate an intimate, concrete essence that would be a justification of the uncommon value of all our images of protected intimacy? This, then, is the main problem.

In order to solve it, it is not enough to consider the house as an 'object' on which we can make our judgments and daydreams react. For a phenomenologist, a psychoanalyst, or a psychologist (these three points of view being named in the order of decreasing efficacy), it is not a question of describing houses, or enumerating their picturesque features and analyzing for which reasons they are comfortable. On the contrary, we must go beyond the problems of description – whether this description be objective or subjective, that is, whether it

---

* In *The Poetics of Space* [1958], translated by Maria Jolas (Boston, MA: Beacon Press, 1994 [1964]), 3–37.

gives facts or impressions – in order to attain to the primary virtues, those that reveal an attachment that is native in some way to the primary function of inhabiting. A geographer or an ethnographer can give us descriptions of very varied types of dwellings. In each variety, the phenomenologist makes the effort needed to seize upon the germ of the essential, sure, immediate well-being it encloses. In every dwelling, even the richest, the first task of the phenomenologist is to find the original shell.

But the related problems are many if we want to determine the profound reality of all the subtle shadings of our attachment for a chosen spot. For a phenomenologist, these shadings must be taken as the first rough outlines of a psychological phenomenon. The shading is not an additional, superficial colouring. We should therefore have to say how we inhabit our vital space, in accord with all the dialectics of life, how we take root, day after day, in a 'corner of the world.'

For our house is our corner of the world. As has often been said, it is our first universe, a real cosmos in every sense of the word. If we look at it intimately, the humblest dwelling has beauty. Authors of books on 'the humble home' often mention this feature of the poetics of space. But this mention is much too succinct. Finding little to describe in the humble home, they spend little time there; so they describe it as it actually is without really experiencing its primitiveness, a primitiveness which belongs to all, rich and poor alike, if they are willing to dream.

But our adult life is so dispossessed of the essential benefits, its anthropocosmic ties have become so slack, that we do not feel their first attachment in the universe of the house. There is no dearth of abstract, 'world-conscious' philosophers who discover a universe by means of the dialectical game of the I and the non-I. In fact, they know the universe before they know the house, the far horizon before the resting-place; whereas the real beginnings of images, if we study them phenomenologically, will give concrete evidence of the values of inhabited space, of the non-I that protects the I.

Indeed, here we touch upon a converse whose images we shall have to explore: all really inhabited space bears the essence of the notion of home. In the course of this work, we shall see that the imagination functions in this direction whenever the human being has found the slightest shelter: we shall see the imagination build 'walls' of impalpable shadow, comfort itself with the illusion of protection – or, just the contrary, tremble behind thick walls, mistrust the staunchest ramparts. In short, in the most interminable of dialects, the sheltered being gives perceptible limits to his shelter. He experiences the house in its reality and in its virtuality, by means of thought and dreams.

[In the rest of Part I, Bachelard discusses how memory and imagination draw from the various dwelling places of our lives to provide material for our dreams and a collective sense of home. The house shelters and inspires daydreaming and protects the dreamer; it has the power to integrate the thoughts, memories, and dreams of all mankind.]

II

Of course, thanks to the house, a great many of our memories are housed, and if the house is a bit elaborate, if it has a cellar and a garret, nooks and corridors, our memories have refuges that are all the more clearly delineated. All our lives we come back to them in our daydreams. A psychoanalyst should, therefore, turn his attention to this simple localization of memories. I should like to give the name of topoanalysis to this auxiliary of psychoanalysis. Topoanalysis, then, would be the systematic psychological study of the sites of our intimate lives. In the theatre of the past that is constituted by memory, the stage setting maintains the characters in their dominant rôles. At times we think we know ourselves in time, when all we know is a sequence of fixations in the spaces of the being's stability – a being who does not want to melt away, and who, even in the past, when he sets out in search of things, wants time to 'suspend' its flight. In its countless alveoli space contains compressed time. That is what space is for.

2.2 MARTIN HEIDEGGER 'Building, Dwelling, Thinking'*

In what follows we shall try to think about dwelling and building. This thinking about building does not presume to discover architectural ideas, let alone give rules for building. This venture in thought does not view building as an art or as a technique of construction; rather it traces building back into that domain to which everything that *is* belongs. We ask:

1 What is it to dwell?
2 How does building belong to dwelling?

---

* [1951]. In *Poetry, Language, Thought*, translated by Albert Hofstadter (New York: Harper and Row, 1971), 145–61.

I

We attain to dwelling, so it seems, only by means of building. The latter, building, has the former, dwelling, as its goal. Still, not every building is a dwelling. Bridges and hangars, stadiums and power stations are buildings but not dwellings; railway stations and highways, dams and market halls are built, but they are not dwelling places. Even so, these buildings are in the domain of our dwelling. That domain extends over these buildings and yet is not limited to the dwelling place. The truck driver is at home on the highway, but he does not have his shelter there; the working woman is at home in the spinning mill, but does not have her dwelling place there; the chief engineer is at home in the power station, but he does not dwell there. These buildings house man. He inhabits them and yet does not dwell in them, when to dwell means merely that we take shelter in them. In today's housing shortage even this much is reassuring, and to the good; residential buildings do indeed provide shelter; today's houses may even be well planned, easy to keep, attractively cheap, open to air, light, and sun, but – do the houses in themselves hold any guarantee that *dwelling* occurs in them? Yet those buildings that are not dwelling places remain in turn determined by dwelling insofar as they serve man's dwelling. Thus dwelling would in any case be the end that presides over all building. Dwelling and building are related as end and means. However, as long as this is all we have in mind, we take dwelling and building as two separate activities, an idea that has something correct in it. Yet at the same time by the means-end schema we block our view of the essential relations. For building is not merely a means and a way toward dwelling – to build is in itself already to dwell. Who tells us this? Who gives us a standard at all by which we can take the measure of the nature of dwelling and building?

It is language that tells us about the nature of a thing, provided that we respect language's own nature. In the meantime, to be sure, there rages round the earth an unbridled yet clever talking, writing, and broadcasting of spoken words. Man acts as though *he* were the shaper and master of language, while in fact *language* remains the master of man. Perhaps it is before all else man's subversion of *this* relation of dominance that drives nature into alienation. That we retain a concern for care in speaking is all to the good, but it is of no help to us as long as language still serves us even then only as a means of expression. Among all the appeals that we human beings, on our part, can help to be voiced, language is the highest and everywhere the first.

What, then, does *Bauen*, building, *mean?* The Old English and High German word for building, *buan*, means to dwell. This signifies: to remain, to stay in a place. The real meaning of the verb *bauen*, namely, to dwell, has been lost to us.

But a covert trace of it has been preserved in the German word *Nachbar,* neighbour. The neighbor is in Old English the *neahgebur; neah,* near, and *gebur,* dweller. The *Nachbar* is the *Nachgebur,* the *Nachgebauer,* the near-dweller, he who dwells nearby. The verbs *buri, büren, beuren, beuron,* all signify dwelling, the abode, the place of dwelling. Now to be sure the old word *buan* not only tells us that *bauen,* to build, is really to dwell; it also gives us a clue as to how we have to think about the dwelling it signifies. When we speak of dwelling we usually think of an activity that man performs alongside many other activities. We work here and dwell there. We do not merely dwell – that would be virtual inactivity – we practice a profession, we do business, we travel and lodge on the way, now here, now there. *Bauen* originally means to dwell. Where the word *bauen* still speaks in its original sense it also says how far the nature of dwelling reaches [...] The old word *bauen,* which says that man *is* insofar as he *dwells,* this word *bauen,* however, *also* means at the same time to cherish and protect, to preserve and care for, specifically to till the soil, to cultivate the vine. Such building only takes care – it tends the growth that ripens into its fruit of its own accord. Building in the sense of preserving and nurturing is not making anything. Shipbuilding and temple-building, on the other hand, do in a certain way make their own works. Here building, in contrast with cultivating, is a constructing. Both modes of building – building as cultivating, Latin *colere, cultura,* and building as the raising up of edifices, *aedificare* – are comprised within genuine building, that is, dwelling. Building as dwelling, that is, as being on the earth, however, remains for man's everyday experience that which is from the outset 'habitual' – we inhabit it, as our language says so beautifully: it is the *Gewohnte.* For this reason it recedes behind the manifold ways in which dwelling is accomplished, the activities of cultivation and construction. These activities later claim the name of *bauen,* building, and with it the fact of building, exclusively for themselves. The sense of *bauen,* namely, dwelling, falls into oblivion [...]

But if we listen to what language says in the word *bauen* we hear three things:

1 Building is really dwelling.
2 Dwelling is the manner in which mortals are on the earth.
3 Building as dwelling unfolds into the building that cultivates growing things and the building that erects buildings.

If we give thought to this threefold fact, we obtain a clue and note the following: as long as we do not bear in mind that all building is in itself a dwelling, we cannot even adequately *ask,* let alone properly decide, what the building of buildings might be in its nature. We do not dwell because we have built, but we build and have built because we dwell, that is, because we are *dwellers.* But in what does the nature of dwelling consist? Let us listen once more to what language says to us. The Old Saxon *wuon,* the Gothic *wunian,* like the old word *bauen,* means to remain, to stay in a place. But the Gothic *wunian* says more distinctly how this remaining is experienced. *Wunian* means: to be at peace, to be brought to peace, to remain in peace. The word for peace, *Friede,* means the free, *das Frye,* and *fry* means: preserved from harm and danger, preserved from something, safeguarded. To free really means to spare. The sparing itself consists not only in the fact that we do not harm the one whom we spare. Real sparing is something *positive* and takes place when we leave something beforehand in its own nature, when we return it specifically to its being, when we 'free' it in the real sense of the word into a preserve of peace. To dwell, to be set at peace, means to remain at peace within the free, the preserve, the free sphere that safeguards each thing in its nature. *The fundamental character of dwelling is this sparing and preserving.* It pervades dwelling in its whole range. That range reveals itself to us as soon as we reflect that human being consists in dwelling and, indeed, dwelling in the sense of the stay of mortals on the earth.

But 'on the earth' already means 'under the sky.' Both of these *also* mean 'remaining before the divinities' and include a 'belonging to men's being with one another.' By a *primal* oneness the four – earth and sky, divinities and mortals – belong together in one.

Earth is the serving bearer, blossoming and fruiting, spreading out in rock and water, rising up into plant and animal. When we say earth, we are already thinking of the other three along with it, but we give no thought to the simple oneness of the four.

The sky is the vaulting path of the sun, the course of the changing moon, the wandering glitter of the stars, the year's seasons and their changes, the light and dusk of day, the gloom and glow of night, the clemency and inclemency of the weather, the drifting clouds and blue depth of the ether. When we say sky, we are already thinking of the other three along with it, but we give no thought to the simple oneness of the four.

The divinities are the beckoning messengers of the godhead. Out of the holy sway of the godhead, the god appears in his presence or withdraws into his concealment. When we speak of the divinities, we are already thinking of the other three along with them, but we give no thought to the simple oneness of the four.

The mortals are the human beings. They are called mortals because they can die. To die means to be capable of death *as* death. Only man dies, and indeed continually, as long as he remains on earth, under the sky, before the divinities. When we speak of mortals, we are already thinking of the other three along with them, but we give no thought to the simple oneness of the four.

This simple oneness of the four we call *the fourfold*. Mortals *are* in the fourfold by *dwelling*. But the basic characteristic of dwelling is to spare, to preserve. Mortals dwell in the way they preserve the fourfold in its essential being, its presencing. Accordingly, the preserving that dwells is fourfold.

II

In what way does building belong to dwelling? The answer to this question will clarify for us what building, understood by way of the nature of dwelling really is [...]

Building puts up locations that make space and a site for the fourfold. From the simple oneness in which earth and sky, divinities and mortals belong together, building *receives the directive* for its erecting of locations [...] To preserve the fourfold, to save the earth, to receive the sky, to await the divinities, to escort mortals – this fourfold preserving is the simple nature, the presencing, of dwelling. In this way, then, do genuine buildings give form to dwelling in its presencing and house this presence.

Building thus characterized is a distinctive letting-dwell. Whenever it *is* such in fact, building already *has* responded to the summons of the fourfold. All planning remains grounded on this responding, and planning in turn opens up to the designer the precincts suitable for his designs [...]

Only if we are capable of dwelling, only then can we build [...] Dwelling, however, is *the basic character* of Being in keeping with which mortals exist [...]

Building and thinking are, each in its own way, inescapable for dwelling. The two, however, are also insufficient for dwelling so long as each busies itself with its own affairs in separation instead of listening to one another. They are able to listen if both – building and thinking – belong to dwelling, if they remain within their limits and realize that the one as much as the other comes from the workshop of long experience and incessant practice.

We are attempting to trace in thought the nature of dwelling. The next step on this path would be the question: what is the state of dwelling in our precarious age? On all sides we hear talk about the housing shortage, and with good reason. Nor is there just talk; there is action too. We try to fill the need by providing houses, by promoting the building of houses, planning the whole architectural enterprise. However hard and bitter, however hampering and threatening the lack of houses remains, the *real plight of dwelling* does not lie merely in a lack of houses. The real plight of dwelling is indeed older than the world wars with their destruction, older also than the increase of the earth's population and the condition of the industrial workers. The real dwelling plight lies in this, that mortals ever search anew for the nature of dwelling, that they *must ever learn to dwell*. What if man's homelessness consisted in this, that man still does not even think of the *real* plight of dwelling as *the* plight? Yet as soon as man *gives thought* to his homelessness, it is a misery no longer. Rightly considered and kept well in mind, it is the sole summons that *calls* mortals into their dwelling.

But how else can mortals answer this summons than by trying on *their* part, on their own, to bring dwelling to the fullness of its nature? This they accomplish when they build out of dwelling, and think for the sake of dwelling.

2.3 HENRI LEFEBVRE 'Social Space'*

The history of space will begin at the point where anthropological factors lose their supremacy and end with the advent of a production of space which is expressly industrial in nature – a space in which reproducibility, repetition, and the reproduction of social relationships are deliberately given precedence over works, over natural reproduction, over nature itself, and over natural time. This area of study overlaps with no other. It is clearly circumscribed, for this history has a beginning and an end – a prehistory and a 'post-history.' In prehistory, nature dominates social space; in post-history, a localized nature recedes. Thus demarcated, the history of space is indispensable. Neither its beginning nor its end can be dated in the sense in which traditional historiography dates events. The beginning alone took up a period traces of which remain even now in our houses, villages, and towns. In the course of this process, which may be properly referred to as historical, certain abstract relations were established: exchange value became general, first thanks to silver and gold (i.e., their functions), then thanks to capital. These abstractions, which are social relations implying forms, become tangible in two ways. In the first place, the instrument and general equivalent of exchange value, namely money, takes on concrete form in coins, in 'pieces' of money. Secondly, the commercial relations which the use of money presupposes and induces attain social existence only once they are projected onto the terrain in the shape of relational networks (communications, markets) and of hierarchically organized centres (towns). It must be presumed that in each period a certain balance is established between the centres (i.e., the functioning of each one) and the whole. One might therefore quite reasonably

* In *The Production of Space* [1974], translated by Donald Nicholson-Smith (Oxford: Blackwell, 1991), 68–168.

speak here of 'systems' (urban, commercial, etc.), but this is really only a minor aspect, an implication and consequence of that fundamental activity which is the production of space.

With the twentieth century, we are generally supposed to have entered the modern era. Despite – and because of – their familiarity, however, such crude terms as 'century,' 'modern' and 'modernity' serve to conceal more than one paradox; these notions are in fact in urgent need of analysis and refinement. So far as space is concerned, decisive changes occurred at this juncture which are effectively obscured by invariant, surviving or stagnant elements, especially on the plane of representational space. Consider the house, the dwelling. In the cities – and even more so in the 'urban fabric' which proliferates around the cities precisely because of their disintegration – the House has a merely historico-poetic reality rooted in folklore, or (to put the best face on it) in ethnology. This *memory,* however, has an obsessive quality: it persists in art, poetry, drama and philosophy. What is more, it runs through the terrible urban reality which the twentieth century has instituted, embellishing it with a nostalgic aura while also suffusing the work of its critics. Thus both Heidegger's and Bachelard's writings – the importance and influence of which are beyond question – deal with this idea in a most emotional and indeed moving way. The dwelling passes everywhere for a special, still sacred, quasi-religious and in fact almost absolute space. With his 'poetics of space' and 'topophilia,' Bachelard links representational spaces, which he travels through as he dreams (and which he distinguishes from representations of space, as developed by science), with this intimate and absolute space [...] The contents of the House have an almost ontological dignity in Bachelard: drawers, chests and cabinets are not far removed from their natural analogues, as perceived by the philosopher-poet, namely the basic figures of nest, shell, corner, roundness, and so on. In the background, so to speak, stands Nature – maternal if not uterine. The House is as much cosmic as it is human. From cellar to attic, from foundations to roof, it has a density at once dreamy and rational, earthly and celestial. The relationship between Home and Ego, meanwhile, borders on identity. The shell, a secret and directly experienced space, for Bachelard epitomizes the virtues of human 'space.'

As for Heidegger's ontology – his notion of building as close to thinking, and his scheme according to which the dwelling stands opposed to a wandering existence but is perhaps destined one day to ally with it in order to welcome in Being – this ontology refers to things and non-things which are also far from us now precisely inasmuch as they are close to nature: the jug [...] the peasant house of the Black Forest [...] the Greek temple.[1] [See Heidegger, section 2.2 in this volume.] And yet space – the woods, the track – is nothing more and nothing other than 'being-there,' than beings, than *Dasein*. And, even if Heidegger asks questions about its origin, even if he poses 'historical' questions in this connection, there can be no doubt about the main thrust of his thinking here: time counts for more than space; Being has a history, and history is nothing but the History of Being. This leads him to a restricted and restrictive conception of production, which he envisages as a causing-to-appear, a process of emergence which brings a thing forth as a thing now present amidst other already-present things. Such quasi-tautological propositions add little to Heidegger's admirable if enigmatic formulation according to which 'Dwelling is the basic character of Being in keeping with which morals exist' [...] Language for Heidegger, meantime, is simply the dwelling of Being.

This obsession with absolute space presents obstacles on every side to the kind of history that we have been discussing (the history of space / the space of history; representations of space / representational space). It pushes us back towards a purely descriptive understanding, for it stands opposed to any analytic approach and even more to any global account of the generative process in which we are interested. More than one specific and partial discipline has sought to defend the stance, notably anthropology (whose aims may readily be gauged from the qualifiers so often assigned to it: cultural, structural, etc.). It is from motives of this sort that anthropology lays hold of notions derived from the study of village life (usually the Bororo or Dogon village, but occasionally the Provençal or Alsatian one), or from the consideration of traditional dwellings, and, by transposing and / or extrapolating them, applies these notions to the modern world.

How is it that such notions can be transferred in this way and still retain any meaning at all? There are a number of reasons, but the principal one is nostalgia. Consider the number of people, particularly young people, who flee the modern world, the difficult life of the cities, and seek refuge in the country, in folk traditions, in arts and crafts or in anachronistic small-scale farming. Or the number of tourists who escape into an elitist (or would-be elitist) existence in underdeveloped countries, including those bordering the Mediterranean. Mass migrations of tourist hordes into rustic or urban areas which their descent only helps to destroy (woe unto Venice and Florence!) are a manifestation of a major spatial contradiction of modernity: here we see space being consumed in both the economic and the literal senses of the word.

The modern world's brutal liquidation of history and of the past proceeds in a very uneven manner. In some cases entire countries – certain Islamic countries, for example – are seeking to slow down industrialization so as to preserve their traditional homes, customs and representational spaces from the buffeting of industrial space and industrial representations of space. There are other

– very modern – nations which also try to maintain their living arrangements and spaces unchanged, along with the customs and representations which go along with them. In Japan, for instance, which is a hyper-industrialized and hyper-urbanized nation, traditional living quarters, daily life, and representational spaces survive intact – and this is not in any merely folkloric sense, not as relics, not as stage management for tourists, but indeed as immediate and practical 'reality.' This intrigues visitors, frustrates Japanese modernizers and technocrats, and delights humanists. There is an echo here, albeit a distant one, of the West's infatuation with village life and rustic homesteads.

This kind of perseveration is what makes Amos Rapoport's book on the 'anthropology of the home' so interesting.[2] The traditional peasant house of the Périgord is indeed just as worthy of study as those anthropological *loci classici*, the Eskimo's igloo and the Kenyan's hut. The limitations of anthropology are nonetheless on display here, and indeed they leap off the page when the author seeks to establish the general validity of reductionistic schemata based on a binary opposition – i.e., does the dwelling strengthen or does it reduce domesticity? – and goes so far as to assert the French people always (!) entertain in cafés rather than at home [...]

Much as they might like to, anthropologists cannot hide the fact that the space and tendencies of modernity (i.e., of modern capitalism) will never be discovered either in Kenya or among French or any other peasants. To put studies such as these forward as of great importance in this connection is to avoid reality, to sabotage the search for knowledge, and to turn one's back on the actual 'problematic' of space. If we are to come to grips with this 'problematic,' instead of turning to ethnology, ethnography, or anthropology we must address our attention to the 'modern' world itself, with its dual aspect – capitalism, modernity – which makes it so hard to discern clearly.

The raw material of the production of space is not, as in the case of particular objects, a particular material: it is rather nature itself, nature transformed into a product, rudely manipulated, now threatened in its very existence, probably ruined and certainly – and most paradoxically – *localized.*

It might be asked at this juncture if there is any way of dating what might be called the moment of emergence of an awareness of space and its production: when and where, why and how, did a neglected knowledge and a misconstrued reality begin to be recognized? It so happens that this emergence can indeed be fixed: it is to be found in the 'historic' role of the Bauhaus [...] For the Bauhaus did more than locate space in its real context or supply a new perspective on it: it developed a new conception, a global concept, of space. At that time, around 1920, just after the First World War, a link was discovered in the advanced countries (France, Germany, Russia, the United States), a link which had already been dealt with on the practical plane but which had not yet been rationally articulated: that between industrialization and urbanization, between workplaces and dwelling places. No sooner had this link been incorporated into theoretical thought than it turned into a project, even into a programme. The curious thing is that this 'programmatic' stance was looked upon at the time as both rational and revolutionary, although in reality it was tailor-made for the state – whether of the state-capitalist or the state-socialist variety. Later, of course, this would become obvious – a truism. For Gropius or Le Corbusier, the programme boiled down to the production of space. As Paul Klee put it, artists – painters, sculptors, or architects – do not show space, they create it. The Bauhaus people understood that things could not be created independently of each other in space, whether moveable (furniture) or fixed (buildings), without taking into account their interrelationships and their relationship to the whole. It was impossible simply to accumulate them as a mass, aggregate or collection of items. In the context of the productive forces, the technological means and the specific problems of the modern world, things and objects could now be produced in their relationships, along with their relationships. Formerly, artistic ensembles – monuments, towns, furnishings – had been created by a variety of artists according to subjective criteria: the taste of princes, the intelligence of rich patrons or the genius of artists themselves. Architects had thus built palaces designed to house specific objects ('furniture') associated with an aristocratic mode of life, and, alongside them, squares for the people and monuments for social institutions. The resulting whole might constitute a space with a particular style, often even a dazzling style, but it was still a space never rationally defined which came into being and disappeared with no clear reason. As he considered the past and viewed it in the light of the present, Gropius sensed that henceforward social practice was destined to change. The production of spatial ensembles as such corresponded to the capacity of the productive forces, and hence to a specific rationality. It was thus no longer a question of introducing forms, functions or structures in isolation, but rather one of mastering global space by bringing forms, functions and structures together in accordance with a unitary conception. This insight confirmed after its fashion an idea of Marx's, the idea that industry has the power to open before our eyes the book of the creative capacities of 'man' (i.e., of social being).

The Bauhaus group, as artists associated in order to advance the total project of a total art, discovered, along with Klee [...] that an observer could move around any object in social space – including such objects as houses, public buildings, and palaces – and in so doing go beyond scrutinizing or studying it under a single or special aspect. Space opened up to perception, to conceptualization, just as it did to practical action. And the artist passed from objects in space to the concept of space itself. Avant-garde painters of the same period reached very similar conclusions: all aspects of an object could be considered simultaneously and this simultaneity preserved and summarized a temporal sequence.

NOTES

1 See the discussion in Martin Heidegger, *Holzwege* (Frankfurt: Klostermann, 1950).
2 Amos Rapoport, *House Form and Culture* (Englewood Cliffs, NJ: Prentice-Hall, 1969).

2.4 TIM INGOLD
'Building, Dwelling, Living: How Animals and People Make Themselves at Home in the World'*

How can we distinguish an environment that is built from one that is not? [...] Why should the products of human building activity be any different, in principle, from the constructions of other animals? [...] Imagine a mollusc shell, a beaver's lodge, and a human house. All have been regarded [...] as instances of architecture. Some authors would restrict architecture to the house, others would include the lodge – as an example of 'animal architecture'[1] – but exclude the shell, others would include all three forms. The usual argument for excluding the shell is that it is attached to the body of the mollusc [...] The beaver, by contrast, works hard to put its lodge together: the lodge is a product of the beaver's 'beavering' [...] Likewise the house is a product of the activities of its human builders [...]

Wherever they are, beavers construct the same kinds of lodges and, so far as we know, have always done so. Human beings, by contrast, build houses of very diverse kinds, and although certain house forms have persisted for long periods, there is unequivocal evidence that these forms have also undergone significant historical change. The difference between the lodge and the house lies [...] not in the construction of the thing itself, but in the origination of the *design* that governs the construction process. The design of the lodge is incorporated into the same programme that underwrites the development of the beaver's own

* In *Shifting Contexts: Transformation in Anthropological Knowledge*, edited by Marilyn Strathern (London: Routledge, 1995), 57–80.

body: thus the beaver is no more the designer of the lodge than is the mollusc the designer of its shell. It is merely the *executor* of a design that has evolved, along with the morphology and behaviour of the beaver, through a process of variation under natural selection. In other words, both the beaver – in its outward, phenotypic form – and the lodge are 'expressions' of the same underlying genotype. Dawkins (1982) has coined the term 'extended phenotype' to refer to genetic effects that are situated beyond the body of the organism, and in this sense, the lodge is part of the extended phenotype for the beaver.[2]

Human beings, on the other hand, are the authors of their own designs, constructed through a self-conscious decision process – an intentional selection of ideas. As Joseph Rykwert has recently put it: 'unlike even the most elaborate animal construction, human building involves decision and choice, always and inevitably; it therefore involves a project.'[3] It is to this project, I maintained, that we refer when we say that the house is *made*, rather than merely constructed [...]

[...] The essential distinction [...] between the respective ways in which the subjective existence of human and non-human animals is suspended lays in 'webs of significance.' For the non-human, every thread in the web is a relation between it and some object or feature of the environment, a relation that is set up through its own practical immersion in the world and the bodily orientations that this entails. For the human, by contrast, the web – and the relations of which it consists – is inscribed in a separate plane of mental representations, forming a tapestry of meaning that *covers over* the world of environmental objects. Whereas the non-human animal perceives these objects as immediately available for use, to human beings they appear initially as occurrent phenomena to which potential uses must be affixed, prior to any attempt at engagement. The fox discovers shelter in the roots of a tree, but the forester sees timber only in his mind's eye, and has first to fit that image in thought to his perception of the occurrent object – the tree – before taking action [...]

[...] Let me now return to my earlier observation, comparing the forms of the beaver's lodge and the human house, that the first is tied, as it were, to the nature of the beaver itself, whereas the second is both historically and regionally variable. Among non-human animals, it is widely supposed, there can be no significant change in built form that is not bound to evolutionary changes in the essential form of the species. With human beings, by contrast, built form is free to vary independently of biological constraint, and to follow developmental pathways of its own, effectively decoupled with the process of evolution. In his famous paper of 1917, on 'the super-organic,' Alfred Kroeber declared: 'Who would be so rash as to affirm that ten thousand generations of example would convert the beaver from what he is into a carpenter or a bricklayer – or, allowing for his physical deficiency in the lack of hands, into a planning engineer!'[4] Yet human beings, through practice, example and a good measure of ingenuity, coupled with their ability to transmit their acquired know-how across the generations and to preserve it in long-term memory, have learned all these trades, and many more besides [...]

But how did it come about that, at some decisive moment, our ancestors began to think about what they built? [...]

The search for the first building continues to this date, though it is informed by a much better knowledge both of archaeological traces left by early human or hominid populations, and of the behaviour of those species of animals – namely, the great apes – most closely related to humankind. One of the most peculiar and distinctive aspects of the behaviour of chimpanzees, gorillas, and orangutans is their habit of building so-called 'nests.' In functional terms, they are not really nests at all: every individual animal builds its own nest afresh, each evening, and uses it for the sole purpose of sleeping. Nor does the nest site mark any kind of fixed point in the animal's movements; it may be built anywhere, and is abandoned the next morning.[5] Nevertheless, assuming that the common ancestor of apes and humans would have had a similar habit, attempts have been made to trace an evolutionary continuum from this nesting behaviour to the residential arrangements of prototypical human groups (of which the camps of contemporary hunter-gatherers have frequently been taken as the closest exemplars, on the grounds of the presumed similarity of ecological context).

Comparing the nesting patterns of apes with the camping patterns of human hunter-gatherers, Colin Groves and J[ordi] Sabater Pi note some striking differences. The human 'nest,' if we may call it that, is a fixed point for the movements of its several occupants, and a place to which they regularly return. In other words, it has the attributes of what the ethologist, Heini Hediger [...] would call 'home': it is a 'goal of flight' and a 'place of maximal security.'[6] There is a difference, too, in the respective ways in which apes and humans go about building their accommodation. For one thing, apes use material that comes immediately to hand, normally by a skilful interweaving of growing vegetation to form an oval-shaped, concave bed; whereas humans collect suitable materials from a distance, prior to their assembly into a convex, self-supporting structure. For another thing, the ape makes its nest by bending the vegetation around its own body; whereas the human builds a hut, and then enters it.[7] There is a sense, as Hediger remarks, in which apes build from the 'bottom up,' seeking support for rest and sleeping, whereas humans build from the 'top down,' seeking shelter from sun, rain or wind.[8] Yet there are also remarkable similarities between ape and human living arrangements, in the overall number and layout of nests or huts, and in the underlying social organisation, and on the grounds of these similarities, Groves and Sabater Pi feel justified in arguing that human campsites are but elaborations of a generalised ape pattern. All the critical differences – the functioning of the site as a home-base, the collection of material prior to construction, the technique of building from the outside – can be put down, they think, to one factor, namely, the human ability 'to visualise objects in new configurations, and to bring these configurations into being on the basis of that mental picture.'[9]

Let me conclude by returning to [Jakob] von Uexküll's oak tree.[10] Suppose that it stands, not in the forest, but in the precincts of a house. Now at first glance we might have no hesitation in regarding the house, not the tree, as a building, or an instance of architecture [...] The tree, on the other hand, has no such debt to humanity, for it has grown there, rooted to the spot, entirely of its own accord. On closer inspection, however, this distinction between those parts of the environment that are, respectively, built and unbuilt seems far less clear [...] For the form of the tree is no more given, as an immutable fact of nature, than is the form of the house an imposition of the human mind. Recall the many inhabitants of the tree: the fox, the owl, the squirrel, the ant, the beetle, among countless others. All, through their various activities of dwelling, have played their part in creating the conditions under which the tree, over the centuries, has grown to assume its particular form and proportions. And so, too, have human beings, in tending the tree's surroundings, or even more directly, in pruning its branches.

But the house also has many diverse animal inhabitants – more, perhaps, than we are inclined to recognise. Sometimes special provision is made for them, such as the kennel, stable, or dovecote. Others find shelter and sustenance in its nooks and crannies, or even build there. And all, in various ways, contribute to its evolving form, as do the house's human inhabitants in keeping it under repair, decorating it, or making structural alterations in response to their changing domestic circumstances. Thus the distinction between the house and the tree is not an absolute but a relative one, relative, that is, to the scope of human involvement in the form-generating process. Houses [...] are living organisms.[11] Like trees, they have life histories, which consist in the unfolding of their relations with both human and non-human components of their environments. To the extent that the influence of the human component prevails, any feature of the environment will seem like a building; to the extent that the non-human component prevails, it will seem less so. Thus does the house, following its abandonment by its human occupants, become a ruin.

Building, then, is a process that is continually going on, for as long as people dwell in an environment. It does not begin here, with a pre-formed plan, and end there, with a finished artefact. The 'final form' is but a fleeting moment in the life of any feature, when it is matched to a human purpose, likewise cut out from the flow of intentional activity [...] We may indeed describe the forms in our environment as instances of architecture, but for the most part we are not architects. For it is in the very process of dwelling that we build.

NOTES

1 Karl von Frisch, *Animal Architecture* (London: Hutchinson, 1975).
2 Richard Dawkins, *The Extended Phenotype* (San Francisco, CA: Freeman, 1982).
3 Joseph Rykwert, 'House and Home,' *Social Research* 58 / 1 (1991): 56.
4 Alfred L. Kroeber, *The Nature of Culture* (Chicago, IL: University of Chicago Press, 1952), 31.
5 Colin P. Groves and Jordi Sabater Pi, 'From Ape's Nest to Human Fix Point,' *Man* 20 (1985): 23.
6 Heini Hediger, 'Nest and Home,' *Folio Primatologica* 28 (1977): 181.
7 Groves and Sabater Pi, 'From Ape's Nest,' 45.
8 Hediger, 'Nest and Home,' 184.
9 Groves and Sabater Pi, 'From Ape's Nest,' 45.
10 Jakob von Uexküll, 'A Stroll through the Worlds of Animals and Men: A Picture Book of Invisible Worlds,' in Claire. H. Schiller, ed., *Instinctive Behavior: The Development of a Modern Concept* (New York: International Universities Press, 1957), 5–80.
11 Suzanne Preston Blier, *The Anatomy of Architecture* (Cambridge: Cambridge University Press, 1987), 2.

2.5 PIERRE BOURDIEU 'The Berber House or the World Reversed'*

The interior of the Kabyle house is rectangular in shape and is divided into two parts at a point one third of the way along its length by a small lattice-work wall half as high as the house. Of these two parts, the larger is approximately 50 centimetres higher than the other and is covered over by a layer of black clay and cow dung which the women polish with a stone; this part is reserved for human use. The smaller part is paved with flagstones and is occupied by the animals. A door with two wings provides entrance to both rooms. Upon the

* *Social Science Information* 9 / 2 (1970): 151–70.

dividing wall are kept, at one end, the small clay jars or esparto-grass baskets in which provisions awaiting immediate consumption, such as figs, flour and leguminous plants, are conserved, at the other end, near the door, the water-jars. Above the stable there is a loft where, next to all kinds of tools and implements, quantities of straw and hay to be used as animal-fodder are piled up; it is here that the women and children usually sleep, particularly in winter [...] Against the gable wall, known as the wall (or, more exactly, the 'side') of the upper part or of the *kanun,* there is set a brick-work construction in the recesses and holes of which are kept the kitchen utensils (ladle, cooking-pot, dish used to cook the bannock, and other earthenware objects blackened by the fire) and at each end of which are placed large jars filled with grain. In front of this construction is to be found the fireplace; this consists of a circular hollow, two or three centimetres deep at its centre, around which are arranged in a triangle three large stones upon which the cooking is done.[1]

In front of the wall opposite the door stands the weaving-loom. This wall is usually called by the same name as the outside front wall giving onto the courtyard (*tasga*) [...], or else wall of the weaving-loom or opposite wall, since one is opposite it when one enters. The wall opposite to this, where the door is, is called wall of darkness, or of sleep, or of the maiden, or of the tomb;[2] a bench wide enough for a mat to be spread out over it is set against this wall; the bench is used to shelter the young calf or the sheep for feast-days and sometimes the wood or the water-pitcher. Clothes, mats and blankets are hung, during the day, on a peg or on a wooden cross-bar against the wall of darkness or else they are put under the dividing bench. Clearly, therefore, the wall of the *kanun* is opposed to the stable as the top is to the bottom (*adaynin,* stable, comes from the root *ada,* meaning the bottom) and the wall of the weaving-loom is opposed to the wall of the door as the light is to the darkness [...] A number of signs suggest [...] that these oppositions are the centre of a whole cluster of parallel oppositions, the necessity of which is never completely due to technical imperatives or functional requirements [...]

The dark and nocturnal, lower part of the house, place of objects that are moist, green or raw – jars of water placed on benches in various parts of the entrance to the stable or against the wall of darkness, wood and green fodder – natural place also of beings – oxen and cows, donkeys and mules – and place of natural activities – sleep, the sexual act, giving birth – and the place also of death, is opposed, as nature is to culture, to the light-filled, noble, upper part of the house: this is the place of human beings and, in particular, of the guest; it is the place of fire and of objects created by fire – lamp, kitchen utensils, rifle – the symbol of the male point of honour (*ennif*) and the protector of female honour (*ḥorma*) – and it is the place of the weaving-loom – the symbol of all protection; and it is also the place of the two specifically cultural activities that are carried out in the space of the house: cooking and weaving. These relationships of opposition are expressed through a whole set of convergent signs which establish the relationships at the same time as receiving their meaning from them [...] The link between the dark part of the house and death is also shown in the fact that the washing of the dead takes place at the entrance to the stable [...]

In front of the wall of the weaving-loom, opposite the door, in the light, is also seated or rather, shown off, like the decorated plates which are hung there, the young bride on her wedding-day. When one knows that the umbilical cord of the girl is buried behind the weaving-loom and that, in order to protect the virginity of the maiden, she is made to pass through the warp, going from the door towards the weaving-loom, then the magic protection attributed to the weaving-loom becomes evident [...] In fact, from the point of view of the male members of her family, all of the girl's life is, as it were, summed up in the successive positions that she symbolically occupies in relation to the weaving-loom which is the symbol of male protection: [...] before marriage she is placed behind the weaving-loom, in its shadow, under its protection, as she is placed under the protection of her father and her brothers; on her wedding-day she is seated in front of the weaving-loom with her back to it, with the light upon her, and finally she will sit weaving with her back to the wall of light, behind the loom. 'Shame, it is said, is the maiden,' and the son-in-law is called 'the veil of shames' since man's point of honour is the protective 'barrier' of female honour [...]

The low and dark part of the house is also opposed to the high part as the feminine is to the masculine: besides the fact that the division of work between the sexes, which is based upon the same principle of division as the organization of space, entrusts to the woman the responsibility of most objects which belong to the dark part of the house – water-transport, and the carrying of wood and manure, for instance [...] – the opposition between the upper part and the lower part reproduces within the space of the house the opposition set up between the inside and the outside. This is the opposition between female space and male space, between the house and its garden, the place par excellence of the *haram*, i.e., of all which is sacred and forbidden, and a closed and secret space, well protected and sheltered from intrusions and the gaze of others, and the place of assembly (*thajma'th*), the mosque, the café, the fields or the market: on the one hand, the privacy of all that is intimate, on the other, the open space of social relations; on the one hand, the life of the senses and of the feelings, on the other, the life of relations between man and man, the life of dialogue and exchange. The lower part of the house is the place of the most intimate privacy within the very world of intimacy, that is to say, it is the place of all that pertains to sexuality and procreation. More or less empty during the day, when all activity – which is, of course, exclusively feminine – is based around the fireplace, the dark part is full at night, full of human beings but also full of animals since, unlike the mules and the donkeys, the oxen and the cows never spend the night out of doors; and it is never quite so full as it is during the damp season when the men sleep inside and the oxen and the cows are fed in the stable. It is possible here to establish more directly the relationship which links the fertility of men and of the field to the dark part of the house and which is a particular instance of the relationship of equivalence between fertility and that which is dark, full (or swollen), or damp, vouched for by the whole mythico-ritual system [...]

Thus, the house is organized according to a set of homologous oppositions: fire : water :: cooked : raw :: high : low :: light : shadow :: day : night :: male : female :: *nif* : *ḥorma* :: fertilizing : able to be fertilized :: culture : nature. But in fact the same oppositions exist between the house as a whole and the rest of the universe. Considered in its relationship with the external world, which is a specifically masculine world of public life and agricultural work, the house, which is the universe of women and the world of intimacy and privacy, is *haram,* that is to say, at once sacred and illicit for every man who does not form part of it [...]

As a microcosm organized according to the same oppositions which govern all the universe, the house maintains a relation with the rest of the universe which is that of a homology: but from another point of view, the world of the house taken as a whole is in a relation with the rest of the world which is one of opposition, and the principles of which are none other than those which govern the organization of the internal space of the house as much as they do the rest of the world and, more generally, all the areas of existence. Thus, the opposition between the world of female life and the world of the city of men is based upon the same principles as the two systems of oppositions that it opposes [...]

The house is also endowed with a double significance: if it is true that it is opposed to the public world as nature is to culture, it is also, in another respect, culture; is it not said of the jackal, the incarnation of all that is savage in nature, that it does not have a home?

The house and, by extension, the village,[3] which is the full country (*la 'mmara* or *thamurth i 'amran*), the precincts peopled by men, are opposed in a certain respect to the fields empty of men which are called *lakhla,* the space that is empty and sterile [...]

It is not possible completely to understand the importance and symbolic value attached to the threshold in the system, unless one is aware that it owes its function as a magic frontier to the fact that it is a place of a logical inversion and that, as the obligatory place of passage and of meeting between the two spaces, which are defined in relation to socially qualified movements of the body and crossings from one place to another, it is logically the place where the world is reversed […]

The orientation of the house is fundamentally defined from the outside, from the point of view of men and, if one may say so, by men and for men, as the place from which men come out. The house is an empire within an empire, but one which always remains subordinate because, even though it presents all the properties and all the relations which define the archetypal world, it remains a reversed world, an inverted reflection.[4] […] The special favour accorded to the movement towards the outside, by which the man affirms himself as man, turning his back upon the house in order to go and face men and choosing the way of the Orient of the world, is but a form of categorical refusal of nature, which is the inevitable origin of the movement away from it.

NOTES

1 All the descriptions of the Berber house […] even the most rich in detail concerning the interior organization of space […] contain in their extreme meticulousness, regular omissions, particularly when it is a question of precisely situating things and activities. The reason for this is that these descriptions never consider objects and actions as part of a symbolic system […]

2 Concerning a father who has many daughters one says: 'He is setting up evil days for himself,' and, in the same way, one says: 'The maiden is the dusk,' or: 'The maiden is the wall of darkness.'

3 The village also has its *ḥorma* which every visitor must respect. Just as one must take off one's shoes before going into a house or a mosque or onto a threshing-floor, so one must set one's feet upon the earth when going into a village.

4 In the interior space also the two opposed parts are hierarchized. Here, beside all the other indications quoted, is one more saying: 'It is better to have a house full of men than a house full of goods (*el mal*),' that is to say, of cattle.

2.6 JUAN EDUARDO CAMPO 'Domestications of Islam in Modern Egypt: A Cultural Analysis'*

The Components of Sacrality in Egyptian Muslim Homes

'Every house has its own sacrality *('ḥurma)*' [...] It would be hard to find a more explicit statement in the Egyptian colloquial Arabic about the sacred, inviolable quality people attribute to their houses. As an adage, it has several levels of meaning. On one level, it indicates that entering someone's house requires a demonstration of respect *(i'ḥtir'ḥm)* toward the people living there. This is particularly important in regard to recognizing that the house is the domain for women in the family. To enter without permission or incorrectly, to call out a woman's personal name so that outsiders can hear it, to speak brazenly, and to look in without permission are violations of the house's *'ḥurma.* They are very reprehensible forms of behavior against which there must be a defense. The intimate connection between domestic sacrality and the female is demonstrated aptly by the fact that *'ḥurma,* as well as its cognate *'ḥaram,* also happens to be a customary way of making respectful reference to a man's wife. She is the foremost repository of a house's sacrality, followed by the daughters. The adage implies, therefore, that not only does every house have a sacral character, but that this sacral character is dependent upon the presence of women [...]

That houses have sacrality, and that this is connected with married women does not mean that domestic space and women must be absolutely segregated from the outside world. The *baladi* Egyptian idea of *'ḥurma* normally accepts access to the house, it permits vision, it allows speech. But it sanctions these actions by setting limits on them. The same idea is evidenced by early Islamic discourses of domestic space, which prohibit unauthorized intrusions at the same time that they place positive sanctions on visitation and hospitality. This may be paradoxical, but the same can be said of *'ḥurma* when identified strictly with women, for they only become fully 'inviolable' through marriage to men. In a sense, inviolability is based on controlled violation [...]

Sharaf 'honor' is the masculine counterpart of *'ḥurma;* they are two sides of the same coin. In spatial terms, we can consider *sharaf* as a sort of cover for *'ḥurma;* providing it with its public face and its defensive mask. The word *sharaf* suggests the idea of height, and of 'overseeing.' Without *'ḥurma, sharaf* loses its

* In *The Other Sides of Paradise: Explorations into the Religious Meaning of Domestic Space in Islam* (Columbia, SC: University of South Carolina Press, 1991), 98–138.

reason for being, however. Likewise, *'ḥurma* cannot be preserved for long without its outward visage […]

'Building a House': Inauguration and Marriage Ceremonies

A house's sacrality consists of *'ḥurma* and *sharaf,* its feminine and masculine qualities. This sacrality cannot be known in itself, but must be manifested in concrete signs communicated by social action, speech, and interior display. The successful establishment of sacrality is linked with the generation of the power of blessing and debilitation of the effects of evil. Concomitantly, were sacrality to be non-existent, violated, or diminished, the well-being of the household would be affected negatively, and the effects of evil increase. Women and men alike are responsible for caring for the sacral character of their houses. They are also its greatest threats.

Among the most important occasions involved in the transformation of an ordinary architectural space into a sacralized place are inauguration ceremonies conducted when a house is built or when a family moves into a new dwelling and marriage ceremonies. In rural areas of northern Africa and the east Mediterranean, including Egypt, the building of new dwellings is marked by a series of ceremonial activities […] When house foundations are laid, builders put dates, grain, flour, salt, and perhaps even small silver or gold objects into them. When a wall, threshold, vault, but most of all when the whole building has been completed, a fowl or sheep is sacrificed and a feast is held by the builders or their patrons. At such times, the blood of the sacrificed animal is smeared on the house, usually on its door posts […] On rare occasions, a copy of the Quran is buried in the foundations or within a house wall. Before a new house is occupied, water or salt might be sprinkled on its floors, and it will be fumigated with incense […]

It is often the case that acquiring a dwelling place coincides with the joining of a man and woman in marriage. Religious law makes marriage a fundamental requirement of Muslim social life; it also makes it the chief context for legitimate sexual relations between men and women […]

Social norms, validated by religious requirements that give men the primary responsibility for maintenance, dictate that a marriage cannot be consummated until the male has acquired a dwelling place. In many cases, due to the influence *of rīfi* tradition and the chronic housing shortage, this may simply mean making new sleeping arrangements in the groom's parents' house [… or] he can bargain with the bride's family to either reside with them, or to occupy a flat that they have set aside for their daughter. In fact, middle and upper class Egyptians use the promise of a new flat to enhance their daughter's marriageability […]

'Death and the Destruction of Houses'

If marriage is instrumental to transforming a house into a place of sacrality, then there must be events that threaten to end that sacrality. Divorce is one way in which domestic sacrality can be destroyed [...] Death, because it strikes households repeatedly and inevitably, is a more formidable threat to domestic sacrality than divorce [...] The Egyptian adage, 'Death and the destruction of houses,'[...] expresses the danger the power of death possesses [...]

As with wedding celebrations, the house of bereavement becomes a 'space of appearance'; it is rearranged and opened to receive condolers (including strangers) during the mourning period. Some families reverse or remove household furnishings that have a high display value like mirrors, pictures, rugs, mats, and the bed of the deceased [...]

Egyptians, like other people, have ambiguous feelings towards cemeteries. On the one hand, they designate them with terms such as *turab, qarāfa,* or *gabbāna.* These names convey notions of dirt, loathing, and fear [...] Egyptian oral traditions are replete with reports and stories about terrible things that have happened to people when they pass by graveyards or dare to go through them at night. In village Egypt, parents warn children against wandering among the tombs. When the government built housing projects near Cairo's southern cemetery in the late 1950s, families were wary about moving in because of the harmful forces to which they feared they would become vulnerable.

On the other hand, the cemeteries of Cairo have traditionally been places for holiday picnics and festivities. Mamluk emirs built religious colleges, hostels, and sufi convents there among the tombs. Today, Cairo's cemeteries have actually become full-fledged residential neighbourhoods [...] It is true that many residential neighbourhoods in Cairo proper still have shrines containing the remains of saints, but in the case of the cemeteries, the situation is reversed. The quick have taken up residence with the dead in greater numbers than ever before.

Contributing to the growth of this phenomenon in recent centuries has been the practice of building family tombs that resemble old-style houses. Surrounded by high walls, these mausoleums stand one or two stories above ground and contain living quarters, open courts, and gardens. Below ground, the bodies of the dead are laid to rest in common vaults. Reflecting the norms for segregation of the sexes in the mundane world, men are buried together on the right side of the crypt and women on the left. Above ground, the living family gathers on Thursdays, Fridays, and holidays to remember the dead, distribute food to the poor, and share meals together. To a great extent, the family mausoleum functions as a kind of domestic space, where past and present generations can be united. It is called *'ḥūsh*, a term that otherwise refers to a courtyard, or to a kind of tenement building organized around such a courtyard.

In the past, families hired caretakers who lived in the mausoleums. Eventually the caretakers were joined by their own families. When Cairo was faced with severe housing shortages in the 1960s and 1970s due to urban population growth, immigration of people from the countryside, and refugees coming from war-torn settlements near the Suez Canal, the tombs began to serve as houses for squatters who were unable to acquire other quarters. The government failed to curtail this process. The result has been the creation of residential districts among the tombs, with public utilities, schools, shops, and police stations to serve the hundreds of thousands of people who now live there.

If tombs are in fact considered to be a form of domestic space by Egyptians, then we should expect to find people making efforts to relate to the dead in ways analogous to those used to relate to the living. This is most obviously the case with visitation (*ziyāra*) customs. Normally, families, neighbours, and friends establish and maintain relations with each other by exchanging visits and presenting small gifts. This is especially true during holidays. Likewise, people visit and converse with the dead during holiday excursions to the cemeteries. Unless the dead person is a saint who can provide *baraka* to guests, he or she is unable to fulfil the duties of hospitality in the same way as a living person. Instead, members of the dead person's family, especially the women, take gifts of food with them to the cemeteries to distribute to the people they meet there on behalf of the dead. It makes no difference whether their dead are buried in grand mausoleums, or in modest individual graves. The atmosphere among the tombs is quite gay, as it is in most *baladi* Egyptian households during holidays.

Given the importance attached to the principle of reciprocity in Egyptian social relationships, we also find strong evidence for the belief that the dead make return visits to their families. Appearing to relatives in dreams and visions, they usually ask for prayers, or request that food be distributed to the unfortunate on their behalf. The medieval scholar al-Qadi, in a popular pamphlet still sold in Cairo, provides an account of this subject that he attributes to Ibn 'Abbas, one of the Prophet's companions:

> On a feast day, 'Ashura, the first Friday of Rajab, the eve of the middle of Sha'ban, the Night of Power (at the end of Ramadan), and Thursday evening the souls of the dead leave their graves and stand at the doors of their houses *(buyūt)*. They say, 'Have mercy on us this blessed eve by giving charitable gifts [or a bite to eat. We need it …] Remember us by reciting the *Fātiha* on this blessed eve.

> ['Is there anyone who will ask that God have mercy on us? Will anyone remember our absence? O you who live in our houses *(dūr)*! You who have married our women! You who reside in our roomiest palaces, while we are now in our narrowest graves! O you who have divided our property! You who disparage our orphans! Do any of you remember our absence and poverty? … The dead have no recompense in the grave. Do not forget us – (offer) a morsel of your bread or (say) a prayer, for we will always need you.']
>
> If the dead obtain charitable gifts and prayers from them, they return (to their graves) happy and joyful. If they obtain nothing, they return sad and hopeless because of them[1] […]

This kind of statement views the situation of the living as more fortunate than that of the dead. Yet, by inventing a discourse of the dead, it ventures to remind the living of their obligations towards them. The implication is that if the living act in the right way and say the correct things, they can influence the quality of 'life' for the dead in their graves. Just as they can establish sacrality in their own houses through action and speech, they can do the same for the houses of the dead.

Again, al-Qadi's account is instructive on this point:

> [It is said that every day the grave exclaims five times: 'I am the house (*bayt*) of solitude,] so let reciting the Quran keep me company. I am the house of darkness, so illuminate me with evening prayers. I am the house of dirt, so put a floor covering on me – that is, righteous deeds. I am the house of vipers, so carry the antidote – that is, (say) 'In the name of God, most compassionate and merciful' [and shed tears]. I am the house of interrogation by Munkar and Nakir, so say often as you walk above me, 'There is no god but God, Muhammad is God's messenger.'[2]

In this text the grave, speaking on behalf of Islamic norms, advises the living how they can improve the quality of their existence in the afterlife until Judgment Day arrives. They should learn that they can transform the grave into a domestic space by correct speech and action in life. Concomitantly, the text reflects the ambiguities of death; it blurs the distinctions between the grave and the house, the dead and the living.

NOTES

1 Insertions in brackets are the author's.

2 Insertions in brackets are the author's.

2.7 DAVID STEA
'House and Home: Identity, Dichotomy, or Dialectic? (With Special Reference to Mexico)'*

I should like to consider the words *home, personal,* and *identity* separately. First, concerning home in a broad sense, some differences between *house,* as a physical artefact, and home as place identity and social construct, will be explored. Second, I will try to break the usually assumed equation of personal and individual: thus, the individual who was once the sole concern of environmental psychology is seen as only one of many social units whose behavior gives identity to home and to which home gives identity. Because individual and social behavior are also related to value systems, house form expresses *values identity,* as well. Third, identity will be examined in two senses: first, in the above house-home relationship; second, in the plural form identities, reflecting the sometimes complementary and often contradictory complexes of social and individual roles that characterize societies.

Fourth, in an attempt to bridge the universality and particularity of behavior, three concepts of global interest will be considered: family, social hierarchy, and mode of activity, and in some examples drawn from Mexico, how both are expressed and related to household and social identity. Finally, the foregoing will be related to certain broader issues concerning the relation between identity, home, and society [...]

Our ideal – often our assumption – is the identity of house and home. This reflects a sedentary, agrarian set of values, and a particular concept of 'rootedness.' Usually ignored is the fact that one's abilities to maintain an identity between house and home – that is, actually to dwell in the place one regards as home – are strongly related to the socio-political economy of the country in question [...]

A case of clear non-choice is that of forced or 'involuntary' resettlement,[1] a phenomenon clearly typical of (but no longer confined to), peasants and indigenous people displaced by large-scale hydroelectric projects and extractive industries. Paradoxically, because individual needs are subordinated to the international political economy, people who would like to move (nomads), are forced to settle, and those who would like to remain settled (no longer just the poor), are often forced to move [...]

Failure to express identity through a house seems to result when: (1) identity with the home base is much stronger than with the place where the house is

* In *The Home: Words, Interpretations, Meanings, and Environments,* edited by David N. Benjamin (Aldershot: Ashgate; Brookfield, VT: Avebury, 1995), 181–201.

located, and (2) perceived control over the house is absent or much attenuated – e.g., [in the case of] American Indian Reservation housing [...] Yet a third factor, repugnant to those of us who see houses as the prime form of personal expression, is that, among those with very limited means, other life priorities may be so much higher that the house is of little importance except as mere shelter. Thus, the outward appearance of housing in otherwise well-planned urban 'squatter' settlements in Latin America is a result neither of innate slovenliness nor the operation of a 'culture of poverty,' rather, it indicates the low priority of the house relative to other needs [...]

An important aspect of this argument involves the nature of ties between the inhabitants of the house and what they conceive as home, between the house and home ground, and the spatio-temporal separations between these. What is necessary, in a transitional society, for a house to become a home? One consideration is the adaptiveness of a given house form to cultural necessities: modern internationalized housing is particularly poor at this. Then there is the element of forced non-adaptiveness, or *coercive housing*, the use of housing as a means of acculturation, to forcibly break the tie between house and traditional home, to establish new concepts of the 'proper house,'[2] and to force the establishment not just of new houses, but often unsuccessfully, of new homes [...]

In the case of Mexican houses, the above model directs us to examine basic value structures [...] as evidenced in both traditional and transitional areas. 'Transition' refers, in Mexico, much more to material culture than to the cultural core, which has proven remarkably resilient to change in the face of enormous external pressures and devastating crises. Primary among Mexican values – so far in front that it often eclipses all others – is the family. To consider personal identity apart from family identity in the Mexican house would be utterly meaningless:

> The family's survival as a powerful and deeply conservative institution has been crucial to maintaining Mexico's ... stability ... In reality, society reflects the family ... the paternalistic and authoritarian structure of the family also seems to prepare Mexicans to accept the hierarchical arrangements that prevail in the country at large.
>
> The continuing strength of the family is all the more remarkable in a country that has been convulsed by social change over the past forty years ... yet the family has changed more than the country. For most Mexicans the family remains the pivot of their lives ... The very insularity of the family teaches Mexicans to distrust society as a whole and they feel safer ... if surrounded by relatives.[3]

But the Spanish word *familia* has a very different meaning in Latin America in general, and Mexico above all, than does family in the U.S.A., or many parts of Northern Europe: the nuclear family has four or five members, the extended *familia,* which exists in symbiotic relationship with the Church, has hundreds. The *familia* is extended beyond grandparents, uncles, aunts, and cousins, in many parts of Latin America, through first, the system of *compadrazgo,* the incorporation into the *familia* of another set of god parents at each of many ceremonies, and second, the incorporation of *cuates* (literally twins), or best friends. The resulting enormous conglomerate is an 'insurance umbrella' encompassing nearly everything of importance to traditional rural Mexicans: members of such extended families live close-by and often constitute entire neighborhoods. But the importance of the *familia* to *urban* Mexicans is not markedly less.

Urban Mexican houses give little hint of the foregoing. Free-standing or attached, they incorporate, primarily, nuclear families. A cursory inspection of the urban Mexican house, coupled with the hasty attachment of environment-behavior labels, therefore leads to the very misleading conclusion that the extended family has been weakened and the separation of nuclear elements somehow strengthened. Nothing could be further from the truth. In fact, linkages in this matrifocal world have been spatially lengthened but not markedly strained, and the ties of these nuclear family dwellings to other *familia*-related dwellings [are,] in general, still infinitely stronger than to neighbors.

Let's consider concepts of 'public and private.' In the traditional Mexican town or village, houses of the middle-class and above are divided from the street by continuous walls. The gradient is hard and abrupt, and there is no exterior semi-public space as such. Unless the street is also an extended family domain, the street is familially non-territorial; this may contribute to some observers' impression of incredible contrasts between littered streets and spotlessly clean, compulsively ordered house interiors. It is also part of a dialectical relationship: certainly, compulsivity is not a general part of Mexican psychology: in fact, it is both sex-linked and place-specific. Inside the house is the responsibility of the mother; the outside is the responsibility of something nebulous, ill-understood: 'the government' [...]

The hard walls define a boundary between the private and public realm, but public and private to whom? In brief [...] hospitality is all-important [and] must be available to any member or members of the extended *familia* at any time. All members of the *familia* have access to all parts of the house but food preparations and laundry areas – these are the only ones that can be considered semi-private. They are semi-permeable alien territories, related to a gender-divided hierarchical society: In brief, they are the servants' territory, and accessible only to the women of the *familia,* who supervise, but do not engage in, the demeaning manual labour they represent [...]

Important objects are always conspicuously displayed, in an array that strikes the careless observer as clutter, but is in fact a highly ordered, closely packed, often museum-like collection having, in most homes, almost no relation to traditional Mexico [...] As there is little physically private space, so there are few private objects. The early internationalized homes even incorporated the automobile as part of this conspicuous display: designs which opened garages into living rooms were extremely popular just a few years ago.

Indeed, the closest equivalents to the English word 'privacy' in the Spanish language are intimacy, isolation, and solitude, of which two are connotatively negative and the other sexual.[4] Octavio Paz'[s] (1950) *Labyrinth of Solitude* exists on psychological and philosophical levels, but not in the physical environment.

Because all non-servant spaces are public to all *familia* members, they must be kept in perfect order at all times: Room doors must be open except when sleeping or dressing and all closet doors closed (although closet interiors must be ordered as the rooms) [...] A mother refers to the bedroom in which she sleeps with her husband not as *nuestro cuarto* (our room) but as *mi cuarto* (my room): some women allow female friends or relatives to enter, but not their maids [...] The entire house is clearly female territory, and the kitchen is exclusively so.

In households such as the above, there is a relatively high tolerance for noise, time is difficult to plan, and 'action chains'[5] can rarely be completed. In terms of [Erving] Goffman's theater model, 'front stage' and 'back stage' shift with time: bedrooms which serve as dressing rooms ('back stage') upon arising in the morning become entertainment spaces ('front stage') during the day.

The nuclear family is always subordinate, in both form and function, to the *familia,* and the duties of husband and wife to both their *familias* transcend duties to each other. It is said that 'in Mexico, one does not marry an individual; one marries a family.' Therefore, while the house is occupied by a nuclear family, it is identified with the extended *familia*.

Social reproduction of the *familia* implies many nested ceremonies: these involve extensive preparation and considerable expense at various significant points in the life of the developing child. The Sunday *comida* (afternoon lunch) at grandmother's house is further replicated by the daily *comida* in the nuclear family dwelling. The ceremonial quality of this is reflected in the observation that the most important elements not just of traditional Mexican society, but everywhere apart from the largest cities are still 'mother and lunch.' Even in large cities, nearly all mothers eat lunch with their children at home; this is the only time, until late at night, that the father is likely to be home. Thus, the space devoted to dining is large and central for two reasons: behaviorally, it must accommodate not just the nuclear family, but members of the *familia* on many weekends; symbolically, it is the formal representation of the society's most important value.

[Susan] Kent quoting Hiller and Hanson, has also noted that domestic space use replicates, on a family level, entire social systems.[6] What this means, astonishingly, is that 'eating lunch' can have repercussions at the metropolitan, national, and international levels. The cultural press to return home for *comida* in one of Mexico City's internationalized homes means four rush hours instead of two: astonishingly 'lunch' is thus a major contributor to the greatest urban pollution problems on earth [...]

Territoriality has been a popular area of study in environmental psychology[7] and we have already stated that the house is primarily the mother's territory (the children have 'their' spaces as well). But Mexico remains a rigidly patriarchal society: 'The idea of a strong family is inseparable from that of a family controlled by a paternalistic figure of authority.'[8] How then does this all-powerful male figure relate to the home?

[...] The adult male, who occupies the top of the familial 'pecking order,' has no domestic territory [...] In the provinces, the man exists in two worlds, but his realm (social rather than individual territory), is the street and the *cantina;* in middle-class urban Mexico it is often the office. A few Mexican men have offices 'at home,' these are either in a separate building on the same lot or in a separate wing of the house. In either case, it usually has no access from the house and is entered only from the outside. Thus, in the domestic sphere, territory and hierarchy do not coincide [...]

Ancient and modern internationalized homes are connected through the values and behavior of the people who dwell in them. Social systems, like all large systems, are inherently conservative, they endeavor to maintain themselves in the face of change. It is this self-maintaining characteristic that bridges the contradiction represented by the ancient and modern institutionalized homes: while striving to adjust to social change, people also strive to maintain cultural continuity.

NOTES

1 Michael M. Cernea, *Involuntary Resettlement in Development Projects* (Washington, DC: World Bank, 1988); Barbara J. Cummings, *Dam the Rivers, Damn the People* (London: Earthscan Publications, 1990).

2 Constance Perin, *Everything in Its Place: Social Order and Land Use in America* (Princeton, NJ: Princeton University Press, 1977).

3 Alan Riding, *Distant Neighbors: A Portrait of the Mexicans* (New York: Vintage Books, 1989), 238–9.
4 [Witold] Rybczynski (1986) points out that rooms in which individuals can be alone, which did not come into being in Europe until the seventeenth century, were at first called 'privacies.' His detailed discussion of early indications of the importance of privacy, interestingly, centres on a seventeenth-century Oslo bookbinder and his family [...] Such events, and the values attached to them, are atypical of Latin America. [See section 3.4 in this volume.]
5 Edward T. Hall and Mildred R. Hall, *Hidden Differences* (New York: Doubleday Anchor Books, 1987).
6 Susan Kent, 'A Cross-Cultural Study of Segmentation, Architecture, and the Use of Space,' in Susan Kent, ed., *Domestic Architecture and the Use of Space: An Interdisciplinary Cross-Cultural Study* (Cambridge: Cambridge University Press, 1990), 127–52.
7 For example, Rachel Sebba and Arza Churchman, 'Territories and Territoriality in the Home,' *Environment and Behavior* 15 / 2 (1983):191–210.
8 Riding, *Distant Neighbors*, 242.

2.8 MARY DOUGLAS 'The Idea of a Home: A Kind of Space'*

The more we reflect on the tyranny of the home, the less surprising it is that the young wish to be free of its scrutiny and control. The evident nostalgia in much writing about the idea of home is more surprising. The mixture of nostalgia and resistance explains why the topic is so often treated as humorous. Dylan Thomas left home at an early age. His *Portrait of the Artist as a Young Dog* has a story about two men, outcasts from seaside suburbia, standing under the pier and wistfully speculating on what would be happening at home. Given that it is five o'clock in the evening, they know quite precisely that curtains are being drawn, the children being called in to tea, and even what tea will comprise. *In Less than Angels* Barbara Pym, that coolly detached recorder of homes, has an ironic passage about the suburban home of two sisters. After supper the dishes are cleared and the house made ready for night; every day before retiring one sister sets the table for tomorrow's breakfast, then both go up to bed; every night, before extinguishing the light, the other sister creeps down again to have one last look at

* *Social Research* 58 / 1 (1991): 287–307.

the breakfast table in case something has been forgotten, and is very relieved if she manages to avert catastrophe by straightening a fork or adding a plate that should be there. These are affectionate images of home as a pattern of regular doings. Other images are frankly hostile. The very regularity of home's processes is both inexorable and absurd. It is this regularity that needs focus and explaining. How does it go on being what it is? And what is it?

Home certainly cannot be defined by any of its functions. Try the idea that home provides the primary care of bodies: if that is what it does best, it is not very efficient; a health farm or hotel could do as well. To say that it provides for the education of the infants hardly covers what it does, and raises the same question about whether specialized schools or orphanages would not do it better. We will dismiss the cynical saying that the function of the home in modern industrial society is to produce the input into the labour market. As to those who claim that the home does something stabilizing or deepening or enriching for the personality, there are as many who will claim that it cripples and stifles. This essay makes a fresh start by approaching the home as an embryonic community. If it sounds platitudinous it is because many sociologists think of the embryonic community as modelled on the idea of a home. This relic of nineteenth-century romantic enthusiasm has been a stumbling block in sociology, where it is assumed too easily that the survival of a community over many vicissitudes does not need explaining. On this line of thought both home and community are supposed to be able to draw upon the same mysterious supply of loyal support, and further, their inner sources of strength are unanalyzable: thanks to a kind of mystic solidarity home and small local community are supposed to be able to overcome the forces of fission that tear larger groups apart [...] This essay will approach solidarity from a more pragmatic point of view. It will try to answer the question, What makes solidarity possible? not by theorizing but by empirical observations on what strategies people adopt when they want to create solidarity.

What Kind of Space?

We start very positivistically by thinking of home as a kind of space. Home is 'here,' or it is 'not here.' The question is not 'How?' nor 'Who?' nor 'When?' but 'Where is your home?' It is always a localizable idea. Home is located in space, but it is not necessarily a fixed space. It does not need bricks and mortar, it can be a wagon, a caravan, a boat, or a tent. It need not be a large space, but space there must be, for home starts by bringing some space under control. Having shelter is not having a home, nor is having a house, nor is home the same as household [...] For a home neither the space nor its appurtenances have to be fixed, but there has to be something regular about the appearance and reappearance of its furnishings. The bedding in a Japanese home may be rolled away, and rolled back, morning and night. The same with the populations; people flow through a home too, but there are some regularities [...] A home is not only a space, it also has some structure in time; and because it is for people who are living in that time and space, it has aesthetic and moral dimensions [...] The minimum home has orientation even if it lacks any inside-outside boundary; usually it has both, so that the cardinal points are not mere coordinates for plotting position but 'directions of existence.'[1] [...] Why some homes should have more complex orienting and bounding than others depends on the ideas that persons are carrying inside their heads about their lives in space and time. For the home is the realization of ideas.

Coordination

The primary problem of a virtual community is to achieve enough solidarity to protect the collective good. If solidarity weakens, individual raids destroy the collective resource base. Though the home, like other not-for-profit institutions, is inefficient on market criteria, in another sense it is remarkably efficient [...]

Much of the burden of organization is carried by conspicuous fixed times. The order of day is the infrastructure of the community. In a home there is no need to look for someone: it should be possible to work out where everyone is at any given time, that is, if it is functioning well. But home is a fragile system, easy to subvert. It is generally well recognized that the main contribution of members to the collective good is to be physically present at its assemblies. An act of presence is a public service [...] Absence is to be deplored. Perhaps the most subversive attack on the home is to be present physically without joining in its multiple coordinations. To leave erratically, without saying where or for how long, to come back and go upstairs without greeting, these lapses are recognized as spoliation of the commons. In one of her autobiographical essays Colette describes her mother coming into the garden and calling: Where are the children? No answer. They are up in the trees, stretched out in the boughs, or curled up in the grass, in the stable, hiding, sleeping, reading. She gets no answer, and her disregarded call bespeaks the weakness of that home shortly to be disbanded.

The time devoted to the common meal is a conclave, used for coordinating other arrangements, negotiating exemptions, canvassing for privileges, diffusing information about the outside world, agreeing on strategies for dealing with it and making shared evaluations. The conclave invents exceptions to its rules: permissions to be late, to skip a meal. A home is a tangle of conventions and totally incommensurable rights and duties. Not a money economy, the home is the typical gift economy described by Marcel Mauss [...] Every service and transfer is part of an ongoing comprehensive system of exchanges, within and between the generations. The transactions never look like exchanges because the gesture of reciprocity is delayed and disguised. No one can know the worth of their own contribution to the home. It is not just that calculation is too difficult, but more that it suits no one to insist on a precise offsetting of one service against another. Debts are remembered well enough, but by keeping them vague there is the hope that repayment may be more than equivalent [...]

Tyrannies of the Home

This is how the home works. Even its most altruistic and successful versions exert a tyrannous control over mind and body. We need hardly say more to explain why children want to leave it and do not mean to reproduce it when they set up house. When we add the possibilities of subversion, the case for rejecting the idea of the home is even stronger [...]

On this account, home as a virtual community is often absurd, and often cruel. We have tried to interrogate its life to understand community sources of solidarity. The result of the inquest is that those committed to the idea of home exert continual vigilance in its behalf [...] If we had to choose an index of solidarity from the time-space structure of homes, the strongest indicator would not be stoutness of the enclosing walls but the complexity of coordination [...] Complexity is more surprising than simplicity or confusion. From an information-theoretic point of view its presence needs to be explained. The persons who devote vigilance to the maintenance of the home apparently believe that they personally have a lot to lose if it were to collapse. This is the point at which biological pressures to provide for the young have to be invoked. Other embryonic communities have more trouble about mustering solidarity and demanding sacrifice. To this extent the sociologists are right who attribute to primordial passions the survival of families and small communities [...]

The type of home that has been taken as exemplary [...] is not authoritarian, but it has authority. It is hierarchical, but it is not centralized. The best name for this type of organization is a protohierarchy. It is recognizable because it springs up, spontaneously, to meet certain recurring conditions of organization. It is a multipeaked, rationally integrated system which we find in villages, districts, kingdoms, and empires. Highly efficient for maintaining itself in being, it is easily subverted and survives only so long as it attends to the needs of its members.

NOTE

1 James Littlejohn, 'The Temne House,' *Sierra Leone Studies* (n.s.), 14 (Dec. 1960): 63–7.

2.9 LINDA MCDOWELL 'Rethinking Place: Thoughts on Spaces of the Home, Absence, Presence, New Connections and New Anxieties'*

The focus of this section is an assessment of the extent to which contemporary patterns of change and mobility are affecting representations and meanings of home. In both sociology and geography, mobility rather than stasis is a central issue. A hybrid, mobile subject is the iconic figure of an increasingly distanciated geography that connects the near and the far, and sociology is now defined, according to John Urry[1] by mobility rather than presence / place. While the concept of home is an idea that unites a range of spatial scales from homeland – the nation – to the home – the house or hearth – I want to concentrate here on the local and the small scale: on the meaning of the home in contemporary Britain, as it is at this local level that mobility perhaps seems least relevant as images of the home as a haven, providing security, safety, and certainty are persistent, in contrast to wider social insecurities. Britain is a society currently anxious about its identity, redrawing its borders in order to exclude those distant non-locals defined as less eligible and less useful, but also where a perhaps less-remarked social revolution is occurring. At the same time as the idea of the nation and citizenship is being challenged by long distance movement and by political shifts, by both the amalgamation and fracturing of nation states, the older associations between home, domesticity, and femininity are being challenged by active labour market policies that insist that the key social responsibility of the ungendered individual at the centre of neo-liberal policies is labour

* *Home Cultures* 4 / 2 (2007): 129–46.

market participation [...] Whereas taken for granted co-presence and co-sanguinity – in particular of a mother and her children – have long been the defining characteristics, indeed constitution, of the idea of a home, the home increasingly is a space marked by absence and / or by the co-presence of people united not by ties of blood and affection but by economic exchange [...]

The Good Mother

In the early twenty-first century, national policies in the UK are actively constructing a new version of the good mother and reshaping the boundaries between the 'private' arena of the home, the state, and the market. While femininity, domesticity, and mothering used to be inextricably intertwined, this relationship has been challenged, even broken apart, in the last five or so years by the assumption in state labour market policies that all women must enter the labour market, regardless of their domestic obligations.[2] [...] This radically changes the meaning of motherhood. The good mother now is a mother who enters the labour market to raise her income and skill levels for the benefit of her children, who no longer occupies the home as a continuous presence, and who hands over the care of children to another for part of the day [...] Child care in recent policies has been recast through a substitution lens into a commodity form, reconstituted as a social responsibility enacted through the market and performed by the labour of socially unrelated others, either in state or market provided specialist facilities or in the homes of individual families. This commodity relation transforms the home into a site of financially recompensed interactions, rather than a locus in which all the social relationships and interactions were assumed to be based on ties of love and affection and largely performed outside a cash nexus. I use the term 'assumed' to acknowledge the well-developed and long-standing feminist critique of the home as simultaneously a site of power relations and inequalities as well as a site of pleasure, love, and reciprocity [...]

But to what extent is this new, neo-liberal individualized version of the good / caring mother as the employed mother reflected in the various discursive constructions of motherhood currently in circulation? Is there, as [Kathy] Pitt has suggested a new discourse of mothering, one that she terms 'being a new capitalist mother' in which striving, personal achievement, and a commitment to life-long learning are paramount?[3] And, what concomitantly are current representations of the home? Is it still defined as a distinctive space, as a place differentiated from other more public spaces / places by relations of love and affection? What versions of the home are now current in new policy discourses, in novels, and popular how-to-parent books [...], for example, in the marketing of new forms of technology and in women's own descriptions of their lives?[4] [...]

How does the disconnection of child care from its naturalized association with mother-love and care in the home, and all the associated feelings of duty, obligation, pleasure, desire, guilt, and ambivalence embodied in the individual care of a child by its mother, affect the meaning of the home for women? How does replacement care – especially if it takes place in individual homes – alter the social meaning of that space for mothers? What are the consequences of increased sharing of private spaces by unrelated others, often differentiated by class and ethnicity? It seems to me that the meaning of these diurnal detailed forms of face-to-face interactions has received insufficient attention. Are new connections between people and places that are the consequence of women's increased labour market participation remaking / reshaping the connections between presence and absence and the meaning of home / community? Are ideas about belongingness, duty, obligation, and love – those relationships of close personal association that thirty years ago Bell and Newby argued defined 'communion' (although their concept applied to a wider space than social relations within the home, including the locality or neighbourhood) – now obsolete? At the time when Bell and Newby were writing, few sociologists were interested in what went on behind the front door, but now it is important to explore how social relations of obligation and love enacted in the home are being challenged, replaced or redefined by new patterns of daily living and divisions of labour.[5] If place, the locality, is defined not as a bordered container but a locus of exchange and interactions across different spatial scales,[6] how should we now define the home as it is both the site and the locus of multiple forms of interchange, both 'real' and virtual, between people who are both physically present and absent at different times?

The particular question that I am interested in at present is one that is stimulated by the recent theoretical return to class inequality among sociologists, geographers, and others, as well as contemporary evidence of growing class antagonism in policy discourses and in social behaviour in cities. In a number of debates in these disciplines, arguments about the nature of class and class divisions that emphasize the connections between economic inequalities and cultural misrecognition are common.[7] Theorizations of class have moved beyond a focus on economic inequalities constituted in the sphere of production to look both at discursive representations of class and at class behaviours in other spheres of social action. Thus, it has been argued that class divisions in the spheres of consumption and in urban space are becoming increasingly marked [...]

[...] How then are these inter-class, and often intergenerational, social relations negotiated within the spaces of the home and the family? [...] Which aspects of everyday social behaviours, attitudes, and mores are tolerated and which are contested as different class patterns are reproduced within the home? How are relations of trust established? [...] And what are the boundaries of the spaces that a care-giver might occupy when the employer – typically the mother – is present and when she is absent? Are there spaces within the home that are off-limits to waged careers, places / rooms that remain 'private' family spaces?

And is the division of space different when the care-giver lives within the family home rather than works on a daily basis? How are movements within the home regulated and controlled? For working-class women who labour in the homes of their middle-class employers, a rhetoric of family belonging or what has been termed false kin or quasi-family relationships in studies of au pairs and other domestic workers who 'live-in'[8] is often used in an attempt both to include the waged worker within the relations of intimacy and caring that are the ideal forms of connection between the carer and the cared for, as well as to reduce the economic obligations – to pay the basic minimum wage, for example, or to regulate hours [...]

But what about working-class women in employment, including the growing child-care workforce? Who looks after their children? As I noted above, their own view of good mothering involves both 'being there' whenever possible and preferring informal and family-based, undertaken especially by grandmothers, to commodified care. But does this lead to inter-generational / intra-familial conflicts in the home? One resolution of the dilemmas about employment and child care for working-class mothers is to become childminders, caring for their own and a small number of additional children in their own home (although perhaps surprisingly the number of childminders seems to be declining – it fell from 102,600 in 1996, for example, to 75,600 by 2000) [...]

The labouring bodies of the care-workers, and to a lesser extent the children or elderly dependants they care for, are subjected to forms of surveillance that are more common in factories and prisons than within the boundaries of the home. And perhaps, in homes where such forms of electronic surveillance have not been installed, nevertheless caregivers may behave as if they were watched, although the employers can never be sure, and micro-scale strategies of resistance may include entering forbidden spaces, breaking dietary rules or permitting children greater degrees of freedom than normal [...]

As service economies are restructured, there is already little doubt that one of the epochal changes lies in the changing nature of care and the spaces in which it is given / exchanged and paid for. Home / family / domestic life has changed for most households and as one of Hochschild's respondents, speaking for many other overstretched working fathers and mothers, noted: 'I am not putting my time where my values are.'[9] [...]

While not wanting to [...] deny the advantages that accrue to individual women and to their families from enhanced incomes and greater independence, it is clear that current so-called work / family reconciliation policies (somewhat inaccurately referred to as work / life balance policies in the UK), in combination with inadequate, high-cost, and too often low-quality child-care provision, fail to address the difficult issue of how to value caring for others.

Finally, what all this means for class relationships, for the increasingly common representations of working-class men and women as backward and feckless is harder to judge. Whether co-presence within the home will modify the evident cultural condescension widely apparent at present or whether growing spatial segregation between the classes at other scales – the local, the urban, the North-South divide in the UK – will further cement class polarization is still an open question.

NOTES

1 John Urry, *Sociology beyond Societies* (London: Routledge, 2000).
2 Jane Lewis, 'Individualisation, Assumptions about the Existence of an Adult Worker Model and the Shift towards Contractualism,' in Alan H. Carling, Simon Duncan, and Rosalind Edwards, eds., *Analysing Families: Morality and Rationality in Policy and Practice* (London: Routledge, 2002), 23–41.
3 Kathy Pitt, 'Being a New Capitalist Mother,' *Discourse and Society* 13 (2002): 251–67.
4 Melissa Benn, *Madonna and Child: Towards a New Politics of Motherhood* (London: Jonathan Cape, 1998).
5 Colin Bell and Howard Newby, 'Community, Communion, Class and Community Action: The Sources of New Urban Politics,' in David T. Herbert and Ronald J. Johnston, eds., *Social Areas in Cities* (London: Wiley, 1976), vol. 2, 189–207.
6 Doreen Massey, *For Space* (London: Sage, 2005).
7 bell hooks, *Where We Stand: Class Matters* (London: Routledge, 2000); Iris Marion Young, *Justice and the Politics of Difference* (Princeton, NJ: Princeton University Press, 1990).
8 Abigail Bess Bakan and Daiva K. Stasiulis, *Not One of the Family: Foreign Domestic Workers in Canada* (Toronto: University of Toronto Press, 1997); Sarah Radcliffe, 'Ethnicity, Patriarchy and Incorporation into the Nation: Female Migrants as Domestic Servants in Peru,' *Environment and Planning D: Society and Space* 8 (1990): 379–93.

9 Arlie Hochschild, *The Commercialization of Intimate Life: Notes from Home and Work* (Berkeley, CA: University of California Press, 2003).

2.10 WILLIAM J. GLOVER 'A Feeling of Absence from Old England: The Colonial Bungalow'*

> I am very much amused to witness English home life. There is no such word as 'home' in our language; [in England] it is a word employed chiefly in the elevated style. And every heart is stirred by it. I had heard the word so often that I was anxious to see an English home and real home life. This is a small cozy house, tastefully furnished.
>
> – Excerpt from the London travel diary of Nawab Mehdi Hasan Khan, 1890

The Indian travel agent quoted above highlights the 'elevated' status of the English home in the minds of that island's inhabitants, just as it alludes to differences between English homes in England and English homes in colonial India.[1] If the typical retired Lieutenant Governor's London row-house (as described by Khan) was notable for being 'small' and 'cozy,' then the active Lieutenant Governor's residence in India at the time was certain to be a much grander affair. Not simply the residence of a loyal and well-placed government servant, such a house in India was, according to one prominent historian of British India, 'a representation of the authority of an imperial power and the residence of that power's representative in the colony.'[2]

While this may have been true for the largest official residences, it would not be true of the far humbler structures that were home to the vast majority of Europeans in colonial India. As a visible feature of the landscape, these simpler homes shared some of the symbolic rhetoric of exclusion and superiority that characterized the empire's largest residences. Most European houses were isolated from the street by walls and gates; they were set in relatively large lots; and they were often raised honorifically above their surroundings on a stepped plinth. Even simple houses were sometimes adorned with neoclassical or gothic revival ornament, features that alluded both to extra-local sources of cultural

---

* *Home Cultures* 1 / 1 (2004): 61–82.

authority and to contemporary fashions in the distant metropole. But the ordinary colonial bungalow was much more than a symbolic visual form. It was also a complicated social and material milieu, the setting for a type of domesticity that was meant to help reflect and instil the values and dispositions that separated rulers from their subjects.

Many scholars have underlined the importance of a discourse on 'domesticity' in the constitution of colonial power [...] The Anglo-European ideal of middle-class domesticity described the home as a refuge from the competitive outside world, an incubator for the moral development of children, and a temple to conjugal sexuality. In colonial settings, the Anglo-European home was seen as both a refuge from the strange and unfamiliar world outside, and a potential catalyst for the social improvement of 'Native' society. Maintaining proper domestic arrangements in the colony was seen as a bulwark against the feared dissolution of character that might come about through prolonged exposure to the tropics [...] The properly ordered home was also thought to be a powerful device for reform, one that could mould and reshape 'Native' habits and customs once it had been imposed on the local population. 'Britons were quite open in their efforts to impose their values on local domestic arrangements ... and they never doubted that buildings embodied particular moral principles of conjugality and kinship.'[3] [...]

The bourgeois ideal of domestic comfort was seldom fully realized in the ordinary colonial domicile, however. In colonial India, evidence suggests that the colonial home was both a familiar and strange place to its occupants; a source of both homely comfort and disquieting anxiety. If the English home in colonial India provided a setting for the cultivation of habits and dispositions that authorized colonial rule, then the same structure often gave presence to a kind of 'Indian-ness' that was a source of discomfort to their European occupants. What tied these two opposed senses of home life together – homely comfort and disquieting anxiety – was the architecture of the colonial domicile itself, a material and social artefact with distinctive qualities. Rather than simply symbolizing an idea of European power and authority, the colonial domicile was a complicated milieu where the attitudes and practices of European authority met with – and never fully overcame – a range of stubborn obstacles.

[...] Most of the evidence presented here is drawn from the city of Lahore, the capital city of Punjab Province in British India (1849–1947) [...] By the late nineteenth century, Lahore was a desirable posting for European officers and civilians due to its large size, moderate climate, and relatively cosmopolitan range of institutions and activities. Although the European community in Lahore never exceeded a few hundred people at any time during the nineteenth century, the city's European residential district was considerably larger in area than the entire older 'City' of Lahore, a mostly Indian district that housed more than 150,000 people at the turn of the twentieth century [...]

In Lahore's Civil Station, the most common type of European residence was a bungalow, a detached single-story house surrounded by a large compound that was fenced or enclosed within walls (see Figure 1). Urban sociologist Anthony King has traced the evolution of the bungalow as a house type from its likely origins in Bengal province, where the term 'bangla' denoted a temporary thatched structure used for residence or storage, usually in an agricultural setting. Over time, both the meaning and physical attributes of the bungalow changed, and during the colonial period the term was increasingly used in India to designate a residential structure used primarily by Europeans.[4]

A small minority of Europeans lived in other types of accommodations in Lahore, including residential hotels [which ...] became popular by the early twentieth century [...] in part because they served well as temporary quarters for incoming residents while they waited for a bungalow to be vacated [...]

Some bungalows, especially those located in military cantonments, were built by the colonial government for its officers and employees, and standard plans were produced by the Public Works Department (PWD) for the purpose [...] In larger cities, however, bungalows were often built by Indian businessmen and landowners who rented them both to government officers and to European civilians [...]

The temporary nature of residence, thus, and the problems this produced, was a product of colonial political economy, British administrative practices, and the control exercised over European residents by their Indian landlords. All of these features gave rise to a number of awkward problems for those who would conceive the home as a space for reflecting and helping instil in its occupants the outward marks of decorum and refinement that helped distinguish status between ruler and ruled [...]

Being more or less constantly on the move meant that whatever one possessed by way of 'household decoration' had to be relatively mobile, disposable, or not liable to be missed when left behind. Furnishings of the proper sort were scarce in most cities, and most were acquired 'on the cheap' at moving sales, or at sales accompanying European funerals in the city. A genre of 'ladies' periodical literature and household decoration guides grew up to address the need for cheap furnishings and economical decoration ideas by the latter half of the nineteenth century [...]

Keeping a proper home, with its requisite furnishings and appliances, was one way of making the bungalow an 'island of Englishness,' in the words of Thomas Metcalf – a social and architectural setting which distanced itself from the promiscuous and degraded content of the Indian city as European residents

1 Rudyard Kipling's bungalow in Lahore c. 1897 (destroyed). Source: Architect unknown. *Review of Reviews,* February 1897. Courtesy of William J. Glover.

perceived it.[5] Even within the White community, however, differences in status were open to view, and the bungalow was an important site of social anchorage for marking and maintaining those differences [...]

If the bungalow was, in part, a setting for the cultivation and display of refined manners and taste, then its physical appearance played a role in the pervasive sense of anxiety about the effects on human character of living in a colony highlighted in European writings. The bungalow's walls, rooms, doors, and furnishings became a focus of comparison between qualities found in English and Indian homes, just as they served as vexing reminders of the co-presence of different sensory qualities, meanings, and values tied to more local histories of production and use.[6]

The Social Organization of Domestic Space

More than material qualities played a role in making bungalows seem inadequate to their purposes, however. The social functions these houses had to accommodate required an orchestrated arrangement of spaces that was difficult to manage in a bungalow. The bungalow's relatively simple layout served a variety of social purposes. Most bungalows were built near the centre of an enclosed plot of sufficient area to insure a free flow of breeze across it. Servants' quarters, animal, vehicle, and other kinds of storage sheds were arrayed along one edge of the plot out of view from the main rooms of the house, and a separate structure placed closer to the main dwelling was used for the kitchen [...]

The 'front' and 'back' of the bungalow established an imaginary axis that divided more public functions in the house from those which were considered to be more private [...] Rooms at the front of the house were used for entertaining visitors or overnight guests, and in the case of a government officer's residence, at least one room was required to be set aside as a place for meeting the area's residents on matters concerning local governance. The presence of an office in the bungalow meant that residence and office functions coexisted in the same structure, adding a further layer of complexity to the building's program of use.

The nineteenth-century European bourgeois ideal of proper domestic arrangements specified clear separations between less- and more-private spaces in the house, between servants and family members, and between people of different sexes and ages. The house plan ideally segregated different activities from one another and provided a separate space for each [...]

Bungalows were organized to serve these needs too, but the relations of domestic labour they were supported by, along with the physical distribution of spaces they housed, constantly worked against the ideal.

One of the key points of conflict was, of course, the disposition of household servants [...] Even a relatively modest European household in India would maintain several specialized servants to conduct most of the daily labour of the house, from cooking, gardening, and cleaning out the house's rooms, to serving as wet nurses and *ayahs* (nannies) for European infants and children [...] The co-presence of Indian servants in the innermost recesses of the home was thought to expose its occupants to a range of social (and physical) dangers that derived, in part, from fears of racial mixing [...] tensions included the possibility that European children would develop overly affective ties to their Indian *ayahs* and acquire bad habits of personality – or even take on their pernicious racial traits through the medium of wet nurses' milk; the fear of servants' sexual profligacy or of their becoming a source of sexual arousal for their colonial masters; and the threat that letting down one's guard over personal demeanour might incite insurrection or ridicule, either of which could dismantle the social distance that justified colonial rule itself [...] The layout of bungalows mediated these threats imperfectly, since one of their key qualities was porosity between the interior rooms of the house and the house's exterior [...]

The history of colonial urbanism has often been written as the incomplete imposition of Western forms of society, politics, and technology in a non-Western setting [...] The role of built form in this history is usually to serve as a backdrop for the telling of events or else to provide incontrovertible material evidence of the intentions of a foreign ruling elite [...] However, a study of the intentions that lay behind the way colonial buildings were constructed, inhabited, and socially organized is never wholly adequate for conducting a history of their use and meaning [...] The grounding of colonial power depended as much on everyday and small-scale practices as it did on the display of monumental buildings or public rituals of statecraft. Indeed, in the colonial context, as Ann Laura Stoler has argued, it was 'the domestic domain, not the public sphere, where [the] essential dispositions of manliness, bourgeois morality, and racial attribute could be dangerously undone or securely made.'[7]

[...] Always imperfect for the task, the bungalow nevertheless formed an important setting for enacting those small-scale and everyday practices [...] the material qualities of the bungalow's construction and the social arrangements they were meant to help constitute problematized the everyday expectations and sensory perceptions that, while matters of commonplace for the English at home were de-familiarized and brought prominently to attention in the colonial setting. If the usual trope for describing the colonial bungalow is that it 'served to impress Indians with the power and authority of the British,' then this is a trope more closely attuned with intention than with an actually realized set of practices.[8] Instead [...] it is more useful to think of the bungalow as a milieu for the cultivation of attitudes and behaviours necessary to evoke authority, than as a building that evoked the same thing.

NOTES

1 Nawab Mehdi Hasan Khan, Chief Justice of Hyderabad, Deccan, reprinted in *The Punjab Magazine* 233 (1890): 28, 31.
2 Thomas Metcalf, *An Imperial Vision: Indian Architecture and India's Raj* (Berkeley, CA: University of California Press, 1989), 9.
3 John Comaroff and Jean Comaroff, *Ethnography and the Historical Imagination* (Boulder, CO: Westview Press, 1992), 289.
4 Anthony D. King, *The Bungalow: The Production of a Global Culture* (London: Routledge and Kegan Paul, 1984).
5 Thomas Metcalf, *Ideologies of the Raj* (Cambridge: Cambridge University Press, 1994), 178.

6 Nadia Serematakis, ed., *The Senses Still: Perception and Memory as Material Culture in Modernity* (Boulder, CO: Westview Press, 1994), 136.
7 Ann Laura Stoler, *Race and the Education of Desire: Foucault's History of Sexuality and the Colonial Order of Things* (Durham, NC: Duke University Press, 1995), 108.
8 Thomas Metcalf writes, for example, that 'the size of the compound, together with its wall, gate, guard, and long entry drive, served to impress Indians with the power and authority of the British, while at the same time affording a way of regulating entry' (*Ideologies of the Raj*, 177–8).

2.11 ALAN PASSES
Loud Women: Creating Community from the Domestic in Amazonia (An Anthropological View)

That the home is existentially and philosophically *in* the world rather than outside it is manifestly true as far as Amazonian people are concerned. For them, as Peter Rivière notes, 'the domestic and supradomestic levels are not divorced from one another but are intrinsically related.'[1] Here I explore this relationship and show how, in the indigenous understanding of *communitas,* the qualities of the domestic extend into the supradomestic, both spheres mutually comprising sociality, understood as the quality of living not only socially but sociably.

Early morning on the frontier between Brazil and French Guiana. Life stirs in the small settlement of Palikur Indians as hammocks emerge like boats from the rising mist, and the first villagers appear and gently begin the ritual exchange of daily greetings.[2] But suddenly, shouting shatters the dawn. O.'s mother is telling him off. She stands in the middle of the communal space in front of her dwelling, chastising the teenager who has just attained the status of *awaig takwié,* 'young adult man.' Her voice rises, loud, irate. Something about O. being lazy. That he should pull his weight, contribute more. That his behaviour is *ka kabai,* 'not good,' 'wrong,' 'improper,' 'ugly.' Impassive, O. submits to the tongue-lashing in silence, his mother aiming her words not just at him but to the whole community, so that all be apprised of his misdemeanour, her anger, and reprimand.

A woman, or sometimes two or more in concert, scolding a hapless kinsman over some transgression is a common, everyday occurrence in a Palikur village. For me, it is also emblematic. As an aspect of the power held by the women generally it is a marker not only of Palikur domestic life, but of their *social* life as well. For it is my contention that actions and events which, from a Eurocentric perspective, are a purely private, family affair, can in fact be inherently social and, moreover, create and sustain the community's very sociality.

The Anthropological Domestic

I realize this claim will be implausible to anyone subscribing to the assumption that the domestic and the social are mutually exclusive. Take, for example, the anthropologist Marshall Sahlins who opposes the domestic, defined as private and asocial (i.e., equated with 'chaotic' nature) to the supradomestic, defined as public and social (i.e., equated with hierarchy, coercion, and politics).[3] However, Western anthropology largely ignores the domestic, judging it irrelevant to the weighty task of searching out and explaining the master principles underlying Society and Culture. Under the influence of various grand narratives of modernist thought that accompanied its rise as an intellectual and academic project, the discipline historically concentrated on the formal structures held to govern people's ways of life. Their everyday activities, concerns, and spaces were bypassed as anthropologists, with few exceptions, attended to more 'important' and 'significant' matters: social organization, prescriptions, and rules; rituals, cosmologies, and myths. These themes continue to dominate mainstream anthropological and ethnographic endeavour at the expense of the poetics and performance of the 'ordinary' lives of the thinking-feeling-doing persons in which we briefly participate. For until very recently the condition of such lives, the informal, unstructured, daily business of dwelling in the world – experiential, emotional, sensory, and sensual, polyphonic and dialogic, and to a great extent domestic – tended to be considered an inappropriate subject for serious study.[4]

The disregard for the domestic life derives from a deep-seated misogynist bias in moral and political philosophy linked, as Joanna Overing explains, to Western theories about kinship and society.[5] Once the key concept of anthropology, kinship was initially equated with society and deemed the cornerstone of its principal institutions (law, morality, economics, politics). However, kinship's stock fell on being associated with nature (i.e., biological reproduction) and, consequently, with the private, and non-social, non-political, non-moral, subordinate world of the family, in opposition to the public and moral superordinate world of society, posed in terms of the controlling and coercive power of the collective. This view was reinforced by the theory of 'domestic' and 'jural' domains. The first, primarily woman's, is characterized by relations of filiation and amity between members. In the second, man's domain, principles of descent and lineage prevail and underlie the structures of dominance which produce the social and political order and determine a member's status, rights, and obligations.

But Western hierarchical models of society are inapplicable to egalitarian Amazonian peoples. Far more apposite and useful theoretically, from an anthropological viewpoint, is the hypothesis, advanced by feminist moral philosophers – for example, of a social ethics based not on rights and obligations but virtues, with the stress on the 'female' ones (trust, care) instead of the 'male' ones (justice, personal autonomy).[6] This resonates with Amazonian practice, where an ethic of care, but in this case ungendered, drives not just the domestic life, but often the sociopolitical one as well.

Amazonian Sociality: Inclusion and the Extension of Domesticity

The preclusion of the domestic from the social and their ranking by gender are alien to the Amazonian understanding of social life. Unlike its Western counterpart, it does not entail a morality of obligation. A strong emphasis on personal freedom, compatible with an equally strong sense of community, means relationships are typically a matter of individual intention and choice rather than coercion, law, or Rousseauesque contract. Also, Amazonian sociality tends to be inclusive, allowing it not only to incorporate men but women, strangers, and even, cosmologically, non-humans.

An Amazonian collective's relationships can be described as domestic ones as, philosophically, what pertains outside the home is patterned on, and grounded in, what pertains inside it. For in Amazonia the distinctive features of family life (intimacy, informality, egalitarianism) provide the sociopolitical blueprint for coexisting peacefully, productively, and 'beautifully' with others *as if they were kin,* in the world beyond the hearth. In societies like the Palikur, the moral criteria, communitarian values, and knowledges and skills involved in daily recreating such a life fall on women and men equally. Key social and political activities from caring for children to governance are ungendered. So, the domestic, private realm is not 'female' or the public realm 'male.' Nor, in a further variance from Western dichotomies, do Amazonians categorize domestic life as emotional and social life as non-emotional. Rather, Palikur sociality, like that of other Amerindian peoples, morally privileges the positive emotions and behaviours Overing and I have glossed as Love.[7] It depends for its social – and political – viability on personal interactions based on such conditions as generosity, friendship, trust, cooperation, and sharing. I include scolding as one such interaction, for while not one of its gentler manifestations, it is nevertheless as expressive of care as sharing food with one's neighbour.

Overing's work with the Piaroa people of Venezuela has spearheaded an approach to Amazonian sociality sometimes labelled the 'moral economy of intimacy.' Highlighting the indigenous perspective on the world, it proposes that it is only in the constant praxis of a productive and sociable communal life that humans can turn the dangerous predatory 'other,' originating in the asocial supernatural sphere, into a safe 'someone like us.' This is done by 'domesticating' its destructive power into the constructive power and skills necessary for the collective creation of a fertile, peaceful, happy social life, or 'conviviality.' The process relies on the personal freedom and autonomy of each member of a 'community of similars'[8] – an individualism of a kind not antithetical to the group, as in the West, but intrinsic and instrumental to it. In indigenous eyes, such a sociality constitutes the Good Life, the Beautiful Life, one informed by notions of consubstantiality, commensality, and consanguinity in the form of actual kinship ties or fictive ones accorded to strangers. It is generated in and through social-moral-affective interrelational acts such as 'growing' children, producing and eating the same foods, and speaking the same language. Non-Palikur incomers who produce a Palikur lifestyle in communality with Palikur people can, over time, become 'kin' and acquire Palikur identity by sociable collaborative everyday practice. The personal autonomy basic to the creation of a 'convivial' community is, like most of the skills and knowledges employed, ungendered. As such, it is part of the sexual and political egalitarianism that is widespread in Amazonia. Among the Palikur, the two sexes enjoy a parity of autonomy, authority, and action in both the domestic and supradomestic arenas, with the women possessing high standing and economic and political power, some of them becoming community leaders and shamans.

The Domestic, Social, and Dramatic Art of Palikur Scolding

Such, then, are some of the contextual factors of Palikur scolding. Ethnolinguistically, the behaviour is a sub-category of 'speaking loud-and-strong,' *auna kihao,* which itself is a feature of 'speaking well,' *auna kabai*. 'Loud-and-strong talk' is the requisite style of speech for Palikur adults and has great moral and aesthetic value. It is held to embody a person's health, strength, and, beyond that, humanness. It also indicates eloquence, a speaker's capacity to use words in a manner expressive of care, knowledge, and persuasiveness. Whereas 'loud-and-strong talk' is ungendered, scolding is a purely female register, part of a Palikur woman's stock of cultural traits. The tone is louder and stronger than for standard 'loud-and-strong speech' and communicates ire, indignation, righteousness, severity. Scolds use it to rebuke, reprove, castigate, and sermonize, to voice grievances and demands. Scolding is always directed at men, mainly husbands, sons, and sons-in-law, and monological. It is improper for scoldees to respond.

Scolding is an act of controlled anger, unlike the incontinent violence of *dagaoné*, 'being cross / angry,' which is an illegitimate, antisocial emotion. The villagers, who are virtually all Protestant-fundamentalist converts, consider *dagaoné* and other improper feelings, such as envy and greed, to be products of the Devil, while the loudness and emotion attached to scolding are sanctioned, and the power of God's Word underlies those of the scold's. Thus, scolding is a socially and morally proper behaviour, expressing strength, knowledge, and positive female personhood. This differs from scolding in many other cultures, including our own, where female anger is represented in terms of negative stereotyping: want of self-control, hysteria, bossiness – the attributes of nags and shrews.

In Amazonia, scolding, like quarrels and greetings, is both a public and private activity. As mentioned, the Palikur version unfolds as often as not in communal space. Sometimes several scolds, a mother-in-law and wife, or two sisters and a sister-in-law, join in a chorus of complaint and condemnation. Mostly though, it's just a lone woman like O.'s mother, whose scolding I recorded in my field notes: 'O.'s mother screams at him to either go hunting or else go earn some more money [he has a part-time job in the local town]. His father is away and they need food. O. stony faced, saying nothing, sheepishly taking it as she goes on and on, her arms raised and throat tilted back as if addressing the entire community and the world beyond.'

Palikur scolding occupies the blurred boundary between the mundane and the ritualistic, the informal and formal. Simultaneously spontaneous and theatrical, the behaviour has a dynamic yet somewhat staged quality. Jointly physical and vocal, visual and aural, the mother's performance belongs to the theatre of expression with the striking of a tableaulike pose through which she projects an archetype such as the Aggrieved Woman or Wrathful Wife. Such an enactment of passion, partly impromptu and partly conventional, is a clear example of an embodied emotion involving learned body techniques employed to social or political ends. Through her culturally constructed, gendered display the scolder-actor effectively calls on her audience, the community at large, to bear witness to her grievance, understand the reason for it, and partake in her disapproval of the scoldee's antisocial failings. The son, meanwhile, gives no less a performance just by standing there motionless and mute under the impact of this dramatic public presentation of his shortcomings. Whether this will lead him to mend his ways and comply with behavioural standards is not the issue here. The main point, rather, is that the Palikur woman has, both personally and institutionally, the right and the power to call a man on his wrong behaviour and, just as important, to bring it to everyone else's attention.

Scolding is sometimes described as a means whereby women can react against their structural powerlessness: a socially disruptive strategy with which to assert their autonomy and redress, if temporarily, the balance between the sexes. But, in the egalitarian context of Palikur society, a woman's scolding is the means not of redressing (since this is not required) but of *maintaining* the balance when a man's antisocial tendencies threaten to upset it. By performing and affirming female power, a woman's scolding, a simultaneously intimate and public act between kin, behaves socially as well as domestically in regenerating sociality.

Conclusion

I have sought to show that the Amazonian conception of the domestic and social belongs to an inclusivist and extensivist perspective in which domestic space and domestic acts are not asocial, as some propose, but, on the contrary, inherently social (and political). Linked to this is the indigenous idea that the philosophical and political basis, and template, of sociality is the home: the meaningful, caring, experiential 'activated place' (to use Michel de Certeau's term) of practical and sociable – albeit sometimes angry – interactions with close kin, and a value of the highest moral, aesthetic, and affective importance.[9] The making and maintaining of the social life, as a Good Life and a Beautiful Life shared with a community of 'loving' similars, relies on not only the interplay between the constructive emotions and behaviours, but also the domestication of the destructive antisocial ones. For the Palikur, scolding is one of the ways by which they can concretely realize this process.

NOTES

1 Peter Rivière, *Individual and Society in Guiana* (Cambridge: Cambridge University Press, 1984), 264.
2 The Palikur, or Pa'ikwené, among whom I carried out research in 1993–95, number some 2,000 people inhabiting north Brazil and French Guiana.
3 Marshall Sahlins, *Stone Age Economics* (Chicago, IL: Aldine, 1972).
4 However, as Ivan Illich, in *H_2O and the Waters of Forgetfulness* (London: Marion Boyars, 1986), 8–9, notes, dwelling and living are etymologically and existentially the same; see also Heidegger (section 2.2) and Ingold (section 2.4) in this volume.

5 Joanna Overing, 'Kinship,' in Nigel Rapport and Joanna Overing, eds., *Social and Cultural Anthropology: The Key Concepts* (London: Routledge, 2000), 217–29; 'Society,' in ibid., 333–43.

6 Annette Baier, *Moral Prejudices* (Cambridge, MA: Harvard University Press, 1995); Seyla Benhabib, *Situating the Self: Gender, Community, and Postmodernism in Contemporary Ethics* (Cambridge: Polity, 1992).

7 Joanna Overing and Alan Passes, 'Introduction,' in Joanna Overing and Alan Passes, eds., *The Anthropology of Love and Anger: The Aesthetics of Conviviality in Native Amazonia* (London: Routledge, 2000).

8 Joanna Overing, 'In Praise of the Everyday: Trust and the Art of Social Living in an Amazonian Community,' *Ethnos* 68 / 3 (2003): 299.

9 Michel de Certeau, *The Practice of Everyday Life,* translated by Steven Randall (Berkeley, CA: University of California Press, 1984).

CHAPTER THREE

Interiors

The selections in this chapter sketch the development and varieties of domestic interiors from Roman to modern times and across different cultural practices. As underscored by these selections, the history of the interior is a history of the mapping and crossing of boundaries. Architectural historian Joseph Rykwert argues that the primitive hut, a key element in myths and rituals and a source of fascination for both Bachelard and Heidegger, is displayed by all peoples at all times (see also Marc in this volume), and continues to serve as a paradigm for judging buildings. Turning to first-century Rome, Clive Knights elaborates on this primeval idea of enclosure as applied to the Pompeian house, which in its spatial arrangements of doors (see Simmel in this volume), fauces, vestibules, and atrii embodied Roman culture, and sought to address the cosmic order – a Heideggerian fourfold of mortal, sky, earth, and divinities. Georges Duby explains how a monastery in ninth-century France was perceived and constructed as a replica of a heavenly abode on earth, and how behind the privacy of the cloister walls, it served as home to the family of monks as they participated in daily rituals of prayer, sleeping, eating, bathing, and working. In his study of the evolution of home in Western bourgeois society from the Middle Ages to the 1980s, Witold Rybczynski emphasizes, like Bachelard, the importance of intimacy, but also the growing desire for and implementation of comfort and privacy as reflected in the structural and technological changes in domestic spaces. Starting from a lexicographic analysis of the word 'comfort,' Rybczynski contends that the emergence of its modern significance in the eighteenth century was determined by the evolution of physical interiors – the furniture of minds appearing in conjunction with the furniture of houses. Ma Thanegi demonstrates how traditions of class hierarchy and Buddhist beliefs and rituals determined the spatial organization of the Burmese house and the strict boundaries between the private household and public display. Frances Borzello addresses the invisibility of the domestic interior in the literature on art up to the eighteenth century and its gradual emergence as artists began to challenge the dominance of religious and historical painting. In his prescription for a gentleman's house directed at the new wealthy middle class in mid-Victorian England, architect Robert Kerr documents the emerging preoccupation with domestic privacy.

For Walter Benjamin writing about nineteenth-century Paris, the privacy of the bourgeois urban private citizen is facilitated by the separation of work and living spaces; the home thus becomes his casing (*étui*); his collection of objects are freed from the bondage of usefulness and evoke a 'phantasmagoria of the interior,' while their traces constitute the content of the detective story, especially as created by Edgar Allan Poe.[1] These phantasmagorias of the interior are evidence of the increasing desire for individuation and perpetuation of the self that the nineteenth century expressed also in the accelerated introduction of first names and in the proliferation of symbols of the self such as the use of visiting cards, the spread of the portrait, and individual burials.[2] Alain Corbin approaches the concept of privacy from a very different angle – through the history of the treatment and effects of odours and the bourgeoisie's desire to distance and protect themselves from the unsanitary, malodorous masses, the proximity of which was deemed to have contributed to the spread of cholera. Corbin's emphasis on the novel worry about the 'hidden dangers in the family' points to the broader philosophical concerns that arguably led both to the preoccupation with heredity and to the birth of psychoanalysis.

In nineteenth-century Paris, as in other European cities, the apartment house became the major form of urban dwelling. Sharon Marcus shows how this new type of vernacular architecture represented a shift in articulations of private and public space; for although the dwelling units were more self-contained, the buildings themselves were more populated and entailed more communal spaces (hallways, stairs, courtyards), and Parisian tenants favoured units that afforded proximity to the density and exchanges of the street. In the twentieth century, privacy, influenced by Freudian concepts, becomes associated with the individual, self-expression, and self-consciousness; thus Dorothy Todd and Raymond Mortimer advocate a new, modern, self-expressive form of interior decoration, unburdened by history and custom, that would assert and reflect the inhabitant's personality. In *Women under Socialism* (1883) the German Marxist August Bebel argued that 'the trend [...] of our social life is not to banish woman back to the house and hearth, as our "domestic life" fanatics prescribe [...] *On the contrary, the whole trend of society is to lead woman out of the narrow sphere of strictly domestic life to a full participation in the public life of the people* [...] and in the task of *human civilization*.'[3] Dolores Hayden describes how the attempts to fulfil Bebel's ideal to promote industrial efficiency by abolishing women's domestic sphere and similar efforts to socialize housework and child rearing in socialist states were thwarted by men's ingrained resistance to women's liberation.

Starting like Ma Thanegi from the premise that rituals are associated with physical boundaries, Ritzuko Osaki demonstrates how the distinctions between inside and outside, dirt and clean, and safety and danger in Japanese culture have shaped the built environment. The influence that Westernization has had on such cultural values, she argues, has in turn been reflected in house forms.

NOTES

1 Walter Benjamin, 'Exposé of 1935,' *The Arcades Project,* translated by Howard Eiland and Kevin McLaughlin; prepared on the basis of the German volume edited by Rolf Tiedemann (Cambridge, MA: Belknap Press, 1999), 15.

2 See Alain Corbin, 'Backstage,' in *A History of Private Life,* translated by Arthur Goldhammer, edited by Michelle Perrot (Cambridge, MA: Harvard University Press, 1990), vol. 4, 457–67.

3 August Bebel, *Women under Socialism* [1910], translated by Daniel De Leon (New York: New York Labor News, 1917); Project Gutenberg Ebook # 30646.

3.1 JOSEPH RYKWERT 'A House for the Soul'*

After all, the penis is only a phallic symbol.

attributed to C.G. Jung

The primitive hut [...] seems to have been displayed by practically all peoples at all times, and the meaning given to this elaborate figure does not appear to have shifted much from place to place, from time to time. I should like to suggest that this meaning will persist into the future and that it will have permanent and unavoidable implications for the relationship between any building and its user.

[...] Writers on architectural theory [...] acknowledged the relevance of the primitive hut directly or indirectly, since it has provided so many of them with a point of reference for all speculation on the essentials of building. These speculations intensify when the need is felt for a renewal of architecture. Nor is this interest limited to speculation: various theorists have attempted to reconstruct such a hut in three dimensions and show the 'natural' form of the building; natural, rational, or divinely revealed according to their lights. Some are content to show this hut in drawings and engravings; but none attempt to suggest where such an original may be found and excavated, since it was built in some remote and primal scene, which we call Paradise, whose location cannot be found on any map.

Moreover, the idea of reconstructing the original form of all building 'as it had been in the beginning,' or as it was 'revealed' by God or by some divinized ancestor, is an important constituent of the religious life of many peoples, so it seems practically universal. In rituals, huts of this kind are built seasonally. They have elaborate and varied connotations; often an identification with a body, whether the human body or some perfect supranatural one, with affinities to the land it is in, to the whole universe. And the building of the primitive huts seems particularly associated with festivals of renewal (New Year, coronations), as well as the passage rites of initiation and marriage [...]

Whether in ritual, myth, or architectural speculation, the primitive hut has appeared as a paradigm of building: as a standard by which other buildings must in some way be judged, since it is from such flimsy beginnings that they

---

* In *On Adam's House in Paradise: The Idea of the Primitive Hut in Architectural History* (Cambridge, MA: MIT Press, 1981), 183–92.

spring. These huts were always situated in an idealized past. Le Corbusier's ideal barbarians built so as to know that they thought. [Adolf] Loos's equally ideal peasants built well because they knew without taking thought, by obeying external necessity and innate ideas alone. Both Loos and Corbusier cite the engineer, uncluttered by cultural baggage and responding to necessity alone in the case of Loos, and reason in Corbusier's, as the true correlative of the early builder. Loos reflects earlier attitudes closely. He is heir to the idea that human nature is in no way discontinuous from animal creation, that right building should also in some way be continuous with nature: Ruskin's belief that the best buildings are an essential part of natural landscape is an instance of this. It has its obverse in [Jean-Nicolas-Louis] Durand's writings, in which the extreme attenuation of eighteenth-century rationalism shades off into a utilitarian conventionalism. And yet in the nineteenth century there are other writers who recognize another drive in man's creative activities: that of echoing the essential rhythms of nature as the spur to the acquisition of all skills, which, in the case of [Gottfried] Semper, makes the daisy chain into the archetype of all human activity. Corbusier may have owed something to this view as well as to earlier ideas formulated before buildings were ideally situated in a continuous nature [...]

[...] The passion for building enclosures, or for 'adopting,' for taking possession of an enclosed volume under a chair or a table as a 'cozy place' for making a 'home,' is one of the commonest of all children's games.[1] Even in this context we have the double parentage of the original house: the 'found' volume of the cave and the 'made' volume of the tent or bower in a radically reduced form [...] Psychologists have often noted the social character of such games. They have associated them – their ambivalent terror / pleasure, their play on exclusion and inclusion – with the child's relation to its mother as it is focused in the fear and desire of the womb [...]

The return to origins is a constant of human development and in this matter architecture conforms to all other human activities. The primitive hut – the home of the first man – is therefore no incidental concern of theorists, no casual ingredient of myth or ritual. The return to origins always implies a rethinking of what you do customarily, an attempt to renew the validity of your everyday actions, or simply a recall of the natural (or even divine) sanction for your repeating them for a season. In the present rethinking of why we build and what we build for, the primitive hut will, I suggest, retain its validity as a reminder of the original and therefore essential meaning of all building for people: that is, of architecture. It remains the underlying statement, the irreducible, intentional core [...]

The desire for renewal is perennial and inescapable. The very continued existence of social and intellectual tensions guarantees its recurrence.

NOTE

1 Susan Isaacs, *Social Development in Young Children* (London: Routledge, 1933), 362–4.

3.2 CLIVE KNIGHTS
'The Spatiality of the Roman Domestic Setting: An Interpretation of Symbolic Content'*

> The undiscoverable house where this lava flower blows, where storms and exhausting bliss are born, when will my search for it cease?
>
> René Cazelles

To engage oneself boldly, as it were, in the situational paradigm that we call the Pompeian house is not to attempt a simulation of what it must have been like, in the literal sense, to be a middle-class Roman in the early Empire; but rather, it is to participate in a mode of dealing with being in the world [...]

The possibility of an encounter with the meaning of the Pompeian house is guaranteed by the persistent condition of its being mortal, on the earth, beneath the sky, in the face of unknowingness.[1] The symbolic representations that human beings make for themselves, as embodied in works of poiesis, become the residual evidence of participation in a common field: the cosmos [...]

The Pompeian house, then, is an embodiment of Roman culture; it is a conglomeration of symbols arranged in a way that testifies to a sense of belonging. Its symbolic organization is rooted with a great degree of complexity to its wider field of reference, the city, which in its turn is rooted to *its* wider field of reference, the Empire, and on to the cosmos. This is not to suggest a series of isolated entities linked by some all-embracing, determinable formulation. The integral rootedness of each mode of embodiment (house, city, empire, if we choose – artificially – to distinguish them) arises from a common urge to address the cosmic order through every avenue of representational possibility. The Pompeian house is not an object amongst others, moulded, smoothed and polished in perfect isolation like some jewel of Roman artistic achievement that

* In *Architecture and Order: Approaches to Social Space*, edited by Michael Parker Pearson and Colin Richards (London: Routledge, 1994), 113–45.

we can slip beneath the lens of an analytical microscope. It is the manifestation of a way of being; it is a paradigm of a human way of acting in the face of the ominous insurmountability of the world. Every aspect of the Pompeian house in some way contributes to an immanentization of this transcendent condition. For the sake of common understanding it articulates, expounds, and bears witness to the cosmic themes dominating the cultural field in which it participates as an expressive medium. Essentially, to discuss the house is to discuss, indirectly, the cosmos; and it is this discourse, this cosmology, that makes it and any other study of artistic production exhilarating and meaningful [...]

The Pompeian house, like all aspects of Roman architectural reality, is to do with the elaboration of 'participation' and 'passage.' It is about being involved in a 'movement-through,' whereby the mundane kinetic understanding of movement is, here, an analogical representation of a spiritual movement, that is, the force of divine activity which, in itself, is analogical in the face of the cosmic 'given' [...]

The succession of spaces – vestibule, fauces, atrium, tablinum, peristyle – betrays an alignment in plan which is a general feature throughout the house type. Formal rigidity, however, is secondary, as many examples indicate – in particular those houses on irregular plots and homes which have been extended at various times. No two houses are the same and yet all evidence would suggest a level of identity arrived at through subtleties which transcend the scope of mere formal repetition, and imply a strong sense of interpretative flexibility.

The street facade of the house is often a simple vertical planar surface with minimal articulation – maybe a small number of openings correspond to minor service rooms, or in a great many cases tabernae line the streets limiting the street facade of the house to its entrance [...] In any case, we find the focus of elaboration clustered about the entrance recess, the vestibule. Little ambiguity accompanies the experience of this primary aspect of the house: the threshold to the scenario of the household, the initial penetrative event. Eliade expounds the spiritual significance of 'threshold' in the context of his discussion of the symbolism of the centre and construction rites. All acts of construction, he suggests, whether of towns or of houses, every act of carving out a dwelling is simultaneously an imitation of the creation of the world and the establishment of its 'centre': 'Every dwelling, by the paradox of consecration of space and by the rite of its construction, is transformed into a "centre." Thus, all houses – like all temples, palaces and cities – stand in the self-same place, the centre of the universe.'[2]

It is the very nature of the transcendent significance of each that makes this multiplicity of centres acceptable, and every act of passage across a threshold meaningful. The establishment of the city boundaries and the sacredness of the pomoerium reinforce this notion.

Passing through the large double doors into the fauces presents the participant with a preludial experience of the depth of the domestic setting. Layered beyond in receding spatial progression are the series of punctured screens, openings, doorways, columnal screens, wells of light and shade, which signify a reciprocal limitation and extension of space, and penetrative possibilities [...] Essentially, what is encountered is a reciprocity between bounded and unbounded spatiality, a boundedness which detains and releases simultaneously by the exercise of creative interpretation. The primary spatial ground comes to us in terms of these territories, with their enclosing walls and soffit, their doorways and columnal screens; but they are at the same time both the creation of an interior closedness and the structuring components of an outward opening onto a metaphorical domain. They are the more persistent, physical attributes of an overall symbolic disclosure of meaning.

Around the enclosing walls of the fauces the pictorial extension of spatiality commences, complementing the directional pull of the dominant axis. In other words, a spatial dimension opens up laterally around the participant which is at odds with the dimension of physical manoeuvrability, denying it predominance whilst offsetting its significance, inviting realignment. This notion is difficult to comprehend with a modern understanding of spatiality. If we cannot physically move into a space we are inclined to conclude that it is not spatial; in the restricted, architectural sense of the term, space is a void that we move around in freely. However, physically to move across the earth 'merely displays spatial and temporal applications in a more striking way.'[3] Movement has no monopoly over being, it is merely one mode of becoming.

Moving into the atrium space, like a domestic 'forum,' with a centralized compluviate opening in the roof enclosure, echoed on the floor plane by the impluvium, we encounter a pool of light, a pool of water and a circumambulatory space surrounded on the two lateral sides by the punctured walls to the adjacent ancillary chambers (which include storerooms and bedrooms: cubiculi), and to the front by the emphasized opening to the tablinum. Often the centrality of the impluvium-compluvium arrangement in the atrium is enhanced by a peripheral row of columns. The main room in the house, the tablinum, is like a study, but used to serve as the master bedroom. It extends the penetrative direction towards the peristyle garden, providing a fundamental link between atrium and peristyle which is elaborated by the articulation of the grand opening from atrium to tablinum and the more subdued, often occular, opening from tablinum to peristyle. The most important side chamber, opening onto the atrium or peristyle, is the triclinium: the dining room. Associated with the whole ceremony of feasting and receiving guests, 'the triclinium was where the master of the house showed who and what he was.'[4] [...]

The vestibule with its tall double entrance doors has been described above as the articulation of the initial penetrative event, and its significance has more avenues of interpretation open to it than immediately evident. To begin with, Ovid makes the etymological connection of vestibule with Vesta, the goddess of the hearth and the eternal fire, and he mentions that the hearth once stood in the porch of the houses, 'Oh Vesta, thou who dost inhabit the foremost place.'[5] Indeed, but how much more evocative is the association of her virginal qualities, her abstinence from violation, her penetrative resistance and the respect it gains her when considered in relation to the main entrance of the private dwelling of a Roman citizen [...] However, this may be a secondary consideration in the light of the true pre-eminence of the sacred fire and the hearth of the household with its fundamental relationship to the Lares, Manes, and Genii of the family. In any event, the significance of the vestibule rests on the fact that it is the primary figuration of threshold, of passage from one domain to another, as a breach in the boundary; it is symbolically 'the place of doors.' In this case it manifests a passage from urban life to domestic life, but its recurrence as a theme throughout the house and in all Roman architecture imbues it with a primacy which cannot be overlooked [...]

The theme continues in Virgil's *Aeneid*.[6] For Aeneas the acts of crossing and entering became a synonymous and persistent engagement. A multiplicity of thresholds besiege his every move, and culminate in the flurry of gates and doors that signify his passage through the underworld: the gates of Cumae's golden temple of Apollo; the vast cavern in the Euboean Rock with its, 'hundred tremendous orifices'; the mighty 'double-doors' that open onto Pluto's infernal kingdom; the 'Entrance Hall in the very jaws of Hades'; the 'gigantic gate with columns of solid adamant' through which Aeneas glimpses the horrors of Hell, and the corresponding 'archway' opposite that gives access to the Fortunate Woods, the joyful domain of Elysium. The climax of Aeneas's subterranean journey, having traversed the seething march of Styx and reached the banks of the Lethe, is the speech of his dead father Anchises (who, incidentally, was delivered to safety when Aeneas carried him out through the gates of burning Troy), whose prophesy describes the opening of the 'golden centuries' of an emerging empire under the auspices of Augustus.

NOTES

1 Martin Heidegger, 'Building, Dwelling, Thinking,' in *Poetry, Language, Thought*, translated by Albert Hofstadter (New York: Harper and Row, 1971). [See section 2.2 in this volume.]

2 Mircea Eliade, *Patterns in Comparative Religion* (London: Sheed and Ward, 1958), 379.
3 Maurice Merleau-Ponty, *Phenomenology of Perception,* translated by Colin Smith (London: Routledge and Kegan Paul, 1962), 275. See also Heidegger ['Building, Dwelling, Thinking,'] (1971), 156 [...]
4 Philippe Ariès and Georges Duby, *A History of Private Life,* translated by Arthur Goldhammer (Cambridge, MA: Harvard University Press, 1987), vol. 1, 365.
5 Ovid, *Fasti,* translated by H.T. Riley (London: George Bell, 1887), 224.
6 Virgil, *The Aeneid,* translated by W.F. Jackson Knight (Harmondsworth: Penguin, 1956), 147–74.

3.3 GEORGES DUBY
'The Aristocratic Households of Feudal France: Communal Living'*

According to the vision of Sunniulf, as reported by Gregory of Tours in the sixth century, souls that survive their trial in Purgatory eventually come to a 'great white house.' Two centuries later another visionary sees much the same sight: 'On the other side of the river loomed huge, high, resplendent walls.' But Saint Boniface, who recounts it, explains: 'this was the heavenly Jerusalem.' Not a house, then, but a city: the metaphor is political and urban; it refers to a city which, though in decay, continued to fascinate with its myriad monuments only recently fallen in ruin, a city to which memories of Rome also attached, a refuge – but a public one, ready to embrace all the children of God. The arches that frame the figures of the evangelists in Carolingian miniatures evoke not a court but the porticoes of a forum. Only later was the image of a house superimposed upon this ancient image: the Roman Catholic Church still wished to see heaven as a mighty city. Primarily, though, people thought of heaven as a kind of house [...] Bernard of Clairvaux, [for example,] apostrophized heaven in these terms: 'O marvellous house, preferable to our beloved tents.' Heaven, then, is a solidly built house, a place to settle down and rest after the vagabond life of *homo viator* – undeniably a place of lodging [...]

* In *A History of Private Life,* vol. 2, *Revelations of the Medieval World,* edited by Georges Duby, translated by Arthur Goldhammer (Cambridge, MA: Belknap Press of Harvard University Press, 1988), 35–85.

The Monastery: Model of Private Life

Imagination was not strictly necessary. Men could see with their own eyes, on earth, exact replicas of the heavenly abode. These were the Benedictine monasteries, which claimed to be the antechambers and prefigurations of heaven in this world. Monasteries were therefore walled cities, 'cloisters' to which access was controlled, with but a single gate which, like city gates, was opened and closed at fixed hours. An important monastic office was the hostelry, which governed all relations with the outside world. Yet monasteries were essentially houses. Each was home to a 'family'; in fact, the families of monks were the most perfect of all families, the most carefully organized. The organization of the monastery was governed by the Rule of Saint Benedict, a clear, well-thought-out, strictly conceived plan for perfection. Since the ninth century, copious resources had been flowing into the monasteries, enabling them to take the lead in developing new agricultural techniques. They are among the best-known medieval residences; quantities of explicit documents tell us a great deal about how they were organized and run [...] At the height of the Carolingian renaissance, between 816 and 820, while Emperor Louis the Pious was putting the finishing touches on a program of monastic reform patterned closely after the Benedictine model, a design was prepared of the ideal monastery. The celebrated plans for Saint-Gall, preserved on five pieces of sewn parchment, consist of a series of scale drawings with legends. They were sent, probably by the Bishop of Basel, to Abbot Gozbert, who was considering rebuilding the abbey. The plans embody a theory of what a monastery should be: a place closely attuned to the harmonies of the spheres, cleaving to the axes of the universe, and perfectly balanced in a mathematical sense. The elementary architectural unit in the drawings measures forty feet on a side, with the nave of the church the centrepiece of the entire composition. The church was the heart of the whole organism, the point of contact between heaven and earth. Here the monks gathered to perform their main function: to sing God's praises in unison with the choir of angels.

The monks' residence was located south of the area reserved for the liturgy. Its arrangement resembles that of an ancient villa. There is an inner court abutting the church. To one side are the wine cellar, the food stores, the kitchen, and the bakery. On the other side is the refectory, above which is storage space for clothing. Along the third side is a hall, flanked by baths and latrines, and above it a dormitory, which communicates with the church. Adjoining the residence are extensive annexes used for agricultural and artisanal purposes, gardens, granges, stables, barns, workshops, and servants' huts. To the north, beyond the church to which it is attached, stands the house of the abbot, equipped with its own kitchen, wine cellar, and baths. To the northeast, novices and monks suffering from disease, temporarily excluded from the community, were confined in a separate residence, divided into two parts; purges and bleedings were administered in the far corner of the building. Finally, near the gate, to the northwest, strangers admitted into the cloister were housed in two buildings as fully equipped as the rest. One, next to the abbot's residence, received the more important guests and pupils from outside the community; the other, closer to the monks, was reserved for pilgrims and the poor.

It is clear that the abbey's organization was intended to reflect the strict hierarchies of the heavenly court. The central place was God's: the sanctuary. On his right, beyond the north bay of the transept, was the place of the abbot, who stood alone; as head of the family he occupied a higher plane. To the left of the Almighty, occupying the third rank, were the members of the family: the monks were the sons, all brothers, all equal, like the angels forming a militia, a garrison sustained by servants who lived next to the refectory, since the ideal was autarchy, self-sufficiency. Farthest from the gate, that fissure open to the world's corruption, were confined the invalids and young recruits still undergoing training – the young, the old, and also the dead, since the cemetery was located here. The most vulnerable part of the community had to be kept separate on account of its weakness, sheltered but also protected by the right hand of God. Here, too, were the areas reserved for spiritual functions, the school and the writing studio; the material functions, those which sustained the body, were relegated to the other side, to the left hand of God. Note that the graves were placed to the east, on the side of the rising sun, symbol of the resurrection, whereas visitors were lodged on the west, the side of the setting sun and worldly perversity […]

The fraternity of monks was divided, as prescribed by the customaries of Cluny, into four groups, each assigned to a distinct quarter of the monastery: the novitiate, the infirmary, the cemetery, and the cloister. Separated from the monks' residence by the church, the novices' residence was a place of transition and gestation. Here the slow process of spiritual reproduction took place. Children sent to the monastery by their families at a very tender age were fed and educated. When their apprenticeship was complete, when they had learned the complexities of monastic behaviour and knew what to do when and how to sing and how to express themselves by signs during the periods of silence, they were solemnly initiated into the community of adult monks […]

The infirmary, too, was a place of waiting, to which some members of the community were sent for a time because tainted by disease. In effect, disease was seen as a mark of sin. Those who suffered from it had to be isolated during their period of purgation. At Cluny two rooms in the infirmary were set aside for purifying ablutions, one for washing feet, the other for washing dishes. Four other rooms were furnished with two beds apiece. The abbot, however, enjoyed the privilege of a private room. Adjoining the infirmary was a separate kitchen, because ailing monks, made less pure by illness, ate a different diet from the rest of the community [...]

Most monks lay for a time in the infirmary before entering the other world. This transition was another occasion for collective ritual. No one died alone; death was perhaps the least private of a monk's acts. The death of a monk was rather like a wedding in profane society. Around the deathbed was staged a sort of festival, in which communal bonds were at their most visible. When his condition worsened, the dying man was carried by two of his brothers out of the infirmary and into the meeting hall known as the capitulary for his last confession, which had to be made public. He was then taken back to the infirmary to receive communion and extreme unction and to bid farewell to the community [...] When the dying man finally yielded up his soul, his body was washed by monks, his peers in the hierarchy of age and office. It then was carried into the church, where psalms were sung, and finally laid to rest in the cemetery, which was located in the most private part of the monastery, the third quarter of its familial place [...]

The fourth and final quarter of the monastery was the residence. In Cluny the monks' residence, which occupied the centre of the *curtis*, was supposed to be the earthly embodiment of an ideal of private life, as far as possible a mirror of heaven. The inner court, what we call the cloister, combined the four elements of the visible universe: air, fire, water, and earth. With its covered walkway it was an introverted version of the public square, entirely given over to private concerns. Here the chaos of time was subdued; everything was strictly regulated according to the seasons, the hours of the day and night. Different parts of the building were assigned different functions. The most ornate and carefully maintained was the section set aside for the *opus Dei*, the work of God, the special office of monks, that is, prayer, which was chanted at the top of the lungs in chorus: this was the church. Alongside it was the hall (*aula*), reserved for discussions and judicial proceedings. This was similar to the ancient basilica, but it, too, was turned inward: whatever was said here was private and secret. Every day, after Prime, all monks well enough to attend and not excluded as a result of some punishment gathered in the hall to renew the bonds of community by reading a chapter of the rule and a list of the names of the abbey's dead. The monks also dealt with temporal affairs in much the same manner as the council of a feudal prince. Finally, as a family they corrected one another's mistakes: the hall was a scene of continual self-criticism. Violations of discipline were denounced either by the guilty party himself or by others, for the purpose of restoring order within the community. The guilty were first flagellated. (This was usually the penalty in private, domestic justice, inflicted by a man upon his wife, children, servants, and slaves.) Then they were separated from the community for a period of purification. They took their meals apart and were made to stand at the church door. Their heads always covered, they lived in retreat, isolated from their brothers. Again it is important to note that solitude was envisioned as an exile, a trial, a punishment.

Their sins purged, the lost sheep rejoined the flock in the refectory. Meals, taken in common every day (and supplemented in some seasons by light snacks), were ceremonial occasions, celebrating the unity of brotherhood. The monks sat in prescribed order around tables whose linen was changed every two weeks. At these princely banquets each monk found a loaf of bread and a knife waiting at his assigned place. Bowls of food were brought in from the kitchen and wine brought from the cellar, served in what were called 'just' measures, each one shared by two monks. The rule prescribed that wine was to be drunk in silence. The monks ate in perfect discipline, modulating their gestures as prescribed by the rule and waiting for the silent signals of the abbot, seated at the centre of the table. Meals were a communion, and during them the spirit was occupied, distracted from the flesh, by the voice of one of the monks, who read out loud.

At dusk the time of danger commenced, for the devil was abroad. It was imperative that the community close its ranks and keep a sharp watch. In the dormitory, the most private part of the residence, located on the second story, high above any creeping menace, no monk was allowed to be alone, and the abbot lived in the midst of his flock. Lights were kept burning throughout the night, as in a military camp. Each monk slept in his own bed, however; the rule strictly prohibited any sharing. The needs of community took second place in this regard, owing to an unarticulated but obsessive fear of homosexuality. Ultimately the communal life of the monastery was gregarious; every secret, every intimacy inevitably became common knowledge, and solitude was held to be a danger and used as a punishment.

3.4 WITOLD RYBCZYNSKI 'Intimacy and Privacy'*

[In this excerpt, Rybczynski explores the evolving notion of comfort, beginning with a discussion of the austere furnishings in Albrecht Dürer's painting, *St Jerome in His Study* (1514).]

A great deal *has* changed in the home. Some of the changes are obvious – the advances in heating and lighting that are due to new technology. Our sitting furniture has become much more sophisticated, better adapted to relaxation. Other changes are more subtle – the way that rooms are used, or how much privacy is afforded by them. Is my study more comfortable? The obvious answer is yes, but if we were to ask Dürer, we might be surprised by his reply. To begin with, he would not understand the question. 'What exactly do you mean by comfortable?' he might respond in puzzled curiosity.

The word 'comfortable' did not originally refer to enjoyment or contentment. Its Latin root was *confortare* – to strengthen or console – and this remained its meaning for centuries. We use it this way when we say 'He was a comfort to his mother in her old age.' It was in this sense that it was used in theology: the 'Comforter' was the Holy Spirit. Along the way, 'comfort' also acquired a legal meaning: in the sixteenth century a 'comforter' was someone who aided or abetted a crime. The idea of support was eventually broadened to include people and things that afforded a measure of satisfaction, and 'comfortable' came to mean tolerable or sufficient – one spoke of a bed of comfortable width, although not yet of a comfortable bed. This continues to be the meaning of the expression 'a comfortable income' – ample but not luxurious. Succeeding generations expanded this idea of convenience, and eventually 'comfortable' acquired its sense of physical well-being and enjoyment, but not until the eighteenth century, long after Dürer's death. Sir Walter Scott was one of the first novelists to use it this new way when he wrote, 'Let it freeze without, we are comfortable within.' Later, meanings of the word are almost exclusively concerned with contentment, often of a thermal variety: 'comforter' in secular Victorian England no longer referred to the Redeemer, but to a long woollen scarf; today it describes a quilted bed coverlet [...]

[Rybczynski then discusses different examples of the power of naming and how the meaning of a word changes over time and in different contexts, including the word 'comfort.']

---

* In *Home: A Short History of an Idea* (New York: Viking, 1986), 14–49.

The appearance of the word 'comfort' in the context of domestic well-being is [...] of more than lexicographic interest. There are other words in the English language with this meaning – 'cozy,' for instance – but they are of later origin. The first use of 'comfort' to signify a level of domestic amenity is not documented until the eighteenth century. How to explain this tardy arrival? [...]

[Rybczynski discusses the different meanings of 'snow' as an example of the power of naming.]

People began to use 'comfort' in a different way because they needed a special word to articulate an idea which previously had either not existed or had not required expression.

Let us start this examination of comfort by trying to understand what happened in Europe in the eighteenth century, and why people suddenly found that they needed a special word to describe a particular attribute of the interiors of their homes. To do this it is necessary to look first at an earlier period – the Middle Ages [...]

[After briefly discussing different views of the Middle Ages, Rybczynski explains that the Middle Ages were quite advanced technologically – producing, for example, illuminated books, eyeglasses, cathedrals, and coal mines. He describes the primitive housing of the poor, the town houses of the bourgeois that combined work and living, the simplicity and mobility of furniture (chairs, chests, beds), the importance of bathing, and the elaborate table manners, noting that the period did not altogether lack comfort.]

Their homes were neither rustic nor crude, nor should we imagine that the persons inhabiting them did so without pleasure. But what comfort there was was never explicit. What our medieval ancestors did lack was the awareness of comfort as on objective *idea* [...]

[Rybczynski concludes his discussion of the Middle Ages and the idea of comfort by referring to John Lukacs's influential observations on the evolution of domestic comfort.]

John Lukacs points out that words such as 'self-confidence,' 'self-esteem,' 'melancholy,' and 'sentimental' appeared in English and French in their modern senses only two or three hundred years ago. Their use marked the emergence of something new in human consciousness: the appearance of the internal world of the individual, of the self, and of the family. The significance of the evolution

2 *St Jerome in His Study* (1514), by Albrecht Dürer. Used by permission of Minneapolis Institute of Arts. Bequest of Herschel V. Jones.

of domestic comfort can only be appreciated in this context. It is much more than a simple search for physical well-being; it begins in the appreciation of the house as a setting for an emerging interior life. In Lukacs's words, 'as the self-consciousness of medieval people was spare, the interiors of their houses were bare, including the halls of nobles and of kings. The interior furniture of houses appeared together with the interior furniture of minds.'[1]

NOTES

1 John Lukacs, 'The Bourgeois Interior,' *American Scholar* 39 / 4 (1970): 623.

3.5 MA THANEGI
The Burmese House

Myanmar, also known as Burma, was ruled by Burmese kings until 1885. During this period in this highly class-conscious society, one's rank or prestige was immediately apparent by the type of house one was entitled to build, the sort of dress one could wear, and the insignia and arms one could bear. Houses of commoners, however wealthy, were forbidden carved decorations on the doorjambs or on window frames. Since non-nobility were not permitted to ride on elephants, the commoner's house would not have an open side on the outside platform for stepping onto an elephant's back.

Apart from rigidly imposed restrictions like the two examples above, the architectural aspects of commoners' houses were similar to those of the nobility, given the preference for and abundance of fine wood construction. Houses were built of teak and sat on stilts with a spacious outside platform consisting of several separate pavilions. Inside, rooms whether for noble or commoner families had similar designs and purposes dictated by cultural and religious aspects of Burmese life such as the importance of the shrine, the entertainment that accompanied celebrations, and superstitions about women's menstrual cycles.

The principal rooms in a Burmese house of the nineteenth century and earlier included a shrine room, parlour and show-watching gallery, family room, strong room for keeping cash and other valuables, bedrooms, birthing room, kitchen, store room, servants' rooms, and stables under the house at the coolest corner, with an attached groom's room.

These domestic space arrangements reflected the importance of religious holidays and functions in Burmese Buddhist society. Thus, the shrine room, which was the most important room in the house, displayed one or more Buddha images made of gold, silver, bronze, marble, wood, or formed with clay composed of thousands of dried flowers. Clean cups of water, and fruits, sweets, or rice as food offerings, which must be offered at dawn and removed at noon, were set in front of the images, while vases of fresh flowers, which must never fade or dry, were placed at the sides. If there was not enough room in the house for a separate shrine room, the image and offerings were placed on a stand tacked high on the southern wall of the house. The same would be true today.

The inhabitants must sleep with heads towards the south, although no one today remembers the source of this custom. The parlour and show-watching gallery were two sides of one room which could also serve as one large parlour. In the show-watching gallery, the family and guests could sit in comfort to watch dance performances put on during a family celebration such as the noviciation of sons, the ear-borings of daughters, an engagement or wedding, or to commemorate a promotion, or show off a son leaving to study in Britain, as well as his return, or to welcome or say farewell to an important official. Usually hundreds of guests would be invited and seated in pavilions of plywood painted in gold and varied colours.

Not class alone, but also gender played a role in the organization of space. So, for instance, a room without windows and barred to men was set aside for giving birth. However, Burmese society is strongly matriarchal and women were/are not treated badly or as chattels. Wives handle the finances and both single and married women can work in business or in professions and possess equal rights of inheritance and division of property in divorce. Even in ancient times there were women administrators who served as heads of villages, and handmaidens in the courts who worked as teachers of the children or as religious instructors for the older princesses. Women poets and composers were greatly appreciated and honoured. A wife was/is expected to manage the household well, though not do the actual work herself. She was expected to save money, which was then secured by both husband and wife in a special strong room to store valuables. Since Burmese Buddhist customary law allowed a man to have more than one wife, in the past, husband and wife slept in separate rooms.[1] The first wife had the highest prestige and, as the 'society' wife, would accompany her husband to social occasions. Since a man of standing had the duty to look after his extended family or the offspring of family retainers, every household except the poorest would have one or more servants. Despite class distinctions, servants were not treated formally and long-time retainers became almost like family. But they had to rise before the family, eat after the family, and go to bed last. These practices continue to this day.

Family meals were taken on a low circular table that could be moved into position, usually in the parlour. The oldest person or the head of household even now is always served first.

Up to the 1960s, in conservative families, sons of the family could sleep alone but daughters who were still single had an aunt or maid sleeping in their bedrooms. It is a modern concept that daughters require privacy and have their own bedrooms.

Houses of well-to-do families usually had a well in the garden but others had to carry water home from the village well, the reservoir at the monastery, or the river.

For bathing, a large stone slab would be placed next to the well at the side of the house furthest from the street, sheltered by bushes. The bather would stand here, sluicing himself or herself with water hauled from the well by a servant. Women would pull their waist garments up under their armpits and cover their breasts. The *longyi* (a cotton wrap worn by men instead of trousers, and by women as long skirts) is also long enough to cover the ankles. The men at their baths wore them as usual, tied around the waist.

The toilet, a bamboo or wooden hut placed over a deep hole in the ground, was located at the far end of the backyard. A jar of water, cleaned and filled every day, was supplied for sanitary purposes. When necessary, the hut would be moved to a new spot and the old hole filled in with earth.

The garden, which was not formally laid out, would be planted with fruit trees, herbs, medicinal plants, and shade trees such as tamarind and mango.

Also located in the compound was a granary for storing rice and Martaban jars with oil, beans, molasses, jaggery, and salted dried fish (Martaban jars are huge bulbous glazed-ware jars). To store rain water these jars are placed under the rain gutters of the roof with the tapered bottom half buried in the ground for stability and coolness.

These traditional wooden houses, with wells, bathing areas, granaries, toilets, Martaban jars, and gardens, still exist in rural areas. But, instead of separate pavilions set on high platforms, they are built on stilts, with a veranda, called the 'slipper-leaving space,' reached by wooden stairs running along the length of the house. Here, at the top of the stairs, porous terracotta pots of drinking water cooled by the breeze welcome thirsty visitors. Inside, the shrine still takes pride of place, and only one room is walled off for storing bedding and dressing in private.

Under the house, there is a wooden or bamboo platform with a smooth reed mat for receiving casual visitors and where the family can rest or do light work in the heat of the afternoon. A cloth or cane baby cradle is hung from a beam. However, people of wealth and high rank no longer desire these elevated houses exposed to the breezes, which are so well suited to the tropical weather. Instead, they prefer huge, ornate, air-conditioned houses made of garishly coloured concrete, without doors and verandas open to the elements and without shady resting spaces.

NOTE

1 The laws still exist but now it is no longer the practice for more than one wife to live with the husband; now minor wives are set up in separate establishments. The influence of Westernized culture after British annexation meant that first wives would no longer willingly submit to having minor wives live with them even if under their authority. Also, minor wives refused to live under the thumb of the first wives. Polygamy, although not illegal, is not accepted by society at large, and the 'younger' wives are usually hidden away.

3.6 FRANCES BORZELLO 'Looking for the Interior'*

Until the 1890s, art history is silent on the subject of the domestic interior [...] At first it seemed to conform to the normal patterns of art history. In the fifteenth century, along with landscape and still life, the domestic interior made its first appearance in art as part of something else, the background to religious images or a clue to character interests in portraiture, put there to reinforce the artist's message.

The genres of painting were born in the seventeenth century when landscape, flower pieces, still life, seascapes, and just to make it confusing, genre, the name given to paintings of incidents from everyday life, fought their way out of the background of paintings to become a type of subject, or genre, in their own right.

At the time it looked as though the domestic interior might make the transition. The paintings done in Holland by [Pieter] de Hooch, with their black-and-white tiled floors and peace and quiet, or the rooms in which Gabriel Metsu and Nicolaes Maes placed their characters, show the domestic interior being taken seriously as a subject. Even more dramatic is *View Down a Corridor* (Figure 3), painted by the ambitious poet, painter, and theorist Samuel van Hoogstraten in 1662, a masterpiece of perspective which shows what we see when we enter the front door of a Dutch home. Probably a fictional construct designed to display his skill at making a two-dimensional surface three dimensional, it is totally convincing, down to the dog in the foreground who appears to sense our presence [...]

After this brief flowering, and unlike the other genres, the domestic interior died down for another hundred and fifty years. Apart from a few *trompe l'oeil* paintings, for example, letters in a rack, by Wallerant Vaillant in 1658, or preparatory sketches for subject paintings, the domestic interior never has a painting to itself. Theoretically, it was possible for the interior to have emerged as a subject in its own right. But though certain subjects, such as the Annunciation or paintings of the Virgin Mary holding the baby Jesus, are set in domestic interiors and certain biblical stories are always set indoors – the birth of Christ and of John the Baptist, Christ in the house of Martha and Mary – the interior never made the leap to centre stage in the manner of the landscape or the flower piece. Always there as a setting, to create a mood, to inform about the subject of a portrait, to help tell the story in a genre painting, to supply a sense of history, it is a background which tends to remain in the background [...] An

---

* In *At Home: The Domestic Interior of Art* (London: Thames and Hudson, 2006), 16–25.

3 *View Down a Corridor* (1662) by Samuel van Hoogstraeten, 1662. *Credit:* Dyrham Park, the Blathwayt Collection (acquired through the National Land Fund and transferred to the National Trust in 1961), ©NTPL/John Hammond. Reproduced by permission of the National Trust Photo Library.

idea of the domestic interior's invisibility in standard art theory can be gleaned from the advice given to students at London's Royal Academy from its foundation in the winter of 1768 […]

The artist-lecturers were concerned with passing on a history of the greatest artists of the past, and the depiction of ordinary people going about their small everyday activities had little importance in this scheme where the themes and compositions of the High Renaissance set the tone. Such thinking ensured that the paintings of the seventeenth-century Dutch, the one place where the domestic interior could be found, were rarely mentioned by the lecturers. In the scheme of artistic respectability, the Dutch paintings were seen as flimsy offerings, filled with detail and figures doing nothing of importance. In the eyes of the lecturers, the relationship of these works to fine art was akin to that of drinking songs to opera. It took a long time to recover from Michelangelo's reported dismissal of the Netherlandish artists as painting 'only to deceive the external eye, things that gladden you and of which you cannot speak ill. Their painting is of stuffs, bricks and mortar, the grass of the fields, the shadows of trees, and bridges and rivers, which they call landscapes, and little figures here and there.'[1]

Sir Joshua Reynolds dismissed Dutch genre, even while he admired the qualities that gave rise to it [...] Reynolds understood that detail and individuality were necessary for 'the lower exercises of the art': 'It would be ridiculous for a painter of domestick scenes ... or of still life, to say that he despised those qualities which has made the subordinate schools so famous.'[2] It was just that in his view it was not proper for historical painting: 'It is the inferior stile that marks the variety of stuffs.' But for painters of history, 'the cloathing is neither woollen, nor linen, nor silk, sattin, or velvet; it is drapery; it is nothing more.'[3]

As well as labelling 'domestick scenes' inferior, the thinking of the day supported the notion of the purity of the genres [...]

The closest that students ever got to the concept of the interior was in lectures about composition where, under the heading of background, the interior rated a mention as a tool to create a mood or tangible environment. In the early nineteenth century, Fuseli was respectful of the power of a well-chosen background to make a painting speak: 'By the choice and scenery of the back-ground we are frequently enabled to judge how far a painter entered into his subject, whether he understood its nature, to what class it belonged, what impression it was capable of making, what passion it was calculated to rouse.'[4] [...] The rule of the day was that the main subject matter had to shine and to this end there was an idea of the balance of figure and background: 'the most effective pictures, have been those where the least subject matter contends with the principal objects, and wherein the forms which divide the portion of the surface unoccupied by the figures, produce agreeable shapes,' lectured Thomas Phillips to the students in 1833.[5]

It all adds up to a picture of discouragement. Domestic scenes are inferior; genres are protected species. Too much detail upsets the balance of composition, risks reducing the point of the painting, and is only suitable for the lowest classes of art. Until the nineteenth century, this silence about the interior and these barriers to its introduction stopped academically trained artists giving shape to any vision they might have had, or even prevented its formation. If you were an academy student aiming to reach the top by competing for your institution's prizes and medals, there would be no doubt in your mind that it was history painting which had to be mastered. It is a lot to ask of an artist attracted by light falling onto the floor, an appealing group of objects on a table, the colour of walls and fabrics, or the beauty and comfort of light in a dark interior to make a painting out of them when it was not a legitimate subject and when there was no precedent for doing so.

But art does not exist in a vacuum. Theory is not practice. The recipients of an academic training are not the only artists in the world. And the disdain the academic thinkers had for Dutch genre painting was not universal.

When the Protestant middle classes and their corresponding economic power emerged in seventeenth-century Holland, the effect on art was explosive. They did not share the upper-class taste for history painting, they did not have small altars in their homes, and they did not want grand portraits of themselves – at least not until towards the century's end when they began to ape their aristocratic betters. They wanted something smaller, more intimate, more related to the lives of which they were so proud.

The Dutch loved paintings. Seventeenth-century visitors to the country were amazed by how many paintings there were and how many people had them in their homes: 'All in generall striving to adorne their houses, especially the street or outer roome, with costly peeces [...] yea many tymes blacksmithes, Coblers, etts., will have some picture or other by their Forge and in their stalle.'[6] [...]

At the heart of Dutch society was the home, the expression of everything good the Dutch believed about themselves. The premium the Dutch placed on the intimacy, privacy, and comfort of family life helped encourage the growth of domesticity as an acceptable subject for paintings. The virtues of cleanliness, godliness, order, and a comfortable but modest lifestyle were all expressed in the home, and it was the artists' genius to make this visible. The interior entered art through genre painting. [Jan] Vermeer's soft grey light, the kitchen scenes, and amorous encounters of Metsu and Maes in rooms with carpets on the tables and beds in the background, de Hooch's internal vistas from room to room or room to courtyard, have furnished our minds with a type of home that seems forever rooted in reality. So powerful is the vision the Dutch created that we forget that true interior scenes make up a fairly small proportion of their art.

As the eighteenth century progressed, genre painting became more self-confident. The theoretical absence of the interior as a subject in its own right was counterbalanced by the growth of the middle classes and their demand for images of their own lives in the paintings they bought. Their interest in seeing their values, their pleasures, and their way of life on canvas provided opportunities for artists who were open to the seductions of the interior to indulge their sensibility. In this way, the middle-class taste for genre encouraged the development of scenes of domesticity. In France in 1728, Jean-Siméon Chardin won a battle to have his quiet paintings of still lifes and the domestic interior accepted by the Académie Royale in Paris, which until then had disparaged such work as lightweight compared to history painting. Towards the end of the century, the appealing rationale of family life popularized by the philosopher Jean-Jacques Rousseau in his novels, *Julie, ou La Nouvelle Héloïse* (1761) and *Emile* (1762), was drawn on by a number of painters, including Jean-Baptiste Greuze and Jean-Honoré Fragonard [...] Almost all are set inside the home in which mothers adore their babies and their husbands, husbands adore their wives and their babies, and everything exhibits the doctrine of separate but equal worlds for men and women, the home as the focus for gentle values, the boy child in the mother's care until the age of seven, the girl until she marries.

As genre painting became more important, it began to challenge the dominance of history painting. Despite the pronouncements of the theorists, most artists of the eighteenth century came no nearer to theoretical ideas than they did to the royal families of their respective countries. Many of those who did this kind of work were not the products of the grand academies. Below the level of the great stars of their day, most artists operated as craft workers, producing what their customers wanted. For every ambitious academy student, there were plenty who learned from other artists, whose education was limited to evening attendance at a candlelit life class, and who benefited neither from foreign travel nor from the high-flown rhetoric of the theorists. If they wanted to get on, they found an artist to apprentice themselves to and learned to paint like him – for it was mostly, but not always, a man. Marguerite Gérard is typical of this practice, coming from Grasse to Paris in 1775 to be taught by her brother-in-law Fragonard. She produced modernized Dutch genre for French buyers in the form of finely dressed women in elegant bourgeois interiors, not in the generalized style of history painting but the individualized one of seventeenth-century Holland.

One of the interesting phenomena of the eighteenth century was the way theorists ran to catch up with the artistic developments of their day. To develop, a genre needs an artistic and social rationale. Genre painting, an important route for the interior's entry into art, had to wait until the eighteenth century for this to happen. As the received ideas began to be questioned, the more open-minded theorists and critics found ways to deal with this artist-and buyer-driven phenomenon. Looking back, we can see on the one hand the conservatives clinging to the old ideas and on the other the modernists attempting to formulate a rationale for the new types of painting that were finding favour. Even in Holland, the home of genre, it was not until Gerard de Lairesse examined the works of the Dutch genre painters in *Groot Schilderboek* (The Art of Painting) in 1707 that they were recognized in theory. Lairesse had made the connection between what is now known as genre painting (but which he broke down into sections – for example, outdoor scenes, merry companies) and the middle class by arguing that such paintings should meet the moral needs of the bourgeoisie, and this became the standard way of dealing with the new paintings. In mid-century France, when the Académie Royale recognized only two classes of painting, history and all the rest, the critic Diderot argued that Greuze was attempting to introduce moral ideas into his scenes of realism [...] In other words, he was annexing history to genre in order to justify it.

It is hard to shake received ideas. Arguing for genre to be taken seriously must have been like the early pleas for detective novels to be read as respectfully as they are today. Jean-Etienne Liotard […] was well aware of the way the accepted wisdom could affect how spectators saw and appreciated works of art. 'I have heard painters give judgements on art which were false to the point of being ridiculous. While looking at a collection of Flemish and Dutch paintings of the highest quality and finish […] one of the most accomplished painters in Rome once said to me: "I find no merit in any of these pictures,"' he wrote in 1781.[7] No doubt Liotard's own choice of minute realism made him feel so strongly on this matter, but it does not deny the truth of the statement.

Liotard's comments are important because they are an attempt to justify a change in taste, an assault on the ideas that 'everyone' accepts. They come at a time when the official history in which the interior has no place and no chance of making its way into the most respected kinds of painting converges with the unofficial history. This [section] began with the absence in the writings of any mention of the domestic interior as a type or genre of art. Even with the development of genre painting, there was still no mention of the domestic interior as a type or genre of art. I think there are two histories of the domestic interior in painting before the nineteenth century. The first history, which has been the subject of this [section], is the official one and is silent on the subject. The second, unofficial, history can be constructed from looking at the paintings.

NOTES

1 Kenneth Clark, *Landscape into Art* (London: John Murray, 1949), 26.
2 Sir Joshua Reynolds, 'Discourse 4' (1771), in *Discourses on Art,* edited by Robert R. Wark (New Haven, CT: Yale University Press, 1975), 70–1.
3 Ibid.
4 Henry Fuseli, fourth lecture, 'Invention,' in *Lectures on Painting* (London: Cadell and Davies, 1820), 185–6.
5 Thomas Phillips, lecture 7, 'On Composition,' in *Lectures on the History and Principles of Painting* (London: Longman, 1833), 329.
6 Jakob Rosenberg, Seymour Slive, and E.H. ter Kuile, eds., *Dutch Art and Architecture, 1600–1800* (Harmondsworth: Penguin, 1966), 18–19.
7 Cited in Lorenz Eitner, *Neoclassicism and Romanticism, 1750–1850* (Englewood Cliffs, NJ: Prentice-Hall, 1970), vol. 1, 53.

3.7 ROBERT KERR 'The Family Apartments'*

General Considerations. – Programme.

Let it be again remarked that the character of a gentleman-like Residence is not matter of magnitude or of costliness, but of design, – and chiefly of plan; and that, as a very modest establishment may possess this character without a fault, all unadorned; so also the stately Seat of a millionaire may perchance have so little of it that the most lavish expenditure shall but magnify its defects.

The points which an English gentleman of the present day values in his house are comprehensively these:

Quiet comfort for his family and guests, –
Thorough convenience for his domestics, –
Elegance and importance without ostentation.

The account which has been given of the history of Plan will pretty clearly show in what manner and by what degrees these principles have come to be established, and how recently it is that they have been fully recognised; but it is none the less certain that at the present moment they must be considered to be fixed and final rules, of which no compromise ought to be offered. However small and compact the house may be, the family must have privacy and the servants commodiousness, and the whole dwelling must display an unassuming grace. If, on the other hand, the circumstances of the owner and his tastes are such that magnitude and refinement ought to expand into state, even grandeur must not be pretentious, or wealth ostentatious, and the attributes of an agreeable English home must never be sacrificed [...]

* In *The Gentleman's House, or, How to Plan English Residences from the Parsonage to the Palace; with Tables of Accommodation and Cost, and a Series of Selected Plans* (London: John Murray, 1864), 73–6; Munby Rare Books Room, Cambridge University Library.

Privacy

Defined and exemplified. – For both family and servants. – Superiority of Elizabethan plan.

The idea here implied has already been hinted at, being the basis of our primary classification. It is a first principle with the better classes of English people that the Family Rooms shall be essentially private, and as much as possible the Family Thoroughfares. It becomes the foremost of all maxims, therefore, however small the establishment, that the Servants' Department shall be separated from the Main House, so that what passes on either side of the boundary shall be both invisible and inaudible on the other. The best illustrations of the want of proper attention to this rule must necessarily be obtained from houses of the smaller sort; and here cases more or less striking are unfortunately by no means rare. Not to mention that most unrefined arrangement whereby at one sole entrance-door the visitors rub shoulders with the tradespeople, how objectionable it is we need scarcely say when a thin partition transmits the sounds of the Scullery or Coal-cellar to the Dining-room or Study; or when a Kitchen window in summer weather forms a trap to catch the conversation at the casement of the Drawing-room; or when a Kitchen doorway in the Vestibule or Staircase exposes to the view of every one the dresser or the cooking range, or fills the house with unwelcome odours. Those who are acquainted with the ordinary class of suburban Speculation Villas, which, by the standard of rent, ought to be good houses, but are not, will at once recognise the unexaggerated truth of these illustrations; whilst, on the other hand, the facility with which houses of the same size and value are arranged by better hands for the express avoidance of all these evils is equally well known.

On the same principle of privacy, in a somewhat larger house, a separate Staircase becomes necessary, for the servants' use. Advancing further in respect of the style of the establishment, the privacy of Corridors and Passages becomes a problem; and the lines of traffic of the servants and family respectively have to be kept clear of each other at certain recognised points. Again, in the Mansions of the nobility and wealthy gentry, where personal attendants must be continually passing to and fro in all parts, it becomes once more necessary to dispose the routes of even this traffic so that privacy may be maintained under difficulties. In short, whether in a small house or a large one, let the family have free passage without encountering the servants unexpectedly, and let the servants have access to all their duties without coming unexpectedly upon the family or visitors. On both sides this privacy is highly valued.

It is matter also for the architect's care that the outdoor work of the domestics shall not be visible from the house or grounds, or the windows of their Offices overlooked. At the same time it is equally important that the walks of the family shall not be open to view from the Servants' Department. The Sleeping-rooms of the domestics ought also to be separated both internally and externally from those of the family, and indeed separately approached.

The idea which underlies all is simply this. The family constitute one community: the servants another. Whatever may be their mutual regard and confidence as dwellers under the same roof, each class is entitled to shut its door upon the other and be alone.

When the question of the privacy of rooms comes into notice more properly, in our examination of the apartments in detail, the development of the principle at large will further appear. We may, however, here refer to one point at least of general application, namely, the comparative merits of Italian and Elizabethan plan. In the Classic model, privacy is certainly less. The Principal Staircase especially is almost invariably an instance of this; so also are the various forms of Cortile, Central Hall, and Saloon; all are in a manner public places. But in the Mediaeval model, privacy is never difficult of accomplishment. The Staircase, for example, is generally secluded; and even a Gallery, if properly planned, becomes almost a Family room. In other words, it may be said that the open central lines of thoroughfare in Italian plan must necessarily favour publicity, whilst the indirect routes of the Mediaeval arrangement must equally favour privacy. Or it may be put thus: the Italian model, legitimately descended from the Roman, still exhibits its origin in the open-air habits of a Southern climate; whilst the old English model, the growth of Northern soil, displays a character of domestic seclusion which seems to be more natural to the indoor habits of a Northern home.

3.8 WALTER BENJAMIN
'Louis-Philippe or the Interior'*

La tête … sur la table de nuit, comme une renoncule,
Repose.
('The head … rests upon the night-table like a ranunculus.')

– Baudelaire, 'Une Martyre'

Under Louis-Philippe, the private citizen entered upon the historical scene. The extension of the apparatus of democracy by means of a new electoral law coincided with the parliamentary corruption that was organized by [François] Guizot. Under cover of this, the ruling class made history while it pursued its business affairs. It encouraged the construction of railways in order to improve its holdings. It supported the rule of Louis-Philippe as that of the managing director. With the July Revolution the bourgeoisie had realized the aims of 1789 (Marx).

For the private citizen, for the first time the living-space became distinguished from the place of work. The former constituted itself as the interior. The office was its complement. The private citizen who in the office took reality into account, required of the interior that it should support him in his illusions. This necessity was all the more pressing since he had no intention of adding social preoccupations to his business ones. In the creation of his private environment he suppressed them both. From this sprang the phantasmagorias of the interior. This represented the universe for the private citizen. In it he assembled the distant in space and in time. His drawing-room was a box in the world-theatre.

Statement on *art nouveau*. The shattering of the interior took place around the turn of the century in *art nouveau*. And yet the latter appeared, according to its ideology, to bring with it the perfecting of the interior. The transfiguration of the lone soul was its apparent aim. Individualism was its theory. With [Henry] Van de Velde, there appeared the house as expression of the personality. Ornament was to such a house what the signature is to a painting. The real significance of *art nouveau* was not expressed in this ideology. It represented the last attempt at a sortie on the part of Art imprisoned by technical advance within her ivory tower. It mobilized all the reserve forces of interiority. They

* In 'Paris – the Capital of the Nineteenth Century,' *Charles Baudelaire: A Lyric Poet in the Era of High Capitalism* [1935], translated by Harry Zohn (London: Verso, 1983), 167–9.

found their expression in the mediumistic language of line, in the flower as symbol of the naked, vegetable Nature that confronted the technologically armed environment. The new elements of construction in iron-girder-forms-obsessed *art nouveau*. Through ornament, it strove to win back these forms for Art. Concrete offered it new possibilities for the creation of plastic forms in architecture. Around this time the real centre of gravity of the sphere of existence was displaced to the office. The de-realized centre of gravity created its abode in the private home. Ibsen's *Master Builder* summed up *art nouveau*: the attempt of the individual, on the strength of his interiority, to vie with technical progress leads to his downfall.

> Je crois ... à mon âme: la Chose.
> ('I believe ... in my soul: the Thing.')
>
> – Léon Deubel, *Oeuvres*

The interior was a place of refuge of Art. The collector was the true inhabitant of the interior. He made the glorification of things his concern. To him fell the task of Sisyphus which consisted of stripping things of their commodity character by means of his possession of them. But he conferred upon them only a fancier's value, rather than use-value. The collector dreamed that he was in a world which was not only far-off in distance and in time, but which was also a better one, in which to be sure people were just as poorly provided with what they needed as in the world of everyday, but in which things were free from the bondage of being useful.

The interior was not only the private citizen's universe, it was also his casing. Living means leaving traces. In the interior, these were stressed. Coverings and antimacassars, boxes and casings, were devised in abundance, in which the traces of everyday objects were moulded. The resident's own traces were also moulded in the interior. The detective story appeared, which investigated these traces. *The Philosophy of Furniture* [see section 6.2 in this volume], as much as his detective stories, shows Poe to have been the first physiognomist of the interior. The criminals of the first detective novels were neither gentlemen nor apaches, but middle-class private citizens.

3.9 ALAIN CORBIN 'Domestic Atmospheres'*

From the mid-eighteenth century onward, domestic architecture in France, concerned to meet the new requirements of comfort, had been anxious to promote a specialized distribution of living spaces and to designate their particular functions. In the new dwellings, and even more in architects' plans, rooms ceased to be intercommunicating; numerous passages ensured their autonomy. Reception areas tended to be separate from private areas. The capacity to be alone in a well-ventilated space was, according to Claude-Nicolas Ledoux, both a physical and moral therapeutic imperative [...]

New sensory requirements directly accompanied this development as early as 1762. Abbé Jacquin had already urged that unpleasant odours in dwellings be combatted and that kitchens be kept clean.[1] He advised against excessive use of water and glazes, release of smoke, and the presence of cats and dogs in the bedroom; he recommended that the 'conveniences' be at a distance from it and that the curtains be kept open. His book shows that well before the nineteenth century the location of smells and the tactics of deodorization had their roots in notions of privacy designed to benefit the ruling classes. But after 1832 the seriousness of the [cholera] scare prompted renewed emphasis on the subject, and the systematic nature of the ensuing proposals underlined the rapid changes taking place in collective psychology.

Once again, what was new tallied with the broad bourgeois aim of both keeping away from and protecting himself against the masses, whom he was in other respects endeavouring to supervise more closely. Deodorization involved a withdrawal into his dwelling, the formation of the private sphere – in short, that process of 'domestication' already begun in the eighteenth century that had led Robert Mauzi to write: 'the bourgeois is happy only in his home.'[2] The implementation of 'domestic hygiene' (which tended to become 'family hygiene'), like the deployment of bodily hygiene, was no more than the complement to the retreat from public life; together, they engendered a type of habitat dependent upon the medicalization of private space. In the shelter of his dwelling, far from the odour of poverty and its menaces, the bourgeois sought to partake of the fashionable narcissistic pleasures and the subtle bodily messages that now wove a new delicacy into emotional exchanges [...]

---

* [1982]. In *The Foul and the Fragrant: Odor and the French Social Imagination* (Cambridge, MA: Harvard University Press, 1986), 161–75.

In the private sphere itself, family odour became obtrusive. Around 1840 a new alarm was sounded on this subject. There were hidden dangers in the family, whose virtues had been so highly praised; a specific hygiene was required. This relatively unnoted aspect of pre-Pasteurian attitudes coincided with the (widely studied) emergence of anxieties about morbid heredity and predisposition.

As early as 1844, one of the greatest sanitary reformers of the day, Dr Michel Lévy, warned of the harmful effects of 'the family atmosphere' and the 'gaseous detritus of the family.'[3] 'The family atmosphere' synthesized the individual atmospheres in the dwelling in the same way that the atmosphere of the city represented the sum of social emanations.[4] The imagination of sanitary reformers transposed to private space the threats that had so often been brandished concerning public space. But a specific danger emerged that had no reference to inadequate volume of respirable air or to the absence of collective hygiene; even without any intrusion from the stench of the masses, 'the family atmosphere' could be deadly. The accumulated noxiousness of miasmic exhalations, which, by virtue of being related through kinship and heredity, were of the same nature, constituted in itself a morbid menace. The unique mix thus formed impregnated that 'habitus vital' of 'the domestic atmosphere.' As a result of this constant familial 'miasmic intercourse,' every house had both its own odour and its 'specific endemic diseases,' kept alive by the mephitism of the walls.[5] Lévy expressed it thus: 'We have in mind, not the known effects of the vitiation of the air by congestion, by the escape of flue- or lightning-gas, etc., but the continual exchange of all the influences composing the atmosphere peculiar to several individuals sprung from the same blood, having the same predispositions ... Cohabitation brings into conflict the personal atmospheres of those who live together; equilibrium results from reciprocal saturation, which strengthens certain morbid predispositions in those who are afflicted with them and develops them in those who were previously exempt from them.'[6]

To counteract the harmful effects of 'the domestic atmosphere,' good family hygiene required creation of an area reserved for the free deployment of individual atmosphere, without risk of reciprocal contamination. The interchange of familial emanations called for a private individual area, in the same way that not so long before the interchange of social emanations had decreed flight from the town or withdrawal into the family dwelling. The revulsion from other people's emanations within the family itself accelerated the process of individualization begun in the mid-eighteenth century. After the successful promotion of the individual bed, the next step was the individual bedroom.

Among the masses such an ambition would, for the moment, have been misplaced; the proletarian family, which sanitary reformers aimed to normalize, was subject to the accumulated efforts of family miasmas and had small chance of escaping the threat of disease. The boy's scrofula, the girl's chlorosis were already embedded in the fabric of smells characteristic of the dwelling. The stench of the poor was identified with hereditary decay [...]

The sudden awareness of the characteristic smells of the rooms that composed the private home created a desire to promote the specific smell of individual rooms and thus abolish the offensive mixture of the family atmosphere; it was an incentive to check as far as possible the formation of the potpourri of domestic odours. Like the promiscuity to which it testified, confusion of smells had become obscene. Apart from eliminating the confined air of the recess, the only way to get rid of troublesome smells and to reserve private space for the delicate effluvia of intimacy was to sort them out and contain the strongest smells in the appropriate places. A new intolerance proscribed the mixing of organic odours and subtle perfumes; preventing such confusion would be the function of the modern kitchen, dressing room, and bathroom.

This demarcation of the intimate spaces of interior monologue liberated the olfactory possibilities of both bedchamber and salon; they sanctioned the emergence of an aesthetic of olfaction within private space. A science of scents designed to embellish places of intimacy accompanied the cautious advance of perfumery. Their progression was governed by the same concern to produce increasingly subtle individual messages, and the same desire to reveal and emphasize the person. Because they obeyed the same imperatives, the skilful arrangement of the background of smells in the boudoir came to be aesthetically inseparable from the odour of the woman to whom one came there for inspiration.

Symbolic of the process was the growing concern to deodorize the individual bedroom, which came to be regarded as the place of the smells of intimacy par excellence. Within this refuge, separated lovers could indulge in solitary respiration of the beloved's perfumes [...] Odours helped make the chamber the mirror of the soul. The skilfully delicate atmosphere of this refuge for secret tears and pleasures tended to replace the sensual animality of the alcove.

NOTES

1 Armand-Pierre Jacquin, *De la santé: Ouvrage utile à tout le monde* (Paris: G. Desprez, 1771), 294–5.

2 Robert Mauzi, *L'Idée du bonheur,* 2nd ed. (Paris: A. Colin, 1965), 281.

3 Quoted in Louis Chevalier, *Classes laborieuses et classes dangereuses de Paris pendant la première moitié du XIXe Siècle* (Paris: Hachette, 1984), 179.

4 Michel Lévy, *Traité d'hygiène publique et privée* (Paris: J.B. Baillière, 1850), vol. 1, 544.
5 Ibid., 545.
6 Ibid.

3.10 SHARON MARCUS 'Seeing through Paris'*

During the Restoration and the July Monarchy, from the 1820s through the 1840s, the characteristic Parisian house took on a new form, that of the modern six- to eight-story apartment building with shops on the ground floor and an imposing entrance supervised by a porter. In terms of both their form and the ways that their form was perceived, apartments embodied an urban domesticity that aligned them simultaneously with private homes and with public structures such as monuments, cafés, and streets.

The new apartment house represented a shift from earlier architectural articulations of private and public space. On the one hand, nineteenth-century apartment units were more self-contained and hence provided more spatial privacy than eighteenth-century housing for the middle and working classes; on the other hand, the increased size of nineteenth-century buildings, and their incorporation of vestibules, lobbies, and elaborate stairways, meant that these edifices brought more strangers into contact, in more places, than earlier ones had [...] The apartment house partly owed its unique synthesis of publicity and privacy to its dual architectural sources, the *maisons à allée* and the *hôtels privés*. Most eighteenth-century apartment houses were *maisons à allée,* which lacked vestibules and were entered either through alleys off the street or through ground-floor shops. Internal apartments were formed by blocking off varying sets of rooms according to the needs of individual tenants and often consisted of suites of rooms distributed over several floors; this arrangement tended to multiply contact with other occupants, since one tenant might have to cross another's room to reach her own [...]

Nineteenth-century apartment *units* were spatially self-contained and thus offered tenants greater seclusion within an individual apartment, but nineteenth-century apartment *buildings* maintained and even extended the public nature of the *maisons à allée,* since their larger scale (five to six stories) gathered greater

* In *Apartment Stories: City and Home in Nineteenth-Century Paris and London* (Berkeley, CA: University of California Press, 1999), 17–50.

numbers of residents together under one roof, while their inclusion of clearly articulated common spaces for entrance and egress formalized interaction among tenants. Like the *maisons à allée,* the new buildings had shops on the ground floor and thus continued to mix commerce and private life, though tradespeople and merchants were more common than artists and manufacturers in more costly buildings.

The nineteenth-century apartment house did not evolve exclusively from earlier models of communal housing. Apartment house architects also drew on the aristocratic private townhouse, the *hôtel privé,* in their designs for the imposing double doors (*portes cochères*), elaborate vestibules, and porter's lodges that stood between the apartment building and the street. Some architectural historians have even identified the *hôtel* as the sole origin and model for the apartment house, but significant differences existed between the two building types.[1] The apartment brought public and private rooms into greater proximity with one another than the *hôtel* had. The *hôtel* separated reception rooms such as salons, which were open to strangers and designed for social occasions and display, from the bedrooms, studies, and cabinets intended for retirement and solitude. The apartment not only placed both types of rooms on a single floor but often placed them in direct communication with one another, so that one might enter an apartment's salon by passing through its main bedroom. Furthermore, the *hôtel* was divided into separate wings for the husband and wife, which included separate bedroom suites for each of them, and thus created autonomous masculine and feminine spaces; the more constricted bourgeois apartment usually accommodated only a single conjugal bedroom and thus promoted a greater degree of spatial heterosociality than the aristocratic *hôtel.*[2]

Apartment buildings and *hôtels privés* also differed in their orientation toward their urban surroundings. *Hôtels privés* occupied a space distinct both from other buildings and from the street. As the historian Roger Chartier points out, because *hôtels* were free-standing structures set back from the thoroughfare by a walled courtyard, they 'interrupted the continuous ribbon of facades' that bordered the typical Parisian street.[3] The *hôtel* turned its back to the street, since its primary, highly decorated front and its most important rooms (dining room, salon, bedrooms) faced a private garden. The part of the *hôtel* facing the street, but separated from it by a walled courtyard, consisted of service rooms such as stables and the kitchen. Apartment buildings, by contrast, were situated directly on the street, entered from the street, made to be viewed from and to provide views of the street. Builders constructed apartment buildings with strong front / back axes, aligned facades with the sidewalk, and emphasized the importance of the street front by lavishing better materials and more intricate designs on it. The most sought-after apartments were those closest to the street, and the most prized rooms of an apartment – living room, dining room, and main bedroom – faced the street, while the kitchen, servant's room, and storage rooms faced the courtyard […]

Apartment-house design also bore a conceptual similarity to urban street systems. The ordered grid of the apartment-house facade, like that of city streets, worked to abstract individual details into an aggregate public form. Their unity and symmetry gave facades a decorative power of generalization over the particularities of the rooms behind them in a process related to the urban consolidation of heterogeneous individuals into a public. The windows in a building's street facade often matched one another in size, shape, and design, even when the rooms behind them were different sizes or belonged to apartments separated from one another by vertical or horizontal partitions […] The apartment did have an area whose external irregularities suggested internal dissymmetries – the courtyard, carved out of the space where the undecorated, cheaply constructed back walls of up to four different buildings met and were irregularly punctuated by variously sized windows. Only the occupants of neighbouring buildings, however, could see the disorganization of the courtyard; the general public saw only the symmetry of a balanced, ordered facade.

Where *hôtels privés* allowed passersby mere glimpses of a circumspect, individualized image of domesticity, apartment buildings displayed and oriented a collective domesticity that communicated fully with the public street. Indeed, the building-street configuration characteristic of Paris from the 1820s through the 1840s – contiguous apartment buildings lining both sides of a street or wider boulevard – made streets and houses spatially interdependent […]

The space of early nineteenth-century Parisian buildings mingled with the space of streets in concrete, quotidian ways. As prefect of Paris after 1833, Claude Rambuteau installed benches on all the major boulevards, a practice that made the comfort and stillness conventionally associated with the home available on the street; he also increased the number of public urinals on the sidewalks.[4] Apartment buildings began literally to enter the street when an 1823 ordinance of Louis XVIII allowed facades to project into the street, albeit in very restricted ways, for the first time since 1607. That ordinance also decreed that street widths would determine the height of a building and whether it could have balconies, thus deriving the facade's dimensions and design from those of the street. And on a daily basis people threw their garbage into the streets, street sellers hawked their goods by yelling up into apartments, and merchants plastered building fronts with advertisements for their products […]

Architectural texts linked the public spaces of the street and the private spaces of the residence by consistently associating apartment houses with the urban progress and modernity that twentieth-century historians have attributed only to public spaces such as boulevards and cafés [...]

Others similarly associated apartment buildings with the modern qualities of contemporaneity and progress. In 1838 Jean-Charles Krafft, describing a recently built apartment house, complete with imposing entrance, ground-floor shops, and balconies, wrote: 'This facade, taken as a whole and in its details, seems to conform perfectly to our modern practices and to fulfil all our current requirements for a residence; ... everything in it could serve as a model for a rental house located in the city [*des maisons de ville dites à loyer*].'[5] And when L. Roux wrote that 'the ground floor of a modern house is invariably left to commerce,' he pointed out the links between modern consumer culture and contemporary domestic architecture.[6]

Over the course of the July Monarchy, architects identified apartments not only with an up-to-date, urban style but also with a financial potential redolent of modernity. Apartment buildings came to occupy an important position in a speculative Parisian real-estate market and provided opportunities for newly rich bourgeois to invest and generate income [...]

English observers often criticized Parisian home life for its lack of privacy, not only because they took the single-family house as an architectural standard, but also because they defined domesticity in opposition to the marketplace, and the *maison de rapport* brought economics close to home. French architects, however, did not consider the apartment house's associations either with the street or with urban speculation to disqualify it from a domestic function; they continued to call apartment buildings and units *maisons* or private houses (*maisons particulières*) even after the late 1840s, when financial speculators had begun to build apartments on an almost industrial scale and landlords were commonly depicted as impersonal administrators who rarely lived in the buildings they owned.

NOTES

1 The *hôtel privé* was also interchangeably called the *hôtel particulier* [...]
2 See Monique Eleb-Vidal and Anne Debarre-Blanchard, *Architectures de la vie privée: Maisons et mentalités XVIIe–XIXe siècles* (Brussels: Archives d'architecture moderne, 1989), 78, 83, 238.
3 Roger Chartier, 'Power, Space, and Investments in Paris,' in James L. McClain, John M. Merriman, and Ugawa Kaoru, eds., *Edo and Paris: Urban Life and the State in the Early Modern Era* (Ithaca, NY: Cornell University Press, 1994), 148.

4 See *Les grands boulevards* (Paris: Musées de la ville de Paris, 1985), 209.
5 J.C. Krafft, *Portes cochères et portes d'entrées des maisons et édifices publics de Paris*, 2nd ed. (Paris: Bance, 1838), vol. 2, 3 [...]
6 L. Roux, *Le Cabinet de lecture* (1838), quoted in *Le Parisien chez lui au XIXe siècle: 1814–1914: [exposition organisée par le Secrétariat d'État à la culture, Direction des archives de France], Hôtel de Rohan, novembre 1976–février 1977 (Paris: Archives nationales, 1976)*, 42.

3.11 DOROTHY TODD AND RAYMOND MORTIMER
The New Interior Decoration: An Introduction to Its Principles, and International Survey of Its Methods*

The oldest form of art of which any record remains is Interior Decoration [...]

It has continued one of the most constant and powerful impulses of the human heart, this desire to adorn the place in which we live, second only to the desire to adorn our own bodies. It is an assertion of personality: like the wax comb of the bee and the thin web of the spider, our homes are in a sense a projection of ourselves. We see the facets of our character mirrored in the objects with which we have surrounded ourselves, and with every purchase that we choose we reveal something of our heart to the perceptive eye. Man's exaggerated sense of private property has been stimulated by this feeling that what he owns, he is; and not content with the reasonable satisfaction of this impulse in the possession of the implements with which he works, the furniture on which he rests, and the ornaments, whether of ormolu or common pottery, which he sets upon his mantelpiece, he has asserted himself by the acquisition of land that he has never seen and mines in countries he has never visited. But the most necessary, as well as the most legitimate, field for this projection of personality remains the home [...] The extraordinary recent increase of interest in interior decoration has largely resulted from a more acute need for self-expression [...]

Until comparatively lately the problem settled itself. Each epoch produced almost unconsciously and automatically the applied art suited to the sensibility of the persons living in it. An eighteenth-century Parisian could provide himself with the interior he required without taking thought. The silk-shop provided curtains, the carpenter, chairs, the china-shop, figurines, and dishes which harmonized not only with each other and with the pictures in the

---

* (New York: Charles Scribner's; London: B.T. Batsford, 1929); Vancouver Public Library.

manner of Boucher or Fragonard, but also with the songs that were being sung to the accompaniment of the harpsichord and with the books by Voltaire that filled the shelves with their calf bindings. Every object that the age produced bore the mark of one congruous civilisation [...] But with the nineteenth century a new tide began to sweep over Western Europe. Taste in the visual arts grew more and more uncertain. A house still furnished itself, almost automatically, but the results became increasingly unsatisfactory. Moreover, the revival of past styles – most dangerous of symptoms – began [...]

The contemporary movement in the arts has now developed a vigour which makes all attempts to disregard it ridiculous. The poets and novelists of the twentieth century, the painters and musicians, are alike engaged in expressing the sensibility of the age in new forms, which they have discovered for this purpose. In architecture and interior decoration the achievements have, until the last few years, been less vigorous and are still less known. But to remain content with old forms in these arts is impossible. And it is the thesis of this book that already work in the applied arts is being produced which can take its place with the fine products of the past, and which at the same time is highly original and characteristic of the present. It is not suggested that the magnificent decorative art bequeathed to us by the great craftsmen of the past should be neglected. A T'ang bowl, a Gothic tapestry, a Renaissance bronze, a Chippendale chair must continue to inspire the appreciation that they deserve. But they are to be used as models to rival, not copy: for inspiration not imitation. It is possible today to revert to the fine decorative tradition of our ancestors by employing, as they did, contemporary craftsmen and artists. And if we do this we can retain in our privacy that individuality which modern conditions are suppressing in our public life, and which the vogue for period decoration has been expelling even from our homes.

3.12 DOLORES HAYDEN
'Nurturing: Home, Mom, and Apple Pie'*

The Industrial Strategy

The German Marxist, August Bebel, in his classic book *Women under Socialism* (1883), wanted to move most traditional household work into the factory, abolishing women's domestic sphere entirely. Bebel argued: 'The small private kitchen is, just like the workshop of the small master mechanic, a transition stage, an arrangement by which time, power and material are senselessly squandered and wasted [...] In the future the domestic kitchen is rendered wholly superfluous by all the central institutions for the preparation of food.'[1] He also predicted that just as factory kitchens would prepare dinners, and large state bakeries would bake pies, so mechanical laundries would wash clothes and cities would provide central heating. Children would be trained in public institutions from their earliest years. Women would take up industrial employment outside the household, and the household would lose control of many private activities. The effects of industrialization would be general, and women would share in the gains and the losses with men, although their new factory work would probably be occupationally segregated labour in the laundry or the pie factory. A life of dedication to greater industrial production and the socialist state would reward personal sacrifice in the Marxist version of the industrial strategy.

In Bebel's version of home life, both nature and biology disappear in favour of industrial efficiency. Bebel believed that nurturing work should be done by women, but he tended to see women as interchangeable service workers. The demand that women nurture with a personal touch, so central to Beecher [see section 6.5 in this volume], was replaced by a sense that any day-care worker could offer a substitute for mother love and any canteen worker could serve up a substitute for home cooking. The spatial container for this interchangeable, industrial nurturing was to be the apartment house composed of industrial components and equipped with large mess halls, recreation clubs, child-care centres, and kitchenless apartments. Of course, service workers would need to be constantly on duty to keep these residential complexes running, but Bebel did not consider this service as labour of any particular value or skill. He underestimated the importance of the socialized home as workplace, even as he recognized the private home as workshop [...]

---

* In *Redesigning the American Dream: The Future of Housing, Work and Family Life* (New York: Norton, 2002), 81–119.

The House for the New Way of Life

The first opportunity for fulfilling Bebel's ideal occurred in the Soviet Union, after the October Revolution of 1917. Lenin and Alexandra Kollontai led Bolshevik support for housing and services for employed women. They argued for the transformation of the home by the state and experimented with these ideas as the basis for national housing policy. Lenin, in *The Great Initiative,* wrote about the need for housing with collective services in order to involve women in industrial production: 'Are we devoting enough attention to the germs of communism that already exist in this area [of the liberation of women]? No and again no. Public dining halls, crèches, kindergartens – these are exemplary instances of these germs, these are simple, everyday means, free of all bombast, grandiloquence and pompous solemnity, which, however, are *truly* such that they can *liberate women,* truly such that they can decrease and do away with her inequality vis-à-vis man in regard to her role in social production and public life.' Lenin conceded that 'these means are not new, they have (like all the material prerequisites of socialism) been created by large-scale capitalism, but under capitalism they have firstly remained a rarity, secondly – and particularly important – they were either hucksterish enterprises, with all the bad sides of speculation, of profit-making, of deception, of falsification or else they were a "trapeze act" of bourgeois charity, rightly hated and disclaimed by the best workers.'[2] Following Lenin's encouragement, the new regime developed a program of building multifamily housing with collective services, beginning with competitions by architects to generate new designs for the 'House for the New Way of Life.'

While the competition had a strong intellectual impact on designers of mass housing all over the world, ultimately, few of the projects were built as intended. The USSR lacked the technology and the funds to follow through on its commitment to urban housing under Lenin. Under Stalin, the commitment itself dissolved. Stalin's ascendancy in the 1930s ended the official policy of women's liberation. Divorce and abortion were made difficult; 'Soviet motherhood' was exalted, and experiments in collective living and new kinds of housing ended. Only the most minimal support for women's paid labor-force participation was provided: day care in large, bureaucratic centres stressing obedience, discipline, and propaganda.

Soviet Motherhood

As a result, women in the USSR were encouraged to join the paid labor force without recognition of their first job in the home. In 1980, Anatole Knopp, a specialist in Soviet housing, concluded that 'Soviet society today has but little connection with the fraternal, egalitarian, and self-managing society dreamed of by a few during the short period of cultural explosion which followed the Revolution.' Workers lived in small private apartments in dreary, mass housing projects, where miles and miles of identical buildings had been constructed with industrialized building systems. Individual units were cramped and inconvenient. Appliances were minimal. Laundry was done in the sink; cooking on a two-burner countertop unit without oven. Refrigerators were rare status symbols for the favoured elite. 'Soviet architecture today well reflects daily life in the USSR [...] It reflects the real condition of women in the Soviet Union – a far cry from the idyllic pictures once painted by Alexandra Kollontai.'[3]

NOTES

1 August Bebel, *Women under Socialism* [1883], translated by Daniel De Leon (New York: Schocken Books, 1971), 338–9.
2 Vladmir I. Lenin, *The Great Initiative,* quoted in Vladimir Zelinksi, 'Architecture as a Tool of Social Transformation,' *Women and Revolution* 11 (Spring 1976): 6–14.
3 Anatole Knopp, 'Soviet Architecture since the 20th Congress of the C.P.S.U.,' paper delivered at the Second World Congress of Soviet and East European Studies, Garmisch-Patenkirchen, 30 Sept. – 4 Oct., 1980, 12–13.

3.13 RITSUKO OZAKI
Purity and Danger from a Japanese Perspective: Culture and House Plan

Inside / Outside in Japanese Homes and Families

The Japanese have a number of rituals to maintain traditional distinctions between 'inside,' which is associated with purity, cleanliness, safety, and intimacy, and 'outside' which is related to impurity, dirt, and danger.[1]

In order to keep the inside of the house clean, various daily hygiene rituals are required: when people come home, they take their shoes off, wash their hands, and gargle; dogs are allowed inside only after having their paws wiped;

in the morning people sweep and water the gate, the vestibule, and the area between the two, for as a circumscribed space where the inside meets the outside, this area requires special care and is often a source of anxiety.

The lower parts of the body are regarded as dirty, too, even though they are washed frequently. Therefore, underwear is usually washed separately and a separate pair of slippers is provided exclusively for use in the toilet.

These rituals and practices show the importance of being 'clean' in Japanese culture, maintaining psychological boundaries. Dirt refers not only to physical and visible dirt, but also to cultural and conceptual dirt. Thus, a person's house must be kept clean to represent the cleanliness and purity of the family who live there.

A person's house is also a safe and intimate place, while the outside is dangerous. Indeed, when parents tell their children off, they lock them out as a punishment.

The distinction between the inside of the group and the outside world is clearly established when a child is still very young. Being a member of a group, such as a family, is of vital importance, as evidenced by the fact that a newborn does not receive a birth certificate, but is registered rather with the family. Collectivist values, such as harmony, loyalty, cooperation, and mutual dependency are highly prized.

Children learn to cooperate with the inside group as the best way to benefit personally, and to subject their individual needs to those of the group; they come to acquire the identity of the group to which they belong. As a consequence, children become willing to depend on and be relied on by others, fearful of making independent decisions, anxious about being isolated from the group, and show indifference to, or appear afraid of, strangers.

While there has been a strong feeling against sharing a wall of the house with others, which is why the detached house is the main form of housing, individual rooms are not as common as in the West. Sleeping arrangements reflect the privileging of physical closeness over privacy. In fact, the closest Japanese word to the English 'privacy,' *uchi,* indicates the inside of the group to which one belongs, not the individual.

It is only after the implementation of the new Civil Code of 1947, guaranteeing individual rights, that the Japanese have gradually come to accept the notion of 'personal privacy,' in contrast to 'familial privacy.' (The English word 'privacy' became a common Japanese word – *puraibashī* – after a former foreign secretary used it publicly to defend his personal life.) Now, family members sleep separately in their own rooms, although sleeping together is still the dominant pattern in families with young children.

Boundaries in Japanese House Plans

These socio-cultural boundaries are reflected in the house plans. In Japan, the 'front' of the house is south- and garden-facing. This orientation, common in farmhouses, where during the harvest festival an altar would be established in the drawing room(s) that faced the garden, is also found in townhouses and samurai housing. For instance, in samurai housing of the feudal era, the space for receiving guests held the best orientation in the house facing the garden and south – that is, the front.

Japanese houses traditionally consisted of *tatami* (straw-matted) rooms, and the walls, made of paper, were removable. Each room had a cupboard where one could put a set of futon during the day; therefore the room could be empty with no furniture except for some chests of drawers, and was multipurpose. The paper walls could be removed to make a large, spacious room for special occasions.

The houses built between 1900 and 1945 typically had traditional *tatami* rooms. In the early twentieth century, the middle class started to live in suburban detached houses enclosed by high fences, although some had already lived in such houses in the late nineteenth century. Houses were typically single-storied, except urban housing, which also had a first floor to get the sun in the crowded urban environment. Every house – large or small – had a vestibule where one would take one's shoes off and climb up a few steps to the floor level. This space contained a cupboard for shoes. The most popular early twentieth-century house type was the 'middle-corridor' house, in which a corridor running through the middle of the house divided areas between those for formal use and for everyday use and between those for the family and for the servants. On the sunny side of the house, facing the garden, were the drawing room(s) and the family living room. The kitchen, the bathroom, the toilet, and the maid's room, on the other hand, were located on the opposite side of the corridor. Rooms for sleeping were also situated in the back. The drawing room(s), family room, and sleeping rooms were separated with removable paper sliding doors. The bathroom consisted of a few smaller sections – rooms for undressing and for bathing – and the toilet was separate.

Houses built between the 1970s and the 1990s also feature a vestibule to take one's shoes off, with a cupboard for storing them. The change in bedroom styles, however, is notable. Japanese-style bedrooms have increasingly been replaced by the Western type of room (i.e., rooms with a door and solid wall, and a bed in place of the *tatami*). In the 1970s, the majority of houses had both types of bedrooms, but by the 1990s the *tatami* bedrooms had virtually disappeared.

Although Western-style bedrooms are increasingly popular, there is still typically a Japanese-style *tatami* room next to the living room on the ground floor. This feature is consistently seen, regardless of the age of houses. By virtue of the multifunctional capacity of a *tatami* room, this space can be used as a drawing room for formal occasions or as a guest bedroom at night.

Without exception, the bathroom and the toilet are kept separate. The bathroom always comprises two rooms: one is the actual bathing room which has a bathtub and a space where one washes and rinses oneself. The other is the washing-dressing room where a wash basin and a washing machine are located and where one takes one's clothes off before entering the bathing section. The bathroom is always found at the side of the house that does not face the garden. More and more houses have toilets on both the ground and first floors.

This demarcation defines pure and impure spaces: placing the most defiled area (the toilet) in the space dedicated to purification (the bathroom) would be inconceivable. For the same reason, houses with a washing machine in the kitchen do not sell well in Japan, because people do not like to mix 'clean' food and 'dirty' clothes in the kitchen. It is out of the question to wash one's clothes in the kitchen, which should be the cleanest place in the house. These illustrate what Mary Douglas called 'matter out of place.'[2]

As we have seen, the inside space is not only related to cleanliness, but also to intimacy. The traditional house did not contain personal spaces because of the lack of a sense of personal privacy; however, the high fences around the house were evidence of the emphasis placed on familial privacy. Although terraced housing was the common house type in the nineteenth century, people increasingly started to live in detached houses in suburbs as it suited the strong idea of familial privacy.

Distinctions between inside and outside, and their relation to purity, danger, dirt, and intimacy, reflect salient cultural norms in Japan, even though influenced by Western styles and modernity, and they have affected the way in which people construct, inhabit, and use their domestic spaces.

NOTES

1 For more detailed discussion, please see: Ritsuko Ozaki, 'Society and Housing Form: Home-Centredness in England vs. Family-Centredness in Japan,' *Journal of Historical Sociology* 14 / 3 (2001): 337–57; Ritsuko Ozaki, 'Le péril de l'impur: L'organisation de l'espace dans les intérieurs japonais,' in Béatrice Collignon and Jean-François Staszak, eds., *Espaces domestiques: Construire, aménager et représenter* (Rosny-sous-Bois: Bréal, 2003), 197–210; Ritsuko Ozaki and J.R. Lewes,

'Boundaries and the Meaning of Social Space: A Study of Japanese House Plans,' *Environment and Planning D: Society and Space* 24 / 1 (2006): 91–104.

2 Mary Douglas, *Purity and Danger: An Analysis of the Concepts of Pollution and Taboo* (London: Routledge and Kegan Paul, 1966).

CHAPTER FOUR

House / Body / Psyche

Whether in painting, literature, or architectural theory, the house has served as a recurring metaphor for the human persona, engendering numerous analogies between the house and the body and the house and the psyche. In 'Representation by Symbols in Dreams – Some Further Typical Dreams,' Sigmund Freud drew attention to the house as a favourite image of oneiric fantasy, and opened the floodgates to multifarious interpretations of domestic spaces.[1] This chapter presents a sampling of the ways in which such interconnections among house, body, and psyche have been inscribed.

Beginning with the Roman architect Vitruvius, who had developed an analogy between the symmetry and proportions of the human body and architecture, Marjorie Garber offers a succinct historical overview of the metaphor of the house as body and its implications concerning gender as well as the effect such figuration has had on the negotiation between public and private spaces in the architectural interior. The phantasm of the female body, polluting and biologically determined by its reproductive powers, haunts the house – and the history and theorization of domestic space. This association is brought to the fore in Annmarie Adams's analysis of the architectural prescriptions for the arrangements of the lying-in room directed at young married middle-class Victorian women. The excerpt from Emily Burbank's *Woman as Decoration* (1917) reflects the view of the female body as extension of the house that became ubiquitous at the beginning of the twentieth century; accordingly, the chapters in that book, with telling titles such as 'Intelligent Expressing of Self in Mise-en-Scène' or 'Follow Colour Instinct in Clothes as Well as House Furnishing' are accompanied by illustrations that underline the performance and theatricality of the presentation. Jean-Christophe Agnew argues how in Edith Wharton's novel *The House of Mirth,* Lily Bart's surrender of her moral interior to the physical interiors of her surroundings exposes Wharton's scathing indictment of the interchangeability of the commodified interior and the commodified body that Burbank so enthusiastically celebrated.

In his interpretation of his dream of a house in which time and space intersect and which to him represents his own psyche – home is 'the universal archetypal symbol of the self'– Carl Jung questions Freudian psychology and describes a dream in which he descends from an upper story, furnished in a rococo style, to a cellar dated from Roman times. He associates the lower regions of the house with a primitive self, the upper with his conscious self. In his seminal essay on the uncanny – the unhomely – Freud investigates the meanings of *heimlich* (homely) and *unheimlich* (unhomely), resulting in the revelation that the homely can contain its very opposite. Anthony Vidler examines how traces of the Freudian uncanny are manifested in bourgeois modernity, the city, and architecture; he invokes the uncanny as the 'quintessential bourgeois kind of fear,' linking it to nostalgia, homesickness, and a transcendental homelessness. Although the uncanny has often found its metaphorical home in architecture, Vidler reminds us that buildings themselves are not uncanny; they are however invested with uncanny qualities at times as the fiction of E.T.A. Hoffman, Edgar Allan Poe, and Stephen King amply demonstrates. Thus, the uncanny can be seen as everything that ought to have remained secret and hidden but has come to light, as a double, as the return of the repressed. This is indeed the stuff of ghost stories and horror movies. With echoes of Corbin (section 3.9 in this volume) and his portrayal of the deleterious effects of odours, and of Freud's uncanny, Georges Teyssot explores the early twentieth-century obsession with house pollution and the breeding of dust. The house was perceived as an extension of the epidermis, which must be cleansed of external impurities, while the interior must be protected by glass and the window (i.e., 'wind' and 'eye') from the dangers of seeping poisonous miasmic vapours and gas.

NOTE

1 Sigmund Freud, 'Representation by Symbols in Dreams – Some Further Typical Dreams' [1900–01], in *The Standard Edition of the Complete Psychological Works of Sigmund Freud*, translated and edited by James Strachey (London: Hogarth Press, 1953), vol. 5, 350–404.

4.1 MARJORIE GARBER 'The Body as House'*

The Body as House

The representation of the house as a human body is a very old idea, one often reinvented in children's drawings, where the bungalow or cottage frequently comes to resemble a face. The roof is a hat or hair, the windows of the upper story are eyes, the door is a mouth. Variations on this figure abound in everything from allegorical writing to toys and animated cartoons. But whether expressed in literature, painting, theology, or architecture, this analogy between the house and the body has usually emphasized one of three elements: proportion, function, or sex and gender roles.

Proportion:

Architectural proportions modelled on human proportions, with the implication of natural design.

The Roman architect and engineer Vitruvius had early on developed the analogy between the human body and architecture: 'for without symmetry and proportion no temple can have a regular plan; that is, it must have an exact proportion worked out after the fashion of the members of a finely shaped human body.'[1] The proportions of the body were measured and used as models for architectural proportions ('The face from the top of the forehead and the roots of the hair is a tenth part; also the palm of the hand from the wrist to the top of the middle finger is as much; the head from the chin to the crown, an eighth part').[2]

Similarly, a stanza of Andrew Marvell's seventeenth-century house poem, 'Upon Appleton House,' expresses the ideal of measurement gleaned from nature:

> Why should of all things man unruled
> Such unproportioned dwellings build?
> The beasts are by their dens expressed,
> And birds contrive an equal nest;
> The low-roofed tortoises do dwell
> In cases fit of tortoise-shell.

---

* In *Sex and Real Estate: Why We Love Houses* (New York: Pantheon Books, 2000), 73–80.

No creature loves an empty space;
Their bodies measure out their place.[3]

The body is an instrument of measurement in the Bible as well as in ancient classical culture. There we find natural measurements like the cubit (from the Latin word for 'elbow'), equal to the length of the forearm from the tip of the middle finger to the elbow. God instructed Noah to build the ark 300 cubits long, 50 cubits wide, and 30 cubits high (Genesis 6:15).

The ark may seem an odd kind of model home, but it was designed according to a highly specific plan, with three stories and various categories of beasts (clean and unclean), fowls, and creeping things. Indeed, Christian authors in the Italian Renaissance went on to allegorize the connection between architecture and the body, making it tell a moral and spiritual as well as a physical story. Noah's ark was described in terms of a parallel between human anatomy and human virtue, with the 'higher, good openings and the lower, bad ones'[4] exemplifying the basic tension within mankind (as well as between man and beast). This kind of interpretation clearly pointed in the direction of a *functionalist* reading, explaining the house as a working body as well as an emblem of natural design.

Function:

Bodily functions and how the house reflects them, metaphorically and literally.

The functionalist metaphor of house as body is hierarchical, dividing it into 'lower' and 'higher' functions overseen by the 'head,' which is both man (husband, patriarch) and mind. We might note that this is usually a single body – '*the* body' – and that it is unmarked by gender difference. Its differences are differences *within* (high, low, thought, feeling, eating, elimination, etc.).

The purpose of such an anatomy of the house (both literally and figuratively) is to point toward organic wholeness; the different parts work together, 'naturally,' to make the organism – and the house/household – function. In medieval and Renaissance literature the house is often a 'body-castle,' fortified against assault by sin and desire, at the same time that it possesses an effective internal economy. The House of Alma in Edmund Spenser's *Faerie Queene* is an extreme and ingenious example played out in great detail: the mouth is a barbican (literally a 'gate-with-holes'), the stomach a big dining hall, and waste is disposed of 'privily' through a small door at the back [...] There is an emphasis on high versus low functions and on reading the well-organized household as a model of the healthy and morally fit body.

This is a figure that goes back at least as far as Plato's *Timaeus,* where the part of the soul 'which is endowed with courage and compassion and loves contention' is located 'nearer the head, between the midriff and the neck,' so that 'being obedient to the rule of reason it might join with it in controlling and restraining those desires when they are no longer willing of their own accord to obey the word of command issuing from the citadel.' By contrast, 'the part of the soul which desires meats and drinks and the other things of which it has need by reason of the bodily nature' is placed 'between the midriff and the navel, contriving in all this region a sort of manger for the food of the body.' Like a wild animal within the human frame, 'who was chained up with man and must be nourished if man was to exist,' this 'lower creature' is confined to a specific place in the body 'in order that he might be always feeding at the manger, and have his dwelling as far as might be from the council chamber [i.e., the brain and mind], and make as little noise and disturbance as possible.'[5]

It's clear from this account that various regions of the house, like the corresponding regions of the body, are imagined in a hierarchical relation. The manger – a feeding place for animals – is as far away as possible from the council chamber, so that the thoughtful deliberations of human beings will not be disturbed by animal appetites. And yet all of these rooms and regions are part of the human body.

Sex-Gender:

Architecture as reflecting and producing sexual law and morality, and guarding (or enshrining) female virtue.

Here the differences are *between,* not within. The number is two, not one. Man is the 'head' of the house; woman is its 'heart.' We may note that it is almost impossible to use the metaphor of woman as house, or to extend the figure, without implying some law about her. Which does not keep the metaphor, whether expressed in painting or in poetry, from being, often, very beautiful.

The body is a house, the house of the soul, claimed a medieval treatise on the interior of the body. But since a woman's body was 'open,' its boundaries convoluted, the inside-out version of a man's, she needed a second 'house,' a building, to contain her and protect her soul.[6] It is not so much that the building is being thought of as a body, says Mark Wigley. 'Rather, the body is thought of as a building. The discourses of space and sexuality cannot be separated.'[7]

The relation between the house and the gender and sexuality of its occupants was the implicit or explicit subject of some architectural treatises, like Leon

Battista Alberti's influential fifteenth-century work, *On the Art of Building in Ten Books.* Women are to be sequestered deep within the house for their own protection: 'any place reserved for women ought to be treated as though dedicated to religion and chastity; also I would have the young girls and maidens allocated comfortable apartments, to relieve their delicate minds from the tedium of confinement. The matron should be accommodated most effectively where she could monitor what everyone in the house was doing.'[8] [. . .] The man moves; the woman remains at home. In essence she *is* the home.

Alberti draws closely upon the ideas of the fourth-century B.C. Greek writer Xenophon, who insisted that the gods made women for indoor, and man for outdoor, pursuits: 'Thus for a woman to bide tranquilly at home rather than roam around is no dishonor; but for a man to remain indoors, instead of devoting himself to outdoor pursuits is a thing discreditable.'[9] As Wigley comments, 'The virtuous woman becomes woman-plus-house, or, rather, woman-as-housed, such that her virtue cannot be separated from the physical space.'[10]

Thus Alberti suggests that the spaces in the house are to be arranged in order to restrain and control sensual 'appetite' and to conceal or regulate the physical nature of the body. Much of its architectural design – like that of the modern house – is concerned with decisions about what is to be shown and what is to be concealed.

NOTES

1 Vitruvius, *De Architectura,* translated by Frank Granger (Cambridge, MA: Harvard University Press, 1955), vol. 1, 159. For more on the human body as image of the world, see Leonard Barkan, *Nature's Work of Art* (New Haven, CT: Yale University Press, 1975).

2 Vitruvius, *De Architectura,* vol. 1, 159.

3 Andrew Marvell, 'Upon Appleton House,' lines 9–16, in *The Selected Poetry,* edited by Frank Kermode (New York: New American Library, 1967).

4 Barkan, describing an argument of Francesco Giorgi (*Nature's Work of Art,* 142n).

5 Plato, *Timaeus,* in *The Collected Dialogues of Plato,* translated by Benjamin Jowett, edited by Edith Hamilton and Huntington Cairns (Princeton, NJ: Princeton University Press, 1961), 70a–e, 1193–4.

6 Henri De Mondeville (fourteenth century). See Carolyn Walker Bynum, 'The Female Body and Religious Practices in the Later Middle Age,' in Michel Feher, ed., *Fragments for a History of the Human Body,* Part I (New York: Zone, 1989), 187; and Mark Wigley, 'Untitled: The Housing of Gender,' in Beatriz Colomina, ed., *Sexuality and Space* (Princeton, NJ: Princeton Architectural Press, 1992), 358.

7 Wigley, 'Untitled,' 357.
8 Leon Battista Alberti, *On the Art of Building in Ten Books*, translated by Joseph Rykwert, Neil Leach, and Robert Tavernor (Cambridge, MA: MIT Press, 1988), vol. 5, 149.
9 Xenophon, *Oeconomicus*, translated by H.G. Dakyns as 'The Economist,' in *The Works of Xenophon* (London: Macmillan, 1897), vol. 3, 231.
10 Wigley, 'Untitled,' 337.

4.2 ANNMARIE ADAMS 'Childbirth at Home'*

Childbirth at Home

The belief that the house and the body were inextricably linked, that ensuring the well-being of domestic space would ensure the health of the inhabitants of that space, and that this relationship between the house and the body should be regulated by women was never more evident than in the 'architectural prescriptions' written by doctors for young married women in the late nineteenth century. In their observations on motherhood's spatial implications, social critics and medical reports articulated a clear conception of both the productive and the destructive powers of Victorian women.

The Victorian middle-class birthing experience was the time when women's bodies and domestic spaces intersected; birth itself was a transgression of the boundaries between the woman's body and the house as the child emerged from the womb. Childbirth was also a prime example of the provision of medical care within the middle-class house. Just as the sanitarians had exposed the inner workings of the house by breaking down the building's walls – in models such as the Insanitary Dwelling at the IHE [International Health Exhibition] and in the sectional illustrations in the popular press – the medical profession tried to dissolve the opaque barriers between the outside and inside of women's bodies in order to see, to explain, and to control women's health. Since the idealized domain of the middle-class Victorian woman was the house, it is not surprising that this breakdown took place in the context of domestic space: the lying-in room. More than an innovation of architectural convenience, the lying-in room was

* In *Architecture in the Family Way: Doctors, Houses, and Women, 1870–1900* (Montreal and Kingston: McGill-Queen's University Press, 1996), 103–28.

both a symbolic and a visible extension of the mother's body, an observable space through which doctors could expand the conceptual limitations of the body [...]

Victorian doctors revealed, time and again, their frustration with the basic fact that pregnancy – as well as other female ailments – was beyond their sight. They could not control what they could not see, they implied, echoing the sanitarians' attitude to domestic architecture. Just as the sanitarians had dissolved the walls of the house, the medical profession tried to break down the opaque barriers between the outside and the inside of women's bodies by confining the pregnant woman to an easily controllable and observable environment [...]

The architecture of confinement was realized through the refurbishing of an ordinary bedroom in the house [...] This birthing room, or 'lying-in room' as it was commonly called, accommodated the mother, her attendant, and the baby, from the onset of labour until one month after delivery. This was the time believed necessary for the womb to return to its normal size and for the body of the newly delivered mother to be 'purified' of the illness and dangers associated with childbirth [...] The preparation of the lying-in room began long before the expected date of birth, coinciding with other social and economic contracts made outside the home. As soon as a woman suspected that she was pregnant, she was advised to employ a 'monthly nurse' to attend her during both childbirth and lying in. The lying-in room and the monthly nurse were expressions of the special status accorded to childbirth within the Victorian household. Pregnancy was not seen as an illness but as an altered condition.[1] The lying-in room was thus clearly distinguished from the sickroom that was such a common feature of Victorian middle-class houses. Similarly, the monthly nurse was a different person from the 'sick nurse' who was employed by a family to attend members while they were ill [...]

From the perspective of the doctors, the health of the house, like the woman's own physical health, was solely the pregnant woman's responsibility. Expectant mothers were urged to check the sanitary state of their houses as soon as they realized they were pregnant, particularly its ventilation and drainage [...] Unventilated rooms poisoned the tiny lives growing inside the womb, Victorian women were told: 'You who breathe such air, breathe in what is poisonous, and this poison is racing through your blood into every limb in your body with every breath you draw!'[2] [...]

The isolation of the lying-in room did not only provide a controlled environment in which the newborn child could begin life; it served another purpose too. The very things that were purposely excluded from the birthing space and were perceived as dangerous to the mother in delivery were also produced inside this protected space. Women in childbirth produced noises and smells. More serious still was the fact that women in childbirth were believed actually to generate disease. The architecture of lying in, in its posture of isolation within the house and its distinct material culture, was as much a way of protecting the family from the woman in childbirth as of isolating her from the family. The special furniture, the newspapers on the floor, and the spatial separation of the lying-in room from the other rooms in the house were ways of sequestering and controlling the polluting power of women's 'interiors.'

This belief that women in childbirth actually fouled the environment they occupied was in fact common to many cultures. Childbirth historian Ann Oakley has explained that the persistence of this belief in small-scale traditional societies is part of a larger belief system that sees 'the reproductive powers of women' in general as dangerous. 'The parturient woman,' says Oakley, 'is subject to a host of regulations which control and isolate her act of birth, so that the rest of society is not contaminated by it.'[3] Although the isolation of middle-class mothers in Victorian London was less extreme than the groups studied by Oakley, the process was identical. Removed from the family at the onset of labour and sequestered in a room or suite of rooms that were completely separate from all other spaces in the house, the newly delivered mother became part of an easily controllable environment and was thus seen as less threatening to other family members and to society in general.

The initiative taken by women for the architectural arrangements surrounding birth and their accountability for this architecture reveal the paradoxical situation of women in the late-Victorian home. By seeing women as 'pollutants,' medical experts expected them to secure the safety of other family members by 'cleaning' their houses and isolating their bodies. This was undoubtedly a natural extension of the mid-century notion of the evangelical mother, the 'angel in the house' who was responsible for purifying the family in moral terms. The paradox was most clearly articulated during pregnancy and childbirth. As late as the 1890s, the Victorian woman, like the house itself, was considered a factor of disease, not only through her own carelessness or ignorance – as many medical experts suggested – but simply through the enigma of her capacity to reproduce. The view of pregnancy as an 'infective malady,' as Oakley has elaborated, is the reason why maternity hospitals developed entirely independently from hospitals for the sick. It was not because of the dangers posed to pregnant women – as is commonly assumed – but because of the dangers women posed to those already vulnerable through illness.[4]

NOTES

1 Ann Oakley, *The Captured Womb: A History of the Medical Care of Pregnant Women* (Oxford: Basil Blackwell, 1984), 14.

2 Florence Stacpoole, 'Maternity Rules for Mothers' Meetings,' *Women's Penny Paper* 6 (July 1889): 4.
3 Ann Oakley, 'Wisewoman and Medicine Man: Changes in the Management of Childbirth,' in Juliet Mitchell and Ann Oakley, eds., *Rights and Wrongs of Women* (London: Penguin, 1976), 32.
4 Ibid., 33.

4.3 EMILY BURBANK
Woman as Decoration*

Foreword

Woman as Decoration is intended as a sequel to *The Art of Interior Decoration* (Grace Wood and Emily Burbank).

Having assisted in setting the stage for woman, the next logical step is the consideration of woman, herself, as an important factor in the decorative scheme of any setting – the vital spark to animate all interior decoration, private or public. The book in hand is intended as a brief guide for the woman who would understand her own type, – make the most of it, and know how simple a matter it is to be decorative if she will but master the few rules underlying all successful dressing. As the costuming of woman is an art, the history of that art must be known – to a certain extent – by one who would be an intelligent student of the subject. With the assistance of thirty-three illustrations to throw light upon the text, we have tried to tell the beguiling story of the decorative woman, as she appears in frescoes and bas reliefs of Ancient Egypt, on Greek vases, the Gothic woman in tapestry and stained glass, woman in painting, stucco and tapestry of the Renaissance, seventeenth, eighteenth and nineteenth century woman in portraits.

Contemporary woman's costume is considered, not as fashion, but as decorative line and colour, a distinct contribution to the interior decoration of her own home or other setting. In this department, woman is given suggestions as to the costuming of herself, beautifully and appropriately, in the ballroom, at the opera, in her boudoir, sun-room, or on her shaded porch; in her garden; when driving her own car; by the sea, or on the ice [...]

---

* (New York: Dodd, Mead, 1917).

The author does not advocate the preening of her feathers as woman's sole occupation, in any age, much less at this crisis in the making of world history; but she does lay great emphasis on the fact that a woman owes it to herself, her family, and the public in general, to be as decorative in any setting, as her knowledge of the art of dressing admits [...]

One may follow Woman Decorative in the Orient on vase, fan, screen, and kakemono; as she struts in the stiff manner of Egyptian bas reliefs, across walls of ancient ruins, or sits in angular serenity, gazing into the future through the narrow slits of Egyptian eyes, oblivious of time; woman, beautiful in the European sense, and decorative to the superlative degree, on Greek vase and sculptured wall. Here in rhythmic curves, she dandles lovely Cupid on her toe; serves as vestal virgin at a woodland shrine; wears the bronze helmet of Minerva; makes laws, or as Penelope, the wife, wearily awaits her roving lord [...]

If one would know the story of Woman's evolution and retrogressions – that rising and falling tide in civilization – we commend a study of her as she is presented in Art [...]

While we state that it is not our aim to make a point of fashion as such, some of our illustrations show contemporary woman as she appears in our homes, on our streets, at the play, in her garden, etc. We have taken examples of women's costumes which are pre-eminently characteristic of the moment in which we write, and, as we believe, illustrate those laws upon which we base our deductions concerning woman as decoration. These laws are: appropriateness of her costume to the occasion; consideration of the type of wearer; background against which costume is to be worn; and all decoration (which includes jewels) as detail with raison d'être [...]

Chapter 10 Woman Decorative in Her Sun-Room

A sun-room, as the name implies, is a room planned to admit as much sun as possible. An easy way to get the greatest amount of light and sun is to enclose a steam-heated porch with glass which may be removed at will. Sometimes part of a conservatory is turned into a sun-room, awnings, rugs, chairs, tables, couches, making it a fascinating lounge or breakfast room, useful, too, at the tea hour. Often when building a house a room on the sunny side is given one, two, or three glass sides. To trick the senses, ferns and flowering plants, birds and fountains are used as decorations, suggesting out-of-doors.

The woman who would add to the charm of her sun-room in Winter by keeping up the illusion of Summer, will wear Summer clothes when in it, that is, the same gowns, hats and footwear which she would select for a warm climate. To be exquisite, if you are young or youngish, well and active, you would

Sketched for "Woman as Decoration" by Thelma Cudlipp
Tappe's Creations

4 Tappé's Creations by Thelma Cudlipp. Courtesy of A.R. Mann Library, Cornell University.

naturally appear in the sun-room after eleven, in some sheer material of a delicate tint, made walking length, with any graceful Summer hat which is becoming [...] The effect of movement got by certain line manipulation, suggesting arrested motion, is of inestimable value, especially when your hat is one with any considerable width of brim. The hat with movement is like a free-hand sketch, a hat without movement like a decalcomania [...]

We assume that the colour scheme of the sun-room was dictated by the owner and is therefore sympathetic to her. If this be true, we can go farther and assume that the delicate tones of her porch gowns and tea gowns will harmonise. If her sun-room is done in yellows and orange and greens, nothing will look better than cream-white as a costume. If the walls, woodwork and furniture have been kept very light in tone, relying on the rugs and cushions and dark foliage of plants to give character, then a costume of sheer material in any one of the decided colours in the chintz cushions will be a welcome contribution to the decoration of the sun-room. Additional effect can be given a costume by the clever choice of colour and line in the work-bag [...]

Souvenirs of an artist designer's unique establishment, in spirit and accomplishment *vrai Parisienne* [can be seen in Figure 4]. Notice the long cape in the style of 1825 [...]

[Fashion designer] Tappé emphasises the necessity of knowing the background for a costume before planning it; the value of line in the physique beneath the materials; the interest to be woven into a woman's costume when her type is recognized, and the modern insistence on appropriateness – that is, the simple gown and close hat for the car, vivid colours for field sports or beach; a large fan for the woman who is mistress of sweeping lines, etc. etc.

Tappé is absolutely French in his insistence upon the possible eloquence of line; a single flower well poised and the chic which is dependent upon *how a hat or gown is put on*. We have heard him say: 'No, I will not claim the hat in the photograph, though I made it, because it is *mal posé*.'

4.4 JEAN-CHRISTOPHE AGNEW 'A House of Fiction: Domestic Interiors and the Commodity Aesthetic'*

As the consumption of mass-produced household furnishings expanded after the Civil War, American novelists, painters, and aestheticians seized upon the goods themselves as the most appropriate and compelling idiom in which to represent their changing sense of the human self and its relations [...] In their hands, the commodified home became something more than a likeness or even an expression of the selves placed within it: it became something interchangeable with those selves, something out of which those selves were at once improvised and imprisoned, constructed and confined. To the extent, then, that a commodity aesthetic may be said to emerge under the brush of, say, Eastman Johnson or William Paxton, or under the pen of Edith Wharton or Henry James, it suggests not just a way of seeing but a way of being as well [...]

* In *Consuming Visions: Accumulation and Display of Goods in America, 1880–1920*, edited by Simon J. Bronner (New York: Norton, 1989), 133–55.

The House of Fiction

For many writers at the turn of the century, the purchased interior became a convenient metaphor with which to convey the new powers and predicaments that they discerned in their own bourgeois existence. Both Edith Wharton and Henry James thought in architectonic terms about their fiction […] Wharton, who entered the literary marketplace in 1897 as co-author of *The Decoration of Houses* [see section 6.4 in this volume], used her writings on the domestic interior as a means of emancipating herself from the confinement of the social role to which she, as a bourgeois woman, had been consigned. In this sense, Wharton was able to draw the kind of boundaries between herself and her commodity environment that Lily Bart, the protagonist of Wharton's great novel *The House of Mirth* (1905) is incapable of achieving.

At the outset of the novel, Wharton presents Lily as a beautiful, self-absorbed woman approaching the end of her eligibility in the marriage market of Gilded Age Society. The reader first sees Lily through the eyes of one of her admirers, Lawrence Selden, as he walks with her down New York's Madison Avenue: 'As she moved beside him with her long, light step, Selden was conscious of taking a luxurious pleasure in her nearness: in the modeling of her little ear, the crisp upward wave of her hair – was it ever so slightly blackened by art? […] He had a confused sense that she must have cost a great deal to make.'

Selden's confusion over the source of Lily's artificiality – did it spring from within or from without? – soon becomes the reader's confusion and, as such, persists throughout the narrative. On the one hand, Lily becomes a figure whose 'impenetrable surface suggested a process of crystallization which had fused her whole being into one hard, brilliant substance.' On the other hand, Lily remains a figure whose boundaries occasionally dissolve into the ornamental world that surrounds her. She is herself an ornament, as she readily acknowledges, a decorative status that is most strikingly demonstrated in the famous *tableaux vivants* scene that comes midway through the novel […] Lily astonishes her jaded audience by posing as herself, by pointing quite deliberately to herself as a work of art and a marriageable commodity. The nominal inspiration for Lily's tableau is a portrait by Joshua Reynolds, but as Wharton describes the scene, 'It was as though she had stepped, not out of, but into, Reynolds' canvas […]'[1]

Lily is forever 'stepping into' the gilded frames of various New York interiors, so it is no surprise that her ultimate downfall should come by being quite literally framed. She is, after all, a temperament notoriously open to the suggestion of her surroundings […] Lily cannot 'figure herself as anywhere but in a drawing-room, diffusing elegance as a flower sheds perfume.' As her name suggests, Lily *is* a flower, but a 'rare flower grown for exhibition' and cultivated indoors.[2] She thrives in the luxuriant, hot-house atmosphere of New York's mansions and begins to die only when she is driven out of them. Their furnishings are her soil; their mirrors are the pools in which she finds the security of her own reflected beauty, so much so that whenever Lily encounters an unexpected reversal of fortune, she invariably rushes to the nearest mirror for reassurance, exchanging electric light for candlelight when the reflection grows too harsh and unflattering. Throughout *The House of Mirth,* Wharton uses the increasingly shabby New York interiors to which Lily is condemned as an index of her inexorable social decline. But Wharton also uses these interiors to bring home, as it were, the arrested character of Lily's emotional development. Because the conditions of Lily's own self-presentation as an ornament – a marriageable commodity – are so overriding, the aesthetic preoccupations of her life almost completely displace the moral perplexities they entail [...] Lily thus pursues an almost caricatured form of situational ethics, one in which her moral interior surrenders entirely to the various physical interiors in which she happens to find herself [... yet] the reader is made to share Lily's immersion, made to step into a personality that, in turn, diffuses itself into every room she enters. 'For all the hard glaze of her exterior,' Wharton concludes, Lily is 'inwardly as malleable as wax.'[3] She dies as she lives, by the pathetic fallacy of a commodity aesthetic.

NOTES

1 Edith Wharton, *The House of Mirth* (1905; reprint, New York: New American Library, 1964), 7, 198, 141–2.
2 Ibid., 29, 106.
3 Joan Lidoff, 'Another Sleeping Beauty: Narcissism in *The House of Mirth*,' in Eric J. Sundquist, ed., *American Realism: New Essays* (Baltimore: Johns Hopkins University Press, 1982), 238–58.

4.5 CARL GUSTAV JUNG
Memories, Dreams, Reflections*

As I have already said, Freud was able to interpret the dreams I was then having only incompletely or not at all. They were dreams with collective contents,

* Recorded and edited by Aniela Jaffé, translated by Richard and Clara Winston (London: Collins, 1989).

containing a great deal of symbolic material. One in particular was important to me, for it led me for the first time to the concept of the 'collective unconscious' and thus formed a kind of prelude to my book, *Wandlungen und Symbole der Libido.*[1]

This was the dream. I was in a house I did not know, which had two stories. It was 'my house.' I found myself in the upper story, where there was a kind of salon furnished with fine old pieces in rococo style. On the walls hung a number of precious old paintings. I wondered that this should be my house, and thought, 'Not bad.' But then it occurred to me that I did not know what the lower floor looked like. Descending the stairs, I reached the ground floor. There everything was much older, and I realized that this part of the house must date from about the fifteenth or sixteenth century. The furnishings were medieval; the floors were of red brick. Everywhere it was rather dark. I went from one room to another, thinking, 'Now I really must explore the whole house.' I came upon a heavy door, and opened it. Beyond it, I discovered a stone stairway that led down into the cellar. Descending again, I found myself in a beautifully vaulted room which looked exceedingly ancient. Examining the walls, I discovered layers of brick among the ordinary stone blocks, and chips of brick in the mortar. As soon as I saw this I knew that the walls dated from Roman times. My interest by now was intense. I looked more closely at the floor. It was of stone slabs, and in one of these I discovered a ring. When I pulled it, the stone slab lifted, and again I saw a stairway of narrow stone steps leading down into the depths. These, too, I descended, and entered a low cave cut into the rock. Thick dust lay on the floor, and in the dust were scattered bones and broken pottery, like remains of a primitive culture. I discovered two human skulls, obviously very old and half disintegrated. Then I awoke.

What chiefly interested Freud in this dream were the two skulls. He returned to them repeatedly, and urged me to find a *wish* in connection with them. What did I think about these skulls? And whose were they? I knew perfectly well, of course, what he was driving at: that secret death-wishes were concealed in the dream. 'But what does he really expect of me?' I thought to myself. Towards whom would I have death-wishes? I felt violent resistance to any such interpretation. I also had some intimation of what the dream might really mean. But I did not then trust my own judgment, and wanted to hear Freud's opinion. I wanted to learn from him. Therefore I submitted to his intention and said, 'My wife and my sister-in-law' – after all, I had to name someone whose death was worth the wishing!

I was newly married at the time and knew perfectly well that there was nothing within myself which pointed to such wishes. But I would not have been able to present to Freud my own ideas on an interpretation of the dream without encountering incomprehension and vehement resistance. I did not feel up to quarrelling with him, and I also feared that I might lose his friendship if I insisted on my own point of view. On the other hand, I wanted to know what he would make of my answer, and what his reaction would be if I deceived him by saying something that suited his theories. And so I told him a lie.

I was quite aware that my conduct was not above reproach, but *à la guerre, comme à la guerre!* It would have been impossible for me to afford him any insight into my mental world. The gulf between it and his was too great. In fact, Freud seemed greatly relieved by my reply. I saw from this that he was completely helpless in dealing with certain kinds of dreams and had to take refuge in his doctrine. I realised that it was up to me to find out the real meaning of the dream.

It was plain to me that the house represented a kind of image of the psyche – that is to say, of my then state of consciousness, with hitherto unconscious additions. Consciousness was represented by the salon. It had an inhabited atmosphere, in spite of its antiquated style.

The ground floor stood for the first level of the unconscious. The deeper I went, the more alien and the darker the scene became. In the cave, I discovered remains of a primitive culture, that is, the world of the primitive man within myself – a world which can scarcely be reached or illuminated by consciousness. The primitive psyche of man borders on the life of the animal soul, just as the caves of prehistoric times were usually inhabited by animals before men laid claim to them.

During this period I became aware of how keenly I felt the difference between Freud's intellectual attitude and mine. I had grown up in the intensely historical atmosphere of Basel at the end of the nineteenth century, and had acquired, thanks to reading the old philosophers, some knowledge of the history of psychology. When I thought about dreams and the contents of the unconscious, I never did so without making historical comparisons; in my student days I always used Krug's old dictionary of philosophy. I was especially familiar with the writers of the eighteenth and early nineteenth century. Theirs was the world which had formed the atmosphere of my first-story salon. By contrast, I had the impression that Freud's intellectual history began with Büchner, Moleschott, Du Bois-Reymond, and Darwin.

The dream pointed out that there were further reaches to the state of consciousness I have just described: the long uninhabited ground floor in medieval style, then the Roman cellar, and finally the prehistoric cave. These signified past times and passed stages of consciousness.

Certain questions had been much on my mind during the days preceding this dream. They were: On what premises is Freudian psychology founded? To what category of human thought does it belong? What is the relationship of its almost exclusive personalism to general historical assumptions? My dream was giving me the answer. It obviously pointed to the foundations of cultural history – a history of successive layers of consciousness. My dream thus constituted a kind of structural diagram of the human psyche; it postulated something of an altogether *impersonal* nature underlying that psyche. It 'clicked,' as the English have it – and the dream became for me a guiding image which in the days to come was to be corroborated to an extent I could not at first suspect.

This was my first inkling of a collective *a priori* beneath the personal psyche. This I first took to be the traces of earlier modes of functioning. Later, with increasing experience and on the basis of more reliable knowledge, I recognized them as forms of instinct, that is, as archetypes.

NOTE

1 *Psychology of the Unconscious* [translated by Beatrice M. Hinkle (Moffat: Yard, 1916)]; rev. ed.: *Symbols of Transformation* (CW 5) [*Collected Works of C.G. Jung,* vol. 5)].

4.6 SIGMUND FREUD
'The Uncanny'*

It is only rarely that a psycho-analyst feels impelled to investigate the subject of aesthetics, even when aesthetics is understood to mean not merely the theory of beauty but the theory of the qualities of feeling. He works in other strata of mental life and has little to do with the subdued emotional impulses which, inhibited in their aims and dependent on a host of concurrent factors, usually furnish the material for the study of aesthetics. But it does occasionally happen that he has to interest himself in some particular province of that subject; and this province usually proves to be a rather remote one, and one which has been neglected in the specialist literature of aesthetics.

The subject of the 'uncanny' is a province of this kind.[1] It is undoubtedly related to what is frightening – to what arouses dread and horror; equally certainly, too, the word is not always used in a clearly definable sense, so that it tends to coincide with what excites fear in general. Yet we may expect that a special core of feeling is present which justifies the use of a special conceptual term. One is

* [1919]. In *The Standard Edition of the Complete Psychological Works of Sigmund Freud,* translated and edited by James Strachey (London: Hogarth Press, 1955), vol. 17, 217–56.

curious to know what this common core is which allows us to distinguish as 'uncanny' certain things which lie within the field of what is frightening.

As good as nothing is to be found upon this subject in comprehensive treatises on aesthetics, which in general prefer to concern themselves with what is beautiful, attractive and sublime – that is, with feelings of a positive nature – and with the circumstances and the objects that call them forth, rather than with the opposite feelings of repulsion and distress. I know of only one attempt in medico-psychological literature, a fertile but not exhaustive paper by Jentsch (1906). But I must confess that I have not made a very thorough examination of the literature, especially the foreign literature, relating to this present modest contribution of mine, for reasons which, as may easily be guessed, lie in the times in which we live;[2] so that my paper [this section] is presented to the reader without any claim to priority.

In his study of the 'uncanny,' Jentsch quite rightly lays stress on the obstacle presented by the fact that people vary so very greatly in their sensitivity to this quality of feeling. The writer of the present contribution, indeed, must himself plead guilty to a special obtuseness in the matter, where extreme delicacy of perception would be more in place. It is long since he has experienced or heard of anything which has given him an uncanny impression, and he must start by translating himself into that state of feeling, by awakening in himself the possibility of experiencing it. Still, such difficulties make themselves powerfully felt in many other branches of aesthetics; we need not on that account despair of finding instances in which the quality in question will be unhesitatingly recognized by most people.

Two courses are open to us at the outset. Either we can find out what meaning has come to be attached to the word 'uncanny' in the course of its history; or we can collect all those properties of persons, things, sense-impressions, experiences and situations which arouse in us the feeling of uncanniness, and then infer the unknown nature of the uncanny from what all these examples have in common. I will say at once that both courses lead to the same result: the uncanny is that class of the frightening which leads back to what is known of old and long familiar. How this is possible, in what circumstances the familiar can become uncanny and frightening, I shall show in what follows. Let me also add that my investigation was actually begun by collecting a number of individual cases, and was only later confirmed by an examination of linguistic usage. In this discussion, however, I shall follow the reverse course.

The German word *'unheimlich'* is obviously the opposite of *'heimlich'* ['homely'], *'heimisch'* ['native'] – the opposite of what is familiar; and we are tempted to conclude that what is 'uncanny' is frightening precisely because it is *not* known and familiar. Naturally not everything that is new and unfamiliar is frightening, however; the relation is not capable of inversion. We can only say that what is novel can easily become frightening and uncanny; some new things are frightening but not by any means all. Something has to be added to what is novel and unfamiliar in order to make it uncanny.

On the whole, Jentsch did not get beyond this relation of the uncanny to the novel and unfamiliar. He ascribes the essential factor in the production of the feeling of uncanniness to intellectual uncertainty; so that the uncanny would always, as it were, be something one does not know one's way about in. The better orientated in his environment a person is, the less readily will he get the impression of something uncanny in regard to the objects and events in it.

It is not difficult to see that this definition is incomplete, and we will therefore try to proceed beyond the equation 'uncanny' = 'unfamiliar.' We will first turn to other languages. But the dictionaries that we consult tell us nothing new, perhaps only because we ourselves speak a language that is foreign. Indeed, we get an impression that many languages are without a word for this particular shade of what is frightening.

I should like to express my indebtedness to Dr Theodor Reik for the following excerpts:

> LATIN: (K.E. Georges, *Deutschlateinisches Wörterbuch,* 1898). An uncanny place: *locus suspectus;* at an uncanny time of night: *intempesta nocte.*
> GREEK: (Rost's and Schenkl's Lexikons). [**Greek: Eéros] (i.e., strange, foreign).
> ENGLISH: (from the dictionaries of Lucas, Bellows, Flügel, and Muret-Sanders). Uncomfortable, uneasy, gloomy, dismal, uncanny, ghastly; (of a house) haunted; (of a man) a repulsive fellow.
> FRENCH: (Sachs-Villatte). *Inquiétant, sinistre, lugubre, mal à son aise.*
> SPANISH: (Tollhausen, 1889). *Sospechoso, de mal aguëro, lúgubre, siniestro.*

The Italian and Portuguese languages seem to content themselves with words which we should describe as circumlocutions. In Arabic and Hebrew 'uncanny' means the same as 'daemonic,' 'gruesome.' [...]

[Freud now provides a list of definitions and uses of *heimlich*; eds.]

What interests us most in this long extract [...] is to find that among its different shades of meaning the word '*heimlich*' exhibits one which is identical with its opposite, '*unheimlich*.' What is *heimlich* thus comes to be *unheimlich*. (Cf. the quotation from Gutzkow: 'We call it "*unheimlich*"; you call it "*heimlich*."') In general we are reminded that the word '*heimlich*' is not unambiguous, but belongs to two sets of ideas, which, without being contradictory, are yet very different: on the one hand, it means what is familiar and agreeable, and on the other, what is concealed and kept out of sight.[3] '*Unheimlich*' is customarily used, we are told, as the contrary only of the first signification of '*heimlich*,' and not of the second. Sanders tells us nothing concerning a possible genetic connection between these two meanings of *heimlich*. On the other hand, we notice that Schelling says something which throws quite a new light on the concept of the *Unheimlich*, for which we were certainly not prepared. According to him, everything is *unheimlich* that ought to have remained secret and hidden but has come to light [...]

Thus *heimlich* is a word the meaning of which develops in the direction of ambivalence, until it finally coincides with its opposite, *unheimlich*. *Unheimlich* is in some way or other a sub-species of *heimlich*.

NOTES

1 The German word, translated throughout this paper [section] by the English 'uncanny,' is *unheimlich*, literally 'unhomely.' The English term is not, of course, an exact equivalent of the German one.
2 An allusion to the First World War only just concluded.
3 According to the *Oxford English Dictionary*, a similar ambiguity attaches to the English 'canny,' which may mean not only 'cosy' but also 'endowed with occult or magical powers.'

4.7 ANTHONY VIDLER
The Architectural Uncanny: Essays in the Modern Unhomely*

> Something is uncanny – that is how it begins. But at the same time one must search for the remoter 'something,' which is already close at hand.
>
> Ernst Bloch, 'A Philosophical View of the Detective Novel'

The contemporary sensibility that sees the uncanny erupt in empty parking lots around abandoned or run-down shopping malls, in the screened *trompe l'oeil* of simulated space, in, that is, the wasted margins and surface

* (Cambridge, MA: MIT Press, 1992).

appearances of postindustrial culture, this sensibility has its roots and draws its commonplaces from a long but essentially modern tradition. Its apparently benign and utterly ordinary loci, its domestic and slightly tawdry settings, its ready exploitation as the *frisson* of an already jaded public, all mark it out clearly as the heir to a feeling of unease first identified in the late eighteenth century.

Aesthetically an outgrowth of the Burkean sublime, a domesticated version of absolute terror, to be experienced in the comfort of the home and relegated to the minor genre of the *Märchen* or fairy tale, the uncanny found its first home in the short stories of E.T.A. Hoffmann and Edgar Allan Poe. Its favourite motif was precisely the contrast between a secure and homely interior and the fearful invasion of an alien presence; on a psychological level, its play was one of doubling, where the other is, strangely enough, experienced as a replica of the self, all the more fearsome because apparently the same.

At the heart of the anxiety provoked by such alien presences was a fundamental insecurity: that of a newly established class, not quite at home in its own home. The uncanny, in this sense, might be characterized as the quintessential bourgeois kind of fear: one carefully bounded by the limits of real material security and the pleasure principle afforded by a terror that was, artistically at least, kept well under control. The uncanny was, in this first incarnation, a sensation best experienced in the privacy of the interior. Ernst Bloch was not the first to remark that 'the setting in which detective stories are enjoyed the most is just too cozy. In a comfortable chair, under the nocturnal floor lamp with tea, rum, and tobacco, personally secure and peacefully immersed in dangerous things, which are shallow.'[1] The vicarious taste for the uncanny has been a constant in modern culture, only intensified by shifts in media.

But the uncanny, as Walter Benjamin noted, was also born out of the rise of the great cities, their disturbingly heterogeneous crowds and newly scaled spaces demanding a point of reference that, while not refuting a certain instability, nevertheless served to dominate it aesthetically. Here the privileged point of view – of Hoffman's observer keeping his careful distance from the marketplace, looking through 'The Cousin's Corner Window' with opera glasses; of Poe and of Dickens watching the crowd; of Baudelaire losing himself in the swarming boulevards – attempted to preserve a sense of individual security that was only precariously sustained by the endless quest of the detective tracking his clues through the apparent chaos of modern urban life.[2]

In the context of the nineteenth-century city, the alienation of the individual expressed by writers from Rousseau to Baudelaire was gradually reinforced by the real economic and social estrangement experienced by the majority of its inhabitants [...] For Marx [...] individual estrangement had become class alienation. As he noted in the *Economic and Philosophic Notebooks* [Manuscripts] *of 1844* the development of the rent system had rendered 'home' a temporary illusion at best.

> We have said … that man is regressing to the *cave dwelling*, etc., – but he is regressing to it in an estranged, malignant form. The savage in his cave – a natural element which freely offers itself for his use and protection – feels himself no more than a stranger, or rather feels as much at home as a *fish* in water. But the cellar-dwelling of the poor man is a hostile element, 'a dwelling which remains an alien power and only gives itself up to him insofar as he gives up to it his own blood and sweat' – a dwelling which he cannot regard as his own hearth – where he might at last exclaim: 'Here I am at home' – but where instead he finds himself in *someone else's* house, in the house of a *stranger* who always watches him and throws him out if he does not pay his rent.[3]

Here the question of 'the stranger,' which was to be a central notion in the sociology of Georg Simmel and his followers after the turn of the century, was joined with political urgency to what Hegel had called *Entfremdung* and Marx named *Entäusserung*.

This sense of estrangement was intellectually reinforced by the disturbingly transient qualities of the twin foundations of certainty for the nineteenth century – history and nature. The uncanny habit of history to repeat itself, to return at unexpected and unwanted moments; the stubborn resistance of nature to the assimilation of human attributes and its tragic propensity to inorganic isolation, seemed, for many, to confirm the impossibility of 'living comfortably' in the world. Estrangement, in these terms, seemed a natural consequence of a conception of history, of the implacable impulsion of time that, while sweeping away the past in favor of the future, was necessarily uncertain only about the present. The remedies to such uncertainty, which ranged from revolution to restoration, from reform to utopia, were equally caught in the dilemmas of temporality, tied to the inhospitable context of the here-and-now at the same time as imagining a there-and-then. This anxiety of time, as expressed in the intellectual attempts to imagine impossible futures or return to equally impossible pasts, was accompanied by a fascination with the consequences of time's errors – the dystopian effects of unwonted interference with the natural development of things, on the one hand, and the psychological effects of the past and future shock on the other.

Gradually generalized as a condition of modern anxiety, an alienation linked to its individual and poetic origins in romanticism, the uncanny finally became public in [the] metropolis. As a sensation it was no longer easily confined to the bourgeois interior or relegated to the imaginary haunts of the mysterious and dangerous classes; it was seemingly as disrespectful of class boundaries as epidemics and plagues. Perhaps this is why, from the 1870s on, the metropolitan uncanny was increasingly conflated with metropolitan illness, a pathological condition that potentially afflicted the inhabitants of all great cities; a condition that had, through force of environment, escaped the overprotected domain of the short story. The uncanny here became identified with all the phobias associated with spatial fear, including 'la peur des espaces' or agoraphobia, soon to be coupled with its obverse, claustrophobia [...]

For Freud, 'unhomeliness' was more than a simple sense of not belonging; it was the fundamental propensity of the familiar to turn on its owners, suddenly to become defamiliarized, derealized, as if in a dream [...] Themes of anxiety and dread, provoked by a real or imagined sense of 'unhomeliness,' seemed particularly appropriate to a moment when, as Freud noted in 1915, the entire 'homeland' of Europe, cradle and apparently secure house of western civilization, was in the process of regression [...] The site of the uncanny was now no longer confined to the house or the city, but more properly extended to the no man's land between the trenches, or the field of ruins left after bombardment.

In a moment when history seemed to have been brutally arrested, the uncanny reinforced its traditional links with nostalgia, joining what for many writers after the war seemed to be the 'transcendental homelessness' that Georg Lukács saw as the modern condition [...] 'Homesickness,' nostalgia for the true, natal home, thus emerges in the face of the massive uprooting of war and ensuing Depression as the mental and psychological corollary to homelessness. It was in this context that philosophers from Martin Heidegger to Gaston Bachelard wistfully meditated on the (lost) nature of 'dwelling,' through nostalgic readings of the poets of the first, romantic uncanny. For Heidegger, the *unheimlich,* or what Hubert Dreyfus prefers to translate as 'unsettledness,' was, at least in its formulation of 1927, a question of the fundamental condition of anxiety in the world – the way in which the world was experienced as 'not a home'[...]

It was, of course, for this security that, following the Second World War, Heidegger himself searched; attempting to trace the roots of preanxious dwelling and exhibiting a profound nostalgia for the premodern, his later writings have formed the basis of a veritable discourse on dwelling that has been taken up by latter-day phenomenologists and postmodernists alike [...]

This coincidence of the sensibility of exile, intellectual and existential, with the forced nomadism and lived homelessness of the Depression only reinforced the growing feeling that modern man was, essentially and fundamentally, rootless: 'Homelessness is coming to be the destiny of the world,' wrote Heidegger in his celebrated 'Letter of Humanism' in 1947.

At the same time, for the modernist avant-gardes, the uncanny readily offered itself as an instrument of 'defamiliarization' or *ostranenie;* as if a world estranged and distanced from its own nature could only be recalled to itself by shock, by the effects of things deliberately 'made strange.' Expressionist artists and writers from Kubìn to Kafka explored the less nostalgic conditions of the modern uncanny, pressing the themes of the double, the automat, the de-realization into service as symptoms of posthistorical existence. Symbolists, futurists, dadaists, and of course surrealists and metaphysical artists found in the uncanny a state between dream and awakening particularly susceptible to exploitation. In this way, the uncanny was renewed as an aesthetic category, but now reconceived as the very sign of modernism's propensity for shock and disturbance [...]

As a concept [...] the uncanny has, not unnaturally, found its metaphorical home in architecture: first in the house, haunted or not, that pretends to afford the utmost security while opening itself to the secret intrusion of terror, and then in the city, where what was once walled and intimate, the confirmation of community – one thinks of Rousseau's Geneva – has been rendered strange by the spatial incursions of modernity. In both cases, of course, the 'uncanny' is not a property of the space itself nor can it be provoked by any particular spatial conformation; it is, in its aesthetic dimension, a representation of a mental state of projection that precisely elides the boundaries of the real and the unreal in order to provoke a disturbing ambiguity, a slippage between waking and dreaming.

In this sense, it is perhaps difficult to speak of an 'architectural' uncanny, in the same terms as a literary or psychological uncanny; certainly no one building, no special effects of design can be guaranteed to provoke an uncanny feeling. But in each moment of the history of the representation of the uncanny, and at certain moments in its psychological analysis, the buildings and spaces that have acted as the sites for uncanny experiences have been invested with recognizable characteristics. These almost typical and eventually commonplace qualities – the attributes of haunted houses in Gothic romances are the most well known – while evidently not essentially uncanny in themselves, nevertheless have been seen as *emblematic* of the uncanny, as the cultural signs of estrangement for particular periods. An early stage of psychology was as a result even prepared to identify space as a *cause* of the fear or estrangement hitherto a privilege of fiction; for an early generation of sociologists, 'spatial estrangement' was more than a figment of the imagination, but represented precisely that mingling of mental projection and spatial characteristics associated with the uncanny [...]

If actual buildings or spaces are interpreted through this lens, it is not because they themselves possess uncanny properties, but rather because they act, historically or culturally, as representations of estrangement. If there is a single premise to be derived from the study of the uncanny in modern culture, it is that there is no such thing as an uncanny architecture, but simply architecture that, from time to time and for different purposes, is invested with uncanny qualities [...]

As a frame of reference that confronts the desire for a home and the struggle for domestic security with its apparent opposite, intellectual and actual homelessness, at the same time as revealing the fundamental complicity between the two, *das Unheimliche* captures the difficult conditions of the theoretical practice of architecture in modern times. As a concept that itself has recurred with differing effects in the last two centuries, it serves as an interpretative model that cuts through the periodizations of historians according to categories such as romanticism, modernism, and postmodernism, as a way of understanding an aspect of modernity that has given a new meaning to the traditional Homeric notion of 'homesickness.'

NOTES

1 Ernst Bloch, 'A Philosophical View of the Detective Novel' [1965], in *The Utopian Function of Art and Literature: Selected Essays,* translated by Jack Zipes and Franck Meckelburg (Cambridge, MA: MIT Press, 1988), 245.

2 Walter Benjamin, *Charles Baudelaire: A Lyric Poet in the Era of High Capitalism,* translated by Harry Zohn (London: New Left Books, 1973), 128–31: 'Fear, revulsion, and horror were the emotions which the big city crowd aroused in those who first observed it' (131).

3 Karl Marx, 'Economic and Philosophic Manuscripts of 1844,' in Karl Marx and Friedrich Engels, *Collected Works,* vol. 3, *Marx and Engels, 1843–1844* (New York: International Publishers, 1975), 314.

4.8 GEORGES TEYSSOT
'"Water and Gas on All Floors": Notes on the Extraneousness of the Home'*

At the beginning of [the twentieth] century, numerous blue and white enamel plaques on the facades of Parisian luxury apartment houses announced 'gas on every floor.' Marcel Duchamp used one of these plaques as a ready-made object in 1958: 'Eau et gaz à tous les étages.' Duchamp was just using a play on words to evoke the two opposite principles of appearance (*l'eau coule, couleur*) and of apparition (illuminating gas, light) in painting. But gas and vapours form the stuff of one of the most widespread fantasies at the end of the last century.

Several authors have shown that the whole of the 19th century inherited a great fear of miasmas, that had developed in the 18th century, a horror aroused by mephitic vapours, by the stuff of fever and pestilence, capable of profoundly disturbing man and the universe. Deleterious vapours – it was thought – made their way into the heart of substances, bringing the seed of their death, the very principle of decomposition. The widespread dislike of gas and of impure vapours made it possible to invent a new fear, centred on the means of infection and contagion. When J.K. Huysmans, in his *Croquis parisiens* of 1880, wished to depict the, for him, repugnant spectacle of the 'European drinking-saloon at Grenelle,' it was on this fear that his images relied: the Brasserie has a ceiling of 'old-fashioned green canvas, now addled by *gas* fires and the leaking of *water*.' Further on, he describes an immense partition of glass separating the public dance-hall from the drinking-saloon, resembling that of a 'small railway station,' a partition 'that quivered with *gas* in a stream of *vapour*.'[1] Another end-of-the-century phantasm was the very insidious one of dust.

In the 'glass house,' in the 'doll's house' and above all in the nursery, the hunt for dust and microbes was on. From 1900 on, the terror aroused by 'nids à poussière,' literally: dustnests, in middle-class apartments and working-class homes mobilised landlords, tenants, philanthropists, architects, and doctors:[2] cleaning, henceforth, meant to drive out corruption by its microscopic causes. Bacteriology turned into religion. 'This was the time when the benefits of hygiene, clean hands and clean sheets, open air, pure air and mountains were discovered,' recounts Michel Serres.[3] 'Comte,' he added, 'looked for stone, hardness and drove out decomposition. Nietzsche also chose the stone, as opposed to the sand and the dust.' Experts on hygiene and the home thought that the

* Special Issue, 'L'inquieto spazio domestico / Disputed Domestic Space,' edited by Pierluigi Nicolin, *Lotus International* 44 (1984): 82–93.

chief agent of propagation of microbes in the house was dust. Today we know that it is not very dangerous.[4] But it allowed a free run to that Western passion for the sharp and glaring dichotomy, which leaves no residue. The contrast of good and evil was replaced by those of healthy and unhealthy, clean and infected, high and low, 'noble' parts and 'low' parts, the hard solid and loose dust.[5]

This obsession with corruption is also to be found in a text of [Paul] Scheerbart: 'Brick becomes rotten. It produces mouldiness ... In the vaults of brick houses, the air is impregnated with these bacilli: the architecture of glass has no need of vaults' ('The discovery of the brick bacillus,' in *Glasarchitektur,* 89). To which one might respond, as did G. Bachelard, that a house without vaults (and therefore without foundations), is a home without archetypes,[6] and that the city of glass, set on the ground like a space-ship, is a city without sewers.

Around the wash-basin, the regenerated worker – ornament of the factory – holds hands with the housewife – ornament of the habitat.[7] In reaction, perhaps, to all this purificative frenzy, Man Ray would photograph the *Élevage de poussière* from *Le Grand Verre* by Marcel Duchamp in 1920.

What is lost in the 'architecture of glass,' in *Glasarchitektur,* is the rightful feeling of possession, of the ownership of objects that are, as Peter Altenberg emphasized in 1899, 'extensions of ourself.' The apartment, the walls of the room, form the outermost epidermis of the human body: getting rid of the wall would be tantamount to exposing the inside of our organism. Instead of epithelial glass, Altenberg suggests we start 'by painting all our walls white,' and then place in one corner a marvellous enamel basin: 'The object set on my table or hung on the wall of my room is an integral part of myself, just like my hair or my skin.'[8]

For all that, this conception of the house as an extension of the epidermis can lead to symptoms of regression, paralysis and dissolution in the emptiness of the inwardness: it is, for instance, the 'return to the mother's womb' ('Zurückkriechen in den Mutterlieb') of which Hofmannsthal gave warning.[9] As Bachelard put it, 'one cannot write the history of the human unconsciousness without writing a history of the house,'[10] and it is no accident that he later devoted an entire book to establishing the law of the isomorphism of images of depth: the cavern, the house, the 'interior' of things, the mother's womb (in *La terre,* 1948); and that, more recently, the psychoanalyst Elvio Fachinelli has written a fine study of 'claustrophilia,' recalling that Freud has distinguished the symbols of female genital organs (boxes, chests, cases, suitcases, etc.) from the symbols of the maternal lap (cupboard, ovens and above all rooms).[11]

It is true that the 'interior' is only established by means of a separation. 'The house gives to the man dreaming *behind* its window ... the sense of an *exterior,* that is so much the more different from the interior, the greater is the intimacy of his room' (Bachelard).[12] The etymology of the English word 'window' reveals a combination between 'wind' and 'eye,'[13] that is to say between an element of the outside and an aspect of innerness. The separation on which dwelling is based is the possibility for a being to settle himself. Going further, the philosopher Emmanuel Levinas stresses that 'the inwardness of the house is made up of extraterritoriality in the middle of the elements of pleasure on which life feeds.' Due to the separation, gathering (any form of human activity) is made concrete as existence-in-a-home, as economic existence. But 'separation does not isolate me, as if I was simply torn away from these elements.' 'It makes possible work and property,' by the postponement and delay that permits and allows staying and gathering in a house. What the hand produces, it deposits, by *bringing it back*, in the home. This gathering, carried out in the *extra-territoriality* of the house, is in no case the fruit of a situation, of a care about a particular site or situation. For Levinas, in contrast to M. Heidegger, 'the house chosen is the complete opposite of a root': it is only accomplished by a disengagement with regard to the situation, by an errancy, 'that is not *a minus* in respect to the settlement.'[14]

Applied successively or simultaneously to housing, all these little clean lines (conjugal, hygienic, aesthetic), all these microtechniques (transparency, privacy, 'fixed movable') were soon going to come together in the debate over the flexibility of living space.

NOTES

1 Joris-Karl Huysmans, *En rade. Un dilemme. Croquis parisiens* (Paris: U.G.E., 1976), 349. [Emphasis added, Eds.]

2 Anne Martin-Fugier, *La Place des bonnes: La domesticité féminine à Paris en 1900* (Paris: Grasset, 1979), 107 onwards.

3 Michel Serres, *Hermes IV: La distribution* (Paris: Minuit, 1977), 174, 178; on this subject, see also Jacques Guillerme et al., Special Issue, 'Le sain et le malsain,' *Dix-Huitième Siècle* 9 (1977).

4 Barbara Ehrenreich and Deirdre English, 'The Manufacture of Housework,' *Socialist Revolution* 5 / 4 (1975): 26.

5 Serres, *Hermes IV,* 184.

6 [Paul Scheerbart, *Glasarchitektur* (Berlin: Verlag Der Sturm, 1914) and] Gaston Bachelard, *La terre et les rêveries du repos* (Paris: Jose Corti, 1982 [1948]), 105. But I think that Scheerbart should not be taken too seriously, as the architects of the 'Gläserne Kette' have done; it would be better to include him, like his contemporary Alfred Jarry, in a new 'anthology of black humour.'

7 Lion Murard and Patrick Zylberman, 'La cité eugénique,' *Recherches* 29 (Dec. 1977): 426.

8 Peter Altenberg, 'In München' (1899), in *Was der Tag mir zuträgt, fünfundsechzig neue Studien* (Berlin: S. Fischer, 1921), 306–9; quoted by Claude Quiguer, *Femmes et machines de 1900: lecture d'une obsession Modern Style* (Paris: Klincksieck, 1979), 395.

9 Hugo von Hofmannsthal, 'Das Bergwerk zu Falun,' in *Gesammelte Werke in Einzelausgaben, Gedichte und lyrische Dramen* (Stockholm: Berman-Fischer Verlag, 1946), 421; quoted by Quiguer, *Femmes et machines*, 386.

10 Bachelard, *La terre*, 115; see too, 6, 55, 121, and 151.

11 Elvio Fachinelli, *Claustrophilia* (Milan: Adelphi, 1983), 84.

12 Bachelard, *La terre*, 115.

13 Ernest Klein, *A Complete Etymological Dictionary of the English Language* (London: Elsevier, 1966); quoted by Ellen Eve Frank, *Literary Architecture: Essays towards a Tradition, Walter Pater, Gerard Manley Hopkins, Marcel Proust, Henry James* (Berkeley, CA: University of California Press, 1979), 263.

14 Emmanuel Levinas, *Totalité et infini: essai sur l'extériorité*, 4th ed. (The Hague: Nijhoff, 1974), 124–47.

CHAPTER FIVE

Gendered Spaces

Because of the enduring and inevitable association of home and woman, many of the selections in this *Reader* naturally allude to issues of gender. In the following selections, however, the relationship and performance of sexuality and gender in domestic spaces come to the fore to be analysed, critiqued, and deconstructed. Thus in the essay that opens this section, Bart Verschaffel enters the interiors of seventeenth-century Dutch painters to probe the unsaid in their narratives and to interrogate the too often taken for granted relationship between femininity and domesticity. Deborah Cohen demonstrates how even though it became a cliché in the nineteenth century to claim that woman was mistress of the house, men continued to control interior decoration. It was not until the Oscar Wilde scandal in 1895 had created an unsavoury association with home furnishing that interior decoration became a female province. If in Britain it took the Wilde scandal to make the home woman's territory, by the 1930s she had free rein on its decor, which, according to journalist Basil D. Nicholson, was unfortunate. Writing two years after Freud in *Civilization and Its Discontents* had made known his views about women's 'retarding and restraining influence' on civilization,[1] Nicholson blamed the survival of obsolete types of architecture on the intellectual torpor induced in women by marriage. Focusing on a British form of modernism – the Amusing Style characterized by theatricality, artifice, playfulness – Christopher Reed exposes the sexual and gender anxiety that underlay Le Corbusier's designs. Both Le Corbusier's masculinist and rationalist functionality and John Betjeman's nationalist ideology, Reed argues, contributed to the suppression of this important aspect of modernist design. Richard A.H. Livett's advocacy of the small-flat developments in urban planning after the First World War is an early and rare example of sensitivity to the requirements of the increasing number of single working women. If in England in the 1930s neither the 'Parlour House' designed for a family nor the lodging house provided an adequate housing solution to the practical needs of businesswomen, in the 1950s United States *Playboy* magazine gloried in imagining sites suitable to accommodate the fantasies of a man yearning 'for quarters of his own.' Thus George Wagner turns his attention to the decor suitable to the penthouses designed for men for whom desire, technological sophistication, and immediate gratification are what matters, and for whom the Bachelardian lived house as a site of memories has no meaning whatsoever. Matt Cook's overview of the history of the relationship between home and homosexuality in the past two centuries in Britain teases out layered meanings of home for homosexual men – a place of exclusion and incompatibility, but also a barometer of identity, identification, socialization, childrearing, and mutual support. Moving beyond the gendered spaces of Britain and North America, Marcia Stephenson's analysis of housing in Bolivia begins with the consideration of how in a stratified society notions of space, race, and gender converge with the reproduction of power to map boundaries and demarcate distinctions between inside and outside. Renée Hirschon offers an analysis of domestic space that focuses on the way in which in urban Greek locality the relationship between 'inside' and 'outside' is mediated by the kitchen and the 'movable chair.' These spatial negotiations are analogous to the ones in which are engaged the inhabitants of the Algerian community studied by Joëlle Bahloul (see section 7.4 in this volume). Iris Marion Young anticipates recent scholars' claims that the unintended by-product of early feminist efforts to 'rescue' women from the alleged degradation of domesticity has connived in the trivialization of women's experiences. Calling attention to the creatively human aspects of women's traditional household work, she argues for an approach that rethinks feminist attitudes to house and home. A similarly positive and empowering approach is undertaken by Aritha van Herk in her spirited and eloquent defence of 'making home' as distinguished from 'housework' and of the surprising fertile history of laundry as an activity of preservation and creation with important political and social valences.

NOTE

1 Sigmund Freud, *Civilization and Its Discontents* [1930], translated and edited by James Strachey (New York: Norton, 1961), 50.

5.1 BART VERSCHAFFEL 'The Meanings of Domesticity'*

What makes a house a home? What does domesticity mean for those who live too late to experience fully what 'dwelling' really is (Heidegger)? What does domesticity mean for adults who have to *remember* home, who have become again the child they carry within, because only children can fully know how a house is a beginning? [...]

A house is more than a place: the *domus* is the principle of an order, it is a device for separating and bringing together animals and humans, the dead and the living, the feelings and gestures of the night and those of the day, meals and digestion, man, woman, children, etc. The house is a device for articulating differences and defining a hierarchy in the meanings one lives by. The house is the place where order is protected and restored when things start wandering around or haphazardly mix, without rules. It is a place that is 'cleaned' every day, where 'symbolic labour' is done in clearing away the mess and the dirt so that everything can start anew and life can go on, so that life is passed on to the next day [...]

What happens to femininity when it is linked to domesticity? At first, femininity seems reduced: linking woman and house could be a means to simplify and control the feminine, out of fear or for whatever reason. Because, indeed, she does not stand just for home and hearth and Ithaca, woman is not just the name for what drives homewards, what brings movement and history to a stop, to rest and peace. Woman also lures into the woods and the sea and the night, she invites to danger and death. Woman also embodies the Virtues, even Truth. The meaning of 'femininity' is very complex, more than 'masculinity' for sure, and nobody, neither man nor woman, can relate to the feminine simply. Does the house dominate femininity? Is woman put in her place there? Linking femininity and domesticity or house can only come down to a simplification and limitation when one presupposes that the house is simple, and that domesticity is simple – that it is nothing more than 'place' and 'centre.'

Is the house what it seems to be: hearth, home, microcosm? The old, premodern world, a landscape of monuments and houses, seems to be a world made of centred and fixed meanings. In the modern conception, it is modernity – the big city and metropolitan life – that slowly undoes this old world and makes everything 'melt into thin air' [...] Modernity introduces exchange, movement and transport, change and openness, it induces the globalisation

* *Journal of Architecture* 7 / 3 (2002): 287–96.

that weakens identity and deconstructs the home. People who live the largest part of their lives in a-topia, who work, communicate and socialise virtually, become automatically those 'nomadic subjects' who at every moment can (re) define their position and belong nowhere – except exactly in that permanent 'in-transit-condition.' This idea of modernity as an almost heroic, rather violent, forced liberation from the closure and fixity of the old world negates, however, the tensions and ambiguities within the old pre-modern conceptions of space and place. There is more to the house than this logic and force that centralises and fixes. More than anything else the house is a space where two equally powerful forces interact, limit each other and create some kind of a balance. This complexity of the meaning of house does not derive from a deconstruction of its centrality, fixity, or safety, by which the familiar then turns strange, the home 'uncanny,' or the house *unheimlich*. Of course, every meaning is a fragile construction, of course no identity is 'full' or saturated. My argument, however, is different: it points to a complexity that is included *in* the representation – in the construction of the meaning – of 'house' and 'home' itself, rather than being an effect of its de-construction [...]

[...] I will illustrate my argument by images taken from the Dutch tradition of interior painting since Pieter de Hooch [...] For a long time the images of seventeenth-century Holland interior paintings were considered as realistic reorientations of peaceful life in the bourgeois homes and towns of Holland. Later, after recognising motives taken from emblem books or from Father Cats, they were seen as moralising pictures representing mostly female virtue. Recently even Peter Sutton wrote about de Hooch: 'The orderly context of de Hooch's interiors and their adjoining courtyards and gardens create an eminently comforting home environment, the objective correlative of domestic virtue.'[1] [...]

The interior paintings by Pieter de Hooch are not portraits, showing faces and people in their environment. They are not like genre paintings that present human situations and anecdotes, in a theatrical mode, so that the 'place of action' is represented, also, as a decor. He situates characters and activities in an interior space, but so that these can never occupy or fill the space [...] For a spectator used to bourgeois culture, his houses do not only feel empty and rather cold, they don't seem cosy, but they are in an almost unrealistic way open and wide and deep. De Hooch opens up his interior spaces through opening perspectives: views through windows and doors, views into halls and siderooms, so that one looks out onto landscapes or facades, or so that passing through outside space – as across streets – one looks into rooms and houses again. He opens up secondary perspectives through figures who look out through doors and windows at views that are not visible for the beholder, he shows light falling in without indicating its origin, he uses staircases to suggest

5 Nicolaes Maes, *The Eavesdropper,* 1657. Photograph © 2012 Museum of Fine Arts, Boston.

vertical depth in the interior space, etc. He often opens up the rooms in two or three directions at once, and so intensifies the sense of depth.

In these interiors de Hooch paints women, most often pursuing their daily, homely activities, sometimes alone, sometimes in the company of their maid or children. But at the same time he does not represent the interiors they are in as hearth. The women are present and 'at home,' but their presence and activities do not fill and do not define the space. Peter Sutton notices this when he writes that de Hooch's paintings praise the mothers and housewives, but 'together with the investigation of complex and subtly observed effects of light in the interior space.'[2] There is more 'space' than the intrigue or situation asks for, but Sutton reduces that surplus to an opportunity for demonstrating the painter's ability in the rendering of light effects, unrelated to the meaning of the image [...] What Sutton does not see here is that in these images the female personage, indeed reduced to a housewife, is *opposed* to and exposed to an inhabited, empty, almost abstract space. De Hooch gives the house the depth and distance (or 'elsewhere') of a landscape, and thereby announces the World to the interior – a World these women seem almost unaware of.

The woman can take on a different meaning and position too. Martha Hollander illustrates this with a series of images by Nicolaes Maes (Figure 5).[3] In these examples Maes divides his painting by means of 'see-through' into two different rooms or scenes, with the woman in two different roles: the housewife catches the maid who in the next room or the kitchen is dreaming away or is flirting. Hollander argues very well that these images do not just illustrate moral lessons or encourage the housewife to take care of the household, but also show and associate two sides of the feminine and thereby suggest a 'structural weakness' and unreliability in every woman – and every housewife. De Hooch too associates in some paintings the depth effect with a sometimes tiny, almost hidden female figure, 'waiting' there in the distance as 'elsewhere.' In a similar logic he often confronts by way of a picture-within-the-picture the bourgeois or homely scene with a mythological, often explicitly erotic nude: the contrast reveals the hidden dimension of woman that is not Hestia. The femininity is, so it shows, so complex that in one and the same image, the female figure can be opposed to the 'distant' but can embody it as well.

NOTES

1 Peter Sutton, *Pieter de Hooch, 1629–1684* (London: Yale University Press, 1988), 30.
2 Ibid.
3 Martha Hollander, 'Nicolaes Maes: Space as Domestic Territory,' in *An Entrance for the Eyes: Space and Meaning in Seventeenth-Century Dutch Art* (Berkeley, CA: University of California Press, 2002), chapter 3, 103–48.

5.2 DEBORAH COHEN
'In Possession: Men, Women, and Decoration'*

Contrary to what most books on the subject have assumed, the Victorian interior was neither chiefly the responsibility, nor even the prerogative of women. Through the late nineteenth century, amid the rage for furnishing that overtook the middle classes, men played a crucial role in the fitting out of the home. Most often, husbands and wives made decorating decisions collaboratively. But men did not merely follow; more often than not, they seem to have led [...] The earliest home decoration manuals were written by married men for married men. Decorators were men; the cause of design reform was led by men; upholsterers were men, as were the clerks on the shop floor [...]

But by the 1920s and 1930s, home decoration had become nearly exclusively a woman's domain. Men played a limited role in choosing possessions for their houses; smart lady decorators such as Syrie Maugham set the fashions. This represented a dramatic change from the Victorian era, but one which has been obscured by the assumption that women's claim on the house remained much the same throughout this period. We begin, therefore, with men such as Mr Winterbottom, in order to investigate why Victorian masters of the house took such pains over their decorative schemes. Why many men seem to have abandoned home decoration after the turn of the century, how women claimed it, and to what degree, if any, a struggle ensued are the questions we take up next. What changed [...] was more than the hand that furnished the house. Along with the emancipated 'New Woman' of the late nineteenth century came a new ethos of domesticity characterized specifically by the novel belief that a woman's décor served to reflect her personality [...]

An Englishman's Home

Before the 1880s, those who wrote about home decoration largely directed their advice to the man of the house. Robert Kerr's 1864 treatise on the dwellings of 'the better sort' was baldly titled *The Gentleman's House*. [See section 3.7 in this volume.] [...]

Why, apart from the expense, did men care so much about grey-felt carpets and nicely arranged mantelpieces? Motivations, we can assume, varied dramatically. There were, for instance, those men who sought through their décor to

---

* In *Household Gods: The British and Their Possessions* (New Haven, CT: Yale University Press, 2006), 89–121.

safeguard the righteousness of their households. The home, as envisioned by evangelicals, had redemptive power; there, the man could throw off the temptations to which his work had exposed him. In very religious households, men were the arbiters of display, though the prevailing asceticism did not provide much scope for manoeuvre. By contrast, the coming of incarnationalism after the mid-nineteenth century, combined with rising prosperity, made decoration a pressing issue for the paterfamilias. If beauty was a moral virtue, as the Reverends Boyd and Loftie had claimed, men were obliged to attend to even the most minute details of room decoration. This was not simply a matter of protecting his family from possessions that might exercise a pernicious influence. It also implicated a man's moral cultivation. In the process of beautifying his surroundings, the house – or so the advice manuals promised – worked a change upon him. Painting one's walls and studying the form of furniture became acts of grace, which 'humanized' the amateur home decorator […]

According to *Furnishings*, the leading trade journal of the 1920s: ' … woman is the purchaser of at least 90 per cent of the furnishings for the home.'[1] Marketing campaigns featured female shoppers, while stores courted their clientele by emphasizing women's preferences in walnut or French china […]

What explains the transformation? The decade of the 1890s witnessed a change in the relationship between a man and his possessions that though gradual was nonetheless significant. Suspicious commentators had long mocked the fad for artistic furnishing as insufficiently masculine […] In the *Saturday Review*'s scathing depiction, the 'aesthetic friend' who insinuated himself into the household 'screams with a pretty feminine horror at the mention of mauve or magenta.'[2] Even before [Oscar] Wilde's trials discredited the public face of the 'House Beautiful,' Mrs Talbot Coke, decorating columnist for *Hearth and Home*, distinguished between two kinds of men. Her preference was for (in her words) a 'real man,' who loved sport and outdoor life. 'As to another class of man, the handy man who "does his own draperies" (I know one who also makes his own lampshades, poor thing) … I could never feel the same unwilling respect I do for one who will have none of my artistic notions in his own den, but only wants to "know where to find his things," and be able to smoke undisturbed and unreproved.'[3]

Oscar Wilde's 1895 conviction on charges of 'gross indecency' transformed Mrs Talbot Coke's innuendo into overt public disapproval. If a whiff of femininity lingered around aesthetes and, by extension, home decoration before Wilde's public humiliation, afterwards the link between effeminacy and homosexuality was forged solid. During most of the nineteenth century, there was of course no homosexual identity or consciousness as we today know it […] Men might have sex with or love other men without thinking of themselves as either embodying or rejecting a set of traits. But in the aftermath of Wilde's trials, it is possible to catch a glimpse of a homosexual identity in the making – one which would, in the twentieth century, turn the home into a place for uncloseted self-expression and allow men to transcend provincial prejudices by allying themselves with good taste […] But the cause of gay liberation, even as it would eventually open the closet door, also led heterosexual men to narrow their aesthetic worlds. Too conspicuous a pursuit of the House Beautiful left a man open to ridicule, possibly even misperception. The men who wrote in to decorating columnists in the 1890s and after, sought, above all, to avoid creating the wrong impression: they wanted manly furniture. 'Little Paddy' aimed at the 'good and plain style of the male apartment,' but it eluded him. Mrs Talbot Coke blamed his cream ground floral paper: 'It is that which gives the "sentimental spinster" look you so amusingly deplore.'[4]

While Wilde's disgrace did much to alter the public perception of masculinity within the home, men's relationships to their houses were already changing. By the end of the nineteenth century, the enthusiastic domesticity that had characterized mid-Victorian men was under increasing strain […] the growth of the suburbs meant that many husbands were increasingly absent from the home […] With their prospects in the wider world of professions finally improved, middle-class women took charge of the home.

NOTES

1 G. Rivington, 'The Sales Department,' *Furnishings* (April 1926): 15 […]

2 'The Saturday Review on Art at Home,' *Furniture Gazette* 7 (Feb. 1874): 138.

3 Mrs Talbot Coke, 'A Man's Room,' *Hearth and Home* (1 Sept. 1892): 520. Of interest, too, are *Hearth and Home*'s leading articles for 30 March 1893 and 6 April 1893: 'Effeminate Men.'

4 Mrs Talbot Coke, 'Home Advice,' *Hearth and Home* (22 Oct. 1891): 737; also Eunice, 'Home Decoration,' *The Lady* (3 Oct. 1985): 460; 'On the Unaffected in Furnishing,' *The House* 5 / 1 (July 1987): 219; Richard Dellamora, *Masculine Desire: The Sexual Politics of Victorian Aestheticism* (Chapel Hill, NC: University of North Carolina Press, 1990), 193–217.

5.3 BASIL D. NICHOLSON 'The Architectural Consequences of Women'*

The blame for the present condition of English domestic architecture and equipment is too ponderous a load to lay on any one section of the community. It belongs equally to everyone who has done nothing active to improve matters. But the source of infection is certainly that vast army of women who take marriage as a signal for dropping their contacts with the outside world in favour of bridge, hats, and the synthetic worries of a mismanaged and unplanned house [...] According to advertising agents, whose sociological opinions are to be respected because their mistakes come home to them in terms of cash, the domination of women in domestic buying habits is complete. It is not the sort of statement that needs expert authority. The contractors, the decorators, the house agents, even the building societies, all direct their barrage against women. There is no doubt of women's responsibility for the English home. And not only are contemporary houses rare in England; where they exist they have been chosen for an unhealthy reason – just because they are exotic, and unexpected, and a good conversation piece. Given the bankruptcy of domestic architecture, there is naturally a tendency for the rest to conform to it. The mass production of obsolete equipment, indeed, makes it ruinous to install any other. The vicious circle has begun to revolve [...]

There is, of course, no foundation for the suspicion with which any new styles and new material are regarded. They involve the acceptance of no theories more extravagant than those implicit in the designs of cam-shafts, or dash-boards, or four-wheel brakes. They postulate, in Le Corbusier's words, that a house is a machine for living in, and subordinate materials, design, and internal detail to that specific purpose. This is, of course, distinct from existing building practice, with its vicious circle of obsolete style involving obsolete material. It does not, for example, say: 'This is a Tudor house. We are committed to beams and plaster. They will rot and flake because the work will be hurried and the materials cheap, but one can't have everything. We had better keep to windows leaded off into small squares or diamonds. They darken the room, and the expensiveness and difficulty of making large areas of glass in a single piece have long ago been overcome; but this is a Tudor house and it will look better. They used, in those days, to be forced by the leakiness of their small units of roofing to make sharply pitched and gabled roofs, so we will do the same. A flat roof with zinc, lead, or concrete covering would be better and

* *Architectural Review* 72/431 (1932): 119–20.

cheaper, and would add another open-air storey to the house, but that is neither here nor there [...]' and so on.

The refusal on the part of these latter-day Luddites to regard the house as a machine has resulted in its equipment on equally archaic lines. Brass is still retained as a metal, not only as an ornament for those who are prepared to face the trouble of polishing it, but as a standard fitment. Letterboxes, door-knockers, electric light switches, and name-plates are overwhelmingly brass; taps, doorknobs, and even large cylindrical geysers are usually the same. A house agent tells me that these fittings are of brass in over seventy-five per cent of the London flats that pass through his hands, and that while some progress has taken place in the equipment which the tenant provides, builders' fitments have remained the same since the introduction of electric light. Housewives think it quite normal for the brasswork or burnished copper of a three-roomed flat to take upwards of 2 1/2 hours to polish.

Built-in furniture and indirect lighting, whose desirability is already acknowledged, have made no headway owing to the enforced survival of the old watertight division between the house and its furniture. Power points and even additional lighting plugs are rare and have most often to be supplied later by the tenant at a cost that surprises him. Wiring is still installed so that its extension or removal is a job for the builder. This effectively limits electrical equipment to refrigerators, vacuum cleaners, irons, and wireless sets, only the last two having penetrated the majority of homes. Neither the individual housekeeping installations of the United States nor their collectivised counterparts in Vienna are approached in this country.

The rut of house slavery combined with pre-war standards of discomfort is so deep here that it is accepted without comment. Those who are caught and broken by it, as thousands of women are every year, do not even know that they have imposed it on themselves by sanctioning with their own ignorance and contempt for progress, that of the housing contractor and the furniture maker. The house layout and equipment survive that were designed when there were squads of housemaids to maintain it.

It is, in part, a vicious circle. However humorous the pursuit of culture by American women may seem to us, the Englishwoman's relapse into intellectual apathy after marriage compares unfavourably with it as an instrument of progress. Drudgery, or the detailed supervision necessary to organise the drudgery of others, takes up so large a proportion of the Englishwoman's time that she is both a reactionary citizen and unable even to lever herself out of her quite unnecessary servitude. At a moderate estimate 100,000,000 hours of work a year could be saved by the rationalisation of housing and its equipment in Great Britain – about four times as many hours as were lost by strikes in 1930.

But the Tudor houses, the magpie arrays of knick-knacks, the traditional cooking arrangements, the ponderous furniture with its garnishing of polish and brocade, the brass, the false privacy that prevents the pooling of work and the introduction of communal services on any scale even in London flats – all remain impregnably entrenched in the vicious circle of ignorant traders, hidebound architects, and tired women. There are interior decorators who pin their faith on the permeation of the public consciousness by shops and theatres which have 'gone modern.' It is possible, but there have been cars with clean lines, rational layout of controls, and refreshing colours existing for so long side by side with the drab lumpiness of designs that imitate the façades without recalling the spirit of other centuries, that it is difficult to pin much faith to that alone. Heartbreak House is more likely to succumb to an unexpected and combined insurrection of all those whom it has ground down – the wives whose lives it wastes, the civilised people who do not like its looks, the progressives who prefer not to live in a museum, and the handful of manufacturers and architects who are producing 1932 goods for a country whose coat-tails have caught in 1907. This cult of coracles cannot much longer stand out against even good taste, let alone the forces of convenience. Heartbreak House must fall; for it relies on sanctions as illusory as the French aristocrat's to enforce an even greater tyranny, and its bluff, for all its seeming success, has the same shadow of a lamp-post falling athwart it.

5.4 CHRISTOPHER REED
'Taking Amusement Seriously: Modern Design in the Twenties'*

To me it seems axiomatic that the history of design – and domestic interior design in particular – has been strongly inflected by broader anxieties over gender and sexuality [...] These anxieties were particularly acute in the late twenties and early thirties, in the wake of political changes signalled by women's achievement of the vote, cultural shifts embodied in the androgynous generation of Bright Young Things, and the economic tensions that followed the

* In *Designing the Modern Interior: From the Victorians to Today,* edited by Penny Sparke, Anne Massey, Trevor Keeble, and Brenda Martin (Oxford: Berg, 2009), 79–93.

Great War, worsening, of course, with the worldwide economic depression of the 1930s […]

An obvious, and highly influential, source of modernism's conservative gendered rhetorics is Le Corbusier's *Towards a New Architecture*. This manifesto opens by linking 'houses and moth-eaten boudoirs' as feminine spaces that undermine the masculinity of the men who live in them, leaving them 'sheepish and shrivelled like tigers in a cage.' Imputations of effeminacy fused with rehearsals of the homophobic rhetorics generated around the Wilde trials as Le Corbusier condemned conventional architecture schools as 'hot-houses where blue hortensias and green chrysanthemums are forced, and where unclean orchids are cultivated.' All this to contrast, of course, with his own designs inspired by the heroic figure of the 'healthy and virile' engineer […][1] [See section 8.4 in this volume.]

Le Corbusier's appeals to anxieties over sexuality and gender were seized upon in the first British manifestoes for modernism. John Betjeman's '1830–1930 – Still Going Strong: A Guide to the Recent History of Interior Decoration,' published in the *Architectural Review* in 1930, is still widely lauded for its prescient advocacy for modernist design. Betjeman's essay is equally prescient of the repressive gender rhetorics that accompanied modernism's introduction in Britain. His opening lines invoking a 'British public' summoned by dinner gongs address modernism to the bourgeoisie. Far from attending to worker housing, modernism, as Betjeman presented it, confronted the problem of the 'recent permission that was given to Germany to thicken English design' with what he called the 'awf'lly modern' style, 'started in 1920 and known as "jazz"' […] Betjeman's nationalist ideology, which turned British women working in the Arts-and-Crafts tradition into a foreign threat to a Britishness embodied by Continental designers, culminates in his conclusion warning that 'French, German, and Swedish' manufacturers, by following Le Corbusier, have usurped a truly British legacy […] To right this wrong, Betjeman asserted, Britain must turn to 'intelligent designers,' – that is to professional men who could suppress the international jazz aesthetic of their amateur daughters (more likely, sisters) by deploying an essentially British style embodied in a Swiss architect.[2]

[…] Betjeman's rhetoric was part of a full-bore assault on what, during the twenties, was actually a home-grown style of British modernism, an assault successful enough to consign this style – simply called modern or contemporary in its own day – to an oblivion so complete it does not have a name in design history […] The characteristics of this style include theatricality, humour and an emphasis on artifice and playfulness exactly opposite to the claims for functional rationality that were used to promote the competing version of modernism of the thirties. To identify this suppressed form of modernism, I have proposed to rehabilitate a ubiquitous adjective of approbation of the twenties, by coining the term 'Amusing Style.'[3]

The ubiquity of 'Amusing' is attested to in Paul Nash's 1932 *Room and Book,* which described the early twenties as a time when 'the adjective "amusing" started on its endless flight from lip to lip.'[4] By 1932, Nash intended this to be pejorative, for he was part of the trend towards the masculine professionalisation of design. Like Betjeman, Nash invoked the spectres of both national and sexual boundary violation in his description of the twenties as a time when 'charming young men and formidable ladies were hopping backwards and forwards between England and the Continent,' importing 'a piece of stuff from Paris, a German lamp, a steel chair, or just a headful of other people's ideas' [...] Ratcheting up the rhetorics of *Room and Book* in an admiring review in the *Architectural Review,* R.H. Wilenski invoked Wyndham Lewis's condemnation of the 'queerer' qualities of the 'amusing' fondness for 'stuffed birds, wax flowers, and so forth.' For Wilenski, too, the solution to the 'parlour pastimes' and 'dilettantish activities' characterising modern British interior design was to be found in the figure of the 'creative professional designer.'[5]

[...] But what if we allow the Amusing Style to speak for itself? To that end, we might turn to the interior design features of British *Vogue,* the primary – though far from the only – forum for coverage of the Amusing Style in the mid-twenties. Here we find the aesthetic of Amusement was promoted as—well, as promiscuous and popular, particularly among emancipated young women. But these qualities were not seen as problems. Promiscuity and popularity were key values for *Vogue,* which in the mid-twenties expanded the rubric of 'fashion' far beyond clothes [...]

When it came to domestic design, the modernity that up-to-date women found in *Vogue* included Corbusian high-tech as one possibility [...] But *Vogue* also presented as modern the *commedia dell'arte* murals commissioned from Gino Severini by the Sitwell brothers as well as whimsical painted furniture and murals by Vanessa Bell, Duncan Grant, and other British artists [...] The 'modern' in *Vogue* was characterised by freedom from conventional constraints and a taste for satiric amusement [...] This was not simply a matter of subject matter, but also of style [...]

To exemplify the dynamics of the Amusing Style of interior design, let me take as a case study the Chelsea home of the Sitwell brothers, Osbert and Sacheverell, as it was featured in *Vogue* in 1924 under the headline 'Unity in Diversity.' [...] 'There are two ways of furnishing a house, the grimly historical and the purely whimsical,' the article begins. The modern man's alternative to the grimness of backwards-looking revival styles is to play with history amusingly: 'For now nothing will be in a room for any reason save that it amused the owner the day he put it there. It is his character, not his possessions, that gives the room its quality. Hence if his character be sufficiently amusing his room will also be lovable.'[6] Here personal identity and its aesthetic manifestation in domestic design are linked, but not as an expression of sober, professional, masculine selfhood on the model of Le Corbusier's 'Engineer's Aesthetic' appropriate to the 'big business men, bankers, and merchants' for whom 'economic law reigns supreme, and mathematical exactness is joined to daring and imagination.'[7] [...] Instead, a dynamic model of identity is embodied in the diversity of what *Vogue* called the Sitwells' 'most unco-ordinated of worlds,' different on any given day. The photo captions draw our attention to the unexpected juxtapositions of an 'extremely modern silver statuette' and 'fruit in Victorian shell-work' that 'jostle each other strangely,' the 'ormulu Dolphin table' before the 'little gallery of pictures by Severini' [...][8]

But the Sitwells' promiscuous inclusion of craftwork by non-professional women (the Victorian bibelots concocted of shells that come 'as a bit of a shock,' *Vogue* says, juxtaposed with Cubist and Futurist art) along with artefacts from the more exuberant periods of European history (that Baroque dolphin-legged table) clearly exceed the restrictions modernists like Paul Nash and Herbert Read would soon use to define modernist design [...] The Sitwells' promiscuous play with foreignness, with women's work, with amateur work – all those 'works' Betjeman disdained – set in rooms that, when they were not the dining room's 'sea-green tinsel,' were painted what *Vogue* described as 'Marie Laurencin pink,' was exactly what subsequent modernists' policing of national and gender boundaries sought to prevent [...] Rather, the rhetorics of what became mainstream modernist design responded to what came to be seen as the wrong kind of modernism, the kind that featured bachelor brothers painting their walls, not just pink, but a pink evocative of a painter both female and foreign. Allusions to Laurencin, specifically, invoked her other appearances in *Vogue* at this era, when she was praised as a 'sister of Sappho' whose art displayed 'a sort of wittiness mixed with wantonness. She will emphasize a pout, an attitude, an expression, a gesture, as character, which is witty; and also as a perverse physical attraction, which is wanton. The spectator is continually being reminded of the peculiar perverse desirability of women.'[9] Challenges to the conventions of masculinity, of professionalism, of Britishness were here linked to the androgynous promiscuity of the Bright Young Things in a compelling conception of what it meant to be modern.

What would it mean to take Amusing domestic design seriously? [...] Let me experiment with a last case study, a cabinet painted by Duncan Grant for the Davidson brothers, whose Sitwellian home was prominently illustrated in both

Vogue and the *Architectural Review* [...] *Vogue*'s article in 1924 illustrated the cabinet with a long caption under the photograph, which read in part:

> *Mr Duncan Grant has restored fantasy to furniture. What – one immediately wonders – does this corner-cupboard contain? Raisins and oranges, wines from Xeres and Oporto? Or music, and the manuscripts of unforgotten songs? Or love-letters, perhaps – for the cupboard has a key? Our questions stay unanswered – still the lover sings, and still the lady listens, and beneath their spell we forget our curiosity. For Mr Grant has turned a cupboard into a romance. He has transformed this Cinderella among furniture into poetic loveliness.*[10]

[...] Even if we accept that *Vogue*'s prose performs a recognisably modernist response to Grant's cabinet, however, we are still justified in asking if the cabinet justifies that reaction. Let me suggest some of the visual characteristics of the Amusing Style that might prompt exactly this kind of reading. To begin, Amusing motifs are often framed by curtains, reinforcing a theatricality evocative of scripts and the repetition of stylised plots [...] This effect of quotation is furthered by other characteristics of the Amusing Style, among them plays with scale, either blatantly incongruous, as in an overmantel Grant also painted for the Davidsons and illustrated in *Vogue* [...] or coy in the way the musician on the cabinet door is scrunched into his space on the panel so as to emphasise that this is an image applied to a surface, thus asserting a reference to other images rather than to musicians in real life. Such visual quotation marks set off the imagery as invocations of pre-existing genres that can be played with by the artist to the delight of the viewer.

This emphasis on the artist's sensibility is reinforced by the Amusing predilection for what *Vogue* called *écriture:* traces of the maker's hand manifest in sponged and scrawled wallpapers as well as in painted surfaces enlivened with the marks of brushes, palette knives, even fingerprints [...] Clive Bell's description of Grant's paint surfaces emphasised their playful sensuality. Grant's 'sensibility of touch,' Bell said, 'has the quality of a thrilling caress' and 'the quality of his paint is often as charming as a kiss.'[11]

This emphasis on eroticism and artifice flies in the face of prescriptions of 'truth to materials,' 'fitness for purpose,' or 'the spirit of living in mass production houses,' all of which were used to dismiss the Amusing Style from the modernist canon. The modernists' insistence that things look like exactly what they are – no secret-concealing painted surfaces, but the masculine engineering know-how of the machine with each component revealed – is diametrically opposed to a cupboard conceived as a 'romance' [...]

Design historians' blindness to the clear archival evidence of modernism's diversity in the twenties bespeaks a continuing defensive reaction to the imputations of modernists of the thirties, who pejoratively associated it with femininity and non-normative sexuality. Stripped of their pejorative intent, however, these associations provide another compelling reason to take the Amusing Style seriously as a form of modernism. Social historians have emphasised, as one of the distinctive features of modernity, the rise of self-identified subcultures – especially youth cultures and cultures based on sexual identity – enabled by urbanisation and the mass media. Although these social formations flourished in the second half of the twentieth century, they have their roots in the twenties in places like London and magazines like *Vogue*. *Vogue*'s theatre coverage and society pages promoted as 'modern' new attitudes that relished plays with identity, especially gender identity. Its cartoons – perhaps the locus classicus of the Amusing sensibility – play constantly on the twin themes of youth and androgyny. A typical series, *Baring the Secrets of the Turkish Bath,* juxtaposes one vignette of the young using the old as rubber rafts, with another showing Gustave, confused by encountering in the men's area, 'Bertie Caraway, one of those plump youngsters whose figure and gestures are just too girlish for anything. Which proves that girls sometimes simply *will* be boys.' [...][12]

So saturated in the rhetorics of Amusement were Britons in the twenties that their first response to Corbusian minimalism was to see it as yet another kind of whimsy. This is true even of a sober-sided professional magazine like the *Architectural Review,* whose reporter, on first encountering Le Corbusier's now-famous *Pavilion de l'Esprit Nouveau* in 1925 at the Art Deco show in Paris, saw it not as a manifestation of the rational functionalism of the Engineer but as a new mode of play:

> *Is not every wall patterned by sunlight and shadow; is not the whole filled with fanciful reality? Ghostly grey at dawn, changing with every fleeting iridescent colour of the sunrise, blatantly, cruelly brilliant at high noon, soothing with restful and deepening tones at the close of day, who is there to say that this room is not decorated?*[13]

[...]To understand that Corbusian modernism competed in the twenties with the already-established Amusing Style helps explain – although perhaps not excuse – the modernists' more pernicious gendered rhetorics [...] Understanding the productive diversity of modernisms that flourished in the twenties may also help design history forge much-needed links with other humanistic disciplines dedicated to the understanding of modernism and its legacies.

NOTES

1 Le Corbusier, *Towards a New Architecture*, translated by Frederic Etchells (1927 rpt. New York: Praeger, 1960), 18, 20, 23.
2 John Betjeman, '1830–1930 – Still Going Strong: A Guide to the Recent History of Interior Decoration,' *Architectural Review* 67 (May 1930): 231–40.
3 Christopher Reed, *Bloomsbury Rooms: Modernism, Subculture, and Domesticity* (London: Yale University Press, 2004), 236–8. In describing the Amusing Style as British, I am signalling its roots in the amateur traditions and whimsical iconographies of the Arts and Crafts Movement. Like the Arts and Crafts Movement, however, the Amusing Style was quickly disseminated by magazines with international readerships and British *Vogue* highlighted manifestations of the aesthetic in France [...] and the United States [...]
4 Paul Nash, *Room and Book* (New York: Scribner's, 1932), 26 [...]
5 R.H. Wilenski, in R.H. Wilenski and John Gloag, 'Two Points of View,' *Architectural Review* 71 (April 1932): 149.
6 'Unity in Diversity,' *Vogue* [London] (late Oct. 1924): 53.
7 Le Corbusier, 22.
8 'Unity in Diversity,' 53–5.
9 Polly Flinders, 'Marie Laurencin,' *Vogue* [London] (late Jan. 1925): 40 [...]
10 'Modern English Decoration,' *Vogue* [London] (1924): 44. The serenade motif echoes the imagery in a painting in the same room of a woman at a balcony, visible in the photograph of the sideboard. The same cabinet appeared in an uncaptioned full-page photograph in an *Architectural Review* special double issue on 'Modern English Interior Decoration' 67 (May 1930): 222.
11 Clive Bell, *Since Cézanne* (London: Chatto and Windus, 1922), 108–9.
12 FISH, 'Baring the Secrets of the Turkish Baths,' *Vogue* [London] (late Oct. 1925): 66–7.
13 Silhouette, 'The Modern Movement in Continental Decoration. IV – The Living Room,' *Architectural Review* 60 (Sept. 1926): 123.

5.5 RICHARD A.H. LIVETT
'Bronte House Scheme'*

The early efforts of state-aided housing in this country too often resulted in the building of large and small groups of houses strictly in accordance with layouts of forced geometrical design showing a total disregard for hill and dale, sun and

---

* *Official Architect* (March 1942): 134–7.

shade and, what is even more important, the actual requirements of the potential tenants. In those days, one thought, designed and built in terms of three and four bedroom Parlour Houses, although occasionally a Local Authority was bold enough to venture upon meeting a real need by building in odd spots a few non-parlour houses but again providing the accepted three bedroom accommodation. For some unaccountable reason these pioneers of housing reform overlooked those unfortunate people who, because of high rents and rates could not afford the luxury of a Parlour.

I am sure that the majority of people who are interested in housing reform strongly support the parlour house, but when it is applied to the real economic need, I think we must agree that although the parlour is desirable in a family house, it is not an absolute necessity.

The pioneers also forgot to cater for the ageing people of the old age pension class, with low incomes and only requiring a one bedroom dwelling, and the large families requiring 5, 6 and, in some cases, 7 bedrooms. The lack of this accommodation on Municipal Housing Estates was undoubtedly one of the principle reasons for the high percentage of overcrowding revealed in the census of overcrowding carried out in this country under the Housing Act of 1935, but the disregard for the needs of the people did not stop here; I can think of only two Cities where Modern Lodging Houses have been provided and in each case these Lodging Houses are a recent contribution to the Housing Programme. Then there is the need for suitable housing accommodation for working women, perhaps, spinsters, perhaps widows. I refer in particular, to the woman who does not wish to live in lodgings or as a Paying Guest or occupy furnished or unfurnished rooms, the woman who wants a dwelling of her own, easy working and inexpensive. Surely this type of accommodation has its place in any modern housing programme, particularly so when there is a big demand for female labour in the neighbourhood.

The planning problems of such a development are in no way difficult, but care must be taken to see that the freedom of the Architect's pencil does not give rise to bitter thinking when the day arrives for fixing rents.

With the idea in mind, a group of 22 One Bedroom Flats have been erected in Leeds, on a well elevated site having a gradual rise from the South.

This group, known as Bronte House, situated a short distance from the City Centre, and served by a frequent bus service, has purposely been designed on a small scale, in order that the tenants will experience the feeling of compactness and privacy, not always found in larger Flat developments. The project consists of 3 small units, 2 and 3 storeys in height, connected by 2 main staircases, giving access to entrance balconies [...]

[The plan] is very straightforward and simple, yet it amply fulfils all the functions necessary to the life of a business woman, who is out for the greater part of the day.

5.6 GEORGE WAGNER 'The Lair of the Bachelor'*

In the fifties and sixties *Playboy* published a number of commissioned designs for apartments, houses, pads, and penthouses as a way of imagining sites for the *Playboy* lifestyle [...] One of the most fascinating aspects of this discussion is how tacitly it is assumed that spaces and objects become charged with the conditions of social and economic gender roles, but also with specific ideas about sexuality as well. These spaces can be understood to constitute a strategy of recovery of the domestic realm by the heterosexual male.

By grounding the bachelor's fantasy away from the suburban family, the urban sites of *Playboy*'s apartments engage the dangerous pleasures of the city's shadows. The penthouse sits above but within the city – in it but not of it – and allows the bachelor a controlling gaze of the urban spectacle. The penthouse implicitly evokes the image of the city at night and its illicit pleasures. These apartments are the fantasy sites of seduction, with the bachelor the wily predator and the woman the prey. All of the apparatus that fill these spaces – the remote controls, the furniture, the bar – are essentially prosthetic devices that expand the effectiveness of the bachelor in his seduction, or, put another way, the predator in conquest of his prey.

Playboy's Penthouse Apartment was published in September and October of 1956 [...] The article began: 'A man yearns for quarters of his own. More than a place to hang his hat, a man dreams of his own domain, a place that is exclusively his. *Playboy* has designed, planned, and decorated, from the floor up, a penthouse apartment for the urban bachelor – a man who enjoys good living, a sophisticated connoisseur of the lively arts, of food and drink and congenial companions of both sexes. A man very much, perhaps, like you.'[1]

The plan of the apartment is fairly simple. It is a penthouse located high in a building of unusual configuration. The plan is open, 'not divided into cell-like rooms, but into function areas well delineated for relaxing, dining, cooking, wooing, and entertaining, all interacting and yet inviting individual as well as simultaneous use.'[2]

There are some things you have to know about the bachelor. He has a lot of friends whom he likes to invite over spontaneously. He has no family; the bachelor is fantasized as a free agent. His apartment is new and facilitates his

---

* In *Architecture and Feminism*, edited by Debra Coleman, Elizabeth Danze, and Carol Henderson (New York: Princeton Architectural Press, 1996), 183–220.

behavior through a dependency on technology. It is a space of imagined liberation, in which technology serves as an extension of sexual desire.

And speaking of entertainment, one of the hanging Knoll cabinets beneath the windows holds a built-in bar. This permits the canny bachelor to remain in the room while mixing a cool one for his intended quarry. No chance of missing the proper psychological moment – no chance of leaving her cozily curled up on the couch with her shoes off and returning to find her mind changed, purse in hand, and the young lady ready to go home, damn it. Here, conveniently at hand, too, is a self-timing rheostat which will gradually and subtly dim the lights to fit the mood – as opposed to the harsh click of a light switch that plunges all into sudden darkness and may send the fair game fleeing.[3]

The primal theme of the male as hunter is further pursued in the decor: 'One entire wall is decorated with bold and vigorous primitive paintings reminiscent of the prehistoric drawings in the caves of Lascaux.'[4] [...] The seduction continues:

> Do we go through the house turning out the lights and locking up? No sir: flopping on the luxurious bed, we have within easy reach the multiple controls of its unique headboard. Here we have silent mercury switches and a rheostat that controls every light in the place and can subtly dim the bedroom lighting to just the right romantic level. Here, too, are the switches which control the circuits for the front door and terrace window locks. Beside them are push buttons to draw the continuous, heavy, pure-linen, lined draperies on sail track, which can insure darkness at morn – or noon. Above are built-in speakers fed by the remotely controlled hi-fi and radio based in the electronic entertainment installation in the living room. On either side of the bed are storage cupboards with doors that hinge downward to create bedside tables. Within are telephone, with on-off switch for the bell, and miscellaneous bedtime items. Soft mood music flows through the room and the stars shine in the casements as you snuggle down.[5] [...]

The woman is never there in the morning, but the eggs and bacon are. We have a picture of the playboy – in the city, but insulated from it by altitude, residing in a space probably not so unlike the office, controlling his world remotely. His actions are not direct, but mediated – he does something that does something to something else. Security, convenience, and desire are electronically intertwined. The world is brought to the bachelor electronically. Everything is reproduced, including the women. The only palpable condition is one of desire, and that for a woman who seems to want to bolt.

The furniture is all new – bought, not inherited. There is no indication of the past; the bachelor lives completely within the world of commodities and the market, and enjoys having no apparent fixity to the social order. The bachelor is nouveau riche. The furniture itself should be marked by an 'exuberance, finesse, and high imagination, to be liberated fanciful and romantic, to reflect good spirits [rather] than high philosophies.'[6] The work of high modernists, of Mies, Le Corbusier, and Marcel Breuer was rejected as 'a belligerent assemblage of mechanical parts [...] thriving on a dogma that rivaled puritan passion.'[7] Preferred designers were Charles and Ray Eames, George Nelson, Edward Wormley.

NOTES

1 'Playboy's Penthouse Apartment,' *Playboy* (Sept. 1956), 54.
2 Ibid., 60.
3 Ibid., 59.
4 'Playboy's Penthouse Apartment – A Second Look,' *Playboy* (Oct. 1956), 70.
5 Ibid., 68–70.
6 'Designs for Living,' *Playboy* (July 1961), 48.
7 Ibid.

5.7 MATT COOK
Queer Domesticities

6 *Fun Home* by Alison Bechdel. Reprinted from *FUN HOME: A Family Tragicomic* by Alison Bechdel, by permission of Houghton Mifflin Harcourt Publishing Company.

So Alison Bechdel introduces her father in her graphic memoir.[1] It is a story of her own 'coming out' and also of her father's queerness, established at the outset through this description of his decorative investment in the family home. Though securing and sustaining home has become tied to the putative masculine role of provider and protector, Bechdel's father's 'flourish' on the home front marks him out as a different sort of man. His particular attention to the home is too aesthetic and intense, diverting him from the family which was meant to be his chief concern. Underscoring this putative betrayal (of masculinity, of family, of the meaning of home itself), he turns the house into an undertaker's; the 'fun home' of the title is funereal not joyous and the homosexual brings death home, troubling the wholesome future promised – queer theorist Lee Edelman might argue – by the child and the nuclear family matrix.[2]

Bechdel's memoir brings into sharp focus multiple dimensions of the fraught relationship between home and homosexuality. Gay men are figuratively both sissy home boys and homeless, caught up in a misogynist discursive bind that belittles attention to domestic detail and housework and yet also constructs home as culturally and socially central and so off-limits to social and sexual outsiders. The story of the 'fun home' as a prelude to Bechdel's own coming out, meanwhile, highlights the centrality of home life to many men's and women's narratives of homosexual becoming: coming-out stories are often as much about experiences in the birth family home as they are about leaving and / or moving on from it to other places that might fulfil the symbolic and practical functions of home more or less queerly.

Focusing on queer men in Britain (by way of illustration and also as a distinctive case), this short piece argues that home has become a key symbol and material indicator of queer alienation, belonging, difference, and 'normalization.' It describes how homosexuality has been figured as both domestic and anti-domestic; how experiences of home could be about self-determination and expression but also about danger and exposure; and how home retained its value for many queer men but also became more mobile – more readily transferable to places which were not associated with permanent residence or the seat of family life. Teasing out these themes highlights the tensions between ideological imperatives and sweeping queer theorizations, on the one hand, and on the other, the pragmatics, problems, and possibilities of being at home and making home for 'ordinary' queer men in a range of different and particular social, cultural, and economic circumstances.

When the 'modern' homosexual began to appear in the pages of sexology books in the late nineteenth century, home and homelessness were marshalled specifically in explanations of the genesis and identification of this figure. In sexological and psychoanalytical theorizations of homosexuality (as opposed to those emphasizing the circumstantial and situational), the invert or homosexual was distinctly the product of the (middle class) family and family home, either through inheritance or deviations in the oedipal drama. Case studies in the works of Richard von Krafft-Ebing, Henry Havelock Ellis, and Sigmund Freud lingered over early home life as a means of explaining this deviance. In adulthood, though, the men in the case studies often described themselves as distant from their family homes. Their sexual and social lives seemed – in these cases and in an increasingly sensational newspaper press – to be more oriented towards public and semi-public space; towards the streets, stations, parks, theatres, and bars of the city rather than new home spaces, queer or otherwise. Reports came too of queer 'goings-ons' in workhouses, prisons, public schools, and universities. In these various places, and away from the wholesome influence of home, men and boys were apparently more likely to stray.

This was, then, an undomesticated passion, produced as alien to putative and always already elusive 'norms' of home and family life and incompatible to all they represented: respectability, restraint, containment, 'true' (middle class) Englishness. This characterization became axiomatic when the binary homosexual / heterosexual understanding of sexuality took more universal hold and the homosexual 'problem' was more widely broached in the 1950s. Poisonous press rhetoric configured more powerfully and specifically than before the domestic, familial, and so national threat posed by this 'minority.' A Law Society memo meanwhile specifically excluded queer men from the domestic scene: 'male persons living together do not constitute domestic life,' it announced.[3]

If home featured prominently in the attack on and rhetorical exclusion of the homosexual, it was also key to calls for legitimization in this period. With home overburdened with symbolism of good citizenship, respectability, relational 'normalcy,' and gender conformity, it is perhaps not surprising that in his tacit argument for reform the sociologist Gordon Westwood touted the 'nice flats' of queer bachelors and the domestic propriety of a middle-class homosexual couple who were 'extremely proud of their home and devote[d] their attention to it like young newly weds.'[4]

The legitimization of homosexuals within the home was always equivocal and partial though. However rhetorically useful the model of the home-loving homosexual was to reformers, it oversimplified established and emerging rhythms of everyday life for many queer men. The dilly boys, queens, and cottagers who took to public spaces their queer sexual and social lives tainted this respectable image, and in the reform of the law on homosexuality advocated by the Wolfenden Committee in 1957 and at length enacted in England and Wales in 1967, these queers were left out in the cold: only those who conducted their sexual relationships in private (a term newly and narrowly defined) and with only one man at a time found themselves within the law.

More and less self-consciously queer men had to work out particular ways of living domestically and of interacting with home as an idea and as a place.

'Home' can thus serve as a barometer of identity, identification, community, sociality, and politics, and it also indicates pragmatic or more ideologically driven negotiations of domineering ideas about the domestic sphere. While romantic socialist Edward Carpenter rejected the upper middle-class trappings of home in his small-holding in Yorkshire in the early twentieth century, for example, the antique collector, B. Charles, continually flagged his domestic rectitude and conventionality in his post–Second World War Mass Observation survey diary.[5] The one signalled his belief that cross-class communication and love in its various forms could only flourish with the stripping back of social convention, including in the home. The other marked out a nationalism and investment in (English) tradition which perhaps sustained a status and sense of self-worth that his queer desires potentially jeopardized. We can similarly identify reflections and productions of particular ideas about queer lives, loves, and sex (as well as signifiers of related class, bohemian, political, and artistic identifications) in the aesthetic 'House Beautiful' of Oscar Wilde; in the darkened, perfumed rooms of Wilde's co-defendant Alfred Taylor; in architect and photographer Montague Glover's carefully positioned miniatures of ancient Greek statuary; in Joe Orton and Kenneth Halliwell's utilitarian bedsit papered with collages of classical and Renaissance art; or in the shared clothes rails and beds of Gay Liberation Front communes in the 1970s. For the men living in these various contexts the home was an important arena in which to affirm a felt difference (as much to themselves as anyone else) and / or to reiterate their conformity despite the sex and relationships they were having.

The very act of producing a 'look' or 'feel' for the home marked queer men out, however. Interior design became a seemingly feminized and queer preserve and profession, and tidiness and domestic care was and is repeatedly used in fiction and film to signal queerness and also to trivialize queer men, to mark them out as all surface and superficiality. Unlike 'normal' men, queers were apparently not looking to the home as a literal and figurative investment in the future.

Though we can look to the homes of queer men for signs and statements of their sense of self, their relative conformity or feeling of difference, and the particular ideas of queer love, culture, and sex they were attuned to, such domestic self-expression did and does not take place in a vacuum. Queer identities and identifications are neither unitary nor exclusive, and these queer engagements with wider discourses of home and domesticity are necessarily modulated by a range of legal, social, cultural, and economic factors. Home was, for example, not always the safest or most comfortable place for queer men to be. Despite the ideas of privacy, retreat, and individualism associated with the British home, such notions were also hedged in by the law, by potent imperatives to respectability and discretion, and by a range of practical and pragmatic considerations. The three men arrested in London in 1927 after dressing up as Salome and other 'exotic' figures were quite wrong when they protested their prosecution on the grounds that 'a man could do what he liked in his own house': the Labouchère Amendment to the Criminal Law Amendment Act of 1885, which criminalized all acts of gross indecency between men, had made clear its reach into private space (a specification which perhaps seemed necessary precisely because of the idealization of the private realm as a haven for individual self-expression).[6] It was often easier for many living in shared accommodation, in boarding houses, and in bed-sits to 'be themselves' and to be 'at home' in other places (in queer bars, in theatre green rooms, in private members clubs). Sex away from home was often not only about the places where opportunities arose but also about the impossibility, inconvenience, or risk of taking sexual partners home. On the other hand, the perils of public sex and socialization, and for some the expense and inhospitability of the commercial gay scene, reinforced the importance of a home base for many men. A group of gay squatters in Brixton, South London, in the 1970s saw their community as an alternative to what they dubbed the 'straight gay scene' of Earls Court in the West.[7] In the early 1990s Ajamu X described how the racism and sexual objectification he encountered in West End gay bars and clubs was part of what led him home to form the black gay men's Breakfast Club and the underground sex club the Black Perverts Network from and in his flat.[8] There was by this time also a higher rate of single occupancy than ever before (29% of the population in Britain in 2001, up 11 percentage points from 1971)[9] and thus a new ease of access to and feeling of safety in private space for many queer men. This, together with the advent of Internet sex and dating sites, brought cruising and sex home for many, reinflecting ideas of immediacy, intimacy, and trust in relation to the domestic space.

Recent work on contemporary queer intimacy has highlighted different queer household configurations and the varied uses of the terminology of family and home. While sometimes this has been about a deliberate refusal of family and wider cultural 'norms,' more often it relates (or *also* relates) to a pragmatic muddling through, and to a range of emotional connections to lovers past and present, friends, children, birth families and so-called families of choice. This is something we can also identify in the past: with Carpenter and his fluid domestic set-up, for example, or with his friend George Ives, who lived in Primrose Hill in London with a former lover, his lover's wife, their two daughters, and a number of working-class men for the first half of the twentieth century. Queer homes have thus been places for socialization, childrearing, friendship, and care in ways that mark them out from – but also connect them to – the home lives of their 'normal' neighbours. Though the care of the sick at home by friends is hardly a queer phenomenon, the particularity of the AIDS crisis in Britain and the wider and often homophobic familial, social, and cultural response made voluntary and friendship networks particularly imperative and also particularly defiant and politicized during this period.

What sometimes gets replayed in these analyses, however, is the tacit presumption of a separation of queer homes in adulthood from those of infancy; singly, or in twos, threes, or more, queer men were and are assumed to live at one remove from birth family homes and cultures – more so than their straight brothers and sisters. This reflects the rifts and tensions many queer men experienced and continue to experience in relation to their home and family of birth. It also, though, reflects the ways in which queer identity has tended to be articulated via white and middle-class men who often had the means to move away and were also often expected to do so for work and education. There are, however, many other life stories of continued co-residence with family, and of continuing physical proximity, interaction, and mutual support. Historian Matt Houlbrook identified this especially in his research on London working-class families in the interwar period, and this has been echoed (in different and particular ways) in more recent sociological work on working-class and black Afro-Caribbean gay men living in the British capital.[10] However tentative and riddled with exceptions, these sociological and historical studies alert us to the difference class, religion, migratory, ethnic, and national cultures can make to the experience and understanding of home for queer men.

Bechdel's *Fun Home* – the graphic memoir discussed at the outset – keys into some commonly circulating ideas about the relationship between home and homosexuality and yet is also a tale of a quirky and unique home and family life. What I have suggested in this piece is the need to hold these two positions in tension. Presumptions about the relationship of home to homosexuality are indeed commonplace and also shape the way many queer men create and have created their home lives and cultures. They have become part of a subcultural identification which queer men might accommodate, live out, and/or react against. The everyday and material lives of queer men in relation to home are, though, predictably more quirky, complex, and diverse, and less easy to describe or theorize homogeneously than any glib caricature might suggest. They are modulated by family background, class, cultural, ethnic and religious background, relationship status, friendship networks, HIV status, and much more. We come up against the tension and also the interplay between the cultural stories we tell (and which are told about us) and the individual lives we lead. What is certain, however, is that 'home' remains a crucial actual and discursive site for queer experiences, understandings, and articulations of the self, community, and subculture. Moreover, because of the wider social and cultural claims on home and a closely related homophobia, queer men have had to be more self-conscious than most in the way they figure home symbolically and practically within their lives.

NOTES

1 Alison Bechdel, *Fun Home: A Family Tragicomic* (London: Jonathan Cape, 2006), 6–7.
2 Lee Edelman, *No Future: Queer Theory and the Death Drive* (Durham, NC: Duke University Press, 2004).
3 Cited in Matt Houlbrook, *Queer London: Perils and Pleasures in the Sexual Metropolis, 1918–1957* (Chicago, IL: University of Chicago Press, 2005), 110.
4 Gordon Westwood, *Society and the Homosexual* (London: Victor Gollancz, 1952), 132.
5 Simon Garfield, ed., *Our Hidden Lives: The Remarkable Diaries of Postwar Britain* (London: Random House, 2004), 400–1 and 406. On Carpenter, see especially Sheila Rowbotham, *Edward Carpenter: A Life of Liberty and Love* (London: Verso, 2008).
6 'Photographs Taken by Police: Men's Fancy Dress Costumes in Flat Incident,' *Reynolds* (27 March 1927): 152.
7 Interview with Alex Beyer (by Ian Townson, 11 May 1997), Hall-Carpenter Collection, London School of Economics.
8 Interview with Ajamu X by Matt Cook, 27 June 2008.
9 U.K. Statistics Authority, 'Census 2001: Key Statistics' http://www.statistics.gov.uk/hub/people-places/housing-and-households/households/index.html.
10 Peter Keogh, Catherine Dodds, and Laurie Henderson, *Working Class Gay Men: Redefining Community, Restoring Identity* (London: Sigma Research, 2004).

5.8 MARCIA STEPHENSON
'The Architectural Relationship between Gender, Race, and the Bolivian State'*

This essay examines [...] the nexus of relations between the Bolivian state and the heterogeneous social body, focusing on the ways by which the state, as a guarantor of order, has sought to contain civil society [...] It argues that the practices of social enclosure and cultural fragmentation are implemented through hegemonic discourses of modernity and citizenship. In Bolivia, discourses of modernity and citizenship continue to be linked to histories of colonialism because they deploy a rhetoric structured by hierarchical notions of racial difference that produce and reproduce an idealized (*mestizo*) citizen-subject and its (indigenous) other.[1] [...] These discursive practices are spatially structured, mapping fixed boundaries and demarcating clear-cut distinctions between inside and outside. Moreover, these racialized spaces of containment are also gendered because they require prevailing ideologies of womanhood for the reproduction of power [...] My analysis, therefore, begins with the consideration of hegemonic depictions of the house, a compelling example of one enclosure where, in a stratified society such as Bolivia's, notions of space, race, and gender converge with the reproduction of power [...] The underlying architectural rhetoric of the house and the accompanying image of the Western white mother depicted as inhabiting this idealized space function as organizing principles of modernity. The door of the house thus serves as a threshold metaphor, one that marks the limits of the racialized space of the selfsame [...]

Critical studies on the relationship between motherhood and the home in Bolivia, written by middle- and upper-class essayists, have changed little throughout the twentieth century. These accounts confirm the notion of an essential feminine nature that is fixed and unchanging, one that is biologically determined by a woman's reproductive activities [...] According to this prevailing representation, the domestic space of the home constitutes the fundamental core of womanhood. Normative depictions of the private, domestic realm emphasize a logic of interiority, a unified spatial order that is enclosed and timeless, where stasis, nostalgia, and security are troped in the figure of the mother

* In *The Latin American Subaltern Studies Reader*, edited by Ileana Rodríguez (Durham, NC: Duke University Press, 2001), 367–82.

[...] Thus, the essence of womanhood, and therefore also of motherhood, is inextricably linked to the socio-spatial arena that is the home.

In his study of Bolivian housing, *El problema social de la vivienda* (1949), Alberto Cornejo elaborates on the metaphorical relationship between motherhood and the home, claiming that both can be linked to the notion of origin. Cornejo frames his argument by citing at length from the work of Ramón Clarés. Clarés, in turn, appears undoubtedly to have been influenced by Freud [... who] defines humankind's original home as the mother's womb.[2] On motherhood, Clarés writes: '[...] [Mother is the living synthesis of space and time ... Beyond the mother, the infant does not feel life, because mother is origin ... The mother is the fundamental woman, symbolically called the "house" in the mystical language of the sacred books] (trans. by author)'[3] [...]

Cornejo argues that legislators must address Bolivia's housing shortage, a shortage that already constituted a problem in 1949 because of the increasing growth of urban populations and economic limitations that prevented many people from buying their own homes.[4] According to Cornejo, the solution to the problem is [...] more affordable housing. However, he cautions, the houses should be constructed according to certain specifics that would enable the reorganization of urban society [...] [The districts where low-income projects offer housing for the polychromatic multitudes, these projects are becoming outdated due to social necessity. It is not enough to build houses; rather, these should meet the needs and objectives of a home.] If mother equals origin equals home, Cornejo clearly advocates a House (Mother) through which the polychromatic poor can be eliminated, thereby establishing a decisive link between motherhood, the home, and the racial formation of the modern nation-state [...]

The equation of a particular kind of house with the formation of acculturated (*mestizo*) citizens suggests that, like clothing, architecture fashions the body politic. Consequently, the house constitutes both the gateway to citizenship and the condition of its possibility, functioning literally and symbolically in a continuous trajectory of identity formation.

As an overdetermined cultural and political site, the house is central to both hegemonic discourses of domesticity and counterhegemonic indigenous practices that continually resist *criollo*[5] efforts to delimit the boundaries of the familiar and the selfsame [...] The critical interrogation of the house from the point of view of its architecture and the implications this has for understanding social, political, and economic relations become a useful lens through which it is possible to read the racialized and gendered boundaries of modernity in the context of Bolivia. These current debates unequivocally indicate that hegemonic depictions of modernity in Bolívia are structured through a rhetoric of domestic space; the house functions as a spatial metaphor through which the 'unruly play of representation' can be controlled precisely because it defines and differentiates the (modern or civilized) inside from the (uncivilized) outside.[6]

The architectural rhetoric that is deployed insistently by *criollo* discourses through the anxious reiteration of boundaries suggests that this domestic regime constitutes both the condition and the very possibility of the hegemonic state itself. Dominant depictions of the house, emphasizing enclosure, the privatization of space, and individualization, become an important mechanism with which hegemonic discourses repeatedly attempt to order and discipline the racially heterogeneous social body throughout the second half of the twentieth century. So-called normative houses domesticate individual bodies and families by forcibly bringing them into the realm of the familiar; therefore, the physical layout of hegemonic houses structures processes of ethnic and racial acculturation at the same time that it organizes dominant constructions of gender. Moreover, because normative houses insistently delineate a series of boundaries between inside and outside, it soon becomes apparent that racially diverse groups position themselves and are positioned differently in relation to these same boundaries. Indeed, different or non-hegemonic houses suggest competing positions about boundaries [...] This essay suggests that the prototypical mother in Bolivia who inhabits the normative house is either white and from the upper class or an acculturated, Westernized *mestiza*. Consequently, the state constitutes itself through specific constructions that not only produce traditional gender roles but also promote racial assimilation by privileging white, Western norms. Non-hegemonic or resistant homes, therefore, have implications not only for gender roles but also for racial and political identities.

The architectural relationship between modernity and racial and gendered identities is at the forefront of architect Jorge Saravia Valle's study *Planificación de aldeas rurales* (1986). Saravia Valle contrasts a drawing of an alleged present-day rural house with a model of a proposed modernized house. In Figure 7 labeled '*vivienda actual*' [present-day dwelling], the house depicted is run down, in a state of advanced disrepair. The cracked walls, falling roof, and lack of a foundation suggest the fragility and permeability of boundaries that define and differentiate the interior from the exterior; the presence of a clay oven on the patio indicates that the woman carries out her domestic activities, literally, outside the confines of the house. A cow pictured in the front yard wanders freely, leaving in

7 *Vivienda actual* by Jorge Saravia Valle, 1986. Planificación de aldeas rurales. La Paz: Juventud. Reproduced by permission of Jorge Saravia Valle.

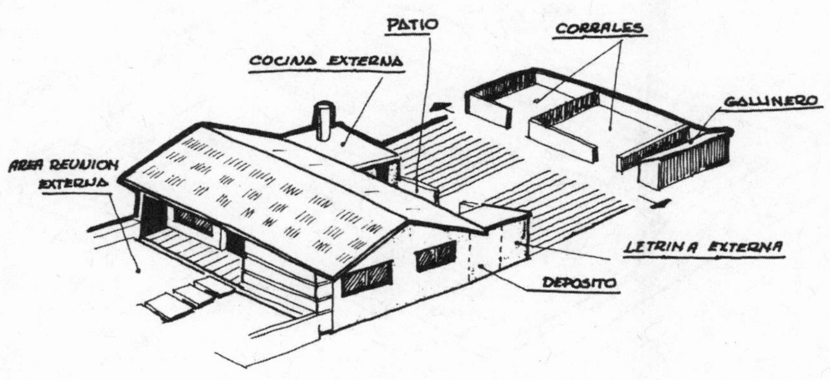

8 Proposed modernized house by Jorge Saravia Valle, 1986. Planificación de aldeas rurales. La Paz: Juventud. Reproduced by permission of Jorge Saravia Valle.

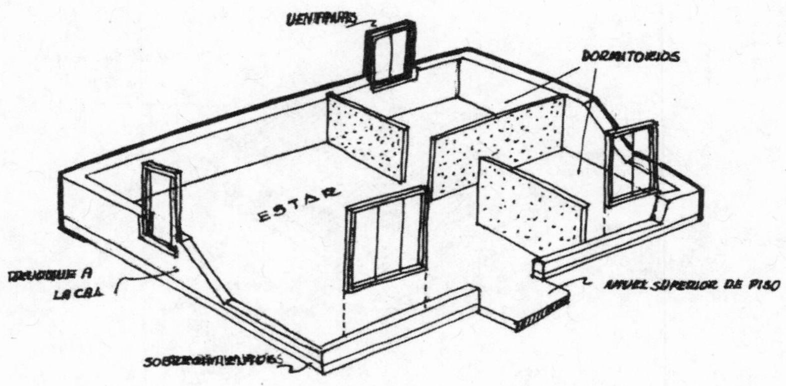

9 Interior of a *vivienda actual* by Jorge Saravia Valle, 1986. Planificación de aldeas rurales. La Paz: Juventud. Reproduced by permission of Jorge Saravia Valle.

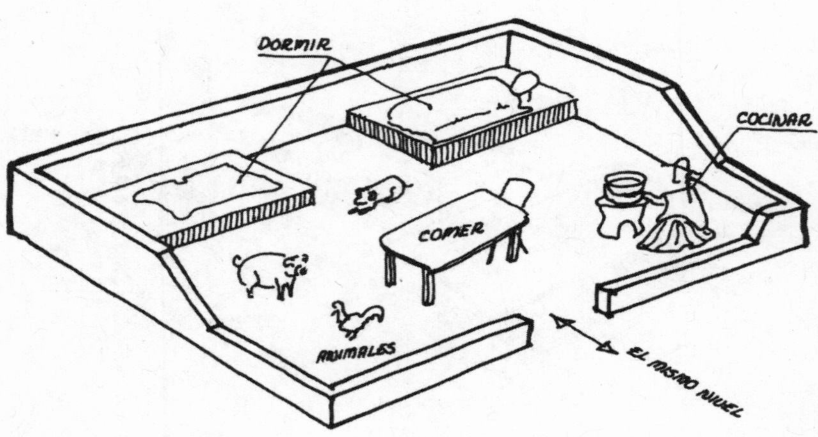

10 Interior of an 'improved' dwelling by Jorge Saravia Valle, 1986. Planificación de aldeas rurales. La Paz: Juventud. Reproduced by permission of Jorge Saravia Valle.

its tracks a pile of manure. A man can be seen just beyond the wall of the corral, squatting and defecating. Next to the house there is a mound of garbage.

In contrast, Saravia Valle's proposed model house (Figure 8) has been emptied of all human and animal presences. The modern house underscores the importance of private rooms, the enclosed latrine, the contained corral, and a state of cleanliness missing in the first drawing. According to the architect, this model house illustrates how '[t]he principal objective of IMPROVING the *campesino* house with technical assistance is to make it a comfortable, hygienic, pleasant, and organic environment]' (trans. by author).[7]

The process by which the Indian woman's identity undergoes transformation is illustrated in a second group of drawings by Saravia Valle. Figures 9 and 10 contrast the interior space of an actual Indian house with that of an 'improved' dwelling. The actual house consists of a single room that serves household needs. An Indian woman squats on the floor, cooking, while another person sleeps. A pig, rooster, and dog share the same domestic space with the family. In contrast, the improved house once again stands out because of the absence of people and animals. Internal walls have been added to emphasize architecturally the containment and privatization of space; now the living room and the kitchen are separate from the bedrooms. The drawings suggest that as the house is modernized and improved, the racial identity of its inhabitants is also transformed. The Indian woman present in the first drawing as a symbol of a collective, native identity but absent in the second, no longer has a place in the refurbished space; instead, we await the arrival of an acculturated housewife to take up residence there [...]

When urban indigenous women and working-class *cholas* circulated freely outside the home, as in the instance of the militant anarchists of the 1930s and 1940s, their bodies threatened the social order because they were out of place (the home) and in the streets. According to the *criollo* oligarchy then, these disorderly, hence polluted and polluting, racialized female bodies were identified with (political) instability and consequently subjected to surveillance and discipline [...] By the 1960s and 1970s, hegemonic womanhood continued to be constructed according to a racial and economic logic that was spatially organized according to the constellation of signifiers ranging between 'order' and 'home' (property).

NOTES

1 [Editors' note: *Mestizo* refers to Latin American people of mixed European and Amerindian ancestry.]

2 Sigmund Freud, 'The Uncanny' [1919], in *The Standard Edition of the Complete Psychological Works of Sigmund Freud,* translated and edited by James Strachey (London: Hogarth Press, 1955), vol. 17, 245. [See section 4.6 this volume.]
3 Ramón Clarés, cited in Alberto S. Cornejo, *El problema social de la vivienda* (Cochabamba: Imprenta Universitaria, 1949), 6.
4 Cornejo, ibid., 5.
5 [Editors' note: *Criollo* refers to Spanish-American people of European, usually Spanish, descent.]
6 Mark Wigley, *The Architecture of Deconstruction: Derrida's Haunt* (Cambridge, MA: MIT Press, 1992), 106–7.
7 Jorge Saravia Valle, *Planificación de aldeas rurales* (La Paz: Juventud, 1986), 82.

5.9 RENÉE HIRSCHON 'Essential Objects and the Sacred: Interior and Exterior Space in Urban Greek Locality'*

This [section] examines aspects of the relationship of urban Greek women to their immediate physical environment through investigating the house and its immediate surroundings. The house is obviously an appropriate focus for the analysis of female activities and spatial organization – the 'woman-environment relationship' (an area usually called 'man-environment studies' [...] – for the domestic *locus* of Mediterranean women in general has become a truism. Most often it carries implications of deprivation and of exclusion from the mainstream of life, but these negative and pejorative connotations may be questioned [...] for [...] in their domestic activities Greek women are concerned with the most vital aspects of physical and social life.

The case of Yerania is an interesting one. The houses were originally designed as units for single family residence, but they have been progressively subdivided through time. This arose from a complex of social, historical, and political factors, among the most important being the provision of dowry for a daughter's marriage. Here, dowry takes the form of separate living quarters in the parental home. Nevertheless the independence of each nuclear family

* In *Women and Space: Ground Rules and Social Maps,* edited by Shirley Ardener (Oxford: Berg, 1993, 70–86).

or 'household' is maintained; it is manifested in the creation of a separate kitchen, the realm of each housewife.

Most houses are thus shared between several households related through women, or have been in the past, and they are characteristically overcrowded. In this context, certain recurrent items of household furniture might seem to an observer to be eminently unsuitable. We find, on consideration, that, although they serve some obvious practical functions, their particular form and their placing in the house can only be understood through the realisation of symbolic attributes and of their 'sacred' connotations. Here the presence of the 'sacred' is embodied in the large dining-table, the double-bed and the *iconostási*, some of the 'essential' objects of Yerania homes [...]

In the wider context of social life the fundamental dichotomy of the 'house' and the 'road,' the inner and outer realms, is the point of orientation for interaction between women in the neighbourhood. This spatial and symbolic division is mediated, however, by two items: the kitchen, which is the diacritical marker of each conjugal household and the exclusive area of each married woman, and the movable chair. The latter is taken out in the late afternoons when people sit on pavements passing the time in conversation and observation of neighbourhood activity. The opposition between 'inside' and 'outside' is bridged through these two 'marginal' items. On the one hand, food brought into the house is processed by the housewife in her kitchen; on the other, social exchange takes place through the extension of the inside realm as the chair is moved out onto the pavement. The association of women with spatial arrangement and objects in the home, and thus with the symbolic order, is seen to be an integral part of their daily activities.

Yerania is a poor district of the city lying a few miles north of the harbour of Piraeus. It was established in 1928 as part of a massive housing programme for over one and a half million refugees from Asia Minor who fled to Greece in the early 1920s. The refugee settlements are today totally integrated in the physical fabric of the city and can be distinguished only where the original housing remains [...] In the face of severe economic constraints, modifications to living space have made manifest, in material form, the priorities of each family which were ultimately culturally defined [...]

The original structures were prefabricated, single-storeyed houses ('prefabs') made from panel board under pitched tiled roofs. They were semi-detached, containing two separate houses, mirror images of one another, under one roof. Each house had two main rooms (3.2 m x 4 m), a third smaller room intended as a kitchen (2 m x 3 m) and a toilet [...] and was set in a courtyard, the size of which depended on its position in the block [...] The crowded conditions characteristic of the localities were already apparent from the earliest days: 550 Yerania houses contained over 650 families at the outset. In the next forty years, densities increased and few houses remained in single-family occupation over this period […]

The Kitchen

Besides the need to provide separate quarters as dowry for daughters, marriage entails another priority in the allocation of living space in the Yerania houses. This is the creation of a separate kitchen, however small, for each married woman. The close kinship between co-resident housewives, that of mothers, daughters, sisters, and the chronic pressure on space in these dwellings, might suggest that food preparation and cooking could be a communal task, or that a single kitchen would be shared by the co-resident families. On the contrary, however, each nuclear family has its own separate cooking area; since most of the houses are subdivided, there are commonly two or three kitchens on any one plot, and even four or five […]

The significance of the kitchen must not be underestimated in spite of its minimal size. Since its primary use is for cooking, the kitchen is the domain of the housewife, for in Yerania food is handled and prepared for consumption solely by the women; rarely do men even purchase food, which once supplied to the home is the concern of the women. In this community culinary ability is highly prized, being one of the main criteria for assessing a woman's worth. Food, its provision, and preparation occupies the housewife's thoughts and actions for much of the day […] Interestingly, the emphasis on preparation of food by women is highlighted in the case of edible raw foods – the abundant fruit of Greece, for example, usually eaten once a day, is never served 'untreated' in its 'natural' form. Oranges, apples, pears, and peaches are not offered whole from a bowl but are first peeled and sliced, then offered on a platter by the woman of the house whose task this is.

As Lévi-Strauss has suggested, the transformation of the raw into the cooked represents a conversion process from nature to culture. The association of women with nourishment, the concept of the woman as a source of sustenance, and her enduring association with food is a theme running through Greek culture […] Transposing the nature / culture opposition to the context of Yerania, it is the woman who, in dealing with the raw 'natural' substances of the 'outside' world, acts as the agent in the cultural process and by extension, the man is designated to 'nature' through his activities outside the home.

The transformation of food takes place on a daily basis in the tiny kitchens of the Yerania homes which provide in this sense the space where the 'inside' world, that of the home and family, intersects with products of the 'outside' world. The kitchen can thus be seen as a zone of transition: it is significant in this respect that the kitchens, among the many modifications in Yerania houses, are always added externally, tacked onto living areas. The association of pollution and cooking may be inferred from this external location of the kitchens [...] certainly, if nothing else, a marginal quality is suggested, as one might expect. The kitchen conveys a sense of its ambivalent character in its peripheral location while in the emphasis on a kitchen for every household it is the physical expression of central cultural notions relating to the family as a unit and to the woman's role within it. It has therefore the force of a major 'condensed symbol.[1] Something of the ambivalent character of the kitchen is shared, albeit in a less emphatic way, by the standard chair common in these houses [...] both link the 'inside' with the 'outside' and provide, or cross, the threshold between these two worlds [...]

This analysis of interior and exterior space in Yerania is founded upon the notion of the house as an exclusive precinct, that of the family, closed to outsiders except under special conditions such as the formal granting of hospitality. Neighbours who are involved in frequent interactions outside their houses seldom enter one another's homes. The house is thus to be understood as conceptually opposed to the 'road,' an image for the 'outside' world, so that by extension a dichotomy of 'inside' and 'outside' is inferred. Although it is itself perceived as a locus of positive values, the house and the family would exist in potential isolation were it not for the clearly defined code of neighbourhood conduct, emphasizing sociability, openness, and requiring frequent interaction from residents in the locality [...] The woman's role in promoting contacts and in creating relationships throughout the locality centred upon her activities in the neighbourhood are thus to be understood as vital in maintaining social life. The object in which social contact beyond the home is embodied is, as we have seen, the movable chair which bridges the separation of the 'house' and 'road' by moving from 'inside' to 'outside.'

Movement across the threshold takes place in the opposite direction too, for food is brought in to be processed first in the kitchen, and then served in the house. The kitchen is thus a marginal zone where the conversion of 'outside' products occurs, and where the two realms intersect. In their activities in the kitchen, the women prepare food which on the one hand provides nourishment, and thus physical life itself is sustained through their efforts, while on the other they offer food at the table where, as we have seen, fundamental symbolic values are expressed.

NOTE

1 Mary Douglas, *Natural Symbols* (Harmondsworth: Penguin, 1973), 29–30.

5.10 IRIS MARION YOUNG
'House and Home: Feminist Variations on a Theme'*

For millennia the image of Penelope sitting by the hearth and weaving, saving and preserving the home while her man roams the earth in daring adventures, has defined one of Western culture's basic ideas of womanhood. Many other cultures historically and today equate women with home, expecting women to serve men at home and sometimes preventing them from leaving the house. If house and home mean the confinement of women for the sake of nourishing male projects, then feminists have good reason to reject home as a value. But it is difficult even for feminists to exorcise a positive valence to the idea of home. We often look forward to going home and invite others to make themselves at home. House and home are deeply ambivalent values [...]

On the one hand, I agree with feminist critics such as Luce Irigaray and Simone de Beauvoir that the comforts and supports of house and home historically come at women's expense. Women serve, nurture, and maintain so that the bodies and souls of men and children gain confidence and expansive subjectivity to make their mark on the world. This homey role deprives women of support for their own identity and projects. Along with several feminist critics, furthermore, I question the yearning for a whole and stable identity that the idea of home often represents. Unlike these critics, however, I am not ready to toss the idea of home out of the larder of feminist values. Despite the oppressions and privileges the idea historically carries, the idea of home also carries critical liberating potential because it expresses uniquely human values. Some of these can be uncovered by exploring the meaning-making activity most typical of women in domestic work [...]

Luce Irigaray makes explicit the maleness of Heidegger's allegedly universal ontology. [See Heidegger, section 2.2 in this volume.] Man can build and dwell in the world in patriarchal culture, she suggests, only on the basis of the materiality and nurturance of women. In the idea of 'home,' man projects onto woman the nostalgic longing for the lost wholeness of the original mother. To fix and keep hold of his identity, man makes a house, puts things in it, and confines there his woman, who reflects his identity to him. The price she pays for supporting his subjectivity, however, is dereliction, having no self of her own.

Irigaray writes about the association of house and home with a male longing for fixed identity in a timeless tone. The property acquisition she describes men

---

* In *Intersecting Voices: Dilemmas of Gender, Political Philosophy, and Policy* (Princeton, NJ: Princeton University Press, 1997), 134–64.

as engaging in as a means of substituting for the lost mother, however, is probably best thought of as characteristic of bourgeois society, whose values became hegemonic in the twentieth century in the West, and increasingly in the world. Thus I explore the specific attachment of personal identity to commodified houses and their contents, in order to find another angle of critique of the longing for home [...]

Like Irigaray, Beauvoir describes women's existence as deprived of active subjectivity because their activity concentrates on serving and supporting men in the home. Unlike Irigaray, however, Beauvoir materializes this account by reflecting on the sexual division of labour. Because she accepts a dichotomy between immanence and transcendence and identifies all of women's domestic labour with immanence, however, Beauvoir misses the creatively human aspects of women's traditional household work, in activities I call preservation.

That aspect of dwelling which Heidegger devalues thus provides a turning point for revaluing home. Preservation makes and remakes home as a support for personal identity without accumulation, certainty, or fixity. While preservation, a typically feminine activity, is traditionally devalued at least in Western conceptions of history and identity, it has crucial human value [...]

Beauvoir is surely right that the bare acts of cleaning bathrooms, sweeping floors, and changing diapers are merely instrumental; though necessary, they cannot be invested with creativity or individuality. She is wrong, however, to reduce all or even most domestic work to immanence. Not all homemaking is housework. To understand the difference we need to reconsider the idea of home, and its relation to a person's sense of identity. Home enacts a specific mode of subjectivity and historicity that is distinct both from the creative-destructive idea of transcendence and from the ahistorical repetition of immanence [...]

Preserving the meaningful identity of a household or family by means of the loving care of its mementos is simply a different order of activity from washing the unhealthy bacteria out of the bathroom. As Beauvoir rightly says, the latter is general, the abstract maintenance of species life. The former, however, is specific and individuated; the homemaker acts to preserve the particular meaning that these objects have in the lives of these particular people. The confusion between these acts and the level of immanence is perhaps understandable, because so many activities of domestic work are both simultaneously. The homemaker dusts the pieces in order to keep away the molds and dirts that might annoy her sinuses, but at the same time she keeps present to herself and those with whom she lives the moments in their lives or those of their forebears that the objects remember [...]

Thus the activity of preservation should be distinguished from the nostalgia accompanying fantasies of a lost home from which the subject is separated and to which he seeks to return. Preservation entails remembrance, which is quite different from nostalgia. Where nostalgia can be constructed as a longing flight from the ambiguities and disappointments of everyday life, remembrance faces the open negativity of the future by knitting a steady confidence in who one is from the pains and joys of the past retained in the things among which one dwells. Nostalgic longing is always for an elsewhere. Remembrance is the affirmation of what brought us here [...]

We should not romanticize this activity. Preservation is ambiguous; it can be either conservative or reinterpretive. The same material things sometimes carry the valences of unique personal identity and status privilege [...] Homemaking consists in preserving the things and their meaning as anchor to shifting personal and group identity. But the narratives of the history of what brought us here are not fixed, and part of the creative and moral task of preservation is to reconstruct the connection of the past to the present in light of new events, relationships, and political understandings [...]

A chain of recent interlinked essays elaborates an argument that feminists should reject any affirmation of the value of home. Biddy Martin and Chandra Mohanty launched this discussion in their reading of Minnie Bruce Pratt's reflections on growing up as a privileged white woman in the American South.[1] Teresa de Lauretis then commented on Martin and Mohanty, enlarging their insights about the connection between home and identity.[2] Most recently Bonnie Honig criticizes what she perceives as a privileged position of withdrawal from politics that the idea of home affords, and she enlarges de Lauretis's ideas about decentred identity and feminist politics.[3]

All these essays express a deep distrust of the idea of home for feminist politics and conclude that we should give up a longing for home. Although I agree with much in their critiques [...] I argue that while politics should not succumb to a longing for comfort and unity, the material values of home can nevertheless provide leverage for radical social critique. Following bell hooks, I shall suggest that 'home' can have a political meaning as a site of dignity and resistance. To the extent that having a home is currently a privilege, I argue, the values of home should be democratized rather than rejected [...] hooks reverses the claim that having 'home' is a matter of privilege.[4] 'Home' is a more universal value in her vision, one that the oppressed in particular can and have used as a vehicle for developing resistance to oppression. As long as there is a minimal freedom of homeplace, there is a place to assemble apart from the privileged and [to] talk of organising; there is a place to preserve the specific culture of the oppressed people. The personal sense of identity supported in the site and things of a homeplace thus enables political agency [...]

Even if people have minimal shelter of their own [...] they need a certain level of material comfort in their home for it to serve as a place of identity-construction and the development of the spirit of resistance that hooks discusses. In this way having a home is indeed today having a privilege.

The appropriate response to this fact of privilege is not to reject the values of home, but instead to claim those values for everyone. Feminists should criticize the nostalgic use of home that offers a permanent respite from politics and conflict, and which continues to require of women that they make men and children comfortable. But at the same time, feminist politics calls for conceptualizing the positive values of home and criticizing a global society that is unable or unwilling to extend those values to everyone [...]

Home is a complex ideal, I have argued, with an ambiguous connection to identity and subjectivity. I agree with those critics of home who see it as a nostalgic longing for an impossible security and comfort, a longing bought at the expense of women and of those constructed as Others, strangers, not-home, in order to secure this fantasy of a unified identity. But I have also argued that the idea of home and the practices of home-making support personal and collective identity in a more fluid and material sense, and that recognizing this value entails also recognizing the creative value of the often unnoticed work that many women do. Despite the real dangers of romanticizing home, I think that there are also dangers in turning our backs on home.

NOTES

1 Biddy Martin and Chandra Talpade Mohanty, 'Feminist Politics: What's Home Got to Do With It?' in Teresa de Lauretis, ed., *Feminist Studies / Critical Studies* (Bloomington, IN: Indiana University Press, 1986), 191–212.

2 Teresa de Lauretis, 'Eccentric Subjects: Feminist Theory and Historical Consciousness,' *Feminist Studies* 16 / 1 (1990): 115–50.

3 Bonnie Honig, 'Difference, Dilemmas, and the Politics of Home,' *Social Research* 61 / 3 (1994): 563–97.

4 bell hooks, 'Homeplace: A Site of Resistance,' in *Yearning: Race, Gender and Cultural Politics* (Boston, MA: South End Press, 1990), 41–9.

5.11 ARITHA VAN HERK
'Cleansing Dislocation: To Make Life, Do Laundry'*

Whether they experience forced, accidental, or chosen dislocation, women seek to make home in various ways. Making home is sharply distinct from 'homemaking,' with all its attendant abjections related to women's confinement within a domestic sphere. Making home is active, determinative, assertive. The agency exercised in making home bespeaks a configuration of belonging, a public declaration of the very opposite of dislocation, location. Home is the frontier that must assert its political, historical, and cultural legitimacy for women to move readily within and between every sphere. And in a world where boundaries shift with every fluid moment, how women make home is key to their strategy for not just survival but sustenance.

One declarative act, a powerful part of making, relates to the seemingly simple domestic task of the refreshment of clothing, doing laundry. The aesthetic of that quotidian commonplace – the cleaning and drying and pressing of clothing – encompasses both an act and composite noun. Laundry serves as a cultural marker, an index of women's position, a metaphor for both secrecy and visibility, a physical labour, a partner to water, and an apparatus of social declension. The representational position that laundry occupies, its implicit association with both filth and the erotic, its picturesque and metaphorical affect, and its sensory allusiveness all underscore the extent to which want of a clean shirt and not a horse might topple a kingdom. For women, the political and social value of laundry remarks a declension that crosses multiple boundaries. The work of laundry visibly addresses how soil and dirt are noticed, addressed, and erased. Clean clothing was ever the marker of order, control, and power. The symbolic associations of white linen with purity and propriety need not be reiterated. But as with the invisible barrier between the social and the political, the extent to which clean clothing demonstrates an at-home-ness is hardly noticed in the register of dislocation's effects. In fact, performing such ablutions signals women's coming to terms with changed circumstances. Historically, when women migrated to a place where even water and soap were difficult to access, they found a way to perform this 'household' task with what was at hand. So women's relation to laundry as marker and performance is then key to both survival and the more quotidian but equally compelling question of character.

---

* Madrid: International and Interdisciplinary Congress on Women's Worlds (Congreso Internacionale / Interdisciplinar Mundos de Mujeres), 2008.

Laundry demonstrates both exhaustion and exuberance, becomes a flag of colourful triumph to a crossed frontier.

A commonplace necessity, laundry as domestic verity has occupied an evasive and evaded position in the material world. Its representation in literature and art underscores the extent to which it has been sidelined, even when it serves as an important metaphor. This work is an inherently political act, not merely a domestic hobby that circulates time. The slippage that ignores the importance of laundry bespeaks a gendered geography in terms of the nature of this work in relation to what it might mean to a dislocated woman. Does laundry merely declare cleanliness, or has it come to occupy a liminal representational space, ever present, but never able to represent itself?

In a universe where women are given little authority, laundry becomes an alertly subversive task, an artistic declaration, an authoritative gesture. A woman who can make clean her own and her family's garments is a woman enacting a revolution within her home, but reaching also beyond that home. Laundry is what is carried out into the public realm on the backs of the women and children and men who centre themselves in a particular home. It is a demonstration and a flaunting, it is a costume or disguise that can help to negotiate an often unfriendly external world. The labour of *nettoyage* then, the cleaning of clothing, is a powerful assertion in any dislocating circumstance. It denotes both control and discipline, it is a creative demonstration of pride, and its accomplishment crosses the permeable barrier between the personal and the public. Part of the mainstream of living, it becomes an art taken for granted.

The very first literary reference to laundry underscores my argument. In Homer's *The Odyssey*, Odysseus, in his peripatetic journey home to his wife Penelope, is shipwrecked and washes ashore on the Phaeacian coast. He awakens to the sound of playful cries, the voices of young women. Athena, Odysseus' protector, the night previous invaded the dreams of the Phaeacian princess, Nausicaa, and persuaded her that she should wash her clothes on the following morning. Filthy and begrimed with salt, he creeps out from his hiding place, and holding a branch to conceal his genitals, begs Nausicaa to pity him, to take him to her city. Here lies Athena's plan: she establishes the situation to provide Odysseus, a dangerous stranger, with a way into what would otherwise be a closed city to him. [Nausicaa] calls back her frightened maids, orders them to give Odysseus food and drink, and to provide him with clean linen. He washes himself (note the connection between clean clothing and clean bodies), and then follows Nausicaa to the fortified city. Admitted under her protection, he tells his tale to her mother, Queen Arete, and her father, King Alcinous, and is granted asylum. Laundry and its accomplishment thus effectively transform Odysseus from dislocated castaway to conquering hero, the man who can return to his home. The manoeuvrings of Athena and Odysseus aside, this ardent and erotic description of washing clothes by the seashore raises intriguing questions. The combination of women and water recites an opportunity to overcome dislocation, to assert female agency, and to relate the domestic duties of women to a broader political realm. This, I would persist, articulates the power of the domestic over the unsettling effects of dislocation.

While some would argue that laundry is a part of an institutional and regulatory discipline that keeps women in line as surely as any overt expression of disapproval,[1] I would argue that laundry can also display a remarkable range of spectacle, disobedience, disclosure, and subversion. By exploring its quotidian erotic, it is possible to disclose a narrative that cleanses dislocation.

Washerwomen have certainly been subject to an artistic gaze, although painterly depictions inevitably present laundry as peripheral, an activity performed at the edges of the central action. Laundry is usually presented as more vehicle than occupation, a means to an end – and an end that is inevitably more significant than the [literal] cleaning of clothes, dirty clothes themselves, or the work at hand. Note, for example, Vincent Van Gogh's *The Drawbridge at Arles with a Group of Washerwomen* (1888) or Eugène-Louis Boudin's *Etretat, Laundresses on the Beach, Low Tide* (1890–94) visual representations that mirror laundry's capacity for transgression, yet also gesture towards the inherent comfort of its accomplishment, how that necessary act becomes itself a survival mechanism.

Historically, of course, domestic servitude served as an instrument of empire. As Anne McClintock has so acutely observed, 'the soap saga captured the hidden affinity between domesticity and empire and embodied a triangulated crisis in value: the undervaluation of women's work in the domestic realm, the overvaluation of the commodity in the industrial market and the disavowal of colonised economies in the arena of empire.'[2] Housewifery, then, configured as a career in vanishing acts (making work and dirt invisible) supports the commodity spectacle of female leisure.[3] The fetish for clean clothes (white, white, white) accompanied a powerful colonial thrust and drove a colonial reading of work (not only laundry) concerned with 'how to discipline the unsightly spectacle of paid women's work.'[4] Despite the extensive critical attention paid to labour history, laundry work continues to be ignored or shunted aside, perhaps because such work does not fit into conventional periods or categories. Laundry is both necessity and pleasure for a family but the work of laundry is relegated to a dislocated space of contingent value. This contingency is both acutely present and acutely historical. The second half of the nineteenth century was the heyday of laundry in Europe. Its documentation was and continues to be sporadic, secondary to investigations of other work, work accorded greater value. Further, because women who needed to make a living often used their homes to do laundry for others, such private labour has not been easily traced, a direct arrow pointing to the present when the value of women's work within the home is seldom accurately measured.

Clean laundry symbolizes order and orthodoxy, a triumph of invention over daily soil; as such, it speaks loudly for the care and concern of women who might be spatially, culturally, or even erotically dislocated. The demonstrably confident aesthetic of laundry as achievement becomes then an enabling instrument, a moment available to unmitigated pride.

Laundry's most subversive association has always been, and still is, that it is a metaphor for secrets. Tied to its amoral reputation is laundry's implicit association with the erotic. Laundry deals with the most private and suggestive articles of apparel. In the past, the physical situation of wash[er]women was seen as a site of possibility (Odysseus again). The world of laundry, both private and public, is thus available as a fascinating discursive site. It can be read as breeding a miasma of exhalations, as a warm and clean refuge from the world, as a space and place of drudgery, or as a cleansing site. In contemporary terms, the laundromat (see [the film] *My Beautiful Laundrette,* [1985]) can become a safe place for cruising, both homosexual and heterosexual.

Relegated to the invisible but necessary, laundry bears the metaphorical weight of the contradictory conjunction between cleanliness and dirt, appearance and admission, private and public, at-homeness in contrast to strangeness. Cleanliness is a display, a declaration; dirt is erased in an almost mysterious enactment, laundry's magic. Women in domestic service, relegated to the back door so that we need not witness their dislocation, become the world's conscience.

NOTES

1 Nancy Armstrong, 'Some Call It Fiction: On the Politics of Domesticity,' in Julie Rivkin and Michael Ryan, eds., *Literary Theory: An Anthology* (Oxford: Blackwell, 2004), 567–83.

2 Anne McClintock, *Imperial Leather: Race, Gender and Sexuality in the Colonial Context* (New York: Routledge, 1995), 207–8.

3 Ibid., 162.

4 Ibid.

CHAPTER SIX

Home Parts

This chapter takes us inside the domestic space to investigate specific objects, rooms, and arrangements. John Crowley's sketch of the development of the chimney fireplace implicitly queries Rybczynski's (see section 3.4 this volume) evolutionary approach to the history of home; Crowley traces the origins of privacy in residential architecture in the requirement to provide a private space for prayer in corporate religious institutions during the Middle Ages. Edgar Allan Poe, in his essay published while editor of *Burton's Gentleman's Magazine*, starts with a sprightly catalogue of various countries' deficiencies in interior decoration – sparing only the English – and launches a vehement attack against the American propensity to mistake ostentation for taste, offering advice on choosing elegant curtains, carpets, mirrors, windows, and paintings.

As Poe sketches the ideal dwelling with loving attention to the most minute detail, the atmosphere of repose he creates may seem odd for a man whose own writings reflected overwrought and gothic settings. However, the pattern of the arabesque, together with references to the grottoes of Stanfield and the Dismal Swamp of Chapman, ruffle this image of repose, suggesting that here, too, terror lurks under the surface. The sections by both Jean Baudrillard and Edith Wharton and Ogden Codman, Jr, discuss household and decorative objects in terms of functionality, aesthetics, and emotions. For, as Oscar Wilde instructed in his 1882 lecture, 'The House Beautiful,' one should have nothing in the house 'that has not given pleasure to the man [or woman] who made it and is not a pleasure to those who use it.'[1] As is apparent from Wharton and Codman's as well as Poe's essays, what gives pleasure is a question of taste, itself an evolving and contested concept. In tune with the spirit of modernity, what Adolf Loos will provocatively call the 'crime of ornament,'[2] Wharton and Codman protest against the clutter that dogged Victorian interior decoration and discuss the art of embellishment or ornaments in late nineteenth-century America in terms of taste and the scale of appropriateness. Anxious to distinguish interior decoration from the vulgar craft of the upholsterer and align it with art,[3] they complain that the substitution of hand-work with cheap machine-made knick-knacks and the unlimited reproduction of works of art debases the quality of decoration. Situating objects within the social relationships in a family, Baudrillard proposes that objects are carriers of emotional value and boundary markers of the symbolic configuration known as home. While the middle-class Western family home was an organism founded on tradition and authority, objects such as mirrors and clocks in the modern house are supple and mobile in their uses and have ceased to exercise or symbolize moral constraint. Catherine Beecher and Harriet Beecher Stowe, like Corbin and Teyssot (see Chapter 3 on Interiors), focus on hygiene and offensive odours. In their endorsement of the plea that 'the soil is not a warehouse to be plundered' and their acclamation of an 'earth-closet' for the elimination of human waste, they offer ecologically minded advice on sanitation for an American audience in the 1860s and 1870s. Katherine Ashenburg further elaborates on this aspect of the home through her lively presentation of the history and literary representations of the bathroom in the West. In her proposal for an ideal nursery, which reflects the emerging concern of the late Victorian period about hygiene in the home, Mrs C.S. (Dorothy Constance) Peel recognizes the importance of lighting, paint colour, and ventilation for the health and comfort of children. In his amusing overview of the changes in the use of the bedroom, Norbert Elias traces its evolution from the Middle Ages to a more private and intimate space in modernity. The pointedly erudite historical excursus on the history of the kitchen that frames Mrs Isabella Beeton's prescriptions to her mid-nineteenth-century British readership for efficient design is suggestive of an anxiety to confer dignity on the subject and on the domestic role of women. On the other hand, as Christopher Wilk describes, labour saving was the main preoccupation behind the mass-produced and efficient fitted kitchen designed by the Austrian communist and anti-fascist resistance fighter Grete Lihotsky (Margarete Schütte-Lihotsky), who drew on ergonomic studies of domestic labour to reduce women's work. By arguing that the application of efficiency principles in the home was propelled by the shortage of domestic service at the end of the nineteenth century and deepened the gulf between servants and their employers, Irene Cieraad provides an important insight into the socio-economic circumstances surrounding the development of the modern kitchen. Interviewed by Kathy Mezei about the appearance and role of the telephone and radio in the home, Stephen Kline explains the effects of media on privacy and family relationships. In 'What's "Home" Got to Do with It?' David Morley focuses on how we can understand the contradictory dynamics through which communications technologies have been domesticated at the same time that domesticity itself has been dislocated through technology.

NOTES

1 Oscar Wilde, 'The House Beautiful,' in Kevin O'Brien, *Oscar Wilde in Canada: An Apostle for the Arts* (Toronto: Personal Library Publishers, 1982), 166.

2 Adolf Loos, 'Ornament and Crime,' an essay in Bernie Miller and Melony Ward, eds., *Crime and Ornament: The Arts and Popular Culture in the Shadow of Adolf Loos* (Toronto: YYZ Books, 2002), 29–36, where he opined, 'the evolution of culture is synonymous with the removal of ornament from objects of daily use,' 30.

3 On the figure of the upholsterer, see Peter Thornton, *Authentic Décor: The Domestic Interior, 1620–1920* (London: Weidenfeld and Nicolson, 1984).

6.1 JOHN E. CROWLEY 'Chimneys and Privacy'*

The English term *chimney* derives closely from the French *cheminée*, whose etymology supposedly depends on the Latin *caminus*, relating to domestic and manufacturing furnaces. Another etymological candidate is *chemise*, referring to a cloth hanging from the mantle to keep smoke in the flue. French use of *cheminée* in its modern sense is documented from the twelfth century; English records begin to use *chimney* two centuries later. These differences of usage indicate both the French origins of the device and its relative infrequency in medieval England. Anglo-Saxon had no equivalent term; *fýr* signified both fire and hearth [...]

The technology of a flue to convey smoke from an open fire – a chimney – is ancient, but it was not used for Roman domestic heating. Roman domestic architecture used completely open and completely enclosed fires for heating. Roman families took their meals in the atrium, a partially roofed court named from the blackening smoke (*ater* = gloomy black) given off by open fires and braziers. The flue (*evaporatio fumi* or *exitus fumi*) was used in antiquity as a means to exhaust smoke from bake ovens and the furnaces of hypocausts (ancient Roman central heating systems), as well as to increase the draft in furnaces for thermal processes such as metalworking and ceramics. The term *caminus* referred to the furnace whose smoke such flues exhausted; it did not have a domestic reference because there were no chimney fireplaces in Roman houses [...]

Ecclesiastical Sources of Domestic Amenity

Plans from the 820s for the remodelling of the monastery of St Gall in Switzerland provide an almost unique, and certainly the richest, early reference in medieval European records to the likely use of fireplaces with chimneys to heat living areas. The plan used various Roman heating technologies. Chimneyless stove ranges heated baths and provided fires for the kitchen. Hypocaust-like facilities heated the plan's infirmary and novitiate. But the plans also called for chimney fireplaces (*caminata*) – in the abbot's house, the guest house, the house for bloodletting, and the physician's house, all of which were relatively private spaces outside the claustral precinct. Most of the officers of the

* In *The Invention of Comfort: Sensibilities and Design in Early Modern Britain and Early America* (Baltimore: Johns Hopkins University Press, 2001), 22–36.

monastery had chimney fireplaces in their quarters, while none of the workmen or monks without office did.[1] [...]

[...] The principle of flues for domestic hearths was known in the early Middle Ages from the technology of antiquity, and northern European building technology was compatible with the use of flues in houses, but apparently most medieval households resisted their adoption [...]

Monastic institutions like St Gall represented a rejection of traditional culture and everyday standards of living. In architecture this rationality articulated distinct spaces for different domestic activities – praying, eating (*frater*), sleeping (dormitory, or *dorter*), washing (*lavatorium*), even defecating (*reredorter*). This articulation of space contrasted sharply with the multipurpose use of space in secular dwellings. Even though monasteries too used hall-like spaces for most of their activities, the halls had specialized purposes. Similarly, the chambers that monasteries appropriated from secular architecture provided more intensive privacy than they did in familial households [...]

The monastic articulation of accommodation provided models for lay people to copy. Parlors were initially simple passageways separating the claustral precincts from outside. The outer parlor connected the cellarer's range with outside supplies, while the inner parlor (*locutorium* or slype), at one end of the *subdorter,* enabled monks to communicate with outsiders while remaining cloistered. In the eleventh century, abbots and priors still slept in the dorter with the other monks, but they had a privileged location at one end, toward the parlour. Since they had to deal with outsiders, they increasingly sought alternative accommodation in the cellarer's range. By the end of the twelfth century, abbots and priors had moved out of the dorter and into separate lodgings that included hall, chamber, and chapel. Once the abbot's accommodation moved out of the dorter, his house took over the parlour's communicative function spatially, and the parlour became a ground-floor room with functions and facilities overlapping those of both the hall and the chamber in secular dwellings. It provided a space to receive visitors with more privacy than was available in the hall but with less intimacy than meeting in the chamber implied. This reception room for visitors to monastic houses apparently provided the model and name for the parlour in secular dwellings. Its defining feature was a decorated fireplace [...]

Early-thirteenth-century monastic architecture frequently introduced chimneys for heating spaces other than the warming room, such as monks' cells and guests' quarters. By the same period the higher secular clergy, such as bishops and deans, had chambers with chimneys, apparently borrowed from monastic examples [...]

Even in the more whole-heartedly communal orders, there was a tendency in the fourteenth and fifteenth centuries to compromise communal life for individual accommodation. From the late fourteenth century until the dissolution of the monasteries, remodelings of monks' accommodation often followed standards previously applicable to monks in need of medical treatment or recuperation. In many monasteries healthy monks increasingly took meals in the infirmary, the misericord, where the enhanced diet included meat. The insertion of new floor levels into refectory halls divided them into meatless fraters, where the order's rule could be followed, while providing equal space for nominal misericorda. In the more indulgent dining area, chimney fireplaces took the place of the refectory's pulpitum. The remodelling of the infirmary at Westminster Abbey in the 1360s added chambers and parlors. Although infirmaries were intended for the 'transient sick,' monks soon occupied them permanently and appointed them with cushions and curtains [...]

A similar process of replacing communal living spaces with small residential units took place in nunneries in the fourteenth and fifteenth centuries. *Familiae,* small groups taking their meals together, effectively formed households within the larger nominal community. Sleeping accommodations became more private still, as separate spaces draped off within the dorter eventually were enclosed solidly as cells. These spaces allowed nuns to entertain visitors in quarters provided with fireplaces and windows, and furnished with wall hangings, chests, cupboards, and beds – just as the prioress had been accommodated all along [...]

Fourteenth-century colleges typically provided two-story ranges of rooms, with several students occupying each room as a sleeping space and each having a partitioned space for study. When heated, such rooms had chimneys, since the rooms' low ceilings precluded open hearths [...]

Chimneys were especially likely to be used in the accommodation of respectable people who lived in small or solitary households, namely the clergy. Numerous houses were built for chantry priests in the fifteenth century. Some of them were collegiate in scale, others had only a few priests and were domestic in scale. The latter typically had a ceiled hall with a wall chimney, and the priests' individual chambers also had chimneys. Such chimneys did not necessarily convey higher status than central hearths. In the late fifteenth century small priests' houses lacked a parlour but were more likely than large ones to have a chimney fireplace, rather than an open hearth, in their hall [...]

Use of chimneys in medieval accommodation corresponds in part with the clergy's increased preference for small, private spaces. This preference was most marked initially among the regular clergy, who already had a rationale for the importance of solitude, for prayer and study. In the twelfth and thirteenth centuries the higher secular clergy began to emulate monastic domestic accommodation and to preach their ideal of a more personal piety conducted in physical privacy. Such prayer called for special books – psalters and books of hours – and for a special place, the oratory, to read them. As oratories came into use for secular as well as pious activities, they became 'closets' – eventually, in the seventeenth century, the focus of amenity in an aristocratic dwelling.

NOTE

1 Walter Horn and Ernest Born, *The Plan of St Gall: A Study of Architecture and Economy of, and Life in a Paradigmatic Carolingian Monastery,* 3 vols. (Berkeley, CA: University of California Press, 1979), vol. 2, 124, 128.

6.2 EDGAR ALLAN POE 'The Philosophy of Furniture'*

In the internal decoration, if not in the external architecture of their residences, the English are supreme. The Italians have but little sentiment beyond marbles and colours. In France, *meliora probant, deteriora sequuntur* – the people are too much a race of gadabouts to maintain those household proprieties of which, indeed, they have a delicate appreciation, or at least the elements of a proper sense. The Chinese and most of the eastern races have a warm but inappropriate fancy. The Scotch are *poor* decorists. The Dutch have, perhaps, an indeterminate idea that a curtain is not a cabbage. In Spain they are *all* curtains – a nation of hangmen. The Russians do not furnish. The Hottentots and Kickapoos are very well in their way. The Yankees alone are preposterous.

How this happens, it is not difficult to see. We have no aristocracy of blood, and having therefore as a natural, and indeed as an inevitable thing, fashioned for ourselves an aristocracy of dollars, the *display of wealth* has here to take the place and perform the office of the heraldic display in monarchical countries. By a transition readily understood, and which might have been as readily foreseen, we have been brought to merge in simple *show* our notions of taste itself [...]

---

* [1840]. In *The Complete Works of Edgar Allan Poe,* edited by James A. Harrison, vol. 14, *Essays and Miscellanies* (New York: AMS Press, 1965), 101–9.

[...] In America, the coins current being the sole arms of the aristocracy, their display may be said, in general, to be the sole means of the aristocratic distinction; and the populace, looking always upward for models, are insensibly led to confound the two entirely separate ideas of magnificence and beauty. In short, the cost of an article of furniture has at length come to be, with us, nearly the sole test of its merit in a decorative point of view – and this test, once established, has led the way to many analogous errors, readily traceable to the one primitive folly.

There could be nothing more directly offensive to the eye of an artist than the interior of what is termed in the United States – that is to say, in Appallachia – a well-furnished apartment. Its most usual defect is a want of keeping. We speak of the keeping of a room as we would of the keeping of a picture – for both the picture and the room are amenable to those undeviating principles which regulate all varieties of art; and very nearly the same laws by which we decide on the higher merits of a painting, suffice for decision on the adjustment of a chamber.

A want of keeping is observable sometimes in the character of the several pieces of furniture, but generally in their colours or modes of adaptation to use. *Very* often the eye is offended by their inartistic arrangement. Straight lines are too prevalent – too uninterruptedly continued – or clumsily interrupted at right angles. If curved lines occur, they are repeated into unpleasant uniformity. By undue precision, the appearance of many a fine apartment is utterly spoiled.

Curtains are rarely well disposed, or well chosen in respect to other decorations. With formal furniture, curtains are out of place; and an extensive volume of drapery of any kind is, under any circumstance, irreconcilable with good taste – the proper quantum, as well as the proper adjustment, depending upon the character of the general effect.

Carpets are better understood of late than of ancient days, but we still very frequently err in their patterns and colours. The soul of the apartment is the carpet. From it are deduced not only the hues but the forms of all objects incumbent. A judge at common law may be an ordinary man; a good judge of a carpet *must be* a genius. Yet we have heard discoursing of carpets, with the air "*d'un mouton qui rêve*," fellows who should not and who could not be entrusted with the management of their own *moustaches*. Every one knows that a large floor *may* have a covering of large figures, and that a small one *must* have a covering of small – yet this is not all the knowledge in the world. As regards texture, the Saxony is alone admissible. Brussels is the preterpluperfect tense of fashion, and Turkey is taste in its dying agonies. Touching pattern – a carpet should *not* be bedizzened out like a Riccaree Indian – all red chalk, yellow ochre, and cock's feathers. In brief – distinct grounds, and vivid circular or cycloid figures, *of no meaning*, are here Median laws. The abomination of flowers, or representations of well-known objects of any kind, should not be endured within the limits of Christendom. Indeed, whether on carpets, or curtains, or tapestry, or ottoman coverings, all upholstery of this nature should be rigidly Arabesque. As for those antique floor-cloths still occasionally seen in the dwellings of the rabble – cloths of huge, sprawling, and radiating devices, stripe-interspersed, and glorious with all hues, among which no ground is intelligible – these are but the wicked invention of a race of time-servers and money-lovers – children of Baal and worshippers of Mammon – men who, to spare thought and economize fancy, first cruelly invented the Kaleidoscope, and then established joint-stock companies to twirl it by steam.

Glare is a leading error in the philosophy of American household decoration – an error easily recognised as deduced from the perversion of taste just specified. We are violently enamoured of gas and of glass. The former is totally inadmissible within doors. Its harsh and unsteady light offends [...]

In the matter of glass, generally, we proceed upon false principles. Its leading feature is *glitter* – and in that one word how much of all that is detestable do we express! Flickering, unquiet lights, are *sometimes* pleasing – to children and idiots always so – but in the embellishment of a room that should be scrupulously avoided. In truth, even strong *steady* lights are inadmissible. The huge and unmeaning glass chandeliers, prism-cut, gas-lighted, and without shade, which dangle in our most fashionable drawing-rooms, may be cited as the quintessence of all that is false in taste or preposterous in folly.

The rage for *glitter* – because its idea has become, as we before observed, confounded with that of magnificence in the abstract – has led us, also, to the exaggerated employment of mirrors. We line our dwellings with great British plates, and then imagine we have done a fine thing. Now the slightest thought will be sufficient to convince anyone who has an eye at all, of the ill effect of numerous looking-glasses, and especially of large ones. Regarded apart from its reflection, the mirror presents a continuous, flat, colourless, unrelieved surface, – a thing always and obviously unpleasant. Considered as a reflector, it is potent in producing a monstrous and odious uniformity: and the evil is here aggravated, not in merely direct proportion with the augmentation of its sources, but in a ratio constantly increasing. In fact, a room with four or five mirrors arranged at random, is, for all purposes of artistic show, a room of no shape at all. If we add to this evil, the attendant glitter upon glitter, we have a perfect farrago of discordant and displeasing effects [...]

But we have seen apartments in the tenure of Americans of modern [moderate?] means, which, in negative merit at least, might vie with any of the *ormolu'd* cabinets of our friends across the water. Even *now*, there is present to our mind's eye a small and not ostentatious chamber with whose decorations no fault can be found. The proprietor lies asleep on a sofa – the weather is cool – the time is near midnight: we will make a sketch of the room during his slumber.

It is oblong – some thirty feet in length and twenty-five in breadth – a shape affording the best (ordinary) opportunities for the adjustment of furniture. It has but one door – by no means a wide one – which is at one end of the parallelogram, and but two windows, which are at the other. These latter are large, reaching down to the floor – have deep recesses – and open on an Italian *veranda.* Their panes are of a crimson-tinted glass, set in rose-wood framings, more massive than usual. They are curtained within the recess, by a thick silver tissue adapted to the shape of the window, and hanging loosely in small volumes. Without the recess are curtains of an exceedingly rich crimson silk, fringed with a deep network of gold, and lined with silver tissue, which is the material of the exterior blind [...] The drapery is thrown open also, or closed, by means of a thick rope of gold loosely enveloping it, and resolving itself readily into a knot; no pins or other such devices are apparent. The colours of the curtains and their fringe – the tints of crimson and gold – appear everywhere in profusion, and determine the *character* of the room. The carpet – of Saxony material – is quite half an inch thick, and is of the same crimson ground, relieved simply by the appearance of a gold cord (like that festooning the curtains) slightly relieved above the surface of the *ground,* and thrown upon it in such a manner as to form a succession of short irregular curves – one occasionally overlaying the other. The walls are prepared with a glossy paper of a silver grey tint, spotted with small Arabesque devices of a fainter hue of the prevalent crimson. Many paintings relieve the expanse of paper. These are chiefly landscapes of an imaginative cast – such as the fairy grottoes of Stanfield, or the lake of the *Dismal Swamp* of Chapman. There are, nevertheless, three or four female heads, of an ethereal beauty – portraits in the manner of Sully. The tone of each picture is warm, but dark. There are no 'brilliant effects.' *Repose* speaks in all. Not one is of small size. Diminutive paintings give that *spotty* look to a room, which is the blemish of so many a fine work of Art overtouched [...] But one mirror – and this not a very large one – is visible. In shape it is nearly circular – and it is hung so that a reflection of the person can be obtained from it in none of the ordinary sitting-places of the room. Two large low sofas of rosewood and crimson silk, gold-flowered, form the only seats, with the exception of two light conversation chairs, also of rose-wood. There is a piano-forte (rosewood, also), without cover, and thrown open. An octagonal table, formed altogether of the richest gold-threaded marble, is placed near one of the sofas. This is also without cover – the drapery of the curtains has been thought sufficient. Four large and gorgeous Sèvres vases, in which bloom a profusion of sweet and vivid flowers, occupy the slightly rounded angles of the room. A tall candelabrum, bearing a small antique lamp with highly perfumed oil, is standing near the head of my sleeping friend. Some light and graceful hanging shelves, with golden edges and crimson silk cords with gold tassels, sustain two or three hundred magnificently bound books. Beyond these things, there is no furniture, if we except an Argand lamp, with a plain crimson-tinted ground-glass shade, which depends from the lofty vaulted ceiling by a single slender gold chain, and throws a tranquil but magical radiance over all.

6.3 JEAN BAUDRILLARD 'Structures of Interior Design'*

The Traditional Environment

The typical bourgeois interior is patriarchal; its foundation is the dining-room / bedroom combination. Although it is diversified with respect to function, the furniture is highly integrated, centring around the sideboard or the bed in the middle of the room. There is a tendency to accumulate, to fill and close off the space. The emphasis is on unifunctionality, immovability, imposing presence and hierarchical labelling. Each room has a strictly defined role corresponding to one or another of the various functions of the family unit, and each ultimately refers to a view which conceives of the individual as a balanced assemblage of distinct faculties. The pieces of furniture confront one another, jostle one another, and implicate one another in a unity that is not so much spatial as moral in character. They are ranged about an axis which ensures a regular chronology of actions; thanks to this permanent symbolization, the family is always present to itself. Within this private space each piece of furniture in turn, and each room, internalizes its own particular function and takes on the symbolic dignity pertaining to it – then the whole house puts the finishing touch to this integration of interpersonal relationships within the semi-hermetic family group.

All this constitutes an organism whose structure is the patriarchal relationship founded on tradition and authority, and whose heart is the complex affective relationship that binds all the family members together. Such a family home is a specific space which takes little account of any objective decorative

* In *The System of Objects* [1968], translated by James Benedict (London: Verso, 1996), 15–29.

requirements, because the primary function of furniture and objects here is to personify human relationships, to fill the space that they share between them, and to be inhabited by a soul [...] The real dimension they occupy is captive to the moral dimension which it is their job to signify. They have as little autonomy in this space as the various family members enjoy in society. Human beings and objects are indeed bound together in a collusion in which the objects take on a certain density, an emotional value – what might be called a 'presence.' What gives the houses of our childhood such depth and resonance in memory is clearly this complex structure of interiority, and the objects within it serve for us as boundary markers of the symbolic configuration known as home. The caesura between inside and outside, and their formal opposition, which falls under the social sign of property and the psychological sign of the immanence of the family, make this traditional space into a closed transcendence. In their anthropomorphism the objects that furnish it become household gods, spatial incarnations of the emotional bonds and the permanence of the family group. These gods enjoyed a gentle immortality until the advent of a modern generation which has cast them aside, dispersed them – even, on occasion, reinstated them in an up-to-date nostalgia for whatever is old. As often with gods, furniture too thus gets a second chance to exist, and passes from a naïve utility into a cultural baroque [...]

The Modern Object Liberated in Its Function

The style of furniture changes as the individual's relationships to family and society change. Corner divans and beds, coffee tables, shelving – a plethora of new elements are now supplanting the traditional range of furniture. The organization of space changes, too, as beds become day-beds and sideboards and wardrobes give way to built-in storage. Things fold and unfold, are concealed, appear only when needed. Naturally such innovations are not due to free experiment: for the most part the greater mobility, flexibility and convenience they afford are the result of an involuntary adaptation to a shortage of space – a case of necessity being the mother of invention. Whereas the old-fashioned dining-room was heavily freighted with moral convention, 'modern' interiors, in their ingeniousness, often give the impression of being mere functional expedients. Their 'absence of style' is in the first place an absence of room, and maximum functionality is a solution of last resort whose outcome is that the dwelling-place, though remaining closed to the outside, loses its internal organization. Such a restructuring of space and the objects in it, unaccompanied by any reconversion, must in the first instance be considered an impoverishment.

The modern set of furniture, serially produced, is thus apparently destructured yet not restructured, nothing having replaced the expressive power of the old symbolic order. There is progress, nevertheless, between the individual and these objects, which are now more supple in their uses and have ceased to exercise or symbolize moral constraint, there is a much more liberal relationship, and in particular the individual is no longer strictly defined through them relative to his family [...] Their mobility and multifunctionality allow him to organize them more freely, and this reflects a greater openness in his social relationships. This, however, is only a partial liberation. So far as the serial object is concerned, in the absence of any restructuring of space, this 'functional' development is merely an emancipation, not (to go back to the old Marxian distinction) a liberation proper, for it implies *liberation from the function of the object only, not from the object itself.* Consider a nondescript, light, foldable table or a bed without legs, frame or canopy – an absolute cipher of a bed, one might say: all such objects, with their 'pure' outlines, no longer resemble even what they are; they have been stripped down to their most primitive essence as mere apparatus and, as it were, definitively secularized. What has been liberated in them – and what, in being liberated, has liberated something in man (or rather, perhaps, what man, in liberating himself, has liberated in them) – is their function. The function is no longer obscured by the moral theatricality of the old furniture; it is emancipated now from ritual, from ceremonial, from the entire ideology which used to make our surroundings into an opaque mirror of a reified human structure. Today, at last, these objects emerge absolutely clear about the purposes they serve. They are thus indeed free as *functional objects* – that is, they have the freedom to function, and (certainly so far as serial objects are concerned) that is practically the *only* freedom they have [...]

Now, *just so long as the object is liberated only in its function, man equally is liberated only as a user of that object.* This too is progress, though not a decisive turning-point. A bed is a bed, a chair is a chair, and there is no relationship between them so long as each serves only the function it is supposed to serve. And without such a relationship there can be no space, for space exists only when it is opened up, animated, invested with rhythm and expanded by a correlation between objects and a transcendence of their functions in this new structure. In a way space is the object's true freedom, whereas its function is merely its formal freedom. The bourgeois dining-room was structured, but its structure was closed. The functional environment is more open, freer, but it is destructured, fragmented into its various functions. Somewhere between the two, in the gap between integrated psychological space and fragmented functional space, serial objects have their being, witnesses to both the one and the other – sometimes within a single interior [...]

Mirrors and Portraits

Another symptomatic change is the disappearance of looking-glasses and mirrors. A psycho-sociology of the mirror is overdue, especially in the wake of so much metaphysics. The traditional peasant milieu had no mirrors, perhaps even feared them as somewhat eerie. The bourgeois interior, by contrast, and what remains of that interior in present-day serially produced furniture, has mirrors in profusion, hung on the walls and incorporated into wardrobes, sideboards, cabinets or panelling. As a source of light, the mirror enjoys a special place in the room. This is the basis of the ideological role it has played, everywhere in the domestic world of the well-to-do, as redundancy, superfluity, reflection: the mirror is an opulent object which affords the self-indulgent bourgeois individual the opportunity to exercise his privilege – to reproduce his own image and revel in his possessions. In a more general sense we may say that the mirror is a symbolic object which not only reflects the characteristics of the individual but also echoes in its expansion the historical expansion of individual consciousness. It thus carries the stamp of approval of an entire social order: it is no coincidence that the century of Louis XIV is epitomized by the Hall of Mirrors at Versailles, nor that, in more recent times, the spread of mirrors in apartments coincided with the spread of the triumphal Pharisaism of bourgeois consciousness, from Napoleon III to Art Nouveau. But things have changed. There is no place in the functional ensemble for reflection for its own sake. The mirror still exists, but its most appropriate place is in the bathroom, unframed. There, dedicated to the fastidious care of the appearance that social intercourse demands, it is liberated from the graces and glories of domestic subjectivity. By the same token other objects are in turn liberated from mirrors; hence, they are no longer tempted to exist in a closed circuit with their own images. For mirrors close off space, presuppose a wall, refer back to the centre of the room. The more mirrors there are, the more glorious is the intimacy of the room, albeit more turned in upon itself. The current proliferation of openings and transparent partitions clearly represents a diametrically opposed approach. (Furthermore, all the tricks that mirrors make possible run counter to the current demand for a frank use of materials.) A chain has definitely been broken, and there is a real logic to the modern approach when it eliminates not only central or over-visible light sources but also the mirrors that used to reflect them; by thus eschewing any focus on or return to a central point, it frees space of the converging squint which gave bourgeois décor – much like bourgeois consciousness in general – such a cross-eyed view of itself [...]

Clocks and Time

Another illusion forsworn by the modern interior is the illusion of time. An essential object has vanished: the clock. It is worth recalling that although the centre of the peasant room is the fire and fireplace, the clock is nevertheless a majestic and living element therein. In the bourgeois or petty-bourgeois interior it takes the form of the clock that so often crowns the marble mantelpiece, itself usually dominated by a mirror above – the whole ensemble constituting the most extraordinary symbolic résumé of bourgeois domesticity. The clock is to time as the mirror is to space. Just as the relationship to the reflected image institutes a closure and a kind of introjection of space, so the clock stands paradoxically for the permanence and introjection of time. Country clocks are among the most sought-after of objects, precisely because they capture time and strip it of surprises within the intimacy of a piece of furniture. There is nothing in the world more reassuring. The measuring of time produces anxiety when it serves to assign us to social tasks, but it makes us feel safe when it substantializes time and cuts it into slices like an object of consumption. Everybody knows from experience how intimate a ticking clock can make a place feel; the reason is that the clock's sound assimilates the place to the inside of our own body. The clock is a mechanical heart that reassures us about our own heart. It is precisely this process of infusion or assimilation of the substance of time, this presence of duration, which is rejected, just like all other returns to inwardness, by a modern order based on externality, spatiality and objective relationships.

6.4 EDITH WHARTON AND OGDEN CODMAN JR 'Bric-à-Brac'*

It is perhaps not uninstructive to note that we have no English word to describe the class of household ornaments which French speech has provided with at least three designations, each indicating a delicate and almost imperceptible gradation of quality. In place of bric-à-brac, bibelots, *objets d'art,* we have only knick-knacks – defined by [James] Stormonth as "articles of small value."

* In *The Decoration of Houses* (New York: Charles Scribner's; London: B.T. Batsford, 1898), 184–195; Munby Rare Books Room, Cambridge University Library.

This definition of the knick-knack fairly indicates the general level of our artistic competence. It has already been said that cheapness is not necessarily synonymous with trashiness; but hitherto this assertion has been made with regard to furniture and to the other necessary appointments of the house. With knick-knacks the case is different. An artistic age will of course produce any number of inexpensive trifles fit to become, like the Tanagra figurines, the museum treasures of later centuries; but it is hardly necessary to point out that modern shop-windows are not overflowing with such immortal toys. The few objects of art produced in the present day are the work of distinguished artists. Even allowing for what [John Addington] Symonds calls the "vicissitudes of taste," it seems improbable that our commercial knick-knack will ever be classed as a work of art.

It is clear that the weary man must have a chair to sit on, the hungry man a table to dine at; nor would the most sensitive judgment condemn him for buying ugly ones, were no others to be had; but objects of art are a counsel of perfection. It is quite possible to go without them; and the proof is that many do go without them who honestly think to possess them in abundance. This is said, not with any intention of turning to ridicule the natural desire to 'make a room look pretty,' but merely with the purpose of inquiring whether such an object is ever furthered by the indiscriminate amassing of 'ornaments.' Decorators know how much the simplicity and dignity of a good room are diminished by crowding it with useless trifles. Their absence improves even bad rooms, or makes them at least less multitudinously bad. It is surprising to note how the removal of an accumulation of knick-knacks will free the architectural lines and restore the furniture to its rightful relation with the walls.

Though a room must depend for its main beauty on design and furniture, it is obvious that there are many details of luxurious living not included in these essentials. In what, then, shall the ornamentation of rooms consist? Supposing walls and furniture to be satisfactory, how put the minor touches that give to a room the charm of completeness? To arrive at an answer, one must first consider the different kinds of minor embellishment. These may be divided into two classes: the object of art *per se,* such as the bust, the picture, or the vase; and, on the other hand, those articles, useful in themselves, – lamps, clocks, fire-screens, bookbindings, candelabra, – which art has only to touch to make them the best ornaments any room can contain. In past times such articles took the place of bibelots. Few purely ornamental objects were to be seen, save in the cabinets of collectors; but when Botticelli decorated the panels of linen chests, and Cellini chiselled book-clasps and drinking-cups, there could be no thought of the vicious distinction between the useful and the beautiful. One of the first obligations of art is to make all useful things beautiful: were this neglected principle applied to the manufacture of household accessories, the modern room would have no need of knick-knacks [...]

An ornament is of course not an object of art because it is expensive – though it must be owned that objects of art are seldom cheap. Good workmanship, as distinct from designing, almost always commands a higher price than bad; and good artistic workmanship having become so rare that there is practically no increase in the existing quantity of objects of art, it is evident that these are more likely to grow than to diminish in value. Still, as has been said, costliness is no test of merit in an age when large prices are paid for bad things. Perhaps the most convenient way of defining the real object of art is to describe it as *any ornamental object which adequately expresses an artistic conception.* This definition at least clears the ground of the mass of showy rubbish forming the stock-in-trade of the average 'antiquity' dealer.

Good objects of art give to a room its crowning touch of distinction. Their intrinsic beauty is hardly more valuable than their suggestion of a mellower civilization – of days when rich men were patrons of 'the arts of elegance,' and when collecting beautiful objects was one of the obligations of a noble leisure. The qualities implied in the ownership of such bibelots are the mark of their unattainableness. The man who wishes to possess objects of art must have not only the means to acquire them, but the skill to choose them – a skill made up of cultivation and judgment, combined with that feeling for beauty that no amount of study can give, but that study alone can quicken and render profitable [...]

Two causes connected with the change in processes have contributed to the debasement of bibelots: the substitution of machine for hand-work has made possible the unlimited reproduction of works of art; and the resulting demand for cheap knick-knacks has given employment to a multitude of untrained designers having nothing in common with the *virtuoso* of former times [...]

It is no longer likely that any collector will be embarrassed by a superfluity of treasures; but he may put too many things into one room, and no amount of individual merit in the objects themselves will, from the decorator's standpoint, quite warrant this mistake. Any work of art, regardless of its intrinsic merit, must justify its presence in a room by being *more valuable than the space it occupies* – more valuable, that is, to the general scheme of decoration.

Those who call this view arbitrary or pedantic should consider, first, the importance of plain surfaces in decoration, and secondly, the tendency of overcrowding to minimize the effect of each separate object, however striking in itself. Eye and mind are limited in their receptivity to a certain number of simultaneous impressions, and the Oriental habit of displaying only one or two objects of art at a time shows a more delicate sense of these limitations than the Western passion for multiplying effects.

To sum up, then, a room should depend for its adornment on general harmony of parts, and on the artistic quality of such necessities as lamps, screens, bindings, and furniture. Whoever goes beyond these essentials should limit himself in the choice of ornaments to the 'labors of the master-artist's hand.'

6.5 CATHARINE E. BEECHER AND HARRIET BEECHER STOWE 'Earth-Closets'*

Earth-Closets

In some particulars, the Chinese are in advance of our own nation in neatness, economy, and healthful domestic arrangements. In China, not a particle of manure is wasted, and all that with us is sent off in drains and sewers from water-closets and privies, is collected in a neat manner and used for manure. This is one reason that the compact and close packing of inhabitants in their cities is practicable, and it also accounts for the enormous yields of some of their crops.

The earth-closet is an invention which relieves the most disagreeable item in domestic labor, and prevents the disagreeable and unhealthful effluvium which is almost inevitable in all family residences. The general principle of construction is somewhat like that of a water-closet, except that in place of water is used dried earth. The resulting compost is without disagreeable odor, and is the richest species of manure. The expense of its construction and use is no greater than that of the common water-closet; indeed, when the outlays for plumber's work, the almost inevitable troubles and disorders of water-pipes in a house, and the constant stream of petty repairs consequent upon careless construction or use of water-works are considered, the earth-closet is in itself much cheaper, besides being an accumulator of valuable matter.

To give a clear idea of its principles, mode of fabrication, and use, we can not do better than to take advantage of the permission given by Mr. George E. Waring, Jr., of Newport, R.I., author of an admirable pamphlet on the subject,

---

* In *The American Woman's Home: or, Principles of Domestic Science; Being a Guide to the Formation and Maintenance of Economical, Healthful, Beautiful, and Christian Homes* (New York: J.B. Ford and Company, 1869), 403–18; British Library, London, England.

published in 1868 by 'The Tribune Association' of New-York. Mr. Waring was formerly Agricultural Engineer of the New-York Central Park, and has given much attention to sanitary and agricultural engineering, having published several valuable works bearing in the same general direction. He is now consulting director of 'The Earth-Closet Company,' Hartford, Ct., which manufactures the apparatus and all things appertaining to it – any part which might be needed to complete a home-built structure [...]

In the brief introduction to his pamphlet, Mr. Waring says:

> It is sufficiently understood, by all who have given the least thought to the subject, that the waste of the most vital elements of the soil's fertility, through our present practice of treating human excrement as a thing that is to be hurried into the sea, or buried in underground vaults, or in some other way put out of sight and out of reach, is full of danger to our future prosperity.
>
> Our bodies have come out of our fertile fields; our prosperity is based on the production and the exchange of the earth's fruits; and all our industry has its foundation in arts and interests connected with, or dependent on, a successful agriculture.
>
> Liebig asserts that the greatness of the Roman empire was sapped by the *Cloaca Maxima,* through which the entire sewage of Rome was washed into the Tiber. The yearly decrease of productive power in the older grain regions of the West, and the increasing demand for manures in the Atlantic States, sufficiently prove that our own country is no exception to the rule that has established its sway over Europe.
>
> The large class who will fail to feel the force of the agricultural reasons in favour of the reform which this pamphlet is written to uphold, will realize, more clearly than farmers will, the importance of protecting dwellings against the gravest annoyance, the most fertile source of disease, and the most certain vehicle of contagion.

Nevertheless, Mr. Waring thinks that the agricultural argument is no mean or unimportant one, and says:

> The importance of any plan by which the excrement of our bodies may be returned to our fields is in a measure shown in the following extract from an article that I furnished for the *American Agricultural Annual* for 1868.
>
> The average population of New-York City – including its temporary visitors – is probably not less than 1,000,000. This population consumes food equivalent to at least 30,000,000 bushels of corn in a year. Excepting the small proportion that is stored up in the bodies of the growing young, which is fully offset by that contained in the bodies of the dead, the constituents of the food are returned to the air by the lungs and skin, or are voided as excrement. That which goes to the air was

originally taken from the air by vegetation, and will be so taken again: here is no waste. The excrement contains all that was furnished by the mineral elements of the soil on which the food was produced.

This all passes into the sewers, and is washed into the sea. Its loss to the present generation is complete.

… 30,000,000 bushels of corn contain, among other minerals, nearly 7000 tons of phosphoric acid, and this amount is annually lost in the wasted night-soil of New-York City […]

Practically the human excrement of the whole country is nearly all so disposed of as to be lost to the soil. The present population of the United States is not far from 35,000,000. On the basis of the above calculation, their annual food contains 200,000 tons of phosphoric acid, being the amount contained in about 900,000 tons of bones, which, at the price of the best flour of bone, (for manure), would be worth over $50,000,000. It would be a moderate estimate to say that the other constituents of food are of at least equal value with the other constituents of the bone, and to assume $50,000,000 as the money value of the wasted night-soil of the United States every year.

In another view, the importance of this waste can not be estimated in money. Money values apply, rather, to the products of labour and to the exchange of these products. The waste of fertilizing matter reaches farther than the destruction or exchange of products: it lessens the ability to produce.

If mill-streams were failing year by year, and steam were yearly losing force, and the ability of men to labor were yearly growing less, the doom of our prosperity would not be more plainly written, than if this slow but certain impoverishment of our soil were sure to continue.

… But the good time is coming, when (as now in China and Japan) men must accept the fact that the soil is not a warehouse to be plundered – only a factory to be worked. Then they will save their raw material, instead of wasting it, and, aided by nature's wonderful laws, will weave over and over again the fabric by which we live and prosper. Men will build up as fast as men destroy; old matters will be reproduced in new forms, and, as the decaying forests feed the growing wood, so will all consumed food yield food again.

[…] The following information and statements are appropriated bodily, either directly or with mere modifications for brevity, from the little pamphlet of Mr. Waring.

The earth-closet is the invention of the Rev. Henry Moule, of Fordington Vicarage, Dorsetshire, England.

It is based on the power of clay, and the decomposed organic matter found in the soil, to absorb and retain all offensive odors and all fertilizing matters; and it consists, essentially, of a mechanical contrivance (attached to the ordinary seat) for measuring out and discharging into the vault or pan below a sufficient quantity of sifted dry earth to entirely cover the solid ordure and to absorb the urine.

The discharge of earth is effected by an ordinary pull-up similar to that used in the water-closet, or (in the self-acting apparatus) by the rising of the seat when the weight of the person is removed.

The vault or pan under the seat is so arranged that the accumulation may be removed at pleasure.

From the moment when the earth is discharged, and the evacuation is covered, all offensive exhalation entirely ceases. Under certain circumstances, there may be, at times, a slight odor as of guano mixed with earth; but this is so trifling and so local, that a commode arranged on this plan may, without the least annoyance, be kept in use in any room.

This statement is made as the result of personal experience. Mr. Waring says:

> I have in constant use in a room in my house an earth-closet commode; and even when the pan is entirely full, with the accumulation of a week's use, visitors examining it invariably say, with some surprise, 'You don't mean that this particular one has been used!'[…]
>
> The truth is, that the machinery is more simple, much less expensive, and far less liable to injury than that of the water-closet. The supply of earth to the house is as easy as that of coals. To the closet it may be supplied more easily than water is supplied by a forcing-pump, and to the commode it can be conveyed just as coal is carried to the chamber. After use, it can be removed in either case by the bucket or box placed under the seat, or from the fixed reservoir, with less offence than that of the ordinary slop-bucket – indeed (I speak after four years' experience), with as little offence as is found in the removal of coal-ashes. So that, while servants and others will shrink from novelty and at first imagine difficulties, yet many, to my knowledge, would now vastly prefer the daily removal of the bucket or the soil to either the daily working of a forcing-pump or to being called upon once a year, or once in three years, to assist in emptying a vault or cesspool.

To the above complete and convincingly apt arguments and statements of fact, we do not care to add any thing. All that we desire is to direct public attention to the admirable qualities of this Earth System, and to suggest that, at least for those living in the country away from the many conveniences of city life, great water power, and mechanical assistance, the use of it will conduce largely to the economy of families, the health of neighborhoods, and the increasing fertility and prosperity of the country round about.

6.6 KATHERINE ASHENBURG
A Short History of the Newest and Sometimes Smallest Room

Thinking about the history of the bathroom brings Oscar Wilde's bon mot about America – 'the only country that passed from barbarism to decadence without civilization in between' – to mind. The bathroom, the newest room, must be the room that passed from birth to decadence most quickly. North American bathrooms have tripled in size since the 1990s, and are equipped with mistless mirrors, scales that calculate muscle / fat ratios, and infinity-edge tubs that seat four and fill in sixty seconds. Bathrooms are promoted as the last word in family togetherness ('the new family room') or as sybaritic fantasy (inspired by Japan or Imperial Rome).

Even for a bath-loving culture such as ancient Rome, these bathrooms would have come as a surprise. A bathroom in a private house was rare and relatively spartan in Rome, reserved for the rich. The best and most luxurious bathing for all classes was the public bathhouse. That belief lasted until the Black Death convinced a terrified Europe that the plague entered the body through pores that had been opened by hot water. From the fourteenth century until the eighteenth or nineteenth, depending on class and country, the best bath was no bath at all, just a change of linen.

When people began to wash again in Europe, in a very gingerly way, most saw no need for a separate room for this dubious practice. Marie Antoinette, who bathed every morning covered modestly in a large flannel nightgown, had her tin tub carried into her bedroom and removed after the bath.[1] So long as maids and menservants were available to transport the tub and water, there was no great urgency to leave the bedroom for a bath. In the 1920s, Lady Fry spoke for many in her class when she declared that 'bathrooms were for servants.'[2]

But for those without a large staff, a room with a fixed bathtub connected to plumbing made sense. First seen in British and American house plans around the 1840s, the new room, spelled 'bath-room,' was just that, a room with a bathtub. At first, the toilet was in a separate and usually more unobtrusively located room, but Americans soon decided that combining the two and consolidating the plumbing was practical. The British continued to think that mixing ablution with evacuation was indelicate: Charles Dickens, designing a very modern and expensive bath-plus-shower for his new London house just off Tavistock Square in 1851, fretted only half-jokingly to his architect that contemplating the W.C. while bathing would affect his bowels.[3] It is still possible to find, in early twentieth-century houses in Commonwealth and European countries, a separate room for the toilet.

The sink, surprisingly, was the last element in what is now the usual bathroom trio. A basin and ewer had been standard bedroom equipment in the nineteenth century, to be used for washing hands and face, strategic spot-cleaning, and even an all-over stand-up bath. The woman in Mary Cassatt's 1891 painting *La Toilette* (ca. 1891) has stripped to the waist to wash her top half in a small basin in her bedroom. Even when there was a room with a bathtub down the hall, it seemed natural to undertake less drastic cleansing in the privacy of the bedroom. As plumbing became more efficient and people more accustomed to using a bathroom, the sink finally took its place there at the very end of the nineteenth century. The new room took hold. At first, it only appeared on the second and higher floors, because no lady could be seen entering it. (When outhouses were the norm, the ladies took a discreet 'turn in the garden' when nature called. In Robertson Davies' novel *What's Bred in the Bone,* Francis Cornish's early twentieth-century Ontario house is mildly scandalous for the number of its bathrooms and especially for the presence of a ground-floor washroom with toilet, 'so that you couldn't decently conceal where you were going when you went.'[4])

In existing houses, the first bathroom was likely to be large, because it was a converted bedroom or dressing room, as in the case of Brideshead. In Evelyn Waugh's novel, *Brideshead Revisited,* the aristocratic Flytes had converted a dressing room at the beginning of the twentieth century into the latest modern improvement by simply replacing a bed with 'a deep, copper, mahogany-framed bath, that was filled by pulling a brass lever heavy as a piece of marine engineering.' Otherwise the room remained unchanged, and its coal fire, paintings, and upholstered furniture are still in place when Charles bathes there in the 1920s. Remembering it two decades later, he writes, 'I often think of that bathroom – the water colours dimmed by steam and the huge towel warming on the back of the chintz armchair – and contrast it with the uniform, clinical, little chambers, glittering with chromium-plate and looking-glass, which pass for luxury in the modern world.'[5]

In new houses at the beginning of the twentieth century, it was 'the smallest room,' a euphemism still in use in Britain. Bathrooms were furnished according to the national spirit: seductive, ultra-feminine lairs in France; clinical marvels of technology in America, cosy and homelike in Britain. But even in Britain, the machinery could be terrifying. In her memoir *Period Piece,* Gwen Raverat describes her uncle's London bathroom at the start of the twentieth century. Uncle William incorporated a few foibles into his bathroom, such as a bookcase filled with literature not suitable for young ladies, and photographs of classical nude statues. But Raverat was not inclined to linger over art or literature in that alarming bathroom. 'The enormous mahogany-sided bath was approached by two steps, and had a sort of grotto containing a shower-bath at one end; this was lined with as many different stops as the organ in King's Chapel. And it was as difficult to control as it would be for an amateur to play that organ. Piercing jets of boiling, or ice-cold, water came roaring at one from the most unexpected angles, and hit one in the tenderest spots. Only Uncle William was not afraid of the monster; but he had perfect physical courage.'[6]

Bathing, which brings together nudity and sparkling water, has always tempted the painter. Medieval artists loved painting the luxurious and often scandalous goings-on in bathhouses, when elaborately jewelled and hatted but otherwise nude women cavorted with men in bathtubs built for two. In the four or five centuries after the Black Death when Europeans shunned washing, those painterly celebrations of water and the body stopped, but as people returned to bathing in the nineteenth century, painters returned to the bath. Ingres, Jean-Léon Gerôme, and others painted exotic and erotic fantasies of the Turkish bath, filled with lavish expanses of decorated tiles and womanly flesh, white in the case of the client and black in the case of the bath attendant. European women, most famously painted by Edgar Degas and Pierre Bonnard, washed themselves in more austere surroundings, often in a sponge bath, a small, low tub that accommodated about six inches of water and a squatting or sitting bather. The sponge bath suited painters better than a bigger tub for it exposed more of the body, which could be interestingly contorted to scrub a foot or peruse a derrière. Sometimes the equipment and the rooms intrigue even more than the bodies: the Japanese pattern on the ewer in Mary Cassatt's *La Toilette;* the copper boiler filled with hot water for the tub in Ramon Casas's *Preparing for the Bath* (1894); the homely, rustic look of the room in Bonnard's photograph of his wife in her sponge bath, called *Marthe in the Tub* (1908).[7]

It is only a century since Bonnard photographed Marthe, but what a transformation from the functional simplicity of the Bonnards' bathroom to the over-the-top *luxe* of the twenty-first-century bathroom. Whether you define decadence as a four-poster bathtub or a waterproof plasma television screen (both are available), the bathroom has now become an inner sanctum where hedonism, narcissism, and hygiene scrupulosity meet.

NOTES

1 Jeanne Louise Henriette Campan, *The Private Life of Marie Antoinette* (New York: Brentano's, 1917), vol. 1, 96. [No translator given.]
2 Jill Franklin, *The Gentleman's Country House and Its Plan, 1835–1914* (London: Routledge and Kegan Paul, 1981), 112.
3 Charles Dickens, *The Letters of Charles Dickens,* edited by Graham Storey and K.J. Fielding (Oxford: Clarendon Press, 1981), vol. 5, 583; vol. 6, 502, 520.
4 Robertson Davies, *What's Bred in the Bone* (Toronto: Macmillan, 1985), 54–5.

5 Evelyn Waugh, *Brideshead Revisited* (London: Penguin, 1962), 148–9.
6 Gwen Raverat, *Period Piece: A Cambridge Childhood* (London: Faber and Faber, 1968), 182–3.
7 The bathing pictures mentioned, and many others, can be seen in Françoise de Bonneville, *The Book of the Bath*, translated by Jane Brenton (New York: Rizzoli, 1998).

6.7 MRS C.S. PEEL
'The Nurseries and the Schoolroom'*

Yet another important point is the lighting of the nurseries. Undoubtedly electric light is the ideal illuminant. It does not poison or overheat the air, is cleanly, safe, and convenient. It should of course be carefully shaded with green shades, otherwise it is too glaring to be good for the eyes of young babies, for whom it always appears to have a marvellous fascination. Next to electric light gas is to be advised, as being far safer than lamps or candles. When the latter are used they should be placed well out of the reach of the children, the best plan being to have iron holders fixed high up on the walls. Having provided the nurseries with dark green blinds, they are now ready to receive the furniture, which should be of a simple description. White enamelled furniture looks fresh and pretty, but it is scarcely to be advised if great economy is necessary. In that case the Austrian bent-wood furniture is excellent, for it is strong and can be washed all over with a disinfectant if needful. As a matter of fact, but little furniture will be required in the day nursery. A good steady table and a sufficiency of chairs, one or two wicker bentwood easy chairs (one of these without arms for the convenience of the person who nurses a small baby), a table on which to place the feeding paraphernalia, a screen, and a good cupboard in which to keep the nursery teathings, toys, etc., a set of fire-irons, high-guard, and coal-box are the principal items. The night nursery should contain a small iron bed with a wire mattress for the nurse, the children's cots, a dressing-chest and hanging cupboard for the nurse, and a large cupboard in which the children's clothes can be kept, a good wash-hand-stand, a couple of chairs, a fire guard, coal

* In *The New Home: Treating of the Arrangement Decoration and Furnishing of a House of Medium Size to Be Maintained by a Moderate Income* (Westminster: Archibald Constable & Co., 1898), 208–20; Munby Rare Books Room, Cambridge University Library.

box and irons, medicine cupboard, thermometer, and small wooden clothes-horse. The linen-basket should on no account be kept in the room.

Now as we aspire (so far as our moderate means will permit) to make the new home thoroughly healthy and comfortable as well as pleasing to the eye, it is to be hoped that both a day and a night nursery can be allowed. If this is impracticable we need not despair, for with careful management it is possible to arrange matters satisfactorily, always supposing that not more than one nurse and one, or at most two, little children have to be housed. It will only be necessary under these circumstances, to attend more carefully than ever to the ventilation of the room, and to avoid an overcrowding of furniture. If on the other hand a room for a night nursery is available, it should be decorated in quiet peaceful colours, such as blue or green.

6.8 NORBERT ELIAS 'On Behavior in the Bedroom'*

Examples

A
Fifteenth century.

From *Stans puer in mensam,* an English book of table manners from the period 1463–1483:

And if that it forten so by
  nyght or Any tyme
That you schall lye with Any man
  that is better than you
Spyre hym what syde of the bedd
  that most best will ples hym,
And lye you on thi tother syde,
  for that is thi prow;
Ne go you not to bede before bot
  thi better cause the,

* In *The Civilizing Process: The History of Manners and State Formation and Civilization* [1939], translated by Edmund Jephcott (Oxford: Blackwell, 1994), 132–8.

For that is no curtasy, thus seys
doctour paler.

223 And when you arte in thi bed,
this is curtasy,
Stryght downe that you lye with
fote and hond.
When ze have talkyd what ze
wyll, byd hym gode nyght in hye
For that is gret curtasy so schall
thou understand.

Let your better choose which side of the bed he'll lie on; don't go to bed first, till he asks you to (says Dr Paler).

When you're both in bed, lie straight, and say "Good night" when you've done your chat.

B

1530. From *De civilitate morum puerilium,* by Erasmus, ch. 12, "On the Bedchamber":

When you undress, when you get up, be mindful of modesty, and take care not to expose to the eyes of others anything that morality and nature require to be concealed.

If you share abed with a comrade, lie quietly; do not toss with your body, for this can lay yourself bare or inconvenience your companion by pulling away the blankets.

C

1555. From *Des bonnes moeurs et honnestes contenances,* by Pierre Broë (Lyons, 1555):

If you share abed with another man, keep still.
Take care not to annoy him or expose yourself by abrupt movements.
And if he is asleep, see that you do not wake him.

D

1729. From La Salle, *Les Règles de la bienséance et de la civilité chrétienne* (Rouen, 1729), p. 55:

You ought … neither to undress nor go to bed in the presence of any other person. Above all, unless you are married, you should not go to bed in the presence of anyone of the other sex.

It is still less permissible for people of different sexes to sleep in the same bed, unless they are very young children …

If you are forced by unavoidable necessity to share a bed with another person of the same sex on a journey, it is not proper to lie so near him that you disturb or even touch him; and it is still less decent to put your legs between those of the other …

It is also very improper and impolite to amuse yourself with talk and chatter …

When you get up you should not leave the bed uncovered, nor put your nightcap on a chair or anywhere else where it can be seen.

E

1774. From La Salle, *Les Règles de la bienséance et de la civilité chrétienne* (1774 ed.) p. 31:

It is a strange abuse to make two people of different sex sleep in the same room.

And if necessity demands it, you should make sure that the beds are apart, and that modesty does not suffer in any way from this commingling. Only extreme indigence can excuse this practice …

If you are forced to share a bed with a person of the same sex, which seldom happens, you should maintain a strict and vigilant modesty …

When you have awakened and had sufficient time to rest, you should get out of bed with fitting modesty and never stay in bed holding conversations or concerning yourself with other matters … nothing more clearly indicates indolence and frivolity; the bed is intended for bodily rest and for nothing else.

Comments on the Examples

1. The bedroom has become one of the most 'private' and 'intimate' areas of human life. Like most other bodily functions, sleeping has been increasingly shifted behind the scenes of social life. The nuclear family remains as the only legitimate, socially sanctioned enclave for this and many other human functions. Its visible and invisible walls withdraw the most 'private,' 'intimate,' irrepressibly 'animal' aspects of human existence from the sight of others.

In medieval society this function had not been thus privatized and separated from the rest of social life. It was quite normal to receive visitors in rooms with beds, and the beds themselves had a prestige value related to their opulence. It was very common for many people to spend the night in one room: in the upper class, the master with his servants, the mistress with her maid or maids; in other classes, even men and women in the same room […] and often guests staying overnight […]

2. Those who did not sleep in their clothes undressed completely. In general, people in lay society slept naked, and in the monastic orders either fully dressed or fully undressed according to the strictness of the rules [...]

This unconcern in showing the naked body, and the position of the shame frontier represented by it, are seen particularly clearly in bathing manners. It has been noted with surprise in later ages that knights were waited on in their baths by women; likewise, their night drink was often brought to their beds by women. It seems to have been common practice, at least in the towns, to undress at home before going to the bathhouse [...]

This unconcern disappeared slowly in the sixteenth and more rapidly in the seventeenth, eighteenth, and nineteenth centuries, first in the upper classes and much more slowly in the lower. Up to then, the whole mode of life, with its greater closeness of individuals, made the sight of the naked body, at least in the proper place, incomparably more commonplace than in the first stages of the modern age [...] People had a less inhibited – one might say a more childish – attitude toward the body, and to many of its functions. Sleeping customs show this no less than bathing habits.

3. A special nightdress slowly came into use at roughly the same time as the fork and handkerchief. Like the other 'tools of civilization,' it made its way through Europe quite gradually. And like them it is a symbol of the decisive change taking place at this time in human beings. Sensitivity toward everything that came into contact with the body increased. Shame became attached to behavior that had previously been free of such feelings. The psychological process which is already described in the Bible by – 'and they saw that they were naked and were ashamed' – that is, an advance of the shame frontier, a thrust toward greater restraint – is repeated here, as so often in the course of history. The lack of inhibition in showing oneself naked disappears, as did that in performing bodily functions before others. And as this sight became less commonplace in social life, the depiction of the naked body in art took on a new significance. More than hitherto it became a dream image, an emblem of wish-fulfilment. To use Schiller's terms it became 'sentimental,' as against the 'naïve' form of earlier phases [...]

4. The examples give a rough idea of how sleep, becoming slowly more intimate and private, is separated from most other social relations, and how the precepts given to young people take on a specific moralistic undertone with the advance of feelings of shame. In the medieval quotation (Example A) the restraint demanded of young people is explained by consideration due to others, respect for social superiors. It says, in effect, 'If you share your bed with a better man, ask him which side he prefers, and do not go to bed before he invites you, for that is not courteous.' And in the French imitation of Johannes Sulpicius by Pierre Broë (Example C), the same attitude prevails: 'Do not annoy your neighbor when he

has fallen asleep; see that you do not wake him up, etc.' In Erasmus we begin to hear a moral demand, which requires certain behavior not out of consideration for others but for its own sake: 'When you undress, when you get up, be mindful of modesty.' But the idea of social custom, of consideration for others, is still predominant. The contrast to the later period is particularly clear if we remember that these precepts, even those of Dr Paler (Example A), were clearly directed to people who went to bed undressed. That strangers should sleep in the same bed appears, to judge by the manner in which the question is discussed, neither unusual nor in any way improper even at the time of Erasmus.

In the quotations from the eighteenth century this tendency is not continued in a straight line, partly because it is no longer confined predominantly to the upper class. But in the meantime, even in other classes, it has clearly become less commonplace for a young person to share his bed with another: 'If you are forced by unavoidable necessity to share a bed with another person … on a journey, it is not proper to lie so near him that you disturb or even touch him,' La Salle writes (Example D). And: 'You ought neither to undress nor go to bed in the presence of any other person.'

In the 1774 edition, details are again avoided wherever possible. And the tone is appreciably stronger. 'If you are forced to share a bed with a person of the same sex, which seldom happens, you should maintain a strict and vigilant modesty' (Example E). This was the tone of moral injunction. Even to give a reason had become distasteful to the adult. The child is made by the threatening tone to associate this situation with danger. The more 'natural' the standard of delicacy and shame appears to adults and the more the civilized restraint of instinctual urges is taken for granted, the more incomprehensible it becomes to adults that children do not have this delicacy and shame by 'nature' […]

The examples on behavior in the bedroom give, for a limited segment, a certain impression of how late it really was that the tendency to adopt such attitudes reached its full development in secular education.

The line followed by this development scarcely needs further elucidation. Here, too, in much the same way as with eating, the wall between people, the reserve, the emotional barrier erected by conditioning between one body and another, has grown continuously. To share a bed with people outside the family circle, with strangers, is made more and more embarrassing. Unless necessity dictates otherwise, it becomes usual even within the family for each person to have his own bed and finally – in the middle and upper classes – his own bedroom. Children are trained early in this isolation from others, with all the habits and experiences that this brings with it. Only if we see how natural it seemed in the Middle Ages for strangers and for children and adults to share a bed can we appreciate what a fundamental change in interpersonal relationships and behavior is expressed in our manner of living. And we recognize how far from self-evident it is that the bed and body should form such psychological danger zones as they do in the most recent phase of civilization.

6.9 MRS ISABELLA BEETON
'Arrangement and Economy of the Kitchen'*

'The distribution of a kitchen,' says Count Rumford, the celebrated philosopher and physician, who wrote so learnedly on all subjects connected with domestic economy and architecture, 'must always depend so much on local circumstances, that general rules can hardly be given respecting it; the principles, however, on which this distribution ought, in all cases, to be made, are simple and easy to be understood,' and, in his estimation, these resolve themselves into symmetry of proportion in the building and convenience to the cook. The requisites of a good kitchen, however, demand something more special than is here pointed out. It must be remembered that it is the great laboratory of every household, and that much of the 'weal or woe,' as far as regards bodily health, depends upon the nature of the preparations concocted within its walls. A good kitchen, therefore, should be erected with a view to the following particulars: (1) Convenience of distribution in its parts, with largeness of dimension; (2) Excellence of light, height of ceiling, and good ventilation; (3) Easiness of access, without passing through the house; (4) Sufficiently remote from the principal apartments of the house, that the members, visitors, or guests of the family, may not perceive the odour incident to cooking, or hear the noise of culinary operations; (5) Plenty of fuel and water, which, with the scullery, pantry, and storeroom, should be so near it, as to offer the smallest possible trouble in reaching them.

The kitchens of the Middle Ages, in England are said to have been constructed after the fashion of those of the Romans. They were generally octagonal, with several fireplaces, but no chimneys; neither was there any wood admitted into the building [...] Some kitchens had funnels or vents below the eaves to let out the steam, which was sometimes considerable, as the

* In *The Book of Household Management* (London: S.O. Beeton, 1861), 25–38; Munby Rare Books Room, Cambridge University Library.

Anglo-Saxons used their meat chiefly in a boiled state. From this circumstance, some of their large kitchens had four ranges, comprising a boiling-place for small boiled meats, and a boiling-house for the great boiler. In private houses the culinary arrangements were no doubt different; for Du Cange mentions a little kitchen with a chamber, even in a solarium, or upper floor.

The simplicity of the primitive ages has frequently been an object of poetical admiration, and it delights the imagination to picture men living upon such fruits as spring spontaneously from the earth, and desiring no other beverages to slake their thirst, but such as fountains and rivers supply. Thus, we are told, that the ancient inhabitants of Argos lived principally on pears; that the Arcadians revelled in acorns, and the Athenians in figs. This, of course, was in the golden age, before ploughing began, and when mankind enjoyed all kinds of plenty without having to earn their bread 'by the sweat of their brow.' This delightful period, however, could not last for ever, and the earth became barren, and continued unfruitful till Ceres came and taught the art of sowing, with several other useful inventions. The first whom she taught to till the ground was Triptolemus, who communicated his instructions to his countrymen the Athenians. Thence the art was carried into Achaia, and thence into Arcadia. Barley was the first grain that was used, and the invention of bread-making is ascribed to Pan [...]

In the primary ages it was deemed unlawful to eat flesh, and when mankind began to depart from their primitive habits, the flesh of swine was the first that was eaten. For several ages, it was pronounced unlawful to slaughter oxen, from an estimate of their great value in assisting men to cultivate the ground; nor was it usual to kill young animals, from a sentiment which considered it cruel to take away the life of those that had scarcely tasted the joys of existence.

At this period no cooks were kept, and we know from Homer that his ancient heroes prepared and dressed their victuals with their own hands. Ulysses, for example, we are told, like a modern charwoman, excelled at lighting a fire, whilst Achilles was an adept at turning a spit [...]

The age of roasting we may consider as that in which the use of the metals would be introduced as adjuncts to the culinary art; and amongst these, iron, the most useful of them all, would necessarily take a prominent place. This metal is easily oxidized, but to bring it to a state of fusibility, it requires a most intense heat. Of all the metals, it is the widest diffused and most abundant; and few stones or mineral bodies are without an admixture of it. It possesses the valuable property of being welded by hammering; and hence its adaptation to the numerous purposes of civilized life [...]

In the arts it is employed in three states: as *cast* iron, *wrought* iron, and *steel*. In each of these it largely enters into the domestic economy, and stoves, grates, and the general implements of cookery, are usually composed of it. In antiquity, its employment was, comparatively speaking, equally universal. The excavations made at Pompeii have proved this [...] [See Knights, section 3.2 in this volume.]

From kitchen ranges to the implements used in cookery is but a step. With these, every kitchen should be well supplied, otherwise the cook must not be expected to 'perform her office' in a satisfactory manner. Of the culinary utensils of the ancients, our knowledge is very limited; but as the art of living, in every civilized country, is pretty much the same, the instruments for cooking must, in a great degree, bear a striking resemblance to each other. On referring to classical antiquities, we find mentioned, among household utensils, leather bags, baskets constructed of twigs, reeds, and rushes; boxes, basins, and bellows; bread-moulds, brooms, and brushes; caldrons, colanders, cisterns, and chafing-dishes; cheese-rasps, knives, and ovens of the Dutch kind; funnels and frying-pans; handmills, soup-ladles, milk-pails, and oil-jars; presses, scales, and sieves; spits of different sizes, but some of them large enough to roast an ox; spoons, fire-tongs, trays, trenchers, and drinking-vessels; with others for carrying food, preserving milk, and holding cheese. This enumeration, if it does nothing else, will, to some extent, indicate the state of the simpler kinds of mechanical arts among the ancients.

6.10 CHRISTOPHER WILK

'Frankfurt Kitchen, 1926–7. Designed by Grete Lihotsky (Margarete Schütte-Lihotsky; 1897 Vienna–2000 Vienna). From the Am Höhenblick Housing Estate, Ginnheim, Frankfurt'*

The vast Frankfurt housing projects built by Ernst May's Municipal Building Department (where architect Grete Lihotsky worked[1]) aimed to standardize building elements and mechanize construction along Taylorist and Fordist lines.[2] These attempts at rationalisation and efficiency applied also to the design of flats and, notably, to the design of this kitchen, versions of which were installed in around 10,000 of the Frankfurt flats. The Frankfurt Kitchen (as it was known at the time) was not the first fitted kitchen, or even the earliest Modernist fitted kitchen, but it was the first to be made in quantity (Figure 11). It was undoubtedly the most successful and influential kitchen of the period, and stood as a symbol of the principles of 'scientific' professionalisation of the domestic workspace.[3]

Like many designers aiming at efficiency in the home, Lihotsky would have been conversant with Erna Meyer's hugely popular manual for the home, *Der neue Haushalt* (The New Household, 1926), which was itself based on the classic American text *The New Housekeeping: Efficiency Studies in Home Management* (1913) by Christine Frederick. In these, the bodily movements and circulation patterns of the housewife as she engaged in daily work were analysed to arrive at new principles for household design and labour. These were reflected in the close analysis of the positioning of each element of the Frankfurt Kitchen in relation to others to minimize unnecessary steps, and in the provision of features aimed at saving labour and providing physical comfort. Among these were the work table for preparing food under a light-giving window and adjacent to the sink, both at a height for using while seated; the storage chutes with handles and pouring spouts for dry comestibles, obviating the need for the steps involved in opening cupboards, then jars, and spooning out the contents, and the drop-down ironing board, omitting the need for another object requiring assembly and storage.

---

* In *Modernism: 1914–1939, Designing a New World,* edited by Christopher Wilk (London: Victoria & Albert Publications, 2006), 180–1.

11 The Frankfurt Kitchen by Margarete Schütte-Lihotsky, 1927. Inv. No. 50/8/FW. Copyright © Universität für angewandte Kunst Wien, Kunstsammlung und Archiv (University of Applied Arts, Vienna, Collection and Archive).

Not only was the idea of labour-saving important to the layout of the kitchen, but it was central to its construction and cheap price. The cabinets had no backs and, owing to the continuity of the units, there was just one side wall required. Financing was offered to flat residents to enable them to buy a kitchen, which they paid off through their monthly rent.[4] The kitchen was made in three sizes, to fit different flats, including those with no servants, one or even two servants (which was possible even for those living in municipal housing, given the low wage costs at the time). The small size of the kitchen reflected a pursuit of efficiency, the belief that eating in the kitchen was unhygienic, and a desire to save space for the living areas of the flat. The principle of the compact kitchen owes much to the design of galleys in ships and trains of the era.[5]

NOTES

1 The kitchen came from a flat at Kurhessenstrasse 132, 2nd floor. The estate was also referred to as the *Siedlung Ginnheimer Hang* (Ginnheim Hillside Estate), in 'Führer durch die Frankfurter Siedlungen,' *Das Neue Frankfurt* 2/78 (1928): 136. [*Das Neue Frankfurt* also published the first article on the kitchen by Grete Lihotsky.]

2 'Internationaler Verband für Wohnungswesen,' *Wohnungspolitik der Stadt Frankfurt am Main* (Frankfurt [1929]), 31, 33.

3 Modernist experiments in rational kitchen design pre-dating the Frankfurt Kitchen included those at the Haus am Horn exhibition house at the Bauhaus exhibition of 1923. Anton Brenner's Vienna Living Machine Project (1924), Gustav Wolf's kitchen for the Westfalian Heimstätte, and Bruno Taut's in Berlin Zehlendorf (1926). See Marjan Boot and Marisella Casciato, *La casalinga riflessiva: La cucina razionale come mito domestico* (exh. cat., Palazzo delle Esposizioni, Rome, 1983), and Bettina Rink and Joachim Kleinmanns, *Küchentraüme* (exh. cat., Lippischen Landesmuseums, Detmold, 2005).

4 The cost of a kitchen has been calculated at 1.5 times the monthly income of a factory worker [...]

5 Susan R. Henderson, in 'A Revolution in the Woman's Sphere: Grete Lihotzky and the Frankfurt Kitchen,' in Debra Coleman, Elizabeth Danze, and Carol Henderson, eds., *Architecture and Feminism* (New York: Princeton University Press, 1996), 235, has pointed out the similar influences on the nineteenth-century authors Catharine Beecher and Harriet Beecher Stowe in their *The American Woman's Home* (1869). [See section 6.5 in this volume.]

6.11 IRENE CIERAAD
'"Out of My Kitchen!" Architecture, Gender and Domestic Efficiency'*

Efficiency Reconsidered

The link between kitchen and the image of the professional housewife is claimed to be a result of the twentieth-century ideology of efficiency. It was in origin an American economic ideology to minimalise time and effort in labour processes in order to save money and to speed up industrial production. An ideology basically comprised as 'time is money.' The names of Americans Frederick Taylor and Henry Ford are inextricably linked with the ideology of efficiency, for Taylor provided the scientific justification and Ford its practical application. By systematically measuring the time of each movement in the performance of a task, the engineer Frederick Taylor demonstrated the effectiveness of his theory of scientific management [...] The factory system of assembly-lines introduced by Henry Ford in the production of motorcars was one of the first and famous examples of industrial efficiency. That is why the ideology of efficiency is also known as Taylorism or Fordism [...]

But how was industrial efficiency related to kitchen design? Household chores seem to have nothing in common with an industrial assembly-line. Moreover, to compare the non-profit labour of love of a mother and full-time housewife with the economic law of 'time is money' would have been an insult to the women involved. Another American, a woman this time, was responsible for the relation between efficiency and kitchen design: Christine Frederick, author of the influential book *The New Housekeeping: Efficiency Studies in Home Management*. The book was published in 191[3] and a year later followed by another book, entitled *Household Engineering: Scientific Management in the Home* [...] In translation the Dutch title of her book was changed into 'The Thinking Housewife.' This abridged title reflected Frederick's scientific aspirations in its stress on thinking before acting.

[Frederick] demonstrated in the book how a kitchen had to be designed to become an efficient workshop requiring the workforce of only one well-trained woman. The secret of kitchen efficiency, according to Frederick, was to arrange all you will need for the cooking of a meal on one side of the kitchen and all you need for dish-washing on the opposite side. By effectively contrasting the efficient, step-saving arrangement of kitchen cabinets, sink and cooking-range

---

* *Journal of Architecture* 7 / 3 (2002): 263–79.

to the inefficient arrangement in which a housewife criss-crosses the kitchen when preparing a meal and doing the dishes, she clarified her point. Without the help of a servant, a professional housewife was capable of managing the household on her own. Providing that the housewife could rely on new electrical appliances like a vacuum cleaner and a washing machine, Frederick claimed that these machines were more reliable and certainly more efficient, than the ever-troublesome domestic servant.

Here we touch upon the real impetus for introducing efficiency in the home. Domestic servants were hard to get and their loyalty was in dispute. They easily switched employers when offered better earnings or working conditions. At the end of the nineteenth century the employment options for girls widened. Domestic service, once the most respectable job for a working-class girl, became the least desirable, compared to the fixed working hours in offices and factories. The shortage of servants had become a true societal problem, first in the United States of America, but a decade later also in most western European countries. With the exception of Germany perhaps, for the economic crisis after World War I forced many well-educated German girls into Dutch domestic service, where they were gladly accepted [...]

That is why the twentieth-century link between housewifery and kitchen had everything to do with the work and domain of the nineteenth-century domestic servant [...] The kitchen was not only the workshop of domestic servants but also their living space. Although nineteenth-century kitchens were not designed according to the principles of efficiency, they were on the whole far more spacious than the cramped, but efficient twentieth-century kitchens. In a nineteenth-century town-house the kitchen was either situated at the back of the house or in the basement: the notorious hierarchy of upstairs-downstairs. The architecture of an upper-class town-house reflected the prevailing social hierarchy, in particular the inferior position of domestic servants. Separate staircases, servant doors and servant rooms were constructed to prevent frequent contact between family members and servants.

At the end of the nineteenth century the architectural separation of family and staff was facilitated by modern technology. With a speaking-tube, the precursor of the telephone, madam – seated in the dining-room upstairs – was able to give orders and communicate with her servant downstairs. Very efficient and step-saving, for the speaking-tube spared the servant the pain of extra walks up and down the stairs to receive her orders. Another efficient, nineteenth-century kitchen technology was the electric bell combined with a panel indicating in what room the service of the domestic servant was required. On the one hand, both the speaking-tube and the bell system were very efficient domestic technologies. On the other, however, they contributed to an instrumental and less personal relation between servant and mistress and in doing so they reinforced in a more subtle way the subordination of servants [...] In short: the first domestic application of efficiency principles was a nineteenth-century solution to economise domestic service and preceded in history the later publication of Christine Frederick's book on efficiency in the home.[1] Moreover, it is often forgotten that efficiency's true principle 'time is money' was born out of a social inequity between wage-labour and capital.

NOTE

1 Research has indicated that Christine Frederick was not the first American woman to apply efficiency standards in the home, but that she was part of a typical American tradition in so-called Christian home-making of which Catharine E. Beecher and Harriet Beecher Stowe, authors of *The American Woman's Home: Or Principles of Domestic Space; Being a Guide to the Formation and Maintenance of Economical Healthful, Beautiful, and Christian Homes* (1869), were the forerunners [see section 6.5 in this volume] [...] In contrast to the efficiency ideology of 'time is money,' the economising principles of the Beecher sisters were morally inspired and attended to the health and well-being of the inhabitants of the home and to the protection of the body as God's temple from evil influences and exhaustion.

6.12 STEPHEN KLINE, INTERVIEWED BY KATHY MEZEI, 2009 The Telephone and the Radio Enter the Home

KM: How did the telephone and the radio enter the home post–First World War? And what significance did this have on family and social relationships?

SK: The first medium to have significant impact on the household and the first one that presented a problem was the telephone. Telephones tended to be wall mounted because they were heavier and more solid than contemporary phones. This caused debates about where in the house to put them (often the hallway was the site of choice), and problems as well since people tended to shout down them and could be heard throughout the house. Thus, the whole notion of privacy within the domestic space was compromised. There is more: the first-wave telephones were mostly on party lines. So historically over the twentieth century the telephone, which we think of as a person-to-person device, was actually a location-to-location kind of technology for multiple users.

KM: Let's take Canada as an example. When did the telephone enter the home in this country?

SK: It depends on where you are talking about in Canada, but in any case before the First World War. But only within the upper middle classes or really wealthy classes; there could be homes that had a telephone fairly soon after their production but they wouldn't have been useful because who could you talk to?

KM: But you could phone a business or the doctor if the doctor had a phone …

SK: That's right – calls to the doctor and such gave impetus for subsequent waves of diffusion. And then interestingly the notion and design of the phone began to change. Phones used to be designed as merely functional things. They were ugly, except in retrospect when we think of them as kitschy, quaint. They were all black, made of classic bakelite, and not meant to be a piece of the furniture. Then after the Second World War, the telephone began to be advertised as part of home decor and came in different colours and configurations; it became more decorative, sleeker, modern.

KM: What was the effect of the phone on the family?

SK: Arguments occurred around the telephone with children and teenagers using it all the time; dilemmas about managing the single phone led to the proliferation of phones, one in each bedroom … or a phone on a long line that could be taken into a private bedroom …

KM: What about the shift from the dial phone, to the push button phone?

SK: This was part of the digital move; the rotary dial system depends on sound, and once you have a digital processor you no longer need the rotary sounds; the digital interface is much easier. The technology listened to the pulses as you dialled and translated those pulses into a representation that could dial out properly.

KM: Think about the role that the sound of dialling played in movies! You made a very interesting point that in the early days there were issues of privacy around the phone. Now that almost everyone has their own telephone, their own cell phone how would you relate this to privacy? Paradoxically, now that the cell phone is so common it is also common for people to speak loudly in public and show no concern for their own – or others' – privacy.

SK: It's one of those McLuhanesque reversals; for although the technology becomes very private, 'this is my phone to your phone,' the way people use it makes it more public. People are behaving as if they were talking in the privacy of their own bedroom but in fact they are out there in public. The technology changes the definitions of public and private space and the 'protocols' or social mores surrounding the use of new technologies need to be redefined. We need a new morality because it's difficult to legislate talking in public – maybe we need social marketing campaigns to 'respect other people's privacy on the bus.'

KM: What about radio?

SK: Radio was probably the next major communication technology and of course it went through a very similar process. It eventually replaced the phonograph – which, in turn, replaced the family piano – but very often during the [19]20s and [19]30s the radio came built into the phonograph. Arguably these were the first multi-media devices. People used to make their own music, but with the phonograph and later the radio you could have Yehudi Menuhin playing in your own living room – the first name for it was 'the home concert hall.'

KM: Yes, [there were] photographs of the family sitting around the radio which had the prominent position in the living room …

SK: Very often the technologies coming into the home are at first appropriated into patterns developed about prior technologies. I believe that is a basic McLuhan point, and it is a very important one to remember. It explains why the radio came into the home in the way it did and was associated with cabinetry and design and never appeared as functional in the way the phone did. Already it was a designed wooden box object with finished decor. From the first mass-produced model it was something you could put on a shelf in the living room as a design object … In McLuhan's analysis the reporting of the Second World War brought new salience to the radio. Its role was to inform the public and impart propaganda; it wasn't just for listening to music, it wasn't just associated with music like the phonograph. It became an item on its own through which information was also being disseminated. Of course it's hard for us again to remember the huge part that radio played within the war unless you go back and watch the old footage. Much later – with digitalization – the radio moved into the bedroom; the merger of the clock and the radio in the 1970s – multimedia – only came with digitalization. Until recently almost everyone had a radio.

KM: Yes, young people don't seem to listen to radios – they have iPhones, iPods, or computers, and Internet.

SK: The radio pattern is interesting but it's history. It becomes more privatized because people are living on different schedules, and so once it takes on that waking function the temporalities of domestic life determine the need for multiple radios … So each child would have one in their room, and the parents would have one, because everyone is on a different schedule. Think of the old grandfather clock: one clock rang the time, and you had uniform time within the house. That one chiming clock marking time for the one family has completely gone. The clocks are on the same time but each person's schedule is different.

KM: How do you see the evolution of the radio in the home – is its evolution similar to the telephone? What about the portable radio, the Walkman, the iPod?

SK: People have done a lot of writing on the Walkman and the transistor radio. Making the radio more portable was hugely important and you get the boom box as an exemplification of that principle of discrete media. But most of the media emerged in some kind of synergy. Now people talk about convergence, and convergence in the phone. But this is a very old pattern. If you trace the history you realize that multimedia or convergence has always been an option and that there is a relationship between these different media. The contents and forms of media change to adjust to other media. My argument is that there are important continuities. The big transition was the initial phonograph or the radio. You shifted from playing music yourself to listening to it; you became a consumer. As for these other media – computers, iPods, etc., we are still consumers.

.13 DAVID MORLEY
'What's "Home" Got to Do with It? Contradictory Dynamics in the Domestication of Technology and the Dislocation of Domesticity'*

Under the impact of new technologies and global cultural flows, the home nowadays is not so much a local, particular or 'self-enclosed' space, but rather, as Zygmunt Bauman puts it, more and more a 'phantasmagoric' place, as electronic means of communication allow the radical intrusion of what he calls the 'realm of the far' (traditionally, the realm of the strange and potentially troubling) into the 'realm of the near' (the traditional 'safe space' of ontological security).[1] Electronic media can thus also be argued to produce a psychic effect which we might describe as that of the 'domestication of elsewhere' – a process whereby Hollywood brings images of the streets of the 'global cities' of the world to people everywhere, without their having ever visited them [...]

But we should still remember that, nonetheless, whatever range of imagery they may be familiar with, for most viewers, their 'horizons of action' – that sense of the scale on which they can act meaningfully in the world – are still very limited [...] Thus, global cultural forms still have to be made sense of within the context of what, for many people, are still very local forms of life [...]

Returning [...] to Foucault's insistence that our analyses must be sensitive both to the 'grand strategies of geopolitics' and the 'little tactics of the habitat,'[2]

---

* *European Journal of Cultural Studies* 6 / 4 (2003): 435–58.

my analysis of the interlinked processes of globalization and domestication will attempt to bring together micro and macro issues. I want here to address questions of identity from the point of view of how we understand the idea of home and to address questions of technology from the point of view of how we can understand the process of domestication.

In doing so, I shall talk at some length about TV – long the principal focus of media studies. However, by way of acknowledging the age of media convergence in which we find ourselves, I will also situate TV within the broader context of the significance of a range of other communications technologies.[3] […]

In this context, I also want to develop a perspective that tries to articulate the symbolic with the material dimensions of analysis. Lynn Spigel puts this point another way when she argues that the 'simultaneous rise of the mass produced suburb and ubiquitous place called "Television-Land" raises a set of questions that scholars have only recently begun to ask.'[4] […]

Spigel argues that, in the North American context at least, we can usefully understand the genealogy of ideas about domesticity in a media-saturated world as developing through three main phases in the post–[Second World] War period. The first phase involved the model of the 'home theatre' […] With the advent of portable TV sets in the USA in the 1960s, designed to symbolize the aspirations of what the industry now figured as a more active and mobile audience of 'people on the go,' this model, Spigel claims, was superseded by the (still dominant) model of the 'mobile home,' characterized not so much by mobile privatization as by what she calls 'privatized mobility.'

In the latest stage of these developments […] we see the model of the digitalized 'smart house' […] which offers not so much an image of mobility but of a 'sentient space,' which, we are often told, so thoroughly transcends the divisions of inside / outside and work / home as to make it unnecessary to actually go anywhere anymore.[5] In its digitalized form, the home itself can then be seen as having become, in Virilio's terms, the 'last vehicle,' where comfort, safety, and stability can happily coexist with the possibility of an instantaneous digitalized 'flight' to elsewhere or the instantaneous importation of desired elements of 'elsewhere' into the home.[6] Nonetheless […] all this 'hi-tech' discourse is often carefully framed and domesticated by a rather nostalgic vision of 'family values.' […]

[…] The dynamics at play in the entry of TV and other media to the home are complicated, as we know. If, as Barthes once argued, TV 'condemns us to the family, whose household utensil it has become, just as the communal stewing pot was, in times gone by,'[7] so too we have to note the ways in which the nature of domestic life itself has effects on how TV is consumed. We also have to attend to the ways in which the nature of TV programming has itself been designed for the specific forms of (distracted) spectator attention routinely available in the home. Moreover, as Spigel points out, the material structure of the home itself was also gradually redesigned, in architectural terms (for example, the invention of the 'through lounge'), to accommodate the needs of TV viewing.[8] There is a complex symbiosis at play here, as TV and other media have adapted themselves to the circumstances of domestic consumption while the domestic arena itself has been simultaneously redefined to accommodate their requirements [...]

The Domestication of TV

[...] My own primary concern [...] is with what Maud Lavin calls the 'intimate histories' of living with a medium such as broadcast TV. This Lavin describes as involving 'a collection of personal memories of growing up with TV [...] [of] how the TV set [has been] gradually incorporated into the home, family and leisure time [...] and [the] history of how we design our spaces, habits and even emotions around the TV.'[9] This is a question of how our personal memories – especially of childhood – are formulated around media experiences such as emblematic programmes and TV characters. In this respect, we might usefully draw a parallel with Gaston Bachelard's analysis of how the material structure of the house provides the 'trellis' around which childhood memory is entwined – but perhaps we now need to extend the analogy so as to think also of how that trellis now has a mediated, as much as a material, structure [...]

From this perspective, we perhaps also need to treat TV not so much as a visual medium, but as a visible object [...] because, as Matthew Geller puts it, too often we simply 'look through' the object of TV to the images it provides, while the set remains, as it were, 'invisible' to us and we ignore its role as a totemic object of enormous symbolic importance in the household.[10] It is in this context that we must also address the long history of TV's domestication, as we trace its journey from its initial position as a singular 'stranger,' allowed only into the most public / formal space of the house (in the living room), through the development of the multiset household and TV's gradual penetration of the more intimate spaces of our kitchens and bedrooms, to the point where the new individualized / personal media delivery systems, in their latest portable and miniaturized forms, might more properly be conceptualized as 'body parts.' [...]

Domesticating the Future

[...] If the future represents, for many people, a troublesome realm of constant change, much of this trouble comes to be symbolized by (and in) technological forms. The question, therefore, is how this problematic technological realm comes to be naturalized and domesticated so as to make it less threatening and more manageable for its inhabitants.

Many years ago, Bausinger argued that the everyday was coming to be characterized in the affluent West by what he called the 'inconspicuous omnipresence of the technical.'[11] In the research on the domestic use of information and communications technologies in which I have been involved,[12] one of the most striking findings was how, in many households, people went to a great deal of trouble to disguise the presence of communications technologies in their homes, often hiding TV sets, computers and wiring in wooden cabinets or behind soft furnishings. The point is that, if an increasing array of technologies has now become naturalized to the point of literal (or psychological) invisibility in the domestic sphere, we need to understand the process of how that has come about.

The other reason why a historical perspective on new media should be central to our approach to these issues is because the dynamic of making technologies consumer-friendly in practice often means inserting them into recognizable forms from previous eras. To this extent, technological innovation often goes along with a continuing drive to make the techno-future safe by incorporating it into familiar formats, icons, and symbols [...]

Moreover, the process of domestication of the media goes further than this [...] With the advent of the electronic 'dreamhouse' – whether in the earlier versions that Spigel describes in the 1950s and 1960s or nowadays in Bill Gates's own 'fully wired' domestic paradise, as analysed by Allon[13] – we arrive at a new situation. Here, rather than technologies being domesticated, as in the case of the 'smart house,' the domestic realm itself is mediated and made fully electronic. In this vision of the household, the technologies are no longer merely supplementary to, but constitutive of, what the home itself is now [...]

And Now? De-Domesticated / ing Media?

Thus far, in my narrative, I have traced the long story of the gradual domestication of a range of media, most particularly TV, and have taken the 'smart house' as the culmination or 'end point' of this story, where the home itself becomes a fully technologised / wired place and comes to be defined by the techniques that constitute it [...] However, it would be argued that we now face the beginning of a quite different story, where the narrative drive runs in the opposite direction, towards the de-domestication of the media and the radical dislocation of domesticity itself. In many countries, TV began as a public medium, watched collectively in public places, and only gradually moved into the home and then in its further interstices [...] However, it is evident that, having thoroughly colonized the home, TV has now re-escaped from its confines. Nowadays, we find TV everywhere, in the public spaces of bars, restaurants, laundrettes, shops, and airports [...]

These developments also need to be understood in the broader theoretical context of debates about the ongoing transformation of the relationships between the public and private spheres [...] If one of the key historical roles of broadcasting technologies has been their transformation of the relations of the public and private spheres, then the questions that face us now concern what these new technologies do to those relations and how they, in turn, may be regulated and domesticated. We now find ourselves in a world where we are all audiences to one or another medium, almost all of the time, and where, after its long process of domestication, TV and other media have now escaped home – to (re)colonize the public sphere. While the domestic home itself might now be said to have become a fully technological artefact, it also seems that domesticity itself has now been dislocated.

NOTES

1 Zygmunt Bauman, *Community: Seeking Safety in an Insecure World* (Cambridge: Polity Press, 2001).

2 Michel Foucault, 'Questions of Geography,' in C. Gordon, ed., *Michel Foucault: Power / Knowledge: Selected Interviews and Other Writings, 1972–1977* (New York: Pantheon, 1980), 63–77.

3 [Editors' note: We acknowledge that the abridged version of this essay does not do justice to the author's declared intent to avoid the 'technologically determinist vision [...] that unfortunately characterizes so much current work on the "new media."']

4 Lynn Spigel, *Welcome to the Dreamhouse* (Durham, NC: Duke University Press, 2001), 15.

5 Lynn Spigel, 'Media Homes: Then and Now,' *International Journal of Cultural Studies* 4 / 4 (2001): 386, 398.

6 Paul Virilio, *Lost Dimension* (New York: Semiotext(e), 1991). Cited in Spigel, 'Media Homes,' 400.

7 Roland Barthes, 'On Leaving the Movie Theatre,' in Theresa Hak Kyung Cha, ed., *Apparatus* (New York: Tanam Press, 1980), 1.

8 Lynn Spigel, *Make Room for TV* (Chicago, IL: University of Chicago Press, 1992).

9 Maud Lavin, 'TV Design,' in Matthew Geller, ed., *From Receiver to Remote Control: The TV Set* (New York: New Museum of Contemporary Art, 1990), 85.

10 Matthew Geller, *From Receiver to Remote Control,* 7.

11 Hermann Bausinger, 'Media, Technology and Daily Life,' *Media, Culture and Society* 6 (1984), 343–51.

12 Roger Silverstone and Eric Hirsch, eds., *Consuming Technologies: Media and Information in Domestic Spaces* (London: Routledge, 1992).

13 Spigel, *Welcome to the Dreamhouse;* Fiona Allon, 'Altitude Anxiety: Being At-Home in a Globalised World,' Ph.D. dissertation, University of Technology, Sydney, Australia, 2000.

CHAPTER SEVEN

Liminal Spaces

This chapter looks at those spaces that negotiate the relationship between inside and outside, private and public, such as doors, gardens, or windows. Georg Simmel describes the functions, metaphysics, and aesthetics of the door in relation to and as a kind of 'bridge.' He differentiates between the door and the window, contending that, although doors and windows are similar in that they both connect the interior to the exterior, the window is only meant for looking out. The door, which forms a link between human space and the outside, is however, a mode of *both* separation and connection. Simmel's perspective is turned around in the interiors of the modernist architect, Adolf Loos, where, as Beatriz Colomina notes, the window is only a source of light that contributes to the theatricality of the interior, directing the gaze of the onlooker, occupant, or voyeur towards the inside. Olivier Marc's Jungian approach leads him to detect in the figure of the door a memory of the maternal womb; the door thus functions as an aperture into the womblike house. In her discussion of how remembrance inhabits the house and is moulded into the material and physical structures of domestic space, Joëlle Bahloul focuses on the way in which the theme of enclosures is articulated through recurring references to doors and windows in domestic memories. Emphasizing the role that such spatial images play in collective memory of her maternal grandfather's multifamily Algerian home, Bahloul explains how the house is perceived as an enclosure of femininity and is structured to contain and control women. Extending beyond the liminality of doors and windows, Robert Mugerauer outlines the history and decline of the American porch as a mediating place between house and exterior and as a site to experience nature in the city. Catherine Alexander's analysis of the English garden is centred on the intimate relationship between the English small back garden and the house, and discusses how the garden acts as a liminal area of separation between the private space of the house and the public area of the road.

Liminal domestic spaces are also found in ships, trains, cars, and other modes of transport. 'The ship is the heterotopia par excellence,' stated Foucault, '[i]n civilizations where it is lacking, dreams dry up.'[1] Focusing on the writings of British and American women travellers from the late nineteenth to the early twentieth centuries, Emma Robinson-Tomsett demonstrates that by mimicking domestic space in their use and decor, as well as in their obeisance to class and gender divisions, accommodations on trains and ships fulfilled the dream of a home away from home. With a view to solving housing problems and densification in Vancouver, Patrick Chan offers alternate models for city dwelling in his innovative proposal for laneway housing.

NOTE

1 Michel Foucault, 'Of Other Spaces,' translated by Jay Miscowiec, *Diacritics* 16 / 1 (1986): 26.

7.1 GEORG SIMMEL 'The Bridge and the Door'*

With respect to nature only humans are given the capacity to relate and to separate in the peculiar fashion that the one is always the pre-condition for the other [...] Things must first be separate in order to be together. Practically and logically, it would be senseless to relate that which was not separate, or to relate that which in some sense does not remain separate. All of our doing may be classified according to the formula in which the two modes of operation [are found] together [...] We are at any moment – in the immediate or symbolic, in the physical or mental sense – beings who separate what is related and who relate what is separate.

The humans who were the first to construct a path between two locations reached one of the greatest achievements [...]

This achievement reaches its high point in the construction of the bridge. Here not only the passive resistance of what is spatially separated, but also the active resistance of a particular configuration, appear to oppose the human will-to-relate. By overcoming this obstacle, the bridge symbolizes the spreading of our will through space. Only to us the banks of the river are not merely apart but >separated<; the concept 'separation' would not have any meaning if we did not relate them first in our purposeful thinking, in our desires, in our imagination. The natural form – as if with positive intention – aids this conception of separateness; here separateness of singular elements appears to be the rule [*gesetzt*; author's translation] but the mind then transcends this separateness in a reconciling and unifying fashion.

The bridge becomes an aesthetic value not only because it in reality achieves the inter-relation of what is separate, and because it achieves practical purposes, it becomes an aesthetic value because it makes the inter-relation immediately visible. The bridge encourages the eye to inter-relate parts of the landscape just as in practical reality it encourages bodies to relate to one another. The mere dynamics of the movement – in the reality of which the 'purpose' of the bridge exhausts itself – has become something concrete and enduring [...] As far as the eye is concerned, the bridge has a relation to the river banks it connects that is much more direct and much less haphazard than the relation a house has to the ground, which to our eyes disappears below the house [...]

With respect to the relation 'separateness – unification,' the bridge emphasizes the latter, and it makes obvious the distance between its resting points, and

* [1909]. Translated and edited by Michael Kaern. *Qualitative Sociology* 17/4 (1994): 407–13.

makes it measurable. By so doing, it also overcomes this distance at the same time. The door, however, in a stricter and more obvious manner demonstrates that the acts of separating and relating are but two sides of the same act. The human being who was the first to build a hut demonstrated – much like the one who was first to build a path – the specifically human know-how (with which he confronts nature) by carving a parcel out of the continuity and infinity of space and by designing this parcel into a separate whole according to *one* meaning. By so doing, a piece of space was unified in itself and separated from the rest of the world. The door cancels the separation of the inside from the outside because it constitutes a link between the space of the human and everything which is outside of it. Exactly because the door can be opened, its being shut gives a feeling of being shut out, that is stronger than the feeling emanating from a solid wall. The wall is silent but the door speaks. It satisfies their deepest nature when humans define their own limitations but do so with freedom, i.e., in such a fashion that they can remove the limitation and put themselves outside of it.

The finiteness into which we have put ourselves always borders somewhere at the infinity of the physical or metaphysical being. In this way the door becomes the symbol for the threshold on which humans always stand or can stand. The door relates the finite unity – as which we have constituted a piece of infinite space designated for us – again to infinite space. The door is the line of demarcation where the limited and limitless meet, but not in the dead geometrical form of merely a partition wall, but rather as the permanent possibility of continuous alternation [...] From the door [...] life flows out of the limitedness of the isolated being-by-yourself, and it flows into the unlimited number of directions in which paths can lead.

On the one hand, the elements of separateness and relatedness meet in the bridge in such a fashion that the former appears to be more a matter of nature and the latter more a matter of humans; on the other hand, both enter human achievement – as human achievement – in more equal proportion through the door. On this rests the richer and livelier significance of the door as compared to the bridge. It manifests itself in the fact that it does not make any difference in meaning in which direction you walk across a bridge, whereas the door with its going-in and going-out function signals a totally different intention. In this respect the door also differs from the window, which in a way is similar to the door – both are a connection of the interior space with the outside world. But the teleological feeling vis-à-vis the window exclusively goes from inside to outside – it is only meant for looking-out-of and not for looking into. The window establishes the relation between the inside and the outside. Because of its transparency it does so – so to speak – necessarily [*chronisch*; author's translation] and continuously; but because of the one-way manner in which this relating works, and because of the limitation of the window to being only a path for the eye, the window is granted only a fraction of the deep significance that the door has in principle [...]

The forms which rule the dynamics of our life are transformed [...] by the bridge and the door into the sturdy permanence of perceptible form. The mere functionality and the telos of our movements are not carried by them as if they were tools, but rather, the function and the telos coagulate in the form of the bridge and the door to an immediately convincing plasticity. If one considers the different emphases of the bridge and the door which dominate their appearance, then the bridge shows how man unifies the separateness of being that exists in nature, and the door shows how man breaks the uniform continuous unity that exists in nature. Through this general aesthetic meaning that the bridge and door gain through their signifying something metaphysical, and through their stabilizing of something merely functional lies the reason for their special value for the arts.

7.2 BEATRIZ COLOMINA
'Interior'*

'To live is to leave traces,' writes Walter Benjamin, discussing the birth of the interior. 'In the interior these are emphasized. An abundance of covers and protectors, liners and cases is devised, on which the traces of objects of everyday uses are imprinted. The traces of the occupant also leave their impression on the interior. The detective story that follows these traces comes into being [...] The criminals of the first detective novels are neither gentlemen nor apaches, but private members of the bourgeoisie.'[1] [See section 3.8 in this volume.]

There is an interior in the detective novel. But can there be a detective story of the interior itself, of the hidden mechanisms by which space is constructed as interior? Which may be to say, a detective story of detection itself, of the controlling look, the look of control, the controlled look. But where would the traces of the look be imprinted? What do we have to go on? What clues?

There is an unknown passage of a well-known book, Le Corbusier's *Urbanisme* (1925), that reads: 'Loos told me one day: "A cultivated man does not look out of

* In *Privacy and Publicity: Modern Architecture as Mass Media* (Cambridge, MA: MIT Press, 1994), 232–81.

the window; his window is a ground glass; it is there only to let the light in, not to let the gaze pass through.'" [...] It points to a conspicuous yet conspicuously ignored feature of Loos's houses: not only are the windows either opaque or covered with sheer curtains, but the organization of the spaces and the disposition of the built-in furniture (the *immeuble*) seem to hinder access to them [...]

In the Moller house (Vienna, 1928; see Figure 12) there is a raised sitting area off the living room with a sofa set against the window. Although one cannot see out the window, its presence is strongly felt. The bookshelves surrounding the sofa and the light coming from behind it suggest a comfortable nook for reading. But comfort in this space is more than just sensual, for there is also a psychological dimension. A sense of security is produced by the position of the couch, the placement of its occupants against the light. Anyone who, ascending the stairs from the entrance (itself a rather dark passage), enters the living room, would take a few moments to recognize a person sitting on the couch. Conversely, any intrusion would soon be detected by a person occupying this area, just as an actor entering the stage is immediately seen by a spectator in a theatre box.

Loos refers to this idea in noting that 'the smallness of a theatre box would be unbearable if one could not look out into the large space beyond.'[2] While [Heinrich] Kulka, and later [Ludwig] Münz, read this comment in terms of the economy of space provided by the *Raumplan,* they overlook its psychological dimension. For Loos, the theatre box exists at the intersection between claustrophobia and agoraphobia [...] This spatial-psychological device could also be read in terms of power, regimes of control inside the house. The raised sitting area of the Moller house provides the occupant with a vantage point overlooking the interior. Comfort in this space is related to both intimacy and control.

This area is the most intimate of the sequence of living spaces, yet, paradoxically, rather than being at the heart of the house, it is placed at the periphery, pushing a volume out of the street facade, just above the front entrance. Moreover, it corresponds with the largest window on this elevation (almost a horizontal window). The occupant of this space can both detect anyone cross-trespassing the threshold of the house (while screened by the curtain) and monitor any movement in the interior (while 'screened' by the backlighting).

In this space, the window is only a source of light, not a frame for a view. The eye is turned toward the interior. The only exterior view that would be possible from this position requires that the gaze travel the whole depth of the house, from the alcove to the living room to the music room, which opens onto the back garden. Thus, the exterior view depends upon a view of the interior.

12 The Moller house (Vienna, 1928) by Adolf Loos. The raised sitting area off the living room. Photograph ALA2455. Reproduced by permission of Albertina, Vienna

The look folded inward upon itself can be traced in other Loos interiors. In the Müller house, for instance, the sequence of spaces, articulated around the staircase, follows an increasing sense of privacy from the drawing room to the dining room and study to the 'lady's room' (*Zimmer der Dame*) with its raised sitting area, which occupies the centre or 'heart' of the house [...] But the window of this space looks onto the living space. Here, too, the most intimate room is like a theater box, placed just over the entrance to the social spaces in this house, so that any intruder could easily be seen. Likewise, the view of the exterior, toward the city, from this 'theater box' is contained within a view of the interior. Suspended in the middle of the house, this space assumes the character both of a 'sacred' space and of a point of control. Comfort is produced by two seemingly opposing conditions, intimacy and control.

This is hardly the idea of comfort that is associated with the nineteenth-century interior as described by Walter Benjamin in 'Louis-Philippe, or the Interior.'[3] [See Benjamin, section 3.8 in this volume.] In Loos's interiors the sense of security is not achieved by simply turning one's back on the exterior and immersing oneself in a private universe – 'a box in the world theater,' to use Benjamin's metaphor. It is no longer the house that is a theater box; there is a theater box inside the house, overlooking the internal social spaces. The inhabitants of Loos's houses are both actors in and spectators of the family scene – involved in, yet detached from, their own space [...] The classical distinction between inside and outside, private and public, object and subject, becomes convoluted.

Traditionally, the theater box provided for the privileged a private space within the dangerous public realm, by reestablishing the boundaries between inside and outside. It is significant that when Loos designed a theater in 1898 (an unrealized project), he omitted the boxes, arguing they 'didn't suit a modern auditorium.'[4] Thus he removes the box from the public theater, only to insert it into the 'private theater' of the house. The public has entered the private house by way of the social spaces [...] but there is a last site of resistance to this intrusion in the domestic 'theater box.'

The theater boxes in the Moller and Müller houses are spaces marked as 'female,' the domestic character of the furniture contrasting with that of the adjacent 'male' space, the library. In these, the leather sofas, the desks, the chimney, the mirrors represent a 'public space' within the house – the office and the club invading the interior. But it is an invasion that is confined to an enclosed room – a space that belongs to the sequence of social spaces within the house, yet does not engage with them. As Münz notes, the library is a 'reservoir of quietness,' 'set apart from the household traffic.' The raised alcove of the Moller house and the *Zimmer der Dame* of the Müller house, on the other hand, not only overlook the social spaces but are exactly positioned at the end of the sequence, on the threshold of the private, the secret, the upper rooms where sexuality is hidden away. At the intersection of the visible and the invisible, women are placed as the guardians of the unspeakable [...]

But the theater box is a device that both provides protection and draws attention to itself. Thus, when Münz describes the entrance to the social spaces of the Moller house, he writes: 'Within, entering from one side, one's gaze travels in the opposite direction till it rests in the light, pleasant alcove, raised above the living room floor. *Now we are really inside the house.*'[5] So, where were we before? we may ask, when we crossed the threshold of the house and occupied the entrance hall and the cloakroom in the ground floor or while we ascended the stairs to the reception rooms on the second or elevated ground floor. The intruder is 'inside,' has penetrated the house, only when his/her gaze strikes this most intimate space, turning the occupant into a silhouette against the light. The 'voyeur' in the 'theater box' has become the object of another's gaze;

she is caught in the act of seeing, entrapped in the very moment of control. In framing a view, the theater box also frames the viewer. It is impossible to abandon the space, let alone leave the house, without being seen by those over whom control is being exerted. Object and subject exchange places. Whether there is actually a person behind either gaze is irrelevant:

> I can feel myself under the gaze of someone whose eyes I do not even see, not even discern. All that is necessary is for something to signify to me that there may be others there. The window if it gets a bit dark and if I have reasons for thinking that there is someone behind it, is straight-way a gaze. From the moment this gaze exists, I am already something other, in that I feel myself becoming an object for the gaze of others. But in this position, which is a reciprocal one, others also know that I am an object who knows himself to be seen.[6]

Architecture is not simply a platform that accommodates the viewing subject. It is a viewing mechanism that produces the subject. It precedes and frames its occupant.

NOTES

1 Walter Benjamin, 'Paris, Capital of the Nineteenth Century,' in *Reflections: Essays, Aphorisms, Autobiographical Writings*, translated by Edmund Jephcott (New York: Schocken Books, 1986), 155–6.
2 Ludwig Münz and Gustav Künstler, *Der Architekt Adolf Loos* (Vienna: Anton Schroll, 1964), 130–1. English translation: *Adolf Loos, Pioneer of Modern Architecture* (London: Thames and Hudson, 1966), 148 [...]
3 .[...] Benjamin, 'Paris,' 154 [...]
4 Münz and Künstler, *Adolf Loos*, 36.
5 Ibid., 149.
6 Jacques Lacan, *The Seminar of Jacques Lacan: Book I, Freud's Papers on Technique, 1953–1954*, edited by Jacques-Alain Miller, translated by John Forrester (New York: Norton, 1988), 215. In this passage, Lacan is referring to Jean-Paul Sartre's *Being and Nothingness*.

7.3 OLIVIER MARC
'Birth of the House'*

The Doors of Orly Airport

When Jung sought to describe the complexity of the human psyche at its deeper levels, he drew on his experience of a dream in comparing it to a building. [See section 4.5 in this volume.] The upper floor, he said, might have been built in the nineteenth century, the ground floor in the sixteenth, and a study of its construction might reveal traces of an eleventh-century tower. In the cellar there could be Roman foundations, with flint tools buried below the top-soil, and Ice Age relics in the lower strata.

I realized then that the entrance door went back to the most ancient part of my inner house. In fact it might claim to be the first element. The most ancient and primitive of huts had an entrance – not a door so much as a hole, a passage: a way in, and a way out. But it was primarily a way in, for the exterior was elaborately decorated. Why should the entrance to such a rudimentary dwelling be so superbly decorated? Was the way to the hut so vital? What could its role have been that it should have been considered an object of such importance? And why was it usually oval-shaped, like a natural opening?

The Mother's Womb

A very deep interior motive must have prompted man to leave the natural shelters which the earth provided in the form of caves and grottoes, in order to build the first house. The motive could not have been external, since a hut does not provide as good protection as a cave from cold, bad weather or wild animals. Why then did he leave it for a more precarious habitation? Why didn't he dig himself a hole like a fox?

These first caves represented the womb in which an embryonic 'humanity' was gradually taking form under the pressure of a consciousness soon to be born into history. That consciousness was manifested as a vaguely defined force of life, which secreted its outer substance in order to establish a form, as shellfish do, whose defining shell was to be humanity. Thus the new man, this subtle and sensitive being, was to rise from the earth to confront the world.

Expelled from the earth's womb as a child is expelled from his mother's, newborn humanity now had to stand up in the full light of day. A baby is too

* In *Psychology of the House*, translated by Jessie Wood (London: Thames and Hudson, 1977), 9–28.

comfortable in his mother's womb ever to want to leave it, but on the contrary struggles wildly to return as soon as he is born. Birth is a break with unity, and the split is caused by an evolutionary demand: A child cannot keep from being born; a mother cannot keep from giving birth.

So it was, I imagine, with the first men. An inner compulsion tore them from the protective earth and forced them to build the house. But that house took form because the potentiality of it already existed within him. Man had to have the idea, the perception, the desire, and finally the need to build it. It had to correspond to something inside himself, to an interior image, since no other house yet existed.

If we are right in thinking that architects today get their inspiration from the past or from people around them, as is the case with even the least talented, what are we to say about the first man? Where did he find his inspiration? Does this not bring us, so to speak, to the threshold of the creative process? For, since no outside model then existed, what inside model could have inspired man's first house?

When a child draws a house, he never refers to an outside model. His use of the environment is limited to those elements alone which help him express a truth he senses within himself. The shape of this rudimentary dwelling may be a clue: roughly symmetrical, vague in outline, almost circular at base, it looks like a kind of pouch poking up from the ground. After looking through numerous photographic documents in the Musée de l'Homme, I selected several pictures of primitive habitations, all of which had been built by African tribes living in extreme isolation from the rest of the world and with an instinctive, almost animal approach to life. In their fashion these people must have had a deep understanding of the origins of man. Their buildings of the present time are so rudimentary that their interior model can have changed very little since man's beginnings. These silent champions of continuity have provided us with visible clues to understand better the origins of man's perceptions. I found myself taking a great liking to them.

Their houses look like slightly attenuated pouches, each with a vertical slit along one side. Seen from a certain angle, they reminded me of enormous breasts pointing up towards the sky. But even more striking than the shape was the entrance, a thick-lipped slit, the only decorated element of the structure.

I was then convinced that the interior model which had presided over the birth of this form had been a mother's womb, seen from the inside. These houses were wombs [...]

Ejected from the cave where he had lived according to the rhythm of natural laws, the first man thought to reconstruct the image of unity which he sensed he had lost. When he went back to the cave it was not to live there but to paint the bison he was about to hunt, so as to secure for himself the bounty of that nature which had become alien, and which he might even, it seemed to him, have in some way destroyed. Thus he sanctified the cave, transforming it into a sanctuary dedicated to the forces of nature, which in his new condition were inaccessible to him, condemned as he was to conscious thought.

What could be more normal than to decorate and honour the aperture leading into the womb-like world which man had built for himself? A house whose form man first conceived inside his mother's womb. To leave the womb is a natural step, but to enter – or re-enter – it is a hope forever doomed to frustration except upon a higher plane of consciousness. Therefore the door of the house assumes a sacred character.

Since then each one of us has been born to follow the way of all humanity by breaking away from that unity in order to build his own universe. For we now know that in his first few years every child repeats the same story, which is that of every man since the beginning, since the time when he was first severed from nature. Today we may no longer have to build our house (though children still build huts with enthusiasm). And yet, what precisely is a child doing when he first starts to draw? Perhaps his activity can help us understand the activity of nascent man [...]

To build a house is to create an area of peace, calm, and security, a replica of our own mother's womb, where we can leave the world and listen to our own rhythm; it is to create a place of our very own, safe from danger. For once we have crossed the threshold and shut the door behind us, we can be at one with ourselves [...]

What Children's Drawings Reveal

A child beginning to draw depicts pouch-like structures with a single opening, strangely resembling the womb-houses of primitive men. The concept of an enclosed space isolated from the rest of the world – here represented by the sheet of paper – follows what Arno Stern calls a pre-figurative stage in a child's creative development, or else appears at the end of the stage, and is the precursor of the house the child will later draw. The child itself has no notion of prefiguration and figuration, which are adult concepts. He draws in order to express himself, and the irregular and more or less concentric lines he draws first of all are just as expressive and significant of his state of being as the house he later draws will be. These vague spirals are quite simply his way of exteriorizing his interior perceptions, not images of the things he sees around him. The child is pleased with the house he draws, if it resembles his inner model, and he is completely indifferent to whether or not it looks like the houses we build. His house may look like ours, but only to the extent that our dwellings reflect the profound and universal language of the house.

After he has given expression to universal impulses in the form of vague spirals, wavy lines, and dots – a kind of pristine rhythm – he then begins to trace the shape of his mother's womb, impelled by an unconscious nostalgia to recreate an indefinable stage of being. Since he cannot reproduce the state itself, he draws the place where it was perceived, in order that the depiction of its exterior form may enable him to re-experience it. The womb thus becomes the symbol of this interior peace. The child draws the container to express the contents. The image of the place reveals the soul. Perhaps this is the significance of Lao Tsu's phrase: 'a void containing everything.' Such is the richness of architectural space. The child uses the language of symbols, whose meaning we have lost, the primordial, essential language which is the means of communication of the child, the primitive and the sage.

The child draws his mother's womb to actualize it, to experience it once more, to make sure he hasn't destroyed it. His drawing appears to him like a magic act which reveals a wonderful other world (that world from which, unknowingly, he derives life). As he draws these wonders they miraculously enter into him, calming his anxieties. Thus he experiences himself as truly creative, capable of producing the universe he aspires to. He doesn't try to enter into the 'pouch' he has drawn, yet he experiences its warmth and tranquil peace. He is reassured, because he knows it still exists. Given a cardboard box of the right dimensions, a child will always try to climb inside.

By means of his drawings, the child becomes a magician in the manner of the primitive man, exteriorizing interior situations the better to experience them. He is reborn through his pictures and liberated from the inevitable anxieties which haunt him.

7.4 JOËLLE BAHLOUL
'Telling Places: The House as Social Architecture'*

Remembering the house in which an uprooted culture originated and developed involves reversing history and sinking symbolic roots into a vanished human and geographical world. The remembered house is a small-scale cosmology

* In *The Architecture of Memory: A Jewish-Muslim Household in Colonial Algeria, 1937–1962,* translated by Catherine du Peloux Ménagé (Cambridge: Cambridge University Press, 1996), 28–50.

symbolically restoring the integrity of a shattered geography. 'The reason members of a group remain united, even after scattering and finding nothing in their new physical surroundings to recall the home they have left, is that they think of the old home and its layout … Thus we understand why spatial images play so important a role in the collective memory.'[1]

The past evoked in the following pages is not one re-created through historical work inscribed in a *literary* medium […] Rather, the things of the past meticulously re-created here are those *experienced* in daily life, in the crowded intimacy of the most familiar objects and people, those one sees on rising in the morning and on going to sleep at night. This remembered past is lodged in the monotonous repetition of the necessary acts of concrete experience. The memory that 'invents' it,[2] and rewrites it, is the product of this relentless repetitiveness. Yet this remembrance of concrete experience is structured in terms of two main fusing dimensions: domestic space and family time. Events are not remembered simply as they were experienced by the family and the domestic community. Memory draws the boundaries of the family and domesticity by shaping within them local, regional, and international events. The domestic and family world makes up the woof of remembrance, of memory. The house is 'inhabited' by memory. Remembrance is moulded into the material and physical structures of the domestic space.

Dar-Refayil's memories are designed as an architecture of memory.[3] The biographies collected tell the personal and collective history of Dar-Refayil's residents from 1937 […] until 1962, when most Jewish residents left for Algiers and then for France. Narratives significantly focus on the descriptions of the domestic life, with special emphasis on female accounts because women spent most of their time at home. These narrative memories provide a great many details on the layout of apartments, household accommodations and furnishings, the rhythm of daily life, eating, sleeping, bodily hygiene, and even sexual activity. At the outset, Dar-Refayil's memories seem to be confined to this enclosed world.

Then, as in Impressionist painting, a marked outward movement emerges. The mental reconstruction of the house proceeds by drawing successive narrative boundaries in the form of concentric circles radiating outward from the courtyard. These circles actually indicate the breadth of residents' social life. Starting from a nucleus comprising the rooms lined up around the courtyard, a sort of womb whose only opening is the house's heavy wooden gate, Dar-Refayil's people go out to participate in the city's multicultural life and in that of the Jewish community. They take part in movements of population that lead them to cities such as Constantine and Algiers to seek their fortunes. Narratives present residents' experiences as if they originated in the courtyard, in the heart of the house – as if the house were a spring from which all personal peregrinations and itineraries flowed. Dar-Refayil's domestic community, though confined in the house's protective enclosure, seems at the same time open to urban life and regional events. This dual nature of the domestic community – both exposed and protected – is apparent in the very structure of the narratives. It reveals the contradictory motives of the former residents, who valued domestic conviviality highly and were at the same time irresistibly attracted by the display of the European lifestyle. Memory transforms the house into the symbolic miniature of the Algerian social world. The remembered house is a sort of 'centre of the world.'

This narrative logic, opposing enclosure to opening, permeates the narrative description of the places – of the physical and social organization of domestic space.

The Logic of Enclosure

Doors and Windows without a View

It is in no way surprising that, in this Maghrebian cultural world, memory's discourse feminizes the house grammatically even though the Arabic word *dar* designates the house of the father and of his lineage. Domesticity is described as an enclosure of [femininity], a mother-house symbolically associated with reproduction. The architecture of the building, traditional in Maghrebian urban societies, above all allows and encourages the physical control of women. Consequently, what female memories retain most powerfully is the organization, the detailed layout, and the material equipment of this enclosed world, as if all these things had been addressed specifically to them [...]

The importance of the theme of enclosure is articulated by the recurring references to doors and windows in domestic memories [...] The spatial and social distribution of doors and windows reflects a minor hierarchy within the domestic community. Those whose apartments had more openings were viewed as higher on the social ladder. Similarly, the owners, who were the only residents to have a view onto the street, were considered the only ones with symbolic access to the town's European community. Doors and windows were a metaphor for an open society; they embodied the desire for social advancement.

Reference to enclosure is ambiguous: it either emphasizes the space's hermetic closure or highlights its internal openness. Memory wavers between openness and enclosure in evoking the domestic space. In this oscillation, memory's discourse reverses itself: the lack of windows opening onto the street becomes a metaphor for the ghettoization of the domestic group and the stifling of the individual. At the same time, the permanent openness of all interior doors is interpreted as giving conviviality and security:

> We always left the doors open. We never closed them, and that's why we lived like one big family. If a neighbour needed anything, she just came in; she didn't need to knock. Here [in France], house doors are closed, but there [in Sétif] all the doors were open. From morning, when we got up, we left the doors open till evening, when we closed them before going to bed. We'd go to the market, we'd leave our doors open, and at night, we closed them with a little bolt; you could open the door with your finger. So we lived as one family, not just as neighbours, and we had a good life, we really had a good life.
>
> Clarisse [interviewed by author]

Dar-Refayil is here portrayed as what Bachelard calls a 'felicitous space.'[4] This 'topophilia' [...] inscribed in the discourse of memory operates as a defence of family values as the *moral* values of the domestic group.[5] Familism is here objectified through an architectural metaphor – a semantic procedure widespread in Mediterranean and European cultures.[6] At the same time, the narratives reveal the ambiguity of these values in a society seeking emancipation. Familism is comfortable as long as it does not interfere with the individual's attempts at social advancement and integration into local society:

> It was a bit of a mess, communal toilets, doors which wouldn't close, spiders and cockroaches all over. It was really awful.
>
> Guy [interviewed by author]

> There were lots of windows, but with no view [...] all looking onto the courtyard. Doors were bits of cardboard, there weren't even locks. So you can imagine what it was for newlyweds [...] no door, just a little curtain to screen them.
>
> Rosette [interviewed by author]

Open doors represent conviviality and good life but also lack of privacy: an open door may be either positive or negative. This oscillation recurs in the comparison between life at Dar-Refayil and life in France. In France doors are closed, and there is little conviviality or mutual help, but at the same time there is a sense of privacy and a better material life. While Setifian life is remembered as communally oriented, French life is viewed as individually oriented. In several narratives, in particular those offered by the residents with the lowest incomes, the symbolic opposition between open and closed is associated with that between clean and dirty. For Guy Bakoushe, a closed door means that light and air cannot come in; it is a sign of social and cultural suffocation. For an adolescent in the fifties, eager to discover the world, doors shut in dirt, impurity, and social backwardness.

Ultimately, narratives translate the opening of doors and windows onto the courtyard rather than the street as the enclosure of the domestic group, a sort of metaphor of endogamy materially represented by burdensome overcrowding and lack of privacy and by the clutter of domesticity.[7] Doors and windows are used metaphorically in narratives with a logic different from that of Proust's *Remembrance of Things Past*. In Proust windows give access to individual secrets, operating as narrative spies.[8] By contrast, the opening of Dar-Refayil's doors and windows is associated with its domestic group's social opening outward – in a sense, towards the future. Narratively, the house's interior represents the past and social backwardness, the outside the future and social advancement. Closed doors are interpreted as the visual expression of entrenched archaic traditions and social stagnation. By contrast, doors are opened to social and cultural progress. As in Edward Hopper's paintings, the windows of narrative memory open onto dreams of social and material achievement. When they talk about windows, Jewish women specifically invest this metaphor with their ideal of female and general autonomy. Their memories visualize Muslim women perpetually behind closed doors and windows and thus in social misery. For these Jews who were teenagers in the fifties, doors and windows are full of promise. The narration of their uprooted lives in the eighties reveals in great detail how they managed to break down the barrier of closed doors and windows. Their voices now resonate from the other side of these barriers. These doors and windows are narrative metaphors for the frontiers – geographical, social, and cultural – that were crossed in reality in the great migration.

NOTES

1 Maurice Halbwachs, *The Collective Memory*, translated by F. Ditter and V.Y. Ditter (New York: Harper and Row, 1980), 130.

2 Bernard Lewis, *History Remembered, Recovered, Invented* (Princeton, NJ: Princeton University Press, 1975).

3 [Editors' note: Dar-Refayil is the multifamily house of the author's maternal grandfather in Sétif, Eastern Algeria.]

4 Gaston Bachelard, *The Poetics of Space* (Boston, MA: Beacon Press, 1994 [1958]), xxxi. [See section 2.1 in this volume.]

5 Ibid.; Yi-Fu Tuan, *Topophilia: A Study of Environmental Perception, Attitudes, and Values* (Englewood Cliffs, NJ: Prentice-Hall, 1974), 93–9.

6 Michael Herzfeld, *Anthropology through the Looking Glass: Critical Ethnography in the Margins of Europe* (Cambridge: Cambridge University Press, 1987), 203–4.
7 This is another significant similarity with the Greek domestic world. [See] Renée Hirschon, 'Open Body / Closed Space: The Transformation of Female Sexuality,' in Shirley Ardener, ed., *Defining Females* (London: Croom Helm, 1978), 66–88. [See section 5.9 in this volume.]
8 Howard Moss, *The Magic Lantern of Marcel Proust* (New York: Macmillan, 1962), 43.

7.5 ROBERT MUGERAUER 'Toward an Architectural Vocabulary: The Porch as a Between'*

The Porch and Nature

The physical and cultural meanings of the porch are partly grounded in the manner by which it relates the house to the natural environment, especially to the weather. The porch provides refuge from frequent showers and relief from overheated interior rooms in summer's oppressive heat. Early on, American architects were aware that the porch offered one easy way to ameliorate contrasts between inside and outside the dwelling [...]

The porch, as a mediating place between house and exterior, seems simple, yet reverberates with levels of meaning and implications [...] it shelters by *holding out* undesirable forms of weather or by *opening up to* moderating breezes [...] A constant throughout the range of design complexity is that the porch allows *lingering* between inner and outer spheres. The porch encourages and is articulated by the interplay of natural and domestic features [...] The porch today may be one of the few remaining places where town and city dwellers have significant access to night sky, atmosphere, and bird and animal activity. The porch enables people to be together with nature by providing an intermediate site.

With the advent of air conditioning, the porch began to disappear from the American house. The change would seem to be technological mastery of weather, a development that rendered the porch obsolete environmentally. The impact of technology alone, however, does not account for the rise or fall of the porch, since the impact of air conditioning varies across regions or has nothing

* In *Dwelling, Seeing, and Designing: Toward a Phenomenological Ecology*, edited by David Seamon (Albany, NY: State University of New York Press, 1993), 103–28.

at all to do with some of the porch's functions. In the upper Midwest, the summers are pleasant without air conditioning and, in southern climates, the spring and fall offer adequate time for the use of porches.

In short, porches are not intelligible solely in terms of weather. It rains no less now than it did when the first porches were built as convenient shelters. Rather, our responses to the weather, through both architecture and technology, are a facet of cultural understanding and experience. Porches were not an inevitable American solution, as is witnessed by alternatives in the rest of the world where it also is hot, cold, and rainy. For example, in some Japanese architecture, an increase in eaves' size provides the same function. Moreover, we do not add porches to every building, though the weather in a given place is the same for them all.

Architectural convention and fashion clearly play a part, as does social behavior. The phenomena of the car port and attached garage may indicate changes in perception and behavior, such as acceptance of the automobile as belonging to the home. No doubt the increased time spent before television sets interiorized American living patterns and spatial forms. The influence of modernism is also part of the story. In the early phase of the Arts and Crafts movement, porches were retained but wide eave overhangs also developed; in the later Machine Age Movement, porches were incompatible with the aesthetic of flat, smooth surfaces [...]

Though porches tended to disappear with shifts in technology and architectural styles, they are still built. Even the much beloved suburban ranch house, for all its modern characteristics, sometimes included a minimal porch area or has had one added to it by the occupants [...] The construction of porches has recently benefited from the desire to get in touch with the outdoors again and with attempts to discard the television and re-establish family and neighbourly communication. On new houses, porches seem to be desired as part of a rejuvenation of tradition and the recovery of something lost [...]

The porch not only provides a place to belong to the natural world but also opens a place for family and friends to *gather* [...] As a place to be alone or with others, the porch is a semi-private space parallel to the semi-public space of the street. The porch does not force one to make the unattractive choice between admitting people to the full intimacy of the home or keeping them in the distanced relation of the formal public realm [...]

As a between and joining, the porch's ability to promote lingering is often illustrated by its furnishings. Typical porch chairs are usually casual, certainly as compared to dining or living room furniture, where people maintain a much more erect and 'proper' posture. On the porch, one may lean on the railing, since casual lounging is allowed in the 'semi-private' intimacy that is not formal. There is also the porch swing, which has its own mode of existence, more free and less upright than even the rocking chair (see Figure 13) […]

The range of social relationships and varieties of porch often correspond. The size and placement of the porch may correlate with the occupants' social relation to other community members. More specifically, the height of the porch above the ground generally articulates and maintains the proper range and mediation between those inside and outside. In an American culture that promotes egalitarian and democratic ideals, it is not surprising that many porches are not elevated more than a half dozen steps. The porch's floor is not above the face of someone standing outside. It reflects and supports a fundamentally *equal* social status […] While the democratic measure for building is commonly maintained in the traditional American houses of working people, there are grander styles of houses, occupied by persons of greater than average wealth, status, or power. These houses not only tend to have a larger porch, but one more elevated above the ground […] Built form and social differential coincide […]

An equal relation of dwelling place to street and natural environment is increasingly difficult to maintain as one moves from the scale of low-rise to high-rise buildings and from traditional to international styles. In large, 'functional' housing forms, with their minimal balconies, distancing inevitably occurs […] Not only are apartments substantially removed from the ground, but the force of winds and the angle of sunlight often force residents to keep openable windows and balcony doors closed. At the upper levels of high buildings, balconies tend to be symbolic and part of the continuity of building design rather than usable. When they are used, the increased size of the building tends to diminish the balcony and remove it from life below. The greater the height, the more participation in street life is replaced by the detached aesthetic attitude of 'a view.' The result is a weakened or indirect relationship between inside and outside […]

The porch marks a threshold. The rise of the porch is the rise to the level of the household, a transition in spatial form and meaning. The shift is from the 'rest of the world' to another place of manner of being. *The porch joins different worlds* […] *The porch brings about and extends a between, reconciling outside and inside* […]

A thorough phenomenology requires consideration of all spaces of betweenness – the character of door, window, vestibule, balcony, gallery, and so forth. One would also need to consider the changes in porches in relation to the entire house, and especially interior rooms such as living room and parlor. Such a phenomenology would also examine porches on buildings other than residences, especially in the civic and public spheres. The examples used here are

13 Greek-revival house, Austin, Texas. The porch swing enhances the porch's casual sociability. Courtesy of Robert Mugerauer.

largely Midwestern and Texas porches; these forms would need to be compared with the full range of American porches as well as with the British veranda or *piazza,* the French *galerie,* the Spanish *portale,* and the Italian *loggia* […]

A key conclusion is that the porch is an architectural opening of a site. The porch, as a between, establishes the site for the emergence of a world. The essential features of the porch disclose the physical, environmental, social, and ontological dimensions of the betweenness in our ways of living and building. The porch simultaneously establishes its own identity and our orientation by differentiating and reconciling inside and outside, above and below, front and back in regard to natural and social worlds. The fundamentally horizontal and egalitarian mode of gathering helps establish the character of democratic private and public spaces. By gathering these dimensions together, in a built place, architecture as a between helps open and sustain a democratic mode of dwelling.

Porches disclose themselves as the scene of the gift of admittance and meeting […] According to Heidegger [see section 2.2 in this volume], the giving of admittance never happens once and for all, nor through architectural elements that would somehow be unchanging [...] This gift is primal, not only because it was necessary to make our dwelling possible in the first place, but because to dwell now and in the future, we always need the gift anew. In a continuous but changing manner, architecture gives what sustains us: sites for the establishment and cultivation of human worlds.

7.6 CATHERINE ALEXANDER 'The Garden as Occasional Domestic Space'*

A Brief History of Garden Boundaries

There is a vast quantity of literature concerned with the English Garden [...] Most of it, however, deals with landscapes, the great painterly eighteenth-century gardens, or the garden as text – plot in both senses – from the enclosed Islamic parks onward [...] Elements from these various botanical discourses linger still in the smallest gardens, their primary explicit references dispersed, etiolated or re-appropriated, the equivalent of dead metaphors in language. To take just one instance, *the boundary* may now summon imagery of the Anglophone instinct for territorialization, mocking the suburban gardener for the enthusiastic fencing in of land, however diminutive. The castle writ small and multiplied invites ridicule. Yet there are multiple resonances in this one gesture of circumscription. The Islamic pleasure garden, domain of kings and conquerors, was closed against the aridity of the desert; the internal environment could be watered and controlled, planted with the fruits of raids and war [...] This gesture of turning away from the outer wilderness was carried back and repeated in the medieval *hortus conclusus* [...] The space within now became a symbolic meditation on, and actualization of, the Christian life, a testament to the Testament, an organic rosary. The internalization of nature was used allegorically to mirror both spiritual journeys and psychological travails [...]

To the experiential construction of the garden was added the perspectival subjugation of land to the gaze from the Renaissance onward [...] The formal boxed flower beds and vistas of the fifteenth to seventeenth centuries gave way to the celebrated openness of the English landscape garden [...] Once more the

---

* Forum: 'Domestic Space,' edited by Kathy Mezei and Chiara Briganti. *Signs: Journal of Women in Culture and Society* 27/3 (2002): 857–71.

notion of boundary was key in the landscaped garden, even though it had apparently vanished. The boundary was in fact inverted and made invisible through the *haha,* the ditch that 'call[ed] in the countryside,' in Alexander Pope's words.[1] [...] Prior to this time, gardens were far more formal and intricate, representing a different kind of polity and social relations [...]

The boundaries of the modern suburban garden then rest on a plethora of foundations [...] Where neighbours live cheek-by-jowl, gardens are clearly bounded round their perimeter. Walls, fences, and hedges block other people's gaze and maintain the privacy of the domestic, the privet hedge (*Ligustrum vulgare*) being *the* indicator and demarcator of English suburbia rampant. It is within these bounds that the view across the gardens is unimpeded. The contemplative and the spiritual, the productive and the consumer display – the garden provides an arena for all these moments. The bounds of the garden therefore designate the land over which the owner has property rights [...] Within the garden there are also separations between different areas and particular functions and activities associated with each. Physical separations and orders aside, there are also the (often contested) boundaries between inside and outside, between dirt and cleanliness and between nature and culture [...] In the particular and peculiar nature of the suburban garden, the dissolution of boundaries and category separation conventionally associated with domestic space co-exist with these boundaries [...]

Order

[...] Gardens take an order from the house, but also reorder and disorder. Houses may have a strip of concrete, a backyard; this is not a garden but indicates that a liminal space is always required between the public space of the road or pavement and the most private, secret part of the ground floor, the back. Front gardens are optional: a house may open straight onto the road or pavement.

The order I refer to is spatial. The typical front-to-back structure of the house is repeated in the garden [...] The Palladian renaissance made the new connection between house and body absolutely explicit, dictating that rooms for baser uses should be hidden away as the baser organs of the body are discreetly placed [...]

The suburban or urban garden reflects this front to back (from *you,* to *us,* to *me*) structure. A graveled or paved area generally separates the house from the rest of the garden. Here, most commonly, a table and chairs are set out in the summer months providing a view over the rest of the garden. The view afforded from this terrace, (sometimes ringed with flowerpots) is of the middle area, possibly punctuated by a pond. This is the most manicured part of the garden, where the tussle between growth and restraint is a constant exertion. In a sense, this is a display of the labour that has gone into the garden. Division of labour in such gardens is partially gendered, care of the lawn, with all its resonances of stately park land, is almost universally a male activity […]

Beyond the lawn there is the third area, and this is where, to borrow Palladio's phrase, the baser functions of the garden are generally located: vegetables (if grown), sheds, and compost heaps. Clotheslines for laundry are generally strung from the house across the garden to allow easy access to the line. In gardens where drying laundry cannot be hidden, lines and laundry are generally removed from sight before formal occasions […] What I have called the baser functions are also those of regeneration and transformation, in line with the back and upper quarters of the house.

Temporally, too, there is a sense in which the back garden can be constructed to follow the developmental cycle of a family unit. The use of the garden varies dramatically according to the composition of the family or household at any one time. The basic spatial composition will remain as described above but different elements may enter, find their place, and disappear again. Sandpits, climbing frames, and paddling pools appear for small children, with barbecues for adults and then, possibly, built-up flower beds for the elderly once bending to weed becomes difficult.

Reorder

The reordering of these spatial and temporal dimensions of the house takes place in two senses. The space of the garden has a transformative element vis-à-vis the house, purifying the unclean; but the garden also shifts the scale of domestic space and time, re-contextualizing the house within a cosmological framework. The garden regenerates and transforms, and thereby restores order to the built domestic space […] The sick may be taken to the garden, or, more commonly, cut flowers are brought to the sick […] Laundry can be seen as soil from the house being cleaned through washing and then dried outside […] Once part of the garden, compost may indirectly re-enter the house as flowers, vegetables, or fruit.

Reordering in these senses is an affirmation of order, a restoration of the clean, the healthy, and the fecund, a regeneration of the stale. But the garden also reorders by shifting the scale within which the house is conceived. From the eighteenth century onward, images of house and body give rise to images of safety and constriction, of inside and outside, of beginnings and endings. Even though it is often in the institutional space of the hospital that the acute moments of birth and death occur in the twentieth century, the process of dying occurs largely in the domestic space, alongside the process of daily life.

The mortal body in the Western tradition follows a linear trajectory from birth to death, and from thence to a somewhat disputed position. The garden, however, connotes a tradition that both repeats that of the house and changes the register. Beginnings and endings are encountered again, not on a mortal but on a cosmological scale [...] The world began and ends with a garden: Eden and Paradise are gardens of inception and finality, but they are also the same place, lost and hidden now but to be regained, a spiritual journey that ends where it began, a kind of self-prefiguring. Andrew Marvell too, in 'The Garden,' suggests the greater cycle within which the seasonal cycle takes place when he describes the garden as 'Annihilating all that's made / To a green thought in a green shade' [...] Here is eternal stillness rather than linear process, but an eternal instant manifested in a series of transient moments as seasonal changes intrude.

Gardens present a nested series of life cycles within the domestic space, from annual plants to trees that may outlive whoever planted them and the houses in which they dwell. Trees may be planted to commemorate a birth or death, summoning a spiritual association, Paradise on earth. But a tree planted for a person, also stands *for* that person and allows the gardener to imagine an intertwining of the human life span with the longer history of the tree, projecting beyond mortality and into the future [...]

Disorder

Thus the garden reflects the spatial and temporal ordering of the house and may suggest functional separations. The garden also returns order to the house through transforming and regenerating processes and shifting the scale of the order within which the domestic is placed. The third relationship [...] is that of disorder. Michel Foucault (1986) describes gardens as *heterotopia*, other places beyond the practice of everyday life.[2] [...] Activities and their spaces are conflated in the garden; here, there is excess, inversion, a festive exuberance. Action here is unrestrained.

Above, I mentioned sand pits, climbing frames, and paddling pools. The average suburban house cannot accommodate these: the scale and mess created are all excessive. Indeed, for children, play in the garden has an element of permissible exuberance, excess, and uncontainment. Play that is messy in the house, quite literally *out of order,* is wholesome and invigorating outdoors [...]

For adults, the garden is also a place of games, relaxation, and repose [...] Cooking can also take place in the garden, but this now takes on a festive air, and becomes an almost exclusively male activity. Typically gendered functions within the house may be inverted or less exclusively gendered when outside. Categories break down, rules are softened and blurred.

Finally the garden is a place of dreams and fantasy. From Mannerist landscapes on, gardens have incorporated jokes and follies and now concept gardens peddled through television and gardening magazines encourage people to create different worlds. *Tristram Shandy*'s Uncle Toby is perhaps the most celebrated gardener of other places – for him the battleground of Belgium, for others a summoning of a childhood environment. Such recreational activity is also a process of re-creation, but these other places, whether dream worlds or geographical lands, are miniaturized and the shift in scale is accompanied by a sense of nostalgia [...]

Conclusion

The garden then is a liminal space between the inside and the greater outside, the wilderness, and liminality admits dissolution, inversion, and Robert Herrick's sweet disorder. Paradise is domesticated, but the domestication is only ever partial; cultural borders, just like the herbaceous, are leaky and cannot be contained without labour. Always there, the garden as a made thing slips and slides in and out of view so that as a thing of culture, most gardens are occasional. The essence of such gardens is that they are partially uncontained. Robert Harbison [...] plays on *model* as being both a paradigm and suggestive of something greater than itself, in which sense the garden is a very model of the cosmos.[3] It is, to quote Foucault 'the smallest parcel of the world and then it is the totality of the world.'[4]

NOTES

1 The *haha* is a ditch intended to prevent cattle straying from their owner's property. It was so called because the unwary, stumbling on the lurking ditch, were supposed to exclaim 'Aha!' The *haha* rendered the need for fences and walls unnecessary, affording an uninterrupted view from the house over the land [...]

2 Michel Foucault, 'Of Other Spaces,' translated by Jay Miscowiec, *Diacritics* 16 / 1 (1986): 22–7.

3 Robert Harbison, *Thirteen Ways: Theoretical Investigations into Architecture* (Cambridge, MA: MIT Press, 1997).

4 Foucault, 'Of Other Spaces,' 26.

7.7 EMMA ROBINSON-TOMSETT
'So Having Ordered My Berth I Lay Me Down to Rest'; Ships and Trains: Travelling Home

> The cabins are very private, boarded up to the ceiling, and a door with a catch lock like our bathroom door at home. Everything seems very clean and new and the lower deck seems much lighter with all the boards being painted white.
>
> Isabel Haigh

This description of the cabin accommodation on the S.S. *Mahana* by Isabel Haigh (c.1890/1891–1962), written during her emigration journey from Liverpool to New Zealand with her husband Samuel in May 1920,[1] suggests one way in which women constructed the spaces of transport in the nineteenth and twentieth centuries.[2] Isabel emphasizes the private nature of their living space, and her comment upon its cleanliness suggests she was reminded of a well-kept domestic space, which is reinforced by her observation that the door's lock was similar to that of their bathroom back home.

Nineteenth- and early-twentieth-century trains and ships can be understood as analogous to domestic, homelike space on several levels. First, the interior spaces of ships and trains were divided by the engineers and designers hired by shipping and rail companies into spaces that echoed the private and domestic, such as the train sleeping compartment or private ship stateroom. The architectural division of much ship space, particularly on the largest ocean liners of the era, echoed some of that of the grander Victorian country home. British stately homes such as Clouds, built in 1886 and owned by the Wyndham family until 1936, commonly contained, among others, a smoking room, drawing room, and library, all of which often had equivalents at sea.[3] The Inman Line's *City of New York* and *City of Paris,* launched in 1888, each had five decks containing cabins, public rooms, staterooms, a saloon 55 wide and 100 feet in length, a ladies' drawing room, smoking room, and a library.[4] Amy Richter usefully notes that late nineteenth-century American trains had library and smoking compartments and parlour cars, which could be found in travellers' real homes.[5]

Alongside the formal division by train and ship designers of the ships' and trains' spaces into some that were domestic, the interior decor of trains and ships also emphasized that these spaces were to be understood as homely. Peter Bailey notes that the Victorian railway compartment carried distinctly domestic, and feminine, associations, most obviously in furnishings that duplicated those of the parlour or boudoir.[6] The *Orient Express* made its maiden journey in 1883;

some of its amenities included gold-embossed leather seats, teak- and mahogany-panelled walls, velvet curtains, Gobelins tapestries, engraved silverware, crystal goblets, silk sheets, steam heat, gas lighting, and running water. This similarity to home interior decor continued into the twentieth century. Traveller Margaret Roberts noted that the furnishings in the train on which she and her brother began their journey from England to India and Burma in 1930 were like those of home: 'We went by the Bombay Express to Folkestone, 1st class, and travelled in luxury. It was more like being in a drawing room than a train for there was a carpet on the floor & each passenger had separate armchairs.'[7]

On both trains and ships, the homelike spaces created for women travellers could therefore be particularly luxurious for those able to afford the more expensive accommodation. Lady Emma Liberty, the wife of the founder of Liberty's department store in London, described the accommodation her party managed to secure on the *Orient Express* at the beginning of their journey around Europe, including Turkey and Greece in the early 1880s: 'Waited more than half-an-hour at the railway station, then possession of our "Wagon Lits." We had secured two compartments in the centre of the carriage, communicating with each other by day, and forming a sitting room furnished with two couches and two tables; the beds open out in the most wonderful manner, one over the other, and are a good size and fairly comfortable.'[8]

However, it is important to recognize here that the comfort and standards of these domestic spaces varied according to passenger class. Within British trains and ships, this division of spaces by different passenger classes came to mimic Britain's social divisions. By the turn of the nineteenth century, ships were typically divided into the accommodation pattern of first, second, and steerage classes, although this hierarchy changed significantly in the mid-twentieth century as steerage class was replaced by 'tourist' class. Trains were often divided into first, second, and third class. The furnishing of these spaces reflected their position within the passenger-class hierarchy, and the cost of travelling within them: those who could afford to travel in first class could expect such luxuries as carpets, couches, and armchairs; those who could only afford to travel in third or steerage class could often expect only wooden tables and benches. Travelling in steerage could be a very unpleasant experience: a 1908 U.S. Immigration Commission investigation of steerage conditions found the only form of cleaning done was sweeping; there were no large receptacles for water; the iron floors were always damp, while the wooden floors stank because they were not washed; and the sleeping quarters were overcrowded and dirty.[9]

However, it was not just transport companies who shaped train and ship spaces into domestic, homelike spaces; women travellers also participated in this process both by making physical alterations to their accommodation and through the material objects they brought with them. Bertha Mason Broadwood (1846–1935), who sailed from England to the West Indies in November 1902, extensively altered her space so that it became a 'home.' At the beginning of her journey, she made her cabin 'fairly shipshape' and described in precise detail how she achieved this.[10] She erected '3/11d. shelves,' which she had bought from an ironmonger, and on which she placed 'my books on the lower shelf, & writing case, & handbag on the top one, the intermediate one being occupied by my mending bag, camera, field glasses, [and] pot of marmalade.'[11]

She displayed an admirable sense of practicality and awareness of the possible effect of journey conditions on this space, adding, 'To prevent things rolling off [the shelves] I rigged up cowl & wires in front.'[12] She then described exactly where she placed her hatboxes, towels, and a net bag for odds and ends, among other items. The personal items she brought into her cabin were those that reminded her of home and enabled her to maintain a connection with home – most notably the marmalade, books, and her writing case. The amount of detail with which she records these changes in her diary also suggests she took considerable pride in adapting her space in such a practical and domestic manner. Amelia B. Edwards (1831–1892), the pioneer of Egyptology, also described the adaptations she made to her cabin on her *dahabeeyah,* the *Philae,* on her journey up the Nile in 1873 and 1874, writing, 'It is wonderful, however, what a few books and roses, an open piano, and a sketch or two, will do. In a few minutes the comfortless hired look has vanished [… and] the *Philae* wears an aspect as cosy and home-like as if she had been occupied for a month.'[13] She commented how the high upper deck on the *Philae* was furnished 'like a drawing-room' with lounge chairs, tables, and rugs.[14] Finally, Isabel and Samuel Haigh made considerable adaptations to their living space on the S.S. *Mahana* to make it more homelike, as Isabel described: 'Ben has put the runners on the black box and the handles on the front and has done many other little things for our convenience in the cabin. He bought some little cups and hooks and things […] and we found two boards and Ben won a few nails from a joiners box that was left about and now we have a good extra shelf and a line to slip up at night so we can have dry towels in the morning.'[15]

Although Isabel did not physically make the alterations herself, it is still likely that she was actively involved in discussing how their cabin could be rearranged.

Finally, passenger and staff practices within ships and trains also transformed these spaces into quasi-domestic spaces. A. James Hammerton claims that the 'shipboard protection practices [such as accommodating single women separately from men in steerage class; author's addition] replicated and magnified the control of women and their incarceration at home under conditions of separate spheres.'[16] Jan Gothard notes that on nineteenth-century emigrant ships bound for Australia the matron was expected to prepare women for their new roles as domestic servants by teaching them key domestic skills such as cooking and sewing.[17]

Travellers also used these spaces in ways that echoed the uses they made of their actual homes. Women used their train and ship living spaces as places of privacy, refuge, and shelter from seasickness, bad weather, and other journeyers, and as spaces in which to rest. Women also pursued leisure activities such as reading and letter writing, and enjoyed social interaction with family and friends in them. Prolific traveller and author Annie Brassey noted that on one occasion during her family's voyage to Canada in 1872, 'we adjourned to the cabin to have some music,' a leisure entertainment that was common in the Victorian middle- and upper-class home.[18] On their return voyage on the S.S. *Russia* she again briefly noted, 'as usual we finished up the evening with whist and supper in our cabin."[19]

However, it is important to note that there was one final complication in women's understandings of ship and train spaces as homely. 'Home' is also understood on an emotional level. While women travellers recognized that these spaces had been constructed in a domestic manner, used them as they used their personal domestic spaces, and some even altered these spaces to make them more homelike, most women travellers never felt the degree of emotional attachment to these spaces that they felt for their homes back in Britain. These spaces can be understood as domestic-like, but they never became 'home-from-homes' for travellers.

NOTES

1 Isabel Haigh and Samuel Haigh, *'Where do all the flies go … ?': The Journal of Isabel and Samuel Haigh as they emigrated to New Zealand in 1920*, researched and edited by Stephen and Margaret Shaw (Malton: Little Ittle Publications, 1996), 29: entry for 29 May 1920, by Isabel Haigh.

2 The phrase 'So Having Ordered My Berth I Lay Me Down to Rest,' is from Bertha Mason Broadwood, Voyage Diary to West Indies, entry for 27 Nov. 1902 (Surrey History Centre, 2185 / BMB / 5 / 17 / 1).

3 Mark Girouard, *The Victorian Country House* (London: Yale University Press, 1979), 31, 33; Caroline Dakers, *Clouds: The Biography of a Country House* (London: Yale University Press, 1993), 89–96.

4 Stephen Fox, *The Ocean Railway: Isambard Kingdom Brunel, Samuel Cunard, and the Revolutionary World of the Great Steamships* (London: HarperCollins, 2003), 299–303.

5 Amy G. Richter, *Home on the Rails: Women, the Railroad and the Rise of Public Domesticity* (Chapel Hill, NC: University of North Carolina Press, 2005), 68, 108, 110.

6 Peter Bailey, 'Adventures in Space: Victorian Railway Erotics, or Taking Alienation for a Ride,' *Journal of Victorian Culture* 9 / 1 (2004): 8.

7 Margaret Ethelwynne Roberts, later Lady Thomas, Diary of Voyage to and from India and Burma, entry for 30 Oct. 1930 (British Library India and Oriental Collection, Mss Eur C546).

8 Lady Emma Lasenby Liberty, *The Levant and Back within Twenty-Eight Days: Extracts From A Diary* (printed for private circulation, 1884), 6: entry for 27 March *c.*1883 / 1884 (City of Westminster Archives, 788 / 184).

9 Stephen Fox, *The Ocean Railway,* 333.

10 Bertha Broadwood, diary entry for 27 Nov. 1902.

11 Ibid.

12 Ibid.

13 Amelia B. Edwards, *A Thousand Miles Up the Nile,* facsimile of the 1888 edition (London: Century, 1993), 36.

14 Ibid., 37.

15 Isabel Haigh and Samuel Haigh, '*Where do all the flies go?*' 30: entry for 31 May 1920. 'Ben' was the name by which Samuel was known, an abbreviation of his middle name, Bennett.

16 A. James Hammerton, 'Gender and Migration,' in Philippa Levine, ed., *Gender and Empire* (Oxford: Oxford University Press, 2004), 163.

17 Jan Gothard, *Blue China: Single Female Migration to Colonial Australia* (Melbourne: Melbourne University Press, 2001), 119.

18 Annie Brassey, *A Cruise in the 'Eothen'* (1872; printed for private circulation, 1873), 10: entry for 7 Sept. 1872.

19 Ibid, 149: entry for 28 Nov. 1872.

7.8 PATRICK CHAN
Vancouver's Laneway Houses: Changing Notions of Home

Home?

A community's identity is often tied to its imagination of what is homely or domestic. In any city, some architectural typologies and urban morphologies are always going to be considered more domestic and homely than others, thus representative of the community's identity. Vancouver is no exception. Modifications to existing urban and suburban forms will be seen as threats to its identity. Thus, it is not surprising that some Vancouverites became upset when city hall's EcoDensity Charter promoted laneway houses – alleyway-oriented secondary houses built at the rear of the primary dwelling unit – as an architectural typology to help support the city's desire for densification.[1]

The laneway house, which can potentially house new demographics, is opposed to the manicured front lawn and pitched-roof facade, conventional signs of a well-tempered Vancouver neighbourhood. An increase in rental-oriented properties like laneway houses, along with an increase in population causes anxiety.[2]

In this essay we will explore ways to look beyond this not-homely view of laneway housing. [3] We will consider how how laneway housing can positively change a Vancouver identity that is often tied to the manicured lawns and pitched-roof craftsman-style houses. We will explore how the understanding and experience of home can be transformed.

What is the Vancouver Neighbourhood?

A laneway house may be considered not-homely because it fronts a service lane frequented by rubbish trucks and city workers who are constantly doing roadwork. Noise and dust are not-homely. The lanes also lead to the ubiquitous North American garages; hence the lanes themselves may be treated as no more than small parking lots. Laneways are also sites for gang and drug violence; and, most importantly, in the case of Vancouver, the lanes are where homeless people walk through at nearly all hours of the day collecting recyclables and engaging in illicit activities. It is not uncommon to find the homeless sleeping behind recycling bins on the laneways in middle- and upper-middle-class neighbourhoods such as Kerrisdale and Kitsilano.

At the same time, an opposite sense of place is felt towards the front street and lawn where each house can be properly numbered. The 'front' is where Vancouver's spatial and social identity is seen to be best secured in its tree-lined streets, single-family craftsman-style houses with generous set-backs, BBQs, and SUVs. Demographically, middle- and upper-middle-class Caucasian and East Asian professionals and landowners inhabit these wealthier west side neighbourhoods. These neighbourhoods are also more likely to oppose laneway housing and the introduction of new demographics such as students, artists, and immigrants needing lower cost rental housing.

The residential lots in Vancouver are spatially divided: the homely front-oriented half with a proper street frontage, a house number, a proper street name, and lines of temperate trees is taken as a sign of resistance against densification, which is often associated with globalism's ills. The not-homely laneway-oriented half, touted to be developed into areas for extra housing to aid densification, represents the ills of globalization and urban development.

Urban theorist William J.V. Neill notes that there is a belief that global processes will scour away distinctiveness and destroy the boundaries of one's identity.[4] Quoting Richard Sennett, Neill further suggests that we live in a 'Protestant ethic of space,' which 'regards the inner life [an assumed stable identity] as the most important and, being fearful of the pleasures, differences and distractions of the "outside", it has a controlling and neutralizing effect on the environment.'[5] A possible cause of this resistance to densification and laneway housing may be owed to a rift between the perceived notion of a home and that which lies outside of home, namely, those elements of difference that threaten fixed spatial and social identities.

Yet neighbourhoods like Kitsilano, Kerrisdale, Cambie-Riley Park, Dunbar, and Shaughnessy – which oppose laneway housing and densification in general – were not always composed the way they are today. Many of the landowners who decide who or what is welcome are Asians. Only a few generations ago they themselves did not fit the profile of the proper Vancouver resident; today they form a model minority who can afford property and thus sit on various neighbourhood visioning committees and are given the chance to voice their displeasure. At these visioning committees and other social outlets they pick which architectural or urban typologies represent 'home' and which ones do not. Another noteworthy fact is that these professionals and landowners are also well-heeled travellers who work within capitalist and globalist economic frameworks. Thus, the binary erected here is not really between capitalism and communalism, or even globalism and localism. It is really an issue of not-home and home.

The way the proper place of Vancouver's residential neighbourhoods can be imagined through the past few generations demonstrates fluidity of place. Here, spatial, cultural, economic, and even racial boundaries are constantly breached and reformed. If boundaries on the scale of the neighbourhood can be reformed, is it not possible for the boundaries between the front-oriented half and laneway-oriented half to be redrawn? If the boundaries of home can spill onto the front lawn and even the street by means of 'neighbourhood-ly' activities like barbecues and street-hockey games, is it not possible that new positive associations of laneways can be made if these laneways are used or inhabited differently? After all, a place becomes good or bad, homely or not, through inhabitation and use. It is a matter of how one relates to it that produces meanings – positive or negative. Lot lines do not define 'home.'

Interiorizing the Laneway House

How can we think of this transformation from not-home to home? One common definition of interiority is that it is something – a place or selfhood – which is produced through interiorization. What is interiorization? For Christine McCarthy, to interiorize something or some space is to control, limit, and restrain it.[6] Interiorization is an action of exclusion, as much as one of inclusion. Interiorization involves categorization and discrimination, and how each psychical or architectural interior space may be occupied. It is about containment and expulsion.[7]

In short, interiority is a form of regulation. Producing an interiority or identity of a place or neighbourhood involves the management of the natural, built, and social environments.[8] Interiorization is a form of place making in a wider sense. Place making is the act of assigning meaning to the place where people inhabit, work, and entertain. Meaning assignment is a process of equating socio-historical, cultural, and political values to things – buildings, trees, streets, laneways, parks, and even the relationships between these built forms. No buildings, trees, laneways, parks, and streets are inherently bad or good. As Neill notes, place making 'involves an emotionally charged spatial imagination extending from the personal to various collective manifestations, including spiritual and symbolic identifications.'[9] At some point this involves equating some buildings, streets, or parks to the notion of good place and others to bad place.

Place making is a process of imagining both good place and bad place, not just the former. Place making is also a matter of asking *when* a site is good – expressive of the neighbourhood's current value system – and *when* it is not. It is about what can be included in one's interior, one's home, and what can be expelled. Yet there is a temporal dimension to place making. Controlling, limiting, and restraining the place-ness of a neighbourhood is always a product of the conditions of that moment in time. This is why Neill notes that there is 'a need not to fetishize place but to see place-construction as a social process' that takes place in passing time.[10]

This temporal condition of a place is best expressed by the fragility of its boundaries. McCarthy notes that between the interior and the exterior is a fragile, porous, and flexible boundary. Interiority is conditioned less by a permanent predetermined spatial enclosure and more by a temporal / temporary enclosure that breaks and reforms over time.[11] The different compositions of forces that at one point define a particular 'good' interiority or enclosure can recompose differently to produce other kinds of interiorities and enclosures *in time*. Other kinds of forces can be incorporated, and hence, other kinds of identities and experiences of home can thus be produced.

To give an example of this spatial and social fragility, one may look at Vancouver's Chinatown and Japantown. They were sites of racial violence not more than a century ago, but are today visited by millions and touted as sites that represent Vancouver's ideal(ized) multicultural-scape. The varying socio-historical, cultural, and political values associated with these spaces point to the fragile boundary between what is considered rightly interior to Vancouver's identity and what is exterior to it. *Time produces this variation in boundaries.*

In this sense, McCarthy notes, an interiority – spatial and / or subjectival – may be engaged as a 'temporal manifestation, subject to the volatile temperament of its boundaries.'[12] It is possible that even the proper streets and front lawns can become not-homely during a severe snowstorm or when night falls. McCarthy further elaborates: 'changes in boundary location (temporal or spatial) breed [other kinds of] interiorities. "Day" and "night," identifiably discrete and bracketed by the setting and rising sun, become seasonally shifting instances of interior containment.'[13]

Following this line of thought that interiority and home are malleable, is it not possible that a laneway can become a homely space when neighbours working on their cars in the garage during the summer months start to communicate and produce new positive social and interpersonal relations? Is it not possible that laneway housing can increase positive human activities in the laneways, in turn increasing the chances for interaction and positive associations with the laneways over time? Moreover, laneway houses functioning as residences as well as artist studios, small businesses, and housing for the aged introduce opportunities for social diversity – which can lead residents to rethink the limits of home and community. An interior's limit or boundary is malleable through *diversifying* engagement and events.

The subjectivity or interiority of both the single-family house occupants and the potential laneway housing occupants can change when their static imaginations of Vancouver and of each other dissipates. Interiority and exteriority are two modalities of the same thing. From a temporal turn, any interiority holds the potential within it to become an exterior and vice versa.

14 Craftsman-style laneway houses in the Arbutus Ridge area of Vancouver, British Columbia. Courtesy of Patrick Chan.

There must be a will, public and private, to allow time to bring in new and sometimes even unfamiliar forces that can enable a reconstitution of how we imagine home and not-home; this in turn may change the quotidian imagination of a laneway. In other words, as McCarthy suggests, a will to inhabit the exterior differently brings about 'a *possibility* of [new] interiority.'[14] This is evident in the growing number of laneway-oriented houses being proposed and constructed in Vancouver. In fact, this process of 'home-making' via laneway housing is already taking place in resistive neighbourhoods like Arbutus Ridge, Cambie-Riley Park, and Kitsilano (see Figure 14). These include already-built housing for young professional couples by firms like LaneFab[15] as well as proposed emergency housing for seniors designed by various community groups.[16]

The not-home is not always exterior to or antithetical to the home. Likewise, the home can be a potential interiority of the not-home. Place- or home-making is always happening-in-time. As Vancouver urbanist Gordon Price commented recently, 'Everyone has to recognize that change, guaranteed by time, will come in some form.'[17]

NOTES

1 See www.ecodensity.ca (accessed 25 June 2009).
2 City of Vancouver, *Ecodensity Summary Report*, http://vancouver.ca/commsvcs/ecocity/pdf/EcoDensity%20Summary%20Report%20_web%281%29.pdf.
3 The concept of the un-homely (*unheimlich*) is explored by writers such as Anthony Vidler, *The Architectural Uncanny: Essays in the Modern Unhomely* (Cambridge, MA: MIT Press, 1992). (See also section 4.7 in this volume.) However, for the purpose of this section, 'not-homely' will be considered to simply mean that which is not considered homely rather than exhibiting a sense of the uncanny.
4 William J.V. Neill, *Urban Planning and Cultural Identity* (London: Routledge, 2004), 4.
5 Ibid, 15.
6 Christine McCarthy, 'Toward a Definition of Interiority,' *Space and Culture* 8 / 2 (2005): 113.
7 Ibid.
8 Ibid.
9 Neill, *Urban Planning*, 112.
10 Ibid.
11 McCarthy, 'Toward a Definition of Interiority,' 115.
12 Ibid., 120.
13 Ibid.
14 Ibid., 119.
15 See www.lanefab.com (accessed 10 Aug. 2010).
16 See http://lestersarmy.com/shelterproject/?page_id=74 (accessed 10 Aug. 2010).
17 See http://pricetags.wordpress.com/2010/08/12/face-off-at-perception-gap/ (accessed 10 Aug. 2010).

CHAPTER EIGHT

Contested Spaces

This chapter presents a selection of domestic spaces that are sites of appropriation, rebellion, or subversion in which normative or conventional views and uses of home and house are challenged. In her astute critique of the home at the turn of the twentieth century, Charlotte Perkins Gilman, the famous advocate of a domestic revolution that would allow for women's full participation in public life, frames her criticism of female unpaid labour through economic and social arguments that show up present domestic arrangements as anachronistic and wasteful. Paige Raibmon notes how, paradoxically, Aboriginal domestic space in the Canadian and American northwest was brought into public domain because of pressure to adopt Victorian ideas of privacy. Discussing the colonial transformation of this domestic space into spectacle in the 1893 Chicago World's Fair, her essay exposes the long-lasting and harmful impact of colonial ideas of home on Aboriginal communities. Rebecca Ginsburg suggests that despite the destructive consequences of apartheid, domestic female workers in Johannesburg in the 1960s and 1970s found opportunities to exert power and independence in their own domestic arrangements and to take charge of the conditions of their family life. Attacking the traditional house structure, Le Corbusier's manifesto famously advocates the house as a machine for living and as a form of mass production. Like Le Corbusier, Swedish architect Lars Lerup disrupts the myth and hegemony of single-family house design – the design that is modelled in Baudrillard's 'bourgeois interior' (see section 6.3 in this volume). But if for modernist Le Corbusier the house was a machine for living, for postmodernist Lerup it is a machine for dreaming; Lerup seeks to liberate architecture from the family narrative and open up an oneiric and fantasy space for poetic and philosophical meditation.[1] Artistic representations of contested and disruptive space come under scrutiny in Richard Shone's discussion of Rachel Whiteread's controversial 1993 installation, *House*. This iconic concrete cast of the inside of an entire Victorian terraced house (demolished in January 1994) offers the pretext for a meditation on the evocative power of other disused rooms in literature and painting, domestic spaces which, once divested of human significance, become casts / masks of memory. David Morley revisits the notion of homelessness by arguing that traditions are flexible forms that cannot be simplistically opposed to modernity, and by showing how home for migrants may be symbolized not by a key but by a suitcase. In this discussion, the 'migrant's suitcase' substantiates Rosemary Marangoly George's contention that 'the immigrant genre is marked … by excessive use of the metaphor of luggage, both spiritual and material.'[2] Turning to contemporary Vancouver, Leslie Robertson examines the negotiations in 'taming space' engaged in by marginalized women in Vancouver's poverty- and drug-ridden Downtown Eastside.

NOTES

1 The only touches of fantasy, whimsy, or even charm (what Christopher Reed would call 'Amusing'; see Section 5.4 in this volume) to which Le Corbusier conceded were due to a woman designer, Charlotte Perriand, whose rugs exhibited in Cologne in 1931 startled the *Neue Sachlich* German designers. See Mary McLeod, 'Furniture and Femininity,' Special Issue, 'Corbusier 100,' *Architectural Review* 181 / 1079 (1987): 43–7.

2 Rosemary Marangoly George, *The Politics of Home: Postcolonial Relocations and Twentieth-Century Fiction* (Cambridge: Cambridge University Press, 1996), 8.

8.1 CHARLOTTE PERKINS GILMAN The Home, Its Work and Influence*

Domestic Mythology

There is a school of myths connected with the home, more tenacious in their hold on the popular mind than even religious beliefs. Of all current superstitions none are deeper rooted, none so sensitive to the touch, so acutely painful in removal [...]

The domestic hearth, with its undying flame, has given way to the gilded pipes of the steam heater and the flickering evanescence of the gas range. But the sentiment about the domestic hearth is still in play. The original necessity for the ceaseless presence of the woman to maintain that altar fire – and it was an altar fire in very truth at one period – has passed with the means of prompt ignition; the matchbox has freed the housewife from that incessant service, but the *feeling* that women should stay at home is with us yet [...]

The Home as a Workshop

The Housemaid

Men are too busy doing other things, too blinded by their scorn for 'women's work.' Women are too busy doing these things to think about them at all; or if they think, stung by the pain of pressing inconvenience, they only think personally, they only feel it for themselves, each one blindly buried in her own home, like the crafty ostrich with its head in the sand.

The question is a public one; none could be more so. It affects in one of its two branches every human being except those who board; every home, without exception. Perhaps some impression may be made on the blank spaces of our untouched minds by exhibiting the economic status of home industry.

We Americans are credited with acuteness and good business sense. How can we reconcile ourselves to the continuance of a system not only so shamefully inadequate, but so ruinously expensive? If we are not mortified to find that our bloated industrial progress carries embedded in its very centre this stronghold of hoary antiquity, this knotted, stumpy bunch of amputated rudiments; if

* (London and New York: McClure, Philips and Co., 1903), 36–61, 82–123; Cambridge University Library.

we are not moved by the low standard of general health as affected by food, and the *no* standard of general education as affecting the baby, perhaps we can be stimulated somewhat by the consideration of expense.

The performance of domestic industries involves, first, an enormous waste of labour. The fact that in nine cases out of ten this labour is unpaid does not alter its wastefulness. If half the men in the world stayed at home to wait on the other half, the loss in productive labour would be that between half and the fraction required to do the work under advanced conditions, say one-twentieth. Any group of men requiring to be cooked for, as a ship's crew, a lumber camp, a company of soldiers, have a proportionate number of cooks. To give each man a private cook would reduce the working strength materially. Our private cooks being women makes no difference in the economic law. We are so accustomed to rate women's labour on a sex-basis, as being her 'duty' and not justly commanding any return, that we have quite overlooked this tremendous loss of productive labour [...]

Is it not time that the home be freed from these industries so palpably out of place? That the expense of living be decreased by two-thirds and the productive labour increased by nine-twentieths? That our women cease to be an almost universal class of house-servants; plus a small class of parasitic idlers and greedy consumers of wealth? That the preparation of food be raised from its present condition of inadequacy, injury, and waste to such a professional and scientific position that we may learn to spare from our street corners both the drug-store and the saloon? That the care of children become at last what it should be – the noblest and most valuable profession, to the endless profit of our little ones and progress of the race? And that our homes, no longer greasy, dusty workshops, but centres of rest and peace; no longer gorgeous places of entertainment that does not entertain, but quiet places of happiness; no longer costing the laborious lives of overworked women or supporting the useless lives of idle ones, but properly maintained by organised industries; become enjoyed by men and women alike, both glad and honourable workers in an easy world?

8.2 PAIGE RAIBMON
'Living on Display: Colonial Visions of Aboriginal Domestic Spaces'*

Notions of domesticity were central to colonial projects around the globe. They were part of the fray when metropole and colony collided and transformed one another [...] The colonial desire to order domestic space had its correlate in broader attempts to impose discipline in the public sphere [...] On the late nineteenth-century Northwest Coast [of North America], this process took shape for Aboriginal people who increasingly lived not only overseas from, but within, the society of the colonizing metropoles. Aboriginal people experienced extreme pressure to bring their lives into conformity with Victorian expectations about private, middle-class, bourgeois domesticity. This pressure came not only from isolated missionaries posted in lonely colonial outposts but also from a broad swath of colonial society. So intense was the interest in Aboriginal domestic arrangements, however, that colonial society brought Aboriginal domestic space into the public domain as never before, even as it urged Aboriginal communities to adopt the Victorian values of the domestic private sphere. While missionaries and government officials pressured Aboriginal families to replace multifamily longhouses with Victorian-style nuclear family dwellings, anthropologists and tourists invaded Aboriginal homes, alternately in search of a rapidly receding ('savage') past or a slowly dawning ('civilized') future [...] In a sense, as they transformed Aboriginal domestic spaces into spectacle, all of the members of these non-Aboriginal groups became sightseers.

Domestic space was transformed into spectacle, and attempts to effect greater separation between private and public spaces simultaneously blurred the two, creating a hybrid public / private domain. Colonialism is riven with such invariably ironic contradictions. But the importance of such contradictions runs deeper than postmodern irony. While with one hand colonial society held out the promise of assimilation, with the other it impressed upon Aboriginal people its lack of good faith. The history of Aboriginal people in North America is replete with 'sweet' promises gone sour; with 'final' promises turned final solutions [...] How did colonizers reconcile these contradictions, these 'tensions of empire'? [...] A review of their views of Aboriginal domestic space provides an opportunity to address this question.

---

* Special Issue, 'Domestic Spaces,' edited by Kathy Mezei, *BC Studies*, no. 140 (Winter 2003): 69–89.

When curious, often nosy, sometimes aggressive members of colonial society entered Aboriginal homes, they brought the things they needed to make sense of the room around them. The significance of cultural practice may lie in the story we tell ourselves about ourselves, but the insight that the metropole has been defined by the colonies, and the 'self' by the 'other,' forces us to acknowledge that culture is also the story we tell ourselves about others [...] The colonial preoccupation with the domestic spaces of Aboriginal people provides a window onto stories that worked in both of these ways simultaneously. The stories that members of colonial society told themselves about Aboriginal people were also stories they told themselves about themselves. The stories that Canadians and Americans told themselves differed, as did specific policies and conditions on both sides of the border. However, during the late nineteenth century, public interest in 'authentic' Indians and pride in successful Indian policy were important components of both countries' sense of nationalism. Differences in policy did not preclude continuities in attitudes and assumptions. Colonizers' fascination with the domestic spaces of Aboriginal people offer us an important moment of cultural convergence.

The colonial narration of Aboriginal domestic space as spectacle generated a multiplicity of stories about, among other things, Aboriginal savagery, White civilization, colonial legitimacy, and modernity. Two assumptions of colonial thought recur in these stories. First, from their various, and admittedly diverse, vantage points, members of late nineteenth-century colonial society cast domestic spaces and domestic goods as material markers of civilization. But this alone cannot explain the sway that these markers of domesticity held over the colonial imagination. The second assumption takes us this additional step. The evidence suggests that members of colonial society assumed that the significance of these markers was more than skin deep. They assumed that the markers were straightforward reflections of the inner state of the individual's soul and the family's moral state. They extrapolated from fixed material form to fixed immaterial self. If the space was civilized, then likewise its inhabitants; if the space was uncivilized, then so were its inhabitants.

Aboriginal domestic spaces were put on display in a variety of contexts and along a continuum of consent [...] Whether they suffered public scrutiny willingly or not, most Aboriginal families could ill afford to forgo the material benefits that accompanied submission to the colonial view. Some form of direct or indirect remuneration usually accompanied the performance of everyday life. This sometimes came as wages, at other times it came from the sale of souvenirs to sightseers hoping to commemorate their excursions into Aboriginal domestic space [...]

Exposition Space

[...] While live exhibits at European fairs tended to come from distant overseas colonies, North American fairs, beginning with the 1893 Chicago World's Fair, featured displays of internally colonized Aboriginal people. While most of these performers spent at least some time in scripted song and dance performances, the bulk of their time as live exhibits was given over to the performance of everyday life.

The live exhibits at the 1893 Chicago World's Fair invariably revolved around domestic dwellings. Millions of tourists flocked to see Aboriginal people supposedly living 'under ordinary conditions and occupying a distinctive habitation.'[1] These dwellings fed into the fair's organizational theme: progress. They offered a relief against which visitors could measure the architectural achievements not only of the rest of the fair but also of dominant society in general. As one reporter wrote, the Aboriginal dwellings stood 'in amazing contrast to the white palaces stretching away to the north, that evidence[d] the skill and prosperity of their successors in this western domain.'[2] Against this backdrop of modernity, the Aboriginal dwellings lent themselves to a social evolutionist narrative that legitimated colonial endeavours.

Anthropologists and other exhibitors erected a 'great Aboriginal encampment,'[3] consisting of the living spaces of Aboriginal people from across North America. While newspaper reporters might concede that Aboriginal people lived in 'stone, brick and frame houses'[4] when they were at home, they imagined 'authentic' Aboriginal dwellings as something quite different. For the duration of their time at the fair, Inuit families lived in skin tents; Penobscot families in birchbark wigwams; Navajo families in hogans; Menominee families in skin tepees; Winnebago families in 'sugar-loaf' woven reed mat wigwams; Chippewa families in birchbark longhouses; Iroquois families in elm and birchbark huts and longhouses; and Kwakwa̲ka̲'wakw families in cedar plank longhouses [...] [See Figure 15]. Anthropologists simultaneously created and fulfilled expectations of authenticity among visitors to the fair by carefully stage managing the forms of dwelling put on display [...]

The Kwakwa̲ka̲'wakw performers from northern Vancouver Island were, in several respects, typical of the live exhibits. Frederic Ward Putnam, Harvard professor and organizer of the anthropology display, explained that the sixteen Kwakwa̲ka̲'wakw participants would 'live under normal conditions in their natural habitations during the six months of the Exposition.'[5] In order to reinforce the aura of ordinary life, Putnam and his assistants worked to ensure that the Kwakwa̲ka̲'wakw troupe consisted of family units. This principle was applied to

15 Kwakwa̲ka̲’wakw village at the Chicago Fair, 1893. Negative number 322897, Photo. A. J. Rota, Courtesy of Department of Library Services, American Museum of Natural History.

most of the live exhibits, although the definition of ‘family’ in this context was a non-Aboriginal one. Organizers attempted to limit the performers to couples and their children, even when would-be performers expressed a desire to travel in larger groups [...]

Putnam’s fixation with producing authentic, ‘normal’ conditions extended to his insistence that the domiciles be originals rather than faux reproductions. Thus, when the Kwaka̲ka̲’wakw from Vancouver Island arrived at the Chicago World’s Fair, they reassembled the planks of a cedar longhouse that had been disassembled at a Nuwitti village on the northern coast of Vancouver Island before being shipped by rail to Chicago. The house’s authenticity was heightened by the report that, when it was chosen for the exhibit, it had actually been occupied by a Kwaka̲ka̲’wakw family [...]

The display of everyday life was about domestic goods as well as domestic space. ‘Traditional’ domestic goods completed the tableaux of Aboriginal domesticity presented by the familial scenes. Visitors could see the Kwakwa̲ka̲’wakw living among items representative of everyday and ceremonial life, including canoes, house poles, totem poles, masks, and regalia. And if they strolled past the dairy exhibit to the nearby anthropology building, visitors could inspect hundreds of other implements integral to Northwest Coast Aboriginal life. Like other human performers, the Kwakwa̲ka̲'wakw were living appendages of the vast displays of ethnographic objects, many of them drawn from domestic life. The Kwakwa̲ka̲'wakw exhibit in Chicago was an explicit realization of the colonial assumption that the 'normal' – that is, 'traditional' and 'authentic' – state of these so-called savages was most visible in their 'everyday life.' The enormous trouble and expense that exhibit organizers took to ensure that the mock villages consisted of 'real' houses, filled with 'real' goods was emblematic of their belief that inner meaning was inherent within outward form. They knew that the live exhibits did not 'normally' live beneath the intrusive eyes of millions of visitors. But they nonetheless assumed that the more subjective characteristics of everyday life could be held stable as long as outward conditions and characteristics were replicated as precisely as possible [...]

Colonial society from the nineteenth century through to the present has focused on houses as representative material forms of culture – as culture in practice. And Aboriginal people have consistently inhabited their houses in ways that prove the simplistic nature of this assumption.

NOTES

1 'The Man Columbus Found,' *New York Press,* 28 May 1893, Scrapbook, vol. 2, Frederic Ward Putnam Papers, Harvard University Archives.
2 *The Dream City* (St Louis, MO: N.D. Thompson Publishing, 1893), n.p.
3 'All Kinds of Indians,' *Daily Inter Ocean* (Chicago), 20 June 1893.
4 See, for example, *Daily Inter Ocean* (Chicago), 9 July 1893, Scrapbook, vol. 2, Frederic Ward Putnam Papers, Harvard University Archives.
5 Rossiter Johnson, ed., *A History of the World's Columbian Exposition Held in Chicago in 1893* (New York: D. Appleton, 1897), vol. 1, 315.

8.3 REBECCA GINSBURG
'"Come in the Dark": Domestic Workers and Their Rooms in Apartheid-Era Johannesburg, South Africa'*

Apartheid was good for no one, but there was nobody it was worse for than African women. This was especially true with regard to housing. South Africa's vast collection of policies and regulations governing who could live in which areas under what conditions imposed more hardships upon African women than on any other group. Whether in rural African villages, white farms, or cities, they found themselves disadvantaged by discriminatory laws based on race and restricted because of their gender. Both legal and social structures assumed and demanded female dependence on men for housing and support. African women had few options and little autonomy in deciding where and how to live.

The quiet tree-lined streets of segregated white residential neighbourhoods, miles from the areas where most Africans lived, were an unlikely setting for African women's challenges to this state of affairs. Nonetheless, it was here that significant numbers of them began to exercise control over the terms of their housing and to take charge of the conditions of their family life. Indeed, as apartheid became even more repressive, with the government making even harsher attempts to squeeze Africans from the cities and into so-called homelands, women found themselves holding increasingly greater power over their domestic arrangements. This tension – between the oppression of apartheid and the opportunities it provided women to alter the conditions of home life – reached a peak during the height of apartheid, in the 1960s and 1970s [...]

At the centre of the story was a humble structure: the live-in domestic worker's quarter, commonly known as a 'back room.' [...] Every middle-class property contained one of these shelters, constructed at the same time as the main house and considered just as essential. These small detached buildings were where a household's live-in African servant retired after completing her day's work in the white house [...] It was because she had access to such a place that an African woman could shift the balance of power in her domestic arrangements. My account of how domestic workers exploited their control over these rooms and the implications of their activities there is based mainly on interviews I conducted between 1995 and 1998 with former domestic workers and their employers in Johannesburg, South Africa's largest city.

---

* *Perspectives in Vernacular Architecture* 8 (2000): 83–100.

The Call of the City

African men and women had worked in white people's homes – as paid employees, indentured servants, or slaves – since the earliest days of European colonization. The attraction of higher paying mine jobs and other considerations gradually pulled men away from such employment, until by the mid-twentieth century domestic service was almost entirely a female-only occupation [...]

Since as early as the turn of the nineteenth century, African marriages had been subject to a series of profound stresses related to increased male migration to the mines and the cities. Men's long terms of absence and the personal and social affronts they endured while living in white society raised their interests in coming home to a family in which their roles as patriarchs and masters were respected. At the same time, the women they had left behind found themselves increasingly disinclined to submit to the authority of someone they only rarely saw and who provided little support towards the day-to-day maintenance of the household [...]

Rates of adultery, divorce, desertion, and premarital pregnancy increased as women and men tried to work out new ways of relating to one another. Many women made the move to the city precisely to escape the increasingly stressed gender and familial relations of rural areas, and this exodus continued well into the 1960s and 1970s [...]

The rural women who reached the city understood that their employment options were effectively limited to domestic service. After all, most lacked education, proficiency in English or Afrikaans, and experience other than house or field work – not to mention a valid work permit, which would have been required by any reputable corporate employer. They also recognized that their housing needs could most efficiently and easily be met by taking a back room on a white employer's property. For that reason, most found themselves heading directly to the white suburbs upon their arrival in the city.

Suburban Johannesburg

Johannesburg's white residents lived in comfortable, racially exclusive neighbourhoods [...] Typically, a main house designed for nuclear family occupation by white residents sat facing the street [...] A driveway might lead to a garage and a walkway to the front door. In the backyard was a cluster of service buildings – toolshed, storage bin, a servant's back room or two, and a toilet and shower stall for African staff. Back rooms varied only slightly in size and plan, generally measuring about eight by ten feet, almost always constructed of brick, with concrete floors and no ceilings. They rarely had electricity. Furnishings consisted usually of the cast-offs of the employer. A twin bed, wardrobe, and small bench were standard. Not much more could fit inside. There was a single door that locked with a key, usually held by both the worker and her white employers, and, typically, a single, small window [...]

A minority of suburbs were high-density areas that contained large apartment buildings [...] On the top of each apartment building – in a few cases, in their basements – was a dormitory for workers. Along narrow hallways open to the skies were rows of single rooms, communal toilets, and bathing facilities. Each room was owned or rented by the white resident for whom its occupant worked; servants' rooms were included in the purchase or lease of a flat. The quarters were about the same size as back rooms, each also with a single door and window. The 'skylight locations' were accessible from stairs that ascended from the top floor of the building. Elevators did not travel this high and were reserved anyway for white passengers only. Entry to the building itself was gained from a separate servants' entrance on the ground floor. Officially, about 100,000 African servants lived in Johannesburg during this period, about three-quarters of them in back rooms and the rest in skylight locations. By comparison, white Johannesburg had a population of about 400,000 and nearby Soweto of approximately 750,000 [...]

Domestic Service

[...] The ease with which they could be fired – expressed specifically in terms of an eviction – was only one problem faced by servants. They had to deal as well with financial worries, physical fatigue, and the preservation of their dignity in conditions that conspired to undermine it. Domestic workers' greatest concern, though, on a daily basis, was fighting loneliness. They spent most of their waking hours inside the white house. If the sole employee of this household, they passed much of this time in relative isolation. The habit of some employers of locking their workers in the house during the day to ensure they did not leave, in addition to being a dangerous practice, accentuated these women's feelings of being removed from others [...]

Night-time could be even worse. For many, the communal life among strangers in the skylight location was alienating and frightening after the accustomed order of their rural communities. Many retreated to their rooms, though there was little to do there [...] What women seemed to miss most of all were intimate and sustained relationships with men. Although it meant breaking the law and, usually, the explicit rules of their employers, and therefore risking their jobs; they arranged to sneak African men onto white properties and into their back rooms to stay with them there [...]

There was no shortage of males looking desperately for lodging. African men had been making their ways to Johannesburg since the earliest days of European settlement in the region, following the discovery of gold in 1867 [...] Men who arrived in the city without the proper documentation and without a job in hand were in the least favourable housing position. They qualified for none of the official African housing in townships or workers' hostels. Johannesburg's hotels and boarding residences were strictly 'whites only.' African newcomers to the area found themselves essentially homeless. Some found shelter in public spaces, for instance, on city streets, public toilets, parks, mine dumps, and train stations. The possibility of spending time in a servant's room while trying to secure one's own job and, possibly, independent accommodation offered a much more pleasant alternative [...] Even some men who had their own township houses – in nearby Soweto, for example – preferred to stay instead in the back rooms with their girlfriends [...] One attraction was no doubt the lure of the mistress over the wife and the children, but living with a domestic servant also offered material amenities. Far from the dirt roads of the townships or the noxious noises of industry, back rooms sat in green gardens in quiet neighbourhoods [...] Compared to other housing alternatives, and even in its own right, the back room offered a pleasant spot to return to in the evenings.

The physical setting of the back room was matched favourably by its amenities. Beds, though often the rejects of employers, were an improvement over the concrete slabs of the hostels. Some backyard bathrooms had hot and cold running water, unlike either township houses or the compounds. And the toilet and bathroom would be shared by only two instead of ten or two hundred. A few rooms even had electricity [...]

Every domestic worker that I interviewed had engaged, at some point during this period, in the practice of secretly hiding people in the back room. Several of them seem to have run virtual boarding houses. 'You [would] find that in the rooms, we [slept] like sardines.'[...] Though they also housed their children, friends, and, sometimes, absolute strangers, the most common guests, by far, were male lovers. And while practical necessity and pangs of loneliness were often the driving forces in bringing two people together, these relationships were by no means completely mercenary affairs [...] Love did exist in the back rooms. However, the forms that it assumed were subject to change. In these settings that they controlled, women began to ask for new forms of attachment from their partners [...]

Significance

The practice of hiding people carried multiple significances for domestic workers. At the most basic level, it provided warm human contact. These women were often miserably lonely. Many were ill-treated. Their rooms were cold and dark. Having a roommate offered assurance that at the end of a long day, there was […] 'somebody to talk to.'[…]

Clearly, though, once a person made a commitment to hiding someone, for a weekend or for months at a time, she found that the comforts of companionship carried a whole host of problems. Would the dogs bark? Was the new watchman bribable? When would the police next raid? […] Nonetheless, it was partly just because there were so many pressures associated with hiding others that the practice provided meaning on a second level. It gave these women the satisfaction of taking control of their lives and making bearable hard conditions […] There was pleasure in designing a room to accommodate secret visitors, plotting escape routes, and devising schedules of entry and egress […] In addition […] these practices allowed domestic workers a means of resisting individually and privately what they saw as unfair labour practices, at the same time their menfolk were organizing into trade unions and engaging in collective action to assert themselves within their own employment spheres.

'Come in the Dark'

What most distinguished the use of domestic workers' quarters from other historical examples of surreptitious use of space – for example, from the hiding of black slaves in the United States or Jews during the Holocaust – was that women controlled these places and set the terms for their use. It was the meaning that the practice held for domestic workers *as women* that was ultimately most significant. Many domestic workers, as we have seen, sought what some called 'modern' relationships, unions that offered fewer restrictions and, as they saw it, greater personal dignity. City life offered many favourable conditions for achieving this. Women's potential for financial independence there and their release from the control of authoritative family members made it easier for them to negotiate domestic relations on terms that suited their interests.

However, at the same time, women in the city encountered a significant new obstacle. An African woman needed a man to register for a township house. This requirement, first introduced in the 1930s and strongly reinforced by the apartheid regime in the 1960s, often cut against women's efforts to establish themselves independently. Indeed, many women tolerated severe marital hardships rather than risk losing their rights to urban residence. 'Women did everything to save their houses. They … married their own cousins or relatives, or even men they did not like.'[…] Domestic workers had another advantage over their township and country sisters in their shared efforts to create personally satisfying relationships. Their distinct and intimate exposure to white families helped broaden their vision of what marriage could be. It encouraged them to consider new options for themselves and, perhaps most importantly, provided them a model to assert against their partners for negotiating purposes […] Their impressions of white marriage may have sometimes been rose-hued […] but it was not as important that African women were accurate in their perceptions of white marriage, sometimes confusing the privileges of class with those of race, as that they were moved and empowered by them […]

For men who believed that the old rules still applied – that 'when I get to my house … I must feel I am being welcomed and everything is done to make me feel back home – a husband feels he should be appreciated when he gets home' – life in a back room could prove a rude awakening […] There were frequent cases of domestic abuse in the servants' quarters; women did not have absolute power there. But even this violence may have been less a sign of men's continuing control over their women than a symptom of its disintegration. In the rooms that they controlled, and by virtue of the fact that they controlled them, African women took giant steps in their efforts to acquire a new sense of their own dignity […]

Conclusion

By housing their men, workers opened the doors of the city to 'illegal' African immigration from the countryside, thus undermining one of the basic assumptions of apartheid, that of white control over urban space. By the mid-1980s, even before the dismantling of apartheid, the National Party government abolished influx control. Its proven impracticability was an important factor in its eventual elimination. Ironically, much of the movement of Africans that so undermined the intent of apartheid's planners took place literally under the noses of domestic workers' white employers. Equally ironically, it was just because this activity took place on private property that it could happen at all.

Most English-speaking whites, even if they disagreed with the government's position on African influx control, did not like the idea of boarding African families in their backyards. But what many disliked even more was the rough intrusions of police – most of whom were working-class Afrikaners – onto their properties […] On principle, they refused to cede their rights to control entry onto their lots […]

For other homeowners, a different principle was at stake. A small minority felt so strongly opposed to the government's influx control policies that they practised civil disobedience in protest, choosing to fight apartheid as it appeared literally at their doorsteps. Precious M.'s madam not only allowed her children to visit during school holidays, she put them up in her own guest room in the main house.[1] Susanna M.'s employer went to jail for fifteen days in protest of apartheid policy rather than pay a fine for illegally harbouring an unregistered worker [...]

White suburbia, the ostensible nurturing grounds for the white nuclear families that formed the core of the apartheid state, served simultaneously as a vast underground railroad station for Africans. And the least remarkable structure in these places, the simple domestic worker's back room, was the key to the whole operation. By exploiting their control of these structures and their social and physical environments, servants were able to make space in the city for their loved ones. In the process, they also forged important new places for themselves.

NOTE

1 Precious M., interview by author, tape recording, Johannesburg, 19 July 1995.

8.4 LE CORBUSIER
Towards a New Architecture*

Argument

[...] Our eyes are constructed to enable us to see forms in light.

Primary forms are beautiful forms because they can be clearly appreciated.

Architects to-day no longer achieve these simple forms.

Working by calculation, engineers employ geometrical forms, satisfying our eyes by their geometry and our understanding by their mathematics; their work is on the direct line of good art [...]

Architects to-day are afraid of the geometrical constituents of surfaces.

The great problems of modern construction must have a geometrical solution [...]

* [1923]. Translated by Frederick Etchells (London: Architectural Press; New York: Frederick A. Praeger, 1978 [1927]).

A great epoch has begun.

There exists a new spirit.

There exists a mass of work conceived in the new spirit; it is to be met with particularly in industrial production [...]

The problem of the house has not yet been stated.

Nevertheless there do exist standards for the dwelling house.

Machinery contains in itself the factor of economy, which makes for selection.

The house is a machine for living in [...]

The business of Architecture is to establish emotional relationships by means of raw materials.

Architecture goes beyond utilitarian needs.

Architecture is a plastic thing.

The spirit of order, a unity of intention.

The sense of relationships; architecture deals with quantities.

Passion can create drama out of inert stone [...]

We must create the mass-production spirit.

The spirit of constructing mass-production houses.

The spirit of living in mass-production houses.

The spirit of conceiving mass-production houses.

If we eliminate from our hearts and minds all dead concepts in regard to the house, and look at the question from a critical and objective point of view, we shall arrive at the 'House-Machine,' the mass-production house, healthy (and morally so too) and beautiful in the same way that working tools and instruments which accompany our existence are beautiful [...]

The history of Architecture unfolds itself slowly across the centuries as a modification of structure and ornament, but in the last fifty years steel and concrete have brought new conquests, which are the index of a greater capacity for construction, and of an architecture in which the old codes have been overturned. If we challenge the past, we shall learn that 'styles' no longer exist for us, that a style belonging to our own period has come about; and there has been a Revolution.

The Engineer's Aesthetic and Architecture

[...] But men live in old houses and they have not yet thought of building houses adapted to themselves. The lair has been dear to their hearts since all time. To such a degree and so strongly that they have established the cult of the home. A *roof!* then other household gods. Religions have established themselves on dogmas, the dogmas do not change; but civilizations change and religions tumble to dust. Houses have not changed. But the cult of the house has remained the same for centuries. The house will also fall to dust [...]

Mass-Production Houses

[...] One thing leads to another, and as so many cannons, airplanes, lorries and wagons had been made in factories, someone asked the question: 'Why not make houses?' There you have a state of mind really belonging to our epoch. Nothing is ready, but everything can be done. In the next twenty years, big industry will have co-ordinated its standardized materials, comparable with those of metallurgy; technical achievement will have carried heating and lighting and methods of rational construction far beyond anything we are acquainted with [...] Dwellings, urban and suburban, will be enormous and square-built and no longer a dismal congeries; they will incorporate the principle of mass-production and of large-scale industrialization. It is even possible that building 'to measure' will cease. An inevitable social evolution will have transformed the relationship between tenant and landlord, will have modified the current conception of the dwelling-house, and our towns will be ordered instead of being chaotic. A house will no longer be this solidly-built thing which sets out to defy time and decay, and which is an expensive luxury by which wealth can be shown; it will be a tool as the motor-car is becoming a tool. The house will no longer be an archaic entity, heavily rooted in the soil by deep foundations, built 'firm and strong,' the object of the devotion on which the cult of the family and the race has so long been concentrated.

Eradicate from your mind any hard and fast conceptions in regard to the dwelling-house and look at the question from an objective and critical angle, and you will inevitably arrive at the 'House-Tool,' the mass-production house, available for everyone, incomparably healthier than the old kind (and morally so too) and beautiful in the same sense that the working tools, familiar to us in our present existence, are beautiful.

8.5 LARS LERUP
'Planned Assaults: Reflections on the Detached House'*

During the twentieth century the single-family house has been the most prominent domestic aspiration of my class. The conventions of garage, front yard, living room, kitchen, dining room, corridor, bathroom, master bedroom, auxiliary bedrooms, and backyard are the locus of the modern family. It is more important for the house to lack some of its components than it is for it to be complete, since this propels the yearning for a better life. The house plan is thought of as nature – as an unquestionable datum upon which both architecture and family exist. This distinct economy of spatial relations began in the late eighteenth century, only to become full-fledged in this century. The family narrative with its endless flow of birth and death is tattooed into the mythical weave of this plan. The gender mechanics, fear, gloom, and happiness are exercised as if the family was still in paradise. My work is a planned assault on this mythical nature, not ultimately to change it but to expose the little tactics of the habitat.

Villa Prima Facie: The Erased Plan

The first house is a 'heroic' attempt to rescue architecture from the hegemony of the family narrative and the plan. The client wanted no part of the family, no reminder, no memory. He wanted a fresh plan.

Today, the organization of domestic space relies entirely on the plan as the generator. In this process the built material – the substance of architecture – takes a secondary position in favour of the abstract principles of the plan. Walls have become mere spatial definition and the house has become an envelope for behaviour. Thus the plan was erased. Below is the fundament of architecture – the floor. On this floor a row of six walls are erected: a soft wall, a dry wall, a hot wall, a hard wall, a wet wall, and another soft wall. The plan erased, the floor and the walls are the anchors of existence – during an earthquake you rush to the soft wall, during a thunder storm you rush to the dry wall, when you are cold you sit by the hot wall, in the summer you cool off near the wet wall. The hard wall serves as the divider in times of domestic strife. All the walls are set inside a green house. Finally, at the end of the row of walls, just outside the greenhouse, a bedroom is placed. It is one-eighth the size of a suburban house, since sleeping is the only thing the client has in common with the family. This row of walls, the

---

* Special Issue, 'L'inquieto spazio domestico / Disputed Domestic Space,' edited by Pierluigi Nicolin. *Lotus International* 44 (1984): 76–81.

virgin floor and the minimal shelter, bring architecture back to the basics – to the bedrock of architecture.

The No-Family House: The Disrupted Plan

The family narrative, with all its mini-discourses and associated behaviours (feeding the children, taking a nap, going to the bathroom, eating dinner, sleeping, entertaining, and so on) consumes the house with a ruthless disinterest in architecture. The physical house is merely the vehicle for the narrative. The decision to disrupt it is both to delay the narrative, to break it open and to reveal its mechanics, and to bring forth the physical by peeling off its assigned functions. The struggle is between family and architecture.

Symbolically the two symmetrical glass houses stand for the family; they are transparent screens or containers, filled with our daily soap operas. The lion-yellow lump between them stands for architecture. The struggle between the two houses results in penetrations, accretion, and production. This is driven by family power – auto-affection and hetero-affection – here transformed into architectural production, rotation, and lateral shifting. In addition, a series of traps are placed in the new house – the liberated handrail, the useless door, the fresh window, the stair that leads nowhere, and other minor subversions. The result is a house filled with ruptures, cul-de-sacs, displacements, erasures, and collisions. The plan of the single family house is engraved on the entry floor of the glass house.

If the no-family house were to be built, it too would eventually be consumed by its family and the raw surfaces would be bridged over and repaired. These repairs would be the technology of the family.

The Love / House: The Shadow Plan

This house is driven by a singular activity – a single emotion – waiting. But it is of a particular kind of waiting, that of waiting for the lover. This state of mind is described by Roland Barthes in his book *A Lover's Discourse:* 'Tumult of anxiety provoked by waiting for the loved being, subject to delays (rendezvous, letters, telephone calls, returns).'

There is no place in the conventional house plan for this almost clandestine activity. In fact, the whole lover's discourse 'is completely forsaken by surrounding languages: ignored, disparaged, or derided … Once a discourse is driven by its own momentum into the backwater of the "unreal," there is no recourse but to attempt to create a *place* for its 'affirmation.' Most spaces in the single family house are completely exposed, transparent, and designed for everyday life. The fragments of the lover's discourse must therefore hide themselves in the folds and shadows of the plan. But the proper place for waiting is outside the house, in the depth of its shadow, in a true state of unreality.

The place for waiting is thus conceived of as the shadow itself, as a thick sedimentation cast by the double of her house, in the fourth court inside the block in a 'popular' neighbourhood in Paris. The construction of the shadow follows Sigmund Freud's principles of dream transformations: condensation, displacement, and over-determination. The *reality* of her house was transformed using the three mechanisms into a *dream house* – the scaffold for waiting.

Not unlike the unconscious, the black, green, and white shadow house stands as another true reality against the convention of the single family house. This other reality is architecture, in this case a mere dream and a drawing, but still the opposite to the conventions of the plan, and to the lover himself.

8.6 RICHARD SHONE
'A Cast in Time'*

[Rachel Whiteread's] *House* was the death mask of a particular space and a finite period of time. It was the solidification of memory, anonymous history made palpable […] [See Figure 16.]

In choosing the process of casting as the predominant medium for her work, Rachel Whiteread extends one of the oldest sculptural practices. The funerary monuments of Roman nobles and citizens often included a death mask to stand above some suitable inscription, 'for the sake of memory and posterity.' Masks of forebears were hoarded by families so that, as Pliny wrote, 'at a funeral the entire clan was present.' In fifteenth-century Florence, casting became a profitable business, particularly of wax casts made from a plaster mould […]

The mechanically authentic properties of the cast became reserved for waxwork museums and curious, private devotions; the aesthetic high ground was occupied by the often bland and enervated presence of the marble bust. In this context, it is interesting to note that some of the complaints directed against *House* centred on its lifelikeness, that the artist had not done enough to relieve the structure of its unsavoury ordinariness. The house she had cast was already 'an eyesore,' a shabby survival from a time of good riddance; why perpetuate it as such? Others, however, found its inside-out reality its most affecting quality.

---

* In *Rachel Whiteread: House*, edited by James Lingwood (London: Phaidon, 1995), 50–61.

16 Rachel Whiteread, *House,* 1993. © 2010 Rachel Whiteread. Photography by Sue Omerod / Courtesy of Gagosian Gallery.

The magical properties ascribed to casts in earlier ages appeared undiminished in the passionately mixed reactions to *House* […]

In the central section of *To the Lighthouse,* Virginia Woolf pictures the long neglect of the Ramsay family's summer home by the sea. The objects and furniture left within the house take on a life of their own as they submit themselves to the passage of Time. The orderly sense of space containing objects of personal significance – a chair, a chest of drawers, a mirror – is shattered. They no longer maintain their human usefulness. Time re-moulds, decays, transfigures them. They become vessels of memory and touchstones of experience. In order to assume a substantial structure in the mind, they must be divested of their mundane physical presence, as a cast is made by the destruction of its subject.

All of Rachel Whiteread's work, even at its most severely formal, touches this nerve of memory. She casts from basic pieces of furniture and domestic goods – from cupboards and tables to mattresses and sinks. They are the archetypal objects of urgent daily use, nagged and stained by wear and tear. They come to her from wasteland, rubbish tip, street corner, and scrap-yard. Hers is a lowly repertory in which the humblest examples of their kind are commonly linked by their lack of intricacy or ornament. The space they occupy or conceal is measured by the universal requirements of the human body. Its imprint is everywhere – from the indented, nippled mattress to the rusted bathtub. Sounds and gestures are evoked throughout her work – the splash of water through the sink, a body turning on a bed – with an eloquence entirely dependent on the physical properties of the object. We as viewers provide what narrative we must, read where we will among these blocks and sleepers and concavities, these anxious soundings from a reality we thought we knew [...]

Rooms take on a pervasive significance in our lives – their shape, size, light, colours, (in)adequacy, their furnishings (or lack of them). Some remain, for all time, the apple of our eye; others are festooned in our mind with boredom, deterioration, and death. There are rooms remembered for how we viewed ourselves at a certain moment, rooms haunted by other people, etched for us by particular actions or a volley of words, rooms that form rafts of a submerged narrative. We remember how a table was placed just so, a stain was made, how a door wouldn't fully open against a cupboard, how slowly the water drained from a sink, how the bed, once positioned, assumed an authority it held in no other part of the room.

Whiteread suggests all this without resorting to anecdote or blackmailing us with emotional particularity. In this sense, her casts are dumb, her walls bare; we tap round them with our eyes as though with a white stick. Every bump and mark, each soiled underside, each remnant of a human presence becomes collectively significant with the artist's intervention. This concentration on outer materiality guides us to an inner reality, without compromising the formal integrity of the object.

There is a painting by Bonnard of a room in his house, predominantly yellow and a filmy grey. At the far right, through a door that is open towards us, half a figure can be glimpsed; most of the rest of the picture is a representation of woodwork and plaster. Throughout there is a strong vertical emphasis, only interrupted by the central rectangle of a fireplace. Bonnard suggests privacy – for the half-seen figure is a naked woman – with the minimum of means, investing the simple structural features of an 'ordinary' room with the brimming disquiet of the present moment. Yet the room has the look of some part-excavated burial- chamber, as though Mme Bonnard, who had died a few months before the picture was painted, had risen from her sarcophagus-bathtub to hover like a wraith beyond the door.

In another room, dominated by a plaster wall parallel to the picture plane, Vermeer has placed a woman pouring milk. She is clean, comely, capable, and performs her task with care. Pleasure in the immediate moment is suggested as much by her action as by the bread and comestibles on the table and the full morning light from the window. Yet this light reveals a threadbare interior. The wall is pockmarked with nails and nail-holes; the plaster has crumbled above the tiled skirting; damp discolours the wall below the sill. Temporal erosion and the boredom of domestic continuity give tension to this superficially tranquil image of daily life.

In a third room, Henry Wallis has depicted with hallucinatory attention to detail the chamber in which Shakespeare purportedly was born. It is neither rich nor squalid but has a worn plainness suggestive of the mundane origins of the spectacular figure who first saw the light of day there. The furniture, casually displaying books and prints, is pushed to the edges of the room against the graffiti-covered walls. Light rakes the nail-notched floorboards, as if they were the intended focus of our attention. On the window sill are two busts of Shakespeare and, lying face up, a death mask of him, invented by the artist. Pathetic relics on the outskirts of the room allow free play to the symbolic centre, cleared for a public for whom Shakespeare represents a nation and its history. The room, almost empty, becomes both memorial and votive offering, the dead minuteness of its depiction echoed in the mask on the sill.

Each of these works encapsulates the slog of daily life, the tussle between compulsion and habit. *House* conveyed all this – from the mundane outcrop of fireplaces, now become the incinerators of memory, to the isolated structure itself, made almost against all odds and offered as a token of the past.

The close inspection that *House* demanded – as though we were potential tenants or purchasers going round it with a checking eye – generated a succession of speculations and memories. They billowed in the mind as the curtains, on a summer's evening, must have ballooned in and out below the window sash thrown up as high as it could go to catch the breeze. Memory hangs on slight threads such as these. If details of the lives of a house's occupants are unobtainable, then the kind of life lived there slides in sepia between the eyes and the house's imperturbable façade. We provide our own sounds, smells, explanations, add our own commentary to the anonymous sequences of a silent newsreel [...]

When *House* was revealed to the public in late 1993, it stood in pale, forlorn dignity against a vivid backdrop of grass and trees. It had the appearance almost of an apparition, flat yet solid, palpable yet not quite believable, the ambiguous centrepiece, hugging the front of stage, of some curious theatrical performance.

But how modest it was, how discreet, how little space it occupied, shy of an audience that increased day by day, but unperturbed by the squall of comment that swelled around it. By night, in the streetlight, while still holding fast to its secrets, it seemed to take on an animation denied to it in the wide pallid daylight of East London; the protrusions and indentations of its form became sharper, its loftiness above the pavement more imperious, its colour more subtle and diverse. In a nocturnal setting, stimulus to 'gothic' reverie was intensified as the sculpture's features came to resemble more closely the truth of their origins and transcend them. It began to startle, to take you unawares. Skinned of its precarious physical reality, *House* implanted itself on the mind, an unforgettable image of arrested time.

8.7 DAVID MORLEY
'Heimat, Modernity and Exile'*

At Home in Modernity

In his analysis of notions of habitation and belonging in the shifting geography of post-modernity, Roger Rouse argues that the ways in which we now define our identities can no longer be articulated through the traditional terminology of place-based belonging.[1] However, this is not to suggest we have simply all become nomads in some kind of post-modern hyperspace. Thus Rouse suggests that we can find the 'raw materials for a new cartography ... in the details of people's daily lives' in which the idea of home is remapped by migrants, so that it no longer represents simply one particular place (of origin or destination) but rather a dispersed set of linkages across the different places through which they move, 'a single community spread across a variety of sites.'[2] He argues that through their constant back and forth migration and their use of telephones and other long-distance communication media, the residents of the Aguilillan community he studied are able to reproduce their links with people who 'are 2000 miles away as actively as they maintain their relations with their immediate neighbours ... through the continuous circulation of people, money, commodities and information ... [so that] the diverse settlements ... are probably better understood as forming ... one community dispersed in a variety of places.'[3]

* In *Home Territories: Media, Mobility and Identity* (London: Routledge, 2000), 31–55.

These migrants' lives routinely straddle national borders, and they exist in a multi-local social setting, juggling a variety of forms of cultural understandings, economic, political, and legal pressures. Rouse's concern is with 'the widespread tendency to assume that identity and identity formation are universal aspects of the human experience' and with the dangers of ethnocentrically projecting 'onto the lives of people who may think and act quite differently' what are, in fact, quite culturally specific conceptions of personhood developed in the affluent West in the recent period.[4] The experience of the migrants Rouse studied was not so much one in which people possessing one culturally formed identity had to deal with the pressures to take on or accommodate another identity, different in content. Rather, he argues, more fundamentally they moved 'from a world in which [personal] identity was not a central concern to one in which they were pressed with increasing force to adopt' a particular concept for personhood (as bearers of individual identities) and of identity as a member of a collective or 'community' (rather than as a family) which was quite at odds with their own understandings of their situation and their needs [...]

Many contemporary commentators have followed Heidegger's famous dictum that 'homelessness is coming to be the destiny of the world,' without stopping to pose the question that Orvar Lofgren raises, concerning, as he puts it, 'how short the history of homesickness is.'[5] His point is that it may well be that we tend to back-project our own anxieties about homelessness on to a historical past in which, in actuality, many people had a far less sentimental and more pragmatic attitude to the place where they lived, in so far as the home 'had not yet been transformed into a space of longing, for dreams, ambitions, and a project of self realization.' Lofgren's argument is that, in earlier times, people were often less home-centred than we are now, and could feel sufficiently at home on a more pragmatic basis, as they passed through a variety of spaces, as 'life flowed through the house ... [which] was not yet the special place of beginning and endings that we imagine it to be' [...] Contemporaneously the question of who can (literally) afford what degree of sentimentalisation of their idea of home may vary with social, cultural, and economic circumstances: as a Turkish migrant worker interviewed in Germany put it, 'Home is wherever you have a job.'[6]

The Migrant's Suitcase

Sometimes a particular symbolic object – such as the key to the house from which the refugee has been expelled – is taken on the exile's journey and comes to function as a synecdoche for the unreachable lost home, and to act as a focus for memories of the exile's past life.[7] According to George Bisharat, many Palestinian refugee families 'retained the keys to their [original] homes, prominently displaying them in their camp shelters as symbols of their determination to return.'[8] On some occasions, for the migrant, home may perhaps come to be symbolised not by a key but by the suitcase containing their most talismanic possessions [...] Thus, in his analysis of the conditions of life of migrant workers in Europe in the 1970s, John Berger reported that when, in some places, the *Gastarbeiter* were forbidden to keep their suitcases in their dormitories (because these things made their rooms untidy) they went on strike precisely because 'in these suitcases, they keep their personal possessions, not the clothes they put in the wardrobes, not the photographs they pin to the wall, but articles which, for one reason or another, are their talismans. Each suitcase, locked or tied round with cord, is like a man's memory. They defend the right to keep their suitcases.'[9]

Hannah Arendt, having escaped from the Nazis to arrive in New York, is said to have stayed for the rest of her life without unpacking her suitcases [...] Perhaps the most poignant form of the symbolism of the migrant's suitcase appears in Charlotte Salomon's autobiographical paintings of her life as a Jewish refugee, hiding from the Germans in Vichy France. In one of the paintings, her fictional alter ego 'Lotte' is shown sitting dejectedly on the edge of her bed preparing for exile, staring at the debris of her previously cultured life, which she is forlornly failing to pack into the suitcase she will take with her on her flight. As Irit Rogoff has remarked, luggage always functions 'as a sign imbued with an indisputable frisson of unease, displacement, and dislocation,' a double inscription of both 'concrete material belongings and of travel and movement away from the materialised anchorings of those belongings.'[10] In a recent interview, Edward Saïd expressed exactly this anxiety when he said that 'like all Palestinians' he has a tendency to overpack for any journey, because he is always plagued by a 'panic about not coming back.'[11]

Even when migrants arrive at their destination, the suitcase often remains a potent symbol both of the journey they have made, and of the unstable potential for further movement. In her autobiographical novel, describing growing up in the UK of Indian parents, Meera Syal gives us a compelling account of the symbolic significance of the large suitcases which had sat on top of her mother's bedroom wardrobe for as long as she could remember. She explains that as a child she had 'always assumed this was some kind of ancient Punjabi custom, this need to display several dusty, bulging cases, overflowing with old Indian suits, photographs and yellowing official papers, as all my Uncles' and Aunties' wardrobes were similarly crowned with this impressive array of luggage.' Her mother tried to brush off her questions about the significance of the suitcases with the practical observation that they were just a good place to keep 'all the things that do not fit into these small English wardrobes.' However, her daughter was not convinced that matters were so simple, as she had 'already noticed that everything in those cases had something to do with India – the clothes, the albums, the letters from various cousins – and wondered why they were kept apart from the rest of the household jumble, allotted their own place and prominence, the nearest thing in our house that we had to a shrine.'[12] [...]

It is not only the suitcase he carries with him that performs this talismanic function for the migrant. If the suitcase is usually full of things brought from home, for many migrants there is often another crucial physical container, standing empty in their homeland. Thus Lofgren notes that these days, all around the world one can find hundreds and thousands of empty houses, paid for or built by migrants, 'investing a lot of their dreams, ambitions, and resources in building and furnishing houses "back home" [which] may be briefly visited now and then, but really stand as a materialised utopia of returning home ... [which] in all their emptiness ... are full of longing, nostalgia and dreams.'[13]

In a similar vein, Russell King observes that in many places, migrants have transformed their districts of origin by the building of houses in the style of the countries to which they emigrated. As he observes, 'in Southern Italy in the early twentieth century many towns and villages had whole streets of "American houses" – new houses built by the *americani,* the local emigrants who went to America; in Hong Kong houses built with money earned in England are called "sterling houses"; in the Punjab ... *pukka* houses stand out above the local dwellings as testimony to a certain level of success abroad on the part of their owners.'[14]

Similarly, there is a strong tendency for Turkish migrants to Germany to buy apartments in middle-class areas, furnish them and spend their annual holidays there, and to endlessly prepare them for an eventual return which is, in fact, unlikely to ever occur.[15] Beyond the suitcase and the house, there is also a third 'container': the coffin. Writing in the context of France in the 1980s, Azouz Begaz writes that when they die, the bodies of the North African immigrants often make a 'journey home to be buried in their native soil.'[16] Similarly, Alec Hargreaves notes that for many immigrants in France the receding horizon of their much-anticipated return home is often pushed to its ultimate point: 'only after death, with a burial place in the land of their birth, will many immigrants finally accomplish the return journey of which they have dreamed since their initial departure.'[17]

Home is not always symbolised by any physical container – whether suitcase, building, or coffin. At times language and culture themselves provide the migrant with the ultimate mobile home. According to John Berger, in our contemporary mobile world, we need a much more plurilocal concept of home which, for many of the world's mobile population, may be inscribed not in a building or a territory but in 'words, jokes, opinions, gestures, actions, even the way one wears a hat,' in routinised phrases and habitual interactions, in styles of dress and narrative forms.[18] Thus home may not be so much a singular physical entity fixed in a particular place, but rather a mobile, symbolic habitat, a performative way of life and of doing things in which one makes one's home while in movement.[19]

NOTES

1 Roger Rouse, 'Mexican Migration and the Social Space of Postmodernism,' *Diaspora* 1 / 1 (1991), 8–23.

2 Ibid., 9, 14.

3 Rouse quoted in G. Yudice et al., eds., *On Edge: The Crisis of Contemporary Latin American Culture* (Minneapolis, MN: University of Minnesota Press, 1992). [Bracketed insertions are the author's.]

4 Roger Rouse, 'Questions of Identity,' *Critique of Anthropology* 15 / 4 (1995): 352, 363.

5 [Martin] Heidegger, quoted in [Orvar] Lofgren, 'The Nation as home or motel?' unpublished paper, Department of European Ethnology, University of Lund, 1995, 8–9.

6 Shabbir Akhbar, 'Notions of Nation and Alienation,' *Times Higher Education Supplement* (25 April 1997).

7 Cf. Patricia Seed, 'The Key to the House,' in Hamid Naficy, ed., *Home, Homeland, Exile: Film, Media, and the Politics of Place* (London: Routledge, 1999), 85–74.

8 George E. Bisharat, 'Exile to Compatriot: Transformation in the Social Identity of Palestinian Refugees in the West Bank,' in [Akhil] Gupta and [James] Ferguson, eds., *Culture, Power, Place: Explorations in Critical Anthropology* (Durham, NC: Duke University Press, 1997), 214. [Bracketed insertions in the quoted text are the author's.]

9 John Berger, [with photographs by] Jean Mohr, *[A] Seventh Man* (Harmondsworth: Penguin, 1975), 179.

10 Irit Rogoff, 'Terra Infirma,' inaugural lecture, Goldsmiths College, London, 1998. See also her *Terra Infirma* (London: Routledge, 2000).

11 Edward Saïd, quoted in Maya Jaggi, 'Out of the Shadows,' *Guardian* (11 Sept. 1999).

12 Meera Syal, *Anita and Me* (London: Flamingo, 1997), 267.

13 Lofgren, 'The Nation as Home or Motel?' 10. [Bracketed insertions in the quoted text are the author's.]

14 Russell King, 'Migrations, Globalization and Place,' in Doreen Massey and Pat Jess, eds., *A Place in the World? Places, Cultures and Globalization* (Milton Keynes: Open University Press, 1995), 29.

15 Ayse S. Caglar, 'German Turks in Berlin: Social Exclusion and Strategies for Social Mobility,' *New Community* 21 / 3 (1995).

16 Azouz Begag, *North African Immigrants in France* (Loughborough: European Research Centre, Loughborough University, 1989), 18.
17 Alec G. Hargreaves, *Immigration, 'Race' and Ethnicity in Contemporary France* (London: Routledge, 1995), 133. The final shots of Taieb Louichi's 1982 film *L'ombre de la terre (Dhil al-Ardh)* portray exactly this scenario as the migrant's coffin is shipped home to North Africa [...]
18 John Berger, *And Our Faces, My Heart, Brief as Photos* (London: Writers and Readers Press, 1984), 64.
19 Cf. Angelika Bammer, 'Editorial,' *New Formations* 17 (1992): xi.

8.8 LESLIE ROBERTSON
'Taming Space: Drug Use, HIV, and Homemaking in Downtown Eastside Vancouver'*

In what follows, I bring concepts of place making into a constructed dialogue with the narrated realities of women living in Vancouver's DTES [Downtown Eastside], with the intention that understanding their situations will offer insight into the complexities that surround the delivery of homecare nursing for marginalized women.[1] The discussion draws from a secondary analysis of 72 interviews with 14 women who participated in the *Health and Home Research Project* (1999–2001) and who identified themselves as living with HIV. I examine multiple meanings of the idea of *home* that, for these women, evoke complicated negotiations over differently ordered (and patrolled) kinds of space. As residents of a 'skid row' district they are subject to the conflation of persons and place occurring in stigmatized space. As clients of medical and social services, their domestic and public spaces are ordered by official responses to poverty and a health crisis focused on drug use and HIV transmission. Finally, as members of a community of street-involved persons, they inhabit a community space wherein they adhere to particular codes of sociality. What I call 'taming space' refers to women's efforts to actively resist, control, or accommodate these spatial regimes.

Analyses of 'home' are often saturated with nostalgia, with romantic ideals and valorized notions that do not fully apprehend the unstable relationship between places, identities, and experiences. According to Mary Douglas, 'home is

---

* *Gender, Place and Culture* 14 / 5 (2007): 527–49.

located in space but it is not necessarily a fixed space … home starts by bringing some space under control.'[2] [See section 2.8 in this volume.] Home is a site of surveillance and hierarchies of authority that should be analysed through shifting strategies of solidarity negotiated by co-residents or members of shared space.[3] Douglas' approach to home as a space to be brought under control resonates in women's narratives about the DTES. Their process of 'taming space' involves active choice, acquiescence, and negotiation, actions that highlight identity-constituting activities that are themselves shaped by spatial and representational regimes.

While each woman whose story appears here is subject to multiple stigmata, there are differences among women based in individual biographies, their racialized status vis-à-vis the Canadian state, or in their standing as clients of medical services, recipients of social assistance, and subjects of differently ordered housing policies. Attention to such differences breaks the faceless mould that reproduces images of 'wayward women,' 'unfit mothers,' 'the homeless,' 'the urban Indian,' 'addicts,' and 'junkies' – appellations in large part constructed through a perceived break with that treasured domain of female domestic space called home.

Home evokes a feeling, a memory, or a way of being. It may be a 'haven,' a private, intimate space of comfort and safety; conversely, people may feel 'homeless-at-home,'[4] trapped in a space 'of tyranny, oppression, or persecution.'[5] […] Hegemonic representations often overlook the violence, dislocation, and social exclusion that shape the lives of those whom Julia Wardaugh calls 'domestic refugees' and 'gender or culture renegades.'[6] As she writes: 'Those who are not able, or choose not to, conform to the gender, class, and sexuality ideals inherent in establishing a conventional household, find themselves symbolically (and often literally) excluded from any notion or semblance of home.'[7] Clearly, notions of home are ordered by gender and culture expectations and these are anchored to individual biographies, to dynamic relationships among people and between places.

Mobility is especially under-theorized in scholarly considerations of home. Attention to patterns of 'home-leaving' and tenure reinforce a utopian view of family and 'natural' rites of passage. There is little room here for thoughtful consideration of imposed transience, migrancy or nomadism; indeed, these mobile ways of being summon representations that are 'inherently transgressive.'[8] […] Too often, mobility studies disregard social, political, and economic contexts, focusing instead on single, nuclear family households and relying on statistical data that erase the often bumpy 'longitudinal journey' of residence histories […] According to [Daniel] Gutting, a 'presiding fiction' in his work with foreign migrants 'centres on the ever-present desire to return.'[9] While transnational moves conjure larger fields of home, those in a state of domestic exile also have complicated associations with return often tied to perceptions of stigmatized and medicalized identities.

'Skid row' places have long been associated with risk, the specific locales in which dangerous behaviours are enacted and pathology is spatialized [...] With the declaration of a public health emergency in 1997 [...] medicalization of the DTES introduced new regimes of place making mediated through the dominating paradigm of epidemiology [...] Medical journals characterized the DTES using mortality statistics, sero-conversion rates, and high-risk sexual and drug use behaviours [...] Popular media followed, sparking a 'moral panic' about AIDS inextricably linking drug users with a 'tainted' site of criminality, disease, and contagion [...]

As 'feminist urbanists' have theorized for some time, 'the city,' as a conceptual object, presents a number of contradictions for women – it is both constraining and liberating, constructed through emotional experiences and imposed structural forces.[10] [...] Whether they have lived in the neighbourhood for 30 years or barely 6 months, participants' stories of identity, movement and settlement construct home through what Mallett calls 'a repository for memories of the lived spaces.'[11] People actively create *home* in disparate places. 'Being-at-home' is not always grounded in one particular site; it may refer to a state of well-being that extends to communities, cities, nations, or ancestral territories [...] sites where people feel *in place*. For those women in this research, who expressed a sense of 'being-at-home' in the DTES, space was bound to the ephemera of identity grounded variously in health status, multiple forms of marginalization, and the desire for independence.

While a good deal of research addresses homelessness, much of the literature on women who are drug users medicalizes their situations through narrowly conceived categories dictated by public health policy [...]

Home evokes nurturing kin, a space of safety where children grow towards independence, leaving to pursue their lives and establish their own place in the world. In their descriptions of childhood homes, some women expressed a comfortable attachment but for many, histories of rebellion, loss, and abuse suggest homelessness at home [...] Not all women who live a street-involved life, however, hail from what might be termed a broken home. Until she was married, Gina 'grew up in one house [her] whole life.' Helen lived in a middle-class suburb that she described as a 'sheltered' place. Her narrative began as a teenager negotiating the strict authority of her father who prevented her from leaving the area [...] Many women spoke about long-term relationships with foster parents and birth parents; their sense of kinship sometimes extended to fostered peers whom they came to regard as siblings. Others who found themselves in the institutional settings of places of reform recounted genealogies of attachment to co-residents with whom they ventured 'out into the world.' Narrated turning points in women's travels are complicated. They are shaped by financial constraints, by familial ties, income-generating opportunities, and the availability of services and shelter in a city that has one of the nation's most inflated housing markets [...]

Once in the neighbourhood, women moved in and out as they had children or entered into different relationships. Periods of sobriety or affluence, spontaneous opportunities to travel, returns to home communities, or the need for a change each appear in the narratives, reflecting active choices, imposed constraints, and ascribed identities. Structural barriers, including housing and social service policies, enforcement activities, and the allocation of health and social services often shaped their options [...]

There is a turning point common to many narratives when women consciously chose to live in the neighbourhood and began to call it home. This turning pivots on what phenomenological scholars call a state of 'being at home in the world' [...] Some women who come to experience the DTES as home share what Sara Ahmed [...] calls 'patterns of estrangement' in their lives, a relationship between mobility and identity that forges community through absence of shared knowledge or common origins [...][12] In a place demarcated by individual and collective histories of social suffering, women arrive at a sense of belonging through recognition of mutual (albeit distinct) journeys to the social margins [...]

For women who are drug users, arrival in the DTES facilitated access to drugs and improved their options for affordable housing and for generating an independent income. For some of the women in this research it also signalled failure, and was the beginning of a journey from hotel to hotel, negotiating relationships with building managers and other residents, boyfriends, husbands, street associates, agency and government workers, the police, johns, pimps, and dealers. Moves within the DTES corresponded with evictions; decreased or increased cash flow; periods of hospitalization for drug and alcohol treatment, mental and physical illness, and / or injury; disgust with sanitary conditions; or a response to the degree of violence and drug use. In their peregrinations, women have spent time in shelters and transition houses; some lived with 'tricks' or 'sugar daddies'; they 'couch surfed' with acquaintances; slept in doorways, on benches, in churches, and in drop-in centres [...]

By their own accounts, women who live in SRO [single room occupancy] hotels experience few conditions of security. A typical hotel room is approximately 108 square feet. Participants spoke a good deal about their buildings where health codes, tenants' rights, and safety regulations held little sway.

Deploring the sanitary conditions in some hotels, they referred to used needles, excrement, and blood in communal areas such as hallways, stairwells, and bathrooms. They spoke about exposure to HIV, TB, and HCV [respectively, human immunodeficiency virus, tuberculosis, and hepatitis C virus] and described elevated noise levels, drug use in shared areas, deaths, and frequent intruders. Everyone spoke about witnessing and experiencing violence in their buildings.

The household is the 'core' domestic and economic unit structured by dimensions of gender and age.[13] Economically speaking, women's households extend beyond the threshold of their living space into the broader community and, for many, beyond the city where they have families. While they may not share the same space with others, women carry the greater part of the financial burden, often supporting partners, relatives, and friends through income generated by underground economies or by the expert utilization of food banks, soup kitchens, and clothing depots [...] People leave relationships, die, are incarcerated or hospitalized, or they 'clean up' and leave; others arrive in search of family members or the fast pace of the street, but for women living singly in SRO hotels, their household rarely expands or contracts. Rigid, minimal shelter allowances, guest fees, and nightly charges dissuade women from living with their children, relatives, or friends who may be in need of shelter. Most hotels are equipped with surveillance cameras, and residents risk eviction when they sneak people into their rooms [...]

The average social housing unit offers 450 square feet [...] in a self-contained apartment with private bathroom and kitchen, as well as separate living and sleeping areas. Obtaining social housing is the stated goal of many in the research, but their stories about long waiting lists, discrimination, and sheer serendipity provide insight into the barriers they face. Once in social housing, women spoke of taking control over their lives and their spaces [...]

Following Mary Douglas, women who obtain stable housing begin to speak a language of 'solidarity.' Their narratives depict a 'complex coordination and consultation' involved in 'bringing [their] space under control.'[14] Taming space here signals a sea change: women have the option to be alone, uninterrupted by (invited and uninvited) intrusions and, when regulations permit, they are free to choose who enters their home. For many, it is the first time that they have wielded control over the physical thresholds of their households, but they have to unlearn the ways of the street, recognizing how deeply they have shared the stigma of having lived in 'skid row' housing.

Moving into secure housing, some reconciled relationships; after years of estrangement, they resumed roles as mothers, grandmothers, aunties, sisters, or daughters. Transitions were not easy; most had difficulty negotiating renewed relationships and generating any interest in their new surroundings. At issue was the loss of street identity that engendered a fierce independence often at odds with health and housing regimens that require accepting assistance, respecting authority, and acquiescing to surveillance that go hand in glove with secure housing in the neighbourhood [...]

Clearly, the DTES is, if not always a chosen home, a richly inhabited place. Some women found a sense of being at home in unlikely places – on the street or in hotels. For many others, *home* symbolized a social distance from that world, and from the debilitating affects of stigmatization. A state of *being at home* in the DTES generated contradictions for most of the research participants; they were embittered by the exploitative nature of street-based relationships and their acquiescence to them. Developing a sense of belonging may be an oppositional strategy enabling autonomy at the margins, but women also actively worked to transform meanings that surround their spaces and identities.

Marginally housed women live alone in frequently violent, unsanitary, and unregulated buildings, negotiating that blind spot in the civic field of vision. Like SRO hotels, social housing also imposes spatial regimes, albeit medicalized and government scripted, requiring accommodation to dictates of time (through curfews and health routines), and sociality (through surveillance and housing policies). Social, political, and economic circumstances play a role in determining women's mobility, where they live, the financial strategies they adopt, and the kinds of health risks to which they are exposed. Colonialism and neo-liberal policies circumscribe spaces and delineate populations through the assertion of fiercely exclusionary and largely hegemonic ideologies. Meagre (and decreasing) social assistance rates force women into contested spaces like the DTES, where they negotiate gendered and racialized terrains and where they face the many-sided trials of taming space.

NOTES

1 The analysis contributes to a study of health care for marginally housed people living with HIV. Homecare for Homeless People with HIV: An Ongoing Research Project, principal investigator Cindy Patton, Simon Fraser University.

2 Mary Douglas, 'The Idea of a Home: A Kind of Space,' *Social Research* 58 / 1 (1991): 289.

3 Ibid., 287–95.

4 Julie Wardaugh, 'The Unaccommodated Woman: Home, Homelessness and Identity,' *Sociological Review* 47 / 1 (1999): 92.

5 Shelley Mallett, 'Understanding Home: A Critical Review of the Literature,' *Sociological Review* 52 / 1 (2004): 64.
6 Wardaugh, 'The Unaccommodated Woman,' 93–9.
7 Ibid., 97.
8 Sara Ahmed, 'Home and Away: Narratives of Migration and Estrangement,' *International Journal of Cultural Studies* 2 / 3 (1999): 329–48.
9 Daniel Gutting, 'Narrative Identity and Residential History,' *Area* 28 / 4 (1996): 484.
10 Liz Bondi and Demaris Rose, 'Constructing Gender, Constructing the Urban: A Review of Anglo-American Feminist Urban Geography,' *Gender, Place and Culture* 10 / 3 (2003): 229–45.
11 Mallett, 'Understanding Home,' 63.
12 Ahmed, 'Home and Away,' and Wardaugh, 'The Unaccommodated Woman,' 97.
13 Ibid., 68.
14 Douglas, 'The Idea of a Home,' 289, 295.

CHAPTER NINE

Literary Spaces

From the Bible through fairy tales to the contemporary Japanese manga, all genres and periods of world literature are permeated and shaped by representations of houses and the concept of home. Writers and critics have repeatedly described literature and the process of writing in architectural terms and images. Moreover, many literary terms, features, and genres are linked to domestic architecture: structure, aspect, outlook, character, interior, content (contents of the house, content of the novel), liminal, threshold, entry point, style, perspective. In addition, literary genres are named after architectural features and domestic spaces and objects such as closet dramas, gothic novel, drawing-room comedy, kitchen sink drama, the locked room detective story, country house poem and novel, the domestic novel, Aga sagas, and postmodern (a term that literature appropriated from architecture). Mindful of a venerable literary tradition of symbiosis between architecture and literature, the selections in this chapter examine the potent conjuncture of house, home, novel, and poem and their symbolization and encoding across periods and cultures. Focusing on interwar domestic novels, Chiara Briganti and Kathy Mezei argue that houses are stories and narratives of hauntings by memories, ghosts, traces of selves and others, while stories are haunted by fictional and lived and imagined houses, which frequently mimic the psyche and bodies of their inhabitants as well as social practices and political ideologies. They analyse the spectral relation of the novel and the house with reference to the English domestic novel of the interwar years, a period in which the domestic was particularly validated and critiqued.

Positing a relationship between architectural change and patterns of behaviour in the eighteenth century as reflected in literary expression, Cynthia Wall investigates the way in which the heroine's life trajectory in Daniel Defoe's novel *Roxana* is expressed through her efforts and failures to control her domestic spaces. In her reading of the significance of spatial configurations in *Jane Eyre*, Karen Chase shows how the arrangements of rooms in Jane's three different dwelling places convey the threat of confinement and exposure, and play a psychological role in revealing the relations of self and other, love and restraint, wish and fear.

Julian Wolfreys's Heideggerian reading of *Dombey and Son* demonstrates how the uncanny in Charles Dickens's novel is not only grounded in the psyche but is also a product of industrial capitalist Victorian England. Observing the intricate connection between architecture and nineteenth-century French literature, Philippe Hamon outlines how both were venues for the staging of everyday life, the rituals that expose social behaviour, and the effects of industry and commerce. Noting how Emily Dickinson's domestication of the human mind coincided with the historical moment that saw the privatization of the residential dwelling in North America, Diana Fuss seeks to recompose the bifurcation between architecture and literature through her reading of the figure of the door in Dickinson's poetry and letters as a metaphor for loneliness, loss, death and memory, secrecy and safety. Hanna Scolnicov examines how Henrik Ibsen set up the drawing room – 'a gilded shell of an impossible social decorum' – to express women's constricted position in society in the theatrical space of *A Doll's House*. 'The novel, for a long while, has been overfurnished,' said Willa Cather, inviting her contemporaries to 'throw the furniture out of the window.'[1] As Supriya Chaudhuri demonstrates, the Bengali writer Rabindranath Tagore would have been happy to comply. Tagore, Chaudhuri argues, entertained a vexed relationship with Western modernity both in life and in writing. His search for the ideal living space divested of the encumbrances of bourgeois materialism found a literary equivalent in the ambivalence detectable in his longer fiction between a yearning for an unconfined space and the crowded interiors of the nineteenth-century realist novel. Homi Bhabha turns to literary texts to relate the unhomely to the effect of cultural relocation of the home and to the disjunctions of political existence; he explores the unhomely condition of the modern and post-colonial world. In her study of Korean novelist, Sŏk-kyŏng Kang's 'A Room in the Woods,' Jini Watson probes how a young woman's private room represents the tragic conflict between tradition and modernity. Proposing that domestic spaces are a pivotal site of tension between the everyday and the fantastic and that they play a crucial role in children's fantasy literature, Wendy Thompson discloses the often uncanny role of houses in Jonathan Stroud's Bartimaeus Trilogy and R.K. Rowling's Harry Potter series.

The selection with which we conclude, *Designs for a Happy Home* by Matthew Reynolds, is the point of entry into the world of Elizia Tamé, famous for sofas that run on rails and furniture that can be hooked on the ceiling to make room on the floor. The novel starts in a deliberately light manner as a spoof on how-to books and the modern obsession with interior decoration, and a gentle mockery of the heroine, to become more poignant as we move from the hallway into her interior.

NOTE

1 Willa Cather, 'The Novel Démeublé,' in *Not under Forty* (New York: Knopf, 1936), 43–51.

9.1 CHIARA BRIGANTI AND KATHY MEZEI
House Haunting: The Domestic Novel of the Interwar Years

Reflecting on home, Jean-François Lyotard wrote cryptically, 'Thought cannot want its house. But the house haunts it.'[1] Indeed, as strongly as thought might resist its house, the house does haunt it, as the very etymology of the verb suggests. For if in English one of the meanings of 'haunt' is a 'place or abode that one frequents' (its origins lie in the Old English *hamettan,* to provide with a home or house), in French, *hantise* carries the connotation of an obsession, a nagging memory. Jacques Derrida's concept of the logic of hauntology (*hantise*), which points to the relationship between the first time and the last time of an event, to repetition and return, and to the spectral sense of the presence of 'someone as someone other,' resonates with the repetitions, returns, and hauntology of the act of writing and reading the novel and of being in the house.[2]

The House of Fiction

Both home and novel are constructions that represent, imitate, and enable people to live, interact, engage publicly, or retreat into privacy since, as Diana Fuss remarked about nineteenth-century French writers, 'by describing every corner, every object, and every feature of the domestic interior, these writers [...] sought to convey through language [...] "the interior experience of interiority."'[3] Thus, for writers like Virginia Woolf and Katherine Mansfield, who foreground home culture in their experimental fictions, novels *and* houses furnish a dwelling place that invites the exploration and expression of private and intimate relations and thoughts. Their use of private domestic space as frame and metonym of inner, psychological space reflects the recent (nineteenth-century) validation of privacy and intimacy. For example, in Woolf's *To the Lighthouse* (1927), the reader mounts the stairs to the nursery with Mrs Ramsay, where the encounter with everyday, domestic objects triggers Mrs Ramsay's sense of self and continuity:

> They would, she thought, going on again, however long they lived, come back to this night; this moon; this wind; this house; and to her too [...] going upstairs, laughing but affectionately, at the sofa on the landing (her mother's) at the rocking-chair (her father's); at the map of the Hebrides [...] She felt, with her hand on the nursery door, that community of feeling with other people which emotion gives as if the walls of partition had become so thin that practically (the feeling was one of relief and

> happiness) it was all one stream, and chairs, tables, maps, were hers, were theirs, it did not matter whose, and Paul and Minta would carry it on when she was dead.[4]

Similarly, at the end of a long day in the Ramsay summer house, the reader, along with Mrs Ramsay, moves into the drawing room with Mrs Ramsay as she joins her husband and into the intimacy of their marriage. For, as Victoria Rosner observed, Virginia Woolf, in keeping with other Bloomsbury artists, 'attempted to depict an interiority anchored in the home.'[5] In modern and contemporary novels, representations of the domestic interior mirror the inner thoughts of women, children, servants, those 'spectral' dwellers within the house who may appear to be at home but in a space not of their designing.

Readers repeatedly encounter the architectural in fiction, the importance of the home, and houses as personae. For not only do writers place a 'building at the center of a book in order to provide the scaffolding of automatic organization' but they also frequently refer to their work as a built form and their writing in terms of building.[6] Walter Pater talks of 'literary architecture,' Henry James of the 'house of fiction,' Emily Dickinson imagines herself as a carpenter. Explaining her radical 'method' in *Mrs Dalloway,* Woolf resorts to an architectural image: '[For the novelists of the preceding generation] the novel was the obvious lodging, but the novel it seemed was built on the wrong plan,'[7] while contemporary Canadian author Alice Munro compares the construction of her short stories to building up a house.

In her analogical model, Philippa Tristram describes the novel as invincibly domestic because it functions like the house as a little world we think we can control.[8] Tristram calls attention to the correspondences between domestic architecture, which can reveal hidden aspects of the novelist's art and of novels; these correspondences are manifest in terms like structure, aspect, outlook, character, content, liminal, threshold, entry point, perspective, kitchen sink drama, drawing-room comedy, Aga saga (English domestic novels of the 1990s), country house mysteries, cosies (detective novels), the locked room mystery, and the domestic novel.

The Interwar Cult of the House

In their turn to domestic spaces many female domestic novelists were negotiating, in their technique and their subject matter, the modernist antipathy to the home as exemplified by Le Corbusier, the brilliant celebration of domestic decoration and house objects by the Bloomsbury artists of the Omega Workshop, and government-sponsored, market-driven, consumer-fuelled propaganda for a postwar 'cult of domesticity.'

The turn to the home and the domestic interior between the wars and a corresponding turn in the novel form is hardly surprising. Similarly to the eighteenth century, which saw the rise of the novel, the interwar period also experienced a domestication, feminization, and privatization of society. Social historian John Burnett notes that new recruits to the middle class, which increased from 20.3 per cent of the total population of England in 1911 to 30.4 in 1951, 'shared with the older members of the class the belief that family and home were the central life interests, and that the house, which enshrined these institutions, had an importance far beyond other material objects.'[9] The demand for middle-class housing and council estates, the growth of suburbs and garden cities outside London – an attempt to protect the countryside from suburban sprawl with its concomitant proliferation of detached, single-family houses, engendered a taste for home life and an economy of homemaking. As many women were guided towards the design of houses and contributed to concepts of social and communal housing (see Beecher, Cieraad, Hayden, and Wilk in this volume), so female novelists in the interwar years became increasingly preoccupied with the home. The experience of the First World War, the resultant trauma of instability and the desire for recuperation, which coexisted with a resistance to a 'return to normality,' both enhanced the idea and meaning of home for returning soldiers and the home front and accentuated that crisis of gender relations that had been brewing for decades.

A 'return to the home' was energetically promoted through the commercial sphere – advertisements and the growing number of women's magazines dedicated to promoting women's domestic role. Featuring articles that focused on homemaking rather than on high society, and advertisements on interior decoration and labour-saving devices, they were informed by the same ideology that supported the government-sponsored postwar program of social reconstruction. As a random sample, the April 1932 (vol. 31, no. 2) issue of *Good Housekeeping* ran articles on 'Suburban Flats Planned to Save Labour,' 'The Art of Waiting at Table,' while in response to this trend, *The Lady* and *The Queen* shifted their emphasis from society women to the middle class. Events like the Ideal Home Exhibitions and programs like the BBC's 'Woman's Hour' also glorified the idea of home and women's domestic sphere. With the marriage bar,[10] women were forced to turn and return to the home after marriage; symptomatically, *The Lady* cut its employment features and substituted homemaking articles.[11] In 1932, *Good Housekeeping* published a story by Prudence O'Shea, 'The Happiest Way of Things,' the story of a wife who had to choose whether to run a job or a home, and chose to be a wife; however, in April 1930, it had also published articles by Vera Brittain on the subject 'Why I think Mothers Can Have Careers' and by Storm Jameson in June 1927 on 'Marriage,' which she calls 'The Most Difficult Profession in the World.'

Resisting the facile glamorization of the housewife, however, domestic novelists engaged in a thoughtful, often witty reclamation of domesticity and the home. They simultaneously privileged and critiqued the home and homemaking, at times resenting the demands of the family on the 'domesticated female,' like Norah in Rosamond Lehmann's *A Note in Music* (1930), but often also imbuing the home with lyrical and evocative qualities. The resulting textualization of the house and home offered women writers a pattern within which to write or against which to write.

Hantise

In the works of novelists attuned to the grammar of the home, houses and the material objects they contain are not merely passive expressions of agency or mirrors of the people who live in them or own them, but serve as 'the site of memory and of our formative experiences.'[12] Imprinted by the body, they become a body space, so to speak. The *toutounier,* in Colette's 1939 novella by the same name, the couch to which the Eudes sisters repeatedly 'return' to speak a private language and repair the ravages wrought by poverty and emotional exhaustion, is a veritable womblike nest of female intimacy. In the English tradition of novels by Elizabeth Bowen, Rosamond Lehmann, Elizabeth von Arnim, E.M. Delafield, Virginia Woolf, and Enid Bagnold, houses and their accoutrements become living beings with names and personalities as in the haunted space of Pinderwell House in E.H. Young's *Moor Fires* (1916), where the rooms have been named after Mr Pinderwell's unborn children. But it is in Elizabeth Bowen that we find the most fully articulated expression of *hantise*. In her story, 'The New House,' the spinster protagonist utters a paradigmatic complaint: 'Why, even the way the furniture was arranged at No. 17 held me so that I couldn't get away. The way the chairs went in the sitting-room. And mother.'[13]

If, in comparable and repetitive ways, novels and houses – as structures, constructs, shelters, built forms – endeavour to make sense of the world, to imagine and create ways of being at home in a world where we do not feel at home, they also attempt to represent and reckon with the unhomely and with the possibility that a return to the intimacy of *le toutounier* may be also oppressive and stifling. Indeed, a long tradition of feminist work has pursued the disruption of the resonances of tranquillity so usually associated with home and has exposed the home as the site of exploitation, oppression, and violence.

The ghostly repetition and return of domestic rituals – the gathering at the breakfast table, which begins so many novels, the retreat to the study, and the interruption of tea – shape the narratives of the interwar domestic novel. In Ivy Compton-Burnett's study of patriarchal tyranny, *A House and Its Head* (1930), breakfasts are haunted by the ghosts of a recently deceased mother and wife, an adulterous and runaway wife, and infanticide. In Roland Petwee's 1948 *School for Spinsters,* the tyranny of the tea ritual is such that a mother's death will be announced over a slice of walnut cake. Like the ancestral home, domestic ritual both shelters and nurtures the self and imagination, yet also stifles and oppresses individuality.

The (Re)Turn to Domestic Space

The effort to study and validate domestic life parallels a resurgence and revaluation of the domestic novel and of novelists who have been traditionally marginalized because of their focus on that which has accumulated at the side of the story – the unnoticed, the inconspicuous, the unobtrusive. In their turn to domestic space and the domestic interior, domestic novelists of the interwar years inaugurated a turn to interiority, feminine subjectivity, and the everyday, thus privileging the private and the ordinary and the lives of middle-class women and a new haunting of house and novel.

Acknowledgment

This essay is a revised and abbreviated version of 'House Haunting: The Domestic Novel of the Inter-war Years,' *Home Cultures* 1 / 2 (2004): 147–68.

NOTES

1 Jean-François Lyotard, 'Domus and the Megapolis,' in Neil Leach, ed., *Rethinking Architecture: A Reader in Cultural Theory* (London: Routledge, 1999), 277.
2 Jacques Derrida, *Specters of Marx: The State of the Debt, the Work of Mourning, and the New International,* translated by Peggy Kamuf (New York: Routledge, 1994), 9, 10, 177n2.
3 Diana Fuss, *The Sense of an Interior: Four Writers and the Rooms that Shaped Them* (New York: Routledge, 2004), 10. [See section 9.6 in this chapter.]
4 Virginia Woolf, *To the Lighthouse* (Harmondsworth: Penguin, 1964 [1927]), 130–1.
5 Victoria Rosner, *Modernism and the Architecture of Private Life* (New York: Columbia University Press, 2005), 127.

6 Robert Harbison, *Eccentric Spaces* (Cambridge, MA: MIT Press, 2000), 74.
7 Virginia Woolf, 'Introduction to Mrs Dalloway,' in *Mrs Dalloway* (New York: Modern Library Edition, 1928), 36.
8 Philippa Tristram, *Living Space in Fact and Fiction* (London: Routledge, 1989), 2.
9 John Burnett, *A Social History of Housing, 1815–1985* (London: Methuen, 1986), 251.
10 Women who married were not allowed to continue in professions such as teaching and the civil service; this restriction was in effect in the United Kingdom from the 1800s to 1973, when it was abolished.
11 Cynthia L. White, *Women's Magazines, 1693–1968* (London: Michael Joseph, 1970), 100.
12 Jon Bird, 'Dolce Domum,' in James Lingwood, ed., *Rachel Whiteread: House* (London: Phaidon, 1995), 110–25.
13 Elizabeth Bowen, 'The New House,' in *The Collected Stories of Elizabeth Bowen* (London: Jonathan Cape, 1980), 57.

9.2 CYNTHIA WALL
'Gendering Rooms: Domestic Architecture and Literary Arts'*

In the last quarter of the eighteenth century, the fashionable architects Robert and James Adam articulated and affirmed a social as well as structural change in the interiors of upper and middle-class English houses. The dining-room had become the explicit territory of men, the space for political and other kinds of discourse; the drawing-room came under the supervision of women. But where the dining-room had dominated the floor plan in the late seventeenth and early eighteenth centuries, when men and women tended to co-occupy its space in shared entertainment, by the end of the eighteenth century the division into gendered space between the dining and drawing-rooms corresponded to altered proportions: the drawing-room became the usually symmetrical counterpart to the dining-room, both architecturally and socially [...] It would appear that a bargain of sorts had been struck, consciously or unconsciously: in exchange for increasing exclusion from formerly shared space, women were given or (assumed) a separate (but equal?) space of their own.

* *Eighteenth-Century Fiction* 5/4 (1993): 349–72.

The changing significance of and relationship between drawing-room and dining-room mark new patterns of behaviour between women and men, and these changes surface in a diachronic sampling of eighteenth-century novels through characters acting both within and against the evolving patterns of domestic interiors [...] In *Roxana* (1724), *Clarissa* (1747–48), and *Pride and Prejudice* (1813),[1] the central characters all work to define, protect, or resist the boundaries of inhabited space, although the actions and reactions of each are shaped by the changing dimensions and significations of her domestic interiors [...]

The connection between architectural change and literary expression in the eighteenth century is neither arbitrary nor artificial. The publication in 1715 of *Vitruvius Britannicus* and of Giacomo Leoni's English translation of Palladio caught the public imagination, and a general awareness and appreciation of architectural matters increased significantly throughout the century [...] Nor was that appreciation limited to the upper-class patrons and practitioners of art, to Burlington, Kent, and Pope. Craftsmen as well as architects published a wide selection of books devoted to the theory and practice of architectural design [...] These manuals, together with the new standardization of middle-class townhouse design, meant that almost anyone who could afford a house at all could afford one that conformed to the current notions of Palladian taste and proportion [...] Attention to architectural structure and detail, both interior and exterior, was not simply a matter for the designer and builder, but an issue of great excitement and some knowledge to the occupant and observer. Defoe, Richardson, and Austen were themselves each knowledgeable occupants and acute observers of architectural space.[2]

The distribution and the gendering of interior domestic space also excited popular interest, but neither so early nor (at first) so explicitly. Robert Adam notes in the preface to *Works in Architecture* that 'within these few years [there has been] a remarkable improvement in the form, convenience, arrangement, and relief of apartments.'[3] He credits this latter-day awakening to the growing influence of French architectural theory, for it had been in the 'proper arrangement and relief of apartments ... [that] the French have excelled all other nations' (vol. 1, 8). The idea of gendered space may have been imported with the French influence: earlier in the century Jacques-François Blondel had insisted upon a sober character for the dining-room, designed with an '*architecture mâle*' – a masculine decor, deliberately and distinctly different from rooms designed for other forms of receiving and entertaining.[4] But unlike the French, the English architects began to take the figurative characterization of a masculine style quite literally, to create a space not simply 'masculine' in design or decor (a trope long known in classical architecture),[5] but a space designed explicitly *for* men – 'in which "we" are to pass a great part of "our" time.'

In the late-seventeenth century, entertainment in the formal house, whether town or country, meant that by and large the guests followed each other through a pattern of room-centred activities; dining in the saloon (the architecturally and linguistically anglicized counterpart of the French *salon*) or dining-parlour, withdrawing to an antechamber for tea or dessert, cards, or music, and then returning to the dining-room for dancing and supper. A handsome dining-room was socially and architecturally prominent, usually one of the largest and grandest rooms in the house. By the middle of the century, however, fashionable entertaining required a series of rooms offering diverse but simultaneous activities [...]

As popular awareness and knowledge of architectural matters gathered energy and sophistication throughout the eighteenth century, it is not surprising that literary attention to architectural detail should become more concentrated and precise [...] But many of these concerns about the significance of interior domestic space are to be found in Defoe's novels. *Roxana*, published in 1724 and allegedly set in the Restoration, differs strikingly from *Clarissa* and *Pride and Prejudice*, since Roxana's interest in defining and controlling formal interior space is aggressively self-conscious. At a time when such space had no specifically gendered contours or prescriptions, Roxana quite literally draws *all* her rooms around her to generate and consolidate forms of power. Her story enacts a prelude to the gendering of rooms: she dramatizes the larger, constant, generally human desire to define and control space (and, implicitly, its occupants). Yet in the end she forfeits that power by misdefining and misoccupying that space. Her story pivots on the most socially powerful arrangement and employment of London lodgings, but it begins in an empty house and ends in a haunted one. The first and final spaces of the novel invalidate her command of its centre and punish her for the attempt. In the end, all her inhabited space – psychological as well as architectural – becomes haunted space.

Roxana regards all rooms not as general or gendered spaces for men and women, but as the potential property or extension of herself. Her psychological story begins when her first husband abandons her and she confronts the poverty of a naked room: 'I was ... in Rags and Dirt, who was but a little before riding in my Coach; thin, and looking almost like one Starv'd, who was before fat and beautiful: The House, that was before handsomely furnish'd with Pictures and Ornaments, Cabinets, Peir-Glasses, and everything suitable, was now stripp'd, and naked ... in a word, all was Misery and Distress, the Face of Ruin was everywhere to be seen' (17–18).

Roxana's body and her house are bound together by parallel clauses in an identity she will learn to exploit. Within this chilling interior emptiness she begins a series of invisible occupancies, secretly inhabiting (and learning to control) spaces that appear closed and empty to the rest of the world […]

The central scene of the novel, in terms of narrative, psychological, and architectural control, is Roxana's ball in London, where she dons her Turkish dress and dances for the assembled company. She seems to understand and take full advantage of the sexual power implicit in social space (which implicit power hints at some of the cultural incentives for breaking that space apart later in the century). After acquiring impressive lodgings in Pall Mall [… she] not only anticipates what will become the most fashionable arrangements for upper-class entertainment, she also plots out one possible evolutionary track of the drawing-room : 'I had a large Dining-Room in my Apartments, with five other Rooms on the same Floor, all of which I made Drawing-Rooms for the Occasion, having all the Beds taken down for the Day; in three of these I had Tables plac'd, cover'd with Wine and Sweet-Meats; the fourth had a green Table for Play, and the fifth was my own Room, where I sat, and where I receiv'd all the Company that came to pay their Compliments to me' (173).

[…] As her own description testifies, though the dining-room is structurally prominent, her arrangement and occupation of the rooms for the ball pointedly emphasize her own drawing-room as the socially (sexually) powerful centre […]

But the end of the novel subverts its middle, and undermines the faith we can put here in the extent of Roxana's control of her interior spaces […] In the end, no room, no arrangement of rooms, no prestigious or inconspicuous address offers Roxana interior security or admits her spatial control. Her daughter Susan relentlessly tracks her down, invading her lodgings, demanding acknowledgment, haunting her daily thoughts, and eroding her self-control until all her series of houses seem to entrap rather than empower her […] All Roxana's inhabited space is now haunted space. But in a sense Susan's invisible presence had *already* haunted the apartments of Pall Mall, repeating Roxana's own habits of invisible occupancy, infiltrating spaces that seemed most securely subordinated […] Roxana has lost whatever control she might have had over her interior spaces, both architectural and psychological. All her manipulations of space – her tricks with folding-doors and drawing-room entrances – prove only an illusion of control. She has inhabited her houses on false pretences, and as such she is punished for presuming to command the centres of rooms […]

The fracturing of social interiors into masculine and feminine spaces in the eighteenth century generated changing patterns of resistance within differently accommodating walls. The evolving contours of the drawing-room were on the one hand cultural and ideological constructions shaping the female character. As Simon Varey argues, 'the spaces created (in theory or in practice) by architects and those created by the novelists – whether or not they are the same spaces – express specific ideology … For one who resists the pressure to conform as for one who does not, the self is defined, to a remarkable degree, by space.'[6] The drawing-room, in which women were to pass a great deal of *their* time (as implied by Adam's separate claim for men), would contribute to shaping the social and intellectual habits, manners, and assumptions of upper and middle-class Englishwomen, and to the increasing sense of division and difference between men and women, between public and private, between the political and the domestic.

On the other hand, Heidegger defines space as 'something that has been made room for, something that is cleared and free, namely, within a boundary, Greek *peras.* A boundary is not that at which something stops but, as the Greeks recognized, the boundary is that from which something *begins its essential unfolding.*'[7] Walls as boundaries in Heidegger's sense do more than define and enclose; they imply and even generate alternate space; they establish individual as well as cultural relationships between interiors and exteriors; they suggest ways to resist as well as accommodate their own limits […] As the drawing-room changed, along with its implicit possibilities or restrictions, so did narrative patterns of imaginative opposition.

NOTES

1 References are to the following edition: Daniel Defoe, *Roxana: The Fortunate Mistress,* edited by Jane Jack (Oxford: Oxford University Press, 1964) […]

2 Richardson's and Austen's interest in architecture is well known through their letters. Defoe's equal interest is less well documented and frequently discounted by his biographers and critics. In my doctoral dissertation, 'Housing Defoe's Projects: The Rebuilding of London and "Modern" Literary Space' (University of Chicago, 1992), I have argued that in fact much of Defoe's life and most of his important works are centrally concerned with the psychological and social implications of architectural structures.

3 Robert and James Adam, *Works in Architecture,* 3 vols. (reprinted Dourdan: E. Thézard Fils, 1990 [1773–79]), vol. 1, 9; references are to this edition.

4 Peter Thornton, *Authentic Decor: The Domestic Interior, 1620–1920* (New York: Viking Press, 1984), 93 […] Thornton also points out a striking difference between the gendered spaces of the French and English upper classes: in France, husbands and wives occupied separate apartments, but by mid-century the wife held her court in the larger suites, while her husband retired to the smaller and more private rooms.

5 Vitruvius, for example, explains that when the Athenians erected temples to Apollo and Diana, they invented two kinds of columns in which 'they borrowed

manly beauty, naked and unadorned, for the one [Doric], and for the other [Ionic and later Corinthian] the delicacy, adornment, and proportions characteristic of women.' *The Ten Books on Architecture,* translated by Morris Hicky Morgan (Cambridge, MA: Harvard University Press, 1914; reprinted New York: Dover, 1960), 103–4.

6 Simon Varey, *Space and the Eighteenth-Century English Novel* (Cambridge: Cambridge University Press, 1990), 4.

7 Martin Heidegger, 'Building, Dwelling, Thinking,' in *Basic Writings,* edited by David Farrell Krell (New York: Harper and Row, 1977 [1951]), 332. [See section 2.2 in this volume.]

9.3 KAREN CHASE
'Jane Eyre's Interior Design'*

Few novels are as spatially *articulate* as *Jane Eyre*. Its houses, of which there are many, abound with gardens, galleries, bedrooms, dining rooms, schoolrooms, libraries, attics, halls, and closets. These spaces are in continual upheaval. Characters seem ceaselessly engaged in the opening and closing of windows and doors, the ascending and descending of staircases, the crossing of thresholds. Houses are full then suddenly deserted; they are devotedly cleaned or savagely burnt to the ground. Moreover, these houses preoccupy their inhabitants. Rochester comes to see Thornfield Hall as 'a great plague-house'; Jane sees Moor House as 'a charm both potent and permanent.' Indeed, as [Robert] Martin has shown, the succession of buildings furnishes the broad organisation of the plot; Jane's five principal residences mark the five large movements of her career.[1] And within houses, individual rooms come to have distinct personalities. At Thornfield Hall, the schoolroom becomes a 'sanctum,' while at Gateshead whole areas of the house have become menacing; 'Restricted so long to the nursery,' reflects Jane, 'the breakfast, dining, and drawing-rooms were become for me awful regions, on which it dismayed me to intrude': 'I now stood in the empty hall; before me was the breakfast-room door, and I stopped, intimidated and trembling. What a miserable little poltroon had fear, engendered of unjust punishment, made of me in those days! I feared to return to the nursery, I feared to go forward to the parlour; ten minutes I stood in agitated hesitation: the vehement ringing of the breakfast-room bell decided me, I *must* enter' (ch. 4).

---

* In *New Casebooks: Jane Eyre*, edited by Heather Glen (New York: Macmillan, 1997), 52–67.

Later, when guests have come to Thornfield, Jane engages in architectural contortions in order to remain the unobtrusive governess: 'And issuing from my asylum with precaution, I sought a backstairs which conducted directly to the kitchen. All in that region was fire and commotion ... Threading this chaos, I at last reached the larder; there I took possession of a cold chicken, a roll of bread, some tarts, a plate or two and a knife and fork: with this booty I made a hasty retreat' [...] (ch. 17).

More description is lavished on rooms than on the people who inhabit them. Doubtless, Brontë inherits this devotion to spatial intricacy from her gothic predecessors, but, as I hope to show, her purposes are her own [...] In her hands the elaborate spatial design is not so much a way to arouse sensation as to organise it.

Containers within containers – let us begin with this recurrent and compelling image. Houses often exist less as domiciles than as outer shells; rooms and passages serve as inner and intricate spaces; within rooms there are pieces of furniture, drawers, and caskets, which mark still more interior rings. *Within* Gateshead Hall, *within* the red-room, *within* a coffin, Mr Reed once lay, and that, says Jane, accounted for the 'spell' of the room, and 'guarded it from frequent intrusion.' During a crisis at Thornfield, when Mason lies bleeding after Bertha's attack, Rochester sends Jane to his room. Inside the room, he tells her, she will find a toilet-table; in its middle drawer lies a glass and a phial; the phial contains a 'crimson liquid,' which Mason is to drink [...]

[...] The effect is of a system of Chinese boxes at whose innermost point lies a source of dangerous emotive energy [...] The danger is greatest when that source is a living, desiring, rebellious human being. In *Jane Eyre* one can reach Bertha only by passing along a 'dark, low corridor' into a 'tapestried room'; behind one of the tapestries stands a second door leading to an 'inner apartment,' a room 'without a window,' where Bertha moans and shrieks and laughs.

The attempt to represent personality in literature almost invariably takes the form of an effort to visualise the psyche and its contents. Quite often, this involves the personification of emotions, impulses, or faculties – thus Dickens personifies abstract desire in Jingle, and Brontë embodies lawless passion in Bertha [...] The preoccupation with space in the novel gives Brontë a way to confront emotional urgencies by *displaying* them, locating them in terms of high or low, near or far, inner or outer.

Any number of critics (and, no doubt, any number of common readers) have noticed the parallels between Bertha's imprisonment and Jane's confinement in the red-room. In both cases [...] enclosure is the penalty for passion; rooms are asked to contain desires, notably female desires.[2] When Jane thinks of the Reed sisters, Eliza and Georgiana, she pictures 'one the cynosure of a ball-room, the other the inmate of a convent cell' (ch. 22). Jane herself, like Bertha, refuses to accept such imprisonment, and one of the leading dramatic tensions in the novel assumes the spatial form of a struggle between container and contained, between an enclosure (house, room, body) and an emotional quickening at its central core [...]

Confinement is a grave peril in *Jane Eyre,* but no more grave than its spatial antithesis: exposure. When Jane learns of Rochester's marriage, she flees Thornfield Hall, but if we expect this flight to be a saving corrective to her confinement, we, like Jane, are quickly disappointed. Jane, out of doors, is no closer to stability than Jane confined. She wanders for several days, penniless, hungry, and increasingly wretched, and though she had first looked to nature for solace, her hope gives way to 'this feeling of hunger, faintness, chill, and this sense of desolation – this total prostration of hope' (ch. 28). She comes to the brink of death, until she finds another house, a new confinement. A similar reversal had occurred early in the work. Enclosed through the winter in the gloom of Lowood school, Jane welcomes 'the gentler breathings' of spring: 'Lowood shook loose its tresses; it became all green, all flowery; its great elm, ash, and oak skeletons were restored to majestic life' (ch. 9). Here, for the first time in the novel, the natural world appears in attractive form, but after a long passage of lavish description, Jane reverses the expected conclusion: 'The forest-dell, where Lowood lay, was the cradle of fog and fog-bred pestilence; which, quickening with the quickening spring, crept into the Orphan Asylum, breathed typhus through its crowded school-room and dormitory, and, ere May arrived, transformed the seminary into an hospital' (ch. 9).

But in *Jane Eyre* even more dreaded than the exposure to careless nature is an exposure to human scrutiny. Although Jane obsessively seeks to 'elude observation,' she is continually made to endure the stares of others, which strike her as almost physical assaults [...]

We began by considering a crisis of enclosure, the self separated from the world through a succession of barriers, its range of expression greatly narrowed, its passions severely constrained. But it should now be plain that escape from confinement offers no solution, only a new problem. The absence of barriers leads to a contrary, but no less pressing, crisis: the self stripped of any protective carapace, defenceless before nature and human society. The self exposed thus becomes as vulnerable as the self confined. Indeed, these are the extremes that Jane must avoid, extremes moreover that, though opposed, are closely bound. When Jane recognises that she is drifting toward love of Rochester, she issues herself a stern upbraiding: 'It is madness in all women to let a secret love kindle within them, which, if unreturned and unknown, must devour the life that feeds it; and if discovered and responded to, must lead, *ignus-fatuus*-like, into miry wilds whence there is no extrication' (ch. 16).

No statement of the difficulty could be more evocative. Jane warns herself of the agony of love suppressed and the helplessness of love acknowledged – the one depicted as a devouring inner flame, the other as a wilderness [...]

Brontë employs spatial arrangement, in particular the threats of confinement and exposure, as a dominant method for [...] imaginative organisation. The relations of self and other, love and restraint, wish and fear appear in terms of spatial configuration, and in this regard, Brontë's use of the word 'region' is illuminating. Not surprisingly, it appears first in connection with houses. At Gateshead Hall, the breakfast, dining, and drawing-rooms are 'awful regions' and at Thornfield Jane contrasts the gloom of the third story, 'so still a region,' to the 'light and cheerful region below.' The word retains its more familiar use as a general geographic destination – 'I felt we were in a different region to Lowood' (ch. 11) – but it also extends beyond earthly geography. When Helen Burns first speaks of Heaven, Jane wonders to herself, 'Where is that region? Does it exist?'(ch. 9). Finally, the word is put to psychological purposes. When Jane becomes apprehensive before the festivities at Thornfield, she finds herself 'thrown back on the region of doubts and portents, and dark conjectures' (ch. 17). This casual movement of the concept among such distinct realms points to the common imaginative structure that underlies them in Brontë's work. Heaven, earth, houses, and minds, all are visualised in terms of regions, and this spatial analogy lets Brontë establish provocative connections among them.

Minds, for instance, assume the aspect of houses. When Rochester views Jane's pictures, he asks where she found her models:

> 'Out of my head.'
> 'That head I see on your shoulders?'
> 'Yes, sir.'
> 'Has it other furniture of the same kind within?' (ch. 13)

[...] At issue is a forceful conjunction of realms. Psychic life, spiritual life, domestic life, all appear as matters of arrangement, of architecture, of spatial relation. Jane suggests that we feel God's presence most strongly when we see his works 'spread before us,' but this applies to all existence in *Jane Eyre;* things possess significance in so far as they are spread before us, displayed, arrayed. Moreover, by passing so rapidly from 'region' to 'region,' by employing the same spatial figures in each, Brontë creates the impression of a common space in which mind, body, and spirit all find a place – God just behind Rochester's shoulder, doubts on the third story. Crossing thresholds, descending stairs, opening windows, become therefore extraordinary resonant acts; one never knows when the threshold will turn out to be social, the stair psychological, the window spiritual [...]

Passion and reason, feeling and judgement, and the forty organs of the phrenologists, provide only crude distinctions when set against the intricate rhythm of walls and windows, thresholds and compartments, eclipsed suns and unclouded skies. The novel's charged system of spatial relations serves as more than an adornment: it is the imaginative condition of the novel.

NOTES

1 Robert Martin, *The Accents of Persuasion: Charlotte Brontë's Novels* (London: Faber, 1966), 60–1.
2 Sandra M. Gilbert and Susan Gubar, *The Madwoman in the Attic: The Woman Writer and the Nineteenth-Century Literary Imagination* (New Haven, CT: Yale University Press, 1979), 339–71.

9.4 JULIAN WOLFREYS
Dwelling with Dickens and Heidegger

Dickens is the novelist of home par excellence, as well as being the writer who, more than any other, perceives how precarious a thing is home. At the same time, though, it is this very same vulnerability that gives to the poetics of the home in Dickens a place for the possibility of making appear to his characters their own homelessness, and so the concomitant possibility of learning what it means to dwell in relation to, and in care of, one another. This last remark is traced by Martin Heidegger's reflection on the nature of 'dwelling' in 'Building, Dwelling, Thinking' (see section 2.2 in this volume) as a constituent aspect of one's being, as opposed to mere building or existing, and is germane to this discussion of *Dombey and Son*.[1] For Heidegger, dwelling does not define one's existence in a given place. It is irreducible to any notion of building, construction, or activities producing material habitats. Drawing on the etymology of 'dwelling' (*bauen*) in German, and showing its relation to the conjugated forms of the verb of being (*Ich bin, du bist*), and the imperative form, *bis*, meaning 'be,'[2] Heidegger presents the notion of dwelling as part of being's ontology in its historicity, as that which serves to define what it means to exist as a mortal, or what Heidegger would describe as being-towards-death, on, and in knowing relation to, the earth.

One other aspect of 'dwelling' in Heidegger requires consideration, what the philosopher calls 'the fourfold.' Dwelling, as mortals, places us in the 'fourfold' (148). To be mortal means to die, 'to be capable of death *as* death,' and this capability is given only to humans (148). For Heidegger, only humans have the capability of thinking death, of conceptualizing the notion of death and constructing around this various practices, customs, rituals, and so forth. If earth and being in its mortality are two dimensions of the fourfold, the other two in Heidegger's geometry of dwelling are the sky and what he calls the divinities. The 'divinities' is a collective conceptualization, regardless of a specific religion, given to humans to think of as that which is hoped for beyond all rational hope or empirical experience, that which is other and to come. Thus dwelling is constituted through the human reflection on and reception of – a 'staying with' rather than simply existing (149) – the three dimensions of the fourfold that are not categorized as being.

That *Dombey and Son* begins with death in childbirth indicates the striking intimacy and proximity of life and death within, and as, determinants of what it means to dwell, but, more than this, what is closest to home, what strikes home with the most powerful immediacy, and thus comes to haunt the very idea of the home, from the start *and as an inaugural mutation of homeliness*. While death for Paul Dombey, the son, is 'natural,' part of nature, in the images of death that the train journey encompasses and projects repeatedly for Paul's father, death is a destructive force, imagistically projected from the material experience and phenomena of the Victorian age in particular expressions of its industrial-capitalist manifestations. Death is one more product, an outcome if you will, of steam, mechanization, industrialization, urbanization, mercantile mass-production and systems of exchange, the destruction of the land.

Houses in *Dombey* are ruined materially, but nineteenth-century mercantilism, and the economic system that supports it, destroys homes in other ways also. However for Paul, death arrives 'naturally' (he is, after all 'born to die'; but, then, so are we all), the waves and the sea engulfing the room figuratively. In a gesture of *poiesis,* of making appear through poetic creation, Dickens discloses Paul's being gathered into the natural world, Heidegger's earth and sky, as that which calls us to dwell, to 'think of what is called man's existence by way of the nature of dwelling.' Language measures being in its dwelling, as Heidegger argues.[3]

Houses are prisons in Dickens, but they are also places of sanctuary. As the very first chapter of *Dombey* shows us, a particular room can be a locus of both life and death. A room can be a tomb, even though one is still alive, and there is always the violent possibility that one can be expelled from the home, made an outcast, homeless, in one of the most stereotypical of Victorian narrative effects. More than this, *Dombey*, from its very title, plays on the doubleness and duplicity of the house: there is Dombey's house of business but also his home. *Dombey and Son* names both a family relationship and a professional organization. In chapter 3 of *Dombey and Son*, 'In which Mr Dombey, as a Man and a Father, is seen at the Head of the Home-Department' (74), Dickens's ironic title speaks directly to us of the extent to which the idea of home has been elided, occluded even, by the 'House' of business by the 1840s. Home is merely an extension of capitalist enterprise, a department of the business operation, run on modern lines. The chapter begins with a reflection on Mrs Dombey's funeral in particular and funerals in general, from the point of view of the 'neighbourhood,' 'which is generally disposed to be captious on such a point, and is prone to take offence at any omissions or shortcomings in the ceremonies' (74). The private world of grief and mourning becomes subject to scrutiny as public ritual and a communal perspective on such events.

The 'small world' (74) of the house is thus always implicitly open in its comings and goings in its immediate vicinity, and is defined in this manner, even as it mirrors, in however distorted a fashion, the 'great one out of doors' (74).

Only after the system resumes its proper order does the Dickensian narrator describe the house and its interior spaces. The house, we read, 'was a large one, on the shady side of a tall, dark, dreadfully genteel street in the region between Portland Place and Bryanstone Square' (74). The topographical specificity of the location stands in contrast to the anonymity of the home itself. We are told of the exterior form in its totality that 'It was a corner house, with great wide areas containing cellars frowned upon by barred windows, and leered at by crooked-eyed doors leading to dustbins. It was a house of dismal state, with a circular back to it, containing a whole suite of drawing-rooms looking upon a gravelled yard, where two gaunt trees, with blackened trunks and branches, rattled rather than rustled, their leaves were so smoke-dried' (74–5).

In short, this is a parody of a house; bereft of life, yet uncannily animate, with its crooked-eyed doors and barred windows that frown and leer, Dombey's home has something monstrous about it, to the extent that the trees are blasted and the sun rarely shines there.

Such a dismal and unprepossessing condition is doubled and echoed internally, for, we are informed, 'it was as blank a house inside as outside' (75). This has little to do with the fact that a death has recently occurred or a funeral more recently taken place. All 'consciousness' of home, if it can be expressed thus, is 'dispersed' or 'cast out.' The very blankness suggests that all is surface, that this is the very antithesis of what a home should be. It is also as if the house itself is death, or, at the very least aridity and sterility, the 'great world' of business and capitalism contaminating the domestic 'small world.' Dombey's house becomes an unhomely simulacrum of the home proper, defining itself by what it is not, haunting us through all that we know to be absent. Dickens produces an uncanny house that is all the more discomforting for being so materially *of its epoch,* so much a distilled condensation of the historical moment.

Dickens takes us deeper into this strange place. Dombey orders the furniture to be covered. 'Accordingly,' we are told, 'mysterious shapes were made of tables and chairs, heaped together in the middle of rooms, and covered over with great winding sheets' (75). Furniture becomes its own corpse, remaining in its proper location but becoming improperly other than itself.

Everything is covered, hidden; nevertheless everything 'speaks,' though not as itself but in the fragmentary voices of the dead and the murdered, transcribed for, and reported in, the daily and weekly newspapers. That sense of the external house being an animate but inhuman monstrous form considered earlier, returns here through the 'monstrous' tears, as the house turns its gaze inwards. We can only imagine the home from what is not there. Drawing on all his resources from gothic fiction, Dickens imagines the unimaginable, the modern home, an 'especially favoured site for uncanny disturbances: its apparent domesticity, its residue of family history [as figured in the accusatory painting of Mrs Dombey] and nostalgia, its role as the last and most intimate shelter of private comfort sharpened by contrast' with the remainders and reminders of death.[4] The entire productive economy of Dickensian representation tends towards this making unhomely the home as a complex entity produced through both historical and material and psychic phenomena.

In contrast to the dead rooms of the house, Mr Dombey's rooms are sensuously drawn, comprised of various smells, 'hot-pressed paper, vellum, morocco, and Russia leather … the smells of divers pairs of boots' (75). Arguably, such smells encode the passage with a particularly masculine memory that excludes by implication. A spectre is haunting the house of Dombey; the spectre of capitalist masculinity. Victorian man, the man of the age, has become his own, most uncanny, gothic, double – and Dickens presents us with a disquieting perspective on this, in his portrait of the capitalist as a middle-aged man. Dombey does not understand what it means to dwell, and is surrounded, composed we might say, by the ghosts, the scents of commodities, which announce the secret of Dombey's estranged, unhomely being.

Rooms and homes are thus privileged sites that do double service rhetorically and imaginatively, poetically and ideologically. While, on the one hand, they refigure the monstrous machinery and economy of the greater world beyond their walls, on the other hand, they become the crypts, the sarcophagi, in which are secreted the phantoms and phantasms, the ghosts, if not the skeletons in the closets of family identities. Both Dombey and his daughter Edith have become ghosts, or 'shades' of themselves, in being no longer attached in a proper manner to family or home. In the rooms they haunt, their identities are dispersed, only to be condensed subsequently in the intimate, claustrophobic spaces of the very same rooms, their minds in turn banished from the world and any meaningful future.

NOTES

1 All references are to Charles Dickens, *Dombey and Son,* edited by Peter Fairclough (London: Penguin, 1985).
2 Martin Heidegger, 'Building, Dwelling, Thinking,' in *Poetry, Language, Thought,* translated by Albert Hofstadter (New York: Harper Perennial, 2001), 144–5.
3 Martin Heidegger, ' … Poetically Man Dwells … ' in *Poetry, Language, Thought,* translated by Albert Hofstadter (New York: Harper Perennial, 2001), 213, 219–20.
4 Anthony Vidler, *The Architectural Uncanny: Essays in the Modern Unhomely* (Cambridge, MA: MIT Press, 1992), 17. [See section 4.7 in this volume.] (Bracketed insertions in quoted text are the author's.)

9.5 PHILIPPE HAMON
Expositions: Literature and Architecture in Nineteenth-Century France*

For nineteenth-century writers, architecture was not merely the framing or punctuation of a given space or the scenery that served as the backdrop for plot. Architecture was not reducible to aesthetics, economics, or the laws of gravity. Rather, it produced, permitted, and concretized not only a concept of history (be it collective or individual) but also, the staging of everyday life and of those rituals which expose social behavior. These rituals are founded on impalpable legal and ethical distinctions expressed through such oppositions as movable / immovable, private / public, sacred / profane, inside / outside, and privacy / exhibition. The act of dwelling involves living within these 'distinctions' and inhabiting a system

* Translated by Katia Sainson-Frank and Lisa Maguire (Berkeley, CA: University of California Press, 1992).

of values. These distinctions make up the preferred material of nineteenth-century literature; on the one hand, manners and morals (*moeurs*), or one's social relationship to others, as embodied in the novel (Honoré de Balzac writes at the beginning of *La Fausse Maîtresse* that 'architecture is the expression of a nation's mores'); and on the other hand, the subject or the self's relationship to itself through memory and recollection, as embodied in lyric poetry. In a word, the questions of society and the question of the subject [...]

Yet it would probably be easy to confirm that the selective and anthological memory of the average reader retains above all the architectural spaces or objects present in nineteenth-century literature. Here too it would seem that textual memory or readability were entirely dependent upon inscribed or described places: the Vauquer boarding house in *Le Père Goriot,* Fabrice's prison in *La Chartreuse de Parme,* Proust's steeples in *A la recherche du temps perdu,* Emma Bovary's castle-like wedding cake, the symmetrical phalansteries of the good French and bad German engineers in Verne's *Les Cinq cent millions de la Bégum,* des Esseintes's chamber in Joris-Karl Huysmans's *A rebours,* the sewers of Victor Hugo's *Les Misèrables,* Baudelaire's balconies and alcoves, the sealed room of Edgar Allan Poe's *The Murders in the Rue Morgue,* Stéphane Mallarmé's casement windows and waning mirrors. The two literature genres that were, by all accounts first 'invented' in the nineteenth century – the detective story (Poe, Emile Gaboriau) and the prose poem (Aloysius Bertrand, Baudelaire) – both feature intricate and most often urban decors that stand out by their architectural specificity – be it real or invented, proper or common – or the sign of some particular architectural site: *Le cottage Landor;* [...] *La Maison du chat qui pelote; La Maison Tellier;* [...] *Notre-Dame de Paris; La Cathédrale* [...] Such titles are lapidary in the full sense of this term and bear witness throughout the century to the writer's growing sensitivity to the symbolic power of architecture frameworks. It is as if these writers – individuals whom Barthes characterizes as afflicted with the 'disease' of 'seeing language' – suddenly found themselves afflicted with yet another disease, that of 'seeing architecture.' It is as if the fabrication of fiction were now constrained to gather sustenance systematically from the factories, houses, cities, monuments, and various other habitats that dotted an increasingly urbanized landscape of the real. It is as if the writer henceforth would always have to provide housing for his characters, to make them inhabitants; no longer would he be able to describe any of his heroes' habits [...] without also mentioning their habitat [...]

Significantly, nineteenth-century mass literature was quick to adopt the name of the building most emblematic of the entire era: the magazine (*magasin*) ['store' or 'storehouse'] [...] In the same way, such nineteenth-century terms as *panorama, museum, pantheon, ruin, tomb* (those written by Mallarmé being the best known), *tableau, boulevard, salon, Paris,* and *backstage* refer both to a type of publication, or even a particular literary style or genre, and to specific kinds of constructed spaces.

Writers in the nineteenth century took an active interest in architecture. Prosper Mérimée became an inspector of historical monuments, Victor Hugo travelled around as an antiquary, Gustave Flaubert and Maxime Du Camp photographed monuments in Egypt [...]

The imbrication of literature and architecture thus appears widespread in the nineteenth century and seems to play on a variety of levels with a relevance that goes beyond mere historical, metaphorical, or anecdotal coincidence [...]

Perhaps because literature and architecture are the two most 'visible' arts, since they organize both the everyday practices of reading and the everyday necessities of shelter, the crises and tensions that affect them seem strikingly parallel. This parallel appears to take root by 1850. With the emergence of politicians and appointed bureaucrats such as Haussmann, the architects trained at the Ecole des Beaux-Arts deemed themselves increasingly dispossessed of their right and their competence to create the city. They furthermore deemed themselves dispossessed of their ability to create personally designed monuments, houses, and interior furnishings, given the emergence of the knockdown modules used by engineers such as Eiffel. Industrial architecture, with its buildings that could be easily dismantled, restored, or put to a variety of uses, brought about a crisis of style and of meaning which Hugo registered as early as 1830: How do we 'read' a building? Which in turn leads to another all-encompassing crisis: How do we read the real? [...] These architectural crises came at a time when writers were also confronting difficulties in the practice of their profession. Both writers and architects saw their roles becoming increasingly subordinate or accessory: the architect felt reduced to designing bourgeois vacation houses, or 'secondary' homes, while the writer felt obliged to churn out entertainment for concierges, to produce gossip columns [...] to write newspaper articles, or to engage in what Sainte-Beuve termed the 'industrial literature' of the serial novel [...]

As might be expected, the nineteenth century would produce a series of conjunctions between architecture and literature. But the analysis of these conjunctions should involve more than a thematic inventory of the numerous nineteenth-century literary works that describe buildings of their time, or a certain shared vocabulary (as in the aforementioned case of the *magasin*). Rather, these conjunctions should be analyzed from the perspective of a textual poetics that would attempt to describe the system or structure of such interconnections, while above all highlighting the function of certain specific objects, metaphors, or textual schemas.

9.6 DIANA FUSS
The Sense of an Interior: Four Writers and the Rooms That Shaped Them*

My own study of the literary house challenges the too easy bifurcation between literal and figurative space reinforced by the separate disciplines of architecture and literature. To attribute substance and materiality to architecture, and imagination and metaphor to literature, misreads both artistic forms. It is by no means clear that literature is less embodied than architecture, or that architecture is less visionary than literature. Neither the materiality of writing nor the metaphysics of building can be quite so readily elided. My own view on the relation between literature and architecture is one part Martin Heidegger, one part Gaston Bachelard [see sections 2.2 and 2.1 in this volume]. Whereas Heidegger in 'Poetically Man Dwells' argues that a poem is a special kind of building, the 'original admission of dwelling,' Bachelard in *The Poetics of Space* asserts that a building is a special kind of poetry, 'one of the greatest powers of integration for the thoughts, memories and dreams of mankind.'[1] A building and a poem are not substitutable, but they are not oppositional either; neither synonyms nor antonyms, architecture and literature work in tandem for the writer to create a rich and evolving sense of the interior. I am struck by how the seemingly intractable distinction between literary metaphor and architectural reality, between figure and ground, quickly falls away. For writers at least, the creative act of composition poses its own physical challenges, while the built environment offers up a store of metaphysical questions [...]

Long before Gaston Bachelard began exploring the lyrical recesses of the architectural dwelling, Emily Dickinson was intimately involved in mapping her own 'poetics of space.' [...] There is no architectural figure more important, or more weighted, in Dickinson's poetry than the image of the door. The door serves as the central ontological support upon which Dickinson's entire theory of interiority hangs: 'The Opening and the Close / Of Being' (Poem 1047).[2] [...]

In Dickinson's letters and poems, the door emerges as a richly layered metaphor for loneliness, loss, and death, on the one hand, and memory, secrecy, and safety, on the other. The door is the most reversible of Dickinson's images, and the most complex. It dramatizes a tension at the heart of almost all Dickinson's poems, the tension produced by the terror and excitement of the threshold. Doors represent for the poet the possibility of crossing over or passing through.

* (New York and London: Routledge, 2004).

They are the concrete visualization of the tenuous border between the finite and the infinite, the mortal and the immortal, the human and the divine.

In Dickinson's correspondence, the conceit of the door is most often associated with the theme of departure. Dickinson continually portrays herself in her letters as racing to a door or window to catch a final glimpse of a departing loved one.[3] [...] The doorstep marks the place where the poet first fell in love with Susan Gilbert, the place that continues to remind her of Sue even after her friend has gone 'West' to marry Austin:

> I love you as dearly, Susie, as when love first began, on the step of the front door, and under the Evergreens, and it breaks my heart sometimes, because I do not hear from you. (Letter 177)[4]

[...]

> Dear Susie, I dont forget you a moment of the hour, and when my work is finished, and I have got the tea, I slip thro' the little entry, and out at the front door, and stand and watch the West, and remember all of mine. (Letter 103)

[...]

As she grew older Dickinson was indeed increasingly reluctant to travel forth beyond the doors of the family homestead [...] Yet Dickinson's poems are generally not about the fear of *leaving* interiors but more commonly about the anxiety of *entering* them. The problem of gaining entry is, for Dickinson, a far greater preoccupation:

> I Years had been from Home
> And now before the Door
> I dared not enter, lest a Face
> I never saw before
>
> Stare stolid into mine
> And asked my Business there –
> (Poem 609)

'Home' may signify for the poet her favourite spiritual locale (Eden, Paradise, Eternity), or it may refer to the actual house on Pleasant Street that Dickinson still longed to return to years later. In either case, the speaker's dilemma is the same: terror in the face of an unknown presence hidden behind a familiar barrier.

The interior in Dickinson's poetry does not always inspire fear. Just as often a door may conceal an idealized scene of domestic comfort and plenitude.

A Door just opened on a street –
I – lost – was passing by –
An instant's Width of Warmth disclosed –
And Wealth – and Company.

The Door as instant shut – And I –
I – lost – was passing by –
Lost doubly – but by contrast – most –
Informing – misery –
(Poem 953)

[…] Other Dickinson poems syntactically open and shut on the force of a dash, but 'A Door just opened on a street' makes particularly frequent use of the poet's signature punctuation, both to isolate its speaker internally and to slam the poem shut repeatedly, end-stopping every line […]

The door ajar – half open, half closed – evolves over the corpus of Dickinson's poetry into one of her most positive images. For example, in 'The Soul should always stand ajar' (Poem 1055), a soul stands waiting to receive its divine caller, ready at a moment's notice to leave the interior dwelling of the body that has temporarily housed it. The image of the door ajar also animates what may well be Dickinson's most lyrical, tranquil, and perfect poem.

Noon – is the Hinge of Day –
Evening – the Tissue Door –
Morning – the East compelling the sill
Till all the World is ajar –
(Poem 931)

In a single quatrain, Dickinson chronicles the evolution of a day, emphasizing, through precise temporal sequencing, the dawn beyond the dusk, the east beyond the west, the morning beyond the evening. The World is a domestic dwelling, fortified by movement (hinge), mass (door), and foundation (sill). Hinge, door, and sill are all of a piece, forming a translucent 'tissue' boundary between spatial and temporal worlds. The East that gently pries open the morning, leaving all the world ajar, illuminates life's most basic movement of opening and closing, the meaning of creation.

Ultimately, the door in Dickinson's poetry is a completely indeterminate figure. A door can symbolize loss or gain, absence or presence, loneliness or reunion, separation or connection, life or death. The very instability of the image is what appeals to Dickinson most, immediately elevating the figure of the door over architecture's other apparently more static forms. Not long after Dickinson's death, the German philosopher Georg Simmel argued (in striking Dickinsonian fashion) that the door is far superior to the dead geometric form of the wall. To Simmel, a wall is 'mute,' but a door 'speaks.' [See section 7.1 in this volume.] Moreover, a door more successfully transcends the divide between the inner and the outer; a door is where the finite borders on the infinite; a door marks the plane where separation and connection come together, but still remain apart.[5]

NOTES

1 Martin Heidegger, 'Poetically Man Dwells,' in Neil Leach, ed., *Rethinking Architecture* (New York: Routledge, 1997), 112 and 118; Gaston Bachelard, *The Poetics of Space* (Boston, MA: Beacon Press, 1994 [1958]), 6.
2 All poems are from Emily Dickinson, *The Complete Poems of Emily Dickinson,* edited by Thomas H. Johnson (Boston: Little, Brown, 1955).
3 Jane Donahue Eberwein, *Dickinson: Strategies of Limitation* (Amherst, MA: University of Massachusetts Press, 1987), 53.
4 All letters are from Emily Dickinson, *The Letters of Emily Dickinson,* edited by Thomas H. Johnson (Cambridge, MA: Belknap Press of Harvard University Press, 1958).
5 Georg Simmel, 'Bridge and Door,' in *Rethinking Architecture,* edited by Neil Leach (New York: Routledge, 1997), 66–9.

9.7 HANNA SCOLNICOV
Woman's Theatrical Space*

The momentous move from the outdoor theatre of classical times to the indoor auditorium in the Renaissance and after has been echoed by the evolution of the theatrical space. The scene has shifted from the open air, the front of the palace, the street, the piazza, into the state-room, the parlor, the kitchen, the bedroom, narrowing down the scope and infringing on the privacy of intimate relations. Some contemporary playwrights have gone further, deconstructing the familiar naturalistic room to form a non-mimetic interior or abstracting space altogether.

---

* (Cambridge: Cambridge University Press, 1994).

Seen from a feminist point of view, the articulation of the theatrical space is an expression of woman's position in society. Her relative confinement in traditional societies to the seclusion of her home puts the onus of the action on the man, thus making him into an active agent of time, and her into an element of space [...]

Inside the Drawing-Room

The lengthy stage-directions at the head of Henrik Ibsen's middle-period realistic dramas carefully define their particular theatrical spaces [...] The drawing-rooms called for by *A Doll's House* (1879) and *Hedda Gabler* (1890) are very different from each other, reflecting the difference in social position, upbringing, culture, and character of the two heroines. The furnishings are not just a background of naturalistic objects but a living presence that characterizes the protagonists, their taste, income, and style, all of which are constitutive elements of the action. Nora's inexpensive but tasteful furniture is as relevant to her play as are the missing slip-covers on Hedda's elegant chairs and sofas. The realistic appearance of the drawing-room functions both as an environment for the action and an expressive means of characterization [...]

In terms of the theatrical space, the drawing-room is where Nora plays her 'feminine part' and her unseen room is where she can be herself. In order to heal this rift in her personality, Nora must leave the house altogether. When she reaches that conclusion, the traditional spatial definitions, social as well as theatrical, are thrown into disarray. The woman's passage out of the home and into the world leaves the male in the house and severs the woman's ties with her home as her unique space.

The scene which leads up to Nora's dramatic exit is carefully constructed. It begins with Helmer's flinging his study-door open, the condemning letter in his hand, at the same moment that Nora, wrapped up in her shawl, is about to rush out of the house [...] This is a scene which unsettles the social framework represented by the stage-set and advocated by Helmer, and to which up to now, Nora has acquiesced [...]

The naturalistic drawing-room setting serves Ibsen as a laboratory for testing the premises of bourgeois ideology, and the direct confrontation between husband and wife, with which the play ends, is an experiment investigating the nature of marriage itself. Only in the intimacy of the house can such a conversation take place, and even in this carefully laid out space, Nora notes that this is the first time that the two of them are sitting down to have a serious talk (act 3). Her comment works on two levels: it points to a change in the relations between the genders as well as in dramatic technique. Nora's revelation is shared by the playwright who has discovered the power of simple naturalistic dialogue between a man and a woman sitting in their drawing-room, to probe into the basis of their relationship. George Bernard Shaw saw in this 'discussion' a technical breakthrough [...]

Ibsen's analysis of the modern woman's repression as internal rather than external is expressed directly by the meticulously prescribed bourgeois drawing-room. The physical restraint of previous generations, expressed by the theatrical convention of the house front and locked door, has given way to a much freer and more egalitarian life-style in the shared living-room. Enjoying this greater freedom, Ibsen's heroines discover the more subtle fetters, moral and cultural, that inhibit them and force them to act inauthentically. The social propriety that finds its outward form in the formality and elegance of the *salon* is discovered to exert a deadly influence on woman's ability to find self-fulfilment. The room is the gilded shell of an impossible social decorum, a pretence and an imposture that attempt to cover up the vacuity of the underlying moral justification.

9.8 SUPRIYA CHAUDHURI
Interiors and Interiority in Nineteenth-Century India

Looking back today at Gaston Bachelard's phenomenological classic, *The Poetics of Space* (1958), we may be struck by the distance that separates his excavation of the spatial imaginary, particularly the interior of the oneiric house, organized like an intimate universe from cellar to attic, from the spatial experiences of Indian cultural history. [See section 2.1 in this volume.] The contrast is particularly visible in texts that seek to negotiate the material content of Western modernity within an indigenous idiom of affect.

Historians of material culture in India, overwhelmed by the plenitude of objects, textiles, and ornaments that appear to fill up the space of everyday existence, have perhaps paid too little attention to the transformation of daily life effected by the introduction of European buildings and furniture in the nineteenth century. [See Glover, section 2.10 in this volume.] For bourgeois modernity, this helps to compose what Walter Benjamin, writing about nineteenth-century Paris, called not just the universe, but the *étui* of private man. [See section 3.8 in this volume.] It is well known that Bengali fiction in the nineteenth and early twentieth centuries adapted many of the techniques of realism from the high bourgeois novel as from European history writing. The nature of this realism requires it to be grounded in the precise and substantial representation of material culture, in what modern historians would call the social life of things. Indeed the whole project of colonial modernity involves a new valuation placed upon the world as a collection of objects in use, even as a site of commodity exchange and transfer in Marx's sense, at the same time that colonial subjects begin to acquire a new *habitus* of conspicuous consumption distinguished by the possession and display of a previously unknown range of household goods. C.A. Bayly has commented on a shift in material culture, in Istanbul as in India, at some point in the eighteenth century: 'the embellishment of the inside of buildings with a profusion of objects, pictures, tapestries, and furniture became the order of the day in India, reaching its apogee in the cluttered Marble Palace of Calcutta, with its crowd of Carrara marble statues, and the Salar Jung Palace in Hyderabad, where grandfather clocks jostled with huge French chaise-longues.'[1] Both domestic interiors and social exteriors come to serve the purpose of self-substantiation, that is, of *making representation work for the individual.* This material universe is carefully articulated in the new form of the novel, as instanced in the fiction of Bankimchandra Chattopadhyay. Yet the realism of the early modern Bengali novel is deeply ambivalent in its response to the world of objects, and this ambivalence may be seen as the product of internal tensions between the sumptuary codes of modern mercantile capitalism and a profound suspicion of the world and its goods that is culturally encoded as 'tradition.' Domestic space becomes the site of a struggle between old and new, the struggle of the modern as it is realized in the practices of everyday life.

The hot, damp climate of Bengal, encouraging infestation by pests such as termites and borers, never favoured the preservation of wood or upholstery: clay, stone, and textiles that could be frequently washed were customarily preferred for domestic use. The notions of purity and danger, central to Hindu ritual, involved repeated ablutions and washing of all surfaces in use, which would naturally be of stone, marble, or newly coated clay. Traditionally, and in less well-off households, the practices of everyday life – rites of worship, domestic tasks, sleep, rest, and conversation – took place at floor level. Most of the Bengali words for items of furniture, with a few exceptions like *chouki* and *alna* (for a low stool and a clothes rack, both Hindi) are taken from Arabic (*ashbab, sinduk*) and Portuguese (*kedara, almari:* from *cadeira, armario*), indicating the provenance of the articles themselves, as they come to be introduced from the sixteenth century onwards. Even the terms for a bed, *khat, paryanka,* or *palanka,* from Sanskrit or Prakrit, change meaning before being attached to a wooden, sometimes carved bedstead. But by the nineteenth century the rising middle classes were beginning to furnish their houses either in the Persian-Mughal style of interior decoration, with life still lived close to the floor level, but using ornamental low seats and furniture, or in the newly available British fashion, employing tables and chairs. What survives from that period in the city houses of rich *zamindari* (land-owning) or trading families offers not a history of taste but a bewildering medley – as in the Marble Palace of the Mallicks in north Calcutta, in the houses of the Lahas, or in the Shobhabazar Rajbari.

Allowing for some differences across communities, castes, and regions, the house in nineteenth-century India constitutes a space roughly divided into outer and inner precincts, the outer areas reserved for the men of the house, for male visitors, and for business, and the inner or women's quarters, referred to in northern India as the *antahpur, andarmahal,* or *zenana*. The architecture of the traditional dwelling would reflect this separation, with women not normally entering the front rooms or offices where the men sat, though the distinction could only be strictly maintained in households above a certain economic level (if the dwelling was substantial enough to allow the separation), and was open to modification in the heterotopic sites constituted by religion or pleasure – for instance, in the transgressive space of the brothel, or through the socially sanctioned practice of pilgrimage. For women, the demarcation of household space allowed for a degree of freedom as well as privation, both internalized to become a norm of virtuous conduct.

The building of new bourgeois houses in the European style from the eighteenth century onwards did not obliterate the distinction between outer and inner regions, vital to middle- and upper-class notions of respectability. Yet during the same period, as Rabindranath Tagore movingly chronicles in his novel *The Home and the World* (*Ghare Baire,* 1915), the house becomes the site of a project of social modernization by some enlightened families attempting to bring their women out of the *antahpur* to the public apartments. This passage from inner to outer, attended by extreme risk and difficulty, seeks to reconfigure the values of domestic space by recasting women's lives. Typically, it is a *male* project, like many other social reform movements of the nineteenth century. At the same time, the careful spatial articulation of *The Home and the World* reminds us that physical space can never be treated *merely* as a function of ideology: there is always something in it that exceeds the use to which it is put. In nineteenth-century India as in Walter Benjamin's Paris, the interiors of the bourgeois house are instrumental to the self-representation of the individual, just as they are essential to the representational task of realist fiction. But representation, in this double aspect, must contend with deep feelings of distrust and hermeneutic suspicion.

Tagore's grandfather, Prince Dwarakanath, built a townhouse in the new style in 1823, a *baithak-khana bari* consisting of sumptuously furnished outer apartments and offices added on to an older family residence. A modern visitor to that house in Calcutta's Jorasanko is immediately made conscious of the intricate gradations of domestic space in what survives of the original buildings. Virtually nothing remains of the fabulous European furnishings and ornaments of Dwarakanath's day, lost after the financial collapse of the 1840s. By the time of the poet's own childhood, they had become part of what his nephew, the artist Abanindranath, called 'house-memory.' The architecture of the Jorasanko building is a constant, ghostly presence both in his paintings and those of his brother Gaganendranath. Their uncle's writings, too, vividly recall the covered south veranda of his childhood home, but they express no nostalgia for the house's European furniture. In a letter to his wife Mrinalini in 1901, Tagore wrote: 'My inmost being continually craves emptiness, not just the emptiness of sky, air, and light, but an emptiness within the home, an emptiness of furnishings and arrangements, an emptiness of effort, thought, fuss.'[2] This desire for a void within the home may be understood as the longing for a cleansed, empty interior, an absolute simplicity or clarity against which the filled and arranged space of our ordinary lives is experienced.

In a late novel, *Relationships* (*Jogajog*, 1929), Tagore conveys the full extent of the unease, anxiety, and distrust evoked in him by the furnishings of the bourgeois house and its spatial order, so indicative of the culture and aspirations of his own social class. Early in the novel, there is an extended description of the unused European drawing room in the house of the *zamindar* of Nurnagar, Mukundalal:

> In another wing of the house there was an English drawing-room, furnished with eighteenth-century English furniture. Directly in front there was a huge blackened mirror, its gilt frame flanked by two winged angels holding lamp-stands. On the table below stood a black stone clock chased in gold, and a few English glass figurines. The upright chairs, the sofas, the chandelier suspended from a ceiling-joist – everything was wrapped in holland-cloth. The walls were hung with oil-paintings of ancestors, and with them a few portraits of the family's state patrons. The room was covered with European carpets, patterned with plump flowers in rich colours. This room was unveiled only on special occasions for the entertainment of the district's European residents. It was the only modern room in the house, yet it seemed as though it was the most ancient, most ghost-ridden of all the rooms, filled with the suffocating, choking and musty smell of disuse, denied the contacts of daily life, dumb.[3]

Mukundalal himself prefers the old ways, and sits on a low mattress (*gaddi*) on the floor, in his personal chamber, smoking his hookah, surrounded by courtiers and friends. The deadness of his 'modern,' European sitting room exemplifies the incompatibility of his own traditional way of life with colonial modernity figured in the objects of material culture. In his house, we may note, there is an absolute spatial separation between the two modes of life, though there are contemporary records of rooms where the *gaddi* and European chairs are placed next to each other.[4] But Tagore's decision, in this novel, to tell the story of a marriage, and a clash of interests, that is rooted in the history of class and society in the nineteenth century, makes the European sitting room absolutely integral to his plot. As a form, the nineteenth-century novel was designed to express the monetary and sexual aspirations of a new bourgeoisie, and to record its self-substantiation through material goods. Tagore's choice of this form committed him to a descriptive social realism integral to the ideology of representation in the high bourgeois novel, but which Tagore never uses without irony. This irony is not only a fundamental structural principle in his narrative, but inflects irremediably the authorial third person, casting doubt, as it were, on the realism of textual effects. It thus fills with hermeneutic suspicion a representational technique that had from its origin set a high value on the world and its objects as constitutive of reality: the world which in its profusion of metonymic detail fills the nineteenth-century bourgeois novel with an illusion of solidity and depth. That world is simultaneously established and negated in Tagore's fiction, and never more so than in *Relationships.*

The novel's heroine, Kumudini, is married to Raja Madhusudan Ghoshal, a successful entrepreneur like the author's grandfather Dwarakanath, but unlike him, coarse in his manners and harshly self-disciplined in his personal habits. Nevertheless, Madhusudan has built a townhouse in the new bourgeois style, adding it on to an older building housing the women's quarters (the *antahpur*) which remains shabby and uncared-for:

> The outer house had marbled floors and carpets imported from England; its walls were covered with patterned paper and hung with pictures of various kinds, some engravings, others oleographs or oils. Their subjects were stags being chased by hunting dogs, famous horses which had won the Derby, European landscapes or bathing nudes. In addition, the walls were decorated with chinaware, brass plates of Moradabadi work, Japanese fans, yak-tail whisks from Tibet, and other such ill-assorted objects in useless and ill-placed profusion [...] In addition there was a veritable forest of chairs and sofas covered in velvet and silk. In glass-fronted shelves were ranged richly-bound English books, untouched by human hand other than that of the servant with his dust-cloth. On the low tables lay albums, some containing pictures of the family, others those of foreign *actresses.*[5]

The outer rooms of Madhusudan's house, furnished by his English assistant, thus assemble 'in useless and ill-placed profusion' the evidences of wealth (and of a blinding lack of taste) that substantiate the social claims of the new bourgeoisie. Furniture here carries almost the entire weight of representation: metonymically precise, it is also metaphorically overdetermined. By contrast, the women's quarters are neglected and unmodernized, with the exception of Kumudini and Madhusudan's bedroom, described as newly appointed with European pictures and furniture. Kumudini desperately resists its implicit conversion of her, too, into property. This is powerfully rendered in the treatment of domestic space, as she attempts to delay her entry into the bedroom, taking refuge in even more confined spaces like the storeroom, terrace, or bathroom. If we reflect on the way in which Madhusudan seeks to leave his mark on the world he inhabits, his jealous possessiveness with regard to his goods, such as his glass paperweight, his wife Kumudini, and her sapphire ring, we must view this universe of objects as serving the ends of possessive individualism. Indeed, in this novel, as in those of Henry James, objects are burdened, even overdetermined, by the full weight of affective or emotional investment: thus the ring, Kumudini's handkerchief, or her shawl, come to acquire a dense, fetishistic meaning-excess. Here, Kumudini is threatened by the overwhelming presence of an object-dominated setting that threatens to engulf her as a person. Instead of instantiating her existence, these objects proclaim that their value is above or beyond her own.

Within the phantasmagorias of these interiors, which can never be equated with interiority as such, Tagore places the reclusive inner realm of the individual, especially of women characters such as Kumudini in *Relationships*, or Charulata in *The Broken Nest* (*Nashtanir*, 1901; filmed by Satyajit Ray as *Charulata* [The Lonely Wife], 1964). These private regions of the self are also figured – metaphorically rather than metonymically – in spatial terms as deep recesses or tunnels. Charulata is described as digging a tunnel 'under the entire structure of her domestic tasks and duties,' and Kumudini as building a protective carapace for her interior self.[6] But this impulse to withdraw to a deep interiority exceeding the material contours of the inhabited house coexists with the desire for emptiness and infinitude, the open space that Tagore so desperately sought in his own domestic arrangements. In *Relationships*, the grinding detail of realist representation, focusing upon bourgeois interiors, is countered by the affective power of a remembered landscape where the world is not so much a collection of objects in use, as a set of images imprinted on Kumudini's consciousness. That 'other space,' a *heterotopia* implicit in religious devotion, music, and childhood memory, sustains her in the soulless luxury of her marital home as in her stifling marriage, and constitutes a form of infinitude.

Tagore's revulsion from the crowded interiors of the nineteenth-century colonial mansion, fictionalized in the experiences of his characters, may be related to the real changes he sought to effect in domestic architecture. The artist Surendranath Kar designed (roughly between 1919 and 1935) five houses for Tagore in his *ashram* at Shantiniketan, drawing upon pan-Asian (primarily Japanese), traditional Indian, and primitivist-folk sources of inspiration, and rejecting colonial models for a local and nationalist aesthetics, especially in the mud house called 'Shyamali.' This reform of the interior is linked, in Tagore's poetry, to the desire for infinitude, the yearning for the intimate immensity of 'sky, air, light.' Tagore's *asim* ('unlimited'), not identical with Rilke's 'open,' is equally invested in a voiding of the world. In Rilke's eighth Duino Elegy, the feeling for space becomes an existential determination: the creature-world, gazing at the 'open,' is unaware of death or limitation.[7] Human beings can never be 'unworlded' in this way: for them the familiar contours of land and sky, imbued with love, loss, or longing, are limited by the consciousness of mortality. Yet for Tagore and his characters, especially the women who, in all his fiction, feel most intensely the imprisoning confines of domestic space, intimations of infinitude pierce through the constrictions of physical existence. Kumudini, recalling 'the empty sprawling fields, the copses of wild tamarisks, the tow-path,' or the young girl Subha, sitting under a tree, at noon, looking out at the immense silence of nature, feel the pull of that infinitude.[8]

NOTES

1 Christopher A. Bayly, 'The Origins of Swadeshi (Home Industry): Cloth and Indian Society, 1700–1930,' in A. Appadurai, ed., *The Social Life of Things: Commodities in Cultural Perspective* (Cambridge: Cambridge University Press, 1986), 306.

2 Rabindranath Tagore, *Chithipatra* [Letters], vol. 1, 58, letter 29, cited in Prashantakumar Pal in *Rabijibani* [The Life of Rabindranath Tagore], vol. 5 (Kolkata: Ananda Publishers, 1990), 19. Author's translation.

3 Cited from Rabindranath Tagore, *Relationships,* translated by Supriya Chaudhuri (Delhi: Oxford University Press, 2006), 44.

4 See Swati Chattopadhyay, *Representing Calcutta: Modernity, Nationalism and the Colonial Uncanny* (London: Routledge, 2005; Indian reprint, 2006), 221, citing Bengali Inventory of Deceased Estates, L / AG / 34 / 27 series, London, India Office Library Collection (221 n67).

5 Tagore, *Relationships,* 94.

6 See '*Nashtanir,*' chapter 15, in Rabindranath Tagore, *Rabindra Rachanabali*, vol. 22 (Kolkata: Vishva Bharati, 1957), 254 (my translation); and Tagore, *Relationships*, 131.
7 See Rainer Maria Rilke, *Duino Elegies*, edited with translations by J.B. Leishman and Stephen Spender (London: Hogarth Press, 1968), 77: 'Mit allen Augen sieht die Kreatur / das Offene.'
8 See Tagore, *Relationships*, 53, and 'Subha' (1893), in Sukanta Chaudhuri, ed., Rabindranath Tagore, *Selected Short Stories* (New Delhi: Oxford University Press, 2000), 105–6.

9.9 HOMI K. BHABHA 'The World and the Home'*

In the house of fiction you can hear, today, the deep stirring of the unhomely. You must permit me this awkward word – 'unhomely' – because it captures something of the estranging sense of the relocation of the home and the world in an unhallowed place. To be unhomed is not to be homeless, nor can the unhomely be easily accommodated in that familiar division of the social life into private and public spheres. The unhomely moment creeps up on you as stealthily as your own shadow, and suddenly you find yourself, with Henry James's Isabel Archer, taking the measure of your dwelling in a state of 'incredulous terror.'[1] And it is at this point that the world first shrinks for Isabel and then expands enormously. As Isabel struggles to survive the fathomless waters, the rushing torrents, James introduces us to the 'unhomeliness' inherent in that rite of 'extra-territorial' initiation – the relations between the innocent American, the deep, dissembling European, the masking émigré – that a generation of critics have named his 'international theme.' In a feverish stillness, the intimate recesses of the domestic space become sites for history's most intricate invasions. In that displacement, the border between home and world becomes confused; and, uncannily, the private and the public become part of each other, forcing upon us a vision that is as divided as it is disorienting.

In the stirrings of the unhomely, another world becomes visible. It has less to do with forcible eviction and more to do with the uncanny literary and social effects of enforced social accommodation or historical migrations and cultural relocations. The home does not remain the domain of domestic life, nor does the

* In *Dangerous Liaisons: Gender, Nation and Postcolonial Perspectives,* edited by Anne McClintock, Aamir Mufti, and Ella Shohat (Minneapolis, MN: University of Minnesota Press, 1997), 445–55.

world simply become its social or historical counterpart. The unhomely is the shock of recognition of the world-in-the-home, the home-in-the-world. In a song called 'Whose House Is This?' Toni Morrison gives the problem of the unhomely dwelling a lyric clarity: 'Whose house is this? Whose night keeps out the light in here? Say who owns this house? It is not mine. I had another sweeter … The House is strange. Its shadows lie. Say, tell me, why does its lock fit my key?'[2]

My earliest sense of the unhomely occurred in a prosaic house in Oxford, in a narrow street reserved for college servants and research fellows. It was a noisy, red-brick, terraced house haunted by the hydraulic regurgitations of the Victorian plumbing system, yet strangely appropriate to the task at hand, a thesis on V.S. Naipaul. I was writing about *A House for Mr. Biswas,* about a small-time Trinidadian journalist, the son of an Indian indentured labourer, a devotee of Samuel Smiles and Charles Dickens, who was afflicted with the most noisy and public bouts of nervous dyspepsia. As I contemplated his tragic-comic failure to create a dwelling place, I wrestled with the wisdom of Iris Murdoch's laudable pronouncement, 'A novel must be a house for free people to live in.' Must the novel be a house? What kind of narrative can house unfree people? Is the novel also a house where the unhomely can live? I was straining nervously at the edges of Iris Murdoch's combination of liberalism and 'catholic' existentialism, while Mr. Biswas's gastric juices ran amok. The cistern churned and burped, and I thought of some of the great homes of English literature – Mansfield Park, Thrushcross Grange, Gardencourt, Brideshead, Howards End, Fawlty Towers. Suddenly, I knew I had found, in the ruins of the Biswases' bungalows and their unlikely, unsettled lives, my small corner of the world of letters – a post-colonial place.

Working on *A House for Mr. Biswas,* I found that I couldn't fit the political, cultural, or chronological experience of that text into the traditions of Anglo-American, liberal, novel criticism. The sovereignty of the concept of character, grounded as it is in the aesthetic discourse of cultural authenticity and the practical ethics of individual freedom, bore little resemblance to the over-determined, unaccommodated post-colonial figure of Mr. Biswas. The image of the house has always been used to talk about the expansive, mimetic nature of the novel; but in *Biswas* you have a form of realism that is unable to contain the anguish of cultural displacement and diasporic movement. Although the unhomely is a paradigmatic post-colonial experience, it has a resonance that can be heard distinctly, if erratically, in fictions that negotiate the powers of cultural difference in a range of historical conditions and social contradictions.

You can hear the shrill alarm of the unhomely at the moment when Isabel Archer, in *The Portrait of the Lady,* realises that her world has been reduced to one, high, mean window as her house of fiction becomes 'the house of darkness, the house of dumbness, the house of suffocation.'[3] If you hear it thus at the Palazzo Roccanera in the late 1870's, then a little earlier, in 1873, on the outskirts of Cincinnati, in mumbling houses like 124 Bluestone Road, you hear the indecipherable language of the black and angry dead, the voice of Toni Morrison's Beloved: 'the thoughts of the women of 124, unspeakable thoughts, unspoken.'[4] [...] Much closer to our own times, in contemporary South Africa, Nadine Gordimer's heroine Aila emanates a stilling atmosphere as she makes her diminished domesticity into the perfect cover for gun running: suddenly the home turns into another world, and the narrator notices that 'it was as if everyone found he had unnoticingly entered a strange house, *and it was hers*.'[5]

Gordimer's awkward sentence, with its rapid shift of genders and pronouns ('everyone' – 'he' – 'she'), provides the estranging syntax of the unhomely experience. Gordimer's sign of the woman's sense of possession and self-possession ('it was hers'), her ethical or historical transformation of the world, emerges retroactively, belatedly, *at the end of the sentence, toward the end of the book* [...]

The unhomely moment relates the traumatic ambivalence of a personal, psychic history to the wider disjunction of political existence. Beloved, the child murdered by her own mother, Sethe, is a demonic, belated repetition of the violent history of black infant deaths, during slavery, in many parts of the South, less than a decade after the haunting of 124 Bluestone Road (between 1882 and 1895, from one-third to one-half of the annual black mortality rate was accounted for by children under five). But the memory of Sethe's act of infanticide emerges through 'the holes – the things the fugitives did not say; the questions they did not ask ... the unnamed, the unmentioned.' As we reconstruct the narrative of child-murder through Sethe, the slave mother, who is herself the victim of social death, the very historical basis of our ethical judgments undergoes a radical revision.

In the denouement of her novel, Gordimer provides another example of the complexity of the unhomely when she describes what she calls 'the freak displacement' that has afflicted the world of her characters. 'The biological drive of Sonny's life which belonged to his wife was diverted to his white lover [Hannah] ... He and Hannah had begot no child. The revolutionary movement was to be their survivor ... But Aila, his wife, was the revolutionary now.'[6] In the freak displacements of these novels, the profound divisions of an enslaved or apartheid society (negrification, denigration, classification, violence, incarceration) are relocated in the midst of the ambivalence of psychic identification – that space where love and hate can be projected or inverted, where the relation of 'object' to identity is always split and doubled [...]

The study of world literature might be the study of the way in which cultures recognize themselves through their projections of 'otherness.' Where the transmission of 'national' traditions was once the major theme of a world literature, perhaps we can now suggest that transnational histories of migrants, the colonized, or political refugees – these borders and frontier conditions – may be the terrain of world literature. The center of such a study would neither be the 'sovereignty' of national cultures nor the 'universalism' of human culture but a focus on the 'freak displacements' – such as Morrison and Gordimer display – that have been caused within cultural lives of post-colonial societies. If these were considered to be the paradigm cases of a world literature based on the trauma of history and the conflict of nations, then Walter Benjamin's homeless modern novelist would be the representative figure of an unhomely world literature. For he 'carries the incommensurable to extremes in the representation of human life and in the midst of life's fullness, gives evidence to the perplexity of living.'[7] Which leads us to ask: Can the perplexity of the unhomely, intrapersonal world lead to an international theme? [...]

If we are seeking a 'worlding' of literature, then perhaps it lies in a critical act that attempts to grasp the sleight of hand with which literature conjures with historical specificity, using the medium of psychic uncertainty, aesthetic distancing, or the obscure signs of the spirit-world, the sublime and the subliminal. As literary creatures and political animals we ought to concern ourselves with the understanding of human action and the social world as a moment when '*something is beyond control, but it is ... not beyond accommodation*.' This act of writing the world, of taking the measure of its dwelling, is magically caught in Morrison's description of her house of fiction – art as 'the fully realized presence of a haunting' of history [...]

Each of the houses in Gordimer's *My Son's Story* is invested with a specific secret or a conspiracy, an unhomely stirring. The house in the ghetto is the house of 'colored' collusion; the lying house is the house of Sonny's adultery; then there is the silent house of Aila's revolutionary camouflage; there is also the nocturnal house of Will, the narrator, writing of the narrative that charts the phoenix rising in his home, while the words must turn to ashes in his mouth. But each house marks a deeper historical displacement. And that is the condition of being colored in South Africa, or as Will describes it, 'halfway between ... being not defined – and it was this lack of definition in itself that was never to be questioned, but observed like a taboo, something which noone, while following, could ever admit to.'[8]

This halfway house of racial and cultural origins bridges the 'in-between' diasporic origins of the colored South African and turns them into the symbol for the disjunctive, displaced everyday life of the liberation struggle – 'like so many others of this kind, whose families are fragmented in the diaspora of exile, code names, underground activity, people for whom a real home and attachments are something for others who will come after.' Private and public, past and present, the psyche and the social develop an interstitial intimacy. It is an intimacy that questions binary divisions through which such spheres of social experience are often spatially opposed. These spheres of life are linked through an 'in-between' temporality that takes the measure of dwelling at home, while producing an image of the world of history. This is the moment of aesthetic distance that provides the narrative with a double edge that, like the colored South African subject, represents a hybridity, a difference 'within,' a subject that inhabits a stillness of time and a strangeness of framing that creates a discursive 'image' at the crossroads of history and literature, bridging the home and the world [...]

My subject has been the nest of the phoenix, not its pyre. I have attempted to illuminate the world forcibly entering the house of fiction in order to invade, alarm, divide, dispossess. But I have also tried to show how literature haunts history's more public face, forcing it to reflect on itself in the displacing, even distorting, image of art. When the publicity of the 'event,' or the certainty of 'intention' encounters the silence of the word or the stillness of art, it may lose control and coherence, but it provides a profound understanding of what constitutes human necessity and agency [...] When historical visibility has faded, when the present tense of testimony loses its power to arrest, then the distortions of memory offer us the image of our solidarity and survival. This is a story to pass on, to pass through the world of literature on its thither side and discover those who live in the unhomely house of fiction. In the house of fiction, there is a stirring of the unspoken, of the unhomely ... today.

NOTES

1 Henry James, *The Portrait of a Lady* (New York: Norton, 1975), 360.
2 Toni Morrison, 'Honey and Rue' (from song-cycle for Katherine Battle), *Carnegie Hall Stagebill* (Jan. 1992): 12c.
3 James, *Portrait*, 360.
4 Toni Morrison, *Beloved* (New York: Knopf, 1987), 198–9.
5 Nadine Gordimer, *My Son's Story* (London: Bloomsbury, 1990), 241–2.
6 Ibid.
7 Walter Benjamin, *Illuminations* (New York: Schocken Books, 1969), 86.
8 Gordimer, *My Son's Story,* 21–2.

9.10 JINI KIM WATSON
A Room in the City: Woman, Interiority, and Post-colonial Korean Fiction

Written in the thick of South Korea's democratizing movement that challenged military rule in 1987, Sŏk-kyŏng Kang's 1985 novella 'A Room in the Woods' ('Supsok ŭi Pang'),[1] may be read as the tragic story of So-yang, whose failure to find a place in the radical student movement leads to her eventual suicide. Yet Kang – one of the major Korean writers of the 1980s – constructs the text in a curious manner: eschewing narrative action and character development, the novel uses one character's search for another – through the medium of domestic space – as its unifying structure. In short, it is formally organized as a detective story, with Mi-yang, the first-person narrator, as the tireless investigator seeking after the 'truth' of her sister's behaviour.

The Yi sisters live comfortably in their middle-class home in Seoul with their family, which includes their industrialist father, dutiful mother, third sister Hye-yang, youngest brother Chŏng-u, grandmother, and half-uncle. Enjoying the material benefits of their father's successful sweater factory, the sisters are intelligent and well-educated. All three are destined for good marriages, attested to by Mi-yang's approaching union with a bank supervisor. The story begins, however, with the alarming news that So-yang has dropped out of her prestigious university, is refusing her parents' wishes to re-enrol, and is staying out at night. Mi-yang, having just quit her job in the bank in readiness for marriage – 'I thought it natural to resign before getting married' (50) – uses her new-found free time to investigate her sister's private life. She calls So-yang's university department, secretly meets with her college friends and boyfriend, and sneaks into her room to read her diary. In actuality, the novel is less about So-yang's character, and more about Mi-yang's *detective work* on the trail of her sister's ever-elusive interiority – work that consists not only of phone calls, interviews, and diary reading, but the frequent study of the sister's room.

In questioning why her sister 'had cut herself off from everyone,' Mi-yang blames the individualism of her family members, an individualism 'made possible by the fact that each of us had a separate room' (39). In her diary, So-yang writes lines such as, 'I'm a castle now. I've broken off all relations with others' (64), and 'I don't want to walk barefoot anywhere outside my room, even in the hallway' (65). Although the two younger sisters shared a room before moving to their spacious, two-storey house, each child now had a room of her own to decorate as she pleased. The decor of So-yang's room – a Beatles poster and later, flowers, candles, and music collection – denotes the shift to a distinctly Western mode of individualism drawing from American youth culture of the 1960s and 1970s. Confirming this new individualized sense of space, Mi-yang complains about her mother's overdeveloped sense of privacy in not letting her daughter use the master bedroom's bathroom.

The designation of private spaces according to the individual (private bedrooms) or the generation (children's versus parents' spaces) reveals a stark departure from traditional notions of Korean domestic space and causes rifts in this erstwhile happy family. In that [traditional] system, the *anbang*, or master bedroom, was conceived not as the private conjugal space of the couple but rather as the women's and children's quarter, which only at night was converted into a bedroom for the married couple. This opposed the *sarangbang*, the male quarter, open to guests and usually located on the edge of the house. The pervasive influence of Confucian thinking in the Chosŏn period (1392–1910) rendered the greatest distinction within Korean domestic space between the sexes, not generations. Accordingly, the *anbang* could function without contradiction as the most intimate space of the couple (at night) and as the area for raising children, an arrangement not easily translated into the Western concept of 'master bedroom.' Moreover, in traditional planning, all rooms and spaces opened out to a common courtyard space, such that there was no need for corridors or halls. While such arrangements were already being challenged in the colonial era, it was not until the 1970s and 1980s that Western planning for the nuclear-family household came to predominance. The Yi household, therefore, epitomizes the new domestic space embraced by the industrial middle class: a two-storey Western-style house with separate, lockable bedrooms and bathrooms, and corridors defined against a shared, more 'public' living area. So-yang's private space is what both enables her individualism and produces familial and social isolation; furthermore, her troubling relationship to her room is a spatial allegory of the broader, ambivalent position of women in post-colonial societies, which both demand and refute individualism.

Mi-yang recalls a night when she was drawn to So-yang's room by a Leonard Cohen song, 'a folk singer I liked': 'I entered the cavelike room cautiously and discovered So-yang lying toward the wall, her back to the candlelight … So-yang was motionless, her eyes closed. Having lapsed into a world of her own, she was unaware I had entered her room. But that's it – a world of her own! Only now has the right expression come to mind' (40).

So-yang's room is a world away from the rest of the household: a sealed-off, cavelike interior, which locks in So-yang's presence. With its occupant 'motionless, her eyes closed,' the room, rather than the character, saturates her body and speaks of her bleak and morbid interiority. The monadic space of the private interior produces a new kind of subjectivity, at the same time as it produces narrator Mi-yang's need to search for her sister.

The Yi girls' bedrooms are filled with the shoes, clothes, books, posters, and records (Mi-yang's even accommodates her own piano) necessary to flesh out their individual personalities. The alienated form of the commodity is thus, paradoxically, what permits 'authentic' individualism; in other words, 'the concentration of selfhood specific to modernity is also self-alienation.'[2] Like So-yang's 'castle,' the appearance of the bourgeois interior in the world seems monadological: it has no history, is indivisible, and exists purely independently from all others. Recall, however, that the Korean economy from the 1960s to the 1980s relied heavily on cheap female labour, and produced two contradictory shifts concerning women: the move outwards to the industrial workplace, and the move inwards to the bourgeois family. So-yang, aware of this contradiction, writes of her father's trading company in her diary: *'I'm afraid to look at how the workers live in the factory dorms'* (66). In this sense, we can view her room as the airless and spaceless chamber replacing the outside world – 'a world of her own' – while collapsing and refuting the relationship between interior and exterior.

This structural account of the interior also seems to explain the organization of 'A Room in the Woods' as a detective story. In the cavelike atmosphere, in the candlelight of So-yang's room, we see how personalized ownership generates a reversion to pre-historical modes of dwelling – the shell, the skin, and the case. As the interior calls up this exquisite psyche, it simultaneously interpolates the figure of the detective: 'the traces of the inhabitant are imprinted on the interior. Enter the detective story, which pursues these traces.'[3] Mi-yang's pursuit of So-yang's interiority may thus be explained as the narrative form demanded by this shift to individualized space.

Over and again, Mi-yang finds evidence of So-yang's irreducible placelessness in the world. Her diary (the objectless interior par excellence) is the only place where So-yang seems to truly reside, though it speaks incessantly of So-yang's spatial dislocation. In one of Mi-yang's attempts to question So-yang directly, their conversation hinges on the problem of occupying space – both internal and external:

> 'Where have you been hiding these days?' I tried to sound as nonchalant as possible.
>
> 'I feel like I'm suffocating when I'm home. So I try to find myself outside.' She didn't appear to suspect anything.
>
> 'Aren't people supposed to look inside to find themselves?'
>
> 'You sound just like Confucius.' (84)

In her reference to Confucius, So-yang demonstrates confusion over 'inside' and 'outside' as psychological and spatial categories. Yet her phrase also refers to the neo-Confucianist ideology that legitimized young female factory work as dutiful 'service' to families and nation and at the same time subordinated feminist concerns in the student democracy movement. Kang's text precisely maps out these contradictions in terms of *psychological* interiority – women's subjective constitution in industrial modernity – through descriptions of *architectural* interiority. The space of the interior can thus be contrasted with the space of the individual. Where the latter is, following Adorno and Benjamin, the sustaining alibi the subject adopts towards consolidating self-ownership, the post-colonial woman's interior is a psychic space that *cannot* find a direct spatial correlative.

In the final scene after Mi-yang discovers her sister's suicide, the dead girl's diary reiterates her inability to properly occupy space:

> A world in which people fight for the sake of business is alien to me, a scene in a bell jar.
>
> The glittering slogans are for someone else.
>
> I'm an island, an island that traps me and touches nowhere. (146)

In this last line, So-yang figures herself as both an island and trapped by the island, invoking a completely sealed-off interiority that has no corresponding exterior. The *unstable* positioning of woman – neither wholly in public nor private, traditional nor modern space – results in her textual construction as trace. So-yang's 'truth' is the missing object both for her own consciousness and for the narrator.

In 'A Room in the Woods,' So-yang's experiential content is precisely *not* available: the text's production of her in absentia allegorizes the conflicted symbolic repositioning of woman around the threshold of private / public space. As So-yang's diary indicates, she refuses both the limited individualism offered by patriarchal society (the domestic role / spaces of the wife) and the libidinized spaces of student radicalism. The end of the story, however, renders the 'work' of detecting (and reading) void. We are led nowhere except back to So-yang's cave / castle / island room and her dead body. Woman's lack of space, her objectless interior, block the resolution of plot promised by the detective tale and by Mi-yang's desire to help her sister. And it is precisely in its failure that we understand the real 'work' of the text.

NOTES

1 Sŏk-kyŏng Kang, 'A Room in the Woods,' translated by Bruce Fulton and Ju-chan Fulton, in Sŏk-kyŏng Kang,Chi-wŏn Kim, and Chŏ-hŭi O, *Words of Farewell: Stories by Korean Women Writers* (Seattle, WA: Seal, 1989), 28–147.

2 Max Pensky, *Melancholy Dialectics: Walter Benjamin and the Play of Mourning* (Amherst, MA: University of Massachusetts Press, 1993), 170.
3 Walter Benjamin, *The Arcades Project*, translated by Howard Eiland and Kevin McLaughlin (Cambridge, MA: Belknap Press of Harvard University Press, 1999), 9.

9.11 WENDY THOMPSON
Domestic Spaces in Children's Fantasy Literature

Domestic spaces form a central part of the world-building that is a key feature of children's fantasy. But, although domestic spaces as a pivotal site of tension between the everyday and the fantastic play a crucial role in children's fantasy literature, little critical attention has been devoted to the relationship between this tension and the structural and thematic organization of children's fantasy texts. However, what Pauline Dewan says of children's literature in general may also be said of children's fantasy in particular: 'throughout children's literature houses dominate the novels in which they are found.'[1] Examining the structural and symbolic roles houses play as characters and settings in a variety of children's literary texts, Dewan argues that one of the reasons that houses have such a dominating role in much of children's fiction is because they constitute a child's 'first universe' and operate as 'a meeting place and mediator between the self and the world.'[2] The idea that the home plays a significant role in shaping a child's character, behaviour, attitude and, potentially, the adult they will become, can be traced back to at least the nineteenth century. Historian Deborah Cohen [see section 5.2 in this volume] locates the emergence of this idea in the late Victorian and Edwardian periods when the concern with interior decoration and domestic material possessions, such as furniture, as a means of expressing individuality and personality began to be focused onto the domestic spaces inhabited by children, such as children's rooms and nurseries.[3] Yet, the idea may extend back even further, in a less material sense: Andrew O'Malley, for example, discusses the role that middle-class domestic ideology played in the emergence of a literature produced and marketed for children in the eighteenth century.[4]

Gaston Bachelard also points to the intimate relationship between ideas of childhood and domestic spaces [see section 2.1 in this volume]. For Bachelard, the oneiric house is constituted through the memory of the spaces in which we have experienced intimacy, particularly the spaces of the childhood house. Yet child protagonists frequently do not perceive domestic spaces as being idyllic and attention is drawn to the way in which they function as microcosms of the world(s) of the text. Jonathan Stroud's Bartimaeus trilogy, for example, makes frequent, self-conscious references to discourses surrounding domestic architecture and interior design and their relationship to wealth, class, gender, nation, and the power structures of society.[5] Stroud goes further than other children's fantasy writers – such as Susan Cooper, Philip Pullman, and J.K. Rowling – in foregrounding the materiality and artificiality of the power structures permeating place and individuals' relationships to them, for in his series, magic is not something inherently possessed by humans; rather, it is a tool and form of knowledge that is learned by a select few and guarded from the majority of the population. Thus, Stroud's London, perhaps more explicitly so than other children's fantasy worlds, foregrounds a critical tension between the recognizable everyday of this world and the fantasy elements that he creates.

However, this tension plays a key role in many works of children's fantasy literature, for, despite the fantastic elements of the worlds and spaces of these texts, their domestic spaces seem for the most part to replicate the features, ideologies, and anxieties of dominant bourgeois ideas of 'house' and 'home,' rather than suggest radical alternatives. Even as they seem to recycle recognizable domestic spaces and ideologies, these spaces provide integral settings and media through which the often problematic moral, social, and political orders of the texts' world(s) (and, by implication, our own) are presented to the reader and learned, negotiated, challenged, or protected by the characters. Yet, the tension between such normative domestic spaces and their fantastic elements, as well as their relative significance within the universe of the fantasy text, perhaps distinguish them from the domestic spaces in other genres of children's literature. While, as Dewan (like Bachelard) argues, these domestic spaces may constitute a child character's first universe, they are also frequently central sites and actors in the worlds or 'moral universes' of the fantasy text.

Stroud draws upon discourses of interior design and architecture to foreground the way the ruling 'class' of magicians attempt to fortify and consolidate their power through urban planning, public and private architecture and interior design, and (magical) domestic security systems. By providing glimpses into the domestic spaces of both commoners and their oppressors, the wizards, Stroud points to the way in which the power structure and ideology of the magician's British Empire permeates the everyday lives and homes of every strata of society. The wizards' preoccupation with private property in the form of luxury condominiums and houses in wealthy, sectioned-off neighbourhoods of London as a means of obtaining and displaying wealth, power, and social status are contrasted with the drastically different world of the Djinns where the ideas of private property and a private, autonomous self do not exist. In this world essence floats freely, intermingling with other essences in undemarcated space. The relationship between private and public architecture is foregrounded through a somewhat stereotypical, yet humorous and poignant, comparison between the public and private architecture of Prague (in this novel, a former world power defeated by the British in a massive, magical battle). The architecture in Prague is described as being old, ornate, and rundown. Yet, Stroud seems to use this section of the novel to emphasize the aggressive modernism of the protagonist's contemporary Britain, which is somewhat reminiscent of Le Corbusier's 'machine for living' [see section 8.4 in this volume], and its link to imperialism and national chauvinism.

Elizabeth Thiel notes that in spite of children's books that 'privilege transnormative family models and assert that alternatives to the "natural" family are a possibility, today's children's literature market displays a loyalty to nineteenth-century family ideology that reflects a broader social desire for so-called Victorian family values.'[6] She demonstrates the extent to which even novels that depict what she has coined 'transnormative families' nonetheless tend to 'incorporate a longing for the familial ideal which is both nostalgic and poignant, a manoeuvre that reinscribes the desirability of the idyllic domestic sphere and introduces a sense of loss into the narrative.'[7] One fantasy series that has been frequently criticized for its use of gender stereotypes and the heteronormativity of its world is J.K. Rowling's Harry Potter series (1997–2007). Responding to critics such as Michael Bronski, who have argued that the texts are 'queer' in the way they problematize normativity, Tison Pugh and David L. Wallace have pointed to the dominance of heteronormativity within the novels despite their flirtation with 'deconstructing normativity.'[8] They argue that the series ultimately erases same-sex relationships and desires and reinscribes heteronormativity and gender stereotypes through the heteronormative heroism narrative and ideology it employs. Thiel notes how throughout the series, Harry longs for his 'natural' family and that the various other transnormative family groupings prove undesirable or unviable. Yet, the heteronormative 'natural' family not only haunts the domestic spaces of the novel by its absence but also by its failure to provide the love and support its children need.

In *Harry Potter and the Order of the Phoenix* (2003), Sirius Black, Harry's godfather, hosts the headquarters of the Order of the Phoenix (a secret group of wizards, organized by Hogwarts Head Master Albus Dumbledore to challenge the villain Voldemort) in a family house he has inherited.[9] However, the house itself is hostile to both the heir and Order via a legacy of household goods. While the house is full of grotesque and dangerous domestic objects which show the darker side of magic and social structures in the wizarding world, their house cleaning is primarily thwarted by cupboards magically bolted shut, domestic objects that are 'reluctant to leave their dusty shelves' (108), and portraits and banners that cannot be removed from walls. The house and its objects not only reflect but also embody and act out the ideology of their original owners, Voldemort supporters. As Harry puts it, rather than cleaning, 'they were really waging war on the house which was putting up a very good fight, aided and abetted by Kreacher,' the house-elf, sneaking into rooms to rescue the domestic objects discarded by the cleaners (109). For Sirius, who cannot leave the house because he is still wanted for a murder he didn't commit, being back in the house is especially uncomfortable and leads him into moodiness and depression. He says to Harry, 'I don't like being back here ... I never thought I'd be stuck in this house again' (106). Harry empathizes with him by imagining 'how he would feel, when he was grown up and thought he was free of the place for ever, to return and live at number four, Privet Drive,' the suburban house of his loveless foster family (106).

Thus, in both series, domestic spaces as a 'first universe' are sites through which the central characters experience up close the ideologies and power structures governing their worlds and come to either challenge or support and participate in these. While many fantasy texts, like Rowling's Harry Potter series, seem to reinscribe the heteronormative 'natural' family and traditional gender roles in their domestic spaces, others, like Stroud's Bartimaeus series, show relatively little nostalgia for these, although gestures towards alternative family structures and gender roles remain tentative.

NOTES

1 Pauline Dewan, *The House as Setting, Symbol, and Structural Motif* (Queenston, ON: Edward Mellen, 2004), 2.

2 Ibid., 4.

3 Deborah Cohen, *Household Gods: The British and Their Possessions* (New Haven, CT: Yale University Press, 2006), 138.

4 Andrew O'Malley, *The Making of the Modern Child: Children's Literature and Childhood in the Late Eighteenth Century* (New York: Routledge, 2003).

5 All references are to the following: Jonathan Stroud, *The Amulet of Samarkand* (London: Corgi, 2004 [2003]); *The Golem's Eye* (London: Corgi, 2004); *Ptolemy's Gate* (London: Corgi, 2006 [2005]).

6 Elizabeth Thiel, *The Fantasy of Family: Nineteenth-Century Children's Literature and the Myth of the Domestic Ideal* (New York: Routledge, 2008), 166.

7 Ibid., 8, 159.

8 Tison Pugh and David L. Wallace, 'Heteronormative Heroism and Queering the School Story in J.K. Rowling's *Harry Potter* Series,' *Children's Literature Association* 31 / 3 (2006): 261; Michael Bronski, 'Queering *Harry Potter*,' *Z Magazine Online* 16 / 9 (2003).

9 All references are to the following: J.K. Rowling, *Harry Potter and the Order of the Phoenix* (London: Bloomsbury, 2004 [2003]).

9.12 MATTHEW REYNOLDS
Designs for a Happy Home: A Novel in Ten Interiors*

I The Threshold

You have opened the door. Take a deep breath. Now step … into the world of Good Design. Have a look around you. Isn't it lovely? So calming, but also so alive. Here, colours always *go* – or, if they don't, they clash in interesting ways. Here shapes are in harmony (or else meaningful *dis*-harmony) like a beautiful musical chord. Look, over here, at this Utzon chair and footstool next to the simplest possible standard lamp from IKEA (design doesn't always have to be expensive). Isn't it magic? Or gaze down there at the re-creation of the classic WilliWear showroom in New York: so functional – and also so *funny*.

Don't worry: I know you probably can't actually see these things in your mind's eye yet. And maybe you have no sense of colour, or are psychotically messy, or rubbish at DIY, or simply feel design is not for you. All of us are on our separate journeys; all of us have different hurdles to hop over. But trust me. I have taken this path ahead of you, and look at me now: Alizia Tamé, lead designer of IntArchitect Home-is-Harmony. Whether you want to merely go on a day trip, or else a wholesale design pilgrimage, this book that I am writing will be your guide.

It is a How-To Book; and also it is my Life Story. Why both together? Because the roots of my Designs go deep into my life and their branches (i.e., their effects) stretch out in all directions. You will see my ideas spring up, and watch me bringing them across the threshold of reality. Testimonials from friends and colleagues will show you the influence that I and my Designs have had on them. Finally, I am going to reveal to you my personal trade secrets – my Magic

---

* (London: Bloomsbury, 2009).

Mottoes – to help you activate the Design potential in your own lives. A beautiful Interior can make you calmer, more generous – and, in a really startling way, more *you* […]

Now: relax. Reach back (will you do this for me?) to the happiest moments in your life. What Design ideas do they summon up for you? What colours? Textures? Forms? Or any particular *objets?* Stillness or movement? Brightness or velvet gloom? Visualise these memories: make them real, let them gleam again, let the feeling of them grow. It may help if you jot down some pointers – anything at all: words, doodles, names, shapes. If you like, you can jot them down here:

Did you manage? I don't mind if you haven't actually scribbled anything. Jem wouldn't have done, for instance (he's my husband) – he's a very private person, he likes to keep his feelings nested safe inside. All I need is for you to have accessed that Emotion. The sparkle in your heart. That is what we want to grow out and then encapsulate in our Interiors. Through Design, your Happiness can flower and spread.

We have arrived at Magic Motto no.1:

✓ *Interior Design Is the Makeover of Minds.*

I know this is a big claim. But little by little you will see it happening. Room by room.

II The Hallway

a. First Steps

Ready for some actual designing? Where shall we start?
In the Hallway – of course!
But how do we start?
With a question. Actually *the* question:

- What is it for?

Take any hallway you can think of: the narrow corridor of a pinched Victorian terrace, the efficient capsule of a modern Barratt-type home, or the spacious entrance of a country house. Ask: What is it for? And let the answer come to you. Can you hear it?

- For getting people into an Interior – and out of it!

Obvious, perhaps. But it would surprise you how many Designers have ignored this basic fact. Some of them think the Hallway is all about creating 'that vital first impression.' So they try to 'add interest' with incongruous decoration: an 'industrial' theme, or jungle-pattern wallpaper. Or else they try to 'signal comfort' by sticking a sofa in there, or a pair of puffy boudoir chairs. Wrong! Wrong! Wrong! A home is not a stage set. Interiors are to be used: a Hallway is to be walked through. As I put it in the second Magic Motto:

✓ *Design – For Life!*

This brings me to a rather delicate point. Delicate, but essential. Many hallways I have seen have been ruined – not by any Design error – but by a personal failing on the part of the inhabitants: Mess. There is a clutter of shoes and boots and brollies on the floor. It is summer, but the clothes pegs are still piled with winter coats. Maybe there is a picnic blanket hanging there too, and shopping bags. You try to get through – but it feels like clambering over an obstacle course *and* shouldering past a herd of pack animals both at the same time. What I want to say to people with Hallways in this state is: just think about it. It doesn't take much. Think of the effort you (or someone) put into decorating the space and screwing those coat-hooks into the wall [...] All it takes is: a bit of tidying up. Then your Interior will be itself again. And you will have more freedom to be *you*.

What this all comes down to, is that Magic Motto no. 2 is meaningless without no. 3:

✓ *And Live – For Design!*

b. The Work of Memory

We have grasped the basic *function* of the Hallway. Now we must think about its *character*. In this new stage of pre-design process we must again draw on our personal experience – but now in a more focused way. The 'Work of Memory' (as I call it) is vital.

As an example, I am going to call up a memory of my own – of when Jem lifted me over the threshold and into the Hallway of the first space we inhabited together. We were not married then, but that did not in any way reduce the significance of the moment. Nowadays marriage is obviously less important than it used to be, and I often feel that the new milestone in people's lives is the purchase of a property – especially joint purchase. That is when you really have to *commit* [...]

c. Design Consequences

OK then: what sense can we make of this Work of Memory? What principles can we discover to guide us in our Designs? Well, for me, the Hallway is always a place of

- Transformation.

This is the key *Feel* I want people to get from a Tamé Hallway, whether it is the rotating 'Dinner Plate' Entrance Space I have created for a kitchenware manufacturer in Worcester or the Airlock Hallway designed for the London house of a billionaire recluse (to protect the privacy of my clients the names and addresses will have to remain confidential). Obviously I am not saying that every time you go into or out of your Hallway it is as much of a revolution as it was for me, that day, about a decade ago. But, if you stop to think about it, you do change a little, don't you, every time? You might put on a coat – or take it off. You might pick up an umbrella or wrap your neck in a scarf. But what interests me are the Feelings you button up around yourself, or shrug off and hang up on a peg. It might be relief: at reaching the harbour of home after a hard day – or else at going out into the fresh air. It might be nervousness or excitement or happiness or resolve. These feelings Transform you. They make you grimmer or smilier, they make you more open to the world, or less. Have you ever wondered why a Mirror is such a common element in the Hallway? You might think it is simply a practical thing to help you check your mascara or adjust the angle of your hat. But the real reason is more profound. It allows you to examine yourself at the crucial moment of Transformation […] Make your 'public face' fit more securely over the private *you*. Or else measure what damage the world has done to you during a day of being out in it: a little bit more sagginess in that bag under the eye? Another hairline crack?

Back in Wood Street I had taken only the very first steps towards discovering these truths. I had had the experience of being lifted into the Hallway; the idea for the Dawson House had come to me there; Jem and I had had a grump and then made up. All this was giving me a strong feeling that the Hallway was going to be our signature room, the space that set the tone for the entire Interior. But inside my head there seemed to be some blockage, some wad of something grey. I could not convert this Feeling I had into a fully visualised Design […]

When I woke in the morning and found his sleeping body safely there again beside me I sneaked out and down to our still-uncompleted ground floor. I walked to and fro, my footsteps echoing. I looked out of the front window at the sun-filled street; and out of the back window at our shadowy courtyard […] How dark it was, how glum. Obviously ceiling spotlights would brighten it up […] but I needed to do more than that to give it movement and life, to get the all-important feel of Transformation.

I thought of waves crashing on the shore; I thought of rivers flowing to the sea. A sunbeam touched me and I thought of flowers blooming. I thought of children running down a hill […] I thought of a see-saw– just maybe, maybe the merest hint of a wobble, a re-orientation as you walked along? No. I thought of roller-coasters, and rafts, and again of rivers. Then I thought of a bridge.

A bridge. Or rather the concept of a bridge. A little slope up, then a plateau, then a little slope down. It would divide the long narrowness of our passage in a rather pleasing way. And it would interrupt the rhythm of our going in and out of the house with just the sort of effect I was after. You would get your coat out of the cupboard under the stairs, you would go up the little slope, and you would pause, in the way people pause to gaze around halfway across a bridge. Only, you wouldn't gaze around, you would look at yourself, because on either side of this central section I would put mirrors. They would be practical, so you could see what you looked like from back as well as front, but also symbolic, because the infinity of reflections would suggest the past, the future, the many things that can happen, the many, many possible ways of being you. And after that pause, that hitch, that moment of contemplation, you would go rushing in or rushing out with renewed energy, a new spark. It could work! It was *definitely* a solution! [...]

✓ *Ideas Can Come from Anywhere!*

So the Hallway Bridge was built. It was a pearl of a Design! Even Fisher Paul said so when I described it at the IntArchitec Brain Exchange – and Fisher of course is synonymous with a very different take on Interiors: high concept, high budget, and very business-oriented. When, in the wake of the Dawson House, I persuaded him to let me launch our new family-friendly brand of design, Home-is-Harmony, the Hallway Bridge became one of the touchstones for what we were all about. A brand that was Feeling-Focused, a little Humorous, comparatively Inexpensive; and that very much put People First.

Even more importantly, the Hallway Bridge worked for Jem and me [...] Often in those early days we crossed our Bridge together to head out to salvage yards, furniture warehouses, the timber merchant, the paint shop. We were like magpies, spotting stuff that no one else had noticed and hauling it back to add sparkle to our nest. When we finally found the keystone sofa for our sitting area – that was a magical moment [...] Jem and I were spiritually launched, in our Hallway House, discovering life together, and one another.

Every Hallway must feel like a beginning. I *so* disagree with the Design Cliché that says the Hallway should be the most polite, least personal room because it is the house's public face. No! It is an introduction, an opening, a passage to the future. When you design a Hallway, let your fantasies explode around you. Create an airlock, an egg, a rubbish chute, a runway. Take your inspiration from arrows, waves, or wheels. Think butterflies emerging from their chrysalises, or flowers in bud. The Hallway is a place of Transformation. Give it life!

Bibliography

Adam, Robert, and James Adam. *Works in Architecture*. Dourdan: E. Thézard Fils, 1990 [1773–79].

Adams, Annmarie. 'Childbirth at Home.' In *Architecture in the Family Way: Doctors, Houses, and Women 1870–1900*, 103–28. Montreal and Kingston: McGill-Queen's University Press, 1996.

Agnew, Jean-Christophe. 'A House of Fiction: Domestic Interiors and the Commodity Aesthetic.' In Simon J. Bronner, ed., *Consuming Visions: Accumulation and Display of Goods in America, 1880–1920*, 133–55. New York: Norton, 1989.

Agrest, Diana, Patricia Conway, and Leslie Kanes Weisman, eds. *The Sex of Architecture*. New York: H.N. Abrams, 1996.

Ahmed, Sara. 'Home and Away: Narratives of Migration and Estrangement.' *International Journal of Cultural Studies* 2 / 3 (1999): 329–48.

Alberti, Leon Battista. *On the Art of Building in Ten Books*. Trans. Joseph Rykwert, Neil Leach, and Robert Tavernor. Cambridge, MA: MIT Press, 1988.

Alexander, Catherine. 'The Garden as Occasional Domestic Space.' Forum: 'Domestic Space,' eds. Kathy Mezei and Chiara Briganti. *Signs: Journal of Women in Culture and Society* 27 / 3 (2002): 857–71.

Alison, Jane, ed. *The Surreal House*. London and New Haven, CT: Barbican Art Gallery, in association with Yale University Press, 2010.

Allan, Graham, and Graham Crow, eds. *Home and Family: Creating the Domestic Sphere*. London: Macmillan, 1989.

Appadurai, Arjun. *The Social Life of Things: Commodities in Cultural Perspective*. Cambridge: Cambridge University Press, 1986.

Appleyard, Donald. 'Home.' *Architectural Association* 11 / 3 (1979): 4–20.

Archer, John. *Architecture and Suburbia: From English Villa to American Dream House, 1690–2000*. Minneapolis, MN: University of Minnesota Press, 2005.

Architectural Review. Double issue on 'Modern English Interior Decoration' 67 (May 1930).

Ardener, Shirley, ed. *Women and Space: Ground Rules and Social Maps*. Oxford: Berg, 1993.

Ariès, Philippe, and Georges Duby, eds. *A History of Private Life*. 5 vols. Trans. Arthur Goldhammer. Cambridge, MA: Belknap Press of Harvard University Press, 1987–1991.

Armstrong, Nancy. *Desire and Domestic Fiction: A Political History of the Novel*. New York: Oxford University Press, 1987.

– 'Some Call It Fiction: On the Politics of Domesticity.' In Julie Rivkin and Michael Ryan, eds., *Literary Theory: An Anthology*, 567–83. Oxford: Blackwell, 2004.

Ashenburg, Katherine. *The Dirt on Clean*. Toronto: Knopf, 2007.

Attfield, Judy. *Wild Things: The Material Culture of Everyday Life*. Oxford: Berg, 2000.

– *Bringing Modernity Home: Writings on Popular Design and Material Culture*. Manchester: Manchester University Press, 2007.

Attfield, Judy, and Pat Kirkham, eds. *A View from the Interior: Women and Design*. London: Women's Press, 1995.

Aynsley, Jeremy, and Charlotte Grant, eds. *Imagined Interiors: Representing the Domestic Interior since the Renaissance*. London: Victoria & Albert Publications, 2006.

Bachelard, Gaston. 'The House from Cellar to Garret. The Significance of the Hut.' In *The Poetics of Space*, 3–37. [1958].Trans. Maria Jolas. Boston, MA: Beacon Press, 1994.

Bahloul, Joëlle. 'Telling Places: The House as Social Architecture.' In *The Architecture of Memory: A Jewish-Muslim Household in Colonial Algeria, 1937–1962*, 28–50. Trans. Catherine du Peloux Ménagé. Cambridge: Cambridge University Press, 1996.

Bammer, Angelika. 'Editorial: The Question of "Home."' *New Formations* no. 17 (1992): xi.

Barley, Maurice W. *The English Farmhouse and Cottage*. London: Routledge and Kegan Paul, 1961.

– *Houses and History*. London: Faber and Faber, 1962.

Baudrillard, Jean. 'Structures of Interior Design.' In *The System of Objects*, 15–29. [1968]. Trans. James Benedict. London: Verso, 1996.

Bauman, Zygmunt. *Seeking Safety in an Insecure World*. Cambridge: Polity, 2001.

Baumgarten, Murray, and H.M. Daleski, eds. *Homes and Homelessness in the Victorian Imagination*. New York: AMS Press, 1998.

Bausinger, Hermann. 'Media, Technology and Daily Life.' *Media, Culture and Society* 6 (1984): 343–51.

Baydar, Gülsüm, 'Tenuous Boundaries: Women, Domesticity and Nationhood.' *Journal of Architecture* 7 / 3 (2002): 229–44.

Bechdel, Alison. *Fun Home: A Family Tragicomic*. London: Cape, 2006.

Beecher, Catharine E., and Harriet Beecher Stowe. 'Earth-Closets.' In *The American Woman's Home: or, Principles of Domestic Science; Being a Guide to the Formation and Maintenance of Economical, Healthful, Beautiful, and Christian Homes*, 403–18. New York: J.B. Ford, 1869.

Beeton, Mrs Isabella. 'Arrangement and Economy of the Kitchen.' In *The Book of Household Management*, 25–38. London: S.O. Beeton, 1861.

Benhabib, Seyla. *Situating the Self: Gender, Community, and Postmodernism in Contemporary Ethics*. Cambridge: Polity, 1992.

Benjamin, David N., ed. *The Home: Words, Interpretations, Meanings, and Environments*. Aldershot: Ashgate; Brookfield, VT: Avebury, 1995.

Benjamin, Walter. *Illuminations*. Ed. Hannah Arendt. Trans. Harry Zohn. New York: Schocken, 1969.

– 'Louis-Philippe or the Interior.' In 'Paris – the Capital of the Nineteenth Century,' *Charles Baudelaire: A Lyric Poet in the Era of High Capitalism*, 167–9. [1935]. Trans. Harry Zohn. London: Verso, 1983.

– *The Arcades Project*. Ed. Roy Tiedermann. Trans. Howard Eiland and Kevin McLaughlin. Cambridge, MA: Belknap, 1999.

Bennett, Tony. 'Home and Everyday Life.' In Tony Bennett and Diane Watson, eds., *Understanding Everyday Life*, 1–50. London: Blackwell, 2002.

Beppu, Keiko. 'The Moral Significance of Living Space: The Library and Kitchen in the House of Mirth.' *Edith Wharton Review* 14 / 2 (1997): 3–7.

Bermingham, Ann, and John Brewer, eds. *The Consumption of Culture 1600–1800: Image, Object, Text*. London: Routledge, 1995.

Best, Victoria. 'Between the Harem and the Battlefield: Domestic Space in the Work of Assia Djebar.' Forum: 'Domestic Space,' eds. Kathy Mezei and Chiara Briganti. *Signs: Journal of Women in Culture and Society* 27 / 3 (2002): 873–9.

Betjeman, John. '1830–1930 – Still Going Strong: A Guide to the Recent History of Interior Decoration.' *Architectural Review* 67 (1930): 231–40.

Betsky, Aaron. *Queer Space: Architecture and Same-Sex Desire*. New York: Morrow, 1997.

Bhabha, Homi K. 'The World and the Home.' In Anne McClintock, Aamir Mufti, and Ella Shohat, eds., *Dangerous Liaisons: Gender, Nation and Postcolonial Perspectives*, 445–55. Minneapolis, MN: University of Minnesota Press, 1997.

Birdwell-Pheasant, Donna, and Denise Lawrence-Zúñiga, eds. House *Life: Space, Place and Family in Europe*. Oxford: Berg, 1999.

Blier, Suzanne Preston. *The Anatomy of Architecture*. Cambridge: Cambridge University Press, 1987.

Blunt, Alison. 'Imperial Geographies of Home: British Domesticity in India, 1886–1925.' *Transactions* 24 (1999): 421–40.

– *Domicile and Diaspora: Anglo-Indian Women and the Spatial Politics of Home*. Malden, MA: Blackwell, 2005.

Blunt, Alison, and Robyn Dowling, eds. *Home*. London: Routledge, 2006.

Bondi, Liz, and Damaris Rose. 'Constructing Gender, Constructing the Urban: A Review of Anglo-American Feminist Urban Geography.' *Gender, Place and Culture* 10 / 3 (2003): 229–45.

Boradkar, Prasad. *Designing Things: A Critical Introduction to the Culture of Objects*. Oxford: Berg, 2010.

Borzello, Frances. 'Looking for the Interior.' In *At Home: The Domestic Interior of Art*, 16–25. London: Thames and Hudson, 2006.

Bourdieu, Pierre. 'The Berber House or the World Reversed.' *Social Science Information* 9/2 (1970): 151–70.

Bowlby, Rachel. 'Domestication.' In Diane Elam and Robyn Wiegman, eds., *Feminism beside Itself*, 71–91. London: Routledge, 1995.

Braunstein, Susan L., and Jenna Weissman Joselit. *Getting Comfortable in New York: The Jewish Home*, 1880–1950. New York: Jewish Museum, 1990.

Briganti, Chiara, and Kathy Mezei. 'House Haunting: The Domestic Novel of the Inter-War Years.' *Home Cultures* 1/2 (2004): 147–68.

– *Domestic Modernism: The Interwar Novel and E.H. Young*. Aldershot: Ashgate, 2006.

Brink, Stefan. '"Home": The Term and the Concept from a Linguistic and Settlement-Historical Viewpoint.' In David N. Benjamin, ed., *The Home: Words, Interpretations, Meanings, and Environments*, 17–24. Aldershot: Ashgate; Brookfield, VT: Avebury, 1995.

Brooker, Graeme, and Sally Stone. *From Organisation to Decoration: An Interior Design Reader*. London: Routledge, 2011.

Brown, Julia Prewitt. *The Bourgeois Interior: How the Middle Class Imagines Itself in Literature and Film*. Charlottesville, VA: University of Virginia Press, 2008.

Bryden, Inga, and Janet Floyd, eds. *Domestic Space: Reading the Nineteenth-Century Interior*. Manchester: Manchester University Press, 1999.

Bryson, Bill. *At Home: A Short History of Private Life*. Toronto: Doubleday, 2010.

Buchli, Victor. *Material Culture: Critical Concepts in the Social Sciences*. London: Routledge, 2004.

Buchli, Victor, ed. *The Material Culture Reader*. Oxford: Berg, 2002.

Burbank, Emily. *Woman as Decoration*. New York: Dodd, Mead, 1917.

Burman, Barbara, ed. *The Culture of Sewing: Gender, Consumption and Home Dressmaking*. Oxford: Berg, 1999.

Burnett, John. *A Social History of Housing, 1815–1985*. London: Methuen, 1986.

Busch, Akiko. *Geography of Home: Writings on Where We Live*. New York: Princeton Architectural Press, 1999.

Calloway, Stephen. *Twentieth-Century Decoration: The Domestic Interior from 1900 to the Present Day*. London: Weidenfield and Nicolson, 1988.

Campo, Juan Eduardo. 'Domestications of Islam in Modern Egypt: A Cultural Analysis.' In *The Other Sides of Paradise: Explorations into the Religious Meaning of Domestic Space in Islam*, 98–138. Columbia, SC: University of South Carolina Press, 1991.

Candlin, Fiona, and Raiford Guins. *The Object Reader*. London: Routledge, 2009.

Carrington, Christopher, ed. *No Place Like Home: Relationships and Family Life among Lesbians and Gay Men*. Chicago: University of Chicago Press, 1999.

Carsten, Janet, and Stephen Hugh-Jones, eds. *About the House: Lévi-Strauss and Beyond*. Cambridge: Cambridge University Press, 1995.

Cather, Willa. 'The Novel Démeublé.' In *Not under Forty*, 43–51. New York: Knopf, 1936.

Chandler, Marilyn, R. *Dwelling in the Text: Houses in American Fiction*. Berkeley, CA: University of California Press, 1991.

Chapman, Dennis. *The Home and Social Status*. London: Routledge and Kegan Paul, 1955.

Chapman, Tony. *Gender and Domestic Life: Changing Practices in Families and Households*. Basingstoke: Palgrave Macmillan, 2004.

Chapman, Tony, and Jenny Hockey, eds. *Ideal Homes? Social Change and Domestic Life*. New York: Routledge, 1999.

Chase, Karen. 'Jane Eyre's Interior Design.' In Heather Glen, ed., *New Casebooks: Jane Eyre*, 52–67. New York: Macmillan, 1997.

Chattopadhyay, Swati. '"Goods, Chattels and Sundry Items": Constructing 19th-Century Anglo-Indian Domestic Life.' *Journal of Material Culture* 7 / 3 (2002): 243–71.

– *Representing Calcutta: Modernity, Nationalism and the Colonial Uncanny*. London: Routledge, 2005.

Cheney, Elsa M., and Mary Garcia Castro. *Muchachas No More: Household Workers in Latin America and the Caribbean*. Philadelphia, PA: Temple University Press, 1989.

Chippendale, Thomas. *The Gentleman and Cabinet-Maker's Director*. London: Thomas Chippendale, 1754.

Cieraad, Irene. '"Out of My Kitchen!" Architecture, Gender and Domestic Efficiency.' *Journal of Architecture* 7 / 3 (2002): 263–79.

Cieraad, Irene, ed. *At Home: An Anthropology of Domestic Space*. Syracuse, NY: Syracuse University Press, 1999.

Clark, Clifford Edward. *The American Family Home, 1800–1960*. Chapel Hill, NC: University of North Carolina Press, 1986.

Clark, Hazel, and David Brody, eds. *Design Studies: A Reader*. Oxford: Berg, 2009.

Clausen, Christopher. 'Home and Away in Children's Fiction.' *Children's Literature: Annual of the Modern Language Association Division on Children's Literature and the Children's Literature Association* 10 (1982): 141–52.

Cline, Ann. *A Hut of One's Own: Life Outside the Circle of Architecture*. Cambridge, MA: MIT Press, 1997.

Cohen, Deborah. 'In Possession: Men, Women, and Decoration.' In *Household Gods: The British and Their Possessions*, 89–121. New Haven, CT: Yale University Press, 2006.

Coleman, Debra, Elizabeth Danze, and Carol Henderson, eds. *Architecture and Feminism*. New York: Princeton Architectural Press, 1996.

Collignon, Béatrice, and Jean-François Staszak, eds. *Espaces domestiques: Construire, aménager et répresenter*. Rosny-sous-Bois: Bréal, 2003.

Colomina, Beatriz. *Sexuality and Space*. New York: Princeton Architectural Press, 1992.

– 'Interior.' In *Privacy and Publicity: Modern Architecture as Mass Media*, 232–81. Cambridge, MA: MIT Press, 1996.

– *Domesticity at War*. Barcelona: ACTAR; Cambridge, MA: MIT Press, 2007.

Corbin, Alain. 'Domestic Atmospheres.' [1982]. In *The Foul and the Fragrant: Odor and the French Social Imagination*, 161–75. Cambridge, MA: Harvard University Press, 1986.

– 'Backstage.' In *A History of Private Life*, vol. 4, 457–67. Trans. Arthur Goldhammer. Ed. Michelle Perrot. Cambridge, MA: Harvard University Press, 1990.

Cowan, Susanne. 'The Gendered Architecture of the Home in Cinematic Space.' *Built Environment* 26 / 4 (2000): 303–15.

Craik, Jennifer. 'The Making of Mother: The Role of the Kitchen in the Home.' In Graham Allen and Graham Crow, eds., *Home and Family: Creating the Domestic Sphere*, 48–65. London: Macmillan, 1989.

Cranz, Galen. *The Chair: Rethinking Culture, Body and Design*. New York: Norton, 1998.

Cresswell, Tim. *Place: A Short Introduction*. Malden, MA: Blackwell, 2004.

Cromley, Elizabeth Collins. 'A History of American Beds and Bedrooms, 1890–1930.' In Jessica H. Foy and Thomas J. Schlereth, eds., *American Home Life, 1880–1930: A Social History of Spaces and Services*, 120–41. Knoxville, TN: University of Tennessee Press, 1992.

Cromley, Elizabeth Collins, and L. Hudgins, eds. *Gender, Class, and Shelter: Perspective in Vernacular Architecture*. Knoxville, TN: University of Tennessee Press, 1995.

Cross, Alexander. 'Creating Domestic Space in 1950s Canada.' *Architecture and Ideas* 1 (1996): 90–9.

Crowley, John E. '"In Happier Mansions, Warm, and Dry": The Invention of the Cottage as the Comfortable Anglo-American House.' *Winterthur Portfolio: A Journal of American Material Culture* 32 / 2–3 (1997): 169–88.

– 'Houses, Gender, and the Picturesque Landscape: The Designs of Catharine Beecher and Jackson Downing.' In Moira Donald and Linda Hurcombe, eds., *Gender and Material Culture in Historical Perspective*, 158–74. London: Macmillan; New York: St Martin's Press, 2000.

– 'Chimneys and Privacy.' In *The Invention of Comfort: Sensibilities and Design in Early Modern Britain and Early America*, 22–36. Baltimore, MD: Johns Hopkins University Press, 2001.

Csikszentmihalyi, Mihaly, and Eugene Halton-Rochberg. *The Meaning of Things: Domestic Symbols and the Self*. Cambridge: Cambridge University Press, 1981.

Cwerner, Saulo B., and Alan Metcalfe. 'Storage and Clutter: Discourses and Practices of Order in the Domestic World.' *Journal of Design History* 16 / 3 (2003): 229–39.

Dakers, Caroline. *Clouds: The Biography of a Country House*. London: Yale University Press, 1993.

Daniels, Inge. *The Japanese House: Material Culture in the Modern Home*. Oxford: Berg, 2010.

Darling, Elizabeth, and Lesley Whitworth. *Women and the Making of Built Space in England, 1870–1950*. London: Ashgate, 2007.

Das, Veena, et al. 'On the Modalities of the Domestic.' *Home Cultures* 5/3 (2008): 349–71.

Daunton, Martin. *House and Home in the Victorian City: Working-Class Housing, 1850–1914*. London: Edward Arnold, 1983.

Davies, Philip. *Splendors of the Raj: British Architecture in India, 1660 to 1947*. London: J. Murray, 1985.

Davison, Jane. *The Fall of a Doll's House: Three Generations of American Women and the Houses They Lived In*. New York: Holt, Reinhart and Winston, 1980.

de Bonneville, Françoise. *The Book of Bath*. Trans. Jane Brenton. New York: Rizzoli, 1998.

de Botton, Alain. *The Architecture of Happiness*. London: Hamish Hamilton, 2006.

de Certeau, Michel. *The Practice of Everyday Life*. Trans. Steven Randall. Berkeley, CA: University of California Press, 1984.

de Sousa, Geraldo U. *At Home in Shakespeare's Tragedies*. Aldershot: Ashgate, 2010.

De Wolfe, Elsie. *The House in Good Taste*. New York: Century, 1913.

Dennis, Flora. 'Sound and Domestic Space in Fifteenth- and Sixteenth-Century Italy.' *Studies in the Decorative Arts* 16/1 (2008/2009): 7–19.

Dennis, Michael. *Court and Garden: From the French Hotel to the City of Modern Architecture*. Cambridge, MA: MIT Press, 1986.

Derrida, Jacques. *Specters of Marx: The State of the Debt, the Work of Mourning, and the New International*. Trans. Peggy Kamuf. New York: Routledge, 1984.

Després, Carole. 'The Meaning of Home: Literature Review and Directions for Future Research and Theoretical Development.' *Journal of Architectural and Planning Research* 8/2 (1991): 96–115.

Dewan, Pauline. *The House as Setting, Symbol, and Structural Motif*. Queenston, ON: Edward Mellen, 2004.

Dickens, Charles. *The Letters of Charles Dickens*. Ed. Graham Storey and K.J. Fielding. Oxford: Clarendon, 1981.

– *Dombey and Son*. Ed. Peter Fairclough. London: Penguin, 1985.

Dickerson, Vanessa D. *Keeping the Victorian House: A Collection of Essays*. New York: Garland, 1995.

Dickinson, Emily. *The Complete Poems of Emily Dickinson*. Ed. Thomas H. Johnson. Boston, MA: Little, Brown, 1955.

Dixon, Simon. 'Ambiguous Ecologies: Stardom's Domestic *Mise-en-scène* (Film Stars, Roles, Homes).' *Cinema Journal* 42/2 (2003): 81–100.

Dore, Ronald. *The City Life in Japan: A Study of a Tokyo Ward*. London: Routledge, 1958.

– *Shinohata: A Portrait of a Japanese Village*. Berkeley, CA: University of California Press, 1978.

Douglas, Mary. *Purity and Danger: An Analysis of the Concepts of Pollution and Taboo*. London: Routledge and Kegan Paul, 1966.

– 'The Idea of a Home: A Kind of Space.' *Social Research* 58 / 1 (1991): 287–307.

– *The World of Goods: Towards an Anthropology of Consumption*. London: Routledge, 1996.

Dowling, Robin, and Kathleen Mee. 'Home and Homemaking in Contemporary Australia.' *Housing, Theory and Society* 24 / 3 (2007): 161–5.

The Dream City. Introduction by Halsey C. Ives. St Louis, MO: N.D. Thompson, 1893.

Dripps, Robin D. *The First House: Myth, Paradigm, and the Task of Architecture*. Cambridge, MA: MIT Press, 1997.

Duby, Georges. 'Communal Living.' In Georges Duby, ed., *A History of Private Life, vol. 2, Revelations of the Medieval World*, 35–85. Trans. Arthur Goldhammer. Cambridge, MA: Belknap, 1988.

Dunbar, Olivia H. 'Mrs Gilman's Idea of Home.' In Joanne B. Karpinski, ed., *Critical Essays on Charlotte Perkins Gilman*, 103–5. New York: G.K. Hall, 1992.

Duncan, James S. 'Housing as Presentation of Self and the Structure of Social Networks.' In Gary T. Moore and Reginald G. Golledge, eds., *Environmental Knowing*, 247–53. East Stroudsburg, PA: Dowden, Hutchinson and Ross, 1976.

– 'The House as Symbol of Social Structure: Notes on the Language of Objects among Collectivist Groups.' In Irwin Altman and Carol M. Werner, eds., *Home Environments*, 133–51. New York: Plenum, 1985.

Duncan, James S., ed. *Housing and Identity: Cross-Cultural Perspectives*. London: Croom Helm, 1981.

Duncan, James S., and Nancy G. Duncan. *Landscapes of Privilege: The Politics of the Aesthetic in Suburban America*. New York: Routledge, 2003.

Duncan, James S., and David S. Lambert. 'Landscapes of Home.' In James S. Duncan, Nuala Johnson, and Richard Schein, eds., *A Companion to Cultural Geography*, 382–403. Oxford: Blackwell, 2004.

Duncan, Nancy G., ed. *Bodyspace: Destabilizing Geographies of Gender and Sexuality*. London: Routledge, 1996.

Dyck, Isabel. 'Space, Time and Renegotiating Motherhood: An Exploration of the Domestic Workplace.' *Environment and Planning D: Society and Space* 8 / 4 (1990): 459–83.

Edmonds, Susan. *Grotesque Relations: Modernist Domestic Fiction and the U.S. Welfare State*. New York: Oxford University Press, 2008.

Edwards, Clive. *Turning Houses into Homes*. Aldershot: Ashgate, 2005.

Elbourne, Elizabeth. 'Domesticity and Dispossession: The Ideology of "Home" and the British Construction of the "Primitive" from the Eighteenth to the Early Nineteenth Century.' In Wendy Woodward, Patricia Hayes, and Gary Minkley, eds., *Deep HIStories: Gender and Colonialism in Southern Africa*, 27–54. Amsterdam: Rodopi, 2002.

Eleb, Monique. 'Modernity and Modernization in Postwar France: The Third Type of House.' *Journal of Architecture* 9 / 4 (2004): 495–514.

Eleb-Vidal, Monique, and Anne Debarre-Blanchard. *Architectures de la vie privée: Maisons et mentalités XVII*[e]*–XIX*[e] *siècles*. Brussels: Archives d'architecture moderne, 1989.

Elias, Norbert. 'On Behavior in the Bedroom.' In *The Civilizing Process: The History of Manners and State Formation and Civilization*, 132–38. Trans. Edmund Jephcott. Oxford: Blackwell, 1994.

Ennals, Peter, and Deryck W. Holdsworth. *Homeplace: The Making of the Canadian Dwelling over Three Centuries*. Toronto: University of Toronto Press, 1998.

Farr, Marie T. 'Home Is Where the Heart Is – Or Is It? Three Women and Charlotte Perkins Gilman's Theory of the Home.' In Jill Rudd and Val Gough, eds., *Charlotte Perkins Gilman: Optimist Reformer*, 93–110. Iowa City: University of Iowa Press, 1999.

Ferris Motz, Marilyn, and Pat Browne, eds. *Making the American Home: Middle-Class Women and Domestic Material Culture*. Bowling Green, OH: Bowling Green State University Popular Press, 1988.

Fiffer, Sharon Sloan, and Steve Fiffer. *Home: American Writers Remember Rooms of Their Own*. New York: Vintage, 1996.

Finighan, W.R. 'Some Empirical Observations on the Role of Privacy in the Residential Environment.' *Man-Environment Systems* 10 (1980): 153–9.

Flanders, Judith. *The Victorian House*. London: HarperCollins, 2003.

– *Inside the Victorian Home: A Portrait of Domestic Life in Victorian England*. New York: Norton, 2004.

Forty, Adrian. *Objects of Desire: Design and Society, 1750–1980*. New York: Pantheon, 1986.

Foucault, Michel. 'Questions of Geography.' In Colin Gordon, ed., *Michel Foucault: Power / Knowledge*, 63–77. New York: Pantheon, 1980.

– 'Of Other Spaces.' Trans. Jay Miscowiec. *Diacritics* 16 / 1 (1986): 22–7.

Fox, Stephen. *The Ocean Railway: Isambard Kingdom Brunel, Samuel Cunard and the Revolutionary World of the Great Atlantic Steamships*. London: HarperCollins, 2003.

Foy, Jessica H., and Karal Ann Marling. *The Arts and the American Home, 1890–1930*. Knoxville, TN: University of Tennessee Press, 1994.

Foy, Jessica H., and Thomas J. Schlereth, eds. *American Home Life, 1880–1930*. Knoxville, TN: University of Tennessee Press, 1992.

Fraad, Harriet S., Stephen Resnick, and Richard Wolff. *Bringing It All Back Home: Class, Gender and Power in the Modern Household*. London: Pluto Press, 1994.

Frances, Mark, and Randolph T. Hester Jr, eds. *The Meaning of Gardens: Idea, Place, and Action*. Cambridge, MA: MIT Press, 1990.

Frank, Ellen Eve. *Literary Architecture: Essays towards a Tradition: Walter Pater, Gerard Manley Hopkins, Marcel Proust, Henry James*. Berkeley, CA: University of California Press, 1979.

Franklin, Jill. *The Gentleman's Country House and Its Plan, 1835–1914*. London: Routledge and Kegan Paul, 1981.

Fraser, Nancy. *Scales of Justice: Reimagining Public Space in a Globalizing World*. New York: Columbia University Press, 2008.

Freestone, Robert. 'Planning, Housing, Gardening: Home as a Garden Suburb.' In Patrick Troy, ed., *A History of European Housing in Australia*, 125–41. Cambridge: Cambridge University Press, 2000.

Freud, Sigmund. *Civilization and Its Discontents*. [1930]. Trans. and ed. James Strachey. New York: Norton, 1961.

– 'Representation by Symbols in Dreams – Some Further Typical Dreams.' [1900–01]. In *The Standard Edition of the Complete Psychological Works of Sigmund Freud*, vol. 5, 350–404. Trans. and ed. James Strachey. London: Hogarth Press, 1953.

– 'The Uncanny.' [1919]. In *The Standard Edition of the Complete Psychological Works of Sigmund Freud*, vol. 17, 217–56. Trans. and ed. James Strachey. London: Hogarth Press, 1955.

Friedman, Alice T. *Women and the Making of the Modern House: A Social and Architectural History*. New York: H.N. Abrams, 1998.

Friedman, Avi, and David Krawitz. *Peeking through the Keyhole: The Evolution of the North American Home*. Montreal and Kingston: McGill-Queen's University Press, 2002.

Fritze, Tamara. 'Growing Identity, Growing a Home: Contrasting Functions of Two Nineteenth-Century Gardens.' *Studies in the History of Gardens and Designed Landscapes* 22 / 4 (2002): 335–44.

Fryer, Judith. *Felicitous Space: The Imaginative Structures of Edith Wharton and Willa Cather*. Chapel Hill, NC: University of North Carolina Press, 1986.

Fukutake, Tadashi. *The Japanese Social Structure*. Tokyo: University of Tokyo Press, 1993.

Fuss, Diana. *The Sense of an Interior: Four Writers and the Rooms that Shaped Them*. New York: Routledge, 2004.

Gallagher, Winifred. *House Thinking: A Room-by-Room Look at How We Live*. New York: HarperCollins, 2007.

Gan, Wendy. *Women, Privacy and Modernity in Early Twentieth-Century British Writing*. New York: Palgrave Macmillan, 2009.

Garber, Marjorie. 'The Body as House.' In *Sex and Real Estate: Why We Love Houses*, 73–80. New York: Pantheon, 2000.

Gardiner, Stephen. *Evolution of the House*. New York: Macmillan, 1974.

– *The House: Its Origins and Evolution*. Rev. ed. [of *Evolution of the House*, 1974]. London: Constable, 2002.

Gardner, Ernest. 'The Greek House.' *Journal of Hellenic Studies* 21 (1901): 293–305.

Garrett, Elizabeth D. 'The American Home. Part 1. Centre and Circumference: The American Domestic Scene in the Age of the Enlightenment.' *Antiques* 123 / 1 (1983): 214–25.

Garvey, Pauline. 'How to Have a "Good Home": The Practical Aesthetic and Normativity in Norway.' *Journal of Design History* 16 / 3 (2003): 241–51.

Gathorne-Hardy, Flora. 'Home.' In Linda McDowell and Joanne Sharp, eds., *A Feminist Glossary of Human Geography*, 124–5. London: Arnold, 1999.

Geeta, Patel. 'Marking the Quilt: Veil, Harem / Home, and the Subversion of Colonial Civility.' *Colby Quarterly* 37 / 2 (2001): 174–88.

Geldin, Sherri. 'On the House.' [Editorial]. *Assemblage* 24 (1994): 6–7.

Geller, Matthew, ed. *From Receiver to Remote Control: The TV Set*. New York: New Museum of Contemporary Art, 1990.

Gender & History. Special issue on: Gendering histories of home and homecoming. 21 / 3 (2009).

George, Rosemary Marangoly. *The Politics of Home: Postcolonial Relocations and Twentieth-Century Fiction*. Cambridge: Cambridge University Press, 1996.

George, Rosemary Marangoly, ed. *Burning Down the House: Recycling Domesticity*. Boulder, CO: Westview, 1998.

Gerard, Jessica. *Country House Life: Family and Servants, 1815–1914*. Cambridge, MA: Blackwell, 1994.

Gere, Charlotte. *Nineteenth-Century Decoration: The Art of the Interior*. London: Weidenfeld and Nicolson, 1989.

Gere, Charlotte, ed., with Lesley Hoskins. *The House Beautiful: Oscar Wilde and the Aesthetic Interior*, 109–36. London: Lund Humphries, in association with the Geffrye Museum, 2000.

Gerstein, Alexandra, ed. *Beyond Bloomsbury: Designs of the Omega Workshops 1913–19*. London: Courtauld Gallery, in association with Fontanka, 2009.

Gilbert, Sandra M., and Susan Gubar. *The Madwoman in the Attic: The Woman Writer and the Nineteenth-Century Literary Imagination*. New Haven, CT: Yale University Press, 1979.

Giles, Judy. 'A Home of One's Own: Women and Domesticity in England, 1918–1950.' *Women Studies International Forum* 16 / 3 (1993): 239–53.

– *The Parlour and the Suburb: Domestic Identities, Class, Femininity and Modernity*. Oxford: Berg, 2004.

Gill, Richard. *Happy Rural Seat: The English Country House and the Literary Imagination*. New Haven, CT: Yale University Press, 1972.

Gill, Valerie. 'Catharine Beecher and Charlotte Perkins Gilman: Architects of Female Power.' *Journal of American Culture* 21 / 2 (1998): 17–24.

Gilman, Charlotte Perkins. *Home, Its Work and Influence*. London: McClure, Philips, 1903.

Ginsburg, Rebecca. '"Come in the Dark": Domestic Workers and Their Rooms in Apartheid-Era Johannesburg, South Africa.' *Perspectives in Vernacular Architecture* 8 (2000): 83–100.

– *At Home with Apartheid*. Charlottesville, VA: University of Virginia Press, 2011.

Girouard, Mark. *Life in the English Country House: A Social and Architectural History*. Oxford: Clarendon, 1978.

– *The Victorian Country House*. London: Yale University Press, 1979.

– *Robert Smythson and the Elizabethan Country House*. New Haven, CT: Yale University Press, 1983.

Glover, William J. 'A Feeling of Absence from Old England: The Colonial Bungalow.' *Home Cultures* 1 / 1 (2004): 61–82.

Gordimer, Nadine. *My Son's Story*. London: Bloomsbury, 1990.

Gordon, Beverly. 'Woman's Domestic Body: The Conceptual Conflation of Women and Interiors in the Industrial Age.' *Winterthur Portfolio* 31 / 4 (1996): 281–301.

Gore, Alan, and James Chambers. *The English House*. New York: Norton, 1985.

Gorman-Murray, Andrew. 'Gay and Lesbian Couples at Home: Identity Work in Domestic Space.' *Home Cultures* 3 / 2 (2006): 145–68.

– 'Homeboys: Uses of Home by Gay Australian Men.' *Social and Cultural Geography* 7 / 1 (2006): 53–69.

– 'Queering Home or Domesticating Deviance? Interrogating Gay Domesticity through Lifestyle Television.' *International Journal of Cultural Studies* 9 / 2 (2006): 227–47.

– 'New Perspectives on the Public Power and Political Significance of Home.' *Australian Geographer* 38 / 1 (2007): 133–43.

Gow, Ian, and Alistair Rowan. *Scottish Country Houses, 1600–1914*. Edinburgh: Edinburgh University Press, 1995.

Gowans, Alan. *The Comfortable House: North American Suburban Architecture, 1890–1930*. Cambridge, MA: MIT Press, 1986.

Gram-Hanssen, Kirsten, and Claus Bech-Danielsen. 'House, Home and Identity from a Consumption Perspective.' *Housing, Theory and Society* 21 / 1 (2004): 17–26.

Graves, Jane. *The Secret Lives of Objects*. Bloomington, IN: Traffond, 2010.

Greenfield, Jill, Sean O'Connell, and Chris Reid. 'Gender, Consumer Culture and the Middle-Class Male, 1918–1939.' In Alan J. Kidd and David Nicholls, eds., Gender, *Civic Culture and Consumerism*, 183–97. Manchester: Manchester University Press, 1999.

Gregson, Nicky, Louise Crewe, and Kate Brooks. 'Shopping, Space and Practice.' *Environment and Planning D: Society and Space* 20 / 5 (2002): 597–617.

Gregson, Nicky, and Michelle Lowe. *Servicing the Middle Classes: Class, Gender and Waged Domestic Labour*. London: Routledge, 1994.

Grenville, Jane. 'Houses and Households in Late Medieval England: An Archeological Perspective.' In Jocelyn Wogan-Browne, Rosalyn Voaden, Arlyn Diamond, Ann Hutchison, Carol M. Meale, and Lesley Johnson, eds., *Medieval Women: Text and Contexts in Late Medieval Britain: Essays for Felicity Riddy*, 309–28. Turnhout, Belgium: Brepols, 2000.

Grewal, Inderpal. *Home and Harem: Nation, Gender and Cultures of Travel*. London: Leicester University Press, 1996.

Grier, Katherine C. *Culture and Comfort: Parlor Making and Middle-Class Identity, 1850–1930*. Washington, DC: Smithsonian Books, 1997.

– '"The Eden of Home": Changing Understandings of Cruelty and Kindness to Animals in Middle-Class American Households, 1820–1900.' In Mary J. Henninger-Voss, ed., *Animals in Human Histories: The Mirror of Nature and Culture*, 316–62. Rochester, NY: University of Rochester Press, 2002.

Griffiths, Jason. 'What about My Things? "The House of Things."' *Journal of Architecture* 7 / 4 (2002): 375–81.

Groves, Colin P., and Jordi Sabater Pi. 'From Ape's Nest to Human Fix Point.' *Man* 20 (1985): 22–47.

Haberer, P., J. Kapteijins, and K. Geevers. 'When Is a Dwelling a Home?' *Open House International* 2 (1984): 15–21.

Habermas, Jürgen. *The Structural Transformation of the Public Sphere: An Inquiry into a Category of Bourgeois Society*. Cambridge, MA: MIT Press, 1991.

Hadjiyanni, Tasoulla, and Kristin Helle. 'Re / claiming the Past: Constructing Ojibwe Identity in Minnesota Homes.' *Design Studies* 30 / 4 (2009): 462–81.

Halbwachs, Maurice. *The Collective Memory*. Trans. F. Ditter and V.Y. Ditter. New York: Harper and Row, 1980.

Hall, Catherine. *Civilizing Subjects: Metropole and Colony in the English Imagination, 1830–1867*. Oxford: Polity, 2002.

Hall, Edward T. *The Hidden Dimension, Man's Use of Space in Public and Private*. London: Bodley Head, 1966.

Hall, Edward T., and Mildred R. Hall. *Hidden Differences*. New York: Doubleday, 1987.

Haltutten, Karen. 'From Parlor to Living Room: Domestic Space, Interior Decoration, and the Culture of Personality.' In Simon J. Bronner, ed., *Consuming Visions: Accumulation and Display of Goods in America, 1880–1920*, 157–89. New York: Norton, 1989.

Hamilton, Sheryl N. 'The Home of the Future, Then and Now.' *Canadian Home Economics Journal / Revue Canadienne d'économie familiale* 52 / 2 (2003): 6–9.

Hamlett, Jane. *Material Relations: Domestic Interiors and Middle-Class Families in England, 1850–1910*. Manchester: Manchester University Press, 2010.

Hamon, Philippe. *Expositions: Literature and Architecture in Nineteenth-Century France*. Trans. Katia Sainson-Frank and Lisa Maguire. Berkeley, CA: University of California Press, 1992.

Hand, Martin, and Elizabeth Shove. 'Orchestrating Concepts: Kitchen Dynamics and Regime Change in Good Housekeeping and Ideal Home, 1922–2002.' *Home Cultures* 1 / 3 (2004): 235–56.

Handlin, David P. *The American Home: Architecture and Society, 1815–1915*. Boston: Little Brown, 1979.

Hanson, Julienne. *Decoding Homes and Houses*. New York: Cambridge University Press, 1998.

Harbison, Robert. *Thirteen Ways: Theoretical Investigations into Architecture*. Cambridge, MA: MIT Press, 1997.

– *Eccentric Spaces*. Cambridge, MA: MIT Press, 2000.

Hareven, Tamara K. 'The Home and the Family in Historical Perspective.' *Social Research* 58 / 1 (1991): 253–85.

Harris, Dianne. 'Cultivating Power: The Language of Feminism in Women's Garden Literature, 1870–1920.' *Landscape Journal* 13 / 2 (1994): 113–23.

Harris, John, Kimberly Kostival, and Sarah Orchart. *The Artist and the Country House: From the Fifteenth Century to the Present Day*. London: Sotheby's Institute, 1995.

Harris, Steven, and Deborah Berke, eds. *Architecture of the Everyday*. New York: Princeton Architectural Press, 1997.

Harvey, David. *Spaces of Capital: Towards a Critical Geography*. New York: Routledge, 2001.

Hayden, Dolores. *The Grand Domestic Revolution: A History of Feminist Designs for American Homes, Neighborhoods, and Cities*. Cambridge, MA: MIT Press, 1981.

– *The Power of Place: Urban Landscapes as Public History*. Cambridge, MA: MIT Press, 1997.

– 'Nurturing: Home, Mom, and Apple Pie.' In *Redesigning the American Dream: The Future of Housing, Work and Family Life*, 81–119. New York: Norton, 2002.

– *Building Suburbia: Green Fields and Urban Growth, 1820–2000*. New York: Pantheon, 2003.

Haytock, Jennifer. *At Home, at War: Domesticity and World War I in American Literature*. Columbus, OH: Ohio State University Press, 2003.

Hegglund, Jon. 'Defending the Realm: Domestic Space and Mass Cultural Contamination in *Howards End* and *An Englishman's Home*.' *English Literature in Transition* 40 / 4 (1997): 398–423.

Heidegger, Martin. 'Building, Dwelling, Thinking.' [1951]. In *Poetry, Language, Thought*, 145–61. Trans. Albert Hofstadter. New York: Harper and Row, 1971; reprinted by Harper Perennial, 2001.

– 'Poetically Man Dwells.' In Neil Leach, ed., *Rethinking Architecture: A Reader in Cultural Theory*, 109–19. New York: Routledge, 1997.

Henderson, Susan R. 'A Revolution in the Woman's Sphere: Grete Lihotzky and the Frankfurt Kitchen.' In Debra Coleman, Elizabeth Danze, and Carol Henderson, eds., *Architecture and Feminism*, 221–53. Princeton, NJ: Princeton University Press, 1996.

Hendon, Julia A. *Houses in a Landscape: Memory and Everyday Life in Mesoamerica*. Durham, NC: Duke University Press, 2010.

Herzfeld, Michael. *Anthropology through the Looking Glass: Critical Ethnography in the Margins of Europe*. Cambridge: Cambridge University Press, 1987.

Heynen, Hilde. *Architecture and Modernity: A Critique*. Cambridge, MA: MIT Press, 1999.

Heynen, Hilde, and Gülsüm Baydar, eds. *Negotiating Domesticity: Spatial Productions of Gender in Modern Architecture*. London: Routledge, 2005.

Heynen, Hilde, and Karina van Herck. 'Introduction.' *Journal of Architecture* 7 / 3 (2002): 221–8.

Highmore, Ben, ed. *The Design Culture Reader*. New York: Routledge, 2008.

Hillier, Bill, and Julienne Hanson. *The Social Logic of Space*. Cambridge: Cambridge University Press, 1984.

Hirschon, Renée. 'Essential Objects and the Sacred: Interior and Exterior Space in Urban Greek Locality.' In Shirley Ardener, ed., *Women and Space: Ground Rules and Social Maps*, 70–86. Oxford: Berg, 1993.

Hirschon, Renée, and S. Thakurdesai. 'Society, Culture and Spatial Organization: An Athens Example.' *Ekistics* 30 / 178 (1970): 187–96.

Hochschild, Arlie. *The Commercialization of Intimate Life: Notes from Home and Work*. Berkeley, CA: University of California Press, 2003.

Hollander, Martha, 'Nicolaes Maes: Space as Domestic Territory.' In *An Entrance for the Eyes: Space and Meaning in Seventeenth-Century Dutch Art*, 103–48. Berkeley, CA: University of California Press, 2002.

Hollis, Edward. '*The House of Life* and the Memory Palace: Some Thoughts on the Historiography of Interiors.' *Interiors: Design, Architecture and Culture* 1 / 1–2 (2010): 105–17.

Hollis, Edward, John Gigli, Frazer Hay, Andrew Milligan, Alex Milton, and Drew Plunkett, eds. *Thinking Inside the Box: A Reader in Interiors for the 21st Century*. London: Middlesex University Press, 2007.

'Home.' Camberwell. Available at www.Igihome.co.uk.

Home Economics Archive. Available at http://hearth.library.cornell.edu/h/hearth.

Honig, Bonnie. 'Difference, Dilemmas, and the Politics of Home.' *Social Research* 61 / 3 (1994): 563–97.

hooks, bell. 'Homeplace: A Site of Resistance.' In *Yearning: Race, Gender and Cultural Politics*, 41–9. Boston, MA: South End Press, 1990.

Horn, Walter, and Ernest Born. *The Plan of St Gall: A Study of Architecture and Economy of, and Life in a Paradigmatic Carolingian Monastery*, vol. 2. Berkeley CA: University of California Press, 1979.

Hosagrahar, Jyoti. 'Mansions to Margins: Modernity and the Domestic Landscape of Historic Delhi, 1847–1910.' *Journal of the Society of Architectural Historians* 60 / 1 (2001): 26–45.

Humble, Nicola. *The Feminine Middlebrow Novel, 1920s–1950s: Class, Domesticity, and Bohemianism*. Oxford: Oxford University Press, 2001.

Hummon, David M. 'House, Home, and Identity in Contemporary American Culture.' In Setha M. Low, Erve Chambers, and Amos Rapoport, eds., *Housing, Culture, and Design: A Comparative Perspective*, 207–28. Philadelphia, PA: University of Pennsylvania Press, 1989.

Humphrey, Caroline. 'No Place like Home in Anthropology: The Neglect of Architecture.' *Anthropology Today* 4 / 1 (1988): 16–18.

Illich, Ivan. *$H_2$0 and the Waters of Forgetfulness*. London: Marion Boyers, 1986.

Ingold, Tim. 'Building, Dwelling, Living: How Animals and People Make Themselves at Home in the World.' In Marilyn Strathern, ed., *Shifting Contexts: Transformation in Anthropological Knowledge*, 57–80. London: Routledge, 1995.

Inoue, Mariko. 'Regendering Domestic Space: Modern Housing in Prewar Tokyo.' *Monumenta Nipponica* 58 / 1 (2003): 79–102.

Inouye, Jukichi. *Home Life in Tokyo*. London: KPI, 1995.

Ishteeaque, Ellahi M., and Fahd A. Al Said. 'The Story of the Courtyard House: Middle Eastern–Arab Case Study.' *International Journal for Housing Science and Its Applications* 27 / 3 (2003): 213–24.

Jenkins, Virginia Scott. *The Lawn: A History of an American Obsession*. New York: Princeton Architectural Press, 1994.

Jeremiah, David. *Architecture, Design and the Family in Twentieth-Century Britain, 1900–1970*. Manchester: Manchester University Press, 2000.

Johnson, Lesley. 'As Housewives We Are Worms: Women, Modernity and the Home Question.' *Cultural Studies* 10 / 3 (1996): 449–63.

Johnson, Louise. 'Text-ured Brick: Speculations on the Cultural Production of Domestic Space.' *Australian Geographical Studies* 31 / 2 (1993): 201–13.

– 'Browsing the Modern Kitchen – A Feast of Gender, Place and Culture (Part 1).' *Gender, Place and Culture* 13 (2006): 123–32.

Johnson, Matthew. *Housing Culture: Traditional Architecture in an English Landscape*. Washington, DC: Smithsonian Institution, 1993.

Johnston, Lynda, and Gill Valentine. 'Wherever I Lay My Girlfriend, That's My Home: The Performance and Surveillance of Lesbian Identities in Domestic Environments.' In David Bell and Gill Valentine, eds., *Mapping Desire: Geographies of Sexualities*, 99–113. London: Routledge, 1995.

Johnston, Susan. *Women and Domestic Experience in Victorian Political Fiction*. Westport, CT: Greenwood, 2001.

Jones, Elizabeth H. *Spaces of Belonging: Home, Culture and Identity in 20th Century French Autobiography*. Amsterdam: Rodopi, 2007.

Jones, Suzanne W. 'Edith Wharton's "Secret Sensitiveness," the Decoration of Houses, and Her Fiction.' *Journal of Modern Literature* 21 / 2 (1997–1998): 177–200.

Jordan, John O. 'Domestic Servants and the Victorian Home.' In Murray Baumgarten and H.M. Daleski, eds., *Homes and Homelessness in the Victorian Imagination*, 79–90. New York: AMS Press, 1998.

Joselit, Jenna Weissman. '"A Set Table": Jewish Domestic Culture in the New World, 1880–1950.' In Susan L. Braunstein and Jenna Weissman Joselit, eds., *Getting Comfortable in New York: The Jewish Home, 1880–1950*, 19–73. New York: Jewish Museum, 1990.

Jung, Carl Gustav. *Psychology of the Unconscious*. Trans. Beatrice M. Hinkle. Moffat: Yard, 1916.

– *Memories, Dreams, Reflections*. Trans. Clara Winston and Richard Winston. Ed. Aniela Jaffé. London: Collins, 1989.

Kagawa, Keiko P. 'Jane Austen, the Architect: (Re)Building Spaces at Mansfield Park.' *Women's Studies* 35 (2006): 125–43.

Kaluzynska, Eva. 'Wiping the Floor with Theory – A Survey of Writings on Housework.' *Feminist Review* 6 (1980): 27–54.

Kaplan, Caren. 'Deterritorialization: The Rewriting of Home and Exile in Western Feminist Discourse.' In Abdul R. Jan Mohamed and David Lloyd, eds., *The Nature and Context of Minority Discourse*, 357–68. Oxford: Oxford University Press, 1991.

Kearns, Kevin C. *Dublin Tenement Life: An Oral History*. Dublin: Gill & Macmillan, 1994.

Keightly, Keir. '"Turn It Down!" She Shrieked: Gender, Domestic Space, and High Fidelity, 1948–59.' *Popular Music* 15 / 2 (1996): 147–77.

Kelsall, Malcolm Miles. *The Great Good Place: The Country House and English Literature*. New York: Harvester Wheatsheaf, 1993.

Kent, Susan, ed., *Domestic Architecture and the Use of Space: An Interdisciplinary Cross-Cultural Study*. Cambridge: Cambridge University Press, 1990.

Keogh, Peter, Catherine Dodds, and Laurie Henderson. *Working-Class Gay Men: Redefining Community, Restoring Identity*. London: Sigma Research, 2004.

Kerr, Robert. 'The Family Apartments.' In *The Gentleman's House, or, How to Plan English Residences from the Parsonage to the Palace; with Tables of Accommodation and Cost, and a Series of Selected Plans*, 73–6. London: John Murray, 1864.

Kilickiran, Didem. 'Migrant Homes: Ethnicity, Identity and Domestic Space Culture.' In Sarah Menin, ed., *Constructing Place: Mind and Matter*, 99–110. London: Routledge, 2003.

Kinchin, Juliet. 'Interiors: Nineteenth-Century Essays on the "Masculine" and the "Feminine" Room.' In Pat Kirkham, ed., *The Gendered Object*, 12–29. Manchester: Manchester University Press, 1996.

– 'Performance and the Reflected Self: Modern Stagings of Domestic Space, 1860–1914.' *Studies in the Decorative Arts* 16 / 1 (2008 / 2009): 64–91.

King, Anthony D. *Buildings and Society: Essays on the Social Development of the Built Environment*. London: Routledge and Kegan Paul, 1980.

– *The Bungalow: The Production of a Global Culture*. London: Routledge and Kegan Paul, 1984.

– *Urbanism, Colonialism, and the World-Economy: Cultural and Spatial Foundations of the World Urban System*. London: Routledge, 1991.

Klimasmith, Betty. *At Home in the City: Urban Domesticity in American Literature and Culture, 1850–1930*. Durham, NH: University of New Hampshire Press, 2005.

Kline, Stephen. *Out of the Garden: Toys and Children's Culture in the Age of TV Marketing*. Toronto: Garamond, 1993.

Knapp, Bettina L. *Archetype, Architecture, and the Writer*. Bloomington, IN: Indiana University Press, 1986.

Knapp, Ronald G. *China's Vernacular Architecture: House Form and Culture*. Honolulu, HI: University of Hawaii Press, 1989.

– *The Chinese House: Craft, Symbol, and the Folk Tradition*. Hong Kong: Oxford University Press, 1990.

Knights, Clive. 'The Spatiality of the Roman Domestic Setting: An Interpretation of Symbolic Content.' In Michael Parker Pearson and Colin Richards, eds., *Architecture and Order: Approaches to Social Space*, 113–46. New York: Routledge, 1994.

Krasner, James. 'Accumulated Lives: Metaphor, Materiality, and the Homes of the Elderly.' *Literature and Medicine* 24 / 2 (2005): 209–30.

– *Home Bodies: Tactile Experience in Domestic Space*. Columbus, OH: Ohio State University Press, 2010.

Kroeber, Alfred L. *The Nature of Culture*. Chicago, IL: University of Chicago Press, 1952.

Kron, Joan. *Home-Psych: The Social Psychology of Home and Decoration*. New York: Clarkson N. Potter, 1983.

Kruger, Linda M. 'Home Libraries: Special Places, Reading Spaces.' In Jessica H. Foy and Thomas J. Schlereth, eds., *American Home Life, 1880–1930: A Social History of Spaces and Services*, 94–119. Knoxville, TN: University of Tennessee Press, 1992.

Kurg, Andres. 'Empty White Space: Home as a Total Work of Art during the Late-Soviet Period.' *Interiors: Design, Architecture, Culture* 2 / 1 (2011): 45–68.

Kutzer, M. Daphne. 'A Wildness Inside: Domestic Space in the Work of Beatrix Potter.' *Lion and the Unicorn: A Critical Journal of Children's Literature* 21 / 2 (1997): 204–14.

Ladsun, Susan, and Mark Girouard. *Victorians at Home*. London: Weidenfeld and Nicolson, 1981.

Lambert, Phyllis. 'The House and Its Environment.' In Phyllis Lambert and Alan Stewart, eds., *Opening the Gates of Eighteenth-Century Montréal*, 69–78. Montreal: Canadian Centre for Architecture, 1992.

Lane, Barbara Miller. *Architecture and Politics in Germany, 1918–1945*. Cambridge, MA: Harvard University Press, 1985 [1968].

– *National Romanticism and Modern Architecture in Germany and the Scandinavian Countries*. Cambridge: Cambridge University Press, 2000.

Lane, Barbara Miller, ed. *Housing and Dwelling: Perspectives on Modern Domestic Architecture*. London: Routledge, 2007.

Lavin, Maud. 'TV Design.' In Matthew Geller, ed., *From Receiver to Remote Control: The TV Set*, 85–94. New York: New Museum of Contemporary Art, 1990.

Lawlor, Anthony. *The Temple in the House: Finding the Sacred in Everyday Architecture*. New York: Putnam, 1994.

Lawrence, Jane, and Rachel Hurst. 'The Sexual Science of the Kitchen: Representations of Australian Domesticity.' *IDEA: Interior Architecture Design Educators Association Journal* 1 / 3 (2002): 45–54.

Lawrence, Roderick J. 'Transition Spaces and Dwelling Design.' *Journal of Architectural Planning and Research* 1 (1984): 261–71.

– 'Domestic Space and the Regulation of Daily Life.' *Recherches Sociologiques* 17 / 1 (1986): 147–69.

– 'The Meaning and Use of Home.' Special Issue, 'The Meaning and Use of Home,' ed. Roderick J. Lawrence. *Journal of Architectural and Planning Research* 8 / 2 (1991): 91–5.

– 'Deciphering Home: An Integrative Historical Perspective.' In David N. Benjamin, ed., *The Home: Words, Interpretations, Meanings, and Environments*, 53–68. Aldershot: Ashgate; Brookfield, VT: Avebury, 1995.

Lawton de Torruella, Elena. 'Caribbean Domestic Spaces in Four Modes: Walcott, Hippolyte, Brathwaite and Rhys.' *Torre: Revista de la Universidad de Puerto Rico* 7 / 26 (2002): 657–62.

Leach, Neil, ed. *Rethinking Architecture: A Reader in Cultural Theory*. London: Routledge, 1997.

Le Corbusier. *Towards a New Architecture*. [1923]. Trans. Frederick Etchells. London: Architectural Press; New York: Frederick A. Praeger, 1978 [1927].

Lees-Maffei, Grace, and Rebecca Houze, eds. *The Design History Reader*. Oxford: Berg, 2010.

Lefebvre, Henri. *Everyday Life in the Modern World*. Trans. Sacha Rabinovitch. New Brunswick, NJ: Transaction Books, 1986 [1968].

– 'Social Space.' In *The Production of Space*, 68–168. [1974]. Trans. Donald Nicholson-Smith. Oxford: Blackwell, 1991.

Leonard, L., H. Perkins, and D. Thorns. 'Presenting and Creating Home: The Influence of Popular and Building Trade Print Media in the Construction of Home.' *Housing, Theory and Society* 21 / 3 (2004): 97–110.

Lerup, Lars. 'Planned Assaults: Reflections on the Detached House.' Special Issue, 'L'inquieto spazio domestico / Disputed Domestic Space,' ed. Pierluigi Nicolin. *Lotus International* 44 (1984): 76–81.

Leslie, Deborah, and Suzanne Reimer. 'Gender, Modern Design, and Home Consumption.' *Environment and Planning D: Society and Space* 21 / 3 (2003): 293–316.

Leslie, Michael, and John Dixon Hunt, eds. *A Cultural History of Gardens*, 6 vols. Oxford: Berg, 2011.

Levinas, Emmanuel. *Totalité et infini: Essai sur l'extériorité*. The Hague: Nijhoff, 1974.

Lévy, Michel. *Traité d'hygiène publique et privée*. Paris: J.B. Baillière, 1850.

Lewis, Bernard. *History Remembered, Recovered, Invented*. Princeton, NJ: Princeton University Press, 1975.

Light, Alison. *Mrs Woolf and the Servants: The Hidden Heart of Domestic Service*. London: Penguin, 2007.

Livett, Richard A.H. 'Bronte House Scheme.' *Official Architecture* (March 1942): 134–7.

Livingstone, Sonia. 'From Family Television to Bedroom Culture: Young People's Media at Home.' In Eoin Devereux, ed., *Media Studies: Key Issues and Debates*, 302–21. London: Sage, 2007.

Llewellyn, Mark. '"Urban Village" or "White House": Envisioned Spaces, Experienced Places, and Everyday Life at Kensal House, London, in the 1930s.' *Environment and Planning D: Society and Space* 22 / 2 (2004): 229–49.

Lloyd, Justine, and Lesley Johnson. 'The Threes Faces of Eve: The Post-War Housewife, Melodrama, and Home.' *Feminist Media Studies* 3 / 1 (2003): 7–25.

Logan, Thad. *The Victorian Parlour: A Cultural Study*. Cambridge: Cambridge University Press, 2001.

Long, Helen, and Stefan Muthesius. *The Edwardian House: The Middle-Class Home in Britain, 1880–1914*. Manchester: Manchester University Press, 1993.

Low, Setha M., and Denise Lawrence-Zúñiga, eds. *The Anthropology of Space and Place*. Oxford: Blackwell, 2003.

Lower East Side Tenement Museum. Available at www.tenement.org.

Lu, Su-Ju, and Peter Blundell Jones. 'House Design by Surname in Feng Shui.' *Journal of Architecture* 5 / 4 (2000): 355–67.

Lukacs, John. 'The Bourgeois Interior.' *American Scholar* 39 / 4 (1970): 616–30.

Lupton, Ellen. *Mechanical Brides: Women and Machines from Home to Office*. New York: Princeton Architectural Press, for the Cooper-Hewitt Museum, 1993.

Lupton, Ellen, and J. Abbott Miller. *The Bathroom, the Kitchen, and the Aesthetics of Waste: A Process of Elimination*. Cambridge, MA: MIT Press, 1992.

Luria, Sarah. 'The Architecture of Manners: Henry James, Edith Wharton and the Mount.' *American Quarterly* 49 (1997): 298–327.

Lyotard, Jean-François. 'Domus and the Megapolis.' In Neil Leach, ed., *Rethinking Architecture: A Reader in Cultural Theory*, 271–9. London: Routledge, 1999.

Mack, Arien, ed. *Home: A Place in the World*. New York: New York University Press, 1993.

Madigan, Ruth, and Moira Munro. 'Gender, House and Home: Social Meanings and Domestic Architecture in Britain.' *Journal of Architecture and Planning Research* 8 / 2 (1991): 116–32.

– 'House Beautiful: Style and Consumption in the Home.' *Sociology* 66 / 4 (1996): 487–506.

Madigan, Ruth, Moira Munro, and Susan J. Smith. 'Gender and the Meaning of Home.' *International Journal of Urban and Regional Research* 14 / 4 (1990): 625–47.

Maguire, Hugh. 'The Victorian Theatre as a Home from Home.' *Journal of Design History* 13 / 2 (2000): 107–21.

Maldonado, Tomas, and John Cullars. 'The Idea of Comfort.' *Design Issues* 8 / 1 (1991): 35–43.

Mallett, Shelley. 'Understanding Home: A Critical Review of the Literature.' *Sociological Review* 52 / 1 (2004): 62–89.

Manning, Erin. *Ephemeral Territories: Representing Nation, Home, and Identity in Canada*. Minneapolis, MN: University of Minnesota, 2003.

Marc, Olivier. 'Birth of the House.' In *Psychology of the House*, 9–28. Trans. Jessie Wood. London: Thames and Hudson, 1977.

Marcus, Claire Cooper. *House as a Mirror of Self: Exploring the Deeper Meaning of Home*. Berkeley, CA: Conari, 1995.

Marcus, Claire Cooper, Carolyn Francis, and Colette Meunier. 'Mixed Messages in Suburbia: Reading the Suburban Model Home.' *Places* 4 / 1 (1987): 24–37.

Marcus, Sharon. 'Seeing through Paris.' In *Apartment Stories: City and Home in Nineteenth-Century Paris and London*, 17–50. Berkeley, CA: University of California Press, 1999.

– 'Haussmannization as Anti-Modernity: The Apartment House in Parisian Urban Discourse, 1850–1880.' *Journal of Urban History* 27 / 6 (2001): 723–45.

Marken, Ronald. '"From within Outward": Thoreau, Whitman, and Wright on Domestic Architecture.' *Wascana Review* 11 / 2 (1976): 21–36.

Marsh, Margaret. 'From Separation to Togetherness: The Social Construction of Domestic Space in American Suburbs, 1840–1915.' *Journal of American History* 76 / 2 (1989): 506–27.

Marshall, John, and Ian Wilcox. *The Victorian House*. London: Sidgwick and Jackson, 1986.

Martin, Biddy, and Chandra Talpade Mohanty. 'Feminist Politics: What's Home Got to Do with It?' [1986]. In Robin R. Warhol and Diane Price Herndl, eds., *Feminisms: An Anthology of Literary Theory and Criticism*, 293–310. New Brunswick, NJ: Rutgers University Press, 1997.

Martin, Brenda, and Penny Sparke, eds. *Women's Places: Architecture and Design, 1860–1960*. London: Routledge, 2003.

Martin-Fugier, Anne. *La Place des bonnes: La domesticité féminine à Paris en 1900*. Paris: Grasset, 1979.

Massey, Anne. *Chair*. London: Reaktion Books, 2010.

Massey, Doreen. *Space, Place and Gender*. Minneapolis, MN: University of Minnesota Press, 1994.

– *For Space*. London: Sage, 2005.

Matthews, Glenna. *Just a Housewife: The Rise and Fall of Domesticity in America*. New York: Oxford University Press, 1999.

Mauss, Marcel. *The Gift: The Form and Reason for Exchange in Archaic Societies*. Trans. W.D. Halls. London: Routledge, 1990.

Mawer, Simon. *The Glass Room*. London: Little, Brown, 2009.

May, Elaine Tyler. 'Ambivalent Dreams: Women and Home after World War II.' *Journal of Women's History* 13 / 3 (2001): 151–2.

May, Jon. 'Of Nomads and Vagrants: Single Homelessness and Narratives of Home as Place.' *Environment and Planning D: Society and Space* 18 / 6 (2000): 737–59.

McCarthy, Christine. 'Toward a Definition of Interiority.' *Space and Culture* 8 / 2 (2005): 112–25.

McClatchy, J.D., and Erica Lennard. *American Writers at Home*. New York: Library of America, in Association with Vendome Press, 2004.

McClaugherty, Martha Crabill. 'Household Art: Creating the Artistic Home, 1868–1893.' *Winterthur Portfolio* 18 / 1 (1983): 1–26.

McClintock, Anne. *Imperial Leather: Race, Gender, and Sexuality in the Colonial Conquest*. New York: Routledge, 1995.

McDannell, Colleen. 'Parlor Piety: The Home as Sacred Space in Protestant America.' In Jessica H. Foy and Thomas J. Schlereth, eds., *American Home Life, 1880–1930: A Social History of Spaces and Services*, 162–89. Knoxville, TN: University of Tennessee Press, 1992.

McDowell, Linda. 'Women, Gender and the Organization of Space.' In Derek Gregory and Rex Walford, eds., *Horizons in Human Geography*, 131–51. London: Macmillan, 1989.

– *Undoing Place? A Geographical Reader*. London: Arnold, 1997.

– *Gender, Identity and Place: Understanding Feminist Geographies*. Minneapolis, MN: University of Minnesota Press, 1999.

– 'Rethinking Place: Thoughts on Spaces of the Home, Absence, Presence, New Connections and New Anxieties.' *Home Cultures* 4 / 2 (2007): 129–46.

McDowell, Linda, and Doreen Massey. 'A Woman's Place?' In Doreen Massey and James Allen, eds., *Geography Matters! A Reader*, 128–47. Cambridge: Cambridge University Press, 1984.

McDowell, Linda, Diane Perrons, Collette Fagan, Kevin Ward, and Katherine Ray. 'Women's Paid Work and Moral Economies of Care.' *Social and Cultural Geography* 6 (2005): 145–63.

McKay, Sherry. '"Urban Housekeeping" and Keeping the Modern House.' Special Issue, 'Domestic Spaces,' ed. Kathy Mezei. *BC Studies*, no. 140 (Winter 2003): 11–38.

McKellar, Susie, and Penny Sparke, eds. *Interior Design and Identity*. Manchester: Manchester University Press, 2004.

McKeon, Michael. *The Secret History of Domesticity: Public, Private, and the Division of Knowledge*. Baltimore, MD: Johns Hopkins University Press, 2005.

McKnight, Natalie. 'Playing House: The Poetics of Dickens's Domestic Spaces.' *Dickens Quarterly* 20 / 3 (2003): 172–83.

McLeod, Mary. 'Furniture and Femininity.' Special Issue, 'Corbusier 100.' *Architectural Review* 181 / 1079 (1987): 43–6.

Mendelson, Cheryl. *Home Comforts: The Art and Science of Keeping House*. New York: Scribner's, 1999.

Merleau-Ponty, Maurice. *Phenomenology of Perception*. Trans. Colin Smith. London: Routledge and Kegan Paul, 1962.

Metcalf, Thomas. *An Imperial Vision: Indian Architecture and India's Raj*. Berkeley, CA: University of California Press, 1989.

Metraux, Guy P.R. 'Ancient Housing: "Oikos" and "Domus" in Greece and Rome.' *Journal of the Society of Architectural Historians* 58 / 3 (1999): 392–405.

Mezei, Kathy. 'The House of All Sorts: Domestic Spaces in British Columbia.' Special Issue, 'Domestic Spaces,' ed. Kathy Mezei. *BC Studies*, no. 140 (Winter 2003): 3–9.

Mezei, Kathy, and Chiara Briganti. 'Reading the House: A Literary Perspective.' Forum: 'Domestic Space,' eds. Kathy Mezei and Chiara Briganti. *Signs: Journal of Women in Culture and Society* 27 / 3 (2002): 837–46.

Miller, Daniel. *The Comfort of Things*. Cambridge: Polity, 2008.

Miller, Daniel, ed. *Home Possessions: Material Culture behind Closed Doors*. Oxford: Berg, 2001.

Mitchell, Katharyne. 'Conflicting Landscapes of Dwelling and Democracy in Canada.' In Stephen Cairns, ed., *Drifting: Architecture and Memory*, 142–64. Oxford: Taylor and Francis, 2003.

MoDA [Musem of Domestic Design and Architecture]. *Little Palaces: House and Home in the Inter-War Suburbs*. London: Middlesex University Press, 2003.

Moore, Charles, Kathyrn Smith, and Peter Becker, eds. *'Home Sweet Home': American Domestic Vernacular Architecture*. New York: Rizzoli, 1983.

Moran, Joe. 'Housing, Memory and Everyday Life in Contemporary Britain.' *Cultural Studies* 18 / 4 (2004): 607–27.

Morley, David. 'Heimat, Modernity, and Exile.' In *Home Territories: Media, Mobility and Identity*, 31–55. London: Routledge, 2000.

– 'What's "Home" Got to Do with It? Contradictory Dynamics in the Domestication of Technology and the Dislocation of Domesticity.' *European Journal of Cultural Studies* 6 / 4 (2003): 435–58.

Morley, David, and Kevin Robins. *Spaces of Identity: Global Media, Electronic Landscapes, and Cultural Boundaries*. London: Routledge, 1995.

Morris, Jan. *Stones of the Empire: The Buildings of the Raj*. Oxford: Oxford University Press, 1986.

Morse, Edward S. *Japanese Homes and Their Surroundings*. Tokyo: Tuttle, 1972.

Motz, Marilyn Ferris, and Pat Browne, eds. *Making the American Home: Middle-Class Women and Domestic Material Culture, 1840–1940*. Bowling Green, OH: Bowling Green State University Popular Press, 1990.

Mudge, Jean McClure. *Emily Dickinson and the Image of Home*. Amherst, MA: University of Massachusetts Press, 1975.

Mugerauer, Robert. 'Toward an Architectural Vocabulary: The Porch as a Between.' In David Seamon, ed., *Dwelling, Seeing, and Designing: Toward a Phenomenological Ecology*, 103–28. Albany, NY: State University of New York Press, 1993.

Murakami, Takashi. *Privacy versus Mass Media*. Tokyo: Gakuyo Shobo, 1996.

Muthesius, Hermann. *The English House*. Trans. Janet Seligman. London: Crosby Lockwood Staples, 1979.

Muthesius, Stefan. *The Poetic Home: Designing the 19th Century Domestic Interior*. London: Thames and Hudson, 2009.

Myerson, Julie. *Home: The Story of Everyone Who Ever Lived in Our House*. London: HarperCollins, 2004.

Naficy, Hamid, ed. *Home, Homeland, Exile*. London: Routledge, 1999.

Nash, Paul. *Room and Book*. New York: Scribner, 1932.

Nash, Suzanne, ed. *Home and Its Dislocations in Nineteenth-Century France*. Albany, NY: State University of New York Press, 1993.

Naylor, Gillian. 'History of Taste 4: Modernism: Threadbare or Heroic?' *Architectural Review* 162 / 966 (1977): 107–11.

Neill, William J.V. *Urban Planning and Cultural Identity*. New York: Routledge, 2004.

Nicholson, Basil D. 'The Architectural Consequences of Women.' *Architectural Review* 72 / 431 (1932): 119–20.

Nicolin, Pierluigi, ed. 'L'Inquieto Spazio domestico / Disputed Domestic Space.' Special Issue. *Lotus International* 44 (1984).

Noussia, Antonia. 'The use of Domestic Space by Migrants on a Greek Island: Transformation or Translocation of Cultures?' *Built Environment* 30 / 1 (2004): 60–75.

Ochs, Vanessa L. 'What Makes a Jewish Home Jewish?' *Cross Currents: The Journal of the Association for Religion and Intellectual Life* 49 / 4 (1999 / 2000): 491–510.

Oliver, Paul. *Dwellings: The House across the World*. Oxford: Phaidon, 1987.

Olwig, Karen Fog. 'Cultural Sites: Sustaining a Home in a Deterritorialised World.' In Karen Fog Olwig and Kirsten Hastrup, eds., *Siting Culture: The Shifting Anthropological Object*, 17–38. London: Routledge, 1997.

Ota, Hirotaro. *Nihon Jutakushi* [A History of Japanese Housing]. Tokyo: Shokokusha, 1971.

Overing, Joanna, and Alan Passes, eds. *The Anthropology of Love and Anger: The Aesthetics of Conviviality in Native Amazonia*. London: Routledge, 2000.

Ozaki, Ritsuko. 'Society and Housing Form: Home-Centredness in England vs. Family-Centredness in Japan.' *Journal of Historical Sociology* 14 / 3 (2001): 337–57.

– 'Le péril de l'impur: L'organisation de l'espace dans les intérieurs japonais.' In Béatrice Collignon and Jean-François Staszak, eds., *Espaces domestiques: Construire, aménager et représenter*, 197–210. Rosny-sous-Bois: Bréal, 2003.

Ozaki, Ritsuko, and J.R. Lewes. 'Boundaries and the Meaning of Social Space: A Study of Japanese House Plans.' *Environment and Planning D: Society and Space* 24 / 1 (2006): 91–104.

Pader, Ellen Jane. 'Spatiality and Social Change: Domestic Space and Use in Mexico and the United States.' *American Anthropologist* 20 / 1 (1993): 114–37.

Palmer, Phyllis. *Domesticity and Dirt: Housewives and Domestic Servants in the United States, 1920–1945*. Philadelphia, PA: Temple University Press, 1989.

Parkins, Wendy. *Mobility and Modernity in Women's Novels, 1850s–1930s: Women Moving Dangerously*. New York: Palgrave Macmillan, 2008.

Parr, Joy. *Domestic Goods: The Material, the Moral, and the Economic in the Postwar Years*. Toronto: University of Toronto Press, 1999.

Pater, Walter. *The Renaissance: Studies in Art and Poetry*. London: Macmillan, 1873.

– *Appreciations, with an Essay on Style*. New York: Macmillan, 1903.

Pattison, Mary. *Principles of Domestic Engineering: Or the What, Why and How of a Home*. New York: Trow Press, 1915.

Pearlman, Mickey. *A Place Called Home: Twenty Writing Women Remember*. New York: St Martin's Press, 1996.

Peel, Dorothy Constance ('Mrs C.S. Peel'). 'The Nurseries and the Schoolroom.' In *The New Home: Treating of the Arrangement, Decoration and Furnishing of a House of Medium Size to Be Maintained by a Moderate Income*, 208–20. London: Archibald Constable, 1898.

Pennartz, Paul. J.J., and Anke Niehof. *The Domestic Domain: Chances, Choices, and Strategies of Family Households*. Aldershot: Ashgate, 2004.

Pennell, Sara. '"Pots and Pans History": The Material Culture of the Kitchen in Early Modern England.' *Journal of Design History* 11 / 3 (1998): 201–16.

Penner, Barbara, and Charles Rice, eds. 'Constructing the Interior.' Special Issue. *Journal of Architecture* 9 / 3 (2004).

Percival, John. 'Domestic Spaces: Uses and Meanings in the Daily Lives of Older People.' *Ageing and Society* 22 (2002): 729–49.

Perec, Georges. *Espèces d'espace*. Paris: Galilée, 1974–2000.

Pérez-Gómez, Alberto. *Built upon Love: Architectural Longing after Ethics and Aesthetics*. Cambridge, MA: MIT Press, 2006.

Perin, Constance. *Everything in Its Place: Social Order and Land Use in America*. Princeton, NJ: Princeton University Press, 1977.

Petersen, Anna K. C. *New Zealanders at Home: A Cultural History of Domestic Interiors, 1814–1914*. Dunedin: Otago University Press, 2001.

Pevsner, Nikolaus. *The Building of England Series*. Harmondsworth: Penguin, 1952–1983.

– *Pioneers of Modern Design*. Harmondsworth: Penguin, 1960.

– 'The Architectural Setting of Jane Austen's Novels.' *Journal of the Warburg and Courtauld Institutes* 31 (1968): 404–22.

Pink, Sarah. *Home Truths: Gender, Domestic Objects and Everyday Life*. Oxford: Berg, 2004.

Pitt, Kathy. 'Being a New Capitalist Mother.' *Discourse and Society* 13 (2002): 251–67.

Pocius, Gerald L. '"Interior Motives": Rooms, Objects, and Meaning in Atlantic Canada.' *Material History Bulletin* 15 (1982): 5–9.

Poe, Edgar Allan. 'The Philosophy of Furniture.' [1840]. In James A. Harrison, ed., *The Complete Works of Edgar Allan Poe*, vol. 14, *Essays and Miscellanies*, 101–9. New York: AMS Press, 1965.

Ponsonby, Margaret. *Stories from Home: English Domestic Interiors, 1750–1850*. Aldershot: Ashgate, 2007.

Porteous, John Douglas. 'Home: The Territorial Core.' *Geographical Review* 66/4 (1976): 383–90.

Porteous, John Douglas, and Sandra Smith. *Domicide: The Global Destruction of Home*. Montreal and Kingston: McGill-Queen's University Press, 2001.

Potvin, John, and Alla Myzelev, eds. *Fashion, Interior Design and the Contours of Modern Identity*. Surrey: Ashgate, 2010.

Pratt, Geraldine. 'The House as an Expression of Social Worlds.' In James S. Duncan, ed., *Housing and Identity: Cross-Cultural Perspectives*, 137–75. London: Croom Helm, 1981.

Praz, Mario. *An Illustrated History of Interior Decoration: From Pompeii to Art Nouveau*. Trans. W. Weaver. New York: Thames and Hudson, 1982.

Preston, Julieanna. *Interior Atmospheres*. Chichester: Wiley, 2008.

Quiney, Anthony. *House and Home: A History of the Small English House*. London: BBC, 1997.

Raglan, Lord. *The Temple and the House*. New York: Norton, 1964.

Raibmon, Paige. 'Living on Display: Colonial Visions of Aboriginal Domestic Spaces.' Special Issue, 'Domestic Spaces,' ed. Kathy Mezei. *BC Studies*, no. 140 (Winter 2003): 69–89.

Rapoport, Amos. *House Form and Culture*. Englewood Cliffs, NJ: Prentice–Hall, 1969.

Rapoport, Amos, ed. *The Mutual Interaction of People and Their Built Environment*. The Hague: Mouton, 1976.

Rapport, Nigel, and Andrew Dawson. *Migrants of Identity: Perceptions of Home in a World of Movement*. Oxford: Berg, 1998.

Rauchbauer, Otto, ed. *Ancestral Voices: The Big Houses in Anglo-Irish Literature*. Hildesheim: Olms, 1992.

Ravetz, Alison. *The Place of Home: English Domestic Environments, 1914–2000*. London: Spon, 1995.

Rawlings, Irene. *Portable Houses*. Layton, UT: Gibbs Smith, 2004.

Reed, Christopher. *Bloomsbury Rooms: Modernism, Subculture, and Domesticity*. London: Yale University Press, 2004.

– 'Taking Amusement Seriously: Modern Design in the Twenties.' In Penny Sparke, Anne Massey, Trevor Keeble, and Brenda Martin, eds., *Designing the Modern Interior: From the Victorians to Today*, 79–93. Oxford: Berg, 2009.

Reed, Christopher, ed. *Not at Home: The Suppression of Domesticity in Modern Art and Architecture*. New York: Thames and Hudson, 1996.

Reimer, Mavis, and Anne Rusnak. 'The Representation of Home in Canadian Children's Literature / La Representation du chez-soi dans la littérature de jeunnesse canadienne.' *Canadian Children's Literature / Littérature Canadienne pour la jeunesse* 26 / 4 (2000 / 2001): 9–46.

Reinders, Leeke, and Marco Van Der Land. 'Mental Geographies of Home and Place: Introduction to the Special Issue.' *Housing, Theory and Society* 25 / 1 (2008): 1–13.

Rendall, Jane, *The Pursuit of Pleasure: Gender, Space and Architecture in Regency London*. London: Rutgers University Press, 2002.

Rendall, Jane, Barbara Penner, and Iain Borden, eds. *Gender Space Architecture: An Interdisciplinary Introduction*. London: Routledge, 2000.

Reus, Teresa Gómez, and Aránzazu Usandizaga, eds. *Inside Out: Women Negotiating, Subverting, Appropriating Public and Private Space*. Amsterdam: Rodopi, 2008.

Reveyron, Nicholas. 'Houses and Principal Urban Houses: the Domestic Space of Toledo at the End of the Middle Ages.' *Moyen Age* 112 / 2 (2006): 421–3.

Reynolds, Matthew. *Designs for a Happy Home: A Novel in Ten Interiors*. London: Bloomsbury, 2009.

Rice, Charles. *The Emergence of the Interior: Architecture, Modernity, Domesticity*. London: Routledge, 2007.

Rich, B. Ruby. 'The Party Line: Gender and Technology in the Home.' In Jennifer Terry and Melodie Calvert, eds., *Processed Lives: Gender and Technology in Everyday Life*, 221–31. London: Routledge, 1996.

Richardson, A.E., and C. Lovett Gill. *London Houses from 1660 to 1820*. London: B.T. Batsford, 1911.

Richter, Amy G. *Home on the Rails: Women, the Railroad and the Rise of Public Domesticity*. Chapel Hill, NC: University of North Carolina Press, 2005.

Riedinger, Anita R. '"Home" in Old English Poetry.' *Neuphilologische Mitteilungen: Bulletin de la societé neophilologique / Bulletin of the Modern Language Society* 96 / 1 (1995): 51–9.

Riley, Terence. *The Un-Private House*. New York: Museum of Modern Art, 1999.

Robertson, Leslie. 'Taming Space: Drug Use, HIV, and Homemaking in Downtown Eastside Vancouver.' *Gender, Place and Culture* 14 / 5 (2007): 527–49.

Robertson, Lisa. *Occasional Work and Seven Walks from the Office for Soft Architecture*. Astoria, OR: Clear Cut Press, 2002.

Rodríguez, Ileana. *Home, Garden, Nation: Space, Gender and Ethnicity in Postcolonial Latin American Literatures by Women*. Durham, NC: Duke University Press, 1994.

Romines, Ann. *The Home Plot: Women, Writing and Domestic Ritual*. Amherst, MA: University of Massachusetts Press, 1992.

Rose, Gillian. 'Family Photographs and Domestic Spacings: A Case Study.' *Transactions of the Institute of British Geographers* 28 / 1 (2003): 5–18.

Rosedahl, Else. 'The Scandinavians at Home.' In David M. Wilson, ed., *The Northern World: The History and Heritage of Northern Europe, AD 400–1100*, 127–58. New York: H.N. Abrams, 1980.

Rosenberg, Jakob, Seymour Slive, and E.H. ter Kuile, eds. *Dutch Art and Architecture, 1600–1800*. Harmondsworth: Penguin, 1966.

Rosner, Victoria. 'Home Fires: Doris Lessing, Colonial Architecture, and the Reproduction of Mothering.' *Tulsa Studies in Women's Literature* 18 / 1 (1999): 59–89.

– *Modernism and the Architecture of Private Life*. New York: Columbia University Press, 2005.

Rothschild, Joan, ed. *Design and Feminism: Re-Visioning Spaces, Places, and Everyday Things*. New Brunswick, NJ: Rutgers University Press, 1999.

Rowles, Graham D., and Habib Chaudhury. *Home and Identity in Late Life: International Perspectives*. New York: Springer, 2005.

Rowling, J.K. *Harry Potter and the Order of the Phoenix*. London: Bloomsbury, 2004 [2003].

Rudikoff, Sonya. *Ancestral Houses: Virginia Woolf and the Aristocracy*. Palo Alto, CA: Society for the Promotion of Science and Scholarship, 1999.

Ryan, Deborah. *The Ideal Home through the Twentieth Century*. London: Hazar, 1997.

Ryan, Nora. *The Apartment Question: The Avant-garde and the Problem of the Domestic Interior in 1920s Russia*. Charleston, NC: BiblioBazaar LLC, 2011.

Rybczynski, Witold. 'Intimacy and Privacy.' *In Home: A Short History of an Idea*, 14–49. New York: Viking, 1986.

Rykwert, Joseph. 'A House for the Soul.' In *On Adam's House in Paradise: The Idea of the Primitive Hut in Architectural History*, 183–92. Cambridge, MA: MIT Press, 1981.

– 'House and Home.' In Arien Mack, ed., *Home: A Place in the World*, 47–58. New York: New York University Press, 1993.

Sand, Jordan. *House and Home in Modern Japan: Architecture, Domestic Space, and Bourgeois Culture, 1880–1930*. Cambridge, MA: Harvard University Asia Center; distributed by Harvard University Press, 2003.

Saumarez Smith, Charles. *Eighteenth-Century Decoration: Design and the Domestic Interior in England*. London: H.N. Abrams, 1993.

Saunders, Peter. '"The Meaning of Home" in Contemporary English Culture.' *Housing Studies* 4 / 3 (1989): 177–92.

Scarce, Jennifer. *Domestic Cultures in the Middle East: An Exploration of the Household Interior*. Edinburgh: National Museums of Scotland, 1996.

Schiach, Morag. 'Modernism, the City and the Domestic Interior.' *Home Cultures* 2 (2005): 251–68.

Scolnicov, Hanna. *Woman's Theatrical Space*. Cambridge: Cambridge University Press, 1994.

Seddon, Jill, and Suzette Wordon, eds. *Women Designing: Redefining Design in Britain between the Wars*. Brighton: University of Brighton Press, 1994.

Seeley, John R., R. Alexander Sim, and Elizabeth W. Loosley. *Crestwood Heights: A Study of the Culture of Suburban Life*. Toronto: University of Toronto Press, 1956.

Segalen, Martine. 'The Salon des arts *ménagers*, 1923–1983: A French Effort to Instill the Virtues of Home and the Norms of Good Taste.' *Journal of Design History* 7 / 4 (1994): 267–75.

Sennett, Richard. *The Corrosion of Character: The Personal Consequences of Work in the New Capitalism*. New York: Norton, 1998.

Serematakis, Nadia, ed. *The Senses Still: Perception and Memory as Material Culture in Modernity*. Boulder, CO: Westview, 1994.

Sessa, Kristina. 'Holy Households: Domestic Space, Property and Power.' *Journal of Early Christian Studies* 15 / 2 (2007): 129–30.

Sharr, Adam. *Heidegger's Hut*. Cambridge, MA: MIT Press, 2006.

Shone, Richard. 'A Cast in Time.' In James Lingwood, ed., *Rachel Whiteread: House*, 50–61. London: Phaidon, 1995.

Shoul, Michael. 'The Spatial Arrangements of Ordinary English Homes.' *Environment and Behaviour* 25 / 1 (1993): 22–69.

Shove, Elizabeth. *Comfort, Cleanliness and Convenience: The Social Organization of Normality*. Oxford: Berg, 2003.

Silverstone, Roger, and Eric Hirsch. *Consuming Technologies: Media and Information in Domestic Spaces*. London: Routledge, 1992.

Simmel, Georg. 'The Bridge and the Door.' Trans. and ed. Michael Kaern. *Qualitative Sociology* 17 / 4 (1994): 407–13.

Sixsmith, Judith. 'The Meaning of Home: An Exploratory Study of Environmental Experience.' *Journal of Environmental Psychology* 6 / 4 (1986): 281–98.

Smith, Kathryn, and Peter Becker. *Domestic Vernacular Architecture*. Los Angeles, CA: Craft and Folk Art Museum, 1983.

Smith, Neil, and Cindi Katz. *Grounding Metaphors: Towards a Spatialized Politics*. New York: Princeton Architectural Press, 1992.

Smith, Susan, et al. *International Encyclopedia of Housing and Home*. 7 vols. Oxford: Elsevier, 2012.

Smyth, Gerry, and Jo Croft, eds. *Our House: The Representations of Domestic Space in Modern Culture*. Amsterdam: Rodopi, 2006.

Soja, Edward. *Postmodern Geographies: The Reassertion of Space in Critical Social Theory*. London: Verso, 1989.

Somerville, Peter. 'The Social Construction of Home.' *Journal of Architecture and Planning Research* 14 / 3 (1997): 226–45.

Sopher, David E. 'The Landscape of Home: Myth, Experience, Social Meaning.' In Donald William Meinig, ed., *The Interpretation of Ordinary Landscapes: Geographical Essays*, 129–49. New York: Oxford University Press, 1979.

Sorensen, Knut H., and Merete Lie. *Making Technology Our Own: Domesticating Technology in Everyday Life*. Oslo: Scandinavian University Press, 1996.

Southerton, Dale. 'Consuming Kitchens: Taste, Context and Identity Formation.' *Journal of Consumer Culture* 1 / 2 (2001): 179–203.

Spain, Daphne. *Gendered Space*. Chapel Hill, NC: University of North Carolina Press, 1992.

Sparke, Penny. *As Long as It's Pink: The Sexual Politics of Taste*. London: Pandora, 1995.

– *The Modern Interior*. London: Reaktion Books, 2008.

Sparke, Penny, and Susie McKeller, eds. *Interior Design and Identity*. Manchester: Manchester University Press, 2004.

Sparke, Penny, Anne Massey, Trevor Keeble, and Brenda Martin, eds. *Designing the Modern Interior: From the Victorians to Today*. Oxford: Berg, 2009.

Spigel, Lynn. 'From Domestic Space to Outer Space: The 1960s Fantastic Family Sit-Com.' In Constance Penley, Elisabeth Lyon, Lynn Spigel, and Janet Bergstrom, eds., *Close Encounters: Film, Feminism, and Science Fiction*, 205–35. Minneapolis, MN: University of Minnesota Press, 1991.

– *Make Room for TV*. Chicago, IL: University of Chicago Press, 1992.

– 'Media Homes: Then and Now.' *International Journal of Cultural Studies* 4 / 4 (2001): 385–411.

– *Welcome to the Dreamhouse*. Durham, NC: Duke University Press, 2001.

Stamp, Gavin. *Edwin Lutyens: Country Houses: From the Archives of Country Life*. New York: Monacelli, 2001.

Stamp, Gavin, and André Goulancourt. *The English House, 1860–1914: The Flowering of English Domestic Architecture*. Chicago, IL: University of Chicago Press, 1986.

Star, Susan Leigh. 'From Hestia to Home Page: Feminism and the Concept of Home in Cyberspace.' In David Bell and Barbara M. Kennedy, eds., *The Cybercultures Reader*, 632–43. London: Routledge, 2000.

Stea, David. 'House and Home: Identity, Dichotomy, or Dialectic? (With Special Reference to Mexico).' In David N. Benjamin, ed., *The Home: Words,*

Interpretations, Meanings, and Environments, 181–201. Aldershot: Ashgate; Brookfield, VT: Avebury, 1995.

Steedman, Carolyn. *The Tidy House: Little Girls Writing*. London: Virago, 1982.

– *Landscape for a Good Woman: A Story of Two Lives*. London: Virago, 1986.

– *Strange Dislocations: Childhood and the Idea of Human Interiority, 1780–1930*. Cambridge, MA: Harvard University Press, 1995.

Stephenson, Marcia. 'The Architectural Relationship between Gender, Race, and the Bolivian State.' In Ileana Rodríguez, ed., *The Latin American Subaltern Studies Reader*, 367–82. Durham, NC: Duke University Press, 2001.

Stoler, Ann Laura. *Haunted by Empire: Geographies of Intimacy in North American History*. Durham, NC: Duke University Press, 2006.

Stoner, Jill. *Toward a Minor Architecture*. Cambridge, MA: MIT Press, 2012.

Stroud, Jonathan. *The Amulet of Samarkand*. London: Corgi, 2004 [2003].

– *The Golem's Eye*. London: Corgi, 2004.

– *Ptolemy's Gate*. London: Corgi, 2006 [2005].

Sturrock, June. *'Heaven and Home': Charlotte M. Yonge's Domestic Fiction and the Victorian Debate over Women*. Victoria, BC: University of Victoria, 1995.

Styles, John, and Amanda Vickery, eds. *Gender, Taste and Material Culture in Britain and North America, 1700–1830*. London: Yale University Press, 2007.

Sudjic, Deyan. *The Language of Things: Design, Luxury, Fashion, Art: How We Are Seduced by the Objects Around Us*. Harmondsworth: Penguin, 2009.

Sudjic, Deyan, and Tulga Beyerle. *Home: The Twentieth-Century House*. London: Laurence King, 1999.

Sundaram, P.S.A. 'Pavement Dwellers in Bombay.' *Open House International* 13/2 (1988): 37–40.

Tange, Andrea Kaston. *Architectural Identities: Domesticity, Literature and the Victorian Middle Class*. Toronto: University of Toronto Press, 2010.

Taylor, Mark, and Julieanna Preston. *Intimus: Interior Design Theory Reader*. Chichester: Wiley, 2006.

Teyssot, Georges. '"Water and Gas on All Floors": Notes on the Extraneousness of the Home.' Special Issue, 'L'inquieto spazio domestico / Disputed Domestic Space,' ed. Pierluigi Nicolin. *Lotus International* 44 (1984): 82–93.

– 'The Disease of the Domicile.' *Assemblage* 6 (June 1988): 72–97.

Teyssot, Georges, ed. *The American Lawn*. New York: Princeton Architectural Press, 1999.

Thiel, Elizabeth. *The Fantasy of Family: Nineteenth-Century Children's Literature and the Myth of the Domestic Ideal*. New York: Routledge, 2008.

Thompson, Eleanor, ed. *The American Home: Material Culture, Domestic Space, and Family Life*. Winterthur, DE: Winterthur Museum; Hanover, NH: University Press of New England, 1998.

Thornton, Peter. *Authentic Décor: The Domestic Interior, 1620–1920*. London: Weidenfeld and Nicolson, 1984.

Tillotson, G.H.R. *The Tradition of Indian Architecture: Continuity, Controversy and Change since 1850*. New Haven, CT: Yale University Press, 1989.

Titus, Mary. 'The Dining Room Door Swings Both Ways: Food, Race, and Domestic Space in the Nineteenth-Century South.' In Anne Goodwyn Jones and Susan V. Donaldson, eds., *Haunted Bodies: Gender and Southern Texts*, 243–56. Charlottesville, VA: University Press of Virginia, 1997.

Todd, Dorothy, and Raymond Mortimer. *The New Interior Decoration: An Introduction to Its Principles, and International Survey of Its Methods*. New York: Charles Scribner's; London: B.T. Batsford, 1929.

Todd, Pamela. *Bloomsbury at Home*. New York: H.N. Abrams, 1999.

Tognoli, Jerome. 'Differences in Women's and Men's Responses to Domestic Space.' *Sex Roles: A Journal of Research* 6 / 6 (1999): 847–56.

Tosh, John. *A Man's Place: Masculinity and the Middle-Class Home in Victorian England*. London: Yale University Press, 1999.

Tristram, Philippa. *Living Space in Fact and Fiction*. London: Routledge, 1989.

Tuan, Yi-Fu. *Topophilia: A Study of Environmental Perception, Attitudes, and Values*. Englewood Cliffs, NJ: Prentice-Hall, 1974.

Valentine, Gill. *Social Geographies: Space and Society*. New York: Prentice-Hall, 2001.

Valle, Jorge Saravia. *Planificación de aldeas rurales*. La Paz: Juventud, 1986.

van Herck, Karina. 'First Interlude: On the Nuances of Historical Emancipation.' *Journal of Architecture* 7 / 3 (2002): 245–47.

– 'Second Interlude: On the House from All Sorts of Angles.' *Journal of Architecture* 7 / 3 (2002): 281–86.

– 'Epilogue: On Meaning and Experience (or Images Versus Practices).' *Journal of Architecture* 7 / 3 (2002): 297–301.

Varey, Simon. *Space and the Eighteenth-Century English Novel*. Cambridge: Cambridge University Press, 1990.

Venturi, Robert, Denise Scott Brown, and Steven Izenour. *Learning from Las Vegas*. Cambridge, MA: MIT Press, 1972.

Verschaffel, Bart. 'The Meanings of Domesticity.' *Journal of Architecture* 7 / 3 (2002): 287–96.

Vickery, Amanda. *Behind Closed Doors: At Home in Georgian England*. New Haven, CT: Yale University Press, 2009.

Vidler, Anthony. *The Architectural Uncanny: Essays in the Modern Unhomely*. Cambridge, MA: MIT Press, 1992.

– *Warped Space: Art, Architecture and Anxiety in Modern Culture*. Cambridge, MA: MIT Press, 2002.

Virilio, Paul. *Lost Dimension*. New York: Semiotext(e), 1991.

Vitruvius. *The Ten Books on Architecture*. Trans. Morris Hicky Morgan. Cambridge, MA: Harvard University Press, 1914; reprinted New York: Dover, 1960.

– *De Architectura*. Trans. Frank Granger. Cambridge, MA: Harvard University Press, 1955.

Von Frisch, Karl. *Animal Architecture*. London: Hutchinson, 1975.

Von Uexküll, Jakob. 'A Stroll through the Worlds of Animals and Men: A Picture Book of Invisible Worlds.' In Claire H. Schiller, ed., *Instinctive Behavior: The Development of a Modern Concept*, 5–80. New York: International Universities Press, 1957.

Waddey, Lucy. 'Home in Children's Fiction: Three Patterns.' *Children's Literature Association Quarterly* 8 / 1 (1983): 13–15.

Wagner, George. 'The Lair of the Bachelor.' In Debra Coleman, Elizabeth Danze, and Carol Henderson, eds., *Architecture and Feminism*, 183–220. New York: Princeton Architectural Press, 1996.

Walker, Lynne. 'Locating the Global / Rethinking the Local: Suffrage Politics, Architecture, and Space.' *Women's Studies Quarterly* 34 / 1–2 (2006): 174–96.

Wall, Cynthia. 'Gendering Rooms: Domestic Architecture and Literary Arts.' *Eighteenth-Century Fiction* 5 / 5 (1993): 349–72.

– *The Literary and Cultural Spaces of Restoration London*. Cambridge: Cambridge University Press, 1998.

Ward, Peter. *A History of Domestic Space: Privacy and the Canadian Home*. Seattle, WA: University of Washington Press, 1999.

Wardaugh, Julie. 'The Unaccommodated Woman: Home, Homelessness and Identity.' *Sociological Review* 47 / 1 (1999): 91–109.

Watkins, Trevor. 'The Origins of House and Home?' *World Archeology* 21 / 3 (1990): 336–47.

Watson, Janell. *Literature and Material Culture from Balzac to Proust: The Collection and Consumption of Curiosities*. Cambridge: Cambridge University Press, 1999.

Weinthal, Lois. *Toward a New Interior: An Anthology of Interior Design Theory*. New York: Princeton Architectural Press, 2011.

Werner, Carol. 'Home Interiors: A European Perspective.' Special Issue. *Environment and Behaviour* 19 / 2 (1987).

Wharton, Edith, and Ogden Codman, Jr. 'Bric-à-Brac.' In *The Decoration of Houses*, 182–90. New York: Charles Scribner's Sons; London: B.T. Batsford, 1898.

Wigley, Mark. 'Heidegger's House: The Violence of the Domestic.' In M. Lewis, A. Payne, and T. Taylor, eds., *Public* 6, 93–118. Toronto: Public Access, 1992.

– 'Untitled: The Housing of Gender.' In Beatriz Colomina, ed., *Sexuality and Space*, 326–89. Princeton, NJ: Princeton University Press, 1992.

– *The Architecture of Deconstruction: Derrida's Haunt*. Cambridge, MA: MIT Press, 1996.

Wiley, Catherine, and Fiona Barnes R., eds. *Homemaking: Women Writers and the Politics and Poetics of Home*. New York: Garland, 1996.

Wilk, Christopher, 'Frankfurt Kitchen, 1926–7. Designed by Grete Lihotsky (Margarete Schütte-Lihotsky; 1897 Vienna – 2000 Vienna).' In Christopher Wilk, ed., *Modernism: 1914–1939, Designing a New World*, 80–1. London: Victoria & Albert Publications, 2006.

Wilk, Christopher, ed. *Modernism: 1914–1939, Designing a New World*. London: Victoria & Albert Publications, 2006.

Williams, Raymond. *Television: Technology and Cultural Form*. London: Fontana, 1974.

Williams, Tony. 'Thresholds of Desire and Domestic Space in Nineteenth-Century French Fiction.' In Fran Lloyd and Catherine O'Brien, eds., *Secret Spaces, Forbidden Places: Rethinking Culture*, 39–49. New York: Berghahn, 2000.

Wilson, Kristina. *Livable Modernism: Interior Decorating and Design during the Great Depression*. New Haven, CT: Yale University Press, 2004.

Wisker, Gina. '"Honey, I'm Home!" Splintering the Fabrication in Domestic Horror.' *FEMSPEC: An Interdisciplinary Feminist Journal Dedicated to Critical and Creative Work in the Realms of Science Fiction, Fantasy, Magical Realism, Surrealism, Myth, Folklore, and Other Supernatural Genres* 4 / 1 (2002): 108–20.

Wolf, Virginia L. 'From Myth to the Wake of Home: Literary Houses.' *Children's Literature: Annual of the Modern Language Association Division on Children's Literature and the Children's Literature Association* 18 (1990): 53–67.

Wolfe, Tom. *From Bauhaus to Our House*. New York: Farrar Straus Giroux, 1981.

Wolkowitz, Carol. *Bodies at Work*. London: Sage, 2006.

Wood, Sarah, ed. 'Home and Family.' Special Issue. *Angelaki* 2 / 1 (1995).

Woodward, Servanne, ed. *Public Space of the Domestic Sphere / Espace public de la sphère domestique*. London, ON: Mestengo; 1997.

Worsley, Lucy. *If Walls Could Talk: An Intimate History of the Home*. London: Faber and Faber, 2011.

Wright, Frank Lloyd. 'The Cardboard House.' In *Frank Lloyd Wright: Collected Writings, Including an Autobiography*. Ed. Bruce Brooks Pfeiffer, vol. 2, 51–9. New York: Rizzoli and the Frank Lloyd Wright Foundation, 1992.

Wright, Gwendolyn. *Building the Dream: A Social History of Housing in America*. Cambridge, MA: MIT Press, 1983.

– 'Domestic Architecture and the Cultures of Domesticity.' *Design Quarterly* 138 (1987): 12–19.

Wright, Lawrence. *Clean and Decent: The Fascinating History of the Bathroom and the Water-Closet*. London: Routledge and Kegan Paul, 1960.

Young, Iris Marion. 'House and Home: Feminist Variations on a Theme.' In *Intersecting Voices: Dilemmas of Gender, Political Philosophy, and Policy*, 134–64. Princeton, NJ: Princeton University Press, 1997.

Zelinksi, Vladimir. 'Architecture as a Tool of Social Transformation.' *Women and Revolution* 11 (Spring 1976): 6–14.

Zimm, Malin. 'Writers-in-Residence: Goncourt and Huysmans at Home without a Plot.' *Journal of Architecture* 9 / 3 (2004): 305–14.

Index

Aboriginal 12, 285, 289–93; American Indian Reservation 46; domestic space 289, 290; Kwa̱kwa̱ka'wakw people 291–93; longhouses 289

Adam, Robert and James 330–34

Adams, Annmarie 11, 121, 127–30

Africa 12, 41, 257, 294–300, 312, 360–62, *See also* Johannesburg; South Africa

Agnew, Jean-Christophe 11, 121, 133–35

Airport 244, 256

Alexander, Catherine 6, 12, 247, 268–72

Algeria 12, 152, 247, 259–263, *See also* Berber House; Kabyle House

Amazonia 18, 65–71

'Amusing style' 151, 164, 166–67, 168n3, *See also* modernism

Animals 17, 24, 31–35, 36–38, 41, 63, 78, 125, 137, 153, 185, 227, 231, 256–57, 264, 373

Animality 107; animal architecture 31; Ingold, Tim 31–35

Anthropology 3–4, 10, 28–29, 66, 291–93

Apartheid 12, 285, 294–300, 360

Apartments 74, 100–02, 108–11, 114–16, 126, 147–48, 207–08, 213, 230, 260–61, 266, 296, 312, 318, 331, 333–34, 336, 354; male apartment 159, 170–72; nineteenth-century apartment 108; *Playboy's* Penthouse Apartment 170–72; public apartments 353, *See also* flat; *maisons particulières*

Archetypes 69, 78, 138, 148, *See also* Jung, Carl

Architecture 4, 34–35, 77–78, 113, 128–29, 181, 230, 255, 265, 267–68, 303–05; 'animal architecture' 31; colonial 60; and concrete 104; democracy 267–68; Derrida 5; domestic 105, 111, 128–29, 160, 330–331, 357, 368–69; English 206; and gender 125, 151, 236–237; glass 148; and the human body 121, 123–24; and interior design 368–69; and literature 321–22, 326, 334, 338, 343–345, 346, 349, 353, 354; Le Corbusier 163, 300–301; monastic 204; and morality 125; of memory 260; residential 199; Roman 82, 203; secular 204; social 259–61; Soviet 116; uncanny 122, 145–46; vernacular 74

Art nouveau 103–04, 213

Ashenburg, Katherine 6, 11, 200, 221–24

Attics 17, 27, 335, 351, *See also* garret

Bachelard, Gaston 5, 8, 10–11, 15n21, 17, 19–21, 27, 73, 144, 148–49, 152, 243, 262, 346, 351, 367–68
Bachelors 165, 170–72, 175
Back room 294–300
Bahloul, Joëlle 6, 10–12, 152, 247, 259–64
Balcony 110–11, 168n7, 169, 266, 344, *See also* porch
Barthes, Roland 242, 304, 344
Bathing 73, 89, 92–93, 118–19, 221–24, 228, 296, 355
Baudrillard, Jean 6, 11, 199–200, 210–14, 285
Bauhaus 29–30, 235n3
Bathrooms 6, 11, 107, 118–19, 191, 200, 213, 221–23, 273, 297, 303–04, 318, 356, 364, *See also* toilet; water-closet
Bebel, August 74, 114–15
Bechdel, Alison 173–79
Bed, 33, 42, 86–87, 88–89, 97, 106, 118, 171, 176, 205, 210–12, 222, 224, 225–30, 262, 274, 296–97, 307, 311, 333, 352; bedding, 52, 93; deathbed 83; Emin, Tracey 13, *See also* bedroom
Bedroom, 6, 11, 48, 50–53, 81, 91–93, 105–07, 109–10, 118–19, 128, 169–71, 185, 200, 210, 221–22, 225–230, 239–40, 243, 303, 311, 335, 349, 356, 364–65; nursery 224, *See also* bed; sleeping-room
Bedsits, 176–77
Beecher, Catharine E. and Harriet Beecher Stowe 11, 114, 200, 217–20, 235n5, 238n1, 327
Beeton, Mrs Isabella 11, 200, 230–32
Belonging 6, 13, 24, 56, 79, 194, 265, 317, 319, 341; family 57; place-based 309; and postmodernity 309; queer, 174; unhomeliness 144
Benjamin, Walter 5, 8, 11, 74, 103–04, 142, 146n6, 251, 253–54, 351, 353, 361, 366
Berber House 11, 17, 35–39, *See also* Algeria; Kabyle House
Berger, John 311–12
Bhabha, Homi 5, 6, 8, 12, 322, 358–362, *See also* postcolonial
Birthing room 91, 127–28, *See also* lying-in room
Bloch, Ernst 141–42
Boarding-house 14n9, 177, 297, 344
Body 8–12, 18, 39, 53, 69, 77, 85–86, 121, 127–28, 148, 226, 238n1, 243, 269–71, 307, 328, 337–38, 364, 366, 375; and animals 31–33; commodified 122; and death 86, 366; female 8, 121; as house 123–27, 127–29, 269–71, 332, 348; hygiene 117, 221–23; and mind 18, 53, 124, 338; naked 228–30; social 180–82; and time 214
Bolivia 152, 180–85
Bonnard, Pierre 223, 307
Borzello, Frances 11, 73, 94–99
Bourdieu, Pierre 11, 17, 35–39
Bourgeois 60, 63–64, 73–74, 89, 103, 105, 111, 115, 122, 154, 156, 191, 163, 212, 251, 289, 322, 351, 368; apartment 109; fear 122, 134, 142; house 345, 353–55; ideology 350; interior 98, 144, 210, 213–14, 285, 356, 365; novel 351, 355
Bric-à-brac 214–17, *See also* object
Bridges 22, 95, 247, 249–51, 375; Hallway 376
Briganti, Chiara 12, 321, 325–330
Britain 7, 92 151–52, 161, 177; AIDS 178; bathrooms 222; contemporary 54, 369; modernism 163; queerness 174; society 54, 274, 276

Bronte House 168–69
Brothels 353
Bungalows 7, 18, 59–64, 123, 359
Burbank, Emily 8, 11, 121–22, 130–33

Cabinets 27, 109, 165–66, 168n10, 171, 208, 213, 215, 234, 236, 240, 244, 332
Campo, Juan Eduardo 11, 17, 40–44
Canada 239, 276, *See also* Downtown Eastside; Vancouver
Capitalism 7, 29, 115, 279, 342, 352
Carpets 97, 157, 199, 207–09, 274, 354–55
Caves 78, 136–137, 143, 256–58, 364–66; Lascaux 171
Ceiling 147, 205, 210, 230, 234, 273, 296, 323, 354, 375
Cellar 17, 19–21, 27, 84–87, 101,122, 136–37, 143, 204, 256, 341, 351
Cemeteries 42–43, 85–86
Chairs 78, 89, 112–13, 131, 142, 152, 164,187, 189, 209, 212, 215, 224, 227, 265–66, 269, 275, 306, 326, 328, 342, 350, 353–55, 371, 373; armchair 222, 274; rocking 266, 325
Chan, Patrick 6, 12, 248, 272, 278–83
Chandeliers 208, 354
Chase, Karen 12, 322, 335–339
Chaudhuri, Supriya 10, 12, 322, 351–57
Chests 27, 89, 118, 148, 205, 215, 224, 306
Chicago World Fair 285, 291, 292
Childbirth 127–30, 340
Child-care 57–58, 67, 114, 288
Children 7, 36, 42, 48, 50, 52–53, 55, 57, 63, 67–68, 87, 153, 155, 177, 190, 227, 292, 297, 300, 304, 316–18, 328, 360, 375; comfort 193–95, 200; drawings 123, 258–61; education 85, 92,114; games 78, 270–71; literature 322, 367–70; monasteries 85; moral development 60, 117, 229, 239; nurseries 208, 224–25; raising 18, 288, 304, 364; safety 316; spaces 36, 49, 270–71, 364; as spectral dwellers 326
Chimney 11, 199, 203–06, 230, 254
China 217, 219
Cieraad, Irene 6, 9–11, 200, 236–38, 327
Citizenship 54, 175, 180–81
Civilization 74, 113, 131, 144, 151, 216, 221, 228, 230, 248, 290, 302; *and Its Discontents* 151
Class 8, 56–58, 91–92, 101–02,142, 144, 158, 169, 176, 178, 218, 221, 227–29, 239, 248, 299, 303, 315, 354–55, 368; alienation 143; antagonism 56; boundaries 144; distinction 92, 102; hierarchies 73; middle 47–49, 57, 60, 74, 79, 97–98, 104, 118, 121, 127–29, 147, 157, 159, 174–78, 188, 200, 239, 276, 278–79, 289, 294, 312, 316, 327, 329–31, 334, 352, 363–64, 367; passenger 274–76; upper 41, 97, 101, 180, 182, 227–29, 237, 276, 331, 333, 334n4, 353; ruling 103, 105, 368; working 57–58,108, 147, 177–78, 185, 237, 299
Clocks 200, 214–15, 240, 352, 354
Closets 48, 200, 206, 335, 343; closet dramas 321; earth-closets 217–20; water-closet 220
Coffin 312, 314n17, 336
Cohen, Deborah 8, 11, 151, 157–59, 367
Colomina, Beatriz 6, 12, 247, 251–55
Colonialism 180, 289, 319
Comfort 8, 11,15n21, 19, 60, 89–90, 91, 96–7, 100, 105, 110, 126, 142–43, 154, 176, 185, 190–93, 196, 200, 225, 233, 242, 252–53, 262, 274–75, 295, 315, 342, 347, 363, 373; definition of 88–90; and privacy 11, 73, 97, 342

Cook, Matt 8, 11, 152, 173–79
Cooking 36–37, 63, 114, 116, 162, 170, 185, 188–89, 230, 232, 236, 271, 276
Corbin, Alain 11, 74, 105–08, 122, 200
Courtyard 36, 43, 74, 97, 109–10, 154, 187, 260, 262–63, 364, 375
Crowley, John E., 11, 199, 203–06
Crypts, 42, 342, *See also* mausoleum, tombs
Curtains 50, 105, 112, 166, 199, 205, 206–09, 252, 262, 274, 308, *See also* drapery

Dawkins, Richard 32
Death 24, 36–37, 42–44, 86, 88, 136, 147, 153, 174, 270–71, 303, 305–08, 312, 318, 322, 329, 337, 340–42, 346, 348–49, 357, 360; Black Death 221, 223; 'Death of a Hired Man' 5; death-wishes 136
de Beauvoir, Simone 190–91
de Hooch, Peter 94, 97, 154–56
Decoration 121, 216, 373; carved 91; household 61, 157–59; interior 8, 74, 112–13, 151, 162–68, 199–200, 206–09, 323, 326–27, 352, 367; *The Decoration of Houses*, 134, 214–17; woman as decoration 121, 130–33, *See also* design; interior design
Defoe, Daniel 321, 331–334
Derrida, Jacques 5, 325
Design 3, 9–10, 17, 25, 31–32, 48, 61, 84, 91, 100, 109–10, 115, 145, 152, 157,160–65, 167–72, 176, 200, 210, 214, 215–16, 221, 233–35, 236, 239–40; 242–43, 250, 254, 264, 266, 282, 285, 298, 304, 322, 326–27, 331, 335–36, 345, 357, 368, 371–76; architectural 126; modernist 12, 151, 233–35; natural 123–24; reform 157, *See also* decoration; interior design
Detective fiction 74, 99, 104, 141–42, 251, 321, 326, 344, 363, 365–66
Dickens, Charles 142, 221, 322, 336, 339–42, 359
Dickinson, Emily 12, 322, 326, 346–49
Dirt 42, 44, 75, 116, 119, 153, 191, 194, 196–97, 262–63, 269–74, 297, 332
Dining room 81, 101, 109–10, 165, 205, 210–12, 237, 253, 303, 330–38, *See also* triclinium
Disease 85, 106–07, 128–29, 218, 316, 344
Domestic (definition) 3–10
Domestic novel 321, 325–29
Domestic service 197, 200, 237–38, 295–96; workers 57, 294–99
Domesticity 9, 18, 29, 67, 97, 108, 151–52, 153–56, 159, 176, 181, 196, 200, 241–245, 260–63, 289–292, 327–28, 342, 360; bourgeois 214, 289; collective 110–11; and femininity 54–55, 151,157; middle-class 60; scenes of 97
Domus 3, 5, 51, 153
Doors 11–12, 17, 19, 35–38, 41–43, 48, 56, 62, 73, 81–82, 87, 91–93, 94, 98, 101–02, 109, 118, 123–24, 136, 154, 159, 166, 171, 180, 197, 208–09, 247, 249–51, 256, 258, 261–66, 273, 295–96, 299, 304, 307–08, 317, 322, 325, 333, 335–36, 341, 346–49, 350–51, 371; as metaphor 261; servant 237
Douglas, Mary 11, 18, 50–54, 119, 314, 315, 318
Downtown Eastside (DTES), 286, 314–319, *See also* Canada; Vancouver
Drama 27, 301, 321, 326, 350; Oedipal 174

Drapery 96, 207, 209, *See also* curtains
Drawing-room 101, 103, 118, 119, 134, 208, 253, 273–75, 321–22, 326, 330–34, 335, 338, 341, 350–51, 354–55
Duby, George 11, 73, 83–87
Duchamp, Marcel 147–48
Dürer, Albrecht 88, 90
Duncan, James and David Lambert 9
Dwelling 4–5, 10, 14n9, 17, 20–26, 27–30, 31, 34–35, 41, 47, 63, 65–66, 70n4, 80, 82, 100–107, 123, 25, 143–44, 149, 153, 169, 199, 208, 211, 218, 248, 256–59, 266–68, 278, 301–02, 312, 322, 325, 340–44, 346, 49, 353, 358–62, 365; Aboriginal 291; aristocratic 206; family 47–48, 289; 'improved' 184, 185; Insanitary Dwelling 127; secular 204; urban 74, 248, *See also* Heidegger, Martin

Eames, Charles and Ray 172
Earth-closets 200, 217–20
Economy 124, 220, 301, 342, 365; domestic 230, 232, 303, 323, 327; gift 53; global 5; moral 68; political 7, 45, 61
Egypt 17, 40–43, 130–31, 345
Elias, Norbert 6, 11, 200, 225–30
Eliot, T.S. 3
Estrangement 142–46, 317–18
Exile 87, 144, 309–14, 316, 361

Family 6–7, 37, 40–43, 45–49, 57–58, 63, 66, 73–74, 89, 97, 117–19, 128–29, 131, 151, 158, 185, 187–91, 195–96, 229, 238–43, 260, 270, 273, 276, 279, 294–98, 341–43; Amazonian 67; apartments 100–02; celebration 91; in *Fasti 82;* house 14n9, 111, 115, 169, 173–78, 200, 210–12, 221, 281, 285, 304–06, 354, 369; hygiene 105–07, 327–28; Kwakwa̱ka̱'wakw 291–92; monasteries 84–86; nuclear 186, 188–89, 227, 288–89, 315, 364–65; porches 265; room 91, 101–02, 118, 221; and servants 92–93, 237; suburban 170; values 242, 262
Fashion 7–8, 157, 164; architecture 181, 265, 330; British 352–53; contemporary 60; interior decoration 207; women's 130–33
Feminism 8–9, 55, 67, 152, 190–93, 316, 328, 350
Fences 118–19, 269, 272n1
First World War 29, 141n2, 151, 237, 239–40, 327, *See also* Second World War
Flat 41, 151, 162, 169, 175, 233–35, 296, *See also* apartment; *maison particulière*
Floors 39n3, 41, 44, 94, 96, 108, 129, 136, 147–49, 185, 191, 205, 207–09, 222, 269, 274, 296, 303–04, 308, 323, 333, 354, 373; porch 266
Food 7, 12, 42–43, 47, 67–69, 84, 87, 91, 114, 119, 125, 170, 187–89, 195, 218–19, 232, 233, 288, 318, *See also* kitchen
Foucault, Michel 3–6, 241, 248, 271–72
France 29, 73, 83–87, 97–98, 105, 206, 222, 260–62, 311–314, 334n4, 343–46, *See also* Paris
Frankfurt Kitchen 233–35, *See also* Lihotsky, Grete; Schütte-Lihotsky, Margarete
Frederick, Christine 233, 236, 238, 238n1
Freud, Sigmund 8, 11, 15n21, 74, 121–22, 135–38, 138–141, 144, 148,

151, 175, 181, 305; pleasure principle 142; *Civilization and its Discontents* 151–52, *See also* uncanny; unhomely
Frost, Robert 5
Furnishing 30, 42, 52, 61–62, 88, 121, 133, 136, 151, 157–59, 164, 244, 260, 265, 273–74, 296, 307, 312, 345, 350, 354
Furniture 11–12, 30, 73, 88–89, 90, 112, 118, 132, 158–62, 164, 166, 170–72, 187, 206–210, 211–14, 215–17, 224–5, 239, 252–54, 265, 307–08, 322–23, 336, 338, 342, 350–356, 367
Fuss, Diana 4, 12, 322–25, 346–49

Galleries 12, 91, 102, 165, 266, 335
Garber, Marjorie 11, 15n11, 121, 123–127
Gardens 12, 37, 42, 52, 81, 84, 92–93, 118–19, 131, 154, 222, 252, 268–72, 297, 327, 335; English 247, 268; gardening 63, 272; private 109
Garret 19–21, *See also* attic
Gender 3, 8, 18, 121, 175, 180–81, 236, 248, 294–95, 303, 315, 318–19, 360, 368; Amazonian 67–68; anxiety 151, 162–63; boundaries 165; difference 8, 124, 165; division 47, 248; conformity 175; identity 167; and labour 195, 270–72; relations 327, 350; roles 17, 123, 170, 182, 370; and sexuality 125–26, 162; and space 92, 121, 151–52, 330–32; stereotypes 369; studies 10–11
Geography 10, 54, 260, 338; and gender 195; of the house 7; postmodernity 309
Geopolitics 7, 241
George, Rosemary Marangoly 286
Gilman, Charlotte Perkins 10, 12, 285, 287–88
Ginsburg, Rebecca 6, 8, 12, 285, 294–300
Glass 122, 130–1, 147, 160, 208, 210, 252, 304; 'architecture of glass' 148; stained 130
Globalization 241, 279
Glover, William J., 7, 11, 18, 59–65
Good Housekeeping 327
Gordimer, Nadine 360–62
Greece 187–188, *See also* Yerania 274
Guests 36, 43, 63, 81, 85, 91–92, 100, 118–19, 169, 203–04, 227, 230, 297, 318, 332, 336, 364; rooms for 300

Haigh, Isabel 273–75
Haha 269, 272n1
Hallways 74, 238, 296, 318, 363, 373–76
Hamon, Philippe 4, 12, 322, 343–45
Harbison, Robert 272
Harry Potter 322, 369–70, *See also* children's literature; Rowling, J.K.
Haunting 11, 15n21, 121, 140, 144–45, 259, 307, 321, 325–29, 332–33, 340, 342–43, 359–62, 369
Haram 37, 38
Hayden, Dolores 8, 11, 74, 114–16, 327
Health 68, 124, 127–28, 148, 160, 191, 200, 205, 217, 220, 225, 230, 270, 288, 301–02, 314, 316–19
Hegglund, Jon 7
Heidegger, Martin 5, 10–11, 17, 21–26, 27–28, 73, 144, 149, 153, 190–91, 267, 310, 322, 334, 339–41, 346; dwelling 10, 17, 21–26, 28–30, 191, 322, 340–44, 346–49
Heterotopia 4, 248, 271, 356
Hirschon, Renée 6, 8, 11, 152, 186–90, 264n7
Holland 94, 97–8, 154
Hollywood 7, 241
Home 17–18, 20–22, 45–49, 124–127, 151–52, 154–56, 195–97, 260, 285–86,

288, 321–322, 326–29, 347, 354, 367; Aboriginal 290–92; Algerian 247; bourgeois 105, 110–114, 115–19; commodified 133–35; and decoration 158; definitions of 5–6, 51–54, 56–59, 65–69, 73–75, 88–89, 190–93, 210–11, 279–82, 310–12, 314–18, 325, 358–62; Dutch 94, 97–98; and Dickens, Charles 339–343; efficiency 233, 238n1; and ego 27; English 100, 102, 160–61, 164–65, 273–277; etymology of 14n9; family 171, 200; Japanese 116–19; Jung, Carl 122; and modernity 309; and motherhood 180–83; Muslim 40–44; private 104, 107–08; queer 174–78; and technology 239–241, 242–45; traditional 28–29, *See also* unhomely

Homelessness 6, 12–13, 26, 122, 144, 174, 286, 297, 310, 315–16, 319n4, 339

Homer 146, 195, 231

Homesickness 6, 122, 144, 146, 310

Homosexuality 87, 152, 158–59, 174–78, 197, *See also* queer

hooks, bell 192–93

Hospital 4, 129, 317–18, 337, *See also* infirmary

Hospitality 40, 43, 47, 189

Hotels 18, 51, 61, 75, 297, 317–19; *hôtel privé* 108–11

House; American 208, 221, 264, 266, 312; boarding 14n9, 177, 297, 344; and cleanliness 97, 116–117, 119, 185, 269; contemporary 160; country 320–21, 326, 373; Dawson 375–76; detached 117–18, 303–09; etymology of 14n9; Hallway 376; 'House Beautiful' 158–59, 176, 199; lodging 152, 169; Main 101, 294–95, 300; mass-production 301–04, 340; modernized 182–84; oneiric 351, 367; parlour 151, 169; peasant 27, 29; *pukka* 312; religious 14n9, 204–05; 'smart house' 242, 244; suburban 271, 303, 370; temporary 61; terraced 119, 286, 359; townhouse 109, 118, 331, 353, 355; township 294–300; transition 317; Tudor 160, 162; vacation 345, *See also* Bronte House; Kayble House; laneway house; 'machine for living'; Moller House; parlour house; Whiteread, Rachel

Housewife 148, 156, 185, 187, 188, 196, 233, 236–38, 287, 328

Housework 152, 174, 191

Housekeeping 7, 161

Hugo, Victor 344–45

Huysmans, J.K. 147, 344

Hut 11, 17, 19–21, 29, 33, 73, 77–78, 84, 93, 250, 256–58, 291

Hygiene 105–06, 116, 147, 200, 223, 260

Ibsen, Henrik 104, 322, 350–51

Immigration 18, 43, 274, 299

India 18, 59–64, 274, 312, 351–57

Infirmary 85–86, 203–05, *See also* hospital

Ingold, Tim 10–11, 17, 31–35

Interior design 3, 10, 162, 164, 176, 210–14, 335–39, 368, 372, *See also* decoration; design

Interiority 103–04, 180, 211, 280–82, 325–26, 329, 346, 351–57, 363–66

Inuit 291

Irigaray, Luce 190–91

Islam 11, 17, 28, 40–44, 268

James, Henry 133–34, 326, 356, 358

Japan 11, 29, 75, 116–20, 219, 221, 223, 357; architecture 265; fans 355; bedding 52; manga 321

Johannesburg 285, 294–300, *See also* Africa, South Africa
Jung, Carl Gustav 11–12, 77, 122, 135–38, 247, 256, *See also* archetype

Kabyle House 35, *See also* Algeria, Berber House
Kang, Sok-kyong 322, 363–366
Kerr, Robert 74, 100–102, 157
Khan, Nawab Mehdi Hasan 59
King, Anthony 4–7, 61
Kipling, Rudyard 62
Kitchen 6, 48, 63, 84–87, 91, 97, 101, 109–10, 114, 118–19, 152, 156, 185, 187–89, 200, 203, 236–38, 243, 303, 313, 318, 321, 326, 336, 349; cleanliness 105; communal 11; design 236; economy of 230–35; modern 107; utensils 36, 374, *See also* food; Frankfurt Kitchen
Kline, Stephen 11, 200, 238–41
Knights, Clive 11, 73, 79–83, 232
Korea 322, 363–66
Kwakwa̲ka̲'wakw 291–93

Lamps 36, 142, 158, 164, 210, 215, 217, 224, 354, 371
Landscape 59, 78, 94–95, 153–56, 209, 249, 272, 356; English 268; European 355; urbanized 344
Laneway house 3, 12, 248, 278–83, *See also* house
Laundry 47, 114, 116, 152, 194–97, 270
Lawn 270, 278, 280–81
Le Corbusier 6, 12 30, 78, 151, 160, 163, 165, 167, 172, 251, 285, 286, 300–02, 326, 369, *See also* 'machine for living'
Lefebvre, Henri 5, 10–11, 17, 26–31
Leisure 196, 216, 243, 276
Lerup, Lars 12, 285, 303–05
Lévi-Strauss, Claude 188
Lewis, Wyndham 164
Library 254, 273
Light 22, 24, 36–38, 50, 81–82, 87, 88, 96–97, 122, 131, 154–56, 171, 200, 208, 213, 230, 233, 247, 252, 254, 256, 262, 300, 302, 307, 309, 354, 357, 359; candle 135, 364; electric 135, 161, 224; gas 147, 208, 224, 274; sun 167, 266
Lihotsky, Grete 200, 233–35, *See also* Frankfurt Kitchen; Schütte-Lihotsky, Margarete
Linen 87, 96, 171, 194–95, 215, 221, 225
Livett, Richard A.H., 11, 151, 168–69
London 9, 13, 59, 95, 129, 161–62, 167, 177–78, 221–22, 274, 309, 327, 332–33, 368
Loos, Adolf 78, 199, 247, 251–54
Lukacs, John 89–90
Lying-in room 121, 127–29, *See also* birthing room
Lyotard, Jean-François 325

'Machine for living' 6, 160, 285, 301, 369, *See also* Le Corbusier
Maison 19, 344; *à allée* 108–09; *de rapport* 111; *de ville* 111; *femme maison* 8, *particulière* 111, *See also* apartment; flat
Marc, Oliver 6, 12, 73, 247, 256–59
Marcus, Sharon 11, 74, 108–12
Marvell, Andrew 123, 271
Marx, Karl 7, 30 103, 142–43, 352; Marxism 17, 74, 114, 212
Masculinity 11, 153, 163, 165, 174, 342
Maugham, Syrie 157
Mausoleum 42–43, *See also* crypts, tomb
Mauss, Marcel 53

McDowell, Linda 6–8, 11, 18, 54–59
McLuhan, Marshall 239–40
Mexico 11, 45–49
Mezei, Kathy 12, 200, 238–241, 321, 325–330
Middle Ages 73, 89, 199–200, 204, 229–30
Migration 6–7, 28, 263, 295 309, 358
Mirrors 42, 86, 135, 199–200, 208–09, 212–14, 221, 254, 268, 306, 326, 341, 344, 354, 375
Modernism 145–46, 151, 163, 165, 167, 265, 369; British 163, *See also* 'Amusing style'
Moller House 252–54
Monasteries 73; and private life 84–87, 92; St. Gall 203–06
Morley, David 6–8, 10–12, 200, 241–45, 286 309–14
Morrison, Toni 359–61
Motherhood 10, 55, 127, 180–81; Soviet 115–16
Mugerauer, Robert 6, 12, 247, 264–68
Munro, Alice 7–8, 326
Myanmar (Burma) 91–93

Nation 4, 5, 7, 29, 54, 181, 206, 217, 308, 316, 317, 331, 344, 361, 366, 368
Nationalism 176, 290
Neighbourhoods 47, 56, 169, 187, 189, 220, 316–17; Cairo 42; in *Dombey and Son* 341; Downtown Eastside 316–319; London 368; Paris 305; Johannesburg 294–97; Vancouver 278–82
Neighbours 23, 43, 47, 67, 177, 189, 228, 262, 265, 269, 281 309
Nicholson, Basil D. 11, 151, 160–61
Noise 48, 125, 128, 230, 278, 297, 318
Nomadism 45, 144, 154, 309, 315
Nostalgia 8, 28, 50, 122, 144–45, 180, 190, 192–93, 211, 242, 259, 272, 312, 314, 342, 354, 369, 370
Nursery 147, 200, 224–25, 325, 335, *See also* children

Object 3, 11, 13, 19, 29, 30–32, 34, 36–37, 39n1, 41, 48, 74, 96, 104, 112–13, 139–40, 147–48, 170, 186–87, 189, 191, 199, 200, 201n2, 207–08, 213–15, 233, 243, 251, 254–56, 260, 275, 306–07, 316, 321, 325–28, 344–45, 350–52, 355–56, 360; decorative 199, 215–17, 240; domestic 369–70; earthenware 36; ethnographic 293; modern 211–12; symbolic 310, *See also* bric-à-brac
Odour 11, 74, 101, 105–07, 122, 200, 217, 219–220, 230, *See also* smell
Office 7, 49, 84, 102–04, 171, 237, 254, 353–54, *See also* study
Omega Workshop 326, *See also* workshop
Ornament 59, 103–04, 112, 134–35, 148, 161, 199, 201, 214–17, 301, 307, 332, 351, 354
Overing, Joanna 66–68
Ozaki, Ritsuko 6, 11, 116–119

Painting 10, 74, 88, 94–99, 103, 121, 123, 125, 130, 136, 147, 168n7, 199, 207, 209, 222, 286, 342, 354; autobiographical 311; Bonnard 223, 307; Cassatt 222; de Hooch 154–58; Duchamp 147; Hopper 263; impressionist 260; Laurencin 165; Medieval 223; primitive 171
Paris 74, 97, 98, 108–12, 164, 167, 305; Benjamin 74, 103–04, 351, 353; nineteenth-century 351; Parisian 147, *See also* France

Passes, Alan 6, 11, 18, 65–71
Peel, Mrs C. S. 11, 200, 224–25
Performance 66, 69, 91, 121, 151, 194, 236, 288, 290, 308
Phenomenology 266; phenomenological 10–11, 19, 317, 351; phenomenologist 20, 144
Plato 125–26
Playboy 152, 170–72
Poe, Edgar Allan 11,74, 104, 122, 142, 199, 206–10, 344
Poetry 12, 27, 125, 322, 344, 346; Dickinson, Emily 12, 322, 346–49; lyric 344; Tagore 357
Pompeii 11, 73, 79–82, 232
Pope, Alexander 269, 331
Porch 12, 82, 130–132, 247, 264–268, *See also* balcony
Portraits 74, 94, 97, 130, 209, 213–14, 354, 370; de Hooch, Pieter 154; Reynolds, Joshua 134
Postcolonial 5, 11, 322, 358, 361, 363–66, *See also* Bhabha, Homi
Postmodern 289, 309
Postmodernism 144, 146, 285
Poverty 44, 46, 105, 286, 314, 328, 332
Privacy 6, 11, 37–38, 48, 50n4, 73–74, 88–89, 92, 97, 100–02, 105, 108, 111, 113, 117, 119, 142, 149,162, 169, 176, 199–200, 203–06, 222, 238, 253, 262–63, 269, 276, 307, 325, 343, 349, 364, 374; and telephones 239; Victorian 285
Private sphere 105–07, 245, 289, 358, 362, 369, *See also* public sphere
Property 211, 231, 272n1, 279, 294–95, 332, 356, 374; acquisition 190; division of 44, 92, 149, 185; private 112, 299, 368; rights 269
Proust, Marcel 263, 344
Psychoanalysis 9, 15n21, 21, 74
Psyche 8, 11–12, 121–24, 137–38, 256, 321–22, 336, 362, 365
Public sphere 5, 64, 74, 244–45, 266, 289, 358, 362, *See also* private sphere

Queer 164; domesticity 173–79; identities 176; men 174–78; space 11, *See also* homosexuality

Radio 11, 171, 200, 238–41
Raibmon, Paige 6–7, 12, 285, 289–93
Rapoport, Amos 29
Reception room 109, 254
Reed, Christopher 8, 9, 11, 151, 162–68, 286n1
Renaissance 113, 130; art 176, 268, 349; Carolingian 84; High 95; Italian 124; literature 124
Restoration, the 108, 143, 332
Revolution 54, 143, 195, 360–61; and architecture 301, 374; domestic 285; July 103; October 115–16
Reynolds, Joshua 96, 134
Robertson, Leslie 12, 286, 314–19
Robinson-Tomsett, Emma 6, 12, 248, 273–77
Rome 73, 83, 99, 218, 221
Rousseau, Jean-Jacques 67, 97, 142, 145
Rosner, Victoria 326
Rowling, J.K. 322, 368–71, *See also* Harry Potter
Rybczynski, Witold 11, 73, 88–90, 199
Rykwert, Joseph 11, 32, 73, 77–79

Saïd, Edward 311
Salons 12, 107, 109, 136–37, 351; French 332, 345, 351
School 14n9, 43, 51, 85, 96, 337; architecture 163; holidays 300; public 175; rooms 224–25, 335

Schütte-Lihotsky, Margarete 200, 233–35, *See also* Frankfurt Kitchen; Lihotsky, Grete
Scolnicov, Hanna 12, 322, 349–51
Second World War 10, 144, 176, 239–40, 242, *See also* First World War
Servants 11, 47–48, 87, 92, 200, 220–21, 227, 234, 300, 326, 355; African 294–300; domestic 237–38, 276, 288; college 359; government 59; quarters 63, 84–85, 91, 100, 101–02, 110, 118
Sexuality 11, 37, 60, 125, 162–63, 167, 170, 254, 315; homosexuality 87, 152, 158, 174–75, 178; performance 151
Shelter 5–7, 17, 19–22, 32–34, 36, 46, 51, 193, 256, 265, 276, 294, 304, 328–29, 342, 345; bourgeois 105; camp 311; public 297; women's 316–18
Ships 4, 12, 235, 248, 273–277
Shone, Richard 9, 12, 285, 305–09
Shops 4, 43, 108–09, 111–12, 162, 244, 376
Simmel, George 6, 11–12, 73, 143, 247, 249–51, 349
Single room occupancy (SRO), 317–19
Sleep 33, 36, 38, 41, 48, 52, 73, 91–92, 117, 185, 204–05, 209–10, 227–30, 260, 278, 303–04, 352
Sleeping-room 102, 118; trains 273–74, *See also* bedroom
Smell 105, 107, 128, 308, 342, 354, *See also* odour
Sofas 209, 252, 254, 322, 325, 350, 354–55, 373, 376
South Africa 12, 294–300, 360–62, *See also* Africa; Johannesburg
'Spatial turn' 4
Stairs 74, 93, 101–02, 108, 136, 154, 169, 237, 252–54, 296, 304, 318, 325, 335–36, 338–39, 375
Stea, David 6–7, 11, 17, 45–50
Stephenson, Marcia 7–8, 10–11, 152, 180–84
Stove 7, 203, 232
Strangers 42, 67–68, 85, 108–09, 117, 143, 193, 195, 229, 243, 297, *See also* estrangement
Stroud, Jonathan 322, 368–70
Study 81, 88, 90, 101, 253, 329, 350, *See also* office
Suburbs 7, 50, 101, 118–119, 159, 170, 242, 265, 268–69, 270, 271, 278, 295–96, 300, 302–03 316, 327
Sun-room 130, 131–33

Tatami room 118–19
Taylorism 7, 236
Technology 6, 56, 64, 88–89, 104, 171, 200, 222, 237, 238–45, 264–65; antiquity 204; communication 240; family 304; heating 203; modern 236; USSR 115
Technological 30; changes 73; sophistication 152
Telephones 11, 171, 200, 237, 238–40, 304, 309
Temples 23 60, 80, 123, 238n1; Apollo 82, 234n5; Greek 27
Tents 51, 78, 83, 291
Terrace 171, 269, 356, 373
Terraced housing 119, 286, 359
Teyssot, Georges 11, 122, 147–50, 200
Thanegi, Ma 6, 8, 11, 73, 75, 91–93
Theatre 12, 14n9, 103, 162, 167, 175; classical 349; domestic 6, 242; green rooms 177 and memory 21; model 48; outdoor 349; theatre boxes 252–55
Threshold 38, 41, 80, 82, 180, 189, 250, 252, 254, 257–58, 266, 318, 321, 326, 338–39, 346, 366, 371–72, 374;

spiritual significance of 80; and the porch 266
Todd, Dorothy and Raymond Mortimer 11, 74, 112–13
Toilet 93, 117–19, 187, 221–23, 262, 295–97, *See also* bathroom; water-closet
Tomb, 36, 42–43, 340, 345, *See also* mausoleum, crypts
Topoanalysis 21
Topophilia 10, 17, 27, 262
Trains 4, 12, 235, 248, 273–76, 297, 340
Triclinium 81, *See also* dining-room
Tristram, Philippa 326
Trompe l'oeil 94, 141
Turkey 7, 207, 274

Uncanny 122, 138–41, 142–46, 154, 283n3, 322, 342–43, 358, *See also* Freud, Sigmund; unhomely
Unhomely 8, 11, 122, 141, 141n1, 283n3, 322, 328, 342, 358–62, *See also* Freud, Sigmund; home; uncanny
Urbanization 30, 167, 340

Vacuum cleaners 7, 161, 237
Valle, Jorge Saravia 182–85
Vancouver 12, 248, 278–83, 286, 291–92, 314–19, *See also* Downtown Eastside
Van Herk, Aritha 8, 11, 152, 194–97
Vermeer, Jan 97, 308
Verschaffel, Bart 8, 11, 151, 153–56
Vestibule 73, 80, 82, 101, 108–09, 117–18, 266
Vidler, Anthony 8, 11, 122, 141–46, 283n3
Vienna 161, 233–34, 235n3, 252–53
Vitruvius 121, 123, 331, 334n5
Vogue 164–68

Young, Iris Marion 8, 11, 152, 190–93

Wagner, George 8, 11, 152, 170–72
Wall, Cynthia 12, 321, 330–335
Washing machines 7, 119, 237
Water-closet 217, 220, *See also* bathroom; toilets
Waugh, Evelyn 222
Wharton, Edith 11, 121, 133–35, 199, 214–17
Whiteread, Rachel 9, 285, 305–09
Wilde, Oscar 151, 158–59, 163, 176, 199, 221
Wigley, Mark 125–26
Wilk, Christopher 6, 11, 200, 233–35, 327
Windows 12, 17, 92, 101–02, 110, 122–23, 142, 148–49, 154, 160, 171, 199, 205, 209, 215, 233, 247, 250–51, 252–55, 261–63, 266, 296, 304, 308, 322, 335–36, 339, 341, 344, 347, 359, 375
Wolfreys, Julian 10, 12, 322, 339–43
Womb 15n21, 78, 127–29, 148, 181, 247, 256–60, 328
Workshops, 84; home as 114, 287–88; kitchen as 236–37, *See also* Omega Workshop

Yerania 186–9, *See also* Greece